THE
PLACE NAMES
OF NEW MEXICO

THE **PLACE NAMES**

ROBERT JULYAN

OF **NEW
MEXICO**

REVISED EDITION

UNIVERSITY OF NEW MEXICO PRESS / ALBUQUERQUE

WITH LOVE AND HOPE,
I DEDICATE THIS BOOK
TO MY DAUGHTER,
ROBYN

22 21 20 19 18 17   9 10 11 12 13 14

ISBN-13: 978-0-8263-1689-9

Library of Congress Cataloging-in-Publication Data

Julyan, Robert Hixson.
The place names of New Mexico / Robert Julyan.—Rev. ed., 2nd ed.
p. cm.
Includes bibliographical references (p.   ).
ISBN 0-8263-1689-1 (pbk.)
1. Names, Geographical—New Mexico.
2. New Mexico—History, Local.
I. Title.
F794.J84 1998
917.89'0014—dc21   98-25232
CIP

CONTENTS

PLACE NAMES ARE THE LANGUAGE
IN WHICH THE NATION'S
AUTOBIOGRAPHY
IS WRITTEN.

—DONALD ORTH,
former executive secretary of the
U.S. Board on Geographic Names,
Domestic Geographic Names.

INTRODUCTION

This book is the autobiography of New Mexico, as written in the names the state's peoples have placed on its mountains and rivers, its cities and villages, its arroyos, mesas, creeks, springs—any place that people have felt had identity. For place names result from the fundamental and universal human need to label with words, and the concepts of naming and place identity are inextricably linked. As the American names scholar, Kelsie Harder, has observed, a place without a name in one sense isn't really a place.

New Mexico's place-name autobiography began with the Native Americans, more than 10,000 years ago, with names created by paleo-Indians arriving from the north, the first humans to behold the landscape here. What those names were can never be known, but that they existed is beyond doubt. Indeed, long before Europeans arrived, Native American groups constituted a shifting cultural geography here, with the creation and disappearance of many place names. In southwestern New Mexico, the names spoken by the people now known as Mimbres were replaced by names in the Athapascan language spoken by the Apaches. Now the Apaches too are gone from there, but the name Gila, derived from their word for *mountain*, reminds us of their presence. No fewer than seven Native American languages are still spoken in the state, not counting dialects within languages.

Yet despite this linguistic diversity, Indian names not only in New Mexico but throughout North America show certain characteristics. The first is that the names in everyday usage overwhelmingly are descriptive, such as the Navajo name for the Jemez Mountains that means "black-appearing mountains," and the Tewa name for the Rio Grande that like the Spanish name means simply "big river." A major reason for this is that among people without maps or guidebooks, place names tend to serve as identification labels.

Another characteristic of Indian naming is that virtually without exception, Indians do not name places to honor individual people; thus Indians don't put commemorative names on places, as the Spaniards did with Albuquerque and as Anglos did with Mount Taylor. Several reasons exist for this. For one thing, such naming conflicts with Indian concepts of non-linear time and posterity. As Alfonso Ortiz, anthropologist and member of San Juan Pueblo, put it, "Indians want to be remembered, not written about—they're different things."

This is not to suggest that Indian naming is simple. For example, an everyday name for a place often co-exists with other names having ritual or mythological significance; while the Navajo name in everyday usage for Mount Taylor means "big, tall mountain," Navajos also have a ceremonial name for the mountain meaning "turquoise mountain." What's more, within their tribal areas, Indians typically have very high densities of names; within these areas virtually every feature, even a feature that would be ignored by Europeans, has a name. And often a wry humor appears in Indian names; the Navajo name for Fruitland means "burned bread," recalling an unfortunate baking incident there.

So even before Europeans arrived, New Mexico already had a rich and complex namescape. But in 1540, when Don Francisco Vásques de Coronado and his expedition arrived on the banks of the Rio Grande, it became even more rich and complex.

Occasionally, the Spanish-speaking explorers and settlers adopted and adapted Indian names they encountered, passing on names such as Abiquiu, Chama, Chilili, Gila, and Pecos. But more often they created new names, according to their own naming traditions.

Like the Indians, the early Hispanic settlers lived close to the land, in remote rural communities, and thus the names they created, like Indian names, often simply described the place or referred to local plants or animals: Sierra Grande, Bosque Redondo, Chamizal, Piñon, Berrenda, Agua Fria, Corrales, Placitas, La Jara, Alamogordo, Rio Puerco, and so forth.

The Roman Catholic faith was important to the Spaniards, so they named places for saints, not only to honor the saints but also to elicit the saints' patronage and protection. And they created other names expressing their religious faith: Nombre de Dios, Sangre de Cristo, La Concepcion, Belen, Sacramento. Only among the mountains of the Himalayas does such a rich assemblage of religious names exist as in New Mexico.

Families, large and extended, also were important to these early Hispanic people, and thus villages often took family names—Bernal, Los Lunas, Los Montoyas, Gabaldon, Villanueva, Bacaville, Los Trujillos, and many, many more. Frequently such names resulted from a village owing its existence to a land grant, which bore the family name of at least one of the individuals to whom it was given. Very often members of these families still live in the communities bearing their family names.

Sometimes Hispanic names recall specific incidents that happened at the place: Ojo del Perrillo, "spring of the little dog," where the arrival in Oñate's camp on the Jornada del Muerto of a little dog with muddy paws indicated a spring nearby; Cañon del Borracho, where a celebrated yellow steer named Borracho died; Don Carlos Hills, where a Spanish military officer battled Comanches; Fra Cristobal Range, where a pioneer Franciscan died.

New Mexico during the colonial era was at the outer fringes of the Spanish empire, isolated and often alienated from the governments of Spain and New Spain, and the state's Hispanic place names reflect this. Spaniards, unlike Indians, are not averse to using place names to honor people, yet names honoring Spanish royalty or persons prominent in the government of New Spain are all but absent here, Albuquerque being the signal exception. Also virtually absent are names transferred to New Mexico from Spain or Mexico. Sevilleta, Santa Fe, and possibly Talpa are among the few exceptions.

In the 19th century the New Mexico namescape received another seismic shock, with the arrival of Americans speaking English. Characteristically, persons speaking this most accommodating of languages left intact many of the Indian and Spanish names they encountered here, but they created hundreds of new names, particularly on the eastern plains, where Hispanics previously had not settled or only sparsely because of hostile nomadic Indians.

Like the Indians and the Hispanics, the Anglo settlers created many common, everyday descriptive and associative names—Alkali Lake, Elephant Butte, Bible Top Hill, Turkey Creek, Black Range, Brushy Mountain, Bottomless Lakes, Cedar Crest, Red River, Schoolhouse Mesa, Grasshopper Canyon.

And like the Hispanics, the Anglos very often named their settlements for the people who lived there: Abbott, Budville, Causey, Chisum, Clines Corners, Moriarty, Counselors, Dawson, Fenton Lake, Hobbs, Loving, Tatum, Watrous, and Weed.

Also like the Hispanics, the Anglos created names recalling specific incidents: Blacksmith Canyon, where an outlaw gang shoed their horses; Horse Thief Creek, where rustlers hid stolen stock; Massacre Gap, where a family was killed; and Skeleton Canyon, where bones of persons killed in outlaw ambush were found.

But more than the Hispanics, the Anglos used place names to honor people, and thus the New Mexico namescape is populated with the names of persons who never lived here and often never saw the places named for them: Mount Taylor, for President Zachary Taylor; Cleveland, for President Grover Cleveland; Folsom, for Frances Folsom, wife of Grover Cleveland; Fort Fillmore, for President Millard Fillmore; Garfield, for President Garfield; Gladstone, for the British statesmen; and five counties named for U.S. Presidents—Grant, Harding, Lincoln, McKinley, and Roosevelt.

And while the Hispanics were assiduous prospectors, the Anglos were mostly responsible for the mining boom of the late 19th century and the names created then. The names of their mining camps reflect their exuberance and optimism: Bonanza City, Carbonateville, Chance City, Chloride Flats, Gold Dust, Hematite, Molybdenum, and Silver City.

The Anglo settlers also brought railroads to New Mexico, and, like flowers along a stem, new settlements blossomed as the rail lines grew, tendril-like, throughout the state. Many of the settlements took the names of railroad officials, contractors, and workers: Duran, Engle, Grants, Gallup, Grenville, Hagerman, Otis, Ricardo, Torrance, Vaughn, and Willard.

Then in the railroads' wake came homesteaders, creating hundreds of post offices, rural schools, and settlements. These communities, too, often took the names of the people who created them and lived there, frequently the name of the person in whose home the post office was located: Causey, Cliff, Dunken, Dwyer, Floyd, Grady, House, Pendaries, Ragland, Roy, and Watrous. Often the homesteaders' names reflected hope and optimism about a new life in New Mexico: Happy Valley, Pleasant Valley, Eden Valley, Liberty, Paradise Plains, Enterprise, and Harmony.

(A note about names of post offices: in 1889 the postal department forbade two word names, so many pairs were elided into one, e.g., Whitewater; in 1951 this policy was abandoned, and many one-word names reverted to their original two-word forms.)

Humor appears often in Anglo names: Gut Ache Mesa, where a camp cook on a cattle drive tried unsuccessfully to reheat beans; Pitchfork Canyon, near Hay Canyon; Pup Canyon, near Dog Canyon; Rough and Ready, a stage stop; Sunspot, site of a solar observatory; Top o' the World, on the Continental Divide; Badgerville, an early name for Hope, where settlers lived in dugouts, like badgers.

And more than the Spaniards, the Anglos have transferred to New Mexico names from outside the state: Beenham, from Beenham, England; Carlsbad, from Karlsbad, Czechoslovakia; Derry, from Ireland; Regina, from Saskatchewan, Canada; Gascon, from France; Lesbia, from Greece; and names from numerous US states.

Similarly, the Anglos have often been fond of manufacturing names, combining words and names to create new names: Colmor, on the border between Colfax and Mora Counties; Faywood, from the names of two local people, J.C. Fay and William Lockwood; Glenrio, from the English *glen* and the Spanish *río*; Omlee, honoring local rancher Oliver M. Lee; Rutheron, named by a rancher named Heron for his daughter, Ruth; Texico, on the Texas-New Mexico line; and Valmora, in the valley of the Mora River.

Thus, as the centuries have passed, as people, languages, and cultures have intermingled, New Mexico's place-name autobiography has expanded and undergone continuous change.

The autobiography still is being written. New places and thus new names are being created. New communities are springing up, such as Taylor Ranch and Paradise Hills near Albuquerque, Lee Acres in Farmington, and Butterfield Park in Las Cruces. In 1980 seven new wilderness areas were designated in New Mexico. In 1981 a new county, Cibola, was created. In 1987 and 1990 new national monuments, El Malpais National Monument and Petroglyph National Monuments, were established.

At the same time, through institutions such as the NM Geographic Names Committee and the US Board on Geographic Names, names are being changed to reflect more accurately both New Mexico's history and the state's contemporary values. Names such as Niggerhead are being eliminated. Inaccurate or misleading transcriptions of Spanish and Indian names are being corrected. In the Chuska Mountains, Navajos have taken the initiative in replacing the name Washington Pass, honoring an Army colonel whose troops killed a Navajo leader, with the slain leader's name, Narbona.

In the place-name autobiography of New Mexico, this book is but one chapter—and an abridged one at that. The approximately 7,000 names here are but a fraction of all the names that have existed in New Mexico. Yet in this sample can be heard the voices of thousands of individuals—most anonymous and otherwise forgotten—speaking in many languages, telling about their lives, their families, their relation to the land, their faith, their tragedy and humor, the incidents great and small they experienced and through naming remembered.

THE GENESIS OF THIS BOOK

Between 1936 and 1940, N.M. Writers' Project workers collected information for *New Mexico: a Guide to the Colorful State*, but except for what appeared in that book, the place-name information remained in files, unpublished. Then in 1948, at the N.M. Folklore Society's annual meeting, President Ina Sizer Cassidy proposed that the Society sponsor a place-name project; she agreed to chair a place-name committee and to work with T.M. Pearce, the Society's editor of publications, in producing a place-name dictionary. A year later appeared the *First Collection*, a mimeographed publication containing 334 names. Subsequent collections followed, based upon material collected by Folklore Society members and workers with the Spanish Place Name Project at UNM, as well as upon letters solicited through G. Ward Fenley of the UNM News Bureau. Editing was done by Pearce, who in 1950 was elected editor of *New Mexico Place Names*.

From this beginning, and with the support and assistance of his wife, Helen, Pearce assumed the responsibility for recording place-name information in New Mexico. This responsibility Pearce fulfilled with characteristic energy and diligence. He not only edited material collected by others, but he also undertook original research, leading to the publication of *New Mexico Place Names* in 1965 by UNM Press. Until his death in 1986 at the age of 84, Pearce never ceased tracking down place-name information and responding to the voluminous correspondence and inquiries that fall upon a state's place-name-expert-in-residence. For example, I came to him when I was researching *Mountain Names* (The Mountaineers Books, 1984); I found him warm, supportive, and helpful. In working on this present book, I spent several weeks at Special Collections in UNM's Zimmerman Library, going through Pearce's unpublished notes and papers; I was humbled by the breadth and depth of the research he pursued, even when he was quite elderly, and throughout this work I have endeavored not only to incorporate the changes and revisions he would have made but also to give appropriate credit for the information he so painstakingly garnered. I also am gratified to have been able to incorporate into the present work information gathered by George Adlai Feather, linguist at NMSU who spent much of the latter part of his long and productive life visiting and researching towns mentioned by Pearce, with whom he corresponded.

I have been extremely fortunate in having available to me resources Pearce did not have, such as GNIS, USBGN files, improved maps, postal records, recently published county histories, and other sources of information, but I gratefully acknowledge that his are the shoulders upon which I have stood in undertaking my own research.

This book contains approximately 4,400 names, but because the total number of named places in New Mexico very likely exceeds 75,000, throughout this project I was forced to decide which names to include and which to exclude. Clearly, major features would be included, but what about minor features, such as Laney Spring, near Luna in Catron County? Even most local residents have never heard of this place, yet its name recalls the family who brought the first herd of cattle to the area. Could I really exclude it?

Such decisions always were very difficult, and in many cases, as with Laney Spring, I based my decision upon instinct rather than upon formal criteria. Nonetheless, I did establish certain guidelines I attempted, not always successfully, to follow:

❖ Post offices. Since the first US post office was authorized at Santa Fe on Oct. 1, 1849, approximately 1,570 post offices have been established in New Mexico. Because their names usually—but not always—coincided with those of the communities they served, and a post office is a *de facto* insignia of a community, I attempted to include every post office established in New Mexico from 1849 through 1991, though I excluded approved POs that were never actually operated. My source for New Mexico post offices has been Richard A. Helbock's 1981 *Post Offices of New Mexico* because it is the most current and comprehensive listing available.

A post office does not always imply the existence of a distinct settlement, however, as often a post office would be established in a rancher's or homesteader's home to serve a diffuse rural population.

Sometimes a postal name would displace an earlier community name, at least in official records. This happened often in Hispanic New Mexico, where a community's original name might be duplicated on a post office elsewhere in the state and thus be forbidden by postal authorities from being used again. In such an instance, the post office often was given the name of the first postmaster or postmistress, often an Anglo. My research has convinced me, however, that usually the original name survives in local usage.

❖ Mountains. I've included every named summit in New Mexico 10,000 feet or higher, as well as summits of lesser elevation that nonetheless are prominent on the landscape, such as Sierra Grande in Union County, Robledo Mountain in Doña Ana County, and Cabezon in Sandoval County. After that, I've selected according to whether the feature is well-known locally or whether its name is interesting or has historical significance. My source for elevations has been the US Geological Survey's Geographic Information System (GNIS) list. I've also attempted to include most of the state's named mountain ranges.

❖ Water bodies. I've attempted to include every river in New Mexico, even those that sometimes are rivers in name only (the lower Mimbres River rarely has water in it). Similarly, I've attempted to include every sizable lake. But I have not attempted to include every stream, spring, arroyo, or intermittent lake unless the name has special significance or interest.

❖ Land grants. Land grants have been an important part of New Mexico geography, but I've omitted them from this book except where they figure in the history of another named place, such as a settlement.

❖ Railroad sidings. These along with water stops, stations, section houses, and so forth all have had names and once were more important in the pubic consciousness, but I've omitted them except those that once had a post office, that coincided with a settlement, or that gave their name to another feature.

❖ Abandoned settlements. If a name ever was used to designate a place where people lived, regardless of whether anything remains at the site now, I've tried to include it in this book. I've omitted only those names that appeared on but a single map and for which no other information exists, that have vanished not only on the ground but also from the memories and records of knowledgeable local historians.

❖ Administrative areas. I have attempted to include all national parks and monuments, all state parks and monuments, all national forests and wildlife refuges, and all officially designated wilderness areas. Also included are all Indian reservations. Some administrative areas, such as the Warm Springs Indian Reservation and Leonard Wood County, linger only in memory, but their names are part of New Mexico's historical record.

❖ Military sites. I've attempted to include most of New Mexico's named forts and camps, including those, such as Camp Plummer, that were quite ephemeral. Similarly, I've attempted to include past and present military bases.

❖ Housing developments and subdivisions. Simply for practicality, I've excluded all named residential areas within a larger named area, such as the Snowheights Neighborhood in Albuquerque. I have, however, included named developments and suburbs that are geographically outside an affiliated urban area, such as Paradise Hills near Albuquerque and Butterfield Park near Las Cruces.

❖ Just plain interesting names. Some features, though minor, have compellingly interesting names, and if I know the name's origin I have included it. Regrettably, however, the stories behind other intriguing names have eluded me, names such as Cañon de Tio Gordito ("canyon of the fat little uncle"), Dangerous Park, Howinahell Canyon, Granny Mountain, Humbug Creek, Mush Mountain, Piggly Wiggly Canyon, Popping Rock, Salvation Canyon, Sardine Mountain, and Wahoo Peak. Perhaps another time. . . .

HOW TO USE THIS BOOK

This book contains approximately 7,000 names, listed alphabetically according to their specific term, not their generic. Thus an English name such as Mount Taylor is under Taylor, not Mount, and a Spanish name such as Ojo de los Ajuelos, "wild garlic spring," is under Ajuelos and not Ojo. Similarly, definite articles are overlooked in alphabetizing names, especially those of natural features; a name like The Hogback is listed under H, while El Cerro appears under C. Unfortunately, these principles have many exceptions, especially for settlements; Las Cruces is under Las, not Cruces, and Los Alamos is under Los, not Alamos. I also chose to list Spanish river names under Rio.

This book also contains extensive cross-referencing. Regarding a name change, previous names are cross-referenced to the present name; a name with variants is cross-referenced to the most commonly accepted variant (if one exists); and if any confusion exists as to what name is current or what variant is accepted, I have chosen the form approved by the U.S. Board on Geographic Names, as listed in the U.S. Geological Survey Geographic Names Information System (GNIS) Phase I and Phase II inventories. Within the text I have indicated variants, previous names, and names related to the main entry name by italics.

I have not included guides to pronounciation, except where the locally accepted pronunciation is different from what a speaker of standard English or Spanish would expect. Thus I have noted that Thoreau, named for Henry David Thoreau, in New Mexico is pronounced tho-ROO or THROO, and Ledoux, named for a settler of French origin, locally is pronounced la-DOOX.

Regarding Indian place names, with but few exceptions I've presented their meanings but not their sounds; even the best transliterations do no more than approximate the actual sounds of the Indian words, and transliterations encourage the gross corruptions from which Indian names have suffered over the years. Persons who want to hear the sound of the Indian names should consult a native speaker.

After each name is a brief parenthetical summary including the county the feature presently occurs in (county boundaries have changed often in New Mexico), the type of feature if not obvious from the name, its location, and any post office information. While I have attempted to see as many features as possible on the ground and to see all of them on maps, and while I have tried assiduously to make the locations as accurate and current as possible, this book is not intended as a substitute for a good map. In preparing this book I used *The Roads of New Mexico*, based upon the maps of the N.M. Highway Department; these maps are excellent, both for the casual tourist and the more adventurous traveler. I also reviewed each of the more than 2,000 USGS 7.5-minute topographic maps covering New Mexico.

But while this book should not supplant a map, I am aware that T. M. Pearce's *New Mexico Place Names* often has been used as a travel guide, so for each settlement I have tried to indicate its current status; many settlements have vanished completely, others are only ruins, some have only one or two inhabited residences, while others are more active communities, offering services to travelers.

KEY TO ABBREVIATIONS

Railroads:

AE RR	Albuquerque Eastern	PV RR	Pecos Valley
AT&SF RR	Atchison, Topeka, and Santa Fe	PV&NE	Pecos Valley and Northeastern
A&NM RR	Arizona and New Mexico	PD DAWSON RR	Phelps-Dodge Dawson
A&EP RR	Artesia and El Paso	RI RR	Rock Island
A&P RR	Atlantic and Pacific	RGE RR	Rio Grande Eastern
CRI&P RR	Chicago, Rock Island, and Pacific	RGM&P RR	Rio Grande, Mexico, and Pacific
CIM-NW RR	Cimarron and North-western	SFA&P RR	Santa Fe, Albuquerque, and Pacific
C&S RR	Colorado and Southern	SF CENT RR	Santa Fe Central
C&TS RR	Cumbres and Toltec Scenic	SFN RR	Santa Fe Northern
		SFNW RR	Santa Fe Northwestern
D&RG RR	Denver and Rio Grande	SFP RR	Santa Fe Pacific
D&RGW RR	Denver and Rio Grande Western	SFR&DM RR	Santa Fe, Raton, and Des Moines
E&SF RR	Elkhart and Santa Fe	SCD&P RR	Silver City, Deming, and Pacific
EP&NE RR	El Paso and Northeastern	SP RR	Southern Pacific
EP&RI RR	El Paso and Rock Island	StLRM&P RR	St. Louis, Rocky Mountain, and Pacific
EP&SW RR	El Paso and Southwestern	T&NM RR	Texas and New Mexico
NMC RR	New Mexico Central		
NMM RR	New Mexico Midland		
P&SF RR	Panhandle and Santa Fe		

Numbered roads and highways:

I-00	Interstate highway
US 00	US highway
NM 00	State road
CR 00	County road
FR 00	Forest Road

States:

Alaska	AK	Louisiana	LA	Ohio	OH
Arizona	AZ	Maine	ME	Oklahoma	OK
Arkansas	AR	Maryland	MD	Oregon	OR
California	CA	Massachusetts	MA	Pennsylvania	PA
Colorado	CO	Michigan	MI	Rhode Island	RI
Connecticut	CT	Minnesota	MN	South Carolina	SC
Delaware	DE	Mississippi	MS	South Dakota	SD
Florida	FL	Missouri	MO	Tennessee	TN
Georgia	GA	Montana	MT	Texas	TX
Hawaii	HI	Nebraska	NB	Utah	UT
Idaho	ID	Nevada	NV	Vermont	VT
Illinois	IL	New Hampshire	NH	Virginia	VA
Indiana	IN	New Mexico	NM	Washington	WA
Iowa	IA	New York	NY	West Virginia	WV
Kansas	KS	North Carolina	NC	Wisconsin	WI
Kentucky	KY	North Dakota	ND	Wyoming	WY

Other:

BIA	Bureau of Indian Affairs	NPS	National Park Service
BLM	Bureau of Land Management	PO	post office
Co.	Company	Pres.	President
Corp.	Corporation	RR	railroad
Dept.	Department	UNM	University of New Mexico
Gov.	Governor	US	United States
E, W, S, N	east, west, south, north	USBGN	US Board on Geographic Names
ENMU	Eastern New Mexico University	USFS	US Forest Service
GNIS	Geographic Names Information System	USGS	US Geological Survey
NMSU	New Mexico State University	WNMU	Western New Mexico University

THE N.M. GEOGRAPHIC NAMES COMMITTEE

Imagine the chaos if individuals had one name on their driver's license, another on their banking records, another on their medical records, and still others on other documents. In the last century, when vast new areas of the US were being explored and mapped, the confusion of names in government publications was similar to the above situation, so much so that in 1890 the US Board on Geographic Names (USBGN) was created to standardize names appearing on federal maps. Since then the USBGN has continued to set policy and make decisions regarding new names and name changes. The primary criterion for most USBGN decisions is local usage, and to determine which names are indeed recognized and used by local people the USBGN relies heavily on the recommendations of state names authorities. In New Mexico, this responsibility has been given to the Geographic Names Committee of the NM Geographic Information Council. For the past ten years it has been my privilege to chair this committee, and we have tried conscientiously to help ensure that the state's names accurately reflect the history and preferences of the people who live with them. The USBGN publishes its decisions regularly, and all decisions regarding New Mexico names have been incorporated into this book.

The Geographic Names
Information System (GNIS)

Beginning around 1960, the US Geological Survey (USGS) recognized a growing need for a relatively complete inventory of the nation's three to five million place names, and by 1978 the burgeoning of computer technology had made such an inventory possible. Undertaken with the cooperation and support of the US Board on

AND THE U.S. BOARD ON GEOGRAPHIC NAMES

Geographic Names (USBGN), the Geographic Names Information System (GNIS) consists of a two-phase state-by-state inventory of the nation's place names. Phase I consisted of inventorying all names appearing on USGS quadrangles, the basic large-scale maps of the US. In New Mexico, Phase I was completed in 1980 and resulted in a file of approximately 26,000 place names, each identified by county, feature class, coordinate, elevation (where appropriate), and map source. In 1991 the UNM Earth Data Analysis Center began Phase II, a three-year project with me as director; Phase II added to the original database many more names and much more information, gleaned from other federal, state, and local maps, as well as from historic maps, charts, postal records, census records, county histories, oral traditions, and other sources. Phase II also researched and recorded name variants.

While neither Phase I nor Phase II includes detailed historical or anecdotal information about place names, GNIS nonetheless contributes greatly to a more detailed and accurate portrait of New Mexico's namescape, and it has been a great asset in the preparation of this book. GNIS has allowed me to record the distribution of certain common names, as well as to ascertain their locations. For example, it is both revealing and interesting to know that the name element "cottonwood" and its variants appears more than 215 times throughout New Mexico; that the state has at least 20 features in 14 counties named High Lonesome, many of them windmills; and that at least 12 places here are named Hell.

GNIS is an ongoing process, with new names constantly being recorded and added. The numerical total of name occurrences were taken primarily from the Phase I compilation; thus, the actual totals could be higher.

A WORD ABOUT FOLK ETYMOLOGY

Ask someone connected with tourism in Tucumcari about the origin of this curious name, and the chances are great you'll hear a tale about an Apache chief, his daughter Kari, and her lover Tocom. The tale is pure fiction; the name's real origin is obscure but likely is a corruption of a Plains Indian word meaning "lookout," referring to the mountain south of town. Nonetheless, the tale, like most New Mexico legends, not only persists but actually grows stronger each year.

Tucumcari is an excellent example of a process well-known to names scholars whereby people invent, not always consciously, a plausible explanation for a name whose real origin they don't know. The process is called *folk-etymology*, and examples in New Mexico are legion. How often, for example, is it repeated that Puerto de Luna was named when Coronado in 1541 beheld the moon rising over a gap in the mountains and exclaimed, "gate of the moon!"? In fact, Puerto de Luna means "Lunas' gap," for the Luna family that still lives in the area.

This is not to debunk names having colorful origins, as many names indeed do, but rather to encourage a healthy skepticism regarding some of the explanations current in New Mexico. Some of the better-known names often subject to folk-etymology are: Cimarron, High Rolls, La Luz, Las Cruces, Mora, Hatchet Mountains, Tortugas, and Sangre de Cristo.

THE PEOPLE BEHIND THE NAMES

Place names are created by people. When one works with large numbers of names, however, it sometimes is easy to forget this obvious fact, to begin to treat names merely as impersonal records to be noted, cataloged, and filed. But as I traveled the roads of New Mexico and talked to the people who live with the names, I was reminded constantly of my responsibility to show these names not as mere labels on a map but as part of the personal histories of people like myself.

I recall driving north from Clovis one evening to see if I could locate the site of the little homesteader community of Hollene. For some reason the name especially intrigued me, and I wanted to see what was there. I found that Hollene had vanished completely, except for a solitary long-abandoned building—and a cemetery. In the deepening evening light I walked among the graves, looking at headstones, and to my surprise saw one that was very recent. I realized then that while Hollene now is barely a footnote even in local history, to at least some people it will always be home.

I had many such moments during my research:

❖ Listening to Audrey Alpers and her brother, Frank, of Raton recall going to dances at the long-abandoned locality of Hoxie.

❖ Hearing George Dannenbaum of Grants tell of the time he helped a Navajo man in a bar-fight in Correo.

❖ Reading the messages on early 20th-century postcards collected by Wade Shipley of Lovington, sent from places long since vanished.

❖ Sitting in a bar in Mora as Mike Montoya asked the bartender why Mora neighborhoods have names such as Juarez and China Block.

❖ Eating lunch in a cabin in remote Luna County and listening to rancher Alvin Laney tell how his ancestors immigrated from Utah and camped at a spring still called Laney Spring.

❖ Driving with D. Ray Blakely and Bill Wheatley as they explained the proper angle from which Bible Top Hill should be viewed to understand its name.

❖ Sitting in a cafe in Wagon Mound with Anita Wiggins and Margarita Abeyta as they recalled the good times of their childhood in places like Tiptonville and Optimo.

❖ Listening to a tape-recording made by Ray Burrola of 92-year-old Martha Carrillo's recollections of her youth in the Hondo Valley.

❖ Sitting in May Walter's apartment listening to her describe how her husband determined that Wheeler Peak was the state's highest summit.

❖ Seeing in the Aztec Museum an old photo of Peter Knickerbocker, for whom the Knickerbocker Hills were named; the photo shows him at a Fourth of July parade on stilts and in his Uncle Sam costume.

❖ Drinking coffee with Sam Jones of Bingham—he and his wife are the village's only residents—and listening to how selling rattlesnakes enabled him to continue living there.

ACKNOWLEDGMENTS

This book could not have been written without the help and cooperation of many, many people, from librarians who made their collections available, to local people who took time to talk to me, to historians who reviewed my information, to friends and relatives who offered encouragement and support. Here, listed alphabetically along with non-Albuquerque places of residence, are some of the people whose help I wish to acknowledge:

Margarita Abeyta of Wagon Mound
Audrey and Frank Alpers of Raton
Josephine Anderson of the Alamogordo Public Library
Robert Anderson of Los Lunas, Geographic Names Committee member
Anselmo Arrellano of Las Vegas
Derrick Archuleta
Ty Ashlock
Mary Atwood of the Aztec Museum
Martha A. Austin at Navajo Community College, Shiprock
Eldon Baker
George Basabilvaso Jr. and George Basabilvaso Sr. of Lordsburg
Bob Bass, Henry Moore, Tim Larsen at the McKinley County Rural Addressing project in Gallup
Edward C. Beaumont
Richard Becker of Santa Fe

Herbert Benally of Navajo Community College in Shiprock
Susan Berry, Silver City Museum
Lillian H. Bidal
H. B. Birmingham of Reserve
D. Ray Blakeley of Clayton
Denise Bleakly, Geographic Names Committee member
Calvin Boles Jr. of Alamogordo
Jack Boyer of Taos
Ray Burrola and Martha Carrillo of Roswell
David L. Caffey of the Harwood Foundation, Taos
Charles Chapin, NM Bureau of Mines and Mineral Resources in Socorro
Joe Cháves, Geographic Names Committee member
Dan D. Chávez
Flavio and Delfinita Chávez of Aztec

Paige Christiansen, NM Institute of
Mining and Technology, Socorro
Francisco Cisneros of Belen
Ola May Cole of Truth or Consequences
Lurleen Coltharp of El Paso, TX
Kathleen Conant of Belen
Dr. Jolane Culhane of Silver City
Donald Cutter, UNM Department of
History
George Dannenbaum of Grants
Mary Peitsch Davis
William Degenhardt
David Delgado of Santa Rosa
Everett Dennisson of Stanley
Doug Dinwoodie of Carlsbad
Gordon and Ruth Edwards of Quay
Ellen C. Espinosa
Tony Espinoza of Taos
Octavia Fellin of the Gallup Public
Library
Corky Fernandez of Las Vegas
Gene Fifer
Ralph A. Fisher Jr. of Silver City
Elvis E. Fleming of Roswell
Allen Floersheim of Roy
Ed Foster Jr. of Farmington
Albert Franzoy of Salem
T. Wayne Furr, Oklahoma Geological
Survey, Norman, OK
Wanda Fuselier and Elon Yurwit of
Faywood Hot Springs
Ruth Gannaway
Nasario García of Las Vegas
Joseph Gendron of San Lorenzo
Cynthia Geuss, Geographic Names
Committee member

Dr. Dale F. Giese of Silver City
Laura Gleasner of Melrose
David Grant
Janean Grissom of Taiban
Henry Hahn, Roosevelt County Museum
in Portales
Margaret Dismuke Hall
Morrow Hall of Estancia
Winnifred O. Hamilton of Red River
Ellen Harbaugh at the Carlsbad Public
Library
Tom Harmon of the *Albuquerque Journal*
E. Richard Hart
Richard W. Helbock of Oregon, for
making available his postal history
Harvey Hicks of Carlsbad
Allen Hill of Lordsburg
Dorothy Hoard of Los Alamos
Lee Hubbard, Loyd Sadler, and Tanya
White at the Carlsbad Museum
Mike Inglis, UNM Earth Data Analysis
Center
Peter Ives, Geographic Names Committee
member
Carol Jones
Mike Kernodle
Louis Kerschion
John Kessell and the staff at the Vargas
Project at UNM
J. Luree King, librarian in Grants
Amelia Klatt of McIntosh
Jon T. Klingel of Santa Fe
Robert G. Knox of Silver City
Harold W. Kuenstler of Lordsburg
Kay Kunz
Jeanne LaMarca of Lordsburg

Alvin Laney of Luna
Bud and Richard Lawrence of Clayton
Charlie T. Lee of Otero County
Martha Liebert, Sandoval County Historical Society
Carlos Lopopolo of Valencia
Duncan and Gail Major of Mountainair
Don McAlavy in Clovis
Broda McAllister of Portales
Kathryn McKee-Roberts of Bosque Farms
William McPhee of Santa Fe
Connie Meadowcroft
Matías Montoya, Geographic Names Committee member
Michael Montoya of Mora
Ann Mossman
David F. Myrick
Simon O'Rourke of The American University in Cairo Press
David E. Orr of Roswell
Jonathan A. Ortega
Sosimo Padilla of Belen
Louis Page of Santa Rosa
Bob Parsons of Fort Sumner
Alex Paterson of Luna
Roger Payne, Executive Secretary, USBGN
Shawn Penman
Lila Armijo Pfeufer
Michael E. Pitel, NM Tourism and Travel Division
Doug Poulson of the UNM Earth Data Analysis Center
Peggy (Cole) Poulsen
Paxton Price, Dona Ana County Historical Society
Bob Prunty of Red River
Ethel Ramsey of Cimarron

Heather Rex, Mary Winot, and the staff of the UNM Map and Geographic Information Center
Leone R. Reynolds, of Special Collections, Golden Library, ENMSU, Portales
Beryl Roper of Clarendon, TX
J. Richard Salazar, NM State Archivist
Ellanie Sampson and Willy at the Truth or Consequences Public Library
Joseph P. Sánchez, director of the Spanish Colonial Research Center, National Park Service
Gilberto Sandoval, USFS in Jemez Springs
Steve Semken, Navajo Community College, Shiprock
Rita Sue Serna, Hatch Public Library
Sam Servis of Silver City
Wade Shipley of Lovington
Marlene Siepel, Library Director, Lordsburg
E.C. Smith of Tucson
Horace Spurgeon of Reserve
Father Tom Steele
Clarwana Tausworthe and Ruth Daniel
Bill Tefft
Dr. Thomas K. Todsen and his son, Tom, of Las Cruces
Robert J. Torrez, NM State Historian
Cal Traylor of Las Cruces
Herbert L. Traylor of Capitan
Dennis Trujillo, USFS, Jemez Springs
Maria Velasquez, UNM Department of Modern and Classical Languages
Stanton Wallace of Silver City
May Walter of Santa Fe
Gwen Warnick of McIntosh
Bill Watts of Belen

Anita Wiggins of Wagon Mound
Fred Wilding-White of Grants
Jerry Williams, Southwest Institute, UNM
Spencer Wilson, NM Institute of Mining
    and Technology, Socorro
Mary Wyant of MAGIC at UNM
Dr. Karl Wuersching, Sacramento
    Mountains Historical Society,
    Cloudcroft
Stephen Zimmer, Director, Seton
    Museum, Philmont Scout Ranch

All the people at my names talks who have volunteered information and the NM
Endowment for the Humanities for sponsoring my talks

I owe a special debt of gratitude to the following:

Robert R. White, Geographic Names Committee member, historian, and friend,
who started it all

Frank Kottlowski, director emeritus of the NM Bureau of Mines and Mineral
Resources, and Dave Love, Geographic Names Committee member, both visionary
geologists who know how to help make things happen

The unflaggingly cheerful, cooperative, and helpful people at UNM Special
Collections

Ilka Feather Minter, for making available the papers of her father, George Adlai
Feather

Jerold G. Widdison, meticulous editor, tireless researcher, observant traveler, and
generous friend

The members of my family—my wife, Mary, and my daughters, Megan and
Robyn—for their support and encouragement

And especially all those people who graciously and generously have contacted me
with corrections and additions, especially Lillian K. Bidal, Ralph A. Fisher Jr.,
Wade Shipley, and Thomas K. Todsen Sr.

SELECTED BIBLIOGRAPHY

It is beyond the purposes of this book to attempt to include all the sources from which I gleaned information about New Mexico's place names. The following list is intended to provide further references for persons interested in exploring the state or in specific topics.

Chávez, Fray Angélico, *My Penitente Land: the Soul Story of Spanish New Mexico*. Santa Fe: William Gannon, 1979.

Chilton, Lance, et al., *New Mexico: A New Guide to the Colorful State*. Albuquerque: University of New Mexico Press, 1984.

Christiansen, Paige, and Kottlowski, Frank, *Mosaic of New Mexico's Scenery, Rocks, and History*. Socorro: NM Bureau of Mines and Mineral Resources, 1972.

Cobos, Rubén, *A Dictionary of New Mexico and Southern Colorado Spanish*. Santa Fe: Museum of New Mexico, 1983.

Frazer, Robert W., *Forts of the West*. Norman, OK: University of Oklahoma Press, 1965.

Fugate, Francis L. and Roberta B., *Roadside History of New Mexico*. Missoula, MT: Mountain Press Publishing Co., 1989.

Gregg, Josiah, *Commerce of the Prairies*, Max L. Moorhead, ed. Norman, OK: University of Oklahoma Press, 1954.

Horgan, Paul, *Great River*. Austin, TX: Texas Monthly Press, 1984.

Sherman, James E. and Barbara H., *Ghost Towns and Mining Camps of New Mexico*. Norman, OK: University of Oklahoma Press, 1975.

Simmons, Marc, *Albuquerque: A Narrative History*. Albuquerque: University of New Mexico Press, 1982.

Stewart, George R., *Names on the Land*. San Francisco: Lexikos, 1982.

Thompson, Waite, and Gottlieb, Richard M., *The Santa Fe Guide, 2nd Edition*. Santa Fe: Sunstone Press, 1984.

Ungnade, Herbert E., *Guide to the New Mexico Mountains*. Albuquerque: University of New Mexico Press, 1965.

Williams, Jerry L., ed., *New Mexico in Maps, 2nd Edition*. Albuquerque: University of New Mexico Press, 1986.

Young, John V., *The State Parks of New Mexico*. Albuquerque: University of New Mexico Press, 1984.

A MOUNTAIN (Doña Ana). See *Tortugas Mountain.*

ABAJO (general). Spanish, "down, below." In early times, Spanish-speaking people in communities strung along a road or stream often called the localities' extremities *Arriba*, "above," and *Abajo*, "below," the Spanish equivalents of Upper and Lower. This occurred in such communities as Canjilon and Corrales. See *Río Abajo.*

ABBOTT (Colfax; on US 56, 20 mi E of Springer; PO as Abbott 1881, as Sauz 1904–05, as Abbott 1905–35 in Harding County; moved 11 miles to Colfax County, 1935–66, mail to Springer). Abbott was named for its first postmaster, Horace C. Abbott. Horace and his brother, Jerome, were prominent sheep ranchers, and Horace formed a partnership with Sol Floersheim that came to be known as the "King of the Sheep Companies." In 1902–03 the EP&SW RR came through to haul coal from Dawson to Tucumcari, and *Abbott Station*, now abandoned, was established nearby. About this time the community of Abbot briefly was called *Sauz*, Spanish, "willow," but it soon reverted to Abbott. Abbott remained primarily just a PO and mercantile store until homesteaders arrived around 1915, when the population mushroomed. When the PO moved to Colfax County in 1935, the new settlement sometimes was referred to as *New Abbott*. Most houses in New Abbott have been abandoned, but a few inhabited residences survive; Old Abbott is abandoned, the townsite within a ranch. *Abbott Lake* is 9 mi SW of Abbott.

ABEYTAS (Socorro; settlement; on US 85, 14 mi S of Belen; PO 1914–45, mail to Bosque). Also known as *Los Abeytas*, this is one of several small Hispanic settlements along the Rio Grande whose names refer to families. The surname Abeyta evolved from de Veitia, possibly of Basque origin. Persons with this name entered New Mexico in 1692, and a Don Diego de Veitia—the name has been spelled numerous ways—was in Santa Fe in 1701. In 1735 an Antonio de Abeyta was listed as an officer in the militia at Santa Cruz, and as early as 1736 the *Antonio de Abeyta Grant* was made, 5 mi W of Embudo, on the Rio Ojo Caliente. Also in the 18th century, a member of this family married into a Rio Abajo family, and from a cluster of people named Abeyta evolved the place name *Los Abeytas.*

ABIQUIU (Rio Arriba; on US 84, 18 mi NW of Española; PO 1852 to present, with interruptions and temporary change to Joseph in 1884). This Hispanic settlement's name preserves, at least in some form, the name of the Tewa Indian Pueblo upon whose ruins the village originally was built. The name's meaning is obscure, though not for lack of research. All researchers agree the name is a corruption of a Pueblo Indian word, almost certainly Tewa. Some researchers have said it is a corruption of a word used at San Juan Pueblo to mean "ruins." Others have said it means "timber end place." Others have suggested the abandoned pueblo's name was *Abechiu*, said to mean "hooting of an owl." Still others have suggested such meanings as "large grove" and "chokecherry." Stanley Crocchiola summarized the situation best when he said, "With such diversified interpretations we can only say that the proper meaning is lost in antiquity."

The old pueblo was located at a place called *La Puente*, a mesa on the Rio

Chama's south bank, about 3 mi SE of the present village. The pueblo was abandoned, probably in the 1500s, and subsequently the Chama Valley here was shared by Utes, Apaches, and Navajos.

Abiquiu was slow in being settled by the Spanish, despite being fertile, well-watered, and only 40 miles from Santa Fe, the capital. The first settlers arrived at the old pueblo site in the 1740s and called their community *Santa Rosa de Lima de Abiquiú*, for their patron saint. In August, 1747, after devastating Indian raids, the villagers of Abiquiu, along with residents of Ojo Caliente and Pueblo Quemado (now Cordova), petitioned for permission to abandon their village and move to safer locations. That same year the present village of Abiquiu was founded by *genízaros*, Hispanicized Indians. These included some Hopis from north-central Arizona, and the buckskin leggings of these people inspired a nickname, "Big Leggings," for the village. Like the earlier village, the new one had a church and a patron saint, Santo Tomás.

Santa Rosa de Lima de Abiquiu was resettled in 1754, and the new village, Santo Tomás de Abiquiu, more commonly known simply as Abiquiu, grew as well and became a major Indian trade center. Santa Rosa de Lima de Abiquiu continued to be occupied into the 1800s, and its church was used into the 20th century, but now only a crumbling adobe wall remains, though restoration has been undertaken. Modern Abiquiu was made famous by being the longtime residence of artist Georgia O'Keeffe whose paintings often reflect the local landscape. Abiquiu has at least two suburbs, or neighborhoods: *El Curuco*, Spanish, "the tick, louse" to the W; and *La Careda*, Spanish, "the race," to the S.

Abiquiu Creek rises S of Abiquiu and flows through the village into the Rio Chama. *Mesa de Abiquiu* also is S of Abiquiu the village.

Abiquiu Mountain (Rio Arriba). See *Polvadera Peak*.

ABO (Torrance; archaeological/historic site; just N of US 60, 8 mi SW of Mountain-

air). As early as the Rodgríguez expedition of 1581–82 the Spanish were aware of an Indian pueblo at this site, and in 1598 Don Juan de Oñate visited an Indian pueblo here, one he identified as belonging to the Jumanos Indians, a Tompiro-speaking group, and that he called *Abó*. In 1629 Fray Francisco de Acevedo founded the Mission of San Gregorio here by building adjacent to the pueblo a large church and *convento*. But despite the church's massive walls that have survived more than 300 years, the mission and the pueblo could not withstand the persistent Apache raids that also plagued their neighbors at Quarai and Gran Quivira, and like them the mission and the pueblo were abandoned prior to the Pueblo Revolt of 1680. For reasons not known, the Tompiro pueblo bore a name resembling Abo and said to mean "water bowl." *Abo Spring* is 4 mi W of Abo ruins, at Abo Pass. The name *S. Gregorio de Abó* appeared on the Peñalosa map, prepared in 1686–88.

The ancient ruins were made a state monument in 1939; in 1981 the site became a unit of what is now *Salinas Pueblo Missions National Monument*. See also *Tenabo*.

Abo Pass (Valencia; 4 mi W of Abo ruins). A shallow gap separating the Manzano Mountains to the N and the Los Pinos Mountains to the S. Mentioned by Major J.H. Carleton in 1853.

ABO (Torrance; settlement; adjacent to archaeological site; PO 1910–14, mail to Mountainair).

ABREU (Colfax; settlement; on the Rayado River, 23 mi W of Springer, 12 mi S of Cimarron, on NM 21). When Lucien Maxwell, of the famous Maxwell land grant, departed from the pioneer settlement known then as *Rayado*, Maxwell's interests were managed by the Spaniard, José Pley. But when Pley also departed to return to Europe, his interest in the Rayado Ranch fell to Jesús G. Abreu, a son-in-law of Charles Beaubien, one of the original grantees. Abreu (locally pronounced ah-BRAY-yoo) spent the rest of his life in the area, and the Rayado settlement acquired his surname. His descendants still live in Las Vegas, and once a year they return to Abreu/Rayado to tend the Abreu cemetery there. Rayado/Abreu now is managed by the Philmont Scout Ranch. See *Rayado*.

Abreu Canyon (Colfax, heads SE of Beatty Lakes, NW of Cimarron, and flows SE into North Poñil Creek).

ABUELO (Mora; settlement; in the Cebolla Valley, 3 mi SW of Mora). This Spanish name means "grandfather," though in NM Spanish, *abuelo* also can mean "bogeyman," and the *abuelo* is one of the dancers in the *Matachines* ceremonies, terrifying children and exhorting them to say their prayers. Locally, this tiny inhabited Hispanic settlement is said to bear this name because someone's grandfather lived here.

ACEQUIA MADRE (general). Strictly speaking, this Spanish term means "mother ditch," the main canal that supplies irrigation water to smaller distribution ditches, but there's much more to the term than just that. *Acequia* is derived from an Arabic word that originally referred to the irrigation ditches used in North Africa; the Moorish invasion of Spain in the 8th century A.D. introduced the term to Spain, from whence it came to the New World. In NM the term *acequia madre* not only designated the main ditch but also symbolized the importance of water to the region. By 1900, more than 60 *acequias madres* existed in the Rio Grande Valley alone, each controlled by its *mayordomo*, or "ditch boss," a position of considerable influence and prestige as its holder is responsible for distributing the precious water and organizing the community each year to maintain the canal system. The old ditch on the S side of the Santa Fe River in Santa Fe is called specifically *Acequia Madre*, and the name has been transferred to an adjacent street.

ACME (Chaves; just S of US 70, 17 mi NE of Roswell; PO 1906–46, mail to Roswell). Acme was named for the Acme Gypsum Cement Co., which built a mill here that produced plaster and cement blocks until 1936. Now the mill, like the settlement nearby, has all but vanished; only foundations remain. Half a mile away, N of US 70, is the Acme Cemetery. 100 yards to the E is the stone shell of the Frazier School.

ACOMA PUEBLO (Cibola; settlement; 13 mi S of I-40 at Casa Blanca). When Fray Marcos de Niza in 1539 became the first non-Indian to hear of this Keresan village perched atop a 350-foot-high mesa, the name he remembered was *Ahacus*. When Hernando de Alvarado, with Coronado's expedition, the next year actually visited the pueblo, he heard its name as *Acuco*. It was not until 1583, with the visit of Antonio de Espejo, that the current spelling was first used. Acoma is Keresan and means "people of the white rock"; *aco*, "white rock," *ma* "people," though the visitor center at Acoma Pueblo relates an oral tradition that when the Acoma people left the *Shipapu*, the place of emergence into this world, in the north, they traveled south until they found *Hak'u*, "the place prepared."

Tribal traditions tell that the people of Acoma once lived on Enchanted Mesa just to the NE, settling in their present location after being forced to abandon Enchanted Mesa. Though the pueblo of Acoma is a natural citadel, it was beseiged successfully by Governor Oñate's soldiers in 1599 in reprisal for the killing of Oñate's nephew. The mission at Acoma was established in 1629 and dedicated to St. Stephen the Protomartyr, but his feast day, December 26, was so close to Christmas that St. Stephen, king of Hungary, whose feast day is September 2, became the pueblo's patron instead.

Several thousand persons may have lived at Acoma in 1540; today only a small population remains. Most Acoma Indians now live at *McCartys*, *Acomita*, and other Acoma Reservation settlements with better access and living conditions, though the ancient village is likely to survive as an important ceremonial center and tourist attraction. The pueblo's lofty location atop the mesa has led it often to be called *Sky City*.

Acoma Creek heads E of the pueblo to join the Rio San Jose at New Laguna.

ACOMILLA (Socorro; historic site; N of Alamillo and S of Sevilleta). During the colonial period, Acomilla, "little Acoma," was a landmark associated with the basalt-capped mesa of the present San Acacia area. A 1631 reference mentions an *estancia* and a pueblo here. It has been said the pueblo was called *Alamillo*, "little cottonwood," with Acomilla being the hill north of the pueblo. The origin of Acomilla is unknown.

ACOMITA (Cibola; on the Acoma Indian Reservation, approximately 11 mi W of Laguna, S of I–40; PO 1905–06, 1912–58, mail to San Fidel). Acomita, Spanish, "little Acoma," was settled, as its name implies, by residents of Acoma Pueblo to the S around 1870, when the danger of Navajo and Apache raids had passed and the Keresan agriculturalists could safely develop the fertile lands adjacent to the the Rio San Jose.

ADAIR CANYON, SPRING (Catron; 2.5 mi SE of Luna). Newton Adair camped at the spring and developed it. His descendants still live in the area.

ADAM HOAGUE LAKE (Catron; in the Mogollon Mountains, 4 mi SE of Bearwallow Mountain, 20 mi E of Mogollon). A man with this name attempted to homestead here.

ADAMS DIGGINGS (Catron; rural PO; 15 mi NE of Quemado, just E of the Continental Divide; PO 1930–45, mail to Pie Town). Among the Southwest's most celebrated and sought-after legendary lost mines, the Adams Diggings was named for a prospector named Adams who escaped from an Apache massacre of his fellow miners to tell of a fabulously wealthy lode that he never was able to relocate. It has been estimated to be within a triangle with corners at Grants, Silver City, and Alpine, AZ; treasure hunters have spent countless hours searching within this huge area.

But for a time the Adams Diggings was easy to find; one simply had to look on the state highway map where a locality appeared by that name. As a hobby, a NM Highway Dept. employee had spent time looking for the Diggings, finding only rattlesnakes, and when the employee in 1936 temporarily was assigned to mapmaking, as a joke he put on a draft map a small circle in an uninhabited area N of Pie Town where he'd been searching and labeled it Adams Diggings. Through oversight, the site appeared on the new map and remained there for many years, eliciting numerous inquiries to the Highway Dept. A rural post office named Adams Diggings existed NE of Quemado from 1930–45, near the site identified on the map.

ADAMS LAKE (Colfax; in NW part of county, between Castle Rock and Ash Mountain). Named for a prominent local family.

ADBURG (Quay; settlement; on CRI&P RR and US 54, 5 mi NE of Tucumcari). Now primarily a RR siding, Adburg took the name of its first settler.

ADELINO (Valencia; settlement; on NM 47, 3 mi S of Tome; PO 1911–16; mail to Tome). The present name for this small but growing settlement on the Rio Grande's E bank was bestowed by Jesús Sánchez, an early settler and prominent citizen, to honor his first-born son, Adelino Sánchez. But early census records and the recollections of longtime residents indicate that the village originally was called *Los Enlames*, "green moss, slime" such as exists along the Rio Grande in swampy areas, and it was mentioned by this name in Governor Armijo's report of 1840. The village also has been referred to as *Los Ranchos de Tomé*, "the farmsteads of Tome."

ADEN (Doña Ana; settlement; in SW part of county on SP RR; PO, 1894–98). Aden, now just a RR siding, was created and named when the SP RR tapped a spring in the nearby Aden Hills and piped water to a water stop. All the Aden names in the area—siding, Aden Hills, Aden Lava Flow—likely are derived from *Aden Cone*, named by the RR and located, like the famed Rock of Aden on the sea route from Suez to India, in the crater of an extinct volcano, the *Crater of Aden*, 1 mi SE of Aden. Aden Cone was mined for cinders. The *Aden Hills*, 4 mi

NE of Aden, are low, inconspicuous hills.

ADOBE (Socorro; on US 380, 32 mi E of San Antonio; PO, 1933–38, mail to Bingham). Several places in NM have Spanish names referring to the locality's soil, among them Tierra Amarilla (Rio Arriba, "yellow earth"), Arenal (Bernalillo, "sandy"), Negra (Torrance, "black"), and this abandoned settlement. The term *adobe*, Arabic in origin, was brought by the Spanish to the New World, where it sometimes is corrupted by English speakers into *dobe*, or *dobie.*

AEROPLANE MESA (Catron; in Gila Wilderness, near headwaters of Middle Fork of Gila River). As local people tell the story, Claire Chennault, later of Flying Tiger fame in WW II, and other pilots of the US Army mail service would touch down often on this remote mesa, hike down to the Middle Fork of the Gila River, fish, and then return. On at least one occasion, however, Chennault's plane crashed here, hence the name.

AFTON (Doña Ana; postal locality; on SP RR 20 mi SW of Las Cruces; PO, 1924–41). Only loading chutes and foundations mark the site of this former PO along the RR. The name's origin is unknown, though Scots-Irish ancestry was common among RR workers, and the Afton River of Scotland is a likely eponym.

AGRICULTURAL COLLEGE (Doña Ana). See *University Park.*

AGUA (Santa Fe; settlement; 2.5 mi S of Golden, 0.5 mi W of NM 14). Once part of the San Pedro Land Grant, this former settlement took its name from a bountiful spring, which gave a name to *Cañon del Agua* nearby. Local people recognize the locality as the site of the Palo Amarillo Ranch, and while the settlement has vanished, the locality still is inhabited.

AGUA AZUL (Cibola). See *Bluewater.*

AGUA CHIQUITA CREEK (Otero; heads in the Sacramento Mountains, runs NE to join the Rio Peñasco). Spanish, "pretty little water," and numerous summer camps and cabins along the creek, along with the name, testify to the creek's

pleasantness. Most natural features in this region bear names given by Spanish-speaking settlers of the 1800s; later English-speaking settlers often corrupted the Spanish pronunciations; the creek's name sometimes is pronounced AH-wah chi-KEET.

AGUA DEL LOBO (Taos). See *Lobo.*

AGUA FRIA (general). This Spanish name meaning "cold water" occurs 15 times in NM (GNIS), usually on creeks. Names referring to "hot water," especially *ojo caliente*, "hot springs," occur 9 times (GNIS).

AGUA FRIA. (Colfax; settlement; between Angel Fire and Eagle Nest, at junction of US 64 and NM 38; PO 1919–33, mail to Therma). Small inhabited settlement in the southern Moreno Valley, named for *West Agua Fria Creek*, which joins Cieneguilla Creek at the village of Agua Fria. *Agua Fria Peak*, 11,086 ft., is 7 mi SE of the village; *Agua Fria Lake* is NE of Agua Fria Peak.

AGUA FRIA (Santa Fe; settlement; SW of Santa Fe on the Santa Fe River, 3 mi N of I-25). Inhabited community, now a suburb of Santa Fe, that takes its name from frigid water flowing from springs and wells in the village. Some scholars believe Agua Fria occupies the site of an abandoned Indian pueblo called *Quemado*, (Spanish, "burned"), because it had been burned, intentionally; Fray Francisco Atanasio Domínguez knew the locality by that name in 1776, though the site he knew probably was in a slightly different location from the present village.

AGUA NEGRA (Guadalupe; settlement; on Agua Negra Creek, SW of Santa Rosa; PO 1868–69). Abandoned community, named for the creek, whose name locally doesn't refer so much to the water's color as to its being foul-smelling, "sewer water."

AGUA NEGRA (Mora). See *Holman.*

AGUA PIEDRA CREEK (Taos; heads S of Tres Ritos, enters the Rio Pueblo just W of the village). Spanish, "rock water," or simply "rocky creek."

AGUA VIVA (Taos; settlement; on US 64, 10 mi E of Taos in Taos Canyon). Spanish, "living water," probably referring to a spring. Tiny residential cluster.

AGUA ZARCA (general). Spanish, "light-blue water." A common name for water bodies, especially creeks.

AGUA ZARCA (San Miguel; settlement; on NM 283, 4 mi SW of Las Vegas). Tiny Hispanic village, now abandoned, named for its location on *Agua Zarca Creek.*

AGUAJE (general). Spanish, "watering place." For instance, the chronicles of Vargas's 1692 reconquest of NM mention his stopping at *Aguaje del Entretenimiento* "watering place of the amusement," *Aguaje de los Chupaderos,* "watering place of the sinkholes," and *Aguaje de la Magdalena.*

AGUDO (De Baca; settlement; on AT&SF RR, 6 mi S of Fort Sumner; PO 1909–1913, mail to Ricardo). Spanish, "sharp, pointed, keen." Agudo was an active settlement during RR construction in 1906–07 and later was a section house. It since has vanished. Name origin unknown.

AGUILA (San Miguel; settlement; on the E bank of the Gallinas River, 2 mi SE of Chaperito). Abandoned settlement, whose Spanish name means "eagle."

SIERRA AGUILADA (Catron; in W part of county, SE of San Francisco Mountains and W of Glenwood). Small range whose Spanish name likely means "mountains of eagles," and indeed eagles are common in the area. The name appeared on military and other maps of the late 1800s but was dropped from later maps; a 1974 USBGN decision restored it. *Glenwood Brushy,* 7,405 ft., is the highest summit.

AGUIRRE SPRING (Doña Ana; on the E side of the Organ Mountains, about 3.5 mi S of US 70). This popular recreation site, managed by the BLM, bears a Spanish surname. While the specific origin of the name here is unknown, it very likely is related to the Aguirre family that was prominent in Las Cruces at the time of the Civil War.

AHMEGO. See *Lockney.*

AH-SHI-SLE-PAH WASH. (San Juan; heads SW of Kimbeto and runs SW to join Chaco Wash E of Lake Valley). Significant drainage, with a Navajo name meaning "gray silt." The area includes scenic and interesting polychrome eroded land forms; 6,563 acres of it comprise the *Ah-shi-sle-pah Wilderness Study Area,* administered as wilderness by the BLM.

AIR BASE CITY (Lea; settlement; 6 mi NW of Hobbs, at Hobbs Industrial Park). Modern suburban settlement named for the airfield here, which is called *Air Base City Airport.*

CERRO DEL AIRE, 9,023 ft. (Taos; mountain; 6 mi NE of Tres Piedras). Spanish, "breezy," and this isolated extinct volcano would indeed be exposed to the wind. Local English-speakers call it *Wind Mountain.*

AIROLO (Union; settlement; on E bank of Ute Creek, SE of Gladstone; PO 1905–09, mail to Pasamonte). Little is known about this ephemeral community, though it is said to have been christened by Carl Gilg, who also established the Pasamonte PO (see entry).

AKELA (Luna; trading point and RR siding; 22 mi E of Deming, at junction of I-10 and SP RR; PO 1921–40, 1941–43, mail to Cambray). Akela was the leader of the wolf pack in Rudyard Kipling's Mowgli stories, though local people have heard it means "eagle" in an Indian language. Like many names given by RR officials in the 1880s, this name's true origin probably will never be known. The locality survives as a trading point.

ALACRAN HILLS (Eddy; immediately NE of Carlsbad, SE of Avalon Reservoir). Spanish, "scorpion." Though this is the name that appears on most maps, these low hills are more often known locally as the *Cedar Hills.* And while scorpions certainly are found in the area, they are not particularly common in these hills.

ALAMEDA (Bernalillo; pueblo, settlement; on the E bank of the Rio Grande, N of Albuquerque, near the intersection of Alameda Blvd. and Fourth Street; PO 1866–68, 1890–1960, mail to Albuquerque). The Spanish *alameda* means "cottonwood grove"—see *Alamo (general)*—and because cottonwoods require a dependable water source, such groves would have been natural sites for settlement. Coronado found a Tiwa pueblo here when he arrived at the Rio Grande in 1540, and his chronicler mentions Spanish officers trailing stolen stock to this pueblo.

Eventually, the Alameda Tiwas moved to Isleta and were replaced by Spanish settlers. In 1696, a group of settlers petitioned to relocate from *La Villa Nueva de Santa Cruz* to Alameda, and in 1710 Governor Peñuela rewarded Capt. Francisco Montes Vigil with a large grant here. Two years later, Vigil sold the grant to Juan González, who built a chapel; the parish was named *San Carlos,* dedicated to St. Charles Boromeo, 16th-century Cardinal Archbishop of Milan. Other settlers soon followed, most from Albuquerque, and soon a village emerged that is still inhabited.

ALAMILLO PUEBLO (Socorro; settlement; on the E bank of the Rio Grande, NE of its junction with the Rio Puerco). Though he didn't mention it, Don Juan de Oñate doubtless knew of the Piro pueblo called by the Spaniards Alamillo when he journeyed up the Rio Grande in 1598. The name first appears in historical records in 1626, when an unsigned document recorded a conversation at Alamillo in which Governor Eulate took part. Archaeologists have been unable to locate the pueblo's exact site, though they know it was near the Rio Grande, S of *Alamillo Arroyo,* and this is enough to account for the name, for such a well-watered location certainly would have nurtured the "little cottonwood" the name means. Alamillo was closely associated with the nearby Piro pueblo of Seelocu (see entry).

The Piro pueblo was abandoned during the Pueblo Revolt in 1680, and Vargas in 1692 mentioned that it was not reoccupied; very likely the site later was destroyed by floods.

A post-Revolt settlement of Alamillo, named after the pueblo, also was located on the Rio Grande's E bank, but it was not mentioned in documents after 1800.

A territorial village named Alamillo (see entry), located on the W bank and possibly associated with mining in the Sierra Ladrones to the W, appears on an 1859 US War Department map and also on the Wheeler map of 1873–78, where it is shown as the W-bank sister of La Joyita (see entry).

ALAMILLO (Socorro; settlement; on the W bank of the Rio Grande, W of San Acacia). The name of this inhabited settlement probably was taken from earlier settlements in the vicinity named Alamillo, though certainly a "little cottonwood" could easily have inspired the name independently. See *Alamillo* above.

ALAMILLOS (Doña Ana; settlement; S of Las Cruces, exact location uncertain). Spanish, "little cottonwoods." This was a stopping place one day's journey N from El Paso and was mentioned in an 1846 account. It was subject to flooding; in 1884 the old town was abandoned and its residents moved to higher ground. Later the locality was called *Cottonwoods,* translating the Spanish name. While its exact location is subject to debate, many people have put it near Berino.

ALAMITOS (San Miguel; settlement; in NE part of county, W of the Canadian River). Abandoned *comanchero* settlement.

ALAMO (general). Throughout the Southwest, the bright green heart-shaped leaves of the moisture-loving *álamo,* or cottonwood (genus *Populus*), signal the presence of precious water, and thus Spanish place names referring to cottonwoods are among the most common in the region. In NM the variants include *Los Alamos, Alameda, Alamillo, Alamitos, Alamocita,* and *Alamogordo,* appearing on countless canyons, peaks, and settlements but especially on springs, creeks, and other water bodies. GNIS lists 112 names that include *álamo* or one of its variants. The name appears in Navajo as *t'iis,* and the related *t'iistsoh* is what Navajos call the community of *Alamo* (Socorro), an example of parallel names in dissimilar languages. See *Cottonwood (general)* .

ALAMO (Guadalupe; settlement; 17 mi SE of Cuervo; PO 1906–29, mail to Santa Rosa). Abandoned homesteader community.

ALAMO (Socorro; settlement; at the end of NM 169, 32 mi NW of Magdalena). This inhabited settlement, headquarters for the Alamo Band Navajo Indians, likely was named for the Alamo Navajo Band (see below), named in turn for *Alamo Spring*, 3 mi to the SE of the village of Alamo.

ALAMO BAND NAVAJO INDIAN RESERVATION (Socorro; in the NW part of the county). This reservation, along with the Cañoncito and Ramah Navajo Reservations, is separate from the main Navajo Reservation. Removed from the main tribe for more than a hundred years, this group is said to have developed in part from Navajo slaves who fled their Hispanic masters in Socorro; they congregated at *Alamo Spring,* hence their subsequent name. Here they intermarried with Chiricahua and other Apaches, who preferred to be classified as Navajos to avoid being sent to the Apache reservations. The Alamo Navajos also were joined by other Navajos fleeing Kit Carson's campaigns. Between 1912 and 1920, land allotments were made to the Alamo Navajos; these and subsequent land purchases became the basis for the current reservation, which comprises 56,670 acres. Its population is approximately 2,000.

ALAMO CANYON (Otero; on W side of the Sacramento Mountains, just SE of Alamogordo). See *Alamogordo, Alamo Spring.*

ALAMO HUECO MOUNTAINS (Hidalgo; in SE corner of county, 4 mi from Mexico and E of NM 81). The most plausible translation of this Spanish name is "spongy cottonwood." Highest elevation, unnamed summit, 6,838 ft., highest named summit, *Pierce Peak,* 6,149 ft. A tiny ranching settlement named *Alamo Hueco* is in the mountains' western foothills.

ALAMO PEAK, 9,685 feet. (Otero; in Sacra-mento Mountains, 8 mi E of Alamogordo). One of many *álamo*—see *Alamo (general)*—names in this region. This mountain was first called *Hurschburger Peak,* for an early prospector, and had it retained that name it would have avoided being confused with another *Alamo Peak* only 5 mi W.

ALAMOCITA (Sierra; settlement; at the mouth of Cañada Alamosa, near its confluence with the Rio Grande). Abandoned Hispanic community. See *Monticello.*

ALAMOGORDO (Otero; settlement; on US 54-70 and SP RR, at W base of Sacramento Mountains and E side of Tularosa Valley; PO 1898–present). In 1895 a young boy named Carroll Woods accompanied RR developer Charles B. Eddy on Eddy's first visit to *Alamo Spring,* sometimes called *Alamogordo Spring,* in *Alamo Canyon,* just SE of the present town of Alamogordo. Years later, Woods recalled the trip: "When we got to Alamo Spring, we found a beautiful pool of water, eight feet in diameter and possibly four or five feet deep.... Three huge cottonwoods, whose branches spread shade over a space about 150 feet in diameter, grew around the spring in the form of a triangle." A board nailed to one of the trees said, "*Ojo de Alamogordo,*" or "big cottonwood spring."

Soon thereafter Eddy bought the spring from rancher Oliver M. Lee to furnish water for the RR town he and his brother, John Arthur Eddy, were planning nearby. The townsite itself was purchased and laid out in 1898.

In 1923, on the 25th anniversary of the town's founding, J. Arthur Eddy (as he signed his name) wrote about how he named the town: "It devolved upon me to name the stations on the road, and in doing so I sought to apply those of local characteristics or landmarks. It would have been natural, therefore, to use the word *álamo,* but it was objectionable because of its being so common and so many *álamos.* In my cowboy days, one of my favorite camping places between Las

Vegas and Seven Rivers was on a little stream running into the E side of the Pecos called 'Alamo Gordo' [see *Alamogordo Creek*]. I had learned its meaning to be a big or 'Rotund' cottonwood, and upon seeing such a tree or the relic of such a tree, at the mouth of Alamo Cañon, the name came back impressively to me. And that is how Alamogordo got its name."

Alamogordo is the seat of Otero County, created in 1899, in part because of burgeoning RR development. Today, the role of the RR has receded, but Alamogordo has continued to grow because of scientific and military installations in the area, as well as tourism and ranching. And perhaps as a reminder of the city's namesake, large cottonwoods grow along Alamogordo's White Sands Boulevard.

ALAMOGORDO ARMY AIR FIELD. See *Holloman Air Force Base*.

ALAMOGORDO CREEK (Quay, De Baca, Guadalupe; heads in W Quay County, just below the caprock in the Alamogordo Valley, flows SW into the Pecos River at Sumner Lake). Flowing streams are rare in this arid region, making Alamogordo Creek a major landmark and focus for settlement. Named for the large cottonwoods along its banks; see *Alamo (general)*.

ALAMOGORDO LAKE (De Baca). See *Sumner Lake*.

CAÑADA ALAMOSA (Sierra). See *Monticello Canyon*.

ALAMOSA CREEK (Quay, Curry, De Baca; rises in western Quay County, flows SE to Curry County line, turns and flows SW to enter Taiban Creek W of De Baca line). Another "cottonwood" name; see *Alamo (general)*.

ALAMOSA RIVER (Socorro, Sierra; rises on the NW slopes of the San Mateo Mountains, flows S and then SE to enter the Rio Grande at Elephant Butte Reservoir). The villages of Monticello and Placita, as well as numerous farms and ranches and the abandoned Warm Springs Apache Indian Reservation, are located along this flowing stream lined with cottonwoods. *Cañada Alamosa*, also called Monticello Canyon, named for the river, runs from Ojo Caliente to Monticello.

ALASKA (Cibola; settlement; W of the Rio San Jose, 2 mi W of Acomita). Tiny inhabited residential cluster, once a RR station. The name appears on a 1905 map, but its origin is unknown.

ALBEMARLE (Sandoval; settlement; in the SW Jemez Mountains, in Colle Canyon; PO 1901–03, mail to Bland). Of the 13 mining claims that comprised the Albemarle group, four prominent ones were the Albemarle, Pamlico, Ontario, and Huron. Of these names, two—Albemarle and Pamlico—also are the names of coastal features in North Carolina, and they likely were transferred here. The name Albemarle is derived from George Monck, or Monk, a 17th-century professional soldier in England whose successes enabled him to become George, Duke of Albemarle, and in further gratitude the English royalty named several places along the eastern North American seaboard for him, including Albemarle Sound. The mining claims of the Albemarle group were filed in 1894 and later acquired by the Cochiti Gold Mining Co., which developed the mines and created the mining camp. Albemarle often was considered to be part of Bland, a larger mining camp 1.5 miles to the NE in Bland Canyon.

ALBERT (Harding; settlement; on Tequesquite Creek, 13 mi NE of Mosquero; PO as Tequesquite 1879–90, as Albert 1890–1961, mail to a rural station of Mosquero). The first settlers here called this tiny ranching community *Tequesquite*, for it location on Tequesquite Creek, whose name is New World Spanish for "alkali." In 1890, however, the name was changed to honor Albert Mitchell, a prominent cattleman. The Tequesquite Ranch, still owned by Mitchell's descendants, surrounds Albert and uses the former community as its headquarters.

ALBUQUERQUE (Bernalillo; settlement, county seat; on the Rio Grande, W of the Sandia Mountains, on the AT&SF RR and at the junction of I-25 and I-40; PO 1851–82, mail to New Albuquerque, 1882–present). A long and complex history lies behind the name of NM's largest city, a history that in many ways reflects that of the state itself.

The area now occupied by Albuquerque certainly was settled and named by Native Americans before Coronado's arrival in 1540, but their names, like so many prehistoric names, have been lost. Spanish settlers replaced the Indians, and when the Spanish governor of NM, Don Francisco Cuervo y Valdes, early in 1706 sent Juan Ulibarri to the area to determine its suitability for settlement, Ulibarri reported that it was "a very good place for a new villa." At the time of Ulibarri's visit, the locality was called *Bosque Grande de Doña Luisa, Estancia de Doña Luisa de Trujillo, San Francisco Xavier del Bosque Grande*, and, more commonly, simply *Bosque Grande*, "big forest, thicket."

Gov. Cuervo y Valdes accepted Ulibarri's report and soon thereafter authorized the founding of NM's third villa (after Santa Fe and Santa Cruz). He named it *San Francisco de Alburquerque*, in honor of Don Francisco Fernandez de la Cueva Enríquez, Duke of Alburquerque, 34th Viceroy of New Spain, then resident in Mexico City. Don Francisco Fernandez was the second duke titled Alburquerque to serve as Viceroy of New Spain and was the tenth in succession from the first Duke of Alburquerque, Don Beltrán de la Cueva, who received the dukedom in 1464 from King Enríque IV. The city for which the dukedom was named once was encompassed by Portugal, but it now is within the province of Badajoz, Spain, about 10 miles E of the Portuguese border. The dukedom of Alburquerque still exists, and occasionally the current duke visits the NM city.

The name Alburquerque most likely developed from one of several Spanish forms of the Latin *albus quercus*, "white oak" (the trunk of the cork oak is white after the outer layer has been exposed);

the seal of the Spanish city of Alburquerque bears the design of an oak.

It also is remotely possible, however, that the name is Arabic in origin, as the Spanish city is in a region ruled for centuries by the Moors, and the *al* prefix, the definite article in Arabic, is extremely common in Arabic names of all kinds, including place names. Indeed, many Hispanic names in New Mexico have an Arabic etymology: Alcalde, (from Arabic *al-qadi*, "the judge," and Alkali (from *al-qaliy*, "the ashes of saltwort.") Assuming an Arabic origin for Alburquerque, the most likely etymology would be *al burquq*, "the plum."

Gov. Cuervo y Valdes, in choosing St. Francis Xavier, Apostle of the Indies, as the new villa's patron, honored not only his own patron saint but also that of the viceroy. The Duke of Alburquerque, however, fearing the displeasure of King Philip V of Spain, who had not authorized the villa, changed the name to *San Felipe de Alburquerque*, honoring the monarch's patron saint. The church of *San Felipe Neri* on Old Town Plaza honors St. Philip Neri, a 16th-century priest of Rome and founder of a religious congregation. The new name did not gain immediate acceptance, however; according to Fray Angélico Chávez, Franciscans continued using *San Francisco de Alburquerque*, and occasionally, *San Felipe Apostól*, until 1776 when they finally began using *San Felipe Neri* as a title.

Throughout the colonial period and even into the 19th century, as the settlement grew in importance, its name preserved the original spelling, but English-speaking travelers arriving early in the 19th century began to drop the first *r*. Zebulon Pike in 1807, George W. Kendall in 1841, and J.F. Meline in 1866 all spelled it "Albuquerque," even though Escudero's *Noticias* of 1849 continued the original spelling. It's possible that confusion with a titled Portuguese family named Albuquerque, or Alboquerque, contributed to the present spelling. In 1993, the well-known NM author Rudolfo Anaya published a novel about the city he entitled *Alburquerque*, using the original spelling, and upon his urging other people began suggesting the city return to having two *r*'s in the name; in the 1995 state legislature a non-binding resolution was passed also recommending the original spelling, but informal polls showed the public divided over the issue, and in 1995 few, if any, signs had actually been changed.

The matter of the name's form became even more complicated later in the 19th century with the arrival of the RR. In 1879 the NM Townsite Co., a subsidiary of the AT&SF RR, founded a new town in anticipation of the first trains, which entered the new station on April 22, 1880. Soon there were two Albuquerques, and two POs: the old town centered on the plaza and the new town centered on the RR station to the E. As Marc Simmons has described the situation, "Local controversy over who was entitled ownership of Albuquerque's historic name continued for several years. Then, in 1886, the postal authorities effected a compromise by designating the west station, *Old Albuquerque*, and the east station, *New Albuquerque*. It proved an easy way out, particularly since by this time people had developed the habit of referring to the former as *Old Town* and the latter as *New Town*. Later, of course, as New Albuquerque reached out to engulf the plaza, the day came when it could legitimately drop the qualifying adjective."

Though Albuquerque seems a distinctive name, in fact it appears on other towns and features throughout the world in the former Spanish empire. Indeed, the Albuquerque Cays off the Nicaraguan coast even have evolved into the same misspelling as the NM city. What makes the name unique here is that it honors a member of the Spanish nobility and the governmental hierarchy in the New World, something the Spanish namers in NM did with few, if any, other names here.

The name by which Navajos know Albuquerque is simpler; it means "two large bells in place," a reference to an early bell tower.

ALCALDE (Rio Arriba; settlement; on the E side of the Rio Grande, 7 mi N of Española on NM 68; PO as Los Luceros, 1855–70, as Plaza de Alcalde 1877–82, as Alcalde 1890–92, 1894–present). The Spanish word *alcalde* was derived from two Arabic words *al*, "the," and *qadi*, "judge," but in Spanish North America the word also was used to designate the chief civil officer of an area, and the region over which an *alcalde* presided was known as an *alcaldía*. Though no specific *alcalde* has been associated with this small Hispanic community, the name likely was derived from an *alcalde* living here. From 1860 to 1880, this village was the seat of Rio Arriba County.

Three miles N of Alcalde was the settlement originally known as *Plaza de los Luceros*, or simply *Los Luceros*, doubtless from a local family, until it was changed to *Plaza de Alcalde* in 1870. Its relationship to the present village of Alcalde is unclear.

ALCANFOR (Sandoval; settlement; on the W bank of the Rio Grande, in Coronado State Monument, 2 mi NW of Bernalillo). When Coronado and his Spanish army reached the Rio Grande in 1540, they wintered near a Tiwa pueblo the Spaniards called Alcanfor, which some authorities believe to be the pueblo now called Kuaua (see entry), whose ruins are the focus of Coronado State Monument. The Spanish *alcanfor* means "camphor," but why the Spaniards referred to the pueblo by this name is unknown, though possibly they were attempting to reproduce a Tiwa name as they wrote it at least once as *Coofor*.

ALCATRAZ (San Juan; settlement; approx. 0.75 mi S of Turley on NM 511, on the S side of the San Juan River; PO 1892–94, mail to Largo). This Hispanic settlement of the upper San Juan River region began in the 1870s at Manzonares, near where Largo Canyon meets the river. Soon a church was built, and the area near the church became known as Alcatraz. Though the name's origin is a mystery, one local theory is that it was inspired by the location's isolation and difficulty of access, like that of the well-known former federal prison in California. Though a few residences still are at the site of Alcatraz, nothing proclaims the name, and it's not used or recognized except by old-timers.

ALDO LEOPOLD WILDERNESS (Sierra, Grant, Catron; astride the Black Range, between Silver City and Truth or Consequences). Originally part of the Gila Wilderness and administered by the USFS, this 206,016-acre tract includes the wildest portions of the Black Range. It honors longtime USFS employee Aldo Leopold, who as a young ranger was introduced to the wilderness here and became a leading proponent of the designation of the Gila Wilderness (see entry), the nation's first wilderness area. Later, through writings such as *A Sand County Almanac* (1949), Leopold argued eloquently the value of preserving wilderness.

ALEGRES MOUNTAINS, MOUNTAIN, 10,244 ft. (Catron; along the Continental Divide, S of Pie Town). Spanish, "happy, bright." The name here, whose origin is unknown, sometimes is spelled *Alegros* or *Allegros*, but in 1977 the USBGN established Alegres as the accepted form.

ALELLEN (Chaves). See *Orchard Park*.

ALEMAN (Sierra; settlement, campground, RR siding; on the AT&SF RR, on the Jornada del Muerto, 13 mi S of Engle; PO 1869–90, mail to Detroit). This name recalls a German-born trader named Bernardo Gruber who around 1670 was imprisoned in Santa Fe, having been accused of witchcraft; he escaped and was fleeing S over the Camino Real when he perished or was killed. From the discovery of his desiccated corpse the name Jornada del Muerto (see entry) is believed to have evolved. The site of Gruber's death became a *paraje*, or campground for travelers, known as *La Cruz del Alemán*, or "the cross of the German," later simply *El Alemán*.

The campsite was still called La Cruz del Alemán when Josiah Gregg passed through early in the 19th century, and it was still an important stop on the Jornada. During rainy seasons, water collected in low spots, and several wells were attempted. Sometimes the site was known as *Martin's Well*. When the El Paso to Santa Fe stage route began operating on the Jornada in 1860, the name Aleman was continued on a stage stop. Finally, around 1868, a significant well was dug and a ranch established that also served as a PO. A working ranch still exists at the site, its name still recalling the unfortunate German who died here so long ago.

ALGODONES (Sandoval; settlement; 7 mi NE of Bernalillo on US 85; PO 1855–81, 1898–1966, mail to a rural Bernalillo branch). The Spanish word, *algodón*, originally from Arabic, means "cotton," and some records state this inhabited village on the Rio Grande floodplain was named for cotton fields planted soon after the village was settled; an apocryphal story says cotton seeds from the Nile Valley in Egypt were planted here in the early 1700s. Cotton was indeed grown here, but more likely the name was derived from the *algodón* produced by the huge cottonwood trees common in the area.

ALHAMBRA (Grant; settlement; in central part of county, NW of Tyrone; PO 1890–1902, mail to Silver City). This abandoned mining camp took the name of the Alhambra silver mine here, named in turn for the luxurious palace and citadel built in the 13th century by the Moorish kings at Granada. The name comes from the Arabic *al-hamra*, meaning "the red one."

ALIRE (Rio Arriba; settlement; at junction of the Rio Cebolla and Arroyo Blanco, W of Canjilon; PO 1923–25, mail to Cebolla). Little remains of this former settlement; it bears the Hispanic family name, Alire; persons with this name were in NM at least as early as 1790.

ALIRE (Socorro; mining camp; near the former mining camp of Carthage, 13 mi SE of San Antonio). Abandoned mining camp, name origin unknown but possibly associated with Pierre Allaire, a merchant in nearby San Antonio, or with someone bearing the Hispanic surname, Alire.

ALKALI (general). Throughout the Southwest's arid regions, evaporation of mineral-laden water from soil frequently results in extensive white deposits on which only a few plants can live. Early travelers and settlers avoided the barren, poisonous wastes, but alkali deposits became landmarks nonetheless, and thus names such as *Alkali Flat* became common. The word *alkali* comes from the Arabic, *al-qaliy*, "ashes of saltwort." The name element is common in NM, appearing 17 times in GNIS; the Spanish form *tequesquite* appears only twice.

ALLEN (Quay; settlement; in SE part of county, 8 mi SW of Endee; PO 1906–16, mail to Endee). When the community of Endee moved 3 mi N to its present site near the CRI&P RR, the vacuum at the former site was filled by a homesteader community that used the Allen PO for its nucleus. James P. Allen and his wife ran the PO and store, and the community took their name. Today, nothing remains of Allen but some earthen mounds, broken fences, and a graveyard.

ALLERTON (Sandoval; settlement; between Cochiti Pueblo and Bland; 1894–96, mail to Bland). Once a small but active timber and mining camp, likely succeeded by *Woodbury*; name origin unknown. See *Woodbury*.

ALLIE (Roosevelt; settlement; in SE part of county, 3 mi S of Causey; PO 1912–23, mail to Emzy). This abandoned homesteader community was named for its first postmistress, Allie M. Gilmore.

ALLISON (Grant; settlement; in E part of county, W of the Mimbres River, NW of Dwyer; PO 1893–1901, mail to Faywood). John H. Allison, member of a locally prominent ranching family, was the first postmaster of this abandoned settlement.

ALLISON (McKinley; settlement; 2 mi W of Gallup, on local road; PO 1912–37, mail to Gallup). The inhabited community of Allison, originally a company-owned town, was the creation of the Victor American Coal Co., and it was named for Fletcher J. Allison, a company offi-cial. The Allison Mine was acquired by Allison in 1897.

ALMA (Catron; settlement; in SW corner of county, on US 180, 9 mi W of Mogollon; PO 1882–96, 1900–31, mail to Glenwood). Alma was born in 1878 when a party of settlers arrived here from Prescott, AZ. They called their location *Mogollon*, for the Mogollon Mountains (see entry) to the E, and some irreverently referred to it as *Parasite Valley*, "parasite" believed to be a meaning for *mogollón*. But among the early settlers here was Capt. J.G. Birney, and when he purchased the townsite from W.H. McCullough, a native New Mexican, Birney changed the site's name from Mogollon to Alma. Some persons have said the name honored his mother, others have said his wife, and still others have said Birney took the name from the Latin *alma*, "nourishment," because that's what the valley provided the settlers. (Birney later was killed by Indians and Mexicans.) Despite frequent Indian danger, mining and rich farmland caused the community to thrive. At one time Butch Cassidy and some of the Wild Bunch worked at the nearby WS Ranch. Alma has lost population over the years, but the community continues to survive.

ALTAMONT (Rio Arriba; settlement; location unknown; PO 1883–84). Ephemeral locality, exact location unknown, though perhaps the name, manufactured from Spanish words, offers a clue; it is intended to mean "high mountain."

ALTA VISTA (San Miguel; settlement; on NM 104, 3 mi W of Trujillo). Tiny inhabited High Plains community. The name is Spanish, "high view."

ALTO (Lincoln; settlement; on NM 48, 9 mi NW of Ruidoso; PO 1901–present). The Spanish *alto* means "high," and this small farming and ranching community, settled in 1882, was named by postmaster W.H. Walker for its location high in the mountains, at an elevation of more than 7,300 ft. The well-known cowboy writer, Eugene Manlove Rhodes, taught in the rural school here in 1891–92.

When Rhodes was here, the community was known as *Eagle Creek*, for the stream that flows through the community.

CERRO ALTO (Cibola; in W part of county, N of Fence Lake). A prominent volcanic cone whose name in both Spanish and Navajo means "high hill."

ALUM CAMP, ALUMINA (Grant; settlement; at the base of Alum Mountain, 3 mi S of Gila Hot Springs; PO 1890–94, mail to Pinos Altos). Residents of this abandoned mining camp mined meerschaum, the heat-resistant mineral used in tobacco pipes, and not alum, despite its presence in the nearby mountain.

ALUM CANYON, ALUM MOUNTAIN, 6,881 ft. (Grant; in Gila Wilderness, 3 mi S of Gila Hot Springs, E of the Gila River). Alum is abundant in the rocks and soil here.

AMADO (Cibola; settlement; 6 mi NE of San Mateo; PO 1900–05, mail to San Mateo). Though this Spanish name means "loved one, beloved," the name here is said to recall Amado Chávez, one of the owners of the San Mateo Cattle Co.

AMALIA (Taos; settlement; 5 mi SE of Costilla on NM 196; PO as Pina 1900–19, as Amalia 1919–present). The original PO name of *Pina* probably was a corruption of the Spanish *pino*, "pine." The community now bears a Spanish feminine personal name, for reasons unknown.

AMARGO (Rio Arriba). See *Lumberton*.

AMARGO CREEK (Rio Arriba; rises W of the Continental Divide W of Chama and flows NW into the Navajo River). This stream, whose Spanish name means "bitter" and doubtless was derived from bitter-tasting minerals in its water, flows through the town of Dulce, whose Spanish name means "sweet," derived from the taste of spring water there.

AMBROSIA LAKE (McKinley; 21 mi N of Grants). This small, dry lake takes its name from Don Ambrosio Trujillo of San Mateo, who homesteaded here in the 1870s. Trujillo ditched off several watercourses to create the lake, and he and his wife, Serafina Montaño of Cubero, raised seven children here. The contemporary name Ambrosia is a corruption of *Ambrosio*, but despite occasional efforts to change it to reflect the name's true history, it persists on maps. See *Ambrosia Lake* (settlement).

AMBROSIA LAKE (McKinley; settlement; 18 mi N of Grants on NM 509, 3 mi SE of Ambrosia Lake). Small inhabited community associated with uranium mining and milling. Named for nearby Ambrosia Lake (see entry).

AMERICAN VALLEY (Socorro; settlement; location unknown; PO 1887, mail to Socorro). Ephemeral settlement, name origin unknown.

AMISTAD (Union; settlement; in S part of county, on NM 402; PO 1907–present). In 1878 the site of Amistad was a cattle drive stop. Its history as a community dates from 1906, when Rev. Henry S. Wannamaker, a Congregational minister, joined other persons from the East in rushing to homestead on NM's eastern plains. The Reverend Wannamaker, something of a land promoter, believed settlers of high quality could be attracted through advertisements in church newspapers, and among the trainloads of land-hungry immigrants that arrived from 1907 to 1915 to stake claims were more than 40 older ministers. The homesteaders formed "The Improvement Association" to organize the community, and they voted to name their village and PO Amistad—the Spanish word for "friendship"—hoping that a friendly spirit would prevail among its citizens. Amistad grew apace and at one time boasted two newspapers. Later, when hard times struck, much of the population drifted away, but the village of Amistad still remains. Local people pronounce the name AHM-stahd.

AMIZETTE (Taos; settlement; in Rio Hondo Canyon, 14 mi NE of Taos; PO 1893–1902, changed to Twining). Gold fever was epidemic in 1893 when prospectors Al Helphenstine, William Fraser (see Fraser Mountain), and two others established a mining camp here. Later, Helphenstine was joined by his wife, Amizette, the camp's first female resident. They refurbished an old log cabin into a hotel and opened a PO. Other prospectors followed, some proclaiming the booming camp to be the "Cripple Creek of NM." They named the settlement for Mrs. Helphenstine. The prospectors did indeed find gold ore, but transporting it to mills was expensive; by 1895 Amizette was declining, and eventually the boom town of Twining to the E superseded Amizette as the namesake and center of the mining district; see *Twining*.

AMOLES (Doña Ana; settlement; on the Refugio Colony Grant, on the W side of the Rio Grande, near La Union, SE of Las Cruces). Amoles, sometimes *Los Amoles*, was an Hispanic settlement whose Spanish name refers to the soapweed yucca and which likely was named for a local abundance of the dagger-leafed plants. Like many other lower Rio Grande settlements, Amoles was ravaged repeatedly by floods, and it finally was abandoned after 1886, its residents joining with those of Los Ojitos to form the community of La Union; see *La Union*.

AÑAL (De Baca; settlement; about 7 mi N of Fort Sumner; PO 1916–34, mail to Fort Sumner). In 1916 a rural PO was established at the head of *Arroyo de Añil*, a tributary of the Pecos River. *Añil* is NM Spanish for "sunflower," but the postmaster spelled the name as it sounded to him, *añal*. The community has long been abandoned.

ANALCO, BARRIO DE ANALCO (Santa Fe; settlement; neighborhood of Santa Fe on Old Santa Fe Trail at East de Vargas Street). When Spanish settlers came to Santa Fe around 1610, they brought with them from Mexico some 700 Tlascaltec Indians to help them build the new city. The Indians settled here, on the S side of the Santa Fe River, in a *barrio* they named Analco, in their tongue meaning "on the other side of the water." Analco was destroyed during the Pueblo Revolt of 1680, but it was rebuilt following the reconquest of 1692, and after the Plaza it is the oldest area in Santa Fe. The state capitol and other

government buildings are immediately adjacent.

ANALLA (Lincoln). See *Tinnie*.

ANAPRA (Doña Ana; settlement; on the W side of the Rio Grande, across the river from the Sunland Park Race Track and the Sunland Park Airport, just W of the junction of NM 273 and NM 498, just E of the SP RR; PO as Anapra 1907–14, as West El Paso 1914–18, mail to El Paso). Despite the complexity of postal dates and postal names, this longtime inhabited community, once more rural than at present, has preserved its separate identity despite its proximity to an industrial area of El Paso and to the Sunland Park complex, though recently Anapra has had appended to it the *Meadow Vista* residential area. The only explanation offered for the name is that it means "this side of the river."

ANCHETA CREEK (Grant; parallels NM 152 to join the Mimbres River at San Lorenzo). Nepomuceño Ancheta came to NM in 1856 from Mexico. Local legend says he had a secret gold mine here from which he clandestinely extracted ore. His son, Joseph, became an attorney and later a member of the territorial legislature. In 1891, Representative Ancheta was the unintended victim of an apparent attempt to murder Thomas B. Catron.

ANCHO (Lincoln; settlement; on the SP RR, 2 mi E of US 54, 21 mi N of Carrizozo; PO 1902–69, mail to a rural Carrizozo branch). The Spanish *ancho* means "broad, wide," and the *Ancho Valley*, where this tiny inhabited community is located and from which the village takes its name, does indeed fit that description. The RR created a station here in 1899, and it became a shipping and supply point for local ranchers, as well as for gypsum and fire- clay mined from the nearby Jicarilla Mountains; Ancho shipped several hundred tons of plaster for the rebuilding of San Francisco after the 1906 earthquake. Today only a few people live here. *Ancho Peak*, 7,825 ft., is 7 mi SE of Ancho in the Jicarilla Mountains.

ANCHOR (Taos; settlement; NE of Red

River). In 1884 prospectors erected 8 cabins near their claims and at a Christmas meeting organized the Keystone Mining District. At the same meeting they named their fledgling community Anchor, replacing the informal name *Swede Camp*. The camp of Anchor was closely associated with the one named Midnight (see entry), as the Anchor and Midnight mines were but a mile apart. But like most such camps in the area, Anchor's life was brief.

ANCON DE FRAY GARCIA (Doña Ana; about 12 mi N of El Paso, exact location unknown). This site, "the cove of Father García," was mentioned in the account of Vargas's 1692 reconquest of NM.

ANDREWS (Sierra; settlement; 7 mi NE of Hillsboro; PO 1898–1907, mail to Hillsboro). The mining camp of Andrews was named for William Andrews, who had come to NM from Pennsylvania; in addition to managing the Andrews Mine here, he was active in NM politics; he built a sumptuous residence here. The camp of Andrews was overshadowed by its more prosperous neighbor, Hillsboro, though in 1905 Andrews nonetheless had 100 residents, a PO, two store-saloons, and four mining companies. Andrews was short-lived, however, and today only ruins remain.

ANGEL FIRE MOUNTAIN, 11,060 ft. (Colfax; in the SW part of the county, on the E side of the Sangre de Cristo Mountains). Though stories explaining this name differ in their details, most agree the name began with the Moache Utes, who once lived here. One account says lightning ignited a fire on the mountain and threatened an Indian camp. Just as the Indians were about to evacuate, the wind shifted, and a rainstorm extinguished the fire. The Indians began calling the peak "breath of spirits"; when Franciscan friars encountered the legend they Christianized the name to "breath of angels" and later to Angel Fire.

Other accounts attribute the name to the reddish alpenglow on the peak at dawn and dusk, a phenomenon noted by Kit Carson, among others. Christian missionaries again interpreted the glow according to their theology.

When the Moache Utes were removed from the Moreno Valley in the 1870s, their legends regarding the name went with them, and not until the establishment of Angel Fire resort and ski area was interest rekindled in the poetic name.

ANGEL PEAK, 6,989 ft. (San Juan; 13 mi SE of Bloomfield). Early Spanish explorers of the San Juan Basin called this beautiful and dramatic sandstone formation *Nacimiento*, "birthplace." Later Hispanic settlers would refer to the twin-pronged spire as *Los Gigantes*, "the giants."

When English-speaking settlers arrived in the San Juan area in the 1870s, they called the formation variously *Angels Peak*, *Angel Peak*, and *Twin Angel Peak*. T.M. Pearce believed it was named by stockmen for a formation on top resembling two figures at a height only an angel could reach. The surrounding area has been called the *Garden of the Angels*; another nickname is *Little Grand Canyon*. The site has been designated the *Angel Peak National Recreation Area*, administered by the BLM.

ANGLE (Sierra). See *Engle*.

ANGOSTURA (Doña Ana; settlement; 3 mi SE of Hatch). Spanish, "narrows." This tiny inhabited cluster of houses marks the site of a once-important ford, at a narrow spot on the Rio Grande.

ANGOSTURA (Rio Arriba; settlement; 2 mi N of Española, on the Rio Grande). One of Española's many "suburbs," named because an arroyo joins the Rio Grande at a narrow point here.

ANGOSTURA (Sandoval; settlement; just S of Algodones). As early as 1600, this area N of Bernalillo was known as *La Angostura de Bernalillo*. The *Angostura Grant* was given in 1745 to Andrés Montoya, lieutenant and chief *alcalde* of San Felipe Pueblo, but the village of Angostura, still inhabited, was not settled until 1824–25. The name means "narrows" and refers to a constriction of the Rio Grande SW of here.

ANGOSTURA (Taos; settlement; 3 mi SE of

Tres Ritos on NM 518). Inhabited locality named for the confluence here of the *Rito Angostura*, "narrow creek," and the Rio Pueblo. *Angostura Ridge* is just to the NE.

ANGUS (Lincoln; settlement; at junction of NM 34 and NM 48, 7 mi N of Ruidoso; PO 1898–1913, mail to Alto). This inhabited community was settled in 1881 by Amos Eakers, but its name dates from the establishment of the VV Ranch on Little Creek in the late 1880s by James Cree and his family. Cree had come from Scotland, and he attempted to improve the local longhorns by importing 150 Angus bulls from his homeland. Few bulls survived the arduous overland journey from Corpus Cristi to central NM, but enough did to name the Angus VV Ranch, and later a Captain Kirby, a prominent local rancher, gave the name Angus to the nearby little town on the Rio Bonito.

ANIMAS (Hidalgo; settlement; at junction of NM 9 and NM 338, 11 mi S of Cotton City; PO 1909–present). Animas is part of a name-cluster that includes the *Animas Mountains* and the *Animas Valley*; it's unknown which was named first, but the consensus is that the name, Spanish for "souls, specifically those of persons who have died," is short for *ánimas perdidas*, "lost souls, or more specifically, souls lost in hell" and may refer to the numerous people who lost their lives in the area; for much of its history this was Apache country. The settlement dates from 1843, when Hispanic settlers arrived. In 1901 Phelps Dodge Corp. put a RR line through here, and the community expanded. The line was discontinued in 1962, but Animas survives on farming and ranching.

ANIMAS CITY (Sierra; settlement; on Las Animas Creek, on the E side of the Black Range, exact location unknown; PO 1897 but possibly never operated). A short-lived settlement named for the creek.

ANIMAS MOUNTAINS (Hidalgo; in S-central part of county). N-S linear range along the Continental Divide. The range is within the Gray Ranch (see entry).

Highest elevation, *Animas Peak*, 8,519 ft. See *Animas (Hidalgo)* above.

ANIMAS RIVER (San Juan; flows SW from CO into NM, paralleling US 550, joining the San Juan River at Farmington). Before being shortened and Anglicized to its present form, the name borne by this river was the Spanish *Río de las Ánimas*, "river of the souls of the dead," the *ánimas* likely from *ánimas perdidas*, "lost souls, more specifically, lost in hell." The name is very old; it's even possible Coronado gave it when he traveled in the San Juan Valley in 1541 seeking the fabled Cibola. One popular but apocryphal story behind the name is that the Spaniards battled Indians here and tossed their bodies into the river; the Indians, being unbaptized, were damned, their souls "lost." Another popular and more likely story is that the river was named for its treacherous crossings, at which many travelers lost their lives. Or possibly the river was named for other reasons lost in time.

ANIMAS VALLEY (Hidalgo; in S-central part of county). Separates the Animas Mountains from the Peloncillo Mountains to the W. See *Animas (Hidalgo)* above.

ANNISTON (Quay; settlement; 8 mi SE of Logan; PO 1909–13, mail to Logan). Abandoned homesteader community, name origin unknown.

ANNVILLE (Sandoval). See *Domingo*.

ANSONIO (Grant; settlement; location unknown; PO 1890–92, mail to Hanover). Little is known about this abandoned community. T.M. Pearce speculated that the name might have been transferred from Ansonia, Connecticut, named for Anson G. Phelps, senior partner in the Phelps Dodge Corp., which has operations in the area.

ANTELOPE (general). The antelope, or more properly pronghorn (*Antilocapra americana*), found only in North America, is a distinctive creature of the western plains. Its Spanish name is *berrendo*, often *berrenda*, from *berrendo*, meaning "two-colored," which accurately describes the animal's tan and white markings. Place names referring to this swift creature are common throughout the West; GNIS lists 77 Antelope names, 12 Berrendo/Berrenda names for NM.

ANTELOPE (Hidalgo; RR locality; 7 mi E of Animas). This was a point on the SP RR, named for *Antelope Pass* in the Peloncillo Mountains to the W, through which the RR passes; the highway passes through Granite Gap, 12 mi N.

ANTELOPE (Lea; settlement; 6 mi W of Crossroads). An ephemeral boom town that in its brief heyday had a church, dance hall, real estate office, two or three stores, and a school. Its founder, Charles Burks, is said to have named the settlement Antelope for the anticipated "swiftness" of its growth, but like the prairie animal the town swiftly departed.

ANTELOPE (Torrance; settlement; on the AT&SF RR, 5.25 mi N of Estancia; PO 1891–95, mail to Chilili). Antelope, a RR stop now abandoned, was named for *Antelope Springs*, 0.5 mi to the W, named in turn for the antelope that grazed there. The site long had been a stopping place for travelers, and the SF CENT RR built a grand guest house here, complete with chandeliers and paintings, for RR officials and their familiies. A jail nearby accommodated drunks and the unruly.

ANTELOPE WELLS (Hidalgo; settlement; on NM 81, just N of the Mexican border). Settled in 1847 and named for numerous antelope at the water hole here. Now a US Port of Entry.

ANTHONY (Doña Ana; settlement; on NM 478, 20 mi S of Las Cruces, on the Texas border; PO 1884–present). Straddling the NM-Texas boundary, Anthony bills itself as the "Best Little Town in Two States," and throughout its history the town has had something of a dual identity. The area originally was known as *La Tuna*, and when the AT&SF RR built its line through there in 1881 it gave that name to the station it created on the Texas side of the border; the name La Tuna survives on the station and on the federal prison there.

The settlement on the NM side was known as *Half Way House*, because it's approximately half-way between Las Cruces and El Paso. The most widely accepted explanation of the present name says that after a local woman built a chapel in her home, she dedicated it to San Antonio; when the settlement's residents applied for a PO, that was the name they requested. San Antonio, however, duplicated the name of another NM settlement, so the English form, Anthony, was chosen instead.

Another story says the settlement was named by a Catholic priest who established a church here and learned that the rock formation on the mountains to the E was named *St. Anthony's Nose.*

The original settlement was 2 miles N and E of the present border-straddling settlement. No line demarcates the state line, and New Mexicans and Texans co-exist, sharing many services.

Anthony Gap (Doña Ana; pass between NM and Texas segments of the Franklin Mountains, traversed by NM 404, 4 mi E of Anthony). Named for the settlement or for the promontory to the S known as *North Anthonys Nose*, said to resemble the nose of St. Anthony, assuming anyone knew what that looked like.

ANTIOCH (Lea). See *Midway*.

ANTON CHICO (Guadalupe; settlement; in NW part of county, on the Pecos River, 5 mi W of Dilia, on NM 119; PO 1872–present). One of the oldest communities in this part of NM, Anton Chico was founded in 1822 by persons moving down the Pecos River from San Miguel del Bado. Its formal religious name was *La Avocación de Nuestra Señora y Sangre de Cristo*, "the calling of Our Lady and Blood of Christ." But since earliest times this community has been called Anton Chico, originally spelled *Antonchico*, a name whose origin is obscure. It means "little Anthony," but no one with this nickname has been associated with any of the area's early communities or land grants. One writer has speculated that the name refers to St. Anthony the Franciscan, or Friar Minor, as opposed to St. Anthony the Hermit; 200 years ago, *Chico* was an affectionate nickname for Francis. But more likely the name is a corruption of *ancón chico*, "little bend," and indeed the Pecos River makes a little bend around the village here. Just a mile NW from Anton Chico and almost indistinguishable from it is *Upper Anton Chico*, or *Anton Chico Arriba*, said to have been the settlement's original site.

APACHE (general). The Apache Indians entered NM as nomadic hunter-gatherers from the Plains, possibly in the early to middle 1500s, and soon spread throughout the American Southwest and northern Mexico. Though usually depicted as desert dwellers, they in fact prefer mountain environments. They refer to themselves as *N'de*, sometimes spelled *Indeh*, meaning simply, "the people," and they are organized into several bands, the most important in NM having been the Mescalero, Jicarilla, Mimbres, and Chiricahua. The Mescaleros and Jicarillas have reservations in NM.

The name *Apache* likely comes from a Zuni word, *apachu*, meaning "enemies," though the name also is said to come from a Yuman Indian term signifying "fighting men." The first European contact with the Apaches was in 1540, when Coronado encountered them on the eastern plains; he called them *Querechos* and *Teyas*.

Though not numerous today relative to the Navajos, a closely related Athabascan people, the Apaches' impact upon the history and social geography of the Southwest has been enormous, primarily through warfare. Because of this, place names referring to the Apaches are numerous throughout their present and former territories; their name appears 85 times in GNIS, more than twice as often as any other tribal name. Sometimes history has recorded the specific incident or association behind a name, but more often only the name survives, a reminder of the Apaches' wide-ranging presence in the state.

APACHE (Union; settlement; in SW part of county; PO 1877–82, mail to Chico Springs). The location of this abandoned and vanished settlement is imprecise, though most accounts place it N of Gladstone, near Ute Creek and likely associated with the early Goodnight and Chisum cattle trails.

APACHE ARROYO, CANYON (Doña Ana; runs NW-SE, NW of Las Cruces, about 1 mi N of Picacho Mountain). Reported to have been named for the Warm Springs Band of Apaches, who used it as an escape route after raids on the settlements of the Mesilla Valley.

APACHE CANYON (Quay; in N-central part of county, W of Wheatland). Some people say that a small hill near the canyon's mouth was where cattlemen killed the area's last Apache; others say Apaches launched raids from the canyon on wagon trains.

APACHE CANYON (Santa Fe; 6 mi SE of Santa Fe, 4 mi SW of Glorieta). The rugged and craggy stone flanks of this narrow defile through which passed the Santa Fe Trail, as well as other routes both earlier and later, would have been natural lookout and ambush sites for raiding Apaches, though a Tewa informant told the ethnologist John Peabody Harrington that it was Comanches and not Apaches who lurked in the canyon. History has forgotten any specific Apache incident or association behind the name. Actually, the canyon's major historical significance resulted not from the Indian wars but from the Civil War, for it was in Apache Canyon on March 26, 1862, that Union and Confederate troops fought prior to their more decisive battle two days later at Glorieta Pass. See *Cañoncito (Santa Fe)*.

APACHE CREEK (Catron; settlement; on NM 12, at confluence of Apache Creek and the Tularosa River; PO 1928–58, mail to Aragon). Small, inhabited settlement, named for the creek on which it is located. Numerous features named Apache are nearby: *Apache Creek* heads W of Apache Mountain and flows SE to join the Tularosa River at the village of Apache Creek; *Apache Mountain*, 8,868 ft., is a long mountain trending SE-NW, 5 mi N of village of Apache Creek; and *Apache Spring* is S of Apache Mountain, 4 mi N of the village of Apache Creek.

APACHE HILLS (Hidalgo; 6 mi SE of Hachita). Small complex of desert hills, site of early gold-mining; highest elevation, *Rica* (Spanish, "rich"), 5,770 ft.

APACHE KID WILDERNESS (Socorro; in the San Mateo Mountains, SW of Magdalena). The White Mountain Apache who came to be known as the Apache Kid was born near Globe, AZ, about 1860. He spent his youth first as a captive of Yuman Indians, then as a street orphan in Army camps. The name Apache Kid was given to him by Army scout Albert Sieber, who befriended the young Apache and employed him as a scout in the Geronimo campaigns. But whiskey and an Apache feud caused him trouble with the Army, and in 1889 he was convicted of wounding Sieber in a shootout; the Apache Kid denied the charge. While being taken to prison, he escaped. Finding himself outlawed by the Whites and with his Apache friends and relatives in prison, the Apache Kid became a renegade and for four years conducted a one-man reign of terror in the region. Finally, in September 1894 NM cattleman Charles Anderson and some cowboys ambushed some rustlers in the San Mateo Mountains, killing one—the Apache Kid. He was buried near *Apache Kid Peak*, 10,048 ft., located in the heart of the wilderness between Blue Mountain and San Mateo Peak. The Apache Kid Wilderness, administered by the Cibola NF, was designated in 1980 and includes 44,650 acres.

APACHE NATIONAL FOREST (Catron; mostly in Arizona but extends into NM W and N of NM 12). Created in 1898, this unit has since grown with transfers from the former Datil NF. It was named for the Indians who once lived here. The NM portion of the Apache NF is administered by the Gila NF.

APACHE PASS (Taos; in the Sangre de Cristo Mountains, 3 mi NE of Valle Escondido). Named for the Jicarilla Apaches, who used the pass when their

Indian Service agency was within the Maxwell Land Grant at Cimarron.

APACHE PEAK, 10,204 ft. (Colfax-Taos; in the Taos Range, SE of Wheeler Peak, on the Colfax-Taos County line). Doubtless named for the Indians who once hunted in the area. *Apache Spring* is about 1 mi to the W, while another *Apache Peak*, 9,872 ft., is located to the E, in the W part of the Cimarron Range.

APACHE SPRINGS (San Miguel; settlement; just E of US 84, 3 mi SE of Los Montoyas). The settlement and springs are at the base of *Mesa Apache*, a large sprawling mesa SE of Romeroville. *Apache Canyon* runs through the mesa's northern section.

APACHE TEJO (Grant). See *Fort McLane*.

APACHE VALLEY (Union; between Clayton and Rabbit Ear Mountain). This conspicuous valley is an eastward extension of *Apache Canyon*. American settlers arrived here about 1907 and soon established two schools. Though most ranchers and settlers have long since moved into Clayton, the valley still is an important landmark and place name in the area.

APODACA (Rio Arriba; settlement; on the N bank of Embudo Creek, 2.5 mi NE of Dixon, just E of NM 75). Tiny inhabited community bearing a Spanish family name. José González de Apodaca and his wife, Isabel Gutiérrez, and their children, were among colonists who resettled in NM in 1693.

ARABELA (Lincoln; settlement; at the E end of the Capitan Mountains, at the end of NM 368; PO 1901–28, mail to Tinnie). Confusion exists as to whether the name Arabela was preceded by an earlier Hispanic name, but all sources agree the present name was created when Andy Richardson established a PO and named it for a settler's daughter.

ARAGON (general). The Hispanic persons throughout the world named Aragon owe their surname to the province of Aragon in northeastern Spain. In NM, Ignacio de Aragón and his wife, Sebastiana Ortiz, and their two daughters, were among those resettling NM in 1693. A Felix de Aragón also entered NM at this time.

ARAGON (Catron; settlement; on NM 12, 19 mi NE of Reserve, on the Tularosa River; PO as Joseph 1887–98 and 1901–06, as Aragon 1906–present). Aragon's first identity was as the site of *Fort Tularosa*, Indian agency when the Apaches from the Warm Springs Apache Reservation at Ojo Caliente were moved here in 1872; it was abandoned in 1874 when the Apaches were returned to Ojo Caliente. Later the site became *Joseph*, for reasons unknown. Then it took the name Aragon, for a local family whose members still live here.

ARAGON (San Miguel; settlement; in SW part of county, on the Pecos River, about 2 mi S of Villanueva; PO 1884–85, mail to El Pueblo). Ephemeral postal locality, name origin unknown.

ARAGONTOWN (Valencia). See *Valencia*.

ARCH (Roosevelt; settlement; 16 mi SE of Portales, on NM 88; PO 1903–67, mail to Portales). Everyone agrees this small, inhabited farming community was named for a person, not a rock formation, but there agreement ends. Some accounts say the name commemorates Archibald Roosevelt, son of President Theodore Roosevelt, for whom the county was named in 1903, the same year Arch applied for a PO. Others say Arch recalls the first name of Arch Gregg, an early Roosevelt County sheriff. Present-day residents say the name commemorates Arch Williams, an early settler. The community originally was 2 mi E of the present site.

ARCHULETA (general). Ascencio de Arechuleta, a native of the Basque province of Guipúzcoa in Spain, came to NM as a captain in Oñate's 1598 expedition. His children dropped the first *e* in the surname as early as the beginning of the 17th century. Their descendants tended to be clustered in the country N and W of Santa Fe.

ARCHULETA (San Juan; settlement; on S bank of the San Juan River, on NM 511, 16 mi NE of Bloomfield, at Gobernador Wash). The Archuletas were among the first Hispanic settlers in this area in the 1870s, and their descendants still live in and around this tiny community.

ARCHULETA (Sandoval). See *Jemez Springs*.

ARCO DEL DIABLO (Luna; in the N Florida Mountains, SE of Deming). Spanish, "arch of the devil," here a dramatic natural arch rock formation.

ARD (Quay; settlement; on SE edge of Quay County, N of Melrose; PO 1907–14, mail to McAlister). Ard consisted primarily of a PO and a rural school, both now abandoned. Name origin unknown.

ARENAL (Bernalillo; SW suburb of Albuquerque, W of Armijo, just E of Coors Road). Though this Spanish name means "sandy place, sand pit" which certainly could describe the settlement's location on the Rio Grande's floodplain, the name's origins actually may be more complex. When Coronado's men were exploring along the Rio Grande in 1540, they reported passing a pueblo they recorded as Arenal, but whether they gave it that name or whether that was their approximation of the Indian name is unknown. Also unknown is the pueblo's precise location, even though the Spaniards and the pueblo's Indian inhabitants fought a fierce battle at the site. Later, probably about 1703, the present site began to be occupied by Hispanic settlers; their community was known initially as *Los Arenales*, which could have referred to a family. The settlement now has been absorbed into Albuquerque, though the name survives on Arenal Road.

ARENAS (general). Spanish, "sands, sandy." A common descriptive name, especially for intermittent water courses. *Arenoso* and *arenal* are variants.

ARENAS CREEK (Grant; see *Río de Arenas*).

ARENAS VALLEY (Grant; settlement; on US 180, 7 mi E of Silver City, 3 mi W of Central; PO 1947–present). This inhabited settlement takes its name from being in the valley of *Río de Arenas* (see entry).

ARGENTITE (Sierra; settlement; on North Percha Creek, near Hillsboro). This was an abortive settlement during the mining boom of the late 1800s; it was named for a form of silver ore.

ARKANSAS JUNCTION (Lea; trading point; 13 mi W of Hobbs, at the junction of US 62-180 and NM 483). A relatively new settlement, with a filling station and other services. The name's origin is unknown.

ARMENTA CANYON (San Juan; enters San Juan River from the S, 3 mi SW of Blanco). José Armenta and his family settled near the canyon's mouth about 1878.

ARMENTA PLAZA (Harding; settlement; on the E bank of the Canadian River, 3.5 mi N of the San Miguel County line, at the mouth of Armenta Canyon). Of this former settlement, doubtless bearing an Hispanic family name, nothing but the cemetery remains.

ARMIJO (Bernalillo; S suburb of Albuquerque, W of the Rio Grande, centering on the intersection of Isleta Blvd. and Arenal Road; PO 1883–86, changed to Old Albuquerque, 1906–07, 1909–36, mail to Albuquerque). This Albuquerque neighborhood bears the family name of José de Armijo, who in 1695 came to NM from Zacatecas, Mexico, with his wife, Catalina Durán, and their four grown sons. Among their descendants eventually settling in the Rio Abajo was Policarpio Armijo,who with his wife, Petronila Sanchez, in the late 1880s owned land in the Atrisco area; the settlement where the Armijos lived originally was called *Ranchos de Atrisco* (see *Atrisco*), but eventually it came to bear their own name.

ARMIJO DRAW (Santa Fe; heads 5 mi E of Stanley and runs E). Named for José Armijo.

ARMS (Colfax; settlement; in SE part of county, SE of Maxwell, on Chico Creek; PO 1879–80). Ephemeral community, named for Henry M. Arms, its postmaster.

ARNY (Socorro). See *Tiffany*.

ARRASTRE GULCH (Grant; heads SW of Burro Peak in the Big Burro Mountains and runs S and W). An *arrastre* was a primitive device used by Spanish miners in the Southwest for separating miner-als, such as gold, from ore. This gulch in a mining district certainly was named for one.

ARREY (Sierra; settlement; on NM 187 7 mi S of Caballo, 5 mi N of Derry; PO 1901–present). This fertile farming area was known as *Bonito* (Spanish, "pretty") when in 1890 an agent of the Elephant Butte Land and Cattle Co. made a deal with several Hispanic families to homestead here; after the claims were "proved," the lands were to be deeded to the company; descendants of these homesteaders still live in the area. Among the first homesteaders were Tomás Baca and Urbano Arrey, who came from Las Palomas in 1891. When the settlement applied for a PO in 1901, Arrey became the first postmaster and gave his surname, pronounced uh-RAY, to the community.

ARRIBA (general). See *Río Arriba* and *Abajo (general)*.

ARROYO (general). This common Spanish term for stream in the Southwest more commonly refers to a streambed through which water flows only intermittently. Actually it's more complex than that. As Jerold G. Widdison has explained: "In NM, many named arroyos include the term directly in the name, such as Arroyo Chico ('little arroyo') and Arroyo Colorado ('red arroyo'). Other arroyos, however, have come to be called washes or even creeks, though they are normally dry, such as Chaco Wash, Mosquero Creek. By extension, 'arroyo' is sometimes used in the name of a much larger valley or canyon through which an arroyo flows; such is the case with Arroyo Hondo and Arroyo Seco."

ARROYO DEL AGUA (Rio Arriba). See *Coyote*.

ARROYO HONDO (Taos; settlement; on NM 522, 11 mi N of Taos; PO 1885–present). The *Arroyo Hondo*, as its name implies, is a deep valley carved into the Taos Plateau by the *Río Hondo* descending to the Rio Grande from the Sangre de Cristo Mountains. The valley is a conspicuous part of the Taos County landscape, and the fertile, well-watered land along its bottom was a natural site for settlement when Hispanic settlers established outposts on the mountains' western flanks early in the 19th century. In March 1815 Nerio Sisneros and 42 others, responding to an 1813 proclamation inviting settlement on vacant lands, petitioned for a land grant at the "Rio Ondo," and their request was granted a month later. The community they created still survives. Tewa Indians know the arroyo by a name meaning "water cicada arroyo."

ARROYO SECO (Santa Fe; settlement; on the S side of Española, spanning US 84–285). One of many neighborhoods that collectively make up what is more widely known as Española. Arroyo Seco, just S of Sombrillo (see entry), takes its name from the "dry arroyo" passing through it; the full form of the name is *El Valle de Arroyo Seco*, the "valley of the dry arroyo."

ARROYO SECO (Taos; settlement; 7 mi N of Taos on NM 150; PO 1881–1970, changed to Arroyo Seco from Arroyoseco, 1970–present). Like Arroyo Hondo to the W, Arroyo Seco ("dry arroyo") began as one of several Hispanic outposts along the western Sangre de Cristo Mountains early in the 19th century. And like Arroyo Hondo, this tiny farming community, now a crafts center, takes its name from a watercourse, in this case a dry irrigation ditch. Cristóbal Martínez and José Gregorio planted crops here for three years before building homes in 1807. In 1881 a PO named Arroyo Seco was established here, in Alexander Gusdorf's mercantile store, to serve the increasing number of miners and prospectors.

ARTESIA (Eddy; settlement; on the W bank of the Pecos River, at the junction of US 82 and US 285; PO as Stegman 1899–1903, as Artesia, 1903–present). On John Chisum's cattle drives up the Pecos River, which began in 1866, Chisum often stopped and watered at an especially desirable spot on Eagle Draw, near a spring. By 1879 a permanent camp had been established there, and by 1880 the Chisum interests had acquired the site, resulting in the name *Chisum Spring Camp*, or *South Chisum Camp*. Sally Chisum Robert, John's niece, filed a homestead claim here and lived here for many years.

By 1894 a stage line ran through the future townsite of Artesia, where the spring had come to be called *Blakes Spring*. When the RR arrived, a siding was built and named *Miller*. In 1899 the community applied for a PO, and though the settlement was known as Miller, the name requested was *Stegman*, for an early promoter of the area; Sallie L. Stegman was first postmistress.

The first well in the area had been drilled in 1890, for Sally Chisum Robert, but John Richey, a Kansan, was the first person to appreciate the potential for artesian water. In 1903 he formed the Artesia Homesite Company and purchased 80 acres from Robert for a townsite, later expanded to include the entire Robert homestead, as well as that of another early settler, John T. Truitt. Richey suggested that the name of the growing community should reflect its origins—and he suggested Artesia. Ranching and farming dominated the local economy for many years, but since 1923 the oil industry has contributed to the area's development. The spring that first attracted Chisum's attention still flows in the town.

ARVA (Quay; settlement; in SW part of county, 12 mi NW of House; PO 1916–18, mail to Lucille). When residents of this homesteader community, long abandoned, applied for a PO, the name they requested was *Scarbrough*, for the postmaster, John M. Scarbrough. That name was rejected, however, and Arva was chosen instead, for reasons unknown.

ASH (general). Several species of ash trees (genus *Fraxinus*) are found in NM, and because they're often associated with water sources, always important in this arid state, their presence frequently engenders place names, whether in English or in Spanish, as *fresno*.

ASPEN (general). The quaking aspen (*Populus tremuloides*) is a distinctive tree of the NM high country, and it has given its name to many features—it occurs 17 times in GNIS—especially to mountains, where dense stands of aspens turn the autumn hillsides golden. The name appears as *Quaking Asp* on a canyon and creek in Grant and Catron Counties.

Aspen Peak, 11,109 ft. (Santa Fe; just NW of Santa Fe Basin Ski Area and Aspen Basin, 3 mi E of Aspen Hill).

ASTIALAKWA (Sandoval; on Mesa de Guadalupe, separating San Diego and Guadalupe Canyons in the Jemez Mountains N of Cañon). This large Towa pueblo, now in ruins, was inhabited when the Spanish arrived and likely was the site of the mission of San Juan that the Franciscans established early in the 17th century. The etymology of its name, sometimes transcribed *Hastialakwa*, is obscure, though its name has been reported to mean "high view above the water," certainly an accurate description.

ATALAYA MOUNTAIN, 9,121 ft. (Santa Fe; 3 mi E of Santa Fe, S of Nichols Reservoir). The Spanish *atalaya* means "watchtower, height." This summit gave its name to a small land grant surrounding it, referred to in early documents variously as *Atalaya Grant*, *Atalaya Hill Grant*, and *Talaya Grant*. The mountain sometimes has been called *Reservoir Hill*.

ATARQUE (general). *Atarque*, "earthen dam," comes from the Spanish verb *atarquinar*, "to fill up with mud." Small earthen dams in Hispanic NM became distinctive features on the landscape and natural sites for settlements, thus Atarque is a common NM place name.

ATARQUE (Cibola; settlement, trading point; 6 mi N of Fence Lake, 2 mi W of NM 36; PO 1910–55, mail to Fence Lake). In 1882, one year after his father had been killed by Apaches, Juan García took his mother, five younger brothers, and Manuel and Jesús Landavaso, to Jaralosa Canyon, a few miles from the present site of Atarque. In 1885 the Garcías dammed several nearby arroyos

and moved there, calling the site *Los Atarques*, "the dams;" the locality has been called *Atarque de García*. Juan García established a store there, and the settlement eventually became headquarters of the Atarque Sheep Co. The dam has since washed out, and nothing remains of the former settlement but a few ruined buildings—and the name. *Atarque Lake* is 5 mi NW of Atarque.

ATENCIO (Union; settlement; 7 mi from the Texas line, 24 mi N of Clayton; PO 1910–14, mail to Moses). Sometime before 1908 A.C. Miera, Miguel Tixier, and José Merced Gonzáles opened a mercantile store here to serve the numerous families in the area. In 1908 they decided a PO also would serve the local population, as well as increase business, so they petitioned postal officials to establish one. The name they proposed was Atencio, to honor Gabriel Atencio, a prominent local resident. Maggie Atencio, Gabriel's daughter, was the first and only postmistress. Eventually the PO was discontinued, and the mercantile store closed soon after. Today the settlement has gone, though families still live in the area.

ATOKA (Eddy; 5 mi S of Artesia, on US 285). About all that is known for sure about the name of this small, inhabited settlement is that it ultimately was derived from an Indian word, most likely from the language of the Choctaws, who lived in the SE US, where Atoka appears as a place name in several states. The word has been translated as "in, or to, another place," and "ball ground," referring to a game similar to lacrosse played by the Choctaws. In 1830 the Choctaws were forced to leave their homeland and move to a reservation in Oklahoma, which perhaps explains why the name appears in E NM; many early E NM settlers came from Oklahoma, where Atoka is the name of a county, and they likely brought the name with them.

ATRISCO (Bernalillo; SW suburb of Albuquerque, NW of Armijo; PO 1892–93, 1907–08, mail to Albuquerque). Certainly as early as 1703, and perhaps even as early as 1660, before Albuquerque was founded as a villa in 1706, a cluster of farms on the Rio Grande's W bank was known as Atrisco, but the name itself may be much older. It likely is derived from *atlixco*, a Nahuatl word meaning "across the river." From the viewpoint of a traveler on the Rio Grande's E bank, this certainly would have described the community (the name Analco in Santa Fe has been explained similarly; see entry). Alternatively, the name Atlixco could have been transferred to NM from Puebla, Mexico, where it appears on a valley and a city. The locality probably is the *Tousac* Zebulon Pike described as a small village in 1807.

Residents of Atrisco were called Atrisqueños. The settlement lacked municipal organization, and, with the founding and growth of Albuquerque, Atrisco became a satellite of its larger neighbor; it often was referred to as *Atrisco de Albuquerque*. The 1870 US Census showed *Ranchos de Atrisco* with 740 people, Albuquerque with 1,307. Yet despite Atrisco now completely absorbed by Albuquerque, the name and even something of the former settlement's identity persists; the *Atrisco Land Grant*, made by King Charles II of Spain in 1692 to Fernando Durán y Chávez, still includes most of the land on the mesas SW of Albuquerque.

ATSINNA (Cibola; ruins). See *El Morro*.

AUGUSTINE (Socorro; settlement; 2 mi from Catron County line, on US 60; PO 1927–55, mail to Magdalena). Former rural PO, likely named for its location on the *Plains of San Agustin* (see entry). See *San Agustin (general)*.

AURORA (Colfax, Mora; settlement; NW of Ocate; PO as Martinez 1889–1902, as Aurora 1902–21, mail to Ocate). In the late 1800s, friends and relatives of the Taos priest, Padre Antonio José Martínez, settled in a canyon E of Black Lake. The canyon took their surname and so did the PO established there in 1889; Marcelino V. Epimenio Martínez was the first postmaster. Around 1900 the *Martinez* PO moved out of the canyon to a site NW of Laguna Colorada, now called Red Lake, but it retained the name Martinez until 1902, when a Martinez PO was established in Albuquerque. As two POs with the same name would be confusing, postal authorities asked the Colfax County one to submit a list of alternative names. Juan C. Lucero, the Martinez postmaster's assistant, suggested Aurora, the name of his 7-year-old daughter. In 1907 Lucero, then postmaster, moved the store he owned and the Aurora PO S to Wheaton Creek, just within Mora County, 7 mi N of Ocate. Though little remains of the earlier communities, the Mora County Aurora is still inhabited.

AVE MARIA (Rio Arriba; settlement; in NW part of county, exact location unknown; PO 1923–25, mail to Lumberton). An ephemeral settlement, named for the first two words (Latin, "Hail, Mary!") in the angel's salutation to the Virgin Mary. The title of this prayer, an invocation to the Virgin, passed into Spanish usage untranslated from the Latin.

AVIS (Otero; settlement; on NM 24, 7 mi SE of Weed; PO 1903–30, mail to Piñon). *Avis* is Latin for "bird," but why this name was given here—or if indeed the name here is meant to be Latin—is unknown. Once more densely settled, this community still has a few residents.

AZOTEA (general). *Azotea* is a Spanish word referring to a "flat roof" and also referring generally to the architecture found throughout Mexico and the Southwest where in earlier times the flat roof, or *azotea*, served as combination roof-garden, sleeping porch, and defensive structure.

AZOTEA (Rio Arriba; settlement; in N part of county, SW of Chama; PO 1887–1903, mail to Monero). This community was primarily a lumber camp, and while the settlement has vanished, the name Azotea still is applied to its location. See *Azotea (general)*.

AZOTEA MESA (Eddy; approx. 10 mi W of Carlsbad). Large, sprawling mesa whose name describes its flat-roofed appearance; see *Azotea (general)*. *Azotea Peak* and *Azotea Fork* are associated with the mesa.

AZTEC (San Juan; settlement, county seat; on the Animas River, at the junction of US 550 and NM 544; PO 1879–present). The first English-speaking settlers came to this area in 1879, and when in 1890 they selected a name for their community, they chose that of the nearby Anasazi ruins, which were believed at the time to have been built by Indians related to the Aztecs of Mexico. (The D&RGW RR later named a switch on its line NE of Aztec Inca, a name presumably inspired by nearby Aztec, and the Inca Ditch was a major irrigation project.)

When San Juan County was created from Rio Arriba County in 1887, Aztec was the provisional county seat, having buildings ready for occupancy, but several other towns soon petitioned for the designation. The strongest contender was Junction City (see entry), about a mile E of Farmington, and in an election in 1890 to settle the hotly debated issue, Junction City won 255 to Aztec's 246 (Farmington got 1 vote). But in a recount, numerous voters were disqualified, and Aztec, by a vote of 237 to 232, kept its status as county seat, which it still retains. In 1963, the pleasant town was named an "All-American City."

AZTEC RUINS NATIONAL MONUMENT (San Juan; archaeological site; on the W bank of the Animas River, adjoining the town of Aztec). The ruins here don't really have anything to do with the Aztecs of Mexico. On the contrary, this impressive U-shaped 500–room settlement was built by Anasazi people in the early 1100s A.D.; after living at the site less than 100 years, they abandoned it, leaving it to prehistoric Indians of the Mesa Verde culture, who also lived here for a time and then moved on.

The Navajos were the next group to view the site. They called it by names meaning "wide house," "square house," or "oblong house"—names still used by the Navajos.

Europeans first saw the ruins in 1776 when Domínguez and Escalante passed through the area, and their cartographer, Bernardo Miera y Pacheco, put them on his map.

English-speaking settlers arrived in the area in the 1870s, and they, mistakenly assuming the ruins had been built by a northern branch of the Aztecs of Mexico, called them Aztec Ruins. The name stuck. As with most Anasazi settlements, the Anasazi names for them have been lost, leaving it for peoples the Anasazis never knew to give the ruined buildings the names by which we know them today, names that sometimes, as in this instance, are misleading.

AZUL (general). See *Blue (general)*.

BACA (general). This family name and its longer forms, Cabeza de Baca, Cabeza de Vaca, and C de Baca, are said to have originated with an incident during the Moorish wars of 13th-century Spain in which an individual marked a strategic river ford with a cow's skull. (In some versions, a mountain pass, not a ford, was marked.) As a reward, the king dubbed the man Cabeza de Vaca, "cow's head." In the 17th century, the name began appearing as Baca as well as Vaca.

The first member of this family to figure in NM history was Álvar Nuñez Cabeza de Vaca who, along with three others from Cuba, was shipwrecked near the site of today's Galveston and made an overland epic trek to Mexico City (1528–36). And while it generally is agreed Cabeza de Vaca did not actually set foot in what is now NM, his reports inspired the explorations here that followed.

In 1600, Capt. Cristóbal Baca came to NM from Mexico City with his wife, Doña Ana Ortiz, and their three grown daughters and a small son; their descendants figured prominently in the affairs of colonial NM prior to the Pueblo Revolt of 1680. Several members of the Baca family returned with the reconquest of 1692, settling in the Santa Fe area. Around 1800, Don Luis María Baca, one of many sons of Juan Antonio Baca of La Cienega, began using the full name Cabeza de Baca. Bartolomé Baca was governor of NM from 1823 to 1825.

Baca is among NM's most common family eponymns, listed 34 times in GNIS.

BACA (Lincoln; settlement; in the SE Capitan Mountains foothills, N of Lincoln). The site of this former Hispanic community now is a Lincoln NF facility called *Baca Camp*. See *Salazar Canyon*.

BACA (McKinley). See *Prewitt*.

BACA (Union; settlement; exact location unknown; PO 1884–98, mail to Bueyeros). This abandoned settlement took the family name of its first postmaster, Louis A. C de Baca.

BACA LOCATION (Sandoval and elsewhere; land grant). The sprawling Baca Location No. 1, which includes Redondo Peak, Valle Santa Antonio, Valle Grande, and other important features of the E-central Jemez Mountains, resulted from a mistake. In 1835, Juan Maese and 25 other Las Vegas citizens were granted 500,000 acres in the Las Vegas area. But then in 1841 another grant was given to Don Luis María Cabeza de Baca—see *Baca (general)*—born in Santa Fe in 1754. Unfortunately, the two grants seemed to overlap, creating problems. In 1860, the US Congress recognized the primacy of the earlier grant, but to compensate Baca's heirs for their loss Congress allowed them to select an equal amount of vacant, non-mineralized land, to be located in five square parcels anywhere in NM. The Bacas' first choice was the land in the Jemez Mountains, since known as Baca Location No. 1. Baca Location No. 2 was N of Tucumcari, in the area of Fort Bascom, on the Canadian River; this eventually became part of the Bell Ranch. Baca Locations 3 and 4 were in lands later incorporated into Colorado and Arizona. And Baca Location No. 5 was in eastern NM, in territory reserved for Navajo and Apache Indian reservations.

BACAVILLE (Valencia; settlement; suburb of Belen; PO 1909–15, mail to Belen). Bacaville, one of eight *plazas* that comprised early Belen, was named for the Baca family. Juan Rey Baca, a merchant in the late 19th century, was particularly well-known, and in 1874 he constructed the J.R. Baca Store, which contained not only the PO but also some notable murals by Mexican artists. A small school was just S of the store. Bacaville has since been absorbed into Belen, and Baca's famous store was razed in 1972.

BADEÑOS (Torrance; settlement; near Punta de Agua). Abandoned settlement, named for a local family.

BADGERVILLE (Eddy). See *Hope.*

BADO DE JUAN PAIS (Guadalupe; ford; on the Pecos River, just below Dilia). From the Spanish, *vado,* "ford." Once a prominent site on the route between Las Vegas and Santa Rosa, as well as a stage and mail station for early Star Route mail deliveries, this ford was named for the Juan Pais ranch, where stage travelers stopped for dinner.

BAJADA (general). Spanish, "a gradual descent, a gradual slope."

LA BAJADA (Santa Fe; settlement; 7 mi E of Peña Blanca, at the base of La Bajada Hill and La Majada Mesa). The village of La Bajada sits beside the Santa Fe River at the base of *La Bajada Hill* (see entry). Though the hill always has been better known than the village, the settlement dates from before the Pueblo Revolt of 1680; Vargas is said to have visited the site during the reconquest of 1692. For generations the village was an important stopping point for wagons, stages, and, later, automobiles until the construction in 1932 of a route 5 miles S and E, on a longer but more gradual grade. The village once had a peak population of 300; a few people still live here.

LA BAJADA HILL (Santa Fe; 11 mi SW of Santa Fe). From 1598, when Spanish colonists trudged beside lumbering oxcarts, to the early 20th century, when American tourists drove Model A automobiles, the steep and abrupt escarpment of La Bajada Hill was a notorious landmark on the road between Santa Fe and Albuquerque. The old route up La Bajada Hill was barely 1.5 miles long, but it traversed tough volcanic rock; in

the 20th century it included 23 hairpin turns and was the scene of countless frustrations and mishaps, from overturned wagons to boiling radiators. Residents of the village of *La Bajada* (see entry) at the hill's base named a spot on the hill *Florida* because a truck carrying oranges overturned there. In 1932, a new route up the escarpment was laid out, followed today by I-25, and the original route, 5 mi N and W, fell into disuse, though a few drivers still attempt it to test their vehicles' toughness. The name La Bajada now is gradually being transferred to the new route.

During colonial times, La Bajada Hill was the dividing line between the two great economic and governmental regions of Hispanic NM, the *Río Abajo,* "lower river," and the *Río Arriba,* "upper river." The large, sprawling mesa on whose edge La Bajada Hill is located is called *La Majada,* "sheepfold," or "p¹ace where shepherds keep their flocks.')ut because the road from Santa Fe to the Rio Abajo descended from the mesa here, the escarpment took the name La Bajada, "the descent." "Hill" was added to the name much more recently, an addition that often causes confusion to Spanish speakers, as the name now seems to consist of two generics.

BAKER FLAT (Lea; landform; 5 mi W of Crossroads, on the Llano Estacado). This area gave its name to the rural school of Baker Flat that served the abandoned community of Jenkins (see entry). *Baker Flat School* was abandoned before 1927; the name's origin is unknown.

BALD, BALDY, (general). Wherever a mountain's top is naked of trees— through fire, high elevation, or other circumstances—people frequently call it "bald." The name occurs in various Spanish forms: *pelón,* as in *Cerro Pelon* (Jemez Mountains); *pelona,* as in *Pelona Mountain* (Catron County); *peloncillo,* as in *Peloncillo Mountains* (Hidalgo County) and *Peloncillo Peak* (Doña Ana County); and *pelado,* as in *Cerro Pelado* (Jemez Mountains).

BALDWIN (Catron; settlement; 5 mi NE of

Datil). Levi (sometimes spelled Levy) Baldwin was a prominent rancher here in the 1880s, and a tiny settlement and stage stop grew up bearing his family name. Though the settlement has vanished, Baldwin's descendants still live in the area. Some accounts say the settlement of Baldwin occupied the same site as the original site of Datil and that Levi Baldwin was Datil's first postmaster. All accounts agree Levi Baldwin was active in the establishment of Datil.

BALDY (Colfax; settlement; 4 mi NE of Elizabethtown, high on Baldy Mountain; PO 1888–1926, mail to Ute Park). According to tradition, in the 1860s a Ute Indian displayed a piece of rich copper float at Fort Union, and W.H. Kroenig and William Moore paid the Ute to take them to its source. He took them to Baldy Mountain (see entry), and a mining boom soon ensued, with several camps springing up. One of them was called Baldy, for the mountain on which it was located. Two boarding houses accommodated as many as 100 men, and across the barroom wall of the Baldy Hotel was painted, "Altitude 10,000 feet—high, windy, and lusty." Baldy was at its peak in the early 1880s, then declined. About 1941 its buildings were razed, though a few relics still are visible. The site now is on the Philmont Scout Ranch.

BALDY MOUNTAIN, 12,441 ft. (Colfax; in the Cimarron Range, NE of Eagle Nest, at the headwaters of Ute Creek). This and Touch-me-not Mountain (see entry) to the S are the N and S summits along the main ridge of that portion of the Cimarron Range E of Eagle Nest, N of US 64; Baldy Mountain is the highest summit in the entire Cimarron Range. It formerly was called *Elizabeth Peak,* for the nearby mining camp of Elizabethtown (see entry).

BALDY MOUNTAIN, 12,046 ft. (Taos; in the Taos Range, NE of Questa and N of Cabresto Creek).

LOS BALEN BUELAS (Socorro; settlement; next to the RR tracks, S of Socorro and N of Luis Lopez). *Valenzuela* was the name of a family that lived near this now-abandoned settlement, and English speakers later corrupted the name to Los Balen Buelas. The area also was known as *Latear,* derived from the presence here of a large grain winnowing yard; the Spanish verb *latear* means "to winnow."

CERRO BALITAS, 7,935 ft. (Sandoval; in SE Jemez Mountains, just W of Bandelier National Monument). Though the name *Cerro Boletas,* Spanish, "tickets mountain," often appears on maps, the USBGN in 1984 established as the accepted form *Cerro Balitas,* Spanish "little bullets," for numerous bullet-shaped pebbles in the mountain's talus slopes.

BALLEJOS (Cibola). See *San Fidel.*

BANCO JULIAN, 10,413 ft. (Rio Arriba; in the Tusas Mountains, 5 mi NW of Broke Off Mountain.) Spanish, "Julian's bank." *Banco* is an unusual mountain generic term in NM; this name's origin is unknown.

BANDELIER NATIONAL MONUMENT (Los Alamos, Sandoval, Santa Fe; on the Pajarito Plateau, S of Los Alamos). Adolph F. Bandelier was an historian, ethnologist, archaeologist, and novelist who was fascinated by Indian life and lore. Born in Switzerland, he emigrated with his family to the US when he was eight. He lived in Arizona and NM between 1880 and 1886, and during that time he undertook several expeditions to the ruin-studded Pajarito Plateau and especially to the sites of Cañon de los Frijoles. Based upon his visits and also upon his knowledge and acquaintance with contemporary Pueblo Indians, he wrote *The Delight Makers,* published in 1890, a fictionalized account of prehistoric life on the Rito de los Frijoles. Because of all this, when Bandelier National Monument was created in 1916, including Cañon de los Frijoles and other major canyons and uplands, the monument was named in Bandelier's honor, superseding the existing local name for the site, *El Rito. Tyuonyi, Tsankawi,* and *Yapashi* (see entries) are large pueblo ruins within the monument, along with the cliff dwellings in Cañon de los Frijoles.

BANDERA CRATER, 8,309 ft. (Cibola; just

S of NM 53, E of Ice Caves, on the N side of El Malpais National Monument). In the 19th century soldiers at Fort Wingate to the N placed a flag on the highest summit in the area here, and the summit came to be called *Cerro de la Bandera,* "hill of the flag." But when local people indicated the feature called by this name, their ambiguous pointing sometimes included another volcanic hill, nearby to the SW, so David Candelaria, owner of Ice Caves and the southern crater, took this to be his crater's name; he began calling his volcanic cone Bandera Crater, and that name has survived, even though the flag was on the other summit, which still is called *Cerro Bandera,* 8,372 ft.

BANKS (De Baca; settlement; 15 mi NE of Fort Sumner; PO 1909–13, mail to La Lande). Abandoned community, reportedly named for sand banks nearby.

BARCLAYS FORT (Mora; settlement; N of Watrous, at the junction of the Mora and Sapello Rivers; PO 1851–54). Alexander Barclay was an English mountain man who, along with his partner, Joseph P. Doyle, purchased the Scolly Land Grant in 1848 and built a walled adobe fort covering one acre. They built it as an investment, expecting the government would buy the fort, but to their disappointment the US military built Fort Union instead. Barclay died broke at his private fort in 1855 and is buried in an unmarked grave near Watrous. His fort has disappeared.

BARD (Quay; settlement; 28 mi E of Tucumcari, 5 mi NE of San Jon, just N of I-40; PO as Bard 1908–09, as Bard City 1909–13, as Bard 1913–present). Founded in 1906, this tiny community at one time was called *Bard City.* Walter R. Haynes, a longtime resident, has said his father transferred the name Bard to the NM community from a small watermelon-loading site in Texas also named Bard; Haynes said his father felt the name sounded poetic and colorful and also wandering musicians held dances there. Possibly, but the name also has been attributed to a ranch brand, the Bar-D, and names such as this are common in NM; see *Obar.*

BARELA CANYON, SPRING (Taos; 7 mi NW of Tres Piedras). These places bear a Spanish family name.

BARELA MESA, 8,868 ft. (Colfax; NE of Raton, extending into Colorado). This prominent mesa has been called *Chicarica Mesa, Chicorica Mesa* (see *Chicorica*), and *Raton Mesa.* It also has been called *Barilla Mesa,* for a local family in the area, causing considerable confusion and consternation as the Barelas are another local family. In 1983 the USBGN established Barela Mesa as the accepted form, honoring Casimiro Barela, a prominent Hispanic legislator of Trinidad, CO, in the 1890s.

BARELAS (Bernalillo; settlement; locality near downtown Albuquerque, along the E side of the Rio Grande, N of the Barelas Bridge). Today, the community of Barelas has been absorbed into Albuquerque, but in the 19th century it was a distinct settlement. Wagons traveling S on the Valley Road (the old Camino Real) often forded the river near here; the US Census of 1880 showed 350 residents, compared to Albuquerque's 2,135; and Barelas once was mentioned as a possible site for UNM.

The settlement of Barelas likely had its origins in the 17th century, when Pedro Varela, or Barela (in Spanish the letter *v* often is pronounced as *b*), owned an *estancia* in the Albuquerque area, possibly in the South Valley. In 1662 Gov. Diego de Peñalosa, at a meeting at the Varela estate, ordered the establishment of a settlement; the order had approximately 12 signatories, but little came of the effort. In 1809 Don Juan Barela purchased land in the south of Albuquerque at a ranch called *El Torreón,* "the tower"; such towers were common in early NM for defense. By 1870, the rural community had 400 residents.

Though Barelas now is part of Albuquerque, it clings to its distinct identity; its residents conduct a *Las Posadas* through its narrow streets at Christmas, and the *Barelas Bridge* helps preserve the name.

BARKER ARROYO (San Juan; heads in the Ute Mountain Indian Reservation and runs NW into Colorado). A.N. Barker was a well-known stockman who was killed near this arroyo by a member of the Stockton and Ethridge outlaw gangs, who plagued this area around 1880. The names of this arroyo, and nearby *Little Barker Arroyo* and *Barker Dome* recall this rancher and his death.

MOUNT BARKER, 11,455 ft. (San Miguel; in the S Sangre de Cristo Mountains, 1 mi SW of Elk Mountains). In 1991, Dr. Wiley Barker of California proposed renaming 11,180-foot Spring Mountain in the Pecos Wilderness to Mount Barker to honor his uncle, Elliott Barker, noted NM wildlife conservationist and author who wrote about the wilderness.

The proposal was supported throughout the state, but Spring Mountain already had a long-established name and moreover was within a USFS wilderness, where renamings are discouraged. Also, many persons felt the naming should honor the entire Barker family, including Elliott's brother, S. Omar Barker, the noted western writer, and their father, Squire Leandro Barker.

An unnamed peak, outside the wilderness, was found, but some local people feared the naming would displace a traditional but unmapped name, *Valle Alto,* though this later was discovered to be applied to meadows surrounding the peak, not to the peak itself. Eventually, the NMGNC resolved these problems, including getting Valle Alto officially recognized, and in 1994 the USBGN approved Dr. Barker's amended proposal.

BARLEY CANYON (Sandoval; in the Jemez Mountains, runs SW into the Rio Cebolla, just NE of Fenton Lake). Early Hispanic settlers grew barley (Spanish, *sebada*) in this canyon and called it *Cañon de la Sebada.* When the Fentons (see *Fenton Lake*) acquired the property, they also grew barley, and translated the name into English.

BARNEY (Hidalgo; stage stop; 5 mi NE of Lordsburg). Long-vanished stage stop, sometimes called *Barneys Station* and also *Leachs Well,* on the Butterfield Overland Mail route, named for D.M. Barney, a Butterfield company director.

BARNEY (Union; settlement; on Pinabete Creek, 24 mi SW of Clayton; PO 1896–1930, mail to Mount Dora). Sometime after 1880 W.A. Barney settled here and established a PO, which he named for himself. The settlement is abandoned.

BAROMETER MOUNTAIN, 8,042 ft. (McKinley; 6 mi SW of Continental Divide). In the late 1940s and early 1950s, a US Air Force radar station was here, and among its instruments certainly was a barometer.

BARRANCA, BARRANCO (general). Spanish, "gorge, ravine, gully" but sometimes in NM also meaning "hillside."

BARRANCA (Quay; settlement; in S part of county, 8 mi N of Forrest, on Barranca Creek; PO as Barancos 1906–12, mail to Loyd). Located N of and below the Caprock, Barranca, sometimes called *Barrancos,* was named for its location on *Barranca Creek,* named in turn for its steep sides; see *Barranca (general).* The families of Joseph Arnold and A.C. Stephenson came here in 1905; before the PO was established an elderly man occasionally brought mail from Loyd, putting it in a syrup bucket and signifying its delivery by tying a white rag to the bucket. John P. Nelson built and operated the PO and store from 1906 to 1912. Nothing remains of this settlement, but old-timers remember that once it witnessed all the activities that made up so many NM homesteader communities: church get-togethers and ice cream socials, deaths of children, and boundary disputes.

BARRANCA (Taos; railroad station; 4 mi N of Dixon; PO 1881–90, mail to Ojo Caliente). This station on the D&RG RR's Chili Line, now abandoned, owes its name to the steep slope here—see *Barranca (general)*—requiring brakemen on southbound trains to set the retainers before proceeding down the 4 percent grade through Comanche Canyon to Embudo.

BARRANQUITAS (Valencia; settlement; on

E side of the Rio Grande, on NM 304, 4.5 mi SE of Belen). "Little washouts" is how local people translate this Spanish name, describing the location of this tiny but growing community.

BARTLETT MESA (Colfax; immediately N of Raton, extending into Colorado). A large mesa, named for Carlos Bartlett, an early settler and founder in 1906 of the Bartlett Estate in Vermejo Park. The highest point here is a knob called *Raton Mesa,* sometimes *Raton Peak,* 8,868 ft.

BARTON (Bernalillo; settlement; on NM 333, 1 mi W of the Torrance County line; PO 1908–36, mail to Edgewood). A few abandoned buildings are all that remain of this community, whose service station, store, and cabins were well-known landmarks on old US 66. It was named for an early homesteader.

BASCOM (San Miguel). See *Fort Bascom.*

BASCOM CAMP (San Miguel). See *Fort Bascom.*

BASS (Lincoln; postal locality; exact location unknown; PO 1888–90). Ephemeral PO, first postmaster Charles H. Slaughter, name origin unknown.

BATTLESHIP ROCK (Sandoval; landform, picnic area; 3 mi S of La Cueva in the Jemez Mountains on NM 4). A dramatic volcanic rock formation resembling the prow of a battleship, site of a popular trailhead and picnic area.

BAUGHLS STATION (San Miguel; RR locality; 1.25 mi NW of Pecos National Monument). George Adlai Feather reported this to be a station on the AT&SF RR; the station's name clearly resulted from a personal name.

BAXTER MOUNTAIN, 7,285 ft. (Lincoln; 2 mi W of White Oaks). In 1879 George Baxter and two other prospectors discovered the Homestake gold lode on this mountain and thus ignited the mining boom that created the nearby town of White Oaks (see entry). Many other rich strikes also were on this mountain.

BAYARD (Grant; settlement; 2 mi SE of Central, on US 180; PO 1902–present). Inhabited settlement named for *Fort Bayard,* the early fort and Army hospital to the N.

BAYLOR CANYON, PASS, PEAK, 7,721 ft.

(Doña Ana; in the N Organ Mountains, 11 mi NE of Las Cruces). These related features all were named for Lt. Col. John R. Baylor, the Confederate officer who captured Union forces here during the Civil War. Baylor Canyon on the W side of the Organ Mountains leads to the pass, just S of Baylor Peak, which leads to Aguirre Spring and connects the W side of the mountains with the E. Baylor has been described as "a man of vindictive nature, with a sinister look about him," but also as "a decisive and forceful leader." After capturing the Union troops, he proclaimed creation of the Territory of Arizona, with Mesilla its capital and himself its governor.

BEAR (general). Black bears are found throughout NM, and at one time grizzly bears were found here as well. Because any encounter with a bear likely would have been memorable, the place where the encounter occurred easily could have been named for it; thus the numerous "bear" names throughout the state frequently came from specific incidents rather than from a general abundance of bears. The Spanish word is *oso.* GNIS lists approximately 140 Bear names, 32 *oso* names.

BEAR CANYON (Bernalillo; on the W slopes of the Sandia Mountains, N of Embudo Canyon and S of Pino Canyon). Black bears still live in the Sandia Mountain Wilderness, though the specific origin of this name is unknown.

BEAR CANYON (Otero; in the Sacramento Mountains, 9 mi SE of Cloudcroft). In the canyon's lower section is *Bear Springs,* where two battles were fought in 1858 between Army troops and Indians.

BEAR MOUNTAIN, 10,663 ft. (Colfax; in the Cimarron Range, on Philmont Scout Ranch, NW of Tooth of Time Ridge).

BEAR MOUNTAIN, 10,253 ft. (Taos; in the Sangre de Cristo Mountains, in S part of county, 1 mi N of Santa Barbara Campground).

BEARTRAP CANYON, BEARTRAP SPRING (Socorro; on the NW side of the San Mateo Mountains, W of Mount Withington). The Cibola NF's *Beartrap*

Campground is here.

BEARWALLOW MOUNTAIN, 9,920 ft. (Catron; in the Mogollon Mountains, 7.5 mi NE of Mogollon). *Bearwallow Creek* heads here and flows SW. These names sometimes are spelled *Bear Wallow,* but they appear as one word in GNIS.

BEARHEAD PEAK, 8,711 ft. (Sandoval; in SW Jemez Mountains, 11 mi NW of Cochiti Pueblo). The mountain's profile is said to resemble a bear's head.

THE BEAST (McKinley). See *Frog Rock.*

BEATTYS CABIN, BEATTYS (Mora; in the Pecos Wilderness, N of Cowles, at the junction of the Pecos River and the Rito del Padre). Around 1870, prospector George Beatty built a two-room log cabin here. A colorful character, with a distinctive goatee, Beatty would regale visitors with tales of adventures in the wilderness. Nothing remains of the original cabin, but its location has become a major reference point for the Upper Pecos region as several trails intersect here. *Beattys Creek* enters the Pecos River from the W, just S of Beattys Cabin.

BEATTYS FORK OF THE PECOS. See *Rito del Padre.*

BEAUTIFUL MOUNTAIN, 8,388 ft. (San Juan; SW of Shiprock, 2 mi from the Arizona border, 5 mi NW of Sanostee). The English name for this conspicuous 5-mile-long mesa is merely a translation of its Navajo name. In Navajo culture, the concept of "beauty" implies more than mere attractiveness to also include the religious concepts of harmony and balance; the Navajos regard this mesa as sacred. It appeared on an 1860 map as *Mesa Cayateno* and on an 1882 map as *Corona de Giganta,* "giant's crown."

BEAUTY (Lea; settlement; 18 mi NE of Tatum; PO 1916–18, mail to Bronco, TX). Of this short-lived settlement, nothing remains and little is known, including the origin of its name.

BEAVER (general). Primarily because of the commercial value of their fur, beavers once were eagerly sought, and explorers, trappers, and even settlers and farmers noted their presence on creeks and rivers, thus creating the legions of "beaver" names throughout the American West; GNIS lists the term 18 times in NM. The colloquial term used by Spanish-speaking people in NM was *nutria;* this also is common, listed 20 times.

BEAVER (Catron; settlement; on the W side of the San Mateo Mountains, exact location unknown; PO 1880–82). Vanished ephemeral locality. An 1887 map showed this to be on the Tularosa River, below Tularosa.

BEAVERHEAD (Catron; settlement; at the junction of NM 59 and NM 163, in the Gila NF; PO 1922–38, mail to Black Springs). Once the site of the *Beaverhead Lodge,* this place was named by the Evans brothers, local ranchers, because it's near the head of *Beaver Creek.* A Gila NF ranger station is near the settlement site.

BECK (Hidalgo; settlement; in the Steins Pass area). A little mining camp, long abandoned; see *Steins Pass, Kimball,* and *Pocahontas.*

BECKER (Valencia; RR site; on the AT&SF RR, 15 mi SW of Belen). John Becker was among several German immigrants who moved to this area late in the 19th century and established themselves as traders. Together with his partner, Paul B. Dalies, he formed the Becker-Dalies Co. in Belen; their store, long a local landmark, was at the site of the present First National Bank building. Because Becker and Dalies were leaders in having the RR come through Belen, via the Belen Cut-off, the AT&SF RR named the first water tank E of Belen for Becker and the first one NW for Dalies. Their names also appear on streets in Belen.

BEECHATUDA DRAW (San Juan; 6 mi N of Waterflow). The geologists Edward C. Beaumont of Albuquerque and Phil Hayes of Denver claim credit for this delightful pun (say both words rapidly). Accordng to Beaumont, a USGS geologist who worked for many years in the San Juan Basin, Hayes, another USGS geologist, had been mapping some complex stratigraphic geology in this area and on his map wanted to name an unnamed draw Pipeline Draw, because of a pipeline in it (a name was needed so a stratigraphic unit could be labelled). But USGS objected, saying the name was too prosaic, so one night over drinks Beaumont and Hayes concocted the name Beechatuda; when Beaumont submitted this name to USGS, he said it honored a "legendary" Ute chieftain. USGS was suspicious of this name but agreed to accept it if approved by the USBGN, so when Beaumont submitted several names to USBGN he listed them in tabular form; "draw" appeared in the first column and Beechatuda in the second. USBGN, not catching the ruse, approved the name, which irritated USGS for many years but continues to amuse New Mexicans.

BEENHAM (Union; settlement; on a branch of Tramperas Creek, 9 mi SE of Pasamonte; PO 1890–1924, mail to Barney). This community, now abandoned, was founded and named about 1880 by Charles John de Haviland Bushnell, known locally as "Uncle Charley." He was a retired sea captain from Beenham, England, who, according to local lore, wanted to get as far away from the sea as possible.

BECLABITO (San Juan; settlement; in NW part of county, 1 mi from Arizona line). Inhabited Navajo community, with a Navajo name meaning "bottom spring," referring to *Beclabito Spring*. The name has been transliterated many ways— *Biclabito, Bitlabito, Beklabito,* and others—but the USBGN in 1983 settled upon Beclabito.

BELCHER (Roosevelt; settlement; in SE part of county, near Inez; PO 1910–11, mail to Inez). An ephemeral homesteader community, now abandoned, that took the name of its first postmaster, Everett E. Belcher.

BELEN (Valencia; settlement; on the W side of the Rio Grande, on US 85, 31 mi S of Albuquerque; PO 1865–68, 1873–present). The history of the Belen area extends back to the Pueblo Revolt of 1680, for an archive mentions a village destroyed then. But formal settlement and the name Belen date to 1740, when Diego de Torres and Antonio de

Salazar successfully petitioned Don Gaspar Domínguez de Mendoza, Governor and Captain General of NM, for a land grant to be known as *Nuestra Señora de Belén,* "Our Lady of Bethlehem." (In keeping with the biblical theme, a Belen neighborhood later was called *Jerusalem.*)

At the time of the grant, two competing settlements occupied the land, one Hispanic and the other occupied by *genízaros,* Hispanicized Indians formerly captives often ransomed from other Indians. In 1746 the *genízaros* protested the grant, saying they had prior occupancy of the land, but authorities never responded to the lawsuit. Still, *genízaros* continued farming in the area.

Originally, the Belen grant consisted of as many as eight separate *plazas; Bacaville* (see entry) not only had its own name but also its own PO and school. Another plaza was called *Los Trujillos,* for a family there. Eventually Belen grew and absorbed these *plazas,* though some still retain their names and identities.

By the end of the 19th century, Belen had evolved into two rival sections, *Plaza Vieja,* or "old town," and *New Town.* The competition between them finally was resolved by a young priest, Fr. Paulet, who upon seeing the deterioration of the church in Plaza Vieja announced construction of a new church—in New Town.

The completion of the Belen Cut-off of the AT&SF RR in 1907 made Belen a RR center and earned it the nickname "Hub City." The arrival in the 1960s of I-25 has further reinforced Belen's importance as a commercial and population center.

BELL (Colfax; settlement; in NE part of the county, on Johnson Mesa; PO 1891–1933, mail to Sugarite). In the early 1880s, Marion Bell, an AT&SF RR construction worker, led a group of fellow RR workers onto Johnson Mesa to attempt farming. They were successful, at least temporarily, and other farmers followed until a family lived on every 160 acres. When a PO was needed for the diffuse community, it took Bell's name. Marion Bell remained on Johnson Mesa until he moved to Raton in 1914, where he lived until his death in 1930; nothing now remains of the community named for him. See *Johnson Mesa.*

BELL LAKE (Lea; 4 mi E of Lovington). George Bell dug a well and dugout at what became known as Bell Lake. Bell also dug several wells in a salt grass basin 12 miles E of Bell Lake that came to be known as *Bell Wells.*

BELL RANCH (San Miguel; settlement; in E part of county, E of the Canadian River and NE of Conchas Dam; PO 1888–1959, mail to rural station of Conchas Dam). In 1824 Pablo Montoya received a huge grant of land in the Canadian River valley. In 1871, Wilson Waddingham bought almost all this land and established several ranches, one of which was called the Bell Ranch, named for its bell-shaped livestock brand. This, in turn, had been inspired by bell-shaped *Bell Mountain* (see entry), approximately 5 miles N of the ranch headquarters. The mountain also gave its name to a station on the former SP RR line, 14 mi S of Mosquero; its name was *Campana,* Spanish, "bell." Though its PO is gone and its acreage has shrunk, the Bell Ranch is still active.

BELL MOUNTAIN, 5,096 ft. (San Miguel; E of the Canadian River, 2 mi W of Huerfano Mesa). Named for its bell shape. Two smaller prominences nearby to the SW are named *Ding* and *Dong.*

BELL TOP MOUNTAIN, 5,735 ft. (Doña Ana; in the Sierra de las Uvas, 11 mi W of Radium Springs). The name describes the mountain's shape.

BELL VIEW (Curry; settlement; 5 mi S of Grady). Unlike the *Bellview* E of Grady, this Bell View has ceased to exist, except as a memory, and the origin of its name has been lost.

BELLVIEW (Curry; in NE part of county, 6 mi E of Broadview, at the junction of NM 93 and NM 241; PO 1912–present). The tiny inhabited community of Bellview has had a complex history. Soon after the area was settled around

1905, several POs were established at different locations, including *Preston* and *Legansville.* When what is now Bellview was established, the community was called *Rosedale* and the accompanying school was called Bellview. In 1918, however, Bellview was decided upon as the name of the settlement as well, though the name Rosedale survives on the local Baptist Church. (It has been reported that the school was named *Liberty Bell,* the Bell later inspiring the name Bellview.) This Bellview is not to be confused with Bell View (see entry), also in Curry County but located S of Grady and now abandoned.

BELLY ACHE MESA (Catron). See *Gutache Mesa.*

BELMONT (Eddy; settlement; in the vicinity of Seven Rivers). In 1879 promoters laid out a townsite and applied for a PO, but their hopes were premature, as this was the most sparsely settled region of the state at the time, and Belmont was stillborn.

BEN MOORE MOUNTAIN (Grant; large escarpment SE of Santa Rita). US Army Lt. William H. Emory, reporting on his 1846 military reconnaissance, wrote: "We passed at the foot of a formidable bluff of trap, running NW and SE, which I named Ben Moore, after my personal friend, the gallant Captain Moore, of the 1st Dragoons." See *Kneeling Nun.*

BEN SLAUGHTER SPRING (Eddy). See *Slaughter Draw.*

BENNETT (Lea; settlement; 3 mi S of Jal, on NM 205; PO 1940–57, mail to Jal). Sometimes known as *Bennettville,* this inhabited settlement was developed in the 1930s following local oil and gas discoveries; most of its residents have been employees of the El Paso Natural Gas Co. Name origin unknown.

BENNETT PEAK, 6,471 ft. (San Juan; 6 mi N of Newcomb, 1 mi W of US 666). When US Army Lt. James Simpson passed through here on Aug. 30, 1849, he noted in his journal "these splendid peaks." This jagged volcanic formation later was named for another military man, Maj. Frank Tracy Bennett, agent to the Navajos in 1869–71 and 1880–81. The Navajo name for the formation means "traprock sticking up."

BENSON (Roosevelt; settlement; 10 mi W of Floyd; PO 1907–11 as Pearson, 1911–18, mail to Upton). *Pearson* was the first name of the PO in this community, but in 1911, and possibly with a change of location, the name was changed to Benson, for John O. Benson, the first postmaster after the name change.

BENT (Otero; settlement; on US 70, 12 mi NE of Tularosa; PO 1906–present). About 1906 George Bent, miner and promoter, established a mill along the Rio Tularosa, and when a PO was needed it took his name. The mill no longer is active, but the tiny settlement by the river remains.

BERINO (Doña Ana; settlement; on NM 226, 1 mi E of NM 478, 19 mi S of Las Cruces; PO 1902–66, mail to a rural branch). The name *Berino* has been said to be derived from an Indian word meaning "ford," and this old Hispanic settlement's location near the E bank of the Rio Grande would support that. But the name also has been said to be a contraction of *Chamberino,* the name—also of obscure origin—of an Hispanic settlement immediately W of Berino across the river and said to have been founded by residents of Berino seeking to avoid persistent flooding. And George Adlai Feather of Las Cruces, a linguist, believed the name came from a word, related to *merino,* denoting a breed of sheep in northern Mexico. He also said the community had at one time been called *Cottonwoods.* The old part of Berino is located 1 mile E of NM 478, on a small rise, but most businesses have moved to the highway and the AT&SF RR, to the locale known as *Berino Siding.*

BERNAL (San Miguel; settlement; just S of I-25, 17 mi SW of Las Vegas; PO as Serafina 1923–present). This former stage stop, the first that one would meet going from Las Vegas to Santa Fe, bears the Bernal family name. The first person with that surname in NM was Pascuala Bernal, who came with her husband, Juan Griego, as a member of the Oñate expedition of 1598. Some of their sons took the Griego name, but at least one son and several daughters chose Bernal. The PO here has the feminine forename *Serafina,* for reasons unknown. The community also has been referred to as *Bernal Springs,* for local springs. See also *Bernalillo.*

BERNALILLO (Sandoval; settlement, county seat; on NM 313, 17 mi NE of Albuquerque, on the E bank of the Rio Grande; PO 1855–59, 1865–present). The present site of Bernalillo likely was occupied by a southern Tiwa Indian pueblo when Coronado and his troops arrived here in 1540, and many historians believe Coronado wintered here, close to wood and water, and not at *Kuaua* (see entry), 2 mi to the NW at Coronado State Monument. Contemporary Tiwas still remember the pueblo and call it *Stolen Town,* because it was appropriated by the Spaniards.

The area around Bernalillo was among the first settled by the Spanish colonists, and among the families who established estates here were the Bernals; Pascuala Bernal had accompanied her husband, Juan Griego, on the Oñate expedition of 1598, and while some of their sons took the Griego name, at least one son and several daughters chose Bernal. In the town of Bernalillo itself, the consensus is that the name Bernalillo refers to the Gonzáles-Bernal family, whose members lived here before 1680 and also after 1693, though it's obscure why the dimunitive form, "little Bernal," was used; perhaps it referred to a family member small of stature, or perhaps to a "junior." The first appearance of the name Bernalillo is in a 1696 record that mentioned a *Real de Bernalillo* here, *real* meaning "camp, headquarters," though it also is the legal title of a mining camp. Within 50 years of Oñate's expedition, the locality to the N of present Bernalillo was known as *La Angostura de Bernalillo,* "the Narrows of Bernalillo." In 18th century documents, Bernalillo usually is referred to as a *puesto,* a Spanish term meaning literally "place," but in early NM it signified "small town."

Equally obscure is the origin of the name of the Bernalillo neighborhood, *Las Cocinitas*, "the little kitchens," that represents the community's Old Town. Located W of the downtown business district, Las Cocinitas is one of the oldest residential sections in the US, with buildings dating back to the 1690s.

Just N of Bernalillo are two little named "suburbs." *El Chapparral*, "the thicket," is N of the high school. *El Llanito* takes its name, "little plain," from its location on a slight rise; residents of nearby Santa Ana Pueblo jokingly refer to the locality as "Sky City."

BERNALILLO COUNTY (in central NM, astride the Rio Grande; county seat, Albuquerque). Bernalillo County was one of the original nine counties created by the territorial legislature in 1852, but while the county was named for the settlement of Bernalillo, its first county seat was Ranchos de Albuquerque, probably because this was closer to the county's geographic center. In 1854, the seat was moved farther south to Albuquerque, then rapidly growing in importance.

Bernalillo residents, however, coveted the county seat for their community, and in 1875 they arranged for the annexation of Santa Ana County (see entry) to Bernalillo County, which made Bernalillo now closer to the geographic center. At this time, Bernalillo County was NM's largest in population. The legislature denied the Bernalillo residents' request for an outright change of county seat, but it did approve a referendum within the county as to where the seat should be located. The election was held in 1878; Albuquerque lost, Bernalillo won. This was the situation until Sandoval County was created in 1903, which resolved the tug-of-war between Bernalillo and Albuquerque by making each community a county seat.

BERNALILLO PLUG (Sandoval). See *Toe Rock*.

BERNARDO (Socorro; on W bank of the Rio Grande, at junction of US 60 and I-25, 25 mi N of Socorro; PO 1902–19, mail to Bosque). This tiny inhabited settlement was named about 1902 for a friend of John Becker, a prominent Belen merchant. Previously the locality had been called *Picacho*, "peak," because Ladron Peak is just to the west. *Bernardo State Game Refuge* is just E of the settlement of Bernardo.

BERRENDA, BERRENDO (general). See *Antelope (general)*.

BERRENDO (Chaves; settlement; NW of present Roswell, on Berrendo Creek). When this tiny Hispanic village was settled in the 1870s, most likely by people from Missouri Plaza (see entry) on the Rio Hondo, it took the name of the creek on which it was located. Unfortunately, Berrendo came to a tragic and untimely end. In 1878 the village was raided by cowboy ruffians who shot up the town and took everything of value. Discouraged and embittered, the settlers abandoned their homes, and by the time the Milne and Bush ranch headquarters was established later on the site, only one small adobe building remained.

BERRENDO CREEK (Chaves; enters Roswell from the NW). Tributaries include *South Berrendo Creek* and *Middle Berrendo Creek; see Antelope (general)*.

BESS (Guadalupe; settlement; on the W side of the Pecos River, 12 mi SE of Puerto de Luna; PO 1925–30, mail to Fort Sumner). Bess was a PO serving the joint communities of Bess and Los Ojitos, "the little springs," (see entry). It was established by Georgeus Marshall who came from Ireland and in 1972 returned. When water from Sumner Lake covered Los Ojitos, Bess declined as well and has long been abandoned. The origin of its name is unknown.

BETHEL (Lincoln; settlement; on the NE side of the Capitan Mountains). Abandoned community, that once had a store and a schoolhouse. While alive, Bethel often was jocularly referred to as *Hogwaller;* a drunken cowboy attending a dance here during a rainy spell pronounced that the place reminded him of a "hogwaller"—and the epithet stuck.

BETHEL (Roosevelt; settlement; 10 mi W of Portales; PO 1902–07, mail to Portales). This inhabited community was founded in 1901 by homesteaders from Lockney, TX, among whom were several members of the Church of Christ, along with their minister, S.W. Smith. They immediately established a church and a school, and they gave their settlement a Hebrew name meaning "house of God."

BETONNIE TSOSIE WASH (San Juan; in SE part of county, runs SW into Escavada Wash at the abandoned Chaco Canyon Trading Post). Tsosie is a common Navajo surname; the individual whose name appears on this major drainage is unknown.

BEULAH (Rio Arriba; settlement; exact location unknown; PO 1894–95, mail to Abiquiu). Ephemeral locality, likely named for the Land of Beulah; see *Beulah, (San Miguel)*.

BEULAH (San Miguel; settlement; in Sapello Canyon, upstream from San Ignacio, 17 mi NW of Las Vegas; PO 1896–1932, mail to Tecoloteños). Named for the old Methodist hymn, "Beulah Land," named in turn for the Land of Beulah mentioned in John Bunyan's *Pilgrim's Progress* as the land of heavenly joy where the pilgrims tarry before entering the Celestial City. The community has been abandoned.

BIBLE TOP BUTTE, 5,655 ft. (Union; 3 mi W of Rabbit Ear Mountain, N of US 87). A crease centered in the top of this flat-topped butte makes it look like an open book when viewed from the E.

BIBO (Cibola). See *Cebolletita*.

BIG BEAR SPRING (McKinley). See *Fort Wingate*.

BIG COSTILLA PEAK, 12,739 ft. (Taos; in the Sangre de Cristo Mountains, in the Culebra Range, 5 mi S of the Colorado border). Named for its proximity to *Costilla Creek* (see entry), which flows past the mountain on three sides, and also to *Little Costilla Peak* (see entry), 12,580 ft., 8 mi to the SE. The name, Spanish for "rib," described a rib-shaped bend in the creek.

BIG SPRING (Union). See *Seneca Creek*.

BIG WHITE GAP (Doña Ana; in the Sierra de las Uvas, 11 mi W of Radium Springs). Pass likely named for the color of its rocks. Just 1 mi N is *Little White Gap*.

BIGGS (Rio Arriba; settlement; on an abandoned line of the D&RGW RR, 4 mi E of Monero, at the junction of US 64 and US 84). This abandoned lumber camp was named for E.M. Biggs, president of the company that built the lumber road from Lumberton to Hillcrest.

BILL KNIGHT GAP (Catron; between Spur Lake Basin and Luna, in the San Francisco Mountains). A man named Bill Knight lived here.

BILL LEE MESA (Catron; 3 mi NW of Luna). Bill Lee, who once had a store and PO in Luna, ran cattle on this mesa.

BILLING (Socorro; settlement; 5 mi SW of Socorro). This abandoned point on the also-abandoned AT&SF RR between Socorro and Magdalena likely was named for Gustav Billing, a mining engineer.

BILLY THE KID SPRING (Chaves; on San Juan Mesa, 14 mi NW of Kenna). Local lore has it that this small spring in a concavity beneath an overhanging cliff was one of Billy the Kid's hideouts. Located 100 yards from the spring are the ruins of a half-dugout.

BINGHAM (Socorro; settlement; on US 380, 29 mi E of San Antonio; PO 1934–present). Once as many as 300 people lived in the area of Bingham; now a remnant population and the PO keep the community alive. Sam Jones, who with his wife, Vera, were the village's only residents in 1988, said, "Bingham's a healthy place to live: there never was a church, and there never was a graveyard." Bingham takes its name from the homesteader who established the PO; *Old Bingham* was located 2 miles N of the present village.

BIRCHVILLE (Grant). See *Pinos Altos*.

BISHOP PEAK, 8,849 ft. (Catron; 6 mi N of Luna). "Uncle" Henry Reynolds, bishop of the local Mormon church, lived near here.

BISHOPS CAP, 5,419 ft. (Doña Ana; mountain; 12 mi SE of Las Cruces). This peak, shaped like a bishop's cap, is the highest of a series of N-S ridges extending S from the Organ Mountains.

BISHOPS LODGE (Santa Fe). See *Lamy.*

BISTI (San Juan; trading point; 0.50 mi E of NM 371, 32 mi S of Farmington). This locality was named for its proximity to the landforms of the *Bisti* (see entry). Pronounced biss-TY.

BISTI (San Juan; landform; 32 mi S of Farmington, straddling NM 371). *Bisti* approximates the Navajo word for "bad-lands," but the name does little justice to this strange and beautiful natural area, with its polychrome erosional forma-tions and rich assemblage of fossils. The name often appears as *Bisti Badlands,* with a double generic. The *Bisti Oil Field* is here. See *Bisti Wilderness* and *De-na-zin Wilderness.*

BISTI WILDERNESS (San Juan; in the San Juan Basin, 36 mi S of Farmington). Designated in 1984 and administered by the BLM, the 3,946-acre Bisti Wilderness takes its name from the region known as the Bisti, whose features it protects; see also *De-na-zin Wilderness.*

BITTER CREEK BURG (Taos; settlement; on Bitter Creek, NE of Red River). One of several still-born mining camps at-tempted during the boom of 1895. See also *Gysin City, Jellison City.*

BITTER LAKE NATIONAL WILDLIFE REFUGE (Chaves; E of Roswell, just W of the Pecos River and N of US 380). Centered around *Bitter Lake,* which bears a common name in the arid Southwest where dissolved minerals of-ten impart a bitter taste to water. The 24,000-acre refuge provides a wintering area for sandhill cranes, snow geese, and numerous other species of waterfowl, marsh, and shore birds. The *Salt Creek Wilderness* is within the refuge.

BLACK (general). *Black* is a common de-scriptive place name element through-out the world but especially so in NM where widespread volcanism has re-sulted in numerous basalt formations. Black lava, along with dark-appearing conifers and other factors, have resulted in more than 178 places in NM having *Black* in their names. *Black* appears in Spanish as *Negro* or *Negra* 70 times.

BLACK (Bernalillo; extinct volcano; on Albuquerque's West Mesa). See *Vulcan.*

BLACK BUTTE (Socorro; on an open plain, 9 mi E of Bernardo, 1 mi S of US 60). This small but conspicuous knob, easily visible from I-25, is a massive jumble of black basalt, hence the name. It also is referred to as *Turututu,* or *Turato,* names most likely derived from the southern Tiwa Indian language, especially as the butte is a religious landmark to the Tiwas of Isleta Pueblo. But these names also could be related in some way to the Spanish stem, *dura,* meaning "lasting" or "durable."

BLACK CANYON (Grant; a tributary of the Gila River's East Fork, heading in the Black Range). Rocks and timber make this canyon appear dark, especially in its upper reaches.

BLACK HAT (McKinley; settlement; on NM 264, 5 mi E of the Arizona line). This appears as *Top o' the Hill Trading Post* on some maps, but the trading post no longer is active, and the name cur-rently used is Black Hat, most likely de-rived from the locality's Navajo name, meaning "burned through the rock."

BLACK HAWK (Grant; settlement; at the foot of Bullard Peak, at the N end of the Burro Mountains, 15 mi W of Silver City; PO 1884–87, mail to Fleming). In 1881 rich silver ore was discovered near Bullard Peak. Soon mines named Rose and Black Hawk were opened, and be-fore long a mining camp had sprung up. In 1883 a townsite was laid out on a nar-row mesa near the Black Hawk mine. *Carson* was proposed as a name, to honor J.H. Carson, a resident, but the mine's name was adopted instead. Black Hawk thrived from 1885 to 1887, but then mining began to wane, and today mine dumps are about all that remain of Black Hawk.

BLACK HILLS (Harding; in central part of county, E of Mosquero). Small but dis-tinctive group; highest elevation 5,059 ft.

BLACK LAKE (Colfax; in SW part of county, just W of NM 434, 7 mi S of Angel Fire.) Dense conifers on the mountains bordering this lake to the W, when reflected in the lake's waters, give it a dark appearance. Also, decaying vegetation in the broad, marshy swale where the lake is located could give the water a dark hue.

BLACK LAKE (Colfax; settlement; in SW part of county, on NM 434, 7 mi S of Angel Fire, at junction with NM 120; PO as Osha 1894–1903, as Black Lake 1903–27, mail to Ocate). This tiny inhabited settlement originally was called *Osha*, likely for its association with either *Osha Mountain* or *Osha Pass*, both to the W; see *Osha (general)*. (An 1870 map shows the communities of Black Lake and Osha as separate, with Osha being NW of Black Lake.) Black Lake's present name comes from its association with *Black Lake* (see entry) immediately to the W. The first settlers here were Don José María Mares and his wife, Doña Jenara Trujillo, who arrived in 1886. Years earlier, in 1857, Mares had been captured by Indians while he and his brother were hunting. They were taken to Taos and sold to Don Juan Mares, who adopted them and raised them as his own children.

BLACK MESA (general). Throughout much of NM, at various times in the geologic past, black volcanic material has flowed over the earth's surface. Later, the hardened lava—basalt—has been eroded into black-capped mesas, resulting in Black Mesa and its Spanish equivalents, *Mesa Prieta* and *Mesa Negra*, being very common place names.

BLACK MESA, 6,985 ft. (Rio Arriba; W of the Rio Grande, opposite San Juan Pueblo, separating the Rio Grande from the Rio Ojo Caliente). This large mesa, running 12 mi NE-SW, was named for its basalt cap; its Tewa name means "basalt height." Two trails traverse the mesa—the old Ute Trail and the Eagle Gap Trail between San Juan Pueblo and Ojo Caliente. The name appears often in its original Spanish form, *Mesa Prieta,* and in 1743 the *Mesa Prieta Grant* was made to Juan García de Mora and Diego de Medina. The tiny settlement of *Mesa Prieta* is located beneath the mesa to the

W. The mesa also has been called *Mesa de la Canoa,* or in English, *Canoe Mesa,* presumably because of its oblong boatlike shape, though the name possibly is a corruption of *canova,* Spanish, "water trough, sluice."

BLACK MESA, 6,084 ft. (Santa Fe; just N of San Ildefonso Pueblo and E of NM 30). Probably the most famous mesa of this name in NM, Black Mesa resembles a hulking, black fort, and indeed it has served as a refuge more than once. Vargas, in his reconquest of NM in 1692, assaulted the mesa three times, trying to dislodge the San Ildefonso Indians who had retreated there. Black Mesa has religious significance for the Tewas. They call it "very spotted mountain," for the large greenish spots on the N side of the black basalt formation. Other names include *Sacred Fire Mountain,* because of a shrine in its top; *Orphan Mountain,* because it is alone and isolated; *San Ildefonso Mesa,* because of its association with San Ildefonso Pueblo; and *Round Mountain,* because of its rounded summit. The early 20th-century archaeologist Edgar L. Hewett called it *Beach Mesa,* because its top is strewn with pebbles as if it had once been a beach.

BLACK MESA, 6,108 ft. (Socorro; immediately E of the Rio Grande, 16 mi SW of San Antonio). This conspicuous basalt-capped mesa was an important landmark for travelers on the *Camino Real.* Oñate in 1598 mentioned arriving at the marsh of *Mesilla de Guinea,* "so named because it was of black rock." In the 1770s, it appeared on the maps of Bernardo Miera y Pacheco and Nicolas de Lafora as *Mesa de Senecú,* for the Piro Indian Pueblo of Senecú (see entry) to the N. An English-speaker in 1846 called it *Table Mountain.* Around 1854, about the time the village of *La Mesa* at the mesa's northern base was occupied (see *San Marcial*), the mesa was referred to as *La Mesa de San Marcial,* certainly for the village to the NW. Today people refer to it simply as *La Mesa* or Black Mesa.

BLACK MESA OF SANTO TOMAS (Doña Ana; 6 mi S of Las Cruces, immediately W of Santo Tomas). Small lava-flow formation created by the San Miguel Lava Cone on its W side.

BLACK MOUNTAIN, PEAK (general). Dense stands of conifers usually are responsible for this very common mountain name, which appears in GNIS at least 25 times; *Black Hills* appears 11 times.

Black Mountain, 11,302 ft. (Taos; 2 mi SW of the village of Red River).

Black Mountain, 10,390 ft. (Colfax; at the N end of the Cimarron Range, near the NE headwaters of Moreno Creek).

Black Mountain, 10,892 ft. (Colfax; on Philmont Scout Ranch, N of the North Fork of Urraca Creek, W of Tooth of Time Mountain).

Black Peak, 6,792 ft. (Sierra; W of the village of Cuchillo). Also called *Cuchillo Negro Peak* because of its association with the village of Cuchillo Negro, "black knife," named for the Apache chief with that name.

BLACK RANGE (Sierra, Grant; N-S range, extending 100 mi from the Plains of San Agustin S to Thompson Cone, paralleling the Sierra-Grant county line). Because forest-covered mountains often appear darker than the surrounding landscape, names such as Black Range are common worldwide. The name here is especially appropriate, however, because NM's Black Range is conspicuously dark and foreboding; the steep slopes permit few clearings or meadows, and the mountainsides are densely covered with conifers. It's perhaps for these reasons that the range also has been called *Sierra Diablo,* "Devil Range." On some early maps, the Black Range appears as the *Sierra de los Miembres,* "Mimbres Range," after the Mimbres River on its W side, though this name usually is applied only to the extension of the range S of NM 152, an extension now considered part of the main range. Most of the Black Range is within the Gila NF, much in the Aldo Leopold Wilderness. The highest summits are *Reeds Peak,* 10,015 ft., and *Diamond Peak,* 9,850 ft. From Reeds Peak northward, the Continental Divide coincides with the range's crest.

BLACK RIVER (Eddy; rises in the Guadalupe Mountains in the SW corner of the county and flows generally NE into the Pecos River just N of Malaga). This important watercourse likely was named either for dark soil or water. On maps of the 1870s this river was labelled the *Blue River,* or the *Río Azul,* sometimes the *Río Azul Sacramento,* but by the 1880s the name Black River was appearing on maps.

BLACK RIVER VILLAGE (Eddy; settlement; 13 mi S of Carlsbad, 4 mi E of US 62-180 on NM 396, on the Black River). A church now uses tourist cabins here for retreats.

BLACK ROCK (McKinley; settlement; immediately NE of Zuni Pueblo; PO 1904–26, mail to Zuni). Active "suburb" of Zuni Pueblo, named for nearby lava flows. A sub-agency of the Santa Fe Indian Bureau was established here in 1920, followed later by a hospital, government buildings, and a school. The English name translates the Zuni name.

BLACK SPRINGS (Catron; settlement; on NM 61, 5 mi N of Beaverhead; PO 1935–42, mail to Magdalena). Named for nearby springs located in a dense, dark forest. Black Springs was settled in the 1930s, mostly by people from Texas, but they all have departed.

BLACKDOM (Chaves; settlement; 16 mi S of Roswell; PO 1912–19, mail to Dexter). To the African-American homesteaders who came to live in Blackdom, the lure of owning their own farms and having fellowship with other African-American farmers in a tiny Black "kingdom" must have been irresistible. The community was founded around 1900 by Francis Marion Boyer, who had walked to NM from Georgia pursuing the dream of his father, Henry Boyer, a former slave, of a self-sustaining community where African-Americans could own land and live in peace. Years later, Lillian Collins Westfield, who had lived in Blackdom, recalled the beautiful NM sunshine and the company of good friends and neighbors. But irrigation in the Blackdom area was unsuccessful, and the community withered soon after

1920; many of its residents, including Francis Boyer and his wife, Ella Louise McGruder Boyer, migrated to the community of Vado S of Las Cruces, where many of their descendants still live. Only foundations remain of Blackdom.

BLACKSMITH CANYON (Union; 2.5 mi N of Dry Cimarron River, on N side of Black Mesa). The discovery by settlers of an anvil block made from rare hardwood led to the name of this canyon. In the 1860s, the Coe outlaw gang frequented this canyon and did their blacksmithing here.

BLACKTOWER (Curry). See *Portair*.

BLACKWATER DRAW (Roosevelt; runs E-W, 6 mi NE of Portales). Early settlers dug pools to tap the high water table here, and when the water became stagnant it turned dark, hence the name. The draw's significance, however, comes not from the pools but from the paleo-Indian artifacts and remains of extinct mammals found here; since the discovery in 1932 by a highway crew of mammoth bones, the site has revealed important evidence regarding the hunters who lived here 12,000 years ago. *Blackwater Draw Museum* is located on US 70, 6 mi NE of Portales, near the discovery site.

BLAKES SPRING (Eddy). See *Artesia*.

BLANCA, BLANCO (general). The Spanish *blanca, blanco* means "white," and because many NM rocks and mineral deposits, such as alkali, are white or light-colored, these two words are very common in place names; GNIS lists 105 in NM. These terms also appear on snow-capped mountains throughout the Spanish-speaking world. The English form, *White,* also is common, with GNIS listing 202 occurrences, though some reflect the common American surname, White.

BLANCO (San Juan; settlement; 10 mi E of Bloomfield, on US 64; PO 1901–present). When Hispanic settlers moved into the San Juan River Basin in the 1870s, Blanco was among their first communities, and because it was more centrally located with respect to Largo Canyon, site of much farming and ranching, it soon replaced Turley as the area's commercial center. Blanco, still inhabited, was named either for a prominent light-colored rhyolite outcrop in nearby hills or its proximity to *Blanco Canyon*. The Navajo name for the locality means "land into water." When Capt. J.F. McComb passed through here in 1859 he listed the site simply as *Station 44*.

BLANCO CANYON (San Juan; runs NE into Carrizo Creek, 8 mi SE of Blanco). An important area for Navajos, who call the upper canyon "cottonwoods in a wide area," an appropriate descriptive name, and the lower canyon "whiskey wash," for reasons unknown.

BLANCO CREEK (Quay; heads 4 mi W of Forrest and runs S and E into Frio Draw). Named for *Blanco Canyon,* through which it flows.

BLANCO TRADING POST (San Juan; trading point; 8 mi NW of Nageezi on NM 44, at junction with NM 57). This active trading post likely was named for *Blanco Wash* 3 miles to the E.

BLAND (Sandoval; settlement; in the Jemez Mountains, 12 mi NW of Cochiti Pueblo, W of Upper Horn Mesa; PO 1894–1935, mail to Peña Blanca). This abandoned gold-and-silver mining camp, now on private property, was named to honor Richard Parks Bland, congressman from Missouri whose fight against the demonetization of silver gained him national fame and almost a nomination for the US presidency in 1896. Mining at Bland began around 1894, and by 1900 a boom town with 3,000 people was crammed into a narrow canyon only 60 feet wide; the camp had four sawmills, two banks, the *Bland Herald* newspaper, more than a dozen saloons, one church, an opera house, and even a stock exchange; by the end of 1904 the diggings had produced more that $1 million. But soon the deposits were played out; Bland became a ghost town. The site is in *Bland Canyon,* also called *Pino Canyon*.

BLAZERS MILL (Otero). See *Mescalero*.

BLOOMFIELD (San Juan; settlement; on the San Juan River, at junction of US 64 and NM 44; PO as Bloomfield 1879–81, as Porter 1881–82, as Bloomfield 1882–present). Soon after this inhabited and growing town was settled in 1878, it was named Bloomfield, most likely for a settler but also possibly for wildflowers blooming in the lowlands. Soon, however, the name was changed to *Porter,* for a man who had established trading posts in the area. This name lasted little more than a year before the name Bloomfield returned. The Navajos call the locality by a name meaning "where two wide valleys come together."

BLOSSBURG (Colfax; settlement; 5 mi up Dillon Creek, NW of Raton; PO 1881–1905, mail to Gardiner). Though coal deposits had been known in the area since 1820, Blossburg did not begin as a coal-mining camp until 1881 when a Col. Edward Savage opened the Blossburg coal mine; he named it and the settlement for his hometown, Blossburg, PA. The settlement grew rapidly—its promoters called it "The Pittsburg of the West"—and eventually acquired churches, schools, the Blossburg band, and the *Blossburg Pioneer* newspaper. But as demand for coal faded, so did the community, and today Blossburg, like Dawson, Gardiner, Swastika, and other Colfax County coal towns, is abandoned and in ruins.

BLOSSER GAP (Colfax; about 15 mi SW of Raton). A rancher named Blosser once ran cattle through this gap.

BLUE (general). Almost all mountains and most other landforms appear blue when viewed from a distance, and so do most water bodies, when viewed from the right perspective. GNIS lists 91 features in NM with *Blue* as part of their names. The Spanish form, *Azul,* is less common, appearing only 8 times, usually in names of water bodies.

BLUE BIRD MESA (Sandoval; 8 mi SE of Cuba). Both Mountain bluebirds and Western bluebirds are common in this part of NM.

BLUE CANYON (Socorro; heads about 3 mi W of Socorro and runs NE toward the town). Named for mineral deposits that at certain times of the day appear a striking blue.

BLUE HOLE (Guadalupe; spring; in SE Santa Rosa). The name Blue Hole concisely describes this natural spring, a part of the Santa Rosa park system and the source of *Santa Rosa Creek.* The water appears azure, and it flows year-round at the rate of 3,000 gallons a minute into a bell-shaped hole 60 feet in diameter at the top and 91 feet deep, with a constant temperature of 63 degrees F.

BLUE LAKE (Taos; at the head of the Rio Pueblo de Taos, 1 mi SE of Old Mike Peak). Blue Lake, an important symbol for Taos Pueblo, is the site each year of ceremonies and rituals, not to be witnessed by outsiders. Once within the Carson NF, the sacred lake was ceded to the pueblo by the federal government in 1970 after almost 60 years of negotiations.

BLUE MOUNTAIN, 10,336 ft. (Socorro; in the San Mateo Mountains, 3 mi N of San Mateo Peak). This mountain, the highest in the San Mateo Mountains, actually consists of two summits: *West Blue Mountain,* 10,336 ft., and *East Blue Mountain,* 10,319 ft. As many mountains appear blue from a distance, *Blue Mountain* or one of its variants is among the world's most common mountain names.

BLUE RANGE WILDERNESS (Catron; in SW part of county, abutting the Arizona border, 65 mi NW of Silver City). When the NM Wilderness Act of 1980 was passed, this 29,304-acre tract in the Apache NF became the Blue Range Wilderness while an adjoining 173,762 acres in Arizona remained the Blue Range Primitive Area. Traversed from W to E by the Mogollon Rim, this is an area of deep, rugged canyons and extensive timbered slopes. See *Blue River.*

BLUE RIVER (Catron; heads in the San Francisco Mountains and runs into Arizona). Just a few hundred yards before the Arizona border *Dry Blue Creek* becomes the Blue River, whose name likely is related to the Blue Range (see *Blue Range Wilderness*).

BLUEBERRY HILL (Taos; W of Taos Plaza, N of Los Cordovas). The story told to this author by a Taos woman present at the naming is that during the 1950s, when the song "Blueberry Hill" by Fats Domino was popular, a group of Taos high school students skipped school one day and went to party on this hill, naming the hill for the song they listened to on the radio. The author has found no one in Taos with another explanation, and most Taoseños seem to recognize and use the name.

BLUEWATER (Cibola; settlement; just W of I-40, 10 mi NW of Grants; PO 1889–92, 1895–present). This small agricultural community owes its name to its location on *Bluewater Creek;* for the same reason, the settlement has been called *Bluewater Valley.* Local Indians say that long ago, "before the lava came," a great lake existed in this valley, and translating the Indian name for the place Hispanic settlers called the region N of the Zuni Mountains *Agua Azul;* indeed, Agua Azul had been stipulated as the S boundary of Navajo country in the Navajo-Spanish treaty of 1819. In 1870, the American traveler Beadle mentioned Agua Azul and made drawings showing buildings. The Navajos know the place as "large cottonwood trees where water flows out." The first community of Bluewater was created by the A&P RR in 1880–81. When the Mormon settlers Ernest Tietjen and Frihoff Nelson, along with non-Mormon backers, put up an earthen dam at the confluence of Bluewater and Cottonwood Creeks, settlers, both Mormons and non-Mormons, began arriving, and by 1896 a community called *Mormontown* had sprung up 3 mi W of the RR town of Bluewater. Eventually, the RR community died, and the farming community adopted the name. Two recent residential developments—*Bluewater Acres* and *Bluewater Estates,* not adjoining Bluewater village—have been created S of Thoreau on the way to Bluewater Lake.

BLUEWATER CREEK (Cibola; heads in the Zuni Mountains, flows N into Bluewater Lake, then to the village of Bluewater). This simple descriptive name translates the earlier Spanish name, *Agua Azul.* The Navajos' name for the creek also means "blue water."

BLUEWATER LAKE STATE PARK (Cibola, McKinley; on Bluewater Creek, on the Cibola-McKinley line, 7 mi W of the village of Bluewater). Located in Bluewater Canyon and fed by Bluewater Creek, this L-shaped lake is 3 mi long and 0.5 mi wide and when full indeed boasts water conspicuously blue. A dirt dam was built here as early as 1885, by some French ranchers, and other dams followed as earlier ones washed out. The lake and its surrounding piñon-ponderosa forest became a state park in 1955.

Lakes named *Blue Water* also are located in Lincoln and Otero Counties.

BLUE WEED FLAT (Lea; 13 mi NE of Lovington). This area, named for an unknown species of blue "weeds," gave its name to a rural school, discontinued sometime before 1927.

BLUFF SPRINGS (Otero; in the Sacramento Mountains E of Alamogordo, on the Rio Peñasco). A travertine bluff, formed by accretions from the springs, has created a scenic waterfall on the Rio Peñasco here and possibly inspired the name Rio Peñasco (see entry), Spanish, "bluff river" or "rocky river."

BLUITT (Roosevelt; settlement; on NM 262, 9 mi E of Milnesand; PO 1916–44, mail to Milnesand). This abandoned farming and ranching community was named for the Bluitt Ranch in Texas at the suggestion of J.T. Hadaway, who had worked at the ranch before moving to NM.

BLUMNER (Rio Arriba; settlement; near Vallecitos, 20 mi E of Cebolla; PO 1905–07, mail to Vallecitos). Short-lived postal locality, name origin unknown.

BOAZ (Chaves; settlement; 40 mi NE of Roswell on US 70; PO 1907–55, mail to Elida). When W.W. Weatherly established this locality in 1907, he named it for the Boaz mentioned in the Book of Ruth in the Bible. Nothing except perhaps a railroad sign remains to mark the site.

BOBCAT CREEK (Taos; 1 mi SE of village of Red River). Bobcats are indeed abundant in this area. *Bobcat Pass,* 9,820 ft., is at the head of Bobcat Creek, 3 mi SE of the village of Red River.

BOGLE (Lincoln; postal locality; on SP RR, 12 mi N of Carrizozo; PO 1919–25, mail to Carrizozo). Bogle, never more than a RR pumping station and a PO, was established near the site of the former Hurlburt PO (see entry), and like its predecessor it took the name of the RR pumper, James L. Bogle, who also was its first postmaster. Nothing remains at the site today.

LA BOLSA, LA LOMA DE LA BOLSA (Santa Fe; landform; 6 mi SW of Madrid). The name of this basalt-crested mesa on the W side of Stagecoach Canyon, adjacent to NM 14, is Spanish and means "purse, bag," but any resemblance to a *bolsa* is not obvious, and the origin of the name is unknown.

BOLSON (general). The Spanish *bolsón* means "big purse, bag" but in the Southwest, and especially among geologists, the term also refers to basins and valleys lacking outflowing drainage. For example, the Estancia Valley has been called a bolson; see *Playa* (general).

BONANZA CITY (Santa Fe; settlement; in the Cerrillos Mining District, 13 mi SW of Santa Fe, SW of Bonanza Hill on Bonanza Creek, N of Cerrillos; PO 1880–83, mail to Turquesa). Bonanza City, along with the mining camps of *Carbonateville* and *Cerrillos* (see entries), burst into being in 1879 soon after two prospectors, Frank Dimmitt and Robert Hart, discovered rich silver, lead, and zinc ore in this area. In 1880, John J. Mahoney, former US consul to Algiers, laid out the townsite of Bonanza City, and at about the same time Hugh Marshall discovered the Marshall Bonanza two miles from Bonanza City. At one time, as many as 2,000 persons crowded into the camp, seeking the "bonanza" for which the camp optimistically was named, but as happened so often in NM their dreams were not realized; today Bonanza City is little more than a name and a memory. *Bonanza* is a Spanish word meaning "rich ore pocket" and "prosperity."

BOND (Bernalillo). See *Vulcan*.

BONITA, BONITO (general). These Spanish names, meaning "pretty, handsome," have been applied to features throughout NM, particularly streams, valleys, and lakes.

BONITO (Lincoln; settlement; 1 mi E of Bonito Lake, on the Rio Bonito). Small inhabited residential community, named for the Rio Bonito (see entry).

BONITO CITY (Lincoln; settlement; in Bonito Canyon, 6 mi W of Angus; PO 1882–1911, mail to Parsons). In 1880 a small group of prospectors stumbled upon a well-watered, well-timbered site that best of all showed promising signs of mineralization. Though the site technically was on the Mescalero Indian Reservation, the miners were undeterred, especially after silver ore was discovered, and by 1882 a mining camp was burgeoning in *Bonito Canyon*. Because of this location and the rapid growth of the camp, it was called Bonito City, though it more commonly has been called simply *Bonito*.

Eventually, the ore played out, and the miners drifted away, though the PO remained open. Finally, the SP RR constructed a water-supply dam in the canyon, creating *Bonito Lake* and drowning what remained of Bonito City.

BONITO PEAK, 10,616 ft. (Colfax; in the Cimarron Range, on Philmont Scout Ranch). *Bonito Creek* flows SE from here.

BONNER LAKE (De Baca; 12 mi S of Fort Sumner). A playa lake, named because Tom A. Bonner's ranch was on its periphery.

BOOTHEEL (Hidalgo; extreme SW part of state). On maps, the 28-mile jog in the state's southern border here resembles the heel of a boot.

BOOTLEG CANYON (Mora; heads just S of NM 120 E of Wagon Mound and flows SE into the Canadian River). A reminder of the Prohibition era in NM. See *Whiskey (general)*.

BOOTLEG RIDGE (Lea; landform; in W-central part of county). Another reminder of Prohibition. See *Whiskey (general)*.

BOQUILLA (Rio Arriba, Taos?; settlement; along the Rio Grande, exact location unknown). Spanish, "opening, as in an irrigation canal." George Adlai Feather found this long-abandoned locality mentioned often in newspapers from 1875 to 1878 but not after 1900. Feather put it 2–3 mi below Riverside.

BORICA (Guadalupe; settlement; 30 mi S of Santa Rosa, on the mesa 10 mi SE of Puerto de Luna; PO 1916–19, mail to Pastura). Also called *Borica Springs,* this locality was never an actual settlement, though the Charles Ilfeld Co. once had extensive ranching operations here. Ranchers still live in the area. The name appears to be a corruption of the Spanish *borrica,* "jenny donkey," though it possibly could be connected with Diego de Borica, an 18th-century military figure and lieutenant governor in NM.

CAÑADA DEL BORRACHO (Rio Arriba; heads in Valle de los Caballos and runs E into Vallecitos). In the Vallecitos area there once lived a locally famous old yellow steer named Borracho, "the drunken one," and his death in this dry wash resulted in its name.

BORREGO (general). In NM, the Spanish *borrego,* "yearling, lamb," became the general term for sheep; GNIS lists 17 *Borrego* place names.

BORREGO DOME, MESA, SPRING (Sandoval; in the Jemez Mountains, 7 mi E of Jemez Pueblo). Name-cluster associated with the spring. The *Ojo del Borrego Land Grant* here was made to Nerio Antonio Montoya on March 4, 1768.

BORREGO PASS (McKinley; settlement; 9 mi E of Crownpoint, on the Continental Divide). Active Navajo community, named for 7,431-foot *Borrego Pass* just SW of the village. The Navajo name means the same as the Spanish-English name.

BORREGO TRAIL (Santa Fe; runs through Hyde Memorial Park, E of Santa Fe) Before modern roads, this was a major route used by northern NM farmers and ranchers to bring goods and livestock to markets in Santa Fe. Over this route, portions of which now are a hiking trail, passed burro-loads of firewood and large flocks of sheep—hence the name.

BOSQUE (general). *Bosque* is Spanish for "forest, woods," but in NM the term has been used for dense thickets of trees and underbrush—cottonwoods, tamarisk, willows, alders, and others—fringing lakes, rivers, streams, or marshes.

EL BOSQUE (Rio Arriba; settlement; on both banks of the Rio Grande, 18 mi NE of Española). This inhabited community takes its name from being in the brushy floodplain of the Rio Grande; see *Bosque (general).* As ethnologist John Peabody Harrington explained, "This name is applied to the locality on both sides of the river, including Lyden [see entry], which is on the W side. The name Lyden seems never to be applied to the settlement on the E side of the river, which is always called Bosque."

BOSQUE (Valencia; settlement; on NM 304, 7 mi S of Belen; PO 1918–33, 1934–present.) This small, inhabited agricultural community was named for its location in the *bosque* of the Rio Grande. Its first residents were *genízaros,* Hispanicized, detribalized Indians. In 1750, the Bacas, Montaños, Abeytas, Pinos, Cháveses, and Zamoras began farming here.

BOSQUE BONITO (Socorro; settlement; on the W side of the Rio Grande S of Socorro, S of Milligan Gulch). Fort Craig military records mention a settlement named Bosque Bonito, NM Spanish for "pretty forest," and the 1860 US Census listed a "Bosquet Bonito" as having 26 residents. But the settlement has vanished, and few, if any, local residents recall the name.

BOSQUE DEL APACHE NATIONAL WILDLIFE REFUGE (Socorro; 8 mi S of San Antonio, straddling the Rio Grande). Doubtless an incident involving Apache Indians, who frequented the Rio Grande *bosque* until late in the 19th century, resulted in the name Bosque del Apache, but the incident has been forgotten. It certainly occurred before 1845, because in that year Gov. Manuel Armijo gave the *Bosque del Apache Land Grant* to Antonio Sandoval. The grant was purchased by the US government in 1939 as "a refuge and breeding grounds for migratory birds and other wildlife."

Located on the flyways of many migratory birds and offering excellent habitat, the refuge's 57,191 acres now provide sanctuary for numerous wildlife species. Part of the refuge has been designated the *San Pascual Wilderness.*

BOSQUE FARMS (Valencia; settlement; on NM 47, between Isleta Pueblo and Los Lunas). Located on the eastern floodplain of the Rio Grande, this inhabited settlement was called *Bosque de los Pinos,* "forest of the pines," when Spanish-speaking settlers arrived here sometime in the 18th century. An 1848 document mentions a farming community in this area called *Bosque Redondo,* "round forest," where the Cháves *hacienda* once was located. In the 19th century, the prominent stockman and political figure Solomon Luna had large land holdings here; his son, Eduardo Otero, was instrumental in having the Middle Rio Grande Conservancy District established to solve problems of alkalinity and high water table. In 1934–35, as part of a resettlement project, the US government offered 20,000 acres of land, divided into 42 tracts, to families wiped out during the Dust Bowl; names of recipients were drawn by lottery. From that project came the name Bosque Farms. This community is not to be confused with the Valencia County settlement named Bosque located S of Belen.

BOSQUE GRANDE (Chaves; settlement; on the Pecos River, 30 mi S of Fort Sumner). Named by Spanish-speaking settlers about 1860, doubtless for being in a large *bosque*—see *Bosque (general)*—of the Pecos, Bosque Grande was primarily a cow camp. In 1867, the locality became the headquarters for the first herd of "jingle-bob" cattle brought to the valley by John S. Chisum. "Jingle-bob" refers to Chisum's practice of marking his cows not with a body brand but with slits in both ears, so that one part of each ear flopped down while the other stood erect, making his cattle easy to identify.

BOSQUE PEAK, 9,610 ft. (Torrance; in the Manzano Mountains, between Mosca

and Osha Peaks). A small *bosque*—see *Bosque (general)*—is near its summit.

BOSQUE REDONDO (De Baca; 4 mi S of US 60, SE of Fort Sumner, on the Pecos River). This site, whose Spanish name means "round forest," was an Indian campground long before the arrival of Europeans; the name likely refers not to the entire *bosque*—see *Bosque (general)*—which stretches for miles along the Pecos but rather to a round pool or water hole, surrounded by trees. Coronado in 1541 and Espejo in 1583 are said to have passed by here. In 1851, a licensed trading post was established at Bosque Redondo and then a fort, named for Col. Edmond Vose Sumner; see *Fort Sumner.* It was to Bosque Redondo that Kit Carson brought 600 Apaches in 1863 and 7,000 Navajos in 1864, in an attempt to pacify the Indians and convert them to agriculture. Great hardship resulted, however; the Apaches fled the reservation and resumed raiding, while the Navajos, agreeing to forswear raiding forever, returned to their homeland in 1868.

BOSQUE REDONDO (Valencia; near Peralta). Early records mention a settlement here, site of the former Cháves *hacienda.*

BOSQUE SECO (Doña Ana; settlement; S of Las Cruces). Little is known about this abandoned former settlement, except its name, which is Spanish and means "dry forest."

BOSQUECITO (Socorro; settlement; on E bank of the Rio Grande, S of Socorro and N of San Antonio). This Spanish name meaning "little forest" likely describes this settlement's location within the Rio Grande *bosque*—see *Bosque (general)*—though the name "little bosque" might have come from the community having been settled by people from one of the larger communities to the N named Bosque. Established sometime late in the Mexican period, this tiny community appears intermittently on census lists through the 1930s, when it ceases to be mentioned; the flood of 1937 may have contributed to the settlement's decline. The name still appears on road signs, however, and a few people still live in the area.

BOTTOMLESS LAKES STATE PARK (Chaves; 10 mi E of Roswell on US 380 and 6 mi S on NM 409). When 19th-century cowboys measured the depth of these lakes by tying lariats together as a plumb line, they found no bottom and pronounced the pools bottomless, hence the name. But the lakes do have bottoms, at depths ranging from 17 to 90 feet. And to geologists, they are not lakes but sinkholes; groundwater dissolving salt and gypsum deposits created subterranean caverns; when their roofs collapsed, sinkholes resulted, which then filled with water.

The names of the individual lakes are: *Lazy Lagoon; Cottonwood Lake,* for a large cottonwood that once grew beside it; *Mirror Lake,* actually two ponds separated by a narrow neck of land, named for mirror-like reflections when viewed from above; *Devils Inkwell,* named for its steep sides and dark water; *Figure Eight Lake,* a pair of contiguous ponds; *Pasture Lake,* named for wild ducks that once lived here; and *Lea Lake,* named for Capt. Joseph C. Lea. The state park, one of NM's oldest, was established in 1934 as a federal relief project.

BOULDER LAKE (Rio Arriba). See *Stone Lake.*

BOVE (Santa Fe). See *San Ildefonso Pueblo.*

BOWLING GREEN (Socorro; settlement; on the E side of the Rio Grande, S of La Joyita, N of Polvadera). This conspicuously English place name from Ohio or Kentucky seems decidedly out of place on this abandoned settlement that the 1885 US Census listed as completely Hispanic. On early maps and primary sources, however, the name was spelled "Bowlin-green," and only after the settlement was abandoned in 1886 did the name Bowling Green appear. The name likely is an American corruption of *bolón,* an Hispanic-American term referring to a symmetrical hill, and indeed the village was located directly below such a hill; local people in the area refer to the locality as *bolón-guin.*

Bowling Green, or *bolón-guin,* was settled about 1880, coincident with the abandonment of nearby La Joyita because of flooding. The special US census of 1885 counted 145 residents here. Bowling Green itself was destroyed by a flood, in September 1886.

BOX CANYON (general). Narrow canyons created by permanent or intermittent streams and closed or tightly constricted at one end are common throughout NM—and so is this name. See *Rincon (general).*

BOX LAKE (Catron; settlement; SW of Quemado and 6 mi S of US 60; PO 1919–20, mail to Quemado). Abandoned settlement, once called *Cajón,* Spanish for "big box."

BRABA (Taos). See *Taos Pueblo.*

BRACKETT (Colfax; settlement; on the Vermejo River, E of Maxwell; PO 1910–16, mail to Maxwell). A family by this name had a ranch here; the PO took its name from them.

BRAKES (Quay; settlement; SE of Tucumcari; PO 1907–09, mail to Norton). *Breaks* in eastern NM refers to the gullies and shallow canyons incising the Caprock. This abandoned settlement was on the edge of the Caprock and was likely named for the "breaks" here, though the divergent spelling invites other possibilities.

BRAMLETT (Hidalgo; settlement; in S part of county, in the Animas Valley; PO 1911–12, mail to Animas). This ephemeral settlement took the surname of its first postmaster, Nathan N. Bramlett.

BRANCH SEVEN RIVERS (Eddy; river; N of Seven Rivers, N of Carlsbad). See *Seven Rivers.*

BRANTLEY LAKE (Eddy; on the Pecos River, 7 mi NW of Carlsbad). This reservoir was authorized by Congress in 1972 to replace Lake McMillan (see entry); water first flowed from the dam's floodgates in 1987. The reservoir was named to honor John Draper Brantley, better known locally as Draper Brantley. He was born in Carlsbad in 1914. He attended the University of New Mexico but returned to Carlsbad to become a farmer. He was active in numerous agricultural and conservation organizations, especially those concerned with water projects, and he was an enthusiastic promoter of the dam, constructed in the 1980s, creating the reservoir that today bears his name. His family still lives in the area. *Brantley Lake State Park* is located S of the reservoir.

BRAZEL (Doña Ana; settlement; exact location unknown; PO 1894 but likely never operated). George Adlai Feather put this ephemeral mining locality in the Black Mountain Mining District. It was named for W.W. Brazel.

BRAZITO (Doña Ana; settlement; 5 mi S of Las Cruces). The Spanish *brazito* means "little arm, or tributary," and the name of this Hispanic settlement on the Rio Grande has been attributed to "arms," or branches, of the river marshlands near the site, though the name also has been interpreted to mean "little bend on the river." As early as 1776 the locality was called *Huerto* (Spanish, "orchard") *de los Brazitos*. About 1822 the *Brazito Land Grant*, extending 8 miles along the Rio Grande S of Las Cruces, was made to Juan Antonio García. Though only the schoolhouse remains of the settlement, this belies the site's significance in NM history, for here, on Christmas Day 1846, occurred the only battle of the Mexican War to be fought in NM. Col. Alexander W. Doniphan and his Missouri Volunteers defeated a force of 1,200 Mexicans here and went on to occupy El Paso prior to advancing on Chihuahua.

BRAZOS (Rio Arriba; many features). See *Río Brazos*.

BREAD SPRINGS (McKinley; settlement; 9 mi SE of Gallup). Navajos, who have a school and chapter house here, named the springs because nearby rocks resemble loaves of bread.

BREECE (McKinley; settlement; 5 mi SW of Thoreau; PO 1920–27, mail to Thoreau). This abandoned settlement was primarily a lumbering camp; it was named for George E. Breece, who owned Breece Lumber Co. and was responsible for lumbering operations in the Zuni Mountains. Local people called the site *Breecetown*. The Breece Lumber Co. operated until 1931.

BRICE (Otero; settlement; in the Jarilla Mountains W of Orogrande, about 35 mi S of Alamogordo; PO 1904–09, 1913–19). Brice began as a gold-mining camp in the Jarilla Mountains (see entry) and originally was called simply *Jarilla*. In 1904 the EP&NE RR ran a spur line 2 mi W from Jarilla Junction, now Orogrande (see entry), and Jarilla then became Brice, taking the name of a local mining company superintendent. By 1905 the camp had 150 residents, a saloon, general store, hotel, four mining companies, and the area's first school. Further mining activity sent the population to 300 in 1919. Now only ruins remain.

BRIGGS CANYON (Union; heads N of Des Moines and runs into Cimarron Canyon). Named for a family who settled here in 1866.

BRILLIANT (Colfax; settlement; in Dillon Canyon, 3 mi NW of Raton; PO 1906–35, mail to Swastika, 1940–54, mail to Raton). Brilliant, now abandoned, was a company-owned coal town that began when the St. Louis, Rocky Mountain, and Pacific Co. opened the Brilliant Mine in 1906; the name is said to have been inspired by the unusually lustrous sheen of the coal from nearby Tin Pan Canyon. The mine supplied coal for the RRs and also for the coke ovens at Gardiner (see entry) nearby to the S. Operations were suspended in 1908, then resumed in 1912. In the 1920s, Brilliant was joined in the canyon by Swastika (see entry), another company-owned coal town just a mile S of Brilliant, and the two existed together until the Brilliant PO was closed in 1935. During World War II, Swastika changed its name to Brilliant II.

BRIMHALL (McKinley; settlement; 15 mi N of Gallup, 9 mi E of US 666, at Coyote Canyon). The Brimhalls were early Mormon settlers active throughout the Four Corners region, and the PO at Coyote

Canyon bears their family name, doubtless for a trader here. See *Coyote Canyon*. *Brimhall Wash* heads NE of Newcomb and flows W to join the Chaco River.

BROADVIEW (Curry; settlement; 29 mi N of Clovis, at the junction of NM 209, NM 241, and NM 275; PO 1931–89). When Broadview was founded about 1925 it was called *Boney Curve*, for a conspicuous curve in the otherwise ruler-straight highway and a for local family named Boney. When residents applied for a PO in 1931, they proposed the name *Jasper*, for Jasper Anson, one of the original settlers who had a store here, but the name finally settled upon was Broadview, suggested by Barney B. Blackburn. Broadview is an appropriate name, for the community is on a subtle rise, and the view of the surrounding high plains is indeed broad.

BROADVIEW ACRES (Cibola; on NM 605, 4 mi N of Milan). A recent housing development, named for its expansive vistas.

BROIS SPRINGS (De Baca; near La Mora Creek). In 1885, Jim Brois settled on acreage surrounding the springs.

BROKE OFF MOUNTAIN, 10,357 ft. (Rio Arriba; in the Tusas Mountains, 6 mi NE of Hopewell Lake). This name describes a volcanic stump.

BROKEOFF MOUNTAINS (Otero; SE part of county). A small SW spur, rising to an elevation of 6,000 ft., of the Guadalupe Mountains, detached or "broken off" from them and separated by Big Dog Canyon. Most of the chain is in NM, but it joins the Guadalupes just S of the Texas line.

BRONCHO (Torrance; settlement; on AT&SF RR, 6 mi SW of Willard). Now just a siding, this former RR community's name is an American misspelling of the Spanish *bronco*, "wild, unruly," usually referring to horses.

BROOM MOUNTAIN, 7,985 ft. (Cibola; 17 mi S of Acoma Pueblo). This translates the Spanish name *Sierra de la Escoba*. Early settlers came here for the long grasses used in making brooms; they tied the grasses together near the cut end, using the long portion as a broom

for sweeping and the short one for brushing hair.

BROWN (Quay; settlement; 5.5 mi SW of Ragland). George M. Brown applied for a PO here, to be named for himself, but one never operated, and nothing remains at the site now.

BRUSHY (general). "Brushy" accurately if prosaically describes many places in NM and appears in at least 32 place names (GNIS), including 10 Brushy Canyons and 9 Brushy Mountains. A local Spanish equivalent is *Montosa*.

BRUNSWICK (Doña Ana; RR locality; at Berino). According to George Adlai Feather, this locality began as a townsite laid out by land speculators in Las Cruces. They named the town *Lyndon*, sometimes *Linden*. In 1881, when the site became a station on the AT&SF, the name was changed to Brunswick, for an M. Brunswick of Las Vegas.

BRUSHY MOUNTAIN, 6,618 ft. (Socorro; on Chupadera Mesa, E of Socorro). A prominent landmark, named for its vegetation. Often labeled incorrectly as *Bushy Mountain*.

BRYAN (Grant; settlement; on the Gila River, S of Cliff; PO 1912–13, mail to Cliff). Ephemeral settlement, name origin unknown.

BRYANTINE (Harding; settlement; 25 mi SE of Mosquero; PO 1903–20, mail to Logan). Sarah P. Bryant, first postmistress here, gave her name to this abandoned community.

BUCHANAN (De Baca; settlement; on AT&SF RR, 10 mi W of Yeso, 4 mi S of US 60; PO 1907–40, mail to Yeso). Buchanan was founded in 1907 with the building of the RR line and named for President James Buchanan (1857–61). But after the RR was built, the population dwindled, and now the settlement has vanished.

BUCKEYE (Lea; settlement; on NM 8, 17 mi SW of Lovington). Inhabited oilfield community, named for the Buckeye sheep ranch nearby.

BUCKHORN (Grant; settlement; US 180, 36 mi NW of Silver City; PO 1913–present). Inhabited settlement, named for nearby *Buckhorn Creek*.

BUCKHORN (Lincoln; settlement; on the Rio Ruidoso, between Ruidoso Downs and Glencoe). Small residential cluster, name origin unknown.

BUCKLE BAR CANYON (Doña Ana; runs SW to enter the Rio Grande, 4 mi N of Radium Springs). Named for a local ranch brand.

BUCKMAN (Santa Fe; settlement; 5 mi S of San Ildefonso Pueblo, on the E bank of the Rio Grande; PO 1889–1903, 1912–25, mail to Santa Fe). H.F. Buckman was an Oregon lumberman who cut timber and built sawmills on the Pajarito Plateau; he gave his name to this now-abandoned settlement and station on the D&RG RR. His name also has appeared on *Buckman Mesa,* S of San Ildefonso Pueblo, though *La Mesita* was the name accepted by the USBGN in 1984; the mesa also has been known as *Ortiz Mesa.*

BUDAGHERS (Sandoval; settlement; on I-25, NE of Algodones). In the early 1900s, Joseph M. Budagher came to NM from Lebanon. He established businesses here, and his descendants still reside at the site bearing his family name, as well as being active Sandoval County residents.

BUDVILLE (Cibola; settlement; on old US 66, now NM 124, 23 mi E of Grants, 2 mi S of Cubero). Small inhabited community named for H.N. "Bud" Rice, who opened an automobile service and touring business here in 1928. Rice was shot to death in 1967 while resisting a holdup attempt.

BUENA VISTA (Harding; settlement; on NM 39, 28 mi SE of Mosquero). Spanish, "beautiful view." Abandoned community.

BUENA VISTA (Mora; settlement; 20 mi N of Las Vegas, just E of NM 518, on the Mora River). Small inhabited settlement, named for its scenic location.

BUENA VISTA (Rio Arriba; settlement; 1 mi W of Abiquiu). Small inhabited community, overlooking the Rio Chama.

BUEYEROS (Harding; settlement; on NM 102, 29 mi NE of Mosquero; PO as Vigil 1894–98, as Bueyeros 1898–present). About 1878, several Hispanic settlers

from villages of the Sangre de Cristo Mountains brought cattle to the open ranges near Ute Creek. Some of the herders were oxen drivers, or "bueyeros," and the lesser creek on which they built a cluster of homes soon was called Bueyeros Creek. At first the settlement was called *Vigil,* or *Vigil Plaza,* because Leandro and Agustín Vigil ran thousands of cattle here, but later the community took the name Bueyeros.

BUEYEROS CANYON (San Miguel; heads in NE part of county, runs SW to Seco Creek). Spanish, "oxen drivers."

BUFFALO (general). American bison once roamed widely over NM's eastern plains. Castañeda, Coronado's chronicler, in 1540 described the unfamiliar animals as "cows covered with frizzled hair which resembles wool." These first Spanish explorers also called them *cibola; see Cibola (general).* But while the buffalo have vanished, except where they have been reintroduced, their names remain on 17 NM features (GNIS), all in the N and E.

Buffalo Grass Creek (Taos; flows into Rio Pueblo de Taos, 4 mi E of Taos Pueblo).

Buffalo Head (Colfax; rock formation; N of Folsom). Resembles a buffalo's head.

Buffalo Valley (Chaves; valley; six mi E of Lake Arthur, E of the Pecos). *Buffalo Lake* is just to the E.

BUFFALO SPRINGS (McKinley; settlement; on US 666, just S of the San Juan County line). Specific origin unknown. See *Iyanbito.*

BUFORD (Torrance). See *Moriarty.*

BUG SCUFFLE CANYON, HILL, 6,545 ft. (on the W side of the Sacramento Mountains, SE of Alamogordo). This intriguing name, which also labels the geologic formation of the hill, is found in other states besides NM, but its origin here is unknown, even to local people in the area. (There is a town named Bug Tussle in Fannin County, TX, but explanations as to is origin are apocryphal.)

BUGGY TOP HILL, 4,617 ft. (Hidalgo; 4 mi S of Lordsburg, N of Pyramid Peak). This big rock slab is known to local people by this name, but any resemblance to a buggy's top is not obvious.

BULL (general). NM being a ranching state, with open range in the early days, names mentioning bulls are understandably common. Curiously, the Spanish form, *toro,* is uncommon.

BULL CREEK (San Miguel; in the Sangre de Cristo Mountains, 6 mi E of Pecos, flows S to join *Cow Creek* just S of the village of Lower Colonias). This appeared on an 1889 USGS map by its Spanish name, *Toro Creek.*

BULL-OF-THE-WOODS MOUNTAIN, 11,610 ft. (Taos; in the Sangre de Cristo Mountains, 4.5 mi N of Wheeler Peak, 2 mi NE of Taos Ski Valley). Though the details have been lost, this mountain's intriguing name likely relates to a bull elk. During the mining era of the late 19th century, an important horseback route between Twining and Red River went over a pass near *Bull-of-the-Woods Pasture,* located just N of the mountain, and elk often were seen there. Miners working copper claims on the summit of Bull-of-the-Woods Mountain might also have encountered a bull elk. Indeed, elk are still common in the area.

BULLARD PEAK, 7,064 ft. (Grant; in the Big Burro Mountains, 15 mi SW of Silver City). Capt. John Bullard, miner and prospector, was among the founders of *Chloride Flat* (see entry), and during the 1870–71 gold rush here he developed several claims around the peak now bearing his name. In 1871, while leading a campaign against the Apaches, Bullard was shot and killed on another mountain, now also called Bullard Peak, W of Glenwood, just over the Arizona line. One of Silver City's main streets also bears Bullard's name. *Bullard Canyon* heads immediately W of Bullard Peak and runs W.

BULLIS CANYON, LAKE, SPRING (Chaves; in the northern Guadalupe Mountains). In the late 19th century, Captain Bullis and his troops attacked Indians at a stream near here, killing some and driving the others away. The troops then occupied the site, but during the night the Indians returned, killing Bullis and his men. These features have borne his name ever since.

BUNK ROBINSON, 6,241 ft. (Hidalgo; in the S Peloncillo Mountains, just E of the Arizona line). Local lore has it that Apaches trapped a group of soldiers on this peak's summit and only one soldier, an African-American named Bunk Robinson, escaped.

BUNKHOUSE BARE POINT, 11,730 ft. (Colfax; on W boundary of Philmont Scout Ranch, about 2 mi SW of Comanche Peak). A bald peak, presumably named for a bunkhouse located here at one time. Companion summit to *Clear Creek Mountain,* 11,711 ft. (see entry).

BURFORD LAKE (Rio Arriba). See *Stinking Lake.*

BURLEY (Socorro; settlement; in the NW corner of the county, S of the Rio Salado, 15 mi W of Puertocito; PO 1901–18, mail to Puertocito). Abandoned locality, named for the Field and Burley cattle ranch.

BURNED MOUNTAIN, 10,189 ft. (Rio Arriba; in the Tusas Mountains, 5 mi SE of Jawbone Mountain, 4 mi NW of Tusas Mountain). Likely named for a forest fire here.

BURNHAM (San Juan; settlement; on Navajo Rte. 5, 12 mi E of US 666). A cluster of homes near Burnham Trading Post, named for Luther G. Burnham. See also *Fruitland.*

BURNS CANYON (Rio Arriba; runs SW into Vaqueros Canyon, paralleling US 64, W of John Mills Lake). Bears the name of a wealthy sheep-owner near Chama.

BURNS CANYON (Rio Arriba; settlement; location unknown; PO 1923–24, mail to Abiquiu). Short-lived postal locality, name origin unknown, but possibly associated with Burns Canyon, a minor tributary of the Rio Chama at Parkview Fish Hatchery.

BURRO (general). As T.M Pearce put it, "A place name map of NM would not portray faithfully the story of the land if the picture of patient, wood-hauling burros did not appear." These long-suffering beasts of burden are remembered in 52 NM place names (GNIS).

BURRO MOUNTAINS (Grant; W of Silver

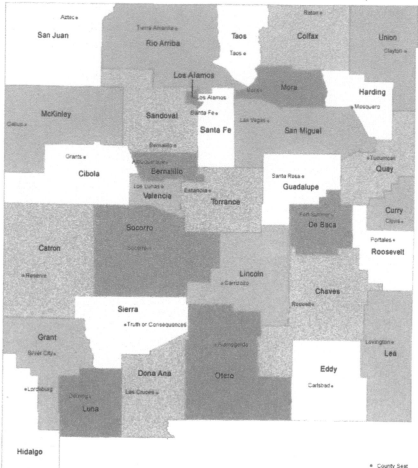

Aztec • • Raton •
San Juan   Tierra Amarilla •   Taos   Colfax   Union
    Rio Arriba   Taos •   Clayton •

    Los Alamos   Mora   Harding
    • Los Alamos   Mora   Mosquero •
McKinley   Sandoval   Santa Fe •
Gallup •   Bernalillo •   Las Vegas •   San Miguel
    Santa Fe
    Grants •   • Tucumcari
Cibola   Albuquerque •   Santa Rosa •   Quay
    Bernalillo
    Los Lunas •   Estancia •   Guadalupe
    Valencia   Torrance   Curry
    Clovis •
    Socorro   Fort Sumner •
Catron   De Baca   Portales •
    Socorro •   Roosevelt

    Lincoln
    • Carrizozo
    Chaves
    Sierra   Roswell •
Grant   • Truth or Consequences
    Lovington •
Silver City •   • Alamogordo   Lea
    Dona Ana   Otero   Eddy
• Lordsburg   Deming •   Carlsbad •
    Luna   Las Cruces •

Hidalgo
    • County Seat
    (c) geology.com

City). These low mountains are separated by Mangas Creek into two parallel sub-ranges, the *Big Burro Mountains* to the W and the *Little Burro Mountains* to the E. Whatever burros inspired this name must have lived a long time ago, because Juan Nentwig's map of 1762 shows *S. [Sierra] de las Burros* just W of *S. del Cobre* and S of the *Río Xila*. *Burro Peak*, 8,035 in the S part of the Big Burro Mountains is the highest point in the Big Burro Mountains; the highest summit in the Little Burro Mountains, 6,637 ft., appears unnamed on most maps but has been said to be called *La Lacha,* meaning obscure, and also *Baldy. Burro Springs,* 15 mi SW of Silver City; was an important watering place in the 1870s.

BURSUM (Catron; settlement; between Willow Creek and the village of Mogollon). An ephemeral settlement, located on the *Bursum Road* (NM 159), initiated by US Sen. Holm Bursum (1921–24) and named for him. The road was first broken through with prison labor, then taken over by the USFS and finally completed in 1936–40 by workmen from the Civilian Conservation Corps at Willow Springs.

BURTCHER CANYON, FLATS (Grant; in W part of county, 3 mi W of Applegate Mountain, flats on W side of canyon). These features originally appeared on maps as *Bircher Canyon* and *Bircher Flats,* but in 1987 descendants of Virgil Burtcher, who homesteaded in the area in 1898, successfully petitioned the USBGN to have the names reflect the family's actual spelling, and the USBGN, following the recommendation of the NM Geographic Names Committee, approved the change.

BURTON FLATS (Eddy; 12 mi NE of Carlsbad). Named for the Burton Ranch. It was in this flat country that V.H. McNutt first discovered the area's potash deposits.

BUSH RANCH (Grant). See *Glenwood.*

BUTTE (Bernalillo). See *Vulcan.*

BUTTERFIELD PARK (Doña Ana; settlement; on US 70, 11 mi NE of Las Cruces). Though the Butterfield stage route did not pass through here but rather passed to the W, this recent residential settlement nonetheless took its name.

BUTTERFIELD TRAIL (Eddy, Otero, Doña Ana, Luna, Hidalgo; entered NM near Popes Crossing on the Pecos River S of Carlsbad and continued W through NM and Texas to exit NM near Steins Peak, N of present I-10). Named for John Butterfield, its developer, the Butterfield Overland Mail route ran 2,701.5 miles from St. Louis, MO, to Stockton, CA. When Butterfield and his associates received the contract for the mail route, they purchased 1,000 horses, 700 mules, 800 harnesses, and 250 coaches and Celerity wagons. Butterfield's instructions to his drivers were, "Remember, boys, nothing on God's earth must stop the United States mail." Though the mail route lasted only from 1857 to 1869, the Butterfield Trail continued to be the major route west until 1881, when the southern-route transcontinental railroad was completed.

BUXTON (San Miguel; settlement; in SE part of county, S of Variadero; PO 1909–14, mail to Variadero). Rural postal locality that took the name of the ranch where it was established. The 1910 US Census tallied 150 people here.

BYNUM (Chaves; settlement; about 10 mi N-NW of Elkins; PO 1907–10, mail to Olive). Abandoned settlement likely named for its first postmaster, John F. Bynum.

BYRIED (De Baca; settlement; in central part of county, W of the Pecos River; PO 1909–20, mail to Ricardo). Abandoned RR settlement, name origin unknown. Pronounced BYE-reed.

C BAR LAKE (Catron; 9 mi NW of Luna). Named for the C Bar Ranch.

CABALLO (general). See *Horse (general)*.

CABALLO (Sierra; settlement; 14 mi S of Truth or Consequences, W of Caballo Reservoir; PO 1916–present). The present community of Caballo, named for the mountains to the E, began in 1908 when John N. Gordon with his wife, two daughters, and their families homesteaded in the Rio Grande *bosque*. In 1938, when the lake behind the newly constructed Caballo Dam began to fill, the waters covered the homes of the earlier settlers, and the community was moved W to its present location.

CABALLO MOUNTAIN, 10,496 ft. (Sandoval; in E Jemez Mountains, W of Santa Clara Pueblo, N of head of Gauje Canyon). See *Horse (general)*.

CABALLO MOUNTAINS (Sierra; N-S range extending S of Truth or Consequences, E of the Rio Grande). This small fault-block range with a dramatic western escarpment appeared as *El Perrillo Sierra*, Spanish, "little dog range," in Nicolás de Lafora's notes of 1766; the name likely was a reference to the spring by that name on the Jornada del Muerto to the E; see *Ojo del Perrillo*. But Zebulon Pike in 1807 mentioned passing the W side of "Horse Mountain," and the range was labeled *Sierra de los Caballos* on the 1828 Mapa de los EUM. The "horse" name is said to come from a resemblance to a horse's head at the range's N end. South Ridge rises to 7,300 ft. See also *Turtleback Mountain*.

LAGUNA DE LOS CABALLOS (Rio Arriba). See *Horse Lake*.

CABALLO LAKE STATE PARK (Sierra; on the Rio Grande, S of Truth or Consequences). Established in 1964 and named for the lake upon which it is based.

CABALLO RESERVOIR (Sierra; on the Rio Grande, S of Truth or Consequences). This storage reservoir was built in 1937–38 and named for the mountains overlooking the lake to the E. The lake, when full, is the third largest in the state, with 11,500 surface acres of water.

CABEZON (Sandoval; settlement; 2 mi N of Cabezon Peak; PO as Cabezon Station, 1879–81; as Cabezon, 1891–1928, 1930–49, mail to Cuba). Cabezon began as one of four tiny Hispanic agricultural settlements in this section of the Rio Puerco Valley, the others being San Luis, Guadalupe, and Casa Salazar (see entries). Cabezon was settled in 1826, when Juan Maestas arrived here from Pagosa Springs, Colorado. It was closely associated with the older Hispanic village of *Rancho de la Posta*, or simply *La Posta*, "the stage stop," a reference to the locale being on what then was a major stage route W from Santa Fe. Another name mentioned early in the 19th century was *San José del Cerro Cabezón*. When English-speaking settlers and traders arrived and applied for a PO, they originally called it *Cabezon Station* and then simply *Cabezon*, both names referring to Cabezon Peak (see entry), which overshadows the village. The development of alternative transportation routes, overgrazing by sheep, and a falling water table along the Rio Puerco caused a general decline in the region, which always was isolated, and Cabezon was finally abandoned in 1934 when the federal government purchased the Ojo de Espiritu Santo Land Grant. The town now is in private ownership; its picturesque abandoned buildings have been used as movie sets for westerns.

CABEZON PEAK, 7,786 ft. (Sandoval; in the Rio Puerco Valley, S of Cuba). The largest of many volcanic plugs, or necks, in the Mount Taylor volcanic field, Cabezon rises nearly 2,000 feet above the surrounding plain. The Navajos call it simply "black rock," but they also identify it as the head of a giant killed by the Twin War Gods; the congealed blood of this giant is believed to be the lava flow to the S of Grants known as El Malpais. Spanish explorers perhaps were aware of this legend, for their name for it, *El Cabezón,* means "the big head." That was how Bernardo Miera y Pacheco labeled the peak on his map based on the 1776–77 Domínguez-Escalante expedition, of which Miera y Pacheco was a member. When Lt. James H. Simpson passed by here in 1849, he recorded seeing "the remarkable peak called *Cerro de la Cabeza." Cerro Cabezón* is another version of the name.

CABRA (general). See *Goat (general).*

CABRA, CABRA SPRING (San Miguel; settlement; 35 mi SE of Las Vegas; PO as Cabra Spring 1878–91; as Cabra 1900–04, mail to Gallinas Spring). This former settlement, now a ranch headquarters, was named for a nearby spring where goats watered. After 1850 many immigrants camped here, as it was located on an old *comanchero* trail and the main route between Forts Bascom and Union.

CABRESTO (general). Spanish, "rope, halter." Many features, especially in northern NM, bear this name, but for reasons unknown.

Cabresto Creek (Colfax; in Taos Range, heads E of Baldy Mountain, runs into Red River from the NE at Questa).

Cabresto Lake (Colfax; in the Taos Range, 6 mi NE of Questa, N of Cabresto Creek).

Cabresto Peak, 12,448 ft. (Taos; in Taos Range, between Venado and Pinabete Peaks, N of Cabresto Creek).

CACHANILLAS (Rio Arriba; settlement; SE part of county, in the Embudo area). Inhabited hamlet that took its name from a northern NM term for a medicinal plant.

CAJON (Catron). See *Box Lake.*

CALAVERAS CREEK (Sandoval; in the NW Jemez Mountains, a tributary of Cebolla Creek). Spanish, "skulls." Local tradition says this name resulted when long ago someone found here the skulls of two male deer, their antlers locked together from a mating battle.

CALIENTE (general). Spanish, "hot." The numerous NM springs and creeks with this word in their names are reminders of the importance of geothermal forces in the state's recent geological history. Caliente appears 13 times in GNIS. See *Hot Springs (general), Frio (general).*

CALUMET (Catron; settlement; in SE corner of county, exact location unknown). This long-abandoned mining camp, 13 mi N of the mining camp of Grafton, took its name from the Calumet Mining Co., active in the late 19th century and into the 20th.

CAMBRAY (Luna; settlement; SP RR, 1 mi W of Doña Ana–Luna County line; PO 1893–1952, mail to Deming). This locality became a water station on the SP RR when a well was drilled here in 1892; years later, as a stop on US 70, Cambray had 75 residents. But its future was truncated when I-10 bypassed it in the early 1960s, and today only a single family remains. Its Spanish name means "cambric, fine linen," but the reason for the name is unknown.

CAMEL MOUNTAIN, 4,687 ft. (Luna; in extreme SE corner of county). Named for its resemblance to a camel.

CAMEL ROCK (Santa Fe; rock formation; between Tesuque and Pojoaque, on the W side of US 84-285). A single glance at this feature explains its name.

CAMERON (Quay; settlement; on NM 469, near Curry County line, 6 mi N of Grady; PO 1908–39 in Curry County, site moved 4.5 mi N, 1939–65 in Quay County). This abandoned rural school and PO took the family name of its first postmaster, Arthur H. Cameron.

CAMINO DEL DIABLO (Chaves). See *Devil's Race Track.*

EL CAMINO REAL (several counties; in NM, along the Rio Grande, with digressions, from El Paso to Santa Fe). Formally called *El Camino Real de Tierra Adentro,* "The Royal Road to the Interior," it was perhaps the greatest road in North America of its day, and it deserved the name by which it most commonly was known, *El Camino Real,* "the Royal Road." In its entirety it stretched from Veracruz in the S, on Mexico's E coast, inland through Mexico City and Durango, thence N to Chihuahua, and finally through the El Paso del Norte into the remote province of *Nuevo México* and its capital, Santa Fe. An extension even took it to Taos, to the trade fairs there.

The first Europeans to pioneer the route in NM were three missionary friars and their escorts, who in 1581 traveled N to convert the Pueblo Indians encountered by Coronado, but the route itself certainly had been traveled by Indians long before. Then in 1598 Oñate followed it on his colonizing expedition into New Mexico. As early as 1609, church and state representatives met in Mexico City to discuss supplying the new province with necessary goods, and soon the Mission Supply began sending wagon trains N over the Camino Real from Chihuahua to Santa Fe, returning with salt, copper, turquoise, blankets, and Indian slaves. Because its main destination S from Santa Fe was Chihuahua, the trail was known in NM as the *Chihuahua Trail.*

The Camino Real continued as the major link between NM and the outside world well into the 19th century, until residents of Santa Fe began trading with the American settlements to the E, and the Santa Fe Trail was opened up. The annexation of NM to the US in 1846, along with the arrival of railroads, meant the end of the Camino Real, though portions of contemporary roads still approximate its route. Wagon ruts still are visible, and place names that were landmarks along it still survive.

CAMP CITY, CAMP (Otero). See *Valmont.*

CAMP CODY (Luna; military installation; NE of Deming; later Camp Cody hospital complex 2 mi W of Deming; PO as Camp Deming Military Branch 1916–17, as Camp Cody Military Branch 1917–19, as Holy Cross Sanatorium 1935–36, as Holy Cross 1936–39, mail to Deming, air base branch to the south 1942–44. This US Army training camp originally was called *Camp Deming* when it was established in 1917, located between the AT&SF and SP RR lines. The name soon was changed to Camp Cody to honor William F. Cody, better known as Buffalo Bill, plainsman and promoter of a Wild West show, who had died that year. More than 30,000 troops passed through Camp Cody during World War I. After the war, the camp moved west and became the Camp Cody hospital complex, treating tuberculosis among veterans. In 1922 the facility was transferred from the Public Health Service to the Deming Chamber of Commerce. The Sisters of the Holy Cross managed the sanitarium until the facilities were destroyed by fire in 1939.

CAMP DATIL (Catron; military installation; at the site of the present village of Datil, an earlier village having been 1 mi S). Built by the US Army around 1884 and manned by a unit of the 6th Cavalry, this fort was intended to protect settlers and travelers from Apaches. It was abandoned in 1886. See *Datil.*

CAMP FRENCH (Sierra; settlement; 1.5 mi N of Hillsboro). Ephemeral mining camp established around 1880; name origin unknown.

CAMP FLEMING (Grant). See *Fleming.*

CAMP FURLONG (Luna; military installation; E of the village of Columbus, S of the old EP&SW RR tracks). During the winter of 1914–15 US Army troops were stationed here to forestall raids by Mexican bandits from across the border. It was a prescient move, because on March 9, 1916, Columbus was attacked by Pancho Villa and his men. Camp Furlong became the base for retaliatory expeditions into Mexico. The camp was dismantled after General John "Black

Jack" Pershing in February 1917 brought his expeditionary force back from Mexico. A few historic buildings and ruins remain, within Pancho Villa State Park. A *furlong* is a unit of measure, about 220 yards, and here probably refers to the camp's location relative to the Mexican border.

CAMP HENLEY (Hidalgo; military installation; in the Lordsburg area). Long-abandoned fort, established during the Apache raids of the late 1800s. Origin of name unknown.

CAMP LUNA (San Miguel; military installation; NW section of Las Vegas, W of the Gallinas River, on NM 65). When this facility, now used by public health agencies, opened in 1920 as a National Guard training camp, it was named for Maximiliano Luna, who during the Spanish-American War was a captain in the regiment of Rough Riders of 1898 and who later died in the Philippines. At Camp Luna was trained the ill-fated 200th Anti-aircraft Battalion of the Coast Artillery, which bore the brunt of the Japanese invasion of the Philippines in 1941.

CAMP MIMBRES (Grant; settlement; on the Mimbres River, opposite Dwyer). Little is known about this locality, labelled on an 1867 Land Office map as *Old Camp Mimbres. See Mowry City.*

CAMP MONARCH (Grant; settlement; on the W side of the Black Range, E of San Lorenzo; 1907–08, mail to Lake Valley). During its brief existence, this mining camp had a school and other services. Among the mines here was the Monarch, hence the name.

CAMP PETERSON (Sierra; settlement; 2 mi from Chloride, in the Black Range). This short-lived mining camp was established around 1895 for miners working the Aspen Mine.

CAMP PLUMMER (Rio Arriba; military camp; 1.5 mi S of Los Ojos). In the winter of 1866 Col. Edward H. Bergman set up camp here to control Indians in the Tierra Amarilla. Los Ojos then was the principal settlement in the area, and the site of what Bergman called Camp Plummer has been known to local

people simply as *El Campo* to this day. The colonel found few Indians; desertions occupied most of his time. In 1868 Camp Plummer was renamed *Fort Lowell,* but its existence remained uneventful, and in 1869 it was abandoned.

CAMP SHERMAN (Catron; settlement; in the vicinity of Beaverhead, exact location unknown). Most information about this locality, established about 1887, has been lost.

CAMP VINCENT (Catron; military installation; in the Gila National Forest, near the confluence of Beaver Creek and Taylor Creek, W of Wall Lake). According to historian Dale Giese of Silver City, Camp Vincent existed in the 1870s as a tent outpost of Fort Bayard intended to protect the North Star Road and prevent Apaches from using the Gila country as a staging area. It was manned by 9th Cavalry "Buffalo Soldiers," black troops.

CAMP WING (Sierra; settlement; in the Black Range, on Mineral Creek between Chloride and Rendezvous). Short-lived mining camp, established around 1894 and named for James Wing, wealthy cutlery manufacturer in Sheffield, England, who had bought an interest in some local mines.

CAMPANA (San Miguel). See *Bell Ranch*

CAMPBELL (Chaves; RR locality; on the AT&SF RR, 25 mi from Roswell). A.E. Campbell is said to have had an experimental station here in the 1890s testing using dust as mulch.

CAMPBELLS PASS (McKinley). See *Continental Divide (McKinley).*

CAÑADA (general). Spanish, "ravine, gulch, canyon." In NM the term most often has been applied to large canyons and valleys.

CAÑADA (Sandoval; settlement; on FR 68, 5 mi NW of the town of Cochiti Lake). The *Cañada de Cochiti Land Grant* was made in 1728, and in 1782 the village of Cañada had 184 inhabitants. In the early 19th century, the settlement was abandoned for several years because of Navajo raids. It was resettled but later abandoned again because of drought; a church remained until the 1920s. The settlement's name has been rendered as

La Cañada de Cochiti or, more often, as *La Cañada* or simply *Cañada.*

CAÑADA ALAMOSA (Sierra; settlement). See *Monticello.*

CAÑADA DE LA CRUZ (Cibola). See *Seama.*

CAÑADA DE LOS ALAMOS (Santa Fe; settlement; 5 mi SE of Santa Fe, E of I-25). A suburban residential area in the piñon-covered foothills of the Sangre de Cristo Mountains, at the head of an arroyo bearing the same name. The *Cañada de los Álamos Grant,* given to Lorenzo Marquez in 1785, originally may have included the present residential area, but because of the way the grant was adjudicated it now includes only a downstream portion of the arroyo's watershed. The upscale suburb of Eldorado at Santa Fe (see entry) occupies part of the land grant.

CAÑADA DEL BUEY (Santa Fe; runs through White Rock into the Rio Grande's White Rock Canyon from the W). Spanish, "canyon of the ox." The canyon's Tewa name means "arroyo of the corner of the chokecherry."

CAÑADA DEL TULE (Curry). See *Tule Lake.*

CANADIAN HILLS (Mora; extend E from Wagon Mound). Named for the Canadian River.

CANADIAN RIVER (NE NM; heads in the Sangre de Cristo Mountains at NM–CO border, flows SE to Raton, then S to Conchas Lake then E into Texas and Oklahoma to join the Arkansas River SE of Tulsa). Few names have been as controversial or spawned as many conflicting explanations as that of the Canadian River, 900 miles long and among the major drainages of the American Southwest. Some persons have claimed the name has an Indian origin, coming from a Caddo name, *Kanohatino,* meaning "red river," and indeed the Mapa de los EUM (1828) of NM labels it the *Canadiano Río.* The Caddoes lived far to the SE of NM, and how the Spanish in NM would have learned of their name is unclear, though the name could have traveled upstream with exploration and

trade. Furthermore, the Caddoes have applied their name not to the Canadian but rather to the Red River, forming the border between Texas and Oklahoma. On the other hand, "Red River" also was the early Spanish name for the Canadian; on Bernardo Miera y Pacheco's 1778 map appears the phrase *Orígen de el RíoRojo,* and in its upper reaches the stream still is called the *Little Red River.* So it is indeed possible the name Canadian preserves a pre-European Indian name.

The Spanish were the first Europeans to know the river. Coronado certainly encountered the Canadian during his 1541 journey onto the Plains; he called it the *Río Cicuyé,* mistakenly believing it was the Pecos River (see entry). Oñate also crossed the Canadian; he called it the *Río de la Magdalena.* Oñate's nephew, Capt. Vicente de Zaldivar, celebrated the feast of San Francisco at a river 40 leagues E of Pecos that possibly was the Canadian; he called it the *Río de San Francisco.*

The likely Spanish origins for the name Canadian have been summarized by the Texas historian Beryl Roper: "According to James Abert and Elliot Coues, 19th-century explorers, the name of that river comes from the Spanish word *cañada,* for the valley through which it flows. To New Mexicans, this river has always been, and still is, the *Colorado,* but mapmakers finally had to give it another name to distinguish it from half a dozen other Red Rivers. *Cañada* usually means a valley with gently sloping walls, though it has been said its meaning sometimes overlaps with *cañaveral,* a place where cane grows. The Canadian fits both these descriptions, as well as a third, that of sheepwalk, the route along which sheep were driven in the great semi-annual migrations from winter shelter in the NM hills to summer pasture on the Llano Estacado."

But the Oklahoma geographer T. Wayne Furr says the name Canadian possibly means just what it says—and refers to Canada. He points out that early in the 17th century, French-Canadian trappers and explorers were active in what is now Oklahoma and that several streams there bear French names. More specifically, in 1739 the brothers Paul and Pierre Mallet led an expedition into NM that included several French-Canadians, and they returned to the Arkansas River via the Canadian River. John Brebner, in his *The Explorers of North America, 1492–1806*, wrote, "It was fitting enough [that] their river has since their day been called the Canadian." But Furr also points out that documentation of this origin is lacking.

The American explorer Maj. Stephen H. Long followed the river in 1820 and called it the *Red River,* only to discover later that the river he thought he was on actually was farther S. In 1822 another American, Jacob Fowler, followed the Canadian and called it the *Kenadean* in his journal.

So the origin of the name Canadian River remains unresolved and likely will remain so.

CANDELARIAS (Bernalillo; settlement; NW Albuquerque). Former settlement, since about 1950 absorbed into Albuquerque, named for early Spanish settlers. *Candelaria Road,* a city street, preserves the name.

LAS MESAS DEL CANJELON (Mora; large, sprawling mesa just E of Wagon Mound). Spanish, "mesas of the antlers." *Los Cuernos,* "the horns," is mentioned as a very early name of the village of Wagon Mound (see entry).

CANJILON (Rio Arriba; 3 mi E of US 84, 16 mi S of Tierra Amarilla; PO 1892–present). Although permanent settlement of this community dates from 1870—by 1880 35 families were in the area—intermittent settlement certainly had occurred much earlier; it is said that on his 1776 expedition Fray Domínguez mentioned that an upper *Cangillon* was distinct from a lower Cangillon, acknowledging that even then the settlement consisted of upper and lower villages. Although several meanings have been given for the name, in the Spanish of northern NM *canjilón* means "deer antler" and in this place name is believed to describe the shape of the nearby mountains.

Canjilon Creek heads at the base of Canjilon Mountain and flows W to the Rio Chama.

Canjilon Lakes, Rio Arriba; 10 mi N and E of the village of Canjilon, are several small lakes named, like the settlement, for the mountain.

Canjilon Mountain, 10,913 ft., 6 mi NE of the village of Canjilon, was named for its resemblance to a deer antler, which is the meaning of the northern NM Spanish word *canjilón.*

CANNON AIR FORCE BASE (Curry; military installation; 4 mi W of Clovis). Established in 1942 as *Clovis Air Base,* it was redesignated in 1957 and named for the late Gen. John K. Cannon.

CANODE (Quay; settlement; on CRI&P RR, 5 mi NE of Logan; PO 1908–14, mail to Logan). Former settlement whose name—origin unknown—now is merely that of a RR siding.

CAÑON, CAÑONCITO (general). Spanish, "canyon, gulch," diminutive, *cañoncito.* While the meaning of *cañon* is clear, there's often confusion as to its orthography, as the English word, *canyon,* derived from Spanish, is pronounced similarly to the Spanish word. Confusion also arises when *cañon* occasionally appears in print as *canon.* In place names, the generic term should match the language of the specific, as in Cañon Blanco and White Canyon.

CAÑON (San Juan; settlement; formerly on the San Juan River, now inundated by Navajo Reservoir; PO 1902–03, mail to La Boca). Doubtless named for being in the canyon of the San Juan River.

CAÑON (Sandoval; settlement; 3 mi N of Jemez Pueblo, on NM 4). The dramatic red canyon walls that are a backdrop for this inhabited village make its name particularly appropriate. The present name may be a contraction of an earlier name, *Cañon de Jemez.* See *Cañones (Sandoval).*

CAÑON (Santa Fe; settlement; in the canyon of the Santa Fe River, 1 mi N of La

Cienega). Tiny residential cluster, named for its location.

CAÑON (Taos; settlement; SE of Taos, at the mouth of the canyon of the Rio Fernando de Taos). Inhabited community, settled about 1700 at the mouth of a canyon that gave the village not only plentiful water but also its name.

CAÑON BLANCO (San Juan; settlement; in E part of county, S and E of Blanco; PO 1917–20, mail to Largo). Abandoned community, named for its association with the canyon of the same name.

CAÑON LARGO (Rio Arriba, San Juan, Sandoval; rises in Sandoval County and flows NW into the San Juan River, entering it near Blanco). A major watercourse in the region, this aptly named "long canyon" is fed by a vast and rugged watershed on the Continental Divide's western slopes. Navajos call its upper part by a name meaning "where the wide canyons meet" and its lower part "spring in the embers," while the entire canyon has been called "valley that extends down to the water." The former settlement of Largo (see entry), on the San Juan River, was named for its location at the mouth of this canyon.

CAÑON DEL NAVAJO (Rio Arriba; NW of Abiquiu, paralleling US 84). US 84 now follows the route through this canyon that for almost two centuries has been the main passage to the Tierra Amarilla; Spanish travelers would have encountered Navajos here; see also *Ojo del Navajo*. Nearby are *Ojito del Comanche*, "Comanche spring," and *Ojito de los Soldados*, "soldiers spring."

CAÑON PLAZA (Rio Arriba; settlement; in E part of county, 5 mi NW of Vallecitos on NM 111). The *plaza* in the name of this tiny, inhabited Hispanic settlement signifies "village" or "town," and the *cañon* refers to its location in the canyon of the Rio Vallecitos.

CAÑONCITO (Bernalillo; settlement; on the E side of the Sandia Mountains, just W of NM 14, between Cedar Crest and San Antonito). Inhabited locality, named for being located in *Cañoncito*, "little canyon"; *Cañoncito Spring* is nearby.

CAÑONCITO, CAÑONCITO NAVAJO INDIAN RESERVATION (Bernalillo, Cibola; Indian reservation; in NW part of Bernalillo County and adjacent part of Cibola County, NW of Albuquerque). Cañoncito, the reservation's main village, is located near the confluence of several canyons, one of which likely accounts for its name, "little canyon." Other Navajos call the Cañoncito Navajos either "enemy people" or "drawing-water-from-a-well people," and several stories attempt to explain why this small band lives as much as 75 miles from the tribe's main reservation. Tradition has it that the Cañoncito Navajos had lived in the Mount Taylor country since at least 1700 and remained here while the main portion of the tribe moved farther W. The name "enemy people" comes from an alleged betrayal by a Navajo named Joaquin in 1818, who revealed to the *alcalde* at Laguna that the Navajos planned to attack the pueblo and nearby Spanish settlements. Joaquin had unsuccessfully opposed the attack. Regarded as traitors by the other Navajos, he and about 200 followers placed themselves under Spanish protection and settled at Cebolleta, near their present location. Despite earlier ostracism by other Navajos, the group now is represented in the Navajo tribal government at Window Rock, AZ. The reservation includes nearly 77,000 acres and is home to about 1,500 people.

CAÑONCITO (Rio Arriba; settlement; on N bank of Embudo Creek, 2 mi SE of Dixon). Inhabited residential community.

CAÑONCITO (Santa Fe; settlement; 15 mi SE of Santa Fe, in a narrow canyon where the old Santa Fe Trail entered Apache Canyon; PO 1879–80). Cañoncito, with one of the most eventful histories in NM, was named simply for its location in a "little canyon." (Signs at the I-25 interchange label the village as *Cañoncito at Apache Canyon*.) Here was located the last station on the Santa Fe Trail before travelers arrived at Santa Fe; the house in which the station at one time was located was called

Johnsons Ranch. At Cañoncito the Mexican governor, Manuel Armijo, failed to hold his troops in August 1846, thus allowing the Americans to occupy NM. And here during the Civil War the supply train of invading Confederates was destroyed by the Union army in 1862, ending Confederate hopes in NM. Cañoncito, still inhabited, leads a quieter life now.

CAÑONES (Rio Arriba; settlement; 3 mi S of NM 96, 7 mi W of Abiquiu, along Cañones Creek). This inhabited community took its name from the creek on which it's located, named in turn for nearby canyons; *Cañones Mesa* is just to the E of the settlement. The Cañones area here is where the earliest Spanish attempts at settlement in the Tierra Amarilla were made. *Cañones Creek* joins Polvadera Creek at Cañones and flows N to the Rio Chama.

CAÑONES (Sandoval; on NM 485, 1 mi NW of its junction with NM 4 and 2 mi NE of Cañon, at the mouth of Cañon de Guadalupe). This tiny but inhabited settlement's location at the junction of two large canyons—Guadalupe and San Diego—accounts for its name. Lt. James H. Simpson, in his journal entry of Aug. 20, 1849, mentioned coming across a "Mexican settlement, which continued sparsely scattered along the [Jemez] river for about 5 miles, the most popular portion of it, called *Cañoncito,* we found to be about 3 mi from camp, at the mouth of Cañon de Guadalupe."

CANTA RECIO (Socorro; settlement; 40 mi S of Socorro, on the W bank of the Rio Grande, S of Milligan Gulch). Nothing remains of this tiny Hispanic village, and the origin of its Spanish name, which means "it sings loudly, or forcefully" is a mystery. The most common interpretation is that it is the Rio Grande that sings, which would duplicate the name Oñate gave a stretch of the Rio Grande S of El Paso, the *Jornada de Cantarecio,* named for springs and pools there. George Gibson, who camped S of Black Mesa in 1846, recorded in his journal that "there was once a settlement here known as the '*Cantarecio,*' but not a

vestige remains that I saw." By 1875, however, the village had been resurrected, and in the 1880s it was the first stage stop out of San Marcial on the way to the Black Range mining districts. Eugene Manlove Rhodes mentioned a '*Cantra Recio*' in a 1919 article. But around 1920 the village apparently came under comdemnation proceedings associated with the creation of Elephant Butte Reservoir and subsequently was inundated.

CANTARA (Curry; railroad siding; 6 mi W of Melrose; PO 1908–12, mail to Melrose). Cantara (Spanish, *cántara,* "pitcher") never was more than a RR siding, though it once had a PO. Today just a metal building by the RR survives; name origin unknown.

CANTON (De Baca; settlement; 15 mi SE of Fort Sumner, N of Buffalo Creek; PO 1910–25, mail to Dereno). Abandoned community, name origin unknown.

CANTONMENT BURGWIN (Taos; military installation; on NM 518, at the confluence of the Rio Grande del Rancho and the Rito de la Olla, 10 mi S of Taos). Construction of this adobe camp began in 1851 to protect the Taos Valley against the Jicarilla Apache and Ute Indians; Cantonment Burgwin, as it was called, was abandoned just 8 years later. Though it was also referred to as *Fort Fernando de Taos,* the post was never large enough to be formally designated a fort. It was named for Capt. John H.K. Burgwin, 1st US Dragoons, who died on Feb. 7, 1847, of wounds received three days earlier during the Taos uprising.

The *Fort Burgwin Research Center* of Southern Methodist University now is at the site.

CANYON ROAD (Santa Fe; heads E from downtown Santa Fe). One of the oldest roads in the US—and possibly the oldest still in use—the present Canyon Road follows a 13th-century Indian trail leading from the pueblo upon whose ruins Santa Fe was built into the Sangre de Cristo Mountains. The Spaniards took over the route, along with the settlement site, and called it *El Camino del Cañon,* the name it bears, rendered into English, today.

CAPILLA DE NUESTRA SEÑORA DE GUADALUPE (Rio Arriba; settlement; 1 mi W of NM 68, 0.5 mi N of Los Luceros). Spanish, "Chapel of Our Lady of Guadalupe," tiny inhabited locality.

CAPILLA DE SAN ANTONIO (Rio Arriba; settlement; 0.3 mi N of Alcalde). Spanish, "Chapel of Saint Anthony," A small residential cluster around the chapel. A traveler who passed through here in 1881 labelled it *Capillita*, "little chapel," and described it as a "small, Mexican village."

CAPILLA PEAK, 9,368 ft. (Torrance; in the S Manzano Mountains, 9 mi NW of village of Manzano). Spanish, "hood, cowl," though it also means "chapel." This name is said to have been given by early Spaniards at the mission of Quarai to the E. The resemblance to a hood is visible from many directions, from the N and W but particularly from the E.

CAPITAN (Lincoln; settlement; at junction of NM 380, 246, and 48, 20 mi E of Carrizozo; PO as Gray 1894–1900, as Capitan 1900–present). In 1884 Seaborn T. Gray homesteaded S of the present site of Capitan; in 1887 he moved to near the present site, on *Salado Flat*, and opened a small store. In 1894 he established a PO, naming it *Gray*, for himself. But the accolade was short-lived, because in 1899 the railroad magnate Charles B. Eddy purchased acreage across from Salado Flat, platted a townsite, and named it Capitan, for Capitan Peak (see *Capitan Mountains*) to the NE—and that name stuck. Capitan's greatest claim to fame is as the home of Smokey Bear; see *Smokey Bear Capitan Historical State Park*.

CAPITAN MOUNTAINS (Lincoln; E-W trending range, N of NM 380, NE of village of Capitan). Named for *Capitan Peak*, 10,083 ft., a commanding summit at the range's E end, whose Spanish name *capitán* means "captain." The mountains are said to have been called the *Sierra Capitana* at least as early as 1780. A 1982 USBGN decision established these mountains as distinct from

the nearby Sacramento Mountains.

CAPITAN MOUNTAINS WILDERNESS (Lincoln; includes the core of the Capitan Mountains). Created in 1980 and administered by the Lincoln NF, this area includes 35,822 acres of very rugged terrain ranging in elevation from 6,500 to 10,000 ft.

CAPITOL DOME, 5,962 ft. (Luna; at the NW end of the Florida Mountains, SE of Deming). Major summit of the Floridas, with a descriptive name.

CAPROCK (E and SE NM; landform). Locally often referred to simply as *The Cap*, the palisaded formation known as the Caprock is aptly named for it effectively "caps" the underlying deposits and is responsible for much of the vast and conspicuously flat landscape of southeastern NM, much of which also is called the *Llano Estacado* (see entry).

CAPROCK (Lea; settlement; on US 380, 47 mi E of Roswell, 0.5 mi from the Chaves County line; PO 1916–present). Persons traveling E over the broken country from Roswell eventually ascend a dramatic uplift to arrive at the table-flat high plains of the Caprock (see entry), a geologic formation associated with the Llano Estacado. And there, at the Caprock's edge, is the tiny settlement named for it in 1913 by Ed Charles E. Crossland—founder, first postmaster, and planter of the cottonwoods that still surround the PO. The settlement's school closed in 1927, but Caprock still has a few residents and a PO. (Ragland (see entry), in southern Quay County, is located, like Caprock, at the brink of the caprock, and also once had that name.)

CAPROCK (Quay). See *Ragland*.

CAPTAIN TOM WASH (San Juan; flows from the Chuska Mountains NE through Newcomb into the Chaco River). Named for the commanding officer under Col. John M. Washington, civil and military governor of NM in 1848. *Captain Tom Reservoir*, 3 mi W of Newcomb, also bears his name.

CAPULIN (general). *Capulín*, pronounced Cah-pyu-LEEN, is Mexican-Spanish for "chokecherry" or wild cherry, *Prunus virginiana;* the Spanish term was derived from the Nahuatl *capolín*. Both the plant and the name are common in NM; GNIS lists 34 occurrences of the name.

CAPULIN (Union; settlement; on US 64-87 28 mi SE of Raton and 9 mi W of Des Moines, near Colfax County line; PO, as Dedman 1909–22, as Capulin 1922–present). Sometime after the Civil War, Hispanic farmers settled here and named their little community Capulin, for Capulin Mountain (see entry), the extinct volcano to the N. When a PO was established here, it and the community took the name *Dedman,* in honor of E.J. Dedman, who in 1909 was superintendent of the AT&SF RR; he died in 1914. Later, in 1922, Dedman became Capulin, returning to its original name.

CAPULIN CANYON (Sandoval; heads in the SW Jemez Mountains, NW of St. Peters Dome, and runs SE through Bandelier National Monument to join the Rio Grande). Spanish, "chokecherry"; see *Capulin (general).* The canyon also has been called *Painted Cave Canyon,* because of the well-known cave in its lower section with polychrome paintings. It also has been called "canyon of the red slope," the same meaning as a Tewa name for the canyon.

CAPULIN VOLCANO NATIONAL MONUMENT (Union; in NW part of county, on NM 325, between Folsom and Capulin). Approximately 60,000 years ago, during one of NM's more recent periods of volcanic activity, a volcano erupted that left a nearly perfect cinder done, rising 1,000 feet above the plain. That cone, today called *Capulin Mountain,* was a prominent landmark for travelers in the region, and from its 8,182-foot summit one can see into 5 states. It is named for the chokecherries that once formed dense stands on the mountain and that still are found in its 45-foot-deep crater. *Capulin Mountain National Monument* was established in 1916; the "mountain" in the name was changed to "volcano" in 1987.

CAPULIN PEAK, 12,200 ft. (Santa Fe; 2 mi N along a ridge from Santa Fe Baldy, at head of the Rio Capulin). Also known as *Redondo Peak,* "round peak"; see *Capulin (general).*

CAPULIN PEAK, 10,470 ft. (Taos; in southern Taos Range, S of the Rio Pueblo de Taos). See *Capulin (general).*

CARBON CITY (McKinley; settlement; 5.5 mi W of Gallup, just N of the Puerco River, about 100 yards NW of Mentmore). Though calling this a "City" was mostly wishful thinking, the name Carbon City still fit this abandoned coal-mining community, associated with the *Carbon City Mine.* The settlement even had a newspaper, the *Carbon City News and McKinley County Democrat.*

CARBONATE CITY (Grant; settlement; in the Burro Mountains, 9 mi from Silver City). A short-lived mining camp laid out in 1882 whose name refers to ores containing carbonized lead and sometimes silver.

CARBONATE CREEK (Sierra; in Black Range, heads just SE of Hillsboro Peak and flows E 3 mi NW of Kingston). *Carbonate* is a prospector's term for ores containing carbonized lead and often silver. The name here is a reminder of the intense mining activity in the Kingston mining district in the late 19th century.

CARBONATEVILLE (Santa Fe). See *Turquesa.*

CARCASS BASIN (Catron; 2 mi W of Glenwood). Animal carcasses once were found here.

CARESSO CREEK (Colfax; flows SE into the Cimarron River E of Springer). This is likely a variant of the Spanish *carrizo,* "reed grass"; see *Carrizo (general).*

CARLISLE (Grant). See *Steeple Rock.*

CARLITO SPRINGS (Bernalillo; in Tijeras Canyon, 5 mi E of Albuquerque, on the SE slope of the Sandia Mountains). Named for Carl Magee, founder and editor of the *Albuquerque Tribune,* who lived here. Formerly called *Whitcomb Springs,* for a Union veteran of the Civil War who homesteaded here. Magee ultimately moved to Oklahoma City, where he invented the parking meter.

CARLSBAD (Eddy; settlement, county seat; on the Pecos River, at the junction of US 285 and US 62-180; PO as Eddy 1888–99, as Carlsbad 1899–present). Carlsbad originally had the same name

as the county for which it is the seat—
Eddy. In 1888, a group of the
settlement's organizers and promoters
gathered at a ford on the Pecos River
called Loving Bend (see entry). There
Lillian Green, a daughter of one of the
promoters, broke a bottle of champagne
and named the town for John A. and
Charles B. Eddy, brothers who held large
ranch interests in the area and promoted
RR development. By 1889 Eddy was calling itself "the Pearl of the Pecos."

The settlement remained Eddy until
a spring NW of town came to be reputed
to have the same mineral content as the
water at the famous European spa
known to Germans as Karlsbad, or
Carlsbad. This spa, now in Czechoslovakia and renamed Karlovy Vary by the
Czechs, was founded in 1349 by Karl IV
and named for him. In 1899, voters in
Eddy agreed to changing their town's
name to Carlsbad, and now the Eddy
brothers are recalled only by the name of
the county; see *Eddy County*.

In its early days Carlsbad had two
suburbs that were hangouts for outlaws:
Phenix (see entry) on the S side of town
and *Lone Wolf* (see *Phenix*) on the N.
Neither name was official, and by 1905
the outlaws had been run out; the settlements later were absorbed into Carlsbad.

Also absorbed into Carlsbad was a
settlement to the N known as *La Huerta*,
Spanish, "the vegetable or fruit garden,"
named for garden plots and orchards
that once supplied food for Carlsbad.

CARLSBAD CAVERNS NATIONAL PARK
(Eddy; 25 mi SW of Carlsbad, in the
foothills of the Guadalupe Mountains).
These caverns, among the world's largest
and most spectacular, were first explored
in 1901 by cowboy Jim White, who
found the cave after seeing bats emerging from its entrance. Prior to being
named for the city to the NE, the caverns were called *Bat Caves*. The national
park, the only one in NM, was created in
1930.

CARMEN, NORTH AND SOUTH (Mora;
settlements; 12 mi S of Mora, in the
Cebolla Valley, on NM 94). Small, inhabited farming communities, about a
mile apart, whose names likely honor
Nuestra Señora de Carmen, "Our Lady of
Carmen," one of many titles of the Virgin Mary.

CARNAHAN (Santa Fe; settlement; E of
San Pedro, S of Golden; PO 1927–30,
mail to Madrid). W.S. Carnahan, prospector and miner, operated the Ana-
conda, Lucky, and Amazon claims at San
Pedro in the late 1920s. He built a store
on a hill E of San Pedro and obtained
postal service there, naming the PO for
himself. Carnahan, his store, and his PO
all are gone.

CARNE (Luna; settlement; on SP RR, 3 mi
N of US 70-80, 14 mi E of Deming; PO
1909–16, mail to Deming). Carne was
the name requested, for reasons unknown, by the first postmaster, Frank H.
Hickman, at this former locality. Encouraged by a series of wet years from
1904 to 1907 and accompanying bountiful harvests, the Mimbres Farm Co. was
established here, but then dry years
came, and crops failed.

CARNERO (general). In NM *borrego* and
borrega were the general terms for sheep,
while *carnero* came to refer to a full-
grown ram, especially one kept for
breeding purposes; variants of the term
included *carnero meso, carnero padre,
carnero toro,* and *carnero terretón;* New
Mexicans used the term *carnero
cimmarón,* "wild ram," to refer to the
Rocky Mountain bighorn sheep.

OJO DEL CARNERO (Quay; near Plaza
Larga Creek, S of Tucumcari). Said to be
named for the wild sheep that watered
here, though the name would seem to
indicate an individual animal rather
than several.

CARNUEL (Bernalillo; settlement; in
Tijeras Canyon, on NM 333, 2 mi E of
Albuquerque). The Spanish-appearing
name of this small inhabited Hispanic
community probably is like Gila, Pecos,
Chama, and others in disguising a much
older Indian name. The Tiwa name for
the site is *Carna-aye* and means "badger
place." Perhaps the name was related to
the pueblo whose ruins have been found
nearby.

The name has appeared on maps as

both *Carnue* and Carnuel (pronounced carn-WELL). Carnue (pronounced carn-WAY) perhaps better approximates the Tiwa word, and the locality appeared as Carnue on Bernardo Miera y Pacheco's *Plano de la Provincia interna del Nueva México* of 1779. On the other hand, the territorial governor L. Bradford Prince cited "Carnue" as an example of a final consonant being lost through evolution, and Carnuel is the form most often used by present-day residents.

The first official settlement of the area occurred on Feb. 12, 1763, when 19 Hispanic men and their families took possession of a land grant. They established a small village they called *San Miguel de Carnué,* but repeated Indian attacks on the village forced its abandonment in 1771; subsequent attempts at resettlement were not successful. The short-lived village is believed to have been on benchland outside the mouth of Tijeras Canyon, within the present Albuquerque city boundary; partially excavated ruins there are preserved within Singing Arrow Park. In 1819 Governor Melgares approved the *Cañon de Carnuel Grant,* giving land to landless persons from Albuquerque. Its boundaries included most of what is now Tijeras Canyon, which also was known as *Cañon de Carnuel.* It was there, within the canyon, that the present village was established.

CAROLITA (Lincoln; settlement; location unknown; PO 1922–24, mail to Capitan). Short-lived postal locality, name origin unknown.

CARPENTER (Bernalillo; settlement; 15 mi E of Albuquerque, between Edgewood and Tijeras, N of I-40; PO 1903–07, mail to Albuquerque). This abandoned and all-but-forgotten settlement took the name of its first postmaster, José R. Carpenter. The name Carpenter had existed earlier in the area, however, as Henry Carpenter operated a large ranch in the Juan Tomas area in the 1880s.

CARPENTER (Grant; settlement; on the W slope of the Mimbres Mountains, exact location unknown). George Adlai Feather reported this to be a small lead-mining camp, established around 1882 and named because many of the prospectors were carpenters.

CARR (Cibola; settlement; near Ramah, exact location unknown; 1893–95, mail to Ramah). Little is known about this ephemeral community, including the origin of its name.

CARR (De Baca; settlement; location unknown; PO 1914, mail to Fort Sumner). Ephemeral postal locality, name origin unknown.

CARRACAS CANYON, MESA (Rio Arriba; mesa in NW part of county, adjacent to the Colorado border; canyon heads on Carracas Mesa and runs N into Colorado). It's unknown why this name appears on these features in Rio Arriba County, but a connection with the capital of Venezuela is unlikely. Rather, the name may be a corruption of the Spanish *carrascas,* "swamp oak." Or perhaps it is derived from the Spanish *carraca,* which can refer to a kind of wooden noise-maker used in Hispanic churches at Easter; perhaps water in the canyon resembled the sound, though in northern NM such a noise-maker is usually called a *matraca.*

CARRACAS (Rio Arriba; settlement; in NW part of county, on the San Juan River, now beneath Navajo Reservoir; PO 1881–82). Named for the mesa or the canyon; see *Carracas Canyon, Mesa.*

CARRISBROOKE (Colfax; settlement; on AT&SF RR, in Sugarite Canyon; PO 1907–08, mail to Raton). Carrisbrooke, sometimes spelled incorrectly without the "e," began as a mansion built in 1898 by A.D. Ensign, an Englishman with mining connections. He furnished the mansion sumptuously, with mahogany imported from England, and he imported its name as well; he called it *Carrisbrooke II,* after the village on the Isle of Wight in whose castle Charles I was imprisoned in 1647–48. Ensign vanished mysteriously, and his mansion was abandoned—only traces of it remain—but among people now living in the area, the name is still used and recognized.

CARRIZALILLO HILLS (Luna; S of Hermanas). These low desert hills bear a name that probably is a diminutive of the Spanish *carrizo;* see *Carrizo (general).*

CARRIZO (general). Spanish, "reed grass." Variants include *Carriso, Caresso, Cariso, Carrissa,* and *Careza* (not to be confused with *cereza,* meaning "cherry").

CARRIZO (Otero; settlement; 4 mi S of Ruidoso, on Carrizo Creek). Small inhabited settlement, likely named for the creek.

CARRIZO CANYON (Rio Arriba, San Juan; flows W into the San Juan River). Also called *Cañon Cereza, Carrizo Creek, Cereza Canyon,* but Carrizo Canyon is the form recognized by federal mapmakers. See *Carrizo (general).*

CARRIZO CREEK (Harding; rises in NW corner of county and flows SE to Tequesquite Creek). See *Carrizo (general).*

CARRIZO CREEK (Union; rises W of Clayton and flows SE into Oklahoma). See *Carrizo (general).*

CARRIZO PEAK, 9,605 ft. (Lincoln; 9 mi NE of Carrizozo). Like the *Carrizo Mountains,* of which this is the dominant summit, this mountain is said to have been named for *Carrizo Springs. Carrizo Cone* is to the E. *Carrizo Canyon* runs from the E between the Patos and Carrizo Mountains. See *Carrizo (general).*

CARRIZOZO (Lincoln; settlement, in SW part of county, at junction of US 380 and US 54; PO 1902–present). Like so many other features in the area, this settlement, the county seat of Lincoln County, was named for *Carrizo Springs,* about 2 mi N of the town, and it was called *Carrizo Flats,* or simply *Carrizo* when founded in 1899 as a new town by the EP&NE RR; at the time, Carrizo was overshadowed by White Oaks, then a mining center, now all but a ghost town. About 1907, when the town finally was platted, James Allcook, foreman of a local cattle ranch, added the second *zo* to Carrizo, making the name Carrizozo, the extra syllable indicating abundance, though the name, or some form of it,

likely had been used previously in the area, as the Carasoso Mining Co. was incorporated at White Oaks in 1880. Another account says W.C. McDonald, a prominent local rancher and later NM's first state governor, urged the RR to change the name from Carrizo to Carrizozo. See *Carrizo (general).*

CARRIZOZO CREEK (Union; heads in NE part of county, flows NE into Dry Cimarron River near Oklahoma border). See *Carrizo (general).*

CARRUMPA CREEK (Union). See *Corrumpa.*

CARSON (San Juan; trading point; 17 mi S of Bloomfield on a local road). This inhabited Navajo settlement was named not for Kit Carson, whose name is anathema among Navajos because of his role in the Long March, but rather for Stokes Carson, a local businessman and trader. The Navajo name for the locality means " (spring) coming out again."

CARSON (Taos; settlement; 15 mi SW of Taos on NM 567; PO 1912–present). The settlement of Carson was named for Christopher "Kit" Carson, who lived and was buried in nearby Taos. Numerous families of dry farmers settled in Carson in the 1920s, and a school was organized here, but the land was unsuitable for dry farming, and the village has all but vanished, though the PO remains active. See *Kit Carson (general).*

CARSON NATIONAL FOREST (Colfax, Rio Arriba, Taos; includes the Sangre de Cristo Mountains, the Tusas Mountains, portions of the Pecos Wilderness, and extensive mesas and uplands). The Carson NF began in 1906 with the *Taos Forest Reserve.* It later was expanded and named for Christopher "Kit" Carson, the trader, frontiersman, government scout, and Indian agent who figured prominently in the history of northern NM and who knew well the forests later named for him. See *Kit Carson (general).*

CARTER (Roosevelt; settlement; 12 mi N of Causey; PO 1906–17, mail to Portales). This abandoned homesteader settlement was named for O.B. Carter, father of Harvey Carter, who resided at the settlement at the time of its naming.

CARTHAGE (Socorro; settlement, mining camp; S of US 380, 10 mi E of San Antonio; PO 1883–93, 1906–50, mail to Bingham). The first coal mining in NM was near Carthage, at the Government Mine, which supplied the smithing needs of Forts Selden, Bayard, and Stanton and was worked by US Army soldiers. A soldier bestowed the name Carthage, for the ancient Tunisian city, to the mining camp that grew up around the mine. Eventually, the SF RR built a bridge across the Rio Grande and laid tracks to Carthage, making it the busiest coal camp in the state. But when Congress denied a patent for the Montoya Grant, where the mines were located, the RR tore up the tracks and moved its operation to Madrid in Santa Fe County. Though the mines at Carthage later were reopened, the locality continued to decline and eventually was abandoned.

CASA BLANCA (Cibola; settlement, N of I-40, 6 mi W of Laguna; PO 1905–present). This inhabited and growing settlement on the Laguna Indian Reservation began as a farming community along the Rio San Jose; it was not settled permanently until the early 1870s when refugees from the bitter factionalism at Laguna arrived. It was named Casa Blanca because some of the community's early houses were coated with white clay. Recently the village has expanded S of I-40. *Casa Blanca Mesa* is about 2.5 mi SE of the village.

CASA BLANCA (Rio Arriba; settlement; on the Brazos River between El Vado and La Puente). George Adlai Feather found this to be a tiny village, no longer indicated on maps.

CASA COLORADA (Valencia; settlement; on the E bank of the Rio Grande, on NM 304, 6 mi SE of Belen; PO as Turn 1927–1938, mail to Belen). Spanish, "red house." During the 18th century, the stage line between Albuquerque and Socorro ran E of the river, following the route of the Camino Real (see entry), and Casa Colorada was a stage stop on the line. It has been reported that the stage depot was in a large adobe general store that had been colored red, hence

the name, although another report mentions an *hacienda* that might also have been colored red. Bishop Tamarón mentioned visiting Casa Colorado in 1760. Josiah Gregg, in his *Commerce of the Prairies* (1844), mentioned passing through Casa Colorada. In the 1920s John W. Conant, whose family had been among the founders of Newkirk (see entry), moved to the community and soon petitioned for postal service. He submitted three names for the PO he sought to establish here; the postal officials chose *Turn*, because the site was on a "turn" in the road. Though the PO has closed, the locality has survived—as has the name Casa Colorada. In 1994 Ramón Baca, from a local family, contacted the NM Geographic Names Committee and proposed officially changing the name from Turn, which appeared on most maps, to Casa Colorada, saying the name Turn was not used—was even resented—by local residents who had never stopped using the original name. Though as of this writing neither the NMGNC nor the USBGN had voted on the proposal, Casa Colorada being long-established and preferred by local usage satisfied two of the most important criteria of both groups.

CASA GRANDE (San Miguel; settlement; E of Las Vegas, NW of Trujillo; PO 1907–12, mail to Cherryvale). Abandoned community, origin of name, Spanish for "big house," unknown. The 1910 US Census recorded 150 people here.

CASA RINCONADA (San Juan; archaeological site; in Chaco Culture National Historical Park, in Chaco Canyon, across the canyon and 0.25 mi S of Pueblo Bonito). Casa Rinconada is the ruin of a "great kiva," a ceremonial chamber built by the Indians who lived here about A.D. 1000–1200. The Spanish name was given because of the site's location in a corner, or *rincón*, of the canyon. The Navajos call the kiva "circular house."

CASA SALAZAR (Sandoval; on the W bank of the Rio Puerco, 4 mi S of Guadalupe; PO as Casa Salazar 1888–95, as Casasalazar 1895–1914, 1915–19). This settlement, named for the Salazar family, was one of four tiny settlements along the valley of the Rio Puerco, the others being *San Luis, Guadalupe,* and *Cabezon* (see entries). Casa Salazar once was a lively place, the scene of numerous dances and fiestas, with 100 residents in 1905; now it's mostly abandoned. See *Salazar (general).*

CASITA DE PIEDRA CANYON (Taos; heads at Capulin Peak and runs S into Taos Canyon, 9 mi E of Taos). Spanish, "little stone house." A family once lived at the mouth of this canyon in a small house made of stone. *Casita Piedra Peak,* 10,210 ft., in the Taos Range, E of Taos and N of Rio Fernando de Taos, at head of Casita Piedra Canyon, 3 mi E of Capulin Peak, was named for the canyon.

CASITAS (Rio Arriba; settlement; 12 mi S of El Rito, near the junction of NM 554 and US 84). Spanish, "little houses." Tiny abandoned Hispanic settlement.

CASS (Eddy; settlement; in SE part of county; PO 1888–90, mail to Lookout). Ephemeral postal locality, name origin unknown.

CASTLE DOME (Catron; just E of NM 32, 14 mi SW of Quemado). Conspicuous, vertical-sided, castle-like formation, also called *Castle Rock.*

CASTLEBERRY (Quay). See *Lesbia.*

CASAUS (Guadalupe; settlement; on Salado Creek, E of Vaughn; PO 1894–1911). Abandoned community, named for the Casaus family; Perfecto Casaus was among the earliest settlers in the area, and members of his family were prominent stockmen in the area. A site SE of Vaughn on the AT&SF RR was known as *Casaus Station.*

CAT MESA (Sandoval; in Jemez Mountains, 2 mi S of Jemez Springs). Likely named for an incident involving a mountain lion here, or perhaps a bobcat; its local Spanish name is *Mesa del Gato.*

CAT MESA (Socorro; 3 mi SE of Monte Prieto and 2 mi E of Chupadera Mesa). Named by sheepherders and known locally as *Cathead Mesa,* for reasons unknown.

CATALPA (Colfax; trading point; in E part of county, on Dry Cimarron River; PO 1882–84, mail to Madison). Michael Devoy, born in Ireland in 1839, came to this area at the age of 26. After being postmaster at Madison on the Dry Cimarron River, he bought a ranch downstream where he built a log cabin and opened a store near his home. He named the store Catalpa, for reasons unknown. Later the cabin housed the public school, until 1918. Devoy died at his ranch in 1914; the store and cabin have been abandoned.

CATCLAW DRAW (Chaves, Eddy; 5 mi W of Hope). This has nothing to do with a feline but rather refers to the catclaw acacia shrub (*Acacia roemeriana*), whose thorns have an obvious resemblance to a cat's claws. In Spanish the name appears here, as elsewhere in NM, as *Uña de Gato.*

CATRON COUNTY (W-central NM, abutting the Arizona line; county seat, Reserve). Created in 1921 from the western part of Socorro County, this county bears the name of Thomas B. Catron, attorney and politician and one of the most influential and controversial figures in NM history. Catron moved to NM in 1866 from Missouri. Almost immediately he became involved in politics, emerging as the leader of the growing Republican party. As a state legislator he was the leader of the "Santa Fe Ring," a circle of overlapping interests that dominated NM politics in the late 19th century. Fluent in Spanish, he acquired 1.5 million acres in former Spanish grant lands; the ethics of his acquisitions have remained controversial. He was an ardent advocate of statehood for NM, and he pushed the issue while US congressman for the territory. Despite frequent disappointments, he lived to see statehood achieved in 1912 and was one of the state's first two US senators. The county named for him is the state's largest, with one of the smallest populations.

CATRON WASH (McKinley; 1.5 mi S of Nakaibito, N of Gallup). Likely named for Thomas B. Catron; see *Catron County.*

CATSKILL (Colfax; settlement; on Vermejo River, NW of Cimarron; PO 1890–1902, 1903–05, mail to Sopris, CO). The lumber camp of Catskill began in 1890 when the Maxwell Land Grant platted the town and leased land for lumbering; it was settled by a group of lumbermen under the company management of H.G. Frankenburger. Soon five major sawmills were operating, along with beehive charcoal ovens, and a RR line was brought in from Trinidad, CO. The burgeoning settlement was named by C.F. Meek, the RR's general manager, for the Catskill Mountains near his hometown in New York State. Catskill is remembered as a fun-loving place, where any event would occasion a celebration. But by the turn of the century timber was becoming scarce. In 1902 the RR tracks were pulled up, and though a few residents tried to substitute stock-raising for lumbering, eventually even this activity ceased, and the town died.

CAUSEY (Lea; trading point; 5 mi S of Lovington). This vanished trading point is where the Causey brothers established the first PO and store on the Llano Estacado of NM, the only such services in a 100-mile radius. The PO, likely never officially sanctioned by the federal government, functioned for about 12 years, from 1884.

T.L. "George" Causey, accompanied by George "Old Jeff" Jefferson, arrived in SE NM in 1882, and his brother, John Causey, soon followed. They became buffalo hunters. When the buffalo were hunted almost to extinction, the Causeys became settlers and ranchers. George Causey built the first permanent dwelling in what is now Lea County, planted the first trees, imported the first windmill, opened the first general store and the first PO, and established the first ranch. By digging the first well, he was the first person to tap the underground reservoirs that have meant so much to the region's development. In 1903, broken in body, suffering from increasingly painful headaches, and with the wild, free life he had loved vanishing because of developments he had helped pioneer, George Causey, age 54, took his own life.

CAUSEY (Roosevelt; settlement; SE of Portales, at the junction of NM 114 and 321, near the Texas border; PO 1907–present). The name of this small inhabited community recalls the Causey brothers, whose lives influenced and symbolized American exploration and settlement of the Llano Estacado. The present village of Causey, begun by Ezra Ball after World War I, is three miles N of an earlier settlement. Ironically, the Causey brothers' own ranch was not located here but farther S, in Lea County; but the Causey brothers—see *Causey (Lea)*—were responsible for opening this part of NM to settlement.

CAVARISTA (Taos; settlement; in NE part of county, in the Sangre de Cristo Mountains; PO 1895, mail to Labelle). Ephemeral settlement, name origin unknown.

CAVE CREEK (San Miguel, Santa Fe; heads in the Sangre de Cristo Mountains, in the Pecos Wilderness, NE of Lake Katherine, flows SE to join Panchuela Creek NW of Cowles). As Elliott Barker described it, "The entire flow of the little creek runs into a descending cave at the side of the canyon and comes out again a half-mile below. This, of course, gives rise to the name, and it is literally a creek in a cave."

CAVE CITY (Catron; settlement; at the mouth of Taylor Creek, S of Beaverhead). According to George Adlai Feather, this long-gone tin-mining camp was named because miners used as offices and living quarters the structures prehistoric Indians here had built in caves.

CAVE CITY (Sierra; settlement; 9 mi NW of Hillsboro at the head of Cave Creek in the Black Range). Short-lived mining camp.

CEBOLLA (general). Spanish, "onion." Spanish-speaking settlers applied this word to numerous places in NM, especially streams and valleys, because of locally abundant wild onions (lily family, genus *Allium*). Occasionally the word described sulphurous water, with an onionlike odor. In NM, *cebolla* often appears in its diminutive forms, *cebolleta* or *cebollita,* though sometimes *cebolleta* has been interpreted to mean "tender onion"; the various forms appear 27 times in NM (GNIS).

CEBOLLA (Rio Arriba; settlement; on US 84 13 mi S of Tierra Amarilla; PO as Sebolla 1907–10, as Cebolla 1910–14). This small community, settled around 1800, was named for the valley where it is located. Sheep and goats grazing in the valley were said to have been especially fond of the wild onions common here, and shepherds came to call the place *El Valle de Cebolla.* The Rio Cebolla, which flows through the village from the NE to enter the Rio Chama, also takes its name from the valley. See *Cebolla (general).*

CEBOLLA VALLEY (Mora; in W part of county, 3 mi S of the village of Mora). The *Rito Cebolla* flows through here, watering fields at North Carmen. See *Cebolla (general).*

CEBOLLA WILDERNESS (Cibola; on the E side of El Malpais National Monument, S of Grants). This is but one of several features in the area named for wild onions; see *Cebollita Mesa* and *Cebolla (general).* The 62,000-acre Cebolla Wilderness, designated in 1987 and administered by the BLM, preserves dramatic mesa, canyon, and rimrock country, as well as nesting sites for raptors; it also includes numerous archaeological features. La Ventana (see entry), NM's second largest natural arch, is here.

CEBOLLETA (Cibola). See *Seboyeta.*

CEBOLLETA MOUNTAINS (Cibola, McKinley; in Cibola NF, NE of Grants). During Spanish colonial times, 11,301-foot Mount Taylor and the volcanic plateau extending 44 miles NE of Grants together were known as *Cebolleta,* but later the features came to have separate names: the plateau was called Mesa Chivato (Spanish, "kid, young male goat"), while in 1849 the mountain was named formally for President Zachary Taylor (see *Mount Taylor*), though the name Cebolleta persisted in local usage. Today, the plateau's NW half is called the *Cebolleta Mountains,* while the southern half, including Mount Taylor and the surrounding plateau is called the *San Mateo Mountains;* the nearby village of San Mateo was named for them.

CEBOLLETITA (Cibola; settlement; 2 mi S of Cebolla and 3 mi N of Paguate; PO as Bibo 1895–1920). Though a literal translation of this Spanish name would be "very little onion," here it means "little Cebolleta," as the village was settled by people from Cebolleta (now Seboyeta) to the N. The inhabited Hispanic settlement of Cebolletita appears on some maps as *Bibo,* for the Bibo brothers who settled in this area in the 1880s; Ben Bibo, the youngest of six brothers, operated a trading post and PO from 1895 to 1920. But while local people use and recognize the name Bibo, many retain a preference for the earlier name, Cebolletita. A military outpost to discourage Navajo raiding was once here.

CEBOLLITA MESA (Cibola; in SE part of county, its edge marking the SW boundary of Acoma Indian Reservation). Large mesa that dominates the surrounding landscape, as does its name: *Cebollita Peak,* 8,765 ft., is on the S part of the mesa; *Cebolla Creek, Cebolla Canyon, Cebolla Spring,* and *Little Cebolla Spring* are immediately to the S, while slightly farther S is *Onion Spring; Cebollita Spring* is just to the N, as is *North Cebollita Mesa.* See *Cebolla (general).*

CEDAR (general). See *Juniper (general).*

CEDAR CREST (Bernalillo; settlement; in the eastern foothills of the Sandia Mountains, 3 mi N of Tijeras, on NM 14; PO as Tijeras 1888–1925, as Cedar Crest 1925—present). In 1922 23-year-old Carl Webb, all but broke and in poor health, left Albuquerque to live in the mountains. He built some rental cabins and soon opened the Webb Trading Post, later the Cedar Crest Trading Post. He also operated the Cedar Crest PO. Webb sold his Cedar Crest holdings in 1955 and moved out of state, though he later returned to Albuquerque in the

1970s. He died in Pennsylvania in 1992 at the age of 93 and is regarded as a founder of Cedar Crest. Presumably the growing settlement with easy access to Albuquerque took its name from the NM "cedars" abundant in the area. See *Juniper (general)*.

CEDAR GROVE (Santa Fe; settlement; E of Albuquerque, on NM 344, N of Edgewood). At one time this was a stage, freight, and military overnight stop, offering wood, water, and grass; later bean farming was important here. Today Cedar Grove is a small residential community. NM "cedars" are abundant here, but not more so than elsewhere in the area. See *Juniper (general)*.

CEDAR HILL (San Miguel; settlement; just E of I-25, 2 mi NE of Tecolote). Tiny residential cluster, named for its location.

CEDAR HILL (San Juan; settlement; on NM 550 and the Animas River, 10 mi NE of Aztec, 4 mi from the Colorado border; PO 1892–1966, mail to Aztec). Cedar Hill certainly describes the setting of this inhabited community, but the name didn't simply evolve from mere description. Sometime between 1887 and 1892, at a meeting of the local Literacy Society, a new name was selected for the growing settlement that until then had been known as *Coxs Crossing*. Members of the Society wrote names upon slips of paper, and the winning name was drawn from a hat. The name drawn—Cedar Hill—had been submitted by Emma Tinker.

CEDAR HILLS (Eddy). See *Alacran Hills*.

CEDAR MOUNTAIN RANGE (Luna; runs SE-NW in SW part of county). Low, gently contoured range; highest points, *Cedar Mountain*, 6,215 ft., in NW part of the range, *Flying W Mountain*, 6,215 ft., in SE part of the range; the latter summit was named for the Flying W Ranch 2 mi E of the summit.

CEDAR SPRINGS (De Baca; settlement; on the Pecos River, 20 mi N of Fort Sumner). Ephemeral settlement, established in 1865 but abandoned after the soldiers were removed from Fort Sumner.

CEDARVALE (Torrance; settlement; in SE part of county, on NM 42, 11 mi NW of Corona; PO 1908–present). Cedarvale was established in 1908 by Ed Smith, William Taylor, and Oliver P. De Wolf and named by them for Cedarvale, KS. Like other small communities in this part of the Estancia Valley, Cedarvale prospered through dry farming and ranching, but the Depression and overgrazing, along with the trend toward large ranches, caused a general decline, and today most houses here are abandoned.

CEDRO (Bernalillo; settlement; in the NE foothills of the Manzano Mountains, just W of NM 337, 5 mi S of Tijeras). This inhabited community likely was named for its location in *Cedro Canyon*. Brothers named Griego and their families homesteaded here in the late 19th century. See *Juniper (general)*.

CEJA (general). Though this Spanish word means, literally, "eyebrow," it also can mean "fringe, border," specifically the escarpment or cliff at the edge of a mesa. *Cejita* is the diminutive.

CEJA DEL RIO PUERCO (Bernalillo, Sandoval, Valencia, W of Albuqerque and Belen). A 70-mile-long escarpment overlooking the Rio Puerco valley to the W, the "eyebrow" stands 500–600 ft. above the valley bottom. Extending E from the escarpment toward Albuquerque and Belen is a grassy flatland often called the *West Mesa* and sometimes *Ceja Mesa;* the latter form originated with geologist Vincent C. Kelly. The term *Llano de Albuquerque* also has been applied to the area.

CEJITA DE LOS COMANCHEROS (Harding; in NE part of county, 2 mi NW of Rosebud). *Comancheros* were Hispanics and later Anglos who traded with the Plains Indians, especially the Comanches. Sometimes the trade, which usually involved buffalo hides, was government sanctioned, but often it was illegal, as it also involved guns and stolen livestock. This particular *cejita* is in broken grassland at the head of both the *Arroyo de la Cejita* and *Arroyo del Cejito,* but if some incident occurred here involving *comancheros,* it has been forgotten.

CENTER (Curry; settlement; on US 70, 2 mi S of Clovis). The farming community of Center owed its existence and its identity to three rural schools; the community was centrally located with regard to them. Though the Center School, which was the nucleus of the community, since has been consolidated with Clovis, Center survives as a residential area; the name is still recognized in the area, and people still identify themselves as residents of Center.

CENTER BALDY, 10,535 ft. (Catron; in the Mogollon Mountains, just S of Whitewater Baldy). Likely named for being in the center of a large complex of peaks and ridges.

CENTER POINT (San Juan). See *Rosing.*

CENTER VALLEY (Doña Ana). See *Vado.*

CENTERFIRE CREEK, BOG (Catron; 5 mi NE of Luna). A long-time resident whose ranch includes the creek and the bog says their name comes from the Spur Cattle Co. once having three camps, the center one being here. "Centerfire" also is the name of a pack-saddle hitch.

CENTERVILLE (Union; settlement; 8 mi S of Amistad, 18 mi N of Nara Visa; PO 1907–44, mail to Nara Visa). This home-steader community was founded by Webster Lamb, who also was first post-master. Local people say he named it Centerville because it was in the "center" of a wide area. Centerville at one time was a substantial settlement; nothing now remains, though the name still is recognized. It appears on some maps as *Centerville Corner,* for a prominent bend in NM 402.

CENTRAL (Grant). See *Santa Clara.*

CENTRAL CITY (Union). See *Hayden.*

CERRILLOS (Santa Fe; settlement; on the Rio Galisteo, just W of NM 14, 20 mi SW of Santa Fe; PO 1880–present). The hills for which this picturesque village was named likely are those 3 mi NW, which appear on some maps under the oxymoron of *Cerrillos Hills* (in translation, "little hills hills). And it was minerals in these and other nearby hills that twice engendered a settlement here. The first time was sometime before 1680;

Indians long had mined turquoise here, and when the Spanish arrived they continued to work the mines. Turquoise from Cerrillos found its way into the crown jewels of Spain. In the 17th and 18th centuries, the names *Cerrillos* and *Cerrito* were applied to *haciendas* near Turquoise Mountain.

Cerrillos experienced a second mining boom in 1879, when two prospectors from Colorado found promising gold and silver ore in the "little hills"; Cerrillos flourished, and the mining camps of Bonanza and Carbonateville (see entries) sprang up nearby. The latter two died soon after the precious metal veins petered out, but Cerrillos still had coal deposits needed by the AT&SF RR, which reached Cerrillos in 1880. Cerrillos often has been called *Los Cerrillos,* probably the original form, but the name accepted by the USBGN in 1975 was simply Cerrillos.

EL CERRITO (San Miguel; settlement; on the Pecos River, 3 mi E of Villanueva; PO 1910–16, mail to Villanueva). The name of this tiny Hispanic village refers to its location on a "little hill." It was settled sometime before 1844 by people from neighboring villages, such as San Miguel del Bado, wishing to be closer to their grazing lands. Though El Cerrito has dwindled over the years, a few residents remain.

CERRITO COLORADO, 10,246 ft. (Taos; in the Fernando Mountains, S of US 64, E of Taos, 3 mi SE of Shadybrook). Spanish, "reddish little mountain." Another *Cerrito Colorado,* 9,661 ft., is 3 mi NE of Valdez.

CERRITO DEL PADRE (Mora). See *Rito del Padre.*

CERRITOS (San Miguel). See *El Cerrito.*

CERRO, CERRILLO, CERRITO (general). *Cerro* is the Spanish term for "hill," though in NM the term has been used to refer to landforms ranging from small lowland hills to high summits of major mountain ranges. Thus the word in some instances is synonymous with "mountain." *Cerrillo* and *cerrito* are the diminutives.

CERRO (Taos; settlement; on NM 522, 3 mi N of Questa). Inhabited farming community, settled in 1854 by persons from Questa and Taos and named for *Cerro Guadalupe* to the SW. The original *plaza* of the community was NE of the present community.

EL CERRO (Valencia; in the Rio Grande Valley, 3 mi NE of Tome). This large volcanic formation, rising abruptly from the surrounding Rio Grande floodplain, is a natural lookout and reference point; petroglyphs are evidence of early Indian presence here. Following the Spanish conquest, Tomé Domínguez de Mendoza (see *Tome*) built his *hacienda* near here, and the hill once was commonly referred to as *El Cerro de Tomé Domínguez*. Today it sometimes is called simply *Tome Hill. Genízaros,* Hispanicized Indians, had a village here, which they called "Rabbit Hill." For local people, El Cerro has acquired religious significance, and pilgrims still hike the rocky trail to crosses and shrines on its summit.

EL CERRO (Valencia; settlement; 3 mi NE of Tome). Growing agricultural and residential community that took the name of nearby *El Cerro* (see entry).

CERRO ALESNA (McKinley; 17 mi NE of San Mateo). The name of this dramatic volcanic neck, one of many in the Mount Taylor volcanic field, is a reminder that NM's Hispanic peoples often named places for their resemblance to common domestic articles. Alesna comes from *la lesna,* "the awl." The sharp-pointed prominence also has been called *Sharks Tooth.*

CERRO DE LA GARITA, 10,610 ft. (Sandoval; in central Jemez Mountains, in N part of Baca Location No. 1, 1.5 mi S of Cerro del Grant). The meanings of *garita* are obscure and varied, but the most likely meaning here is "watchtower" or "government building."

CERRO DE LA OLLA, 9,475 ft. (Taos; 11 mi NW of Questa). A huge volcanic formation named for its resemblance to a pot or jar, for that is the meaning of the Spanish *olla*. Local English-speakers translate the Spanish and call the formation *Pot Mountain.*

CERRO DEL AIRE, 9,023 ft. (Taos; 5 mi NE of Tres Piedras). An isolated volcanic peak, whose Spanish name means "windy mountain." As with Cerro de la Olla, local English-speakers translate the Spanish name and call the peak *Wind Mountain.*

CERRO DEL GRANT, 10,432 ft. (Rio Arriba; in the central Jemez Mountains, just N of Baca Location No. 1). This Spanish-English name, "mountain of the grant," probably refers to the Polvadera Land Grant to the E or the Baca Location No. 1 to the S.

CERRO GRANDE, 10,199 ft. (Sandoval; in the Jemez Mountains, E of the Valle Grande, S of Pajarito Mountain). Spanish, "big mountain."

CERRO MAGDALENA, 6,623 ft. (Doña Ana; 12 mi S of Hatch). A supposed resemblance to Mary Magdalene is said to have inspired the name of this peak, also called *Magdalena Peak.*

CERRO MONTOSO, 8,655 ft. (Taos; 9 mi SW of Questa). An isolated volcanic mountain whose Spanish name means "brushy, or wooded, mountain."

CERRO OLLA 11,932 ft. (Taos; in the Sangre de Cristo Mountains, 15 mi SE of Taos). This mountain at the head of the Rio Grande del Rancho has a Spanish descriptive name meaning "pot-shaped mountain." See also *Cerro de la Olla.*

CERRO PAVO, 10,310 ft. (Rio Arriba; in the central Jemez Mountains, N of Baca Location No. 1). Spanish, "turkey mountain."

CERRO PEDERNAL, 9,862 ft. (Rio Arriba; in the N Jemez Mountains, NW of Abiquiu and SE of Youngsville). This dramatic, chisel-shaped peak was well known to ancient people both for its appearance and even more for its composition. Its name is Spanish and means "flint mountain"; Bernardo Miera y Pacheco on his map of 1779 labeled it *Serra Pedernal* and even drew its distinctive flat top. The nearby abandoned pueblo of *Tsiping* took its name from this peak; the Tewa name means "flaking stone mountain." The Navajo name for the peak also refers to flint. More recently, Cerro Pedernal was made famous through the paintings of Georgia O'Keeffe, who saw the peak from her home in Abiquiu. After O'Keeffe's death in 1986, consideration was given to renaming Cerro Pedernal to honor her, but widespread opposition, as well as O'Keeffe's well-known respect for local traditions, doomed the proposal.

CERRO PELADO, 10,109 ft. (Sandoval; in the Jemez Mountains, in the SE part of the Jemez Caldera, 2 mi S of NM 4). The name is Spanish and means "bald mountain," though it now is forested. It is not to be confused with nearby Redondo Peak (see entry), which on some old maps was labeled Mount Pelado. See *Bald, Baldy (general)*.

CERRO PELON, 9,367 ft. (Rio Arriba; in the NE Jemez Mountains, 4 mi N of Polvadera Peak). Spanish, "bald mountain." See *Bald, Baldy (general)*.

CERRO PICACHO, 10,290 ft. (Mora, Taos; in the Sangre de Cristo Mountains, 2 mi N of NM 518, on the Taos-Mora line). Spanish, "pointed peak."

CERRO RUBIO, 10,449 ft. (Sandoval; in E Jemez Mountains, at the head of Guaje Canyon, SW of Caballo Mountain). Spanish, "blond, or reddish, mountain."

CERRO SARAGATE, 10,641 ft. (Rio Arriba; in the W Tusas Mountains, 10 mi NE of Cebolla). Meaning and origin unknown.

CERRO TOLEDO, 10,925 ft. (Sandoval; in the Jemez Mountains, in the NE part of Baca Location No. 1). This summit shares this Hispanic surname with two other nearby features: *Valle Toledo* and *Sierra de Toledo,* both just to the SW. The identity of the person named Toledo who inspired these names is unknown.

CERRO VISTA, 11,947 ft. (Mora, Taos; in Sangre de Cristo Mountains, on boundary between Mora and Taos Counties, 2 mi NE of Cerro Olla). Spanish, best translated as "mountain with a view." The peak has been called *Cerro Mora,* probably because the Mora River heads S of here.

LOS CERROS CUATES (Sandoval; E of the Rio Puerco, 3 mi SW of Cabezon Peak). This volcanic plug, whose name means "the twin mountains," was an important landmark for the Rio Puerco settlements.

CERROS DEL ABRIGO, 10,332 ft. (Sandoval; in the central Jemez Mountains, in NE part of Baca Location No. 1). Spanish, "mountains of shelter, protection," for reasons unknown.

CERROSOSO (Colfax; settlement; S of US 64, on Cerrososo Creek). Long abandoned locality, named for *Cerrososo Creek,* whose name likely means "hilly."

CERUILITA (Mora; settlement; location unknown). Listed as a *plaza* in 1870.

CHACO (general). This name element, common in NW NM, has passed through at least three languages to reach its present form. Apparently the name began as a Navajo word, *tsegai,* a contraction of Navajo words for "rock" and "white." *Tsegai,* explains the National Park Service archaeologist David M. Brugge, "is the Navajo name that was Hispanicized as *Chaca,* possibly passing through some Pueblo Language to Spanish." The plausibility of this explanation is buttressed by the fact that in most early records, such as Bernardo Miera y Pacheco's map of 1778, the name appears as *Chaca,* and Lt. James H. Simpson, writing during the 1849 military expedition through the region, mentions passing through "Chaca Wash." Brugge continues: "*Chaca* in turn was Anglicized as Chaco and Chacra. All refer to the same general region, but, except for the English Chaco, pertain more to Chacra Mesa than to Chaco Canyon. *Tsegai* is a word that can connote 'home' to some Navajos, in particular to those whose ancestors left most of the remains [in the area]."

The Navajo word *tsekho* also has been suggested as an source for the name; *tsekho* means "canyon" (literally *tse* "rock," *kho* "opening"). And finally, and least likely, the word *chaco* also could be derived from *charco,* a NM Spanish word that means "pool, puddle, mud hole."

CHACO CULTURE NATIONAL HISTORICAL PARK (McKinley, San Juan; mostly in SE part of San Juan County, centered on Chaco Canyon, on NM 57, 38 mi NE of Crownpoint). Chaco Canyon is a cliff-bound arid wilderness, yet here the people known as the Anasazi—forerunners of today's Pueblo Indians—flourished as nowhere else. Thirteen large villages and hundreds of smaller ruins dot the area—the greatest concentration of prehistoric Indian ruins in the US. The earliest structures, pit houses, were constructed here about A.D. 500, but by the 900s the Chaco Anasazi were building on a larger scale, beginning with the construction of Pueblo Bonito, Chetro Kettle, and other large pueblos. During the next 200 years, the site became the center of a vigorous, expansive civilization that extended throughout the Four Corners region. It was a civilization that included roads, irrigation systems, and a complex social structure. But by A.D. 1300, for reasons still not well understood, the people had dispersed; the great structures of Chaco Canyon stood empty and silent.

The ruins at Chaco Canyon were noticed rather late by Spanish explorers; Bernardo Miera y Pacheco drew a tiny picture of them on his 1778 map. They also were visited and described by Lt. James H. Simpson in 1849. The Hyde Exploring Expedition excavated two of the larger ruins, Pueblo Bonito and Pueblo del Arroyo, in 1896–99, and many subsequent archaeological investigations have been made. In 1907, *Chaco Canyon National Monument* was established to preserve the ruins. In 1980 the monument was enlarged and redesignated as Chaco Culture National Historic Park. See also *Pueblo Bonito, Pueblo Alto, Chettro Kettle, Casa Rinconada, Fajada Butte, Kin Kletso, Kin Klizhin,* and *Putnam.*

CHACO CANYON (San Juan; settlement; on NM 57, at Pueblo Bonito in Chaco Canyon; PO 1936–42, mail to Bloomfield). Long vanished, this was a trading post adjacent to Pueblo Bonito.

CHACO RIVER (McKinley, Rio Arriba, San Juan; heads along the Continental Divide in western Rio Arriba County and flows W through Chaco Canyon to join the San Juan River E of Shiprock). A 1963 USBGN decision established Chaco River as the accepted form and not *Río Chaco* or *Tsegilini.* The river seldom has water flowing in it, so it often is called *Chaco Wash.*

CHACON (Mora; settlement; at upper end of Mora Valley, on the Rio Mora, 7 mi N of Holman, on NM 121; PO 1894–present). At the time of the Mora land grant in 1835, this inhabited farming community had 132 residents, in 11 families, and was known as *El Rito de Agua Negra,* "the stream of the black water," a name attributed to sulphur in the water. Later it took the surname of its first postmaster, Diego A. Chacón, whose family members—Albino, Damasco, and Pedro Chacón—were among the Upper Mora Valley's first settlers. (The first Chacóns recorded as being in NM lived near San Juan Pueblo around 1750.) The village of Chacon, surrounded by high mountains and at an elevation of 8,500 ft., has severe winters, thus the local nickname "Little Alaska."

CHACON (Valencia; settlement; between Valencia and Albuquerque, at the foot of the Manzano Mountains). This former community, once the site of the Chacon mineral water bottling company, was named for the Chacón family, who lived here. On a 1769 map, the locality appears as *Laredo.*

CHAMA (general). This is a Spanish approximation of the Tewa Name *Tsama.* A Tewa pueblo by this name was on the W bank of the Rio Chama, just N of modern Abiquiu, and the name has been interpreted to mean "here they wrestled." As such, the *Río Chama* was named for its association with the pueblo on it, as was the Jemez River. But some authorities have said the name is a corruption of the Tewa *tzama,* which has been translated as "red," referring to the color of the river's water, and thus the pueblo might have been named for the river, not vice versa; this explanation is becoming the accepted one.

CHAMA (Rio Arriba; settlement; 8 mi S of

the Colorado line, on NM 17, on the Rio Chama; PO 1880–present). The town of Chama was born in 1880 when the D&RG RR arrived. Earlier the site was occupied by a sawmill and tent town called *Chama Crossing,* for their location on the *Río Chama,* and before that it had been a small Hispanic settlement whose formal name was *San Pedro de Chama.* By 1881 the RR settlement, still mostly tents, was booming and struggling with the lawlessness that characterized such boom towns; holdups and shootings were common. Soon, however, the town became a supply center for area ranches, and the timber industry flourished. Today, Chama is a growing recreation center; a scenic mountainous segment of the old RR is operated as the Cumbres and Toltec Scenic RR.

CHAMA RIVER CANYON WILDERNESS (Rio Arriba; along the Rio Chama, NW of Abiquiu Reservoir). This 50,300-acre wilderness, created in 1978, preserves wild lands on both sides of a 6-mile stretch of the Rio Chama, featuring high polychrome bluffs and riverine habitat. Administered by the Carson NF. See also *Río Chama Wild and Scenic River.*

CHAMBERINO (Doña Ana; settlement; on NM 28, 20 mi S of Las Cruces; PO 1880–82, 1893–present). This name has been said to be a Spanish corruption of an Indian word meaning "deep ford," though corroboration of this is completely lacking. It also has been said to be a colloquial Spanish word for brush that grew here; both are plausible. Whatever the origin, the name clearly is related to that of *Berino* (see entry), E of Chamberino, on the E side of the Rio Grande. The original settlement of Chamberino, still inhabited, was partially destroyed in the flood of 1892 and was rebuilt on higher ground; it is approximately 1 mi SW of the more recent village and is situated on the breaks above the Rio Grande floodplain. When the danger of flooding diminished following the completion of Elephant Butte Dam in 1916, many residents relocated to be closer to the main highway. For a while the community took the name of

its patron saint, San Luis, but the name Chamberino has endured.

CHAMISA, CHAMISO, CHAMISAL, CHAMIZAL (general). *Chamisa* is the name Hispanic New Mexicans have had for several varieties of the shrub *Chrysothamnus nauseosus,* whose English common name is rabbitbrush, though the term *chamiso* also has been applied to the ubiquitous four-wing saltbush (*Atriplex canescens*). As T.M. Pearce suggested, the folk-name *chamisa* may be related to the Spanish *chamuscar,* "to singe or burn," possibly because rural people used the shrub's easily ignited wood as kindling for fires. Chamisa is especially common in northern NM, and the names *chamisal* or *chamizal* mean "overgrown with chamisa." GNIS lists 32 places with Chamisa or one of its variants in their names.

CHAMISAL (Taos; settlement; on NM 76, 3 mi N of Las Trampas; PO 1904–05, 1907–13, 1913–present). Situated within the Picuris land grant, this inhabited Hispanic farming community was established in 1850; it was named like many similar communities, for a feature in the immediate natural environment, in this case the chamisa plant. See *Chamisa (general). Chamizal Creek,* which heads 9 mi SE at Ojo del Oso, flows NW through the village to join the Rio Peñasco.

CHAMITA (Rio Arriba; settlement; on NM 74, 6 mi N of Española and 3 mi NW of San Juan Pueblo, on the E bank of the Rio Chama; PO 1881–1944, name changed to San Juan Pueblo). The name of this small inhabited Tewa Indian settlement means "little Chama," but the origin is obscure. It certainly has little to do with the town of Chama far to the N. Possibly it refers to the ancient Tewa pueblo near Abiquiu—see *Chama (general)*— but possibly it refers to *San José de Chama,* the original name of Hernandez, just across the river to the SW. The site of Chamita has long been inhabited; it's closely associated with the pueblo of Yunque-yunque (see *San Gabriel*), which Capt. Francisco de Barrio-Nuevo encountered while exploring for Coronado; it, like modern Chamita, was located at the mouth of the Rio Chama. Though Chamita and San Juan Pueblo have shared the same PO name, the two settlements are distinct. The *Chamita Grant,* conferred in 1724, is surrounded by lands of San Juan Pueblo. Some maps label the SE part of Chamita *Capilla de San Pedro,* "Chapel of St. Peter."

CHAMIZAL (Socorro; settlement; on NM 408 N of Socorro, between San Acacia and Polvadera). Inhabited Hispanic settlement, named for the shrub; see *Chamisa (general).*

CHANCE CITY (Luna; settlement; 3 mi S of Gage, in the Victorio Mountains; PO as Fullerton 1882–83, as Chance City 1885–86, mail to Gage). Chance City began early in the 1880s when three prospectors found silver ore in the Victorio Mountains, resulting in the Chance and Jessie claim groups. These were purchased and developed by William Randolph Hearst and two associates. Soon a townsite, briefly known as *Victorio,* was laid out 600 yards from the mines. The camp, consisting of 16 frame buildings and two adobes, was called *Fullerton,* but in 1886 this name was changed to Chance City, for the mine. Between 1904 and 1937, $500,000 worth of gold, silver, and other ores flowed from the district. Nothing now remains.

CHAPARRAL (Doña Ana; settlement; 11 mi E of Anthony). Rural subdivision whose name means "overgrown with scrub oak."

CHAPELLE (San Miguel; settlement; on AT&SF RR, 17 mi S of Las Vegas, 2 mi E of Bernal; PO 1895–1939, mail to Serafina). This inhabited village was established as a switch on the AT&SF RR and has been said to have been named for a RR contractor. More likely the name recalls Archbishop of Santa Fe Placidus Louis Chapelle, who was head of the Roman Catholic Church in NM from 1894 to 1897.

CHAPERITO (San Miguel; settlement; 25 mi SE of Las Vegas; PO 1875 intermittently to 1957, mail to Las Vegas). Spanish, "little hat," probably a descriptive metaphor for a nearby landform. Once a major junction on routes along the Gallinas River, Chaperito now has but a few residences.

CHAPERITO KNOB, 10,163 ft. (San Miguel; in the Sangre de Cristo Mountains, 1.5 mi SW of Rosilla Peak, 3 mi SE of Terrero). Spanish, "little hat," likely describing the peak. The *Rito Chaperito* heads here and flows S into Cow Creek.

CHAPMAN (San Miguel; settlement; 0.25 mi S of the Gallinas River, S of Chaperito; PO as Hatchs Ranch 1878–79, as Chapman 1879–80). *Fort Hatch* was a military outpost here in the 1860s. Later, the locality took the name Hatchs Ranch, but the PO, after one year with that name, for another year took the name Chapman, for postmaster John L. Chapman. Hatch's Ranch has been said to have been a dispersal point for livestock stolen by Indians in Texas.

CHARCO (San Miguel; settlement; SE part of county; PO 1893–94, mail to Liberty). Ephemeral community whose Spanish name means "pool, puddle."

CHARETTE LAKE (Mora; E of Ocate and N of Ocate Creek, at the end of NM 569). Name origin unknown; locally pronounced Sha-REHT-ee.

CHARLOTTE (De Baca; settlement; 10 mi N of Taiban; PO 1907–23, mail to Taiban). Abandoned homesteader community; name origin unknown.

CHARILLOS (Torrance; settlement; E of Pinos Wells). George Adlai Feather reported this to be a community settled in the 1890s by sheep ranchers from Galisteo. It long has been abandoned, its name, whose meaning is unknow, all but forgotten.

CHASE CANYON (Colfax; heads NW of Cimarron and opens into Poñil Canyon N of the village). M.M. Chase settled in this canyon. *Chase Mountain* 7,895 ft., NW of Cimarron, also likely bears his name.

CHATFIELD PEAK 7,158 ft. (Otero; on SE slope of the Sacramento Mountains, 2 mi N of NM 508). About 1890 a rancher by this name settled in a canyon at the peak's base.

CHÁVES, CHÁVEZ (general). As Fray Angelico Chávez has explained, in old

Galician Spanish and in Portuguese, the word meant "keys" and was conferred upon two brothers who wrested the ancient town of Cháves from the Moors. Although the name in NM almost always is spelled Chávez, Cháves is the older form. According to Chávez, the ancestor of the NM families with this name was Don Pedro Durán de Cháves, like many *conquistadores* a native of Estremadura Province in Spain, and it's possible he was the person listed as Pedro Gomez Durán in the Oñate roster of 1600. One Don Fernando de Cháves returned with the reconquest of 1692 and settled in the Rio Abajo. Three members of the Chávez lines were NM governors between 1822 and 1834: Francisco Xavier Chávez, 1822–23; José Antonio Cháves, 1828–31; and Mariano Chávez, 1833–34. Col. José Francisco Cháves, son of Don Mariano, was a prominent figure in NM military and political life late in the 19th century, serving three terms as delegate to Congress beginning 1865; Chaves County (see entry) was named for him. The Cháves family, more than most Hispanic families, made their mark on the NM landscape; 69 places bear their name (GNIS).

CHAVES (Chaves; settlement; 30 mi N of Roswell; PO 1932–42, mail to Roswell). In 1929 Mrs. Mattie Griffith opened a store and PO on the Vaughn highway and named the locality for the county in which it was located. Later Mrs. Griffith lived in Roswell; her settlement has vanished.

CHAVES (McKinley; settlement; on AT&SF RR, E of Gallup; PO 1886–92, name changed to Mitchell). This began as a water stop on the RR, taking the name of the Cháves family who kept a store here. Later the PO was moved to Mitchell, which later became Thoreau. *North* and *South Chaves* still are RR sidings. See also *Thoreau*.

CHAVES (San Miguel; settlement; in E part of county, on the SW border of the Pablo Montoya Grant; PO 1901–06, mail to Trementina). This ephemeral com-munity took the name of its first post-master, Francisco S. Cháves.

CHAVES COUNTY (Chaves; SE NM; county seat, Roswell). When Capt. Joseph C. Lea, for whom Lea County was named, in 1889 successfuly persuaded the legislature to create a new county from Lincoln County lands, he insisted that it be named for his close friend and political ally, Col. José Francisco Cháves. (When Lea County was created, Cháves insisted that it be named for Captain Lea!) Cháves, a native of Bernalillo County, was a scion of one of NM's most prominent families. In 1865 he was elected delegate to Congress, where he served three terms, and he also was a speaker of the Lower House of the NM Territorial Legislature. Cháves was assassinated in 1904 at Pinos Wells; his murder was never solved. See *Chaves, Chavez (general)*.

SENATOR WILLIE M. CHAVEZ STATE PARK (Valencia; on NM 6, 2 mi E of Belen). This 107-acre park located in the Rio Grande *bosque* originally was known as *South Valley State Park*, then as *Belen Valley State Park*. It acquired its present name in 1983 as a memorial to NM Sen. William M. Chávez, who had died the year before at the age of 40. Chávez had represented Valencia County since 1974 and was largely responsible for the park's creation in 1976.

CHEECHILGEETHO (McKinley). See *Chi Chil Tah*.

CHEROKEE BILL CANYON (Lincoln, Otero; parallels US 70 S of Ruidoso, enters the Rio Ruidoso just W of Holly-wood). Cherokee Bill Kellam had settled in this canyon from Waco, TX, where he had lived with Indians, claimed to have had some Indian ancestry, and married an Indian woman. He has been described as "a hard-eyed, weather-beaten character, and a real blowhard"; he became involved in the feuds and turbulence of the Tularosa Valley of the late 19th century.

CHEROKEE VALLEY (Quay; in NW part of county). It's unknown why this extensive, vaguely defined area in eastern NM has the name of an Indian tribe originally from the southeastern US, later relocated to Oklahoma.

CHERRY VALLEY, CHERRYVALE (Mora; settlement; NE of Las Vegas, on the Mora River; PO 1910–36, mail to Las Vegas). Abandoned community; the "valley" part of the name likely refers to the community's location in the Mora River valley; the inspiration for the "cherry" is unknown.

CHERRYVILLE (Socorro; settlement; in SW part of county, at Ojo Caliente; PO 1881–86, mail to Monticello). This was the civilian part of the Indian agency at Ojo Caliente (see entry). Name origin unknown.

CHETTRO KETTLE (San Juan; archaeological site; in Chaco Culture National Historical Park, in Chaco Canyon). When Lt. James H. Simpson visited these ruins in 1849, he wrote in his journal: "Continuing down the [Chaco] cañon one and three-quarter miles further [from Hungo Pavi], we came to another extensive structure in ruins, the name of which, according to the guide [the New Mexican Carravahal] is Pueblo Chettro Kettle, or as he interprets it, the Rain Pueblo." Though Simpson's—or Carravahal's—naming has stuck, the linguistic origin of the name remains unexplained. The Navajos call the ruin by a name meaning "covered hole," referring to sealed concavities in the canyon wall behind the ruin, though it has been said the name refers to filled-in niches in the walls of the pueblo. The name is variously spelled—Chetro Ketl, Chettro Ketl, among others—but Chettro Kettle was accepted by the USBGN in 1931.

CHI CHIL TAH (McKinley; settlement; 21 mi SW of Gallup, 8 mi W of NM 602). Navajo, "oak canyon." A trading post, day school, and mission are located here. The locality sometimes is called Cheechilgeetho, Navajo "oak by two waters," but in 1975 the USBGN accepted Chi Chil Tah. Navajos also know the locality by a name meaning "little rabbit." The locality also has been known as Jones Ranch.

CHICAL (Valencia; settlement; within Isleta Indian Reservation, 1.5 mi E of NM 47, NE of Bosque Farms). Small subvillage of Isleta Pueblo, in the farmlands on the Rio Grande's E side. See Chico (general).

CHICAL CREEK (San Miguel; rises 9 mi SE of Bell Ranch, flows S into the Canadian River). See Chico (general).

CHICO (general). This widely applied name element has several meanings. In its formal Spanish usage, chico means "small, little, young" but Stanley Crocchiola said that to the New Mexicans of 200 years ago it also was a nickname for Francis, most often an affectionate term for St. Francis. But in the regional Spanish of NM, chico most commonly has referred to the widespread chicobush, (Sarcobatus vermiculatus), known in English as "black greasewood," and this usually is its meaning in place names. Chical means a thicket of chico bushes.

CHICO (Colfax; settlement; 12 mi N of Abbott and 22 mi E of Maxwell; PO 1877–95 as Chico Springs, 1895–1956 as Chico, mail to Maxwell). Spanish, likely referring to the chico bush, or greasewood; see Chico (general). Chico, also called Chico Springs, was the home of Robert Ingersoll, creator of the Star Route mail system. He also was an associate of US Sen. Stephen W. Dorsey, whose mansion is here; see Clayton, Dorsey. Chico also was the site of a health resort, the Chico Springs Sanatorium. Chico Creek rises nearby and flows SW into the Canadian River. The Chico Hills are between Chico and Abbott.

CHICOMA MOUNTAIN, 11,561 ft. (Rio Arriba; N of the Santa Clara Indian Reservation, in the NE Jemez Mountains, near the Sandoval County line). Also known as Santa Clara Peak, because of its proximity to Santa Clara Pueblo, Chicoma Mountain is the highest summit in the Jemez Mountains. (This is not be to confused with Clara Peak, a summit 8 mi to the E.) Chicoma Mountain has been regarded as the "center of all" not only by the Tewas but also by other tribes. On its summit are remains of a stone shrine, an eliptical enclosure described in 1911 as having seven exits, each pointing to a tribal region. The name approximates a Tewa word meaning "flint, obsidian," often transliterated *Tschicoma,* but the USBGN in 1964 established the Chicoma as the accepted form.

CHICORICA CANYON, CREEK, MESA (Colfax; heads at Lake Maloya 7 mi NE of Raton and flows S). According to T.M. Pearce's research, two possible explanations exist for this name cluster, in which the creek likely was named earliest. The first, suggested by Stanley Crocchiola, is that Chicorica is a corruption of the Spanish *achicoria,* referring to chicory, or wild endive. This is plausible and with numerous precedents. However, a man testified in litigation in 1883 that the canyon, creek, and mesa were named by the Comanches for the great numbers of birds in the pines here. Experts on the Comanche language have suggested that the name might have come from the Comanche *cocora,* referring to wild turkeys, abundant in the area, or roadrunners, also common.

The creek now often is called *Sugarite Creek,* locally pronounced sugar-REET. As Pearce wrote: "The Spanish developed the name [Chicorica] by folk-etymology into Chico Rico, 'rich little bit,' or 'rich little fellow,' which did not have much meaning but made quite as much sense as the Anglo transposition Sugarite." The name Chicorica sometimes is spelled *Chicarica* and *Chicorico,* but the USBGN in 1914 chose Chicorica as the accepted form. Chicorica Mesa now is commonly called *Barela Mesa* (see entry).

CHICOSA LAKE STATE PARK (Harding; off NM 120, 7 mi N of Roy). Located in the grassland plains of NE NM, this state park bears the name local people have for a plant native to the area. The small, shallow lake was a stop on the Loving-Goodnight cattle drives, and a herd of Texas longhorns is a feature of the park.

CHICOSO (Colfax; settlement; location unknown; PO 1876–77). Abandoned community, possibly associated with the community later known as *Chico* (see entry) and *Chico Springs.*

CHIHUAHUA TRAIL (S-central NM, along the Rio Grande). See *El Camino Real.*

CHILI (Rio Arriba; settlement; on US 84, at the junction of the Rio Chama and the Rio Ojo Caliente). This tiny Hispanic community on the W side of the Rio Chama has Spanish and Tewa names equally obscure. It has been said the Spanish name Chili comes from a station on the abandoned D&RG RR line between Antonito, CO, and Santa Fe, known locally as the "Chili Line." But the tracks were several miles from this village, and it's also possible the name refers to the chile pepper (*Capsicum* sp.), in NM usually spelled with an "e", though elsewhere in the US more commonly spelled "chili." The Tewa name for the locality has been translated "flint buttocks," applied for reasons unknown.

CHILILI (Bernalillo; settlement; on NM 337, 20 mi S of Tijeras, in the E foothills of the Manzano Mountains; PO 1882–1937). The Spanish-appearing name of this small, inhabited Hispanic settlement actually comes from a Pueblo Indian word, possibly Tiwa, meaning "very weak spring," or "sound of water barely trickling." It's one of the oldest recorded place names in NM. Chamuscado in 1581 found an inhabited Indian pueblo here, its ruins located near *Arroyo de Chilili,* which runs through the modern village. Oñate 17 years later also visited the site, recording its name as *Chiu Alle;* Fray Alonso de Benavides in 1630 described it as the first pueblo of the Piro Indian group—most other writers believe it was a Tiwa pueblo—and mentioned missionary activity begun by the Franciscans about 1613. But like the other pueblo missions in the Manzano Mountains, this one was subject to persistent Apache attacks, and between 1669 and 1676 it was abandoned. The present Hispanic settlement was established in 1841 after Santiago Padilla and six others, for themselves and 20 more heads of families, successfully petitioned Gov. Manuel Armijo for a land grant. *Old Chilili* is located 2 miles E of the main village.

CHIMAYO (Rio Arriba; settlement; on NM
76, 10 mi E of Española; PO
1894–present). This inhabited settlement takes its name from a Tewa Indian
pueblo once located here; its name,
Tsimayo, meant "good flaking stone,"
though it's unclear what mineral was
refered to: some have suggested flint, not
locally common; others have suggested
mica, found in the mountains to the E.
Spanish settlement here began soon after the reconquest of 1692. The *Plaza of
San Buenaventura* (now the *Plaza del
Cerro*) was built around 1740, and by
1752 the settlement sometimes was
referred to as *San Buenaventura de Chi-
mayó*. This name honors St. Bonaven-
ture, Cardinal Bishop, Doctor of the
Church, pioneer and reorganizer of the
Franciscan Order; he has been the patron of Cochiti Pueblo and Humanas
Pueblo as well. Weaving has always been
important at Chimayo, and around 1900
curio dealers in Santa Fe introduced
commercial looms and yarns to the local
weavers, furthering a tradition of high-
quality woven goods that continues to
this day.

More famous than the village of
Chimayo, however, is the shrine known
as *El Santuario de Nuestro Señor de
Esquipulas*, usually abbreviated to *El
Santuario*. Built in 1813 by Don
Bernardo Abeytas, the shrine is considered a masterpiece of colonial folk art
and architecture. Earth in its floor is
believed to have miraculous healing
powers, like those at the village of
Esquipulas in Guatemala, and pilgrimages to the site are an important part of
Holy Week in northern NM. Also reported to have healing powers is the
nearby chapel of *Santo Niño de Atocha*,
"Holy Child of Atocha." The locality
where these shrines were built originally
was called *El Potrero*, but it now is usually considered part of Chimayo.

CHIMAYOSOS PEAK, 12,841 ft. (Rio
Arriba–Mora; in the Sangre de Cristo
Mountains, E of North Truchas Peak).
This summit was labelled *Jicarilla Peak*
on an 1889 USGS map; the meaning of
the Spanish *jicarilla* is the same as the
peak's name in the Tewa Indian language—"little cup"; both names result
from the peak's outline resembling an
inverted cup. Today the mountain goes
by the name *Chimayosos Peak*, sometimes called *Cerro Chimayosos*, probably
because the *Rito de los Chimayosos* (see
entry) heads near the mountain's SW
slopes.

RITO DE LOS CHIMAYOSOS (Mora; heads
on the E side of Truchas Peak and flows
S to join the Rito del Padre). One of the
main sources of the Pecos River, this
stream's name means "creek of the
Chimayo people." The story is that
people from Chimayo came here first to
hunt and later to pasture their sheep in
the high mountain marshes and meadows.

CHIMNEY (general). Features with this
name usually are narrow, with steep
sides. GNIS lists 22 in NM, including 5
Chimney Canyons and 5 Chimney
Rocks.

CHINA SPRINGS (McKinley; E of US 666,
just N of Gamerco and 5 mi N of
Gallup). In the 19th century, many Chinese laborers lived near a well here,
which served several nearby communities. The Navajo name for the locality,
still inhabited, means "many arrows"
and is said to refer to a Navajo ambush
of a troop of Kit Carson's NM Volunteers in the summer of 1863.

CHINCHONTE ARROYO (Torrance; in
NW corner of county, 4 mi SE of
Chilili). From the Spanish *sinsonte*,
"mockingbird." Located on the
Chinchonte Ranch.

CHINO MESA (Santa Fe; on the S bank of
the Rio Grande, just S of White Rock).
Spanish, "Chinese mesa," origin unknown.

CHIPPEWAY PARK (Otero; in Cox Canyon,
4 mi SW of Cloudcroft). Inhabited residential development, name origin unknown.

CHIQUITA (Otero). See *Sacramento*.

CHISE (Sierra; settlement; 24 mi NW of
Truth or Consequences). Pronounced
CHEEZ and sometimes spelled *Chiz*,
this tiny settlement takes its name from
Cochise, the Chiricahua Apache leader.

Chise, or *Cheis,* has been said to have been his original name, taken from the Apache word for "wood," reportedly because the chief had a tough, springy frame. Bentura Trujillo, born near Montrose, CO, moved to NM before 1832 and came to settle on Cuchillo Negro Creek, W of Cuchillo. Cochise camped near the Trujillos' home and visited them often; Bentura, an active lay member of the Catholic Church, baptized one of Cochise's children and named his farm home for his friend. Raiding Apaches never bothered the Trujillos. Bentura died in 1913 at the age of 105; his descendants still live in the area and own property in Chise.

CHISUM (Chaves; settlement; SE of Roswell, just E of NM 2, 5 mi NW of Dexter; PO 1884–85, mail to Roswell). John Chisum, born in Tennessee, moved to Texas and soon after the Civil War began driving cattle to markets elsewhere. Though his first venture failed, his second, over a Pecos Valley route in NM pioneered by Oliver Loving and Charles Goodnight, succeeded. Realizing the potential of the Pecos Valley, he made it the base of his cattle empire, which stretched from Fort Sumner. This locality owes its name to Chisum ranching operations here; see *South Spring.*

CHIVATO (general). Spanish, "kid, young male goat," a reminder of the importance of goats in the early rural economy of NM.

CHLORIDE (Sierra; settlement; in the foothills of the Black Range, 2 mi SW of Winston; PO 1881–1956, mail to Winston). In 1879 the government freighthauler Harry Pye discovered here an ore that an assay indicated was a chloride of silver—Pye was killed by Apaches soon after—and during the winter of 1880–81 prospectors worked near the mouth of *Chloride Gulch.* John A. Miller of Lake Valley bought a tract of land here, had it surveyed, and had a townsite plat registered. Town lots were awarded by lottery, with a free lot offered to the first woman to settle in Chloride. By the mid-1880s Chloride had 500 residents, and with characteristic miners' optimism the town often was called *Chloride City.* But eventually mining waned, and miners drifted away, though the town and even some mining have survived. *Chloride Creek* heads in the Black Range and flows SE through the village of Chloride.

CHLORIDE FLAT (Grant; settlement; just W of Silver City). The prospector and miner John Bullard (see *Bullard Peak*) in the early 1870s named this mining district for the silver chloride ore mined here. A mining camp once was located here, and the name Chloride Flat still is used for this area.

CHUPADERA, CHUPADERO (general). Though this Spanish term can refer to a sucking insect, such as a tick, from the Spanish *chupar,* "to suck, drink," as a name element in NM *chupadera* or *chupadero* usually means "sinkhole."

CHUPADERA MESA (Socorro; in E part of county extending N of US 380 into Torrance County). This extensive landform was named for its numerous sinkholes; see *Chupadera, Chupadero (general).* A community named *Chupadera* once existed here.

CHUPADERO (Santa Fe; settlement; on NM 22, 3 mi NE of Tesuque and 12 mi NE of Santa Fe). Inhabited settlement likely named for a sinkhole in the area; see *Chupadera, Chupadero (general).* Located on the *Río Chupadero.*

CHURCH MOUNTAIN, 8,802 ft. (Lincoln; in N Sacramento Mountains, 3 mi W of Nogal). In 1882 a prospector named Church announced to companions that he would take his burro to the top of this mountain. Despite their scoffs, he succeeded; he carved his name on a board and stuck it in a monument he built. Soon afterward he returned to Texas. In 1884, living again in NM, he journeyed to Fort Worth, TX, where he bought a government survey map and was astounded to find that government surveyors had been to the top of the mountain, had found the board with his name, and had given his name to the summit.

CHURCH ROCK (McKinley; settlement; 8 mi E of Gallup, one mi N of I-40; PO 1952–present). An inhabited Navajo settlement, sheltered on the N by two red sandstone formations, each named for its shape: *Pyramid Rock* and *Church Rock,* also called *Navajo Church*. It's the latter formation for which the settlement was named. The community's Navajo name means "yellow houses in place."

CHURCHVILLE (Lincoln; settlement; location unknown; PO 1889–90). Ephemeral postal locality that took the name of its postmaster, Harry S. Church, but the PO lasted only six months and was never really in operation.

CHUSKA MOUNTAINS (San Juan, McKinley; range trending NW-SE in SW San Juan County, extending into McKinley County, W of US 666). *Chuska* is an approximation of a Navajo word meaning "white spruce." Escalante in his 1776 expedition referred to the mountains by this name, and it appeared on the 1779 map prepared by Bernardo Miera y Pacheco, a member of the expedition.

According to Richard Van Valkenburgh, the Chuska Mountains are regarded by Navajos as part of a larger grouping, the "Goods of Value Range," that includes the Chuska, Tunicha, Lukachukai, and Carrizo Mountains. Chuska Peak is the head of this mythic range, Narbona Pass the neck, the Tunichas and Lukachukais the body, and the Carrizos the lower extremities.

Chuska Peak, 8,795 ft. (McKinley; 6 mi NW of Tohatchi, at the S end of the Chuska Mountains). Highest summit of the Chuska Mountains, regarded as sacred by the Navajos, who in 1935 blocked erection of a fire tower on its summit.

The Navajo name also carries the meaning "dumping of ash on the side of the hill," a reference to Navajo mythology in which the Holy People built the mountains with layers of ash, and indeed the mountain's sides have a white, ashen appearance.

CIBOLA (general). Pronounced SEE-bo-lah. Like the mythic cities it once named, *cíbola* has been one of the most elusive terms in NM history. Almost everyone agrees it's derived from an In-

dian word for "buffalo," but it is unclear as to how the Spanish explorers first heard it and applied it to the fabled golden cities they sought so hopefully in NM.

In medieval Europe a popular legend told of the Seven Cities of Antilia, located across the Atlantic Ocean. When the Spanish sailed to the New World, it was natural that they try to find the legendary cities, particularly as some Aztec and Incan cities had indeed approached the legend in golden riches. The legend certainly came to their minds when vague reports reached Mexico City hinting of fabulously wealthy cities in the unexplored territory to the N, in what is now NM, and when the Spanish journeyed northward they somehow linked the legend with the word *cíbola,* thus creating the Seven Cities of Cibola.

Some scholars have suggested that *cíbola* comes from a Comanche word and that Nuñez Cabeza de Vaca and his three companions might have heard it from the Plains Indians as they made their long trek across SW Texas in 1529–36; instead of translating it as "buffalo plains" as the Indians meant, the four castaways interpreted it to refer to the wealthy empire—another Mexico, another Peru—that Spaniards wanted to believe lay in the interior of North America. Others have suggested that Fray Marcos de Niza heard it from the Pima tribes of northern Sonora or southern Arizona as he traveled northward in 1539 seeking the cities reported by Cabeza de Vaca; he certainly was using the term before he arrived at the Zuni villages that his guides said were Cibola, and he used the term later when he described the Zuni village he though was Cibola as a magnificent city—the smallest of seven.

The debunking of Fray Marcos's report by Coronado's expedition of 1540–41 did not dissolve the myth; Cibola simply retreated farther into the interior. When Domingo de Castillo's map of the W coast of Mexico appeared in 1541, the only place he bothered to label in the interior of the continent was *La Ciudada de Cíbora;* it was the first place in NM to appear on a map. Similarly, on an untitled 1578 map of North America by Joan Martínes, *Civola* is the map's most conspicuous feature; Martínes sketched the individual cities, complete with towers, gates, battlements, and heraldic banners; no other feature in the interior appears. A 1597 map prepared by Cornelius van Wytfliet shows seven cities surrounding a lake; the Zunis in 1582 had told Antonio de Espejo the lake was ringed with gold.

Eventually, however, successive disappointing expeditions forced the Spanish to accept that Cibola was a place name without a place, and the word began to revert to its original meaning. Fray Alonso de Posada, writing around 1660 about the Pecos River, said, "The latter flows into the interior of the Plains of Cibola.... Due to the river's attractions there are many wild cows called Cibola." *Ciboleros* was a term used later in the colonial period for hardy New Mexicans who ventured onto the plains to hunt buffalo. See *Zuni*.

Cibola Creek (De Baca; heads at *Cibola Spring*, 19 mi SE of Fort Sumner and flows NW into the Pecos).

Cibolo Draw (Rio Arriba; in SW part of county, runs N into Largo Canyon).

CIBOLA COUNTY (western NM; county seat, Grants). Created in 1981 from what formerly had been western Valencia County. It includes the southern portion of the Zuni Indian Reservation.

CIBOLA NATIONAL FOREST (W-central NM). Composed of the Sandia, Mountainair, Mount Taylor, and Magdalena Ranger Districts and including the Sandia, Manzano, Datil, Zuni, Mount Taylor, Gallina, San Mateo, and Magdalena mountains. The Manzano NF was renamed the Cibola NF in 1931.

CICUYE (San Miguel). See *Pecos Pueblo*.

EL CIELO MOUNTAIN, 10,000 ft. (San Miguel; in the Las Vegas Range, W of El Porvenir Canyon, 3 mi NW of the village of El Porvenir). The history and motives behind this poetic Spanish name meaning "the sky, heavens" are unknown.

CIENAGA, CIENEGA (general). Spanish, "marsh, marshy place." Because any marsh would be a good source of scarce water for a settlement in arid NM, numerous communities have this name. Fray Angélico Chávez says that Spanish visitors to NM in 1798 chided the local people for saying *ciénega*, as *ciénaga* is widely regarded as the correct form, "not knowing that with the second *e* it was a good Estremeño word." And many early Spanish explorers and settlers had come indeed from Estremadura in Spain. *Cieneguilla* and *cieneguita* are diminutive forms. English-speakers often corrupt the word in spelling and pronunciation to *sienaga, sinigie, senigie,* and even *seneca*. GNIS lists approximately 30 occurences of *ciénaga* and its variants in the state.

CIENAGA DEL BURRO CREEK (Union). See *Seneca Creek*.

CIENAGA GREGORIO (Rio Arriba). See *Gregorio Lake*.

CIENEGA (Catron; settlement; location unknown; PO 1894–02, mail to Salt Lake). Little is known about this settlement.

CIENEGA (Otero; settlement; in SE part of county, on NM 506, S of Crow Flats and 3.5 mi N of the Texas border; PO 1927–42, mail to Salt Flat, TX). This diffuse rural community has had a school, a PO, and a polling station; people continue to live here.

CIENEGUILLA (Santa Fe; settlement; 9 mi SW of Santa Fe and 3 mi W of I-25). Tiny community settled around 1698 and likely named for nearby *Cieneguilla Creek*. The site previously had been occupied by the Indian pueblo of *Tziguma,* abandoned during the Pueblo Revolt of 1680; Vargas attempted unsuccessfully to restore it in 1695. The *Cieneguilla Land Grant* was centered here; see *La Cienega (Santa Fe)*.

CIENEGUILLA (Taos). See *Pilar*.

CIENEGUILLA DEL BURRO MOUNTAIN (Union). See *Mount Dora*.

CIENEGUILLA MOUNTAIN, 10,613 ft. (Colfax; in the Cimarron Range, S of Agua Fria Creek and E of Angel Fire). Probably named for its association with *Cieneguilla Creek* to the W.

CIMARRON (general). In American Spanish *cimarrón* means "wild, unmanageable," a good meaning for a word whose origins have been conspicuously intractable. As a NM place name, Cimarron was applied first either to the mountains of that name in NE NM or to the river originating in them; the name was then transferred later to other features.

The most widely accepted explanation for the name Cimarron is that it refers to the Rocky Mountain bighorn sheep, once abundant in NM, called in NM Spanish *carnero cimarrón*. Josiah Gregg, in *Commerce of the Prairies* (1844), corroborates this as the local meaning of the term. Wild horses and cattle later also began to be called *cimarrónes*.

Another plausible explanation, espoused by Fray Angélico Chávez, is that the name comes from the wild red-plum that grew profusely along the river and was called *ciruela cimarróna* by Hispanic people. Similarly, the wild rose is called *rosa cimarróna*. Also worth mentioning is that in NM *cimarrón* frequently referred to fugitive Indians. And finally, in Colfax County, they tell the patently apocryphal story of a cowboy cook who, checking his bean pot and finding the beans still hard, exclaimed, "Simmer on!"

CIMARRON (Colfax; settlement; on the Cimarron River, at the junction of US 64 and NM 58 and 21; PO 1861–present). Named for the river, the community of Cimarron began in 1841 with the filing of the Beaubien-Miranda Land Grant, later known as the Maxwell Grant, for which it became headquarters. This designation, together with Cimarron being the principal stop on the Taos branch of the Santa Fe Trail, made the town a natural gathering place for travelers, ranchers, miners, traders, and outlaws; from 1872 to 1882 Cimarron, "cowboy capital of northern NM," was the seat of Colfax County. Cimarron declined in influence when Raton became a RR center in the 1880s, but tourism and resource-based industries have kept the town alive.

CIMMARON CANYON STATE PARK (Colfax; in Cimarron Canyon on US 64, between Eagle Nest and Ute Park). This park stretches 8 miles along the Cimarron River in *Cimarron Canyon* and is surrounded by the 33,116-acre Colin Neblett Wildlife Area (see entry). The *Palisades of the Cimarron* are scenic cliffs within the canyon.

CIMARRON PASS (Union). See *Emery Gap*.

CIMARRON RANGE (Colfax; N-S range forming the eastern boundary of the Moreno Valley, extending nearly to Colorado). Named for the river that heads in the range. The highest summit is *Baldy Mountain*, 12,441 ft. (see entry).

CIMARRON RIVER (Colfax; heads in the Cimarron Range W of Ute Park and flows E through Cimarron Canyon and then SE to join the Canadian River E of Springer). This is not to be confused with the larger Cimarron River of Oklahoma, which actually heads in NM, where it is known as the Dry Cimarron River (see entry). A 1719 reference referred to the river as *La Flecha*, "the arrow," possibly a reference to Palo Flechado Pass (see entry). See *Cimarron (general)*.

CIMARRONCITO (Colfax; settlement; 10 mi SW of Cimarron, in the Cimarron Range). A short-lived mining camp.

CIMARRONCITO PEAK, 10,468 ft. (Colfax; in the Cimarron Range, on Philmont Scout Ranch, NE of Comanche Peak). Likely named nearby *Cimarroncito Creek*.

CIMILORIO (Colfax). See *Vermejo Park*.

CINDER (Bernalillo). See *Vulcan*.

CINIZA (McKinley; settlement; 23 mi E of Gallup, 1 mi N of I-40). From the Spanish *ceniza*, "ash." Currently the site of the Ciniza–El Paso oil refinery, which upon moving here from Prewitt took the existing name of the site, Ciniza.

LA CINTA (San Miguel; settlement; in SE part of county, on the Pablo Montoya Grant; PO 1887–88, mail to Bell Ranch). Spanish, "ribbon, band, strip." This abandoned locality likely was named for *La Cinta Creek*, which heads 16 mi N of Bell Mountain and flows S past the Bell Ranch to join the Canadian River E of Conchas Reservoir.

CIRCLE S MESA (Quay; 12 mi S of Tucumcari and 6 mi W of NM 209). This recalls the Circle S Ranch, long since gone and one of the famous pioneer ranch brands of NM.

CIRCLE SEVEN CREEK (Sierra; heads on E side of Diamond Peak and flows E toward Hermosa). Likely named for a ranch brand.

CIRUELA, CIRUELO (general). Spanish, "plum, plum tree."

Ciruela Creek (Mora; 3 mi SW of Wagon Mound).

Ciruela Mesa (Guadalupe; in extreme NW corner of county).

CIRUELA (Mora; settlement; in the Turkey Mountains NE for Fort Union). A tiny Hispanic community, long abandoned, whose population temporarily swelled with workers cutting ties for the AT&SF RR. The first Spanish-speaking Methodist minister in NM, Benito García, ordained around 1873, came from here.

LOS CISNEROS (Mora). See *Los Sisneros.*

CITY OF ROCKS STATE PARK (Grant; SE of Silver City, 2 mi N of NM 61). As John V. Young put it, "The name City of Rocks is descriptive, so far as it goes, but it does not begin to do justice to the extraordinary charm of this mile-square, mile-high desert hideaway." Stonehenge also would have been a good name, so strong is the impression one has of being transported to an earlier time. This enchanted "city" of rhyolite tuff monoliths, surrounded by spacious vistas, had its origin 33 million years ago; the area became a state park in 1952.

CLAIRMONT (Catron; settlement; 19 mi NW of Glenwood, 5 mi N of Mogollon; PO 1881–83, mail to Alma). Also called *Clermont,* this mining camp was born on Copper Creek around 1878, soon after James C. Cooney discovered silver ore on nearby Mineral Creek. The camp was a cluster of tents and rough log-and-board cabins; it functioned primarily as a supply camp for prospectors and briefly was the population center of the Mogollon Mountains. But when a road was built to Mogollon nearby, Clairmont faded, and today only ruins remain. The origin of its name has been lost.

CLANCY (Guadalupe; settlement; in S part of county, exact location unknown; PO 1908–09, mail to Salado). Little is known about this ephemeral community. It possibly was named for Capt. John G. Clancy, a native of Vermont and a retired sea captain who came to NM in 1879 and developed large ranch holdings on Alamogordo Creek near Fort Sumner. He died in 1916.

CLANTON DRAW (Hidalgo; in extreme SW corner of county, in the Guadalupe Mountains, SW of Cloverdale). Said to have been frequented by the Clanton brothers, of Tombstone, AZ, infamy.

CLAPHAM (Union; settlement; 22 mi SW of Clayton on NM 562, on Major Longs Creek; PO 1888–1954, mail to Clayton). In 1888, Tom Clapham and Jim Davis filed adjoining homestead claims, and they built a long, two-room house arranged so Clapham's room was on his claim, Davis's on his. When a PO was established in this building, it took Clapham's name. A few people still reside in the area, and the name is still used.

CLARK AND BROWN CANYON (Doña Ana; 3 mi N of Organ). Clark and Brown are believed to have been two mining partners in the 1880s.

CLARKS LAKE (Eddy; 6 mi W of Artesia). Called Clarks Lake for being on the former Clark Ranch, though it's often called *Torres Lake* as well, for reasons unknown.

CLARKVILLE (McKinley; settlement; 5 mi NW of Gallup; PO 1898–1908, mail to Gallup). Clarkville, once an important lignite coal mining camp, was operated by the Clark Coal Co. and named for the property's owner, coal magnate W.A. Clark, who also was a US Senator. In 1905 Clarkville had 400 people and was said to be a pretty little town, where liquor sales were forbidden, but by 1907 it had only 200 residents, and soon afterward it was abandoned.

CLAUD (Curry; settlement; 11 mi N of Clovis on NM 209; PO 1909–20, mail to Clovis). Like many High Plains homesteaders, Claud V. Kelly came to eastern NM around 1908 from Oklahoma. While proving up his claim he opened a mercantile store, and the store became the center for the area's early social as well as commercial life; it became known as the *Claud Store,* and soon the community acquired Claud's name as well. Kelly has been credited with growing the first wheat in Curry County. Though the store and the village have vanished, the name survives, and people in the area still identify themselves as residents of Claud.

CLAUDELL (Roosevelt; settlement; 14 mi NW of Elida; PO 1908–35, mail to Elida). This abandoned community's name was created when its first postmaster, Claude D. Wells, melded his first and last names. The name Claudell is still recognized in the area.

CLAUNCH (Socorro; settlement; in NE part of county, on NM 55; PO 1935–present). This tiny settlement takes its name from L.H. Claunch and his Claunch Cattle Co., whose headquarters were nearby. The community of Claunch in the 1910s and 1920s underwent a pinto bean boom, but it is almost a ghost town now.

CLAYTON (Union; settlement, county seat; 8 mi W of the Texas line, on US 56, 64, and 87; PO as Perico 1886–88, as Clayton 1888–present). Clayton began as a dream of several influential and ambitious men. Stephen W. Dorsey was a former US senator (1873–79) from Arkansas who with his lawyer, Bob Ingersoll, started the Triangle Dot Ranch in Colfax and Union Counties. In the late 1880s, Dorsey's range manager, John C. Hill, suggested to Dorsey that they form a company, secure land on a proposed RR right-of-way, and locate a townsite. Dorsey liked the idea, and they chose a site near *Apache Spring,* an important water source. At the time, the only habitation close to the townsite was T.E. Owens's Pitchfork Ranch, 3 mi W of Perico Creek; Homer Byler, Owens's storekeeper, had established a PO called *Perico* there in 1886. By 1887, the settlement that would become Clayton was

primarily a tent town, with a few stores and three saloons; it had neither name nor PO. But early in 1888 Byler moved the Perico PO here, and on March 23, 1888, three days after the first C&S train arrived on newly laid rails, the PO was renamed Clayton to honor Senator Dorsey's son, Clayton Dorsey, who in turn had been named for Senator Clayton of Arkansas. Young Clayton Dorsey eventually became a successful attorney in Denver.

CLAYTON LAKE STATE PARK (Union; on NM 370, 12 mi NW of Clayton). Clayton Lake was created in 1955 when the NM Dept. of Game and Fish dammed Cieneguilla Creek; they named it for the nearby town of Clayton. The state park, established in 1967, offers camping and fishing.

MOUNT CLAYTON (Union; 8 mi W of Mount Dora and 5 mi S of Grenville). Travellers on the Santa Fe Trail passing by here in the middle 1800s called this *Round Mound,* but in 1887 it was renamed Mount Clayton at the request of US Sen. Stephen Dorsey to honor his son, Clayton. See *Clayton.*

CLEAR CREEK (Catron; settlement). See *Glenwood.*

CLEAR CREEK (Colfax; heads on Clear Creek Mountain and flows N to the Cimarron River in Cimarron Canyon). Named for the clarity of its snow-fed waters.

CLEAR CREEK MOUNTAIN (Colfax). See *Waite Phillips Mountain.*

CLEVELAND (Mora; settlement; 3 mi NW of Mora, on NM 518; PO 1892–present). In 1816, encouraged by Gov. Alberto Maynez's policy of promoting new settlements, a group of families moved into the Mora Valley and named their new community *San Antonio lo de Mora,* also sometimes called *El Valle de San Antonio.* The settlement was abandoned briefly in 1833 following Pawnee raids, but it was resettled in 1835 with the authorization of the Mora Land Grant. Like many Hispanic communities here, such as Chacon, Holman, and Ledoux (see entries), its original Hispanic name was changed when it applied for a PO.

The name Cleveland was chosen in 1892 to honor President Grover Cleveland, who served two terms, 1885–89 and 1893–97. The name of the creek that supplies water to Cleveland also has undergone change; see *Río la Casa.*

CLIFF (Grant; settlement; 28 mi NW of Silver City on US 180, at the confluence of the Gila River and Duck Creek, on the river's west side; PO 1894–present). This important area in the Gila country first was occupied by Fort West (see entry), 2 miles SE of the present community. Around 1884 the Cliff family settled here, and the inhabited community bears their name. Actually, Cliff is closely linked with the village of Gila, on the river's east side, and the local residents often refer to the area as *Gila–Cliff* or *Cliff–Gila.*

CLIFFORD (Quay; settlement; 7 mi N of Lockney, at the site of the Clifford Ranch; PO 1913–19, mail to Nara Visa). Abandoned rural PO, named for the ranch where it was located.

CLIFTON (Colfax; settlement; 6 mi S of Raton on the Canadian River; PO 1869–79). *Clifton House* was built in 1867 by Tom Stockton, a rancher, as headquarters for cattle roundups, and soon afterward it acquired a PO, blacksmith shop, and stables, as well as becoming a stop on the Barlow-Sanderson stage line. But with the arrival of the AT&SF RR in 1879, the stage was discontinued, and today nothing remains of Clifton but its cemetery.

CLINES CORNERS (Torrance; trading point; at the junction of US 285 and I-40, E of Albuquerque; PO 1964–present). About 1934, Ray Cline set up a service station on what was then US 66. That highway has been replaced by the larger I-40, and the service center, still with Cline's name, also has expanded.

CLOSSON (Cibola; settlement; in the Zuni Mountains, 30 mi SE of Gallup, on FR 50, just E of the Continental Divide; PO 1916–40, mail to McGaffey). Abandoned locality, named for Ed Closson, who owned a general store and trading post

here.

CLOUDCROFT (Otero; settlement; on US 82 16 mi E of Alamogordo, at the crest of the Sacramento Mountains; PO 1900–present). The village of Cloudcroft had its beginnings in the plans of RR developers Charles B. Eddy and his brother, John A. Eddy, to put in a branch line to bring timber from the forested Sacramento Mountains to their EP&NE RR in the Tularosa Valley below. In 1899 the Alamogordo and Sacramento RR— dubbed the "Cloud-climbing RR" for its steep ascent—finally reached the mountain crest, where a 2,700-acre townsite had previously been set aside. The site was at 8,640 feet, and a survey crew selected the name Cloudcroft because of low-lying clouds and the small clearing there, *croft* being an Old English term for "clearing". Soon after its founding, the settlement's cool summers made it a popular retreat for Alamogordo and El Paso residents, and the benign climate has continued to support the community's prosperity long after the Cloud-climbing RR and its timber demands have vanished.

CLOVERDALE (Hidalgo; settlement; in SW part of county, on NM 338; PO 1912–43, mail to Animas). Sometime in the 1880s the *Cloverdale Ranch* was established, about 1 mi from the present locality. In 1889 the Victorio Land and Cattle Co. acquired the land, other ranches were established, and the diffuse community took the name Cloverdale. In the early 20th century, Cloverdale was the site of a popular annual cowboy camp meeting to which cattlemen and their families would travel long distances to attend. Today the long-abandoned Cloverdale store is all that remains, though the name is still widely used. *Cloverdale Creek* heads in the Guadalupe Mountains to the W and flows E through here; *Cloverdale Peak,* 6,469 ft., is the highest summit of the Guadalupe Mountains.

CLOVIS (Curry; settlement, county seat; at the junction of US 60-84, US 70, and NM 209; PO as Riley 1906–07, as Clovis

1907–present). This locality has been known by two names—*Riley Switch* and Clovis—and the origins of both are controversial. At least three explanations exist for Riley Switch. The first says that in 1903, Leo and Lloyd Riley settled SW of present Cannon Air Force Base and worked on the AT&SF RR; later their mother and brothers also settled in the area. When the RR was completed in 1906, William Palmer established a small store and PO at a siding and switch; he named the PO *Riley* for the family, and the locality became known as *Riley Switch*. The second explanation says the name came from the Riley family that established several ranches in the sandhill country S of Clovis around 1887. And the third says that one Jim Riley of Melrose stopped by Palmer's store in 1906 and, finding him low on groceries, gave him some supplies; in gratitude, Palmer asked RR officials to name the switch for Riley.

The name Clovis also is controversial. Most accounts say the AT&SF RR changed the name from Riley to Clovis after a townsite was established, but as early as March 1906, the AT&SF RR had listed Clovis as the name of its station between Texico and Blacktower—seven months before a townsite was considered. When a town was in fact established, it took that name, replacing Riley. As for the name Clovis, its application here remains a mystery. The naming has been attributed to the wife or daughter of Edward Payson Ripley, president of the AT&SF RR at the time; his family had been touring France and had become interested in Clovis, first Christian king of France, who died in A.D. 511. But the name also has been attributed to a daughter of James Dunn, the RR's chief engineer. Neither origin has been documented.

CLYDE (Socorro). See *Valverde*.

COAL (general). Though a less romantic mineral than gold or silver, coal's economic importance in NM has been far greater and has resulted many place names; GNIS lists 30. The Spanish form is *carbón*, but this does not appear in any NM names.

COAL CANYON (Colfax; heads in Colorado and runs S and E to join the Canadian River at Raton). This, and another *Coal Canyon* about 10 mi to the SW, were named for extensive coal deposits in the area.

COALORA (Lincoln; settlement; 1 mi NW of Capitan; PO 1903–05, mail to Capitan). In 1900 the EP&NE RR began mining coal in the Salado Flat area, and the mining camp of Coalora was born. By 1902 2,000 people lived here, but Coalora was short-lived, and when rail lines were extended to the coal fields at Dawson, Coalora died; the camp has vanished completely.

COANE STAGE STATION (Socorro). See *Ozanne*.

COBERO (Sandoval; trading point; on the W side of the Rio Grande, between San Felipe and Santo Domingo pueblos). This was a stopping point visited by Lt. James W. Abert around 1846. The meaning of the name is unknown.

COBRE (Grant). See *Copper (general)*.

COCA (San Miguel; settlement; in NE part of county, exact location unknown; PO 1899, mail to Sanchez). Ephemeral postal locality, likely bearing a family name.

COCHITI PUEBLO (Sandoval; midway between Albuquerque and Santa Fe, on the W bank of the Rio Grande, on NM 22; PO 1907–08, mail to Thornton). Cochiti is the northernmost of the Keresan-speaking pueblos; its members explain its name thus: "*Kotyete*, which means 'stone kiva,' is our native name. From our oral history we know that our ancestors inhabited Cañon de los Frijoles a few centuries before the Spanish visited us at our present location. When the first Spaniards entered Kotyete in 1581, there were 230 two- and three-story houses; they called our village *Medina de la Torre*." Oñate in 1598 was the first Spaniard to call the pueblo Cochiti, based upon his hearing of the Keresan name.

Cochiti Canyon (Sandoval; 3 mi E of Cochiti Pueblo). The Rio Chiquito flows through the canyon.

Cochiti Springs (Sandoval; on the N bank of the Santa Fe River, just S and W of Cochiti Dam.

COCHITI LAKE (Sandoval; on the Rio Grande, 3 mi N of Cochiti Pueblo). Cochiti Lake was created beginning in 1975 by the US Army Corps of Engineers for flood control, water storage, and recreation. Upon its completion it was the 11th largest earth-filled dam in the world, 5.4 miles long and 251 feet high. The reservoir and dam were named for the pueblo whose lands they occupy.

COCHITI LAKE (Sandoval; settlement; on W side of Cochiti Lake, on NM 22, 3 mi N of Cochiti Pueblo). Built on land leased for 99 years from Cochiti Pueblo, the retirement and vacation community of Cochiti Lake was named for the lake on which it's located. In its early years the community was called *Cochiti Lake City.*

COCKLEBUR (general). The common cocklebur (*Xanthium pennsylvanicum*), found throughout North America, was well-known to early New Mexicans. It grows profusely near bodies of water. The name occurs 5 times in NM (GNIS).

COLD SPRINGS (Cibola; settlement; in the Zuni Mountains; PO 1911–12, mail to Sawyer). Ephemeral logging settlement, named for nearby springs.

COLE (Lincoln; settlement; exact location unknown; PO 1890–92). Ephemeral rural PO that took the name of its only postmistress, Martha A. Cole.

COLE SPRINGS (Bernalillo; on the SE side of the Sandia Mountains). Chauncey Cole and his family moved to NM around 1920 and bought land in this area. He was fond of this spring, and when the USFS established a picnic area here they named it for him.

COLEMAN (Colfax; settlement; near Elkins, W of Raton). Abandoned community established in 1885, bearing the name of a family living near Elkins in the 1870s.

COLFAX (Colfax; settlement; on US 64, 5 mi S of Dawson, just W of the Vermejo River; PO 1908–21, mail to Dawson). Now a ghost town, Colfax had a lot going for it: located in rich farming country, on the Vermejo River, situated on two RRs (the AT&SF and the PD Dawson), near mountains abounding in game, close to other towns. And it was with those assets that the New Mexico Sales Co. promoted the townsite they had laid out in 1908. The town was to be called *Colfax City,* after the county, and while it never fulfilled its developers' expectations, it did survive for 25 years. But, always at the mercy of outside interests and capital and unable to compete with its neighbor, Dawson, Colfax eventually faded, and now only picturesque ruins remain.

COLFAX COUNTY (in NE NM, adjacent to the Colorado line; county seat, Raton). Schuyler Colfax is remembered as US Vice President from 1869 to 1873, but the former Congressman from Indiana was only vice-president-elect when New Mexicans, mostly from Elizabethtown, clamored for a new county to be named for him. The new county was created on January 25, 1869, out of what had been Taos County; at the time it included most of the Maxwell Land Grant and stretched to the Texas-Oklahoma line. Vice President Colfax had a bright political future, but it blinked out when he was implicated in the Credit Mobilier scandal of the times.

COLIN NEBLETT WILDLIFE AREA (Colfax; surrounds Cimarron Canyon and Cimarron Canyon State Park, E of Eagle Nest). This bears the name of a prominent Santa Fe federal judge who also was an ardent sportsman and conservationist. Colin Neblett helped form the first State Game Commission and served as a member in 1936. Wildlife in the state-designated area includes elk, deer, bears, lions, and wild turkeys.

COLLE CANYON (Sandoval; in the SE Jemez Mountains, runs SE into Peralta Canyon). Sometimes appearing as *Colla Canyon* or *Cañon del Coye,* this name comes from a Tewa word meaning "roof-door canyon," and near the canyon's junction with Peralta Canyon is a box-like constriction, almost like a room, that could be construed as being a "roof-door."

COLLINS PARK (Catron; settlement; near the Continental Divide, E of Reserve, between Eagle Mountain and O Bar O Mountain; PO 1951–55, mail to Horse Springs). As the story is told in the area, a man named Graham at the end of the Civil War turned outlaw and changed his name to Collins, eventually becoming known as "Shotgun Collins." To avoid the law and to start a new life, he moved to NM and settled in this remote location. His children later changed their name back to Graham; their descendants still live in the area.

COLLINSVILLE (Quay; settlement; in W part of the county, S of Ima; PO 1908–12, mail to Ima). Abandoned homesteader community that took the name of its first postmaster, Absalom G. Collins.

COLMOR (Colfax; settlement; on AT&SF RR, 11 mi SW of Springer; PO 1887–1963, mail to Springer). The tiny settlement of Colmor, now abandoned and in ruins, was settled in 1887, eight years after the RR came through. Its name was manufactured from the first three letters of the names of Colfax and Mora counties, whose boundary the settlement straddles.

COLONIAS (Guadalupe; settlement; on W side of Pecos River, on NM 379, 16 mi NW of Santa Rosa; PO 1900–51, mail to Santa Rosa). This name is open to several interpretations: "colonies, plantations, ranches, neighborhoods, communities." The settlement, established in the 1830s, originally was called *Las Colonias* and is one of the oldest settlements on NM's eastern plains; early villagers were farmers but hunted buffalo in the fall. A few families still live here.

COLONIAS, UPPER AND LOWER (San Miguel; settlements; about 3 mi apart, on Cow Creek, E of Pecos; PO 1895). Of the two communities, both inhabited, Lower Colonias is the larger. The name most

likely comes from the Spanish word meaning "ranches, neighborhoods, communities." See also *Colonias (Guadalupe)*.

COLORADO (Doña Ana). See *Rodey*.

COLT (general). See *Horse (general)*.

COLUMBINE (Taos; settlement; on NM 38, 5 mi E of Questa). Tiny settlement, named for its location on *Columbine Creek*, at its junction with the Red River. The banks of this clear mountain stream are excellent environment for the blue columbine (*Aquilegia coerulea*).

COLUMBUS (Luna; settlement; 32 mi S of Deming on NM 11, 3 mi N of the Mexican border; PO 1891–93, 1896–present). Columbus began about 1890 as a border station across from Palomas, Chihuahua, but the exact origin of its name is obscure. It has been said it was named by early settlers for Columbus, OH, but Columbus also was the name of a mining district here, and a mining claim named Columbus was in the Tres Hermanas Mountains just to the N. Furthermore, Columbus is a very common US place name, as it honors Christopher Columbus, whose landfall in 1492 launched European settlement of North America. And finally, it has been said the name Columbus was chosen here after postal officials rejected the proposed name *Columbia*, once a popular byname for America, because it was too common in the US, though the name Columbus was in use long before the community applied for a PO. When a RR station was established here in 1903, a new settlement coalesced around it, and the southern site near the border faded; in 1928 an abortive attempt was made to revive the old settlement under the name *Border City*; the plan failed, though maps of that period sometimes show a *South Columbus* there. Columbus entered US history on March 9, 1916, when Pancho Villa raided the town. Two museums and Pancho Villa State Park (see entry) recall the incident.

COMANCHE (general). The Comanches, now living in Oklahoma, were Plains Indians whose hunting, trading, and raiding territory included northern and eastern NM. They did not call themselves Comanches, a corruption of a Ute Indian word meaning "enemies"; rather they called themselves *Nermernuh,* "the People," and they were grouped into several autonomous bands. They also frequently were allied with the Kiowas. Spanish-speaking and later English-speaking traders who carried on an often illegal but widespread trade with the Comanches were called *comancheros.* As with the Apaches, the Comanches' procliivity toward raiding gave them a psychological presence in NM out of proportion to their actual numbers; at least 20 places in NM have *Comanche* in their names (GNIS).

COMANCHE CANYON, CAÑADA DE LOS COMANCHES (Rio Arriba, Taos; marks the county line, 15 mi S of Tres Piedras). Numerous battles between Hispanics and Indians, presumably Comanches, were fought here during the 18th century.

COMANCHE CANYON (Torrance; on W side of the Manzano Mountains, N of Trigo Canyon and JFK Campground). This canyon leads E to *Comanche Pass* and then farther E to *Comanche Ridge,* all along a route used by the Comanches to raid settlements along the Rio Grande. The ridge originally was known as *La Ladera del Bosquecito,* "the slope of the little forest," in association with *Bosquecito Spring,* but the name was changed in 1987 at the instigation of Duncan Simmons, local resident and property owner who felt a more colorful name would encourage tourism in the area. Local citizens supported the change, which was approved by the USBGN. As Simmons pointed out, the ridge, along with Comanche Pass and Comanche Canyon to the W, would have been used by Comanches traveling to the Rio Grande Valley. Simmons also was the proponent of the name Comanche Pass, because it connects Comanche Canyon to the W and Comanche Ridge to the E.

COMANCHE CREEK (Colfax; heads in the Valle Vidal E of Van Diest Peak and flows N to join Costilla Creek). Once frequented by Comanches. A bold rock promontory here is called *Comanche Point.*

COMANCHE PASS, 10,045 ft. (Colfax; in Cimarron Range, on Philmont Scout Ranch, just W of Bear Mountain). Would have been familiar to Comanches traveling W, perhaps to trade fairs in Taos.

COMANCHE PEAK, 11,326 ft. (Colfax; in Cimarron Range, in W part of Philmont Scout Ranch, just E of Waite Phillips Mountain). See *Comanche (general).*

COMANCHE SPRING (Chaves; 4 mi NE of Bottomless Lakes State Park). This was a rendezvous where Comanches and Mescalero Apaches met to trade horses. The spring feeds *Comanche Draw,* which runs SW.

COMANCHE TRAIL (Curry, Quay; ran N-S between Clovis and San Jon). An ancient trail followed by Comanches on hunting parties, later used by Americans despite Indian attacks.

COMANCHEROS CREEK (San Miguel; in SE part of county, on Pablo Montoya Land Grant). See *Comanche (general).*

CONANT (Guadalupe). See *Newkirk.*

CONCEPCION (San Miguel; settlement; 7 mi SE of Las Vegas). This was one of several tiny farm villages along the Gallinas River downstream from Las Vegas. The name may refer directly to the Spanish *Concepción Inmaculada,* "Immaculate Conception," or less likely, it may be from a woman's given name, Concepción.

The Immaculate Conception of Jesus has engendered the names, in various forms, of numerous Catholic churches in NM. For example, the church built in 1630 at Quarai Pueblo was named *La Purísima Concepción.*

CONCHAS (general). Spanish, "shells." From prehistoric times to the present, NM's Native American peoples have used marine shells as ornaments. The *conchas* made by Navajo silversmiths are, in fact, styled to resemble shells.

The word *conchas,* however, often has been confused with *Conchos,* the term that early Spanish chronicles used to label one of several Indian tribes widely dispersed in what is now southern NM and northern Mexico. For example, a 1693 account of Vargas's reconquest mentions an Indian tribe named *Conchos,* as well as the *Río Conchos,* likely the major tributary of the Rio Grande that heads in western Chihuahua and flows into the Rio Grande at Ojinaga, opposite Presidio, TX. The Conchos Indians have long since vanished, but it's possible their name lingers, perhaps corrupted, in some contemporary place names. GNIS lists Conchas 17 times, Conchos none.

CONCHAS LAKE (San Miguel; in SE part of county, on NM 104, 31 mi NW of Tucumcari). *Conchas Dam* was built by the US Army Corps of Engineers in 1937 to impound the Canadian River. It was the state's largest public works project of the Depression era, and the reservoir today is NM's fourth largest lake. The dam and the reservoir take their name from the Conchas River (see entry).

Conchas Lake State Park was designated in 1955, to feature Conchas Lake. The tiny settlement of *Conchas* (PO as Conchas Dam, 1936–1965, mail to Tucumcari rural branch), located at Conchas Lake, houses people associated with the dam and state park.

CONCHAS RIVER (San Miguel; heads in central part of county and flows SE and then E into Conchas Lake). The confluence of the Conchas and Canadian rivers now is submerged by the reservoir (see *Conchas Lake*). A 1939 USBGN decision said Conchas River was the accepted form and not *Río Conchas* or *Conchos River.* See *Conchas (general).*

CONE (Harding; settlement; originally 9 mi W of Hayden, later 8 mi NW of Rosebud; PO 1908–35, mail to Hayden). In 1908 a petition was circulated to establish a PO in central Harding County, and after approval the PO was located at the farm of William W. Cone and his wife, Mystice; she was first postmistress. At one time the settlement associated with the Cone PO had a grocery store, a mercantile store, a gas station, and a school; it was a popular site of regional baseball games. But as ranching replaced homesteading, Cone withered. Only the cemetery remains.

CONEJO (general). See *Rabbit (general).*

CONTADERO (Socorro; settlement; 4 mi S of San Marcial across the Rio Grande from old Fort Craig). The settlement of Contadero, now beneath Elephant Butte Reservoir, began as a simple *paraje,* or stopping place, called *El Contadero,* meaning "a narrow passage where livestock are counted." This *paraje* was an established locality in the pre-Revolt period, functioning as a place where sheep and cattle were impounded, rested, and tallied. Governor Otermín, in his attempted reconquest of 1682, mentions spending the night at El Contadero. Nearby is *Mesa del Contadero* and *El Paso del Contadero,* the latter a narrow trail between the steep sides of the mesa and the river.

The later settlement of Contadero grew out of the paraje, and it appears in US Census records from 1870 to 1920, but it was condemned when Elephant Butte Dam was built and finally flooded out in 1924.

CONTINENTAL DIVIDE (McKinley; settlement; on I-40 5 mi W of Thoreau; PO 1949–present). This community was named for being on the Continental Divide, at 7,247 ft. Locally, the settlement often is called *Top o' the World.* It also has been called *Campbells Pass,* for Albert H. Campbell, civil engineer and surveyor attached to Lt. A.W. Whipple's party of US Topographical Engineers that surveyed the 35th parallel for a RR route; in December 1853 Campbell recommended the pass as the best passage.

CONTINENTAL DIVIDE (western NM). The Continental Divide, separating waters flowing E from those flowing W, enters NM just W of Chama and snakes S to enter Mexico in southern Hidalgo County. Several places in NM are named for being located on this feature.

CONTRERAS (Socorro; settlement; N of Socorro on NM 47, 3 mi N of La Joya; PO 1919–35, mail to La Joya). Matías Contreras raised cattle and sheep here, and the tiny inhabited community he founded bore his name. A 1918 map, however, published just before the PO was established, labels the community

Los Ranchos de la Joya; see La Joya.

COOKES, COOKS (Luna; settlement; 20 mi N of Deming on Cookes Peak; PO 1889–1914, 1915–16, mail to Nutt). Lead-silver ore was discovered on Cookes Peak in 1876 by Edward Orr, and in the summer of 1882 George L. Brooks supervised the grading of a road up the main canyon to the mountain where he chose a campsite and named it for the peak. A bustling mining camp soon developed, divided into eastern and western sections, and it attracted the usual frontier assortment of outlaws and drifters in addition to miners. But eventually the mines played out, and the camp died. The name often appears without the *e*. See *Cookes Canyon, Cookes Peak.*

COOKES CANYON (Luna; heads N of Massacre Peak on the SE side of the Cookes Range and runs SE). Named for *Cookes Peak* to the N, this rugged canyon was called the "Journey of Death" by soldiers to whom it was a gauntlet of Apache ambush sites. The Butterfield Overland Mail stage line ran through here to *Cookes Spring Station,* and as many as 400 travelers—as well as soldiers—were estimated to have died here; at one time in 1867 stage passengers could see at least nine skeletons along the four-mile route; they were removed following protests to authorities. So great was the Apache danger that in 1863 Fort Cummings (see entry) was built at Cookes Spring (see entry) at the canyon's head to protect travelers.

COOKES PEAK, 8,404 ft. (Luna; in the Cookes Range, 18 mi N of Deming). The highest summit in the range named for it, Cookes Peak was named for Capt. Philip St. George Cooke, leader of the Mormon Battalion that passed through here in 1846–47. Earlier, the peak was labeled *Cerro de los Remedios* by the New Mexico mapmaker Bernardo Miera y Pacheco, who worked in the late 1700s. The Butterfield stage line was routed around the mountain because several springs provided water. Lead-silver ore was discovered here in 1876, leading to the mining camp of Cooke (see entry).

Cookes Peak is the dominant summit of the small *Cookes Range.*

COOKES SPRING (Luna; at the head of Cookes Canyon, SE of Cookes Peak and NE of Massacre Peak). This spring, the most important in the Cookes Peak (see entry) area, was named in 1846 by a lieutenant under Capt. Philip St. George Cooke. The Butterfield stage had a station here, and because the spring and the canyon were in Apache territory, Fort Cummings (see entry) was built here in 1863 to protect travelers against ambushes. Earlier, in the late 1700s, in a military expedition coordinated by Governor Juan Bautista de Anza, Capt. Don Francisco Martínez camped by the spring and called it *San Miguel.*

COOLIDGE (McKinley; settlement; on I-40 22 mi E of Gallup, 8 mi W of Thoreau; PO as Cranes 1881, 1888–95, mail to Mitchell, as Coolidge 1926–57, mail to Continental Divide). In the early 1880s, the A&P RR was putting a main line through NM territory, and 3 mi NW of the present inhabited settlement the line passed by a small community named *Cranes.* It was there that William "Uncle Billy" Crane, former scout and teamster for Kit Carson, had established his headquarters, near a site called *Bacon Springs,* and had begun supplying hay and beef to troops at Fort Wingate. With the establishment of a RR station, the Crane locality soon became *Cranes Station,* but in 1882 it became Coolidge, named for Thomas Jefferson Coolidge, president of the RR; Uncle Billy continued to live here until his death in 1904.

The arrival of the RR and the proximity to Fort Wingate made Coolidge a magnet for drifters and rowdies, and one series of killings provoked the lynching of seven outlaws. Numerous writers and artists lived and worked in Coolidge; Charles Lummis lived nearby in 1894. Eventually, the RR transferred most of its business to Gallup, and Coolidge withered, though postal service was maintained under the postal names of *Dewey, Guam,* and *Perea;* sometimes Guam was divided into *North Guam* and *South Guam.* These names still appear on RR signs. About 1926 the present settlement of Coolidge was established with a service station and trading post; the name this time likely was derived from Dane Coolidge (1873–1940), a trader who operated the trading post and who in the 1920s wrote a book about the Navajos. It also has been said, however, the name honors President Calvin Coolidge, then in office. Old Coolidge was bulldozed in 1930. Navajos know Coolidge by a name meaning "tall Chiricahua Apache."

COONEY (Catron; settlement; in the Mogollon Mountains E of Alma, 1.5 mi N of Mogollon; PO 1884–1915, mail to Mogollon). In 1870 James C. Cooney came to Fort Bayard as a sergeant of the 8th US Cavalry, and while on duty as a scout he discovered silver ore on Mineral Creek. After his discharge from the Army in 1876 he returned to the site with two companions to work the claim. In 1880 Cooney was killed by Apaches, and his brother, Capt. Mike Cooney (see *Cooney Canyon*) and friends carved a tomb out of a rock in the canyon where he was killed and sealed it with ore from the mine he'd discovered. Though Cooney the prospector was gone, the mining camp named for him on Mineral Creek (the locality earlier had been called *Canyon City*) thrived, and by 1889 Cooney had 600 residents, three stamp mills, a school, a church, and two hotels. But in 1911 a flood destroyed much of the town, and the decline of mining doomed the rest. Only foundations remain. *Cooney Canyon* is on Mineral Creek, at the settlement of Cooney. *Cooney Peak,* 8,591 ft. is 3 mi E of Cooney settlement.

COONEY CANYON (Grant; in N part of county, in Gila Wilderness; a tributary of Sycamore Canyon). As Henry Woodrow tells the story, Capt. Mike Cooney, brother of James C. Cooney (see *Cooney*), kept returning to the Gila wilderness and especially to Sycamore Canyon searching for a lost gold mine. In 1914, when Cooney was in his 70s, he left Socorro for yet another trip; he never returned. "It was a month or two before his body was found beside a large juniper tree where a side canyon goes into Sycamore Canyon. The tree was marked with a blaze, and Cooney's body was packed out and buried at Socorro. Several years later I named that canyon for him, and it is still known as Cooney Canyon, but the gold mine has never been found."

COONEY PRAIRIE (Catron; 30 mi E of settlement of Cooney). Doubtless named for James or Mike Cooney.

COOPER (Lea; settlement; 6 mi N and 2 mi W of Jal; PO 1914–38, mail to Jal). This abandoned settlement, which once served several oil camps, was named for the Cooper Ranch where the PO was located.

COPELAND CANYON (Chaves; runs N into the Rio Peñasco SE of Elk). This name recalls Sarah Copeland, widow of John Copeland, who briefly in 1878 was Lincoln County sheriff.

COPELAND CANYON (Lincoln; on NE side of the Capitan Mountains). John Copeland, sheriff during the Lincoln County Wars, homesteaded here, and Roy Copeland ranched near here before 1900.

COPPER (general). GNIS lists 26 places named for this mineral. The Spanish form, *cobre,* occurs only 3 times, all near the copper mines at Santa Rita.

COPPER CITY (San Miguel; settlement; in W part of county, exact location unknown; PO as Hamilton 1883, mail to Glorieta). This was a short-lived mining camp in the Hamilton Mining District, from which the PO likely took its name.

COPPER CITY (Sandoval; settlement; 3 mi E of Cuba; PO 1883–90, mail to Cuba). The mineral deposits for which Copper City was named were discovered by Indians and Mexicans early in the 19th century, but the deposits were not worked systematically until the 1880s, when the settlement was born. During its short life Copper City had as many as 500 residents and the usual stores and services, but now even its location is difficult to iden-tify.

COPPERAS PEAK, 7,857 ft. (Grant; in N part of county, 6 mi S of Gila Hot

Springs, W of NM 15, E of the Gila River). Also known as green vitriol, copperas is a crystallized sulphate of various metals, especially copper, iron, and zinc. *Copperas Creek* heads just S of this mountain. *Copperas Vista* on NM 15 just E of the mountain provides a spectacular view of the Gila Wilderness.

COPPERTON (Cibola; settlement; 22 mi SW of Prewitt, 4 mi W of Mount Sedgwick; PO 1901–11, mail to Grants). Copperton, now abandoned, was born when Herbert M. Jones opened a copper mine here in 1900. A year later, with the arrival of the Valencia Mining Corp., a PO was established. But the settlement remained tiny, never more than 10 families, and it died when the copper vein petered out.

COPPINGER (San Juan; settlement; S of Farmington and W of NM 371). Abandoned settlement, named for an early family of sheep ranchers, some of whose descendants still live in the area.

CORAZON (general). Spanish, *corazón,* "heart." This can be a descriptive metaphor, but it also can have religious significance, referring to the "Sacred Heart."

CORAZON (San Miguel; settlement; 12 mi SE of Trujillo; PO 1903–09, mail to Chaperito). Now a ghost town, this community took its name from nearby *El Cerro de Corazón* (see entry).

EL CERRO DEL CORAZON (San Miguel; 1 mi S of NM 104, 12 mi SE of Trujillo). Spanish, "the hill of the heart." Also called *Corazon Hill,* this hill resembles a heart, especially when viewed from the W. El Cerro del Corazón is not to be confused with *Corazon Hill* just to the W, a long, steep highway descent from the mesas around Trujillo to the valley below. *Corazon Creek* in *Cañon de Cerro del Corazón* heads W of El Cerro de Corazón and runs S to the Conchas River.

CORDILLERA (Mora; settlement; on NM 518, 2 mi W of Mora, 1 mi E of Cleveland). Spanish, *cordillera,* "chain of mountains." Tiny residential cluster, name origin unknown.

CORDOVA (Rio Arriba; settlement; 14 mi E of Española, 1 mi S of NM 76, on the Rio Quemado; PO 1900–present). This tiny mountain village was known as *Pueblo Quemado,* Spanish, "burned village," from its founding in 1749 until 1900 when the PO was established. This name may have reflected some long-ago forest fire, perhaps the one that gave the Rio Quemado (see entry) its name. But members of the Córdova family from whom the present name was derived have been here since the village's beginnings, and when postal officials refused to have two towns in NM named Quemado, the town's citizens chose to name the PO for Matías Cordova. Fray Angélico Chávez lists Antonio de Córdoba, a native of Mexico City, as a settler at the new town of Santa Cruz soon after the reconquest of 1692, and his descendants moved up the valley to Chimayo and doubtless to this village, where the spelling of his surname eventually was altered to the present form.

CORDUROY DRAW (Catron; in SE part of county, enters Beaver Creek 1 mi W of Beaverhead). Portions of this long canyon were persistently muddy, so logs were laid across the wet spots, giving them a corduroy appearance.

CORN MOUNTAIN (McKinley). See *Dowa Yalanne.*

CORNUCOPIA DRAW, HILLS (Otero; in SE part of county, paralleling NM 506 W of the Guadalupe Mountains). The exact reasons for this name are unknown, though perhaps it comes from the *Cornucopia Ranch* near the head of the draw. Such names often expressed fanciful hopes for minerals, good crops, or sometimes just reliable water. The *Cornucopia Hills,* elevation 5,575 ft., border the draw on the E.

CORNUDAS MOUNTAINS (Otero; along the NM–Texas line, SE of Otero Mesa and E of US 54). Also known as *Las Cornudas,* Spanish, "the horns," the name Cornudas is said to have been suggested by horn-like rock formations; one summit in the group is called *Horned Mountain,* because its two pinnacles resemble horns. The Cornudas Mountains rise abruptly from a mesa to approximately 7,000 feet. The highest summit is *Wind Mountain,* 7,280 ft.

CORONA (Lincoln; settlement; E of the Gallinas Mountains, at the junction of NM 42 and US 54, 36 mi SE of Willard; PO 1902–present). Corona was born in 1899 when the EP&NE RR, later the SP RR, built its line to the Dawson coal fields, and the company chose the name; it is Spanish for "crown" and was selected because this station was at the highest point—6,724 ft.—on the line. (Another version, less widely accepted, is that the name was inspired by a small peak nearby that appears to have a crown.) But the area was settled before the RR and its village. Before Corona was established, the area was served by the *Red Cloud* PO, located on the Cook and Greathouse Ranch, in Red Cloud Canyon W of Corona; see *Greathouse Tavern.* Corona originally was on the E side of the RR tracks, but when US 54 was laid out in the 1920s the main street moved across the tracks to its present location. Corona was a thriving agricultural and trade center from 1900 to 1940, but since then its economic base has shrunk.

CORONADO NATIONAL FOREST (Hidalgo; in extreme SW part of the state, extending into Arizona). Several US national forests have been expanded, consolidated, and administratively realigned over the years. The Coronado NF is mostly located in Arizona, but it includes portions of the Peloncillo and Guadalupe ranges in NM. When the NM acreage was designated in 1906, it was called the *Peloncillo Forest,* for the mountains. Then in 1910 it became the *Chiricahua Forest,* for the Chiricahua Mountains in Arizona. Then in 1916 it was renamed the Coronado NF, for the *conquistador.*

CORONADO STATE PARK AND MONUMENT (Sandoval; 0.5 mi NW of Bernalillo, on the W bank of the Rio Grande). One of the few places in NM to be named for Francisco Vásquez de Coronado, and perhaps the most appropriate. For it may have been here, at the Tiguex pueblo of *Kuaua* (see entry) that the *conquistador* made his winter headquarters in 1540–41 during his exploration of the Southwest. The state monument features the ruins of Kuaua built around A.D. 1300. It has been thought but not definitely determined that this was the pueblo called *Alcanfor* (see entry) by the Spaniards, the site of Coronado's winter camp. In any case, the famous conqueror certainly was familiar with this pueblo. From the campgrounds and picnic tables of the state park one can look E upon a vista of the Sandia Mountains and the Rio Grande that Coronado and his men would have seen more than 450 years ago. See *Tiguex Province.*

CORRAL (general). From the Spanish, "an enclosed pen for livestock"; the plural is *corrales,* the diminutive *corralito.* GNIS lists 31 places in NM with this element in their names, including 13 Corral Canyons.

CORRAL DE PIEDRA (Rio Arriba; settlement; 1.5 mi N of Española). This tiny community, dating to 1700, takes its name from enormous stone corrals built by the Salazar family. The name used by the Tewas means "stone wall place," approximately the same as the Spanish name.

CORRALES (Sandoval; settlement; on W bank of the Rio Grande, on NM 448, NW of Albuquerque; PO as Corrales 1885–99, as Sandoval 1899–1966, as Corrales 1966–present). Corrales, originally called *Los Corrales,* was the exception to the local custom of naming villages for their leading citizens. The area now known as Corrales was part of the Alameda Land Grant, given to Francisco Montes Vigil in 1701, and it supposedly took its name from extensive corrals built by rancher Juan González, founder of Alameda (see entry); he built an *hacienda* at the S end of Corrales. The grant eventually was divided and sold. *Corrales Alto,* "Upper Corrales," had as its religious name *Santa Rosalia de Corrales.* The lower part went to the Montoyas, a powerful family from Bernalillo; this came to be known as *Corrales Abajo,* "Lower Corrales"; its religious title was *San Ysidro de Corrales,* and it was always the more prosperous of the two communities. For 65 years the community took the name *Sandoval,* for a locally prominent family (see *Sandoval County*), but in 1966 it reverted to its traditional name, which had persisted in local usage.

CORREO (Valencia; settlement; in extreme NW part of county, on NM 6, 2 mi S of I-40, on AT&SF RR; PO 1917–45, 1946–59, mail to Laguna). This RR community originally was called *San Jose,* for the *Río San Jose* to the S, but in 1902 the name was changed to *Suwanee,* sometimes spelled *Suanee,* because there was already a San Jose on the same RR in Oklahoma. With the establishment of a PO, the community took its present name, Spanish for "mail," because this was the only place for many miles where mail could be sent and received. At one time a general store, bar, and PO were here, but now only a few houses remain. As Jerold G. Widdison points out, "'Route 66' enthusiasts recall that the early US 66 W from Los Lunas (now NM 6) was joined at Correo by the later US 66 known as the Laguna Cutoff—built W from Albuquerque. But the cutoff too was eventually replaced by I-40. Remnants of the various old highways at Correo serve as reminders of mid-20th century America."

CORRUMPA (Union; settlement; in N-central part of county, at headwaters of Corrumpa Creek; PO 1905–19, mail to Des Moines). In the early 20th century, a settlement grew up around the headquarters of the sprawling FDW Ranch of Frederick D. Wight, taking its name from the creek on which it was located. A PO was here, and a rural school whose basketball team played in district tournaments. Though ranching still exists in the area, the settlement of Corrumpa has been abandoned.

CORRUMPA CREEK (Union; heads E of Des Moines, on the E slopes of Sierra Grande, and flows E to become the North Canadian River upon entering Oklahoma). Traders on the Santa Fe Trail knew this as *McNees Creek,* recalling an incident in 1828 at a site later known as *McNees Crossing.* Two men, McNees and Monroe, members of an eastbound wagon train, had bathed and fallen asleep here, where they were ambushed and shot by Indians. McNees died here, Monroe at Cimarron. A retaliatory raid by whites intensified hostilities between the two groups. The creek later took the name Corrumpa, sometimes spelled *Currumpaw,* said to be an Indian word meaning, appropriately, "wild, isolated."

The Corrumpa country was made famous by the writings of Ernest Thompson Seton. His story "Lobo, King of the Currumpaw," begins: "Currumpaw is a vast cattle range in northern NM. It is a land of rich pastures and teeming flocks and herds, a land of rolling mesas and precious running waters that at length unite in the Currumpaw River, from which the whole region is named."

COSTILLA (Taos; settlement; at the junction of NM 522 and 196, 1 mi from the Colorado line; PO 1872–present). The settlement takes its name from *Costilla Creek* (see entry), which flows through the village. When James Bennett passed through here in 1854 he noted that this town—he called it *Sostilla*—was just springing up. The community is said to have once had four *plazas.* See also *Big Costilla Peak* and *Little Costilla Peak.*

COSTILLA CREEK (Taos; heads at the Colorado line and flows S into Costilla Reservoir, then NW through the village of Costilla, then back into Colorado to join the Rio Grande). Spanish, "rib," applied to this creek because of a rib-shaped curve along its length, though *costilla* in 18th-century Spanish usage in the Southwest also meant a long slope along a mountain range, which would apply here. The stream often is labeled *Río Costilla* or *Costilla River,* but the form accepted by the USBGN in 1969 was Costilla Creek. *Costilla Reservoir* is in the NE part of Taos County, in the mountain canyon of Costilla Creek; it's also called *Costilla Lake. Little Costilla Creek* heads at Little Costilla Peak and flows SW into Comanche Creek.

COTTON CITY (Hidalgo; settlement; on NM 338, 13 mi S of I-10). Relatively modern community centered around a cotton gin here, supported by local cotton farming.

COTTONWOOD (general). Whether in Spanish as *álamo* or one of its variants, or in English as *cottonwood,* this name element probably is the most common in NM. GNIS lists 127 places named Cottonwood, including 38 Cottonwood Canyons and 29 Cottonwood Springs. See *Alamo (general).*

COTTONWOOD (Colfax; settlement; 10 mi N of Dawson, on Cottonwood Creek). Abandoned community, named for the creek.

COTTONWOOD (Eddy; settlement; 5 mi N of Artesia). Small inhabited settlement, named for a cottonwood grove near a spring on land first settled by Wallace Holt and his cattle company in the 1880s.

COUNCIL ROCK (Socorro; settlement; on FR 10, 11 mi NW of Magdalena, just W of the junction of NM 52 and US 60; PO 1881–83, mail to Alma). In January 1881 a prospector named "Uncle Billy" Hill discovered silver in the Iron Mountain Mining District of Socorro County, and by October a townsite had been staked out with almost 100 cabins. The burgeoning camp was called Council Rock for a large nearby boulder earlier used as a meeting place by Indians and whites. The mines ultimately proved disappointing, and Council Rock was abandoned.

COUNSELOR (Sandoval; trading point; on NM 44, 33 mi NW of Cuba). Jim Counselor began trading with the Navajos in 1916 and established several trading posts, including this one in 1930. His name remains on the settlement here. The Navajo name for the locality means "tall American," a reference to Jim Counselor.

COUSINS (McKinley; settlement, trading point; 28 mi S of Gallup, 7 mi W of Whitewater; PO as Round House 1930–31, mail to Gallup). Two brothers, Bob and Malin Cousins, sons of Charles Cousins who settled here in 1925, be-

came principal operators of the *Cousins Brothers Trading Post,* which is still operated by their descendants. *Round House,* probably translating a Navajo name, was the name of the PO here, but the name Cousins is more widely known.

COW (general). Since the arrival of Europeans, cattle ranching has been important in NM's economy and culture, and place names reflect this; GNIS lists 61 places with *Cow* in their names; the Spanish form *vaca* is less common, appearing 9 times. But as T.M. Pearce pointed out, when *cow* appears in old names, the term may have referred to bison rather than domestic cattle.

COW SPRING (Santa Fe). See *Ojo de la Vaca.*

COW SPRINGS (Luna; stage stop; in NW corner of county, just E of the Luna County line). George Adlai Feather mentioned this as a stop on an 18-century stage route and an isolated water place on the old Santa Rita–Janos road.

COWAN (Quay; settlement; 13 mi N and 5 mi E of Melrose, in Frio Draw; PO 1908–12, mail to Murdock). Cowan, long since abandoned, was primarily a rural PO located in the ranch house of the Cowan family.

COWBOY (general). GNIS shows 9 places in NM named for their association with cowboys, whose individual identities usually have been forgotten. Curiously, no places have *vaquero,* the Spanish equivalent, in their names.

COWLES (San Miguel; settlement; in the Sangre de Cristo Mountains, on the Pecos River, at the end of NM 63; PO 1905–64, mail to rural Glorieta branch). In 1900 a man named Cowles established a hunting and fishing resort here. Though the man is gone, his name survives on the place that still is an important center for outdoor recreation in the Pecos Wilderness.

COX CANYON (Otero; settlement; SE of Cloudcroft, in Cox Canyon, on NM 130). Former community, named for *Cox Canyon,* which heads SW of Cloudcroft and runs SE, paralleling NM 130, to join the Rio Peñasco. Tom Cox homesteaded here about 1883. Another Cox Canyon is located within the S part of Cloudcroft; the old railroad yards, called Spur Landing, were quartered here.

COX PEAK, 8,255 ft. (Catron; 14 mi E of Mangas, 8 mi SE of Pie Town). Three Cox brothers—John, Tom, and Joe—had ranches in the area. John Cox had his ranch at the S end of *Cox Lake,* 3 mi SW of Cox Peak.

COX PEAK, 5,957 ft. (Doña Ana; in SW part of county, just S of Mount Riley). Named for W.W. Cox, pioneer rancher and businessman in the county, as was *Cox Reservoir,* 11 mi NE of Organ.

COX RANCH (Doña Ana). See *Organ Mountains Recreation Area.*

COYOTE (general). As T.M. Pearce observed, "The place which the coyote holds in American experience, among three peoples—Indian, Spanish, Anglo—is emphasized by the frequency of the place name." According to GNIS, 75 NM features, including 4 settlements and 13 Coyote Springs, are named for the ubiquitous coyote, whose name comes from the Nahuatl *coyotl.*

COYOTE (Lincoln). See *Hurlburt.*

COYOTE, LLANO DEL COYOTE (Mora). See *Rainsville.*

COYOTE (Rio Arriba; settlement; on NM 96, 22 mi W of Abiquiu; PO 1915–present). *Coyote Valley* and *Coyote Canyon* were settled around 1862. One mi W, at the confluence of the Rio Puerco and Salitral Creek, is the satellite community of *Arroyo del Agua.* S of Coyote, on Coyote Creek, was the scattered settlement of *Cañon del Coyote.*

COYOTE (Sandoval; settlement; in SE corner of county, 8 mi SE of San Felipe Pueblo, just N of Coyote Arroyo). Like its sister community of Hagan, 3 mi to the SE, Coyote was a coal-mining camp. It was established in 1904, two years after Hagan, with the opening of the Sloan Mine. Both towns fed on hopes of a RR serving the mines, but by the time a line finally reached Hagan in 1924, Coyote already had withered and died. See *Hagan.*

COYOTE CANYON (Bernalillo; mining district; on the W slope of the N Manzano Mountains, S of Carnuel).

During the 1870s, considerable enthusiasm was generated when traces of gold, silver, and copper were discovered here and in nearby Hell Canyon, and a hotel was even proposed for Coyote Canyon. The finds ultimately proved disappointing.

Now within Kirtland Air Force Base, Coyote Canyon is the site of military and US Dept. of Energy testing and training facilities; *Arroyo del Coyote,* also within the base, is 1.5 mi N. See *Coyote Springs.*

COYOTE CANYON (McKinley; settlement; 9 mi SE of Tohatchi). This inhabited Navajo settlement was named for being in *Coyote Canyon,* which heads S of the village. The first trading post at Coyote Canyon was established in 1908 by Charles Baker. The Navajo name for Coyote Canyon translates to "where the coyote got caught in the mud"; Navajos tell of a coyote who, attempting to drink from a deep pothole here, fell in and could not get out. *Brimhall* (see entry) is the PO at Coyote Canyon. *Coyote Wash,* which heads S and W of the village runs N to join the Chaco River at Great Bend.

COYOTE CREEK STATE PARK (Mora; on the E slopes of the Sangre de Cristo Mountains, on NM 434, 14 mi N of Mora). Named for being on *Coyote Creek,* a tributary of the Mora River, this 80-acre state park is in a sheltered valley, with a spectacular display of wildflowers.

COYOTE SPRINGS (Bernalillo; in the NW foothills of the Manzano Mountains, in Arroyo del Coyote, within Kirtland Air Force Base). According to Marc Simmons, Adolph Harsch, who opened the first bakery in Albuquerque's New Town, drilled a well at Coyote Springs and under the name of Harsch's Coyote Bottling Works, marketed the mineral-laden waters. According to Simmons, "His mineral water was long the favorite chaser for whiskey in Albuquerque saloons."

CRAIG (Socorro; settlement; at the site of Fort Craig; PO 1880–85). See *Fort Craig.*

CRANES (Cibola). See *Coolidge.*

CRANKTOWN (Catron; settlement; about 2 mi W of Mogollon). George Adlai

Feather described this as no more than a cluster of prospectors' cabins, but the name has been perpetuated in the Cranktown sandstone formation, which outcrops here.

CRATER (Doña Ana; trading point; on US 80, W of Las Cruces, near the Luna County line; PO 1933–35, mail to Cambray). Former trading point, named for an extinct volcano nearby.

CRAWFORD (Grant). See *Spaulding*.

CRAZY PEAK (Quay). See *Pyramid Peak*.

CREST VIEW (McKinley; settlement; W of Gallup, S of Mentmore). Recent inhabited residential development, likely named for its view of a nearby landform.

CRESTON (Santa Fe; settlement; 8 mi S of Galisteo). In NM the Spanish *crestón* can mean "hillock" or "summit," but it also can mean "cockscomb" or "large crest," and that likely is the meaning applied to the conspicuous rocky spine on the E slope of the Ortiz Mountains called *Creston*. The name was transferred to this nearby mining camp, now abandoned.

THE CRESTON (San Miguel; SW of Las Vegas, bisected by I-25). The Spanish *crestón* here likely means "cockscomb" or "large crest," an appropriate description for this conspicuous hogback ridge. Maps label two gaps in The Creston: *Puerto del Sur*, "south gap," through which I-25 passes, and *Puerto del Norte*, "north gap," 1.5 mi N. See *Kearnys Gap*.

CRIBBENVILLE (Rio Arriba; settlement; NE of Vallecitos and Cañon Plaza, E of NM 111; PO 1884–85 as Cribbensville, 1885–96 as Cribbenville, mail to Vallecitos). In the late 1800s, Cribbenville was a lumber camp, located on a RR spur. The identity of the person named Cribben for whom the settlement was named is unknown.

CRILE (Lea; settlement; 8 mi N of Eunice). Crile was an oil settlement promoted in 1930 by the Singleton and Crile Townsite Co. Lots sold briskly, but despite this the town failed to materialize.

CROMER (Roosevelt; settlement; 10 mi W of Causey; PO 1907–18, mail to Richland). Abandoned homesteader settlement, named for its first postmaster, Richard A. Cromer.

CROOKED CREEK (Eddy; 3 mi N of Carlsbad Caverns). An appropriate descriptive name.

CROSBY CREEK, SPRING (Catron; creek heads at Crosby Spring 5 mi W of Datil and flows E). Named for homesteaders. *South Crosby Peak*, 9,095 ft., is 3 mi S of Crosby Springs, in the ridge-like complex known as the *Crosby Mountains*, 6 mi W of Datil.

CROSSROADS (Lea; settlement; at the junction of NM 206 and 508, 18 mi N of Tatum; PO 1925–present). Lora Miller, a widow, homesteaded here, and when she applied for a PO she submitted the name *Cross Roads*, for the intersection of NM 206 and NM 508; at the time the postal department frowned on two-word names, so it became Crossroads. The highways are still here (one of them renumbered), and so is the community. *Junction* (see entry), in San Juan County, has a similar associative name.

CROW CREEK (Colfax; heads N of US 64 and flows SE to join the Canadian River N of Maxwell). Great flocks of crows once nested in the cottonwoods along this and nearby streams. The creek flows across *Crow Creek Flat*.

CROW FLATS (Otero; settlement; in SE part of the county, W of the Brokeoff Mountains; PO 1898–1900, mail to Van Horn, TX). This inhabited community was named for *Crow Flats*, named in turn for *Crow Springs*, a stage stop on the Butterfield Overland Mail route at the foot of the Guadalupe Mountains in Texas. Stage drivers, apprehensive of Indian attacks, named the spring. As they approached the stop there, they watched the behavior of the local crows. If the crows were resting in the trees, all likely was well. But if the crows were flying, the drivers were on their guard. The flats earlier had been called *Salt Basin*.

CROWNPOINT (McKinley; settlement; 25 mi N of Thoreau, immediately W of NM 371; PO 1911–present). This Navajo community was named for a crown-shaped butte nearby. Its Navajo name means "narrow-leafed cottonwood gap." Crownpoint, established in 1909 as the

Pueblo Bonito Agency, with an Indian school, has become an important administrative center of the BIA and the Navajo Nation. On early maps the name appeared as *Crown Point,* but the name became one word, probably at the urging of postal officials who then disliked two-word names.

CROZIER (San Juan). See *Two Grey Hills.*

LA CRUZ DE ANAYA (Sierra; campground; on the Jornada del Muerto). This was a 17th-century Spanish campground on the Jornada del Muerto, named because a cross here marked the grave of an unfortunate traveler named Anaya.

CRUCES BASIN WILDERNESS (Rio Arriba; in N part of county, just S of the Colorado border, including most of the headwaters of the Rio de los Pinos). Administered by the Carson NF and named because it includes the drainage of *Cruces Creek,* this 18,000-acre wilderness is a rolling mountain plateau, 8,600 to 10,900 feet in elevation, cut by perennial streams. It is important summer range for elk.

CRUZVILLE (Catron; settlement; on NM 12, 3 mi SW of the village of Apache Creek). Members of the Cruz family no longer live in this diffuse inhabited community, but their name remains.

CRYSTAL (San Juan; settlement; 18 mi SW of Sheep Springs on NM 134, at the W entrance to Narbona Pass; PO 1903–41, mail to Fort Defiance, AZ). The inhabited Navajo settlement of Crystal began in 1884 when a trading post was established here. The English name likely is based on the Navajo name, meaning "crystal water flows out."

CRYSTAL SPRINGS (Sierra; settlement; near Lake Valley). An ephemeral mining camp, named for springs that supplied water to Lake Valley early in its development.

CUATES (Union; settlement; 20 mi N of Clayton; PO 1903–38, mail to Des Moines). Only ranches remain at the site of this former settlement, but the name is still recognized and used. It means "twins" in NM Spanish (said to be derived from the Nahuatl *coatl,* "twin") but also can mean "close friends, companions." The origin of the name here is unknown.

CUBA (Sandoval; settlement; on NM 44, 55 mi NW of Bernalillo; PO 1887–present). The inhabited village now called Cuba began in the 18th century as *Nacimiento* and was located to the E of the present settlement. The name came most likely from the *Sierra Nacimiento* (see entry) immediately to the E; the village was labelled Nacimiento on Bernardo Miera y Pacheco's map of the Domínguez-Escalante Expedition of 1776. It also is possible the name of the mountains inspired the settlers to give to their community the title *El Nacimiento de Nuestra Señora,* "The Birthday of Our Lady," and indeed the Nativity Feast on September 8 continues to be observed in the community. The original settlement later was abandoned, most likely because of Navajo raids. It was resettled in 1879, at a site then called *Laguna,* by two families from Jemez, the McCoys and the Atencios, whose descendants still live in the area; Laguna had a suburb to the SW called *Lagunitas,* a name still used locally. But the name Cuba also was likely in use, and when a PO was established in 1887, that was the name it took. The Spanish *cuba* can be translated as "trough, tank," but also as "sink, draw." A small locality across the Rio Puerco was called *Cubeta.*

The coincidental identification of this settlement with the Caribbean island nation often causes confusion, as when visitors say they spent the weekend in Cuba. It also has spawned the apocyrphal story that the village was named by some veterans who had served with Teddy Roosevelt's Rough Riders in Cuba; actually the village was named a full decade before the Spanish-American War.

The Navajo name for Cuba means "gopher water" and is said to come from the name of an elderly Navajo chief called Hastin Na'zisih who lived by a spring where there were many gophers.

CUBERO (Cibola; settlement; N of I-40, 8 mi NW of Laguna; PO 1879–present).

The consensus is that the name of this small settlement recalls Pedro Rodríguez Cubero, who succeeded Diego de Vargas as governor of NM and who served from 1697 to 1703; Cubero passed through here in 1697 on an expedition to Zuni, and it's possible the name originated then. It's also possible the name comes from a local family, though one no longer living in the community. The village appears as *Cubera* on Bernardo Miera y Pacheco's map of the Domínguez-Escalante Expedition of 1776 but as Cubero on most subsequent maps. The village was located on an Indian trail and once was a notorious hangout for Mexican traders in slaves, whiskey, and guns. Indian attacks were frequent here, and in the 18th and 19th centuries, Cubero was a Spanish military outpost; American troops later were stationed here. *Villa de Cubero,* 1 mi W on former US 66, is an abandoned outlier. The Navajo name for Cubero means "water in the crevice," doubtless a reference to the trickling spring here.

RIO CUBERO (Cibola). See *Río San José.*

CUCHILLA, CUCHILLO (general). Spanish, "knife," but in NM it also has become a descriptive metaphor for a geological formation with a sharp edge.

CUCHILLO (Sierra; settlement; 8 mi W of US 85 on NM 52; PO 1883–present). Cuchillo began around 1850 when farmers settled on the banks of *Cuchillo Negro Creek* (see entry). Later, during the Black Range mining boom of the 1870s and 1880s, Cuchillo became an important stage and mail stop on the route to the mining camps.

CUCHILLO NEGRO CREEK (Sierra; heads in the Black Range SW of Chloride and flows SE to join the Rio Grande just N of Truth or Consequences). Baishan was the Apache name for the chief of the Warm Springs Apache Band, whose territory was here, but his Spanish name was Cuchillo Negro, "black knife." He was a leader in the Apache raid on Ramos in Mexico, an important event in Apache history. Numerous features in his former homeland bear his name.

SIERRA CUCHILLO (Sierra; long, narrow range between Ojo Caliente and Cuchillo). Also known as the *Cuchillo Negro Mountains;* highest summit, *Jaralosa Mountain* (Spanish, "with abundant willows"), 8,326 ft.; *Cuchillo Mountain,* in the S part of the range, is 7,895.

CUERVO (Guadalupe; settlement; on I-40, 17 mi E of Santa Rosa; PO 1902–present). This inhabited settlement began when the CRI&P RR line came through here around 1901. The name's origin (Spanish, "crow") is unknown, though it may be related to 5,366-foot *Cuervo Hill* 9 mi to the NW; *Cuervito Peak,* 4,984 ft., is 1 mi NW of the village. English-speakers in the area sometimes pronounce the name CUHR-voh.

CUESTA (general). Spanish, "slope, hill, ridge, escarpment." See *Questa.*

CULBERTSONS SAWMILL (Otero). See *Lower Peñasco.*

CULEBRA (general). See *Rattlesnake (general).*

CULEBRA RANGE (Taos; a subrange of the Sangre de Cristo Mountains, mostly in Colorado but extending into the northern part of Taos County). Spanish, "snake." The name may have been transferred from Culebra Creek in Colorado, a tributary of the Rio Grande that winds snake-like into the river. Highest elevation *Culebra Peak,* 14,069 ft., in Colorado.

CULP PEAK, 7,050 ft. (Otero; at the SW end of the Sacramento Mountains, 3.5 mi SW of Timberon). This peak and the canyon bear the surname of John Culp, who settled here about 1893. *Culp Canyon* heads at Culp Peak and runs S and then W.

CUMBERLAND (Chaves). See *Midway.*

CUMMINGS (Luna). See *Florida.*

CUNDIYO (Santa Fe; settlement; 22 mi N of Santa Fe on NM 503; PO 1922–64, to a rural station of Chimayo). The name is a Spanish corruption of a word used by the nearby Nambe Tewas to mean "round hill of the little bells." The ruins of an ancient pueblo are here—possibly a predecessor of Nambe—but the present inhabitants are almost all Hispanic.

CUNICO (Colfax; settlement; SE of Raton, S of US 64-87; PO 1927–42, mail to Raton). Although members of the Cunico family still live in Colfax County, the settlement that took their name died soon after the Depression, and only an abandoned schoolhouse remains.

CUNNINGHAM (Colfax; settlement; 15 mi SE of Raton). Abandoned community named for Dr. J.M. Cunningham of Las Vegas. *Cunningham Butte* to the NW also likely bears his name.

CUNNINGHAM CREEK, GULCH, HILL (Santa Fe; all on the E side of the Ortiz Mountains, S of Madrid). Named for an early settler.

CURRY (Quay; settlement; 13 mi NW of House; PO 1907–21, mail to Lucille). Abandoned settlement, presumably named for George Curry. See *Curry County.*

CURRY COUNTY (eastern NM, adjacent to the Texas border; county seat, Clovis). George Curry, for whom this county was named, came to NM in 1877 from Dodge City, KS, served as Lincoln County sheriff in 1892, and was territorial governor from 1907 to 1910. He was still in office when Charles Adolphus Scheurich in 1909 almost singlehandedly persuaded the legislature to create a new county from N Roosevelt and S Quay Counties,

CURTIS CREEK (Colfax; heads 12 mi NW of Maxwell and flows SE to enter the Canadian River). Named for "Dad" Curtis, pioneer who started the Curtis Ranch.

CURUCO TOWN (Rio Arriba; settlement; near Santa Cruz). Inhabited neighborhood whose NM Spanish name means "tick." See *El Curuco.*

CUSTER MOUNTAIN, 3,232 ft. (Lea; 7.5 mi WNW of Jal). Local legend says this low landform was named because soldiers under Gen. George Armstrong Custer's command recaptured some escaped Mescalero Apaches, burying in a trench SW of the hill the bodies of the Indians killed in the engagement. This clearly is apocryphal, and other local people say the name is a corruption of *Custard Mountain,* given because the hill resembles a mound of the dessert, custard. A rural school to the N took its name from this hill.

CUTTER (Sierra; settlement; on the AT&SF RR, 9 mi S of Engle; PO 1907–56, mail to Engle). Cutter began as a stop on the RR, and like Crocker, Upham, and Engle (see entries) it was named for a RR engineer. Mining booms, especially vanadium mining in the Caballo Mountains, contributed to Cutter's growth as a community, and at one time 3,500 people were here. But as mining faded, so did Cutter, and ultimately its existence depended on ranching and homesteading. A few ranches remain in the area, but a RR sign is the only reminder of the settlement that once was Cutter.

CUYAMUNGUE (Santa Fe; settlement; 12 mi N of Santa Fe on US 84). This inhabited settlement takes its name from a Tewa word meaning "place of sliding rocks," and nearby are landforms that fit this description. The name likely was applied originally to a Tewa pueblo here; in 1731 Gov. Juan Domíngo de Bustamente granted land to several persons at the site of the pueblo, which had been abandoned.

CYBAR (Luna; settlement; on AT&SF RR, halfway between Nutt and Deming; PO 1900–04, mail to Deming). When Jonas Joseph Morrison applied for a PO here in 1900, he asked that it be called *Florida,* for the nearby mountains, but the postal authorities crossed out Florida and instead inserted Cybar, for reasons unknown.

D

DAHLIA (Guadalupe; settlement; 9 mi N of I-40, just E of the San Miguel County line, on Cañon Blanco). At one time a school served the community here; ranches remain. Once called *Cañon Blanco*, for a nearby canyon; origin of present name unknown.

DALE (Harding; settlement; in E part of county, SW of Rosebud; PO 1908–15, mail to Ione). Ephemeral homesteader community that took the name of its postmistress, Mrs. D. B. Dale.

DALIES (Valencia; RR site; on AT&SF RR, 7 mi NW of Belen). See *Becker*.

DALTON PASS (McKinley; N of Mariano Lake). Once the site of an important wagon and horse trail leading N to the San Juan River, Dalton Pass since has been superseded by US 666. The origin of its English name is unknown. Its Navajo names mean "pass coming down" and "where the horse pulls uphill."

DALY (Sierra). See *Lake Valley*.

DANLEY (Quay; settlement; 10 mi NW of Grady; PO 1917–20, mail to Plain). Abandoned community, name origin unknown.

DANOFFVILLE (McKinley). See *Pinehaven*.

DANVILLE (Sierra; settlement; in the Black Range, on Cave Creek, 7 N of Kingston). An ephemeral silver-mining camp, active around 1884, named for Dan McWilliams.

DARK CANYON (general). A common descriptive name, derived either from dark rocks, dark vegetation, or absence of sunlight. GNIS lists 12 Dark Canyons.

DARK CANYON DRAW (Eddy; heads in hills SE of Carlsbad and empties into the Pecos River just S of Carlsbad). Said to be named for dark ravines near its head.

DATIL (Catron; settlement; at intersection of US 60 and NM 12, 34 mi W of Magdalena; PO 1886–present). This community was named for the nearby *Datil Mountains* (see entry). The settlement began in 1884 as a stop on the wagon road between Magdalena and Quemado and originally was a mile S of its present location. Soon afterward the US Army built *Camp Datil* (see entry) at the site of the present village of Datil to protect settlers from Apache raids. The community and nearby *Datil Well* (see entry) also were where the "Beefsteak Trail" livestock route forked, one prong heading W to Quemado, the other SW through Horse Springs. Datil still is a convenient stop for travelers. See also *Baldwin*.

CAMP DATIL (Catron; military installation; at the site of the present village of Datil). Built by the US Army around 1884 and manned by a unit of the 6th Cavalry, this fort was intended to protect settlers and travelers from Apaches. It was abandoned in 1886.

DATIL FOREST (Catron). See *Apache NF.*

DATIL MOUNTAINS (Catron; in Cibola NF, in NE part of county). Spanish, "date." Two explanations exist for this name. The most likely is that the seedpods of the broad-leafed yucca sufficiently resembled dates to account for the name. The other is that the Spanish applied the name to the fruit of the prickly pear cactus. The name *Sierra del Dátil* appears on Bernardo Miera y Pacheco's 1779 map, based on the Domínguez-Escalante Expedition of 1776–1777. The highest summit is *Madre Mountain*, 9,560 ft.

DATIL WELL NATIONAL RECREATION SITE (Catron: just W of Datil, off NM 60). This facility, managed by the BLM, takes its name from a well that was a water stop on the "Hoof Highway," or "Beefsteak Trail," a route over which thousands of cattle and sheep were driven from Springerville, AZ, to the stockyards at Magdalena. The trail was used from the 1880s to the 1950s.

DAUGHERTY RIDGE (Lincoln; on W slopes of the Sacramento Mountains, 10.5 mi S of Carrizozo). This and *Daugherty Spring* were named for Jasper Newton Daugherty, government trapper and rancher in the area.

DAVID (Harding; settlement; 10 mi E of Mosquero; PO as Ramon 1911–14, as David 1914–21, mail to Mosquero). Sometime before 1911 Benito Cordova opened a store in his home, and by 1911 he'd established a PO, which he called *Ramon*. Three years later Cordova gave up the PO, and the Field family took it into their home, a few miles north. Soon after, the PO went to the home of Fields' son, David C. Fields, and the PO took his name, as did *David Hill*, a precipitous descent on NM 39 just E of Mosquero.

DAWSON (Colfax; settlement; 14 mi NE of Cimarron, on the Vermejo River, 5 mi NW of US 64; PO 1895–1900 as Mountainview, 1900–54 as Dawson). In 1867 two brothers, J. (John) Barkley Dawson and L.S. Dawson, settled on the Vermejo River, and in 1869 John bought 23,000 acres here. About 30 years later, rich coal deposits were discovered, and in 1899 a mine formally was opened on Dawson's ranch. Soon after, in 1901, the Dawson Fuel Co. was organized, with heavy involvement by the El Paso, TX, RR entrepreneur Charles B. Eddy.

A RR was constructed connecting Tucumcari, and a townsite was laid out on the Dawson ranch. The site briefly was called *Mountview,* but soon it took the Dawson name. The Phelps Dodge Corp. purchased the property in 1906, and the burgeoning demand for coal made the community prosper; Dawson eventually had 9,000 residents, one of NM's largest cities at the time. But eventually the market for coal faded; Phelps Dodge sold the property and the company town to the National Iron and Metals Co., who agreed to dismantle it. In 1950 Dawsonites were summarily given 30 days to abandon the only homes many of them had ever known,

and the town was razed.

Today, the major remaining evidence of the company town is the *Dawson Cemetery,* which was placed on the National Register of Historic Places in 1992. With its rows of gray iron crosses, the cemetery is a reminder of two of the worst accidents in the history of American coal mining. On October 22, 1913, an underground explosion killed all 263 men working in Mine No. 2. Then on February 8, 1923, an explosion in Mine No. 1 killed 120 men. Most of the miners at Dawson were from southern and eastern Europe.

Dawson Canyon heads NW from the site of Dawson.

DAYTON (Eddy; settlement; 8 mi S of Artesia and 1 mi E of US 285; PO 1903–44, mail to Artesia). Dayton was founded in 1902 by J.C. Day, for whom it was named, on land he had claimed NE of the Rio Peñasco. In the winter of 1904–05 he laid out a new townsite W of the RR, and everything but the PO and a store moved to the new location. The community at one time boasted a school, a hotel, and a weekly newspaper, but today only oil tanks remain; the *Dayton Road* preserves the name.

DE BACA COUNTY (E-central NM; county seat, Fort Sumner). Ezequiel Cabeza de Baca was NM's second state governor. He died in office in 1917, and this county, created from Roosevelt County, was named a few days after his death. When establishing the county was being considered, *Sumner County* was proposed as a name, but having the new county named for the current governor probably improved its chances in the legislature. Yeso and Guadalupe (see entries) once were proposed for the county seat.

DEAD MAN (general). NM's history often has been violent, the state's natural environment often is harsh, and thus death not surprisingly has resulted in numerous place names. In GNIS are 29 places named Deadman or Dead Man, as well as Dead Horse, Dead Cow, and Dead Dog. Sadly, history usually has forgotten the identities of those whose demise named these places, as well as the circumstances of their deaths.

DEAD MAN (Union; settlement; E of Sierra Grande, near Dead Mans Arroyo; PO 1909–12). Abandoned community, named for *Dead Mans Arroyo* (see entry).

DEAD MAN CANYON (Doña Ana; on the E side of the San Andres Mountains, just NE of White Sands National Monument). This area, at the S end of the Jornada del Muerto, was the site of many Apache raids. This name, as well as that of *Lost Man Canyon*, immediately to the N, possibly resulted from one of them.

DEAD MAN CANYON (Lincoln; in the Sacramento Mountains, near Nogal). In 1886, in this canyon, Indians chased Billy Gill, founder of the American Mine, and killed his partner.

DEAD MAN DRAW (Eddy; runs E through the Seven Rivers Hills to enter Rocky Arroyo from the NW). This is said to owe its name to a dispute that resulted in burials here.

DEAD MAN PEAK, 8,786 ft. (Rio Arriba; 12 mi S of El Vado Reservoir, 6 mi NE of Llaves). Said to have been named because a gambler was slain here after he had run away with another man's wife.

DEAD MAN SPRING (Catron; just S of Lost Lake Mountain, NE of Alma). A man's skeleton once was found here.

DEAD MANS ARROYO (Union; a few miles E of Sierra Grande, in W part of county). On July 4, 1874, a party of Utes came through this area on the warpath, killing several persons on Corrumpa Creek and two persons here, hence the name. It was the last Indian raid in what is now Union County.

DEAD MANS CANYON (Quay; in E part of county, SE of San Jon and S of Bard). Around 1908 in this canyon was found a skeleton, that of a man in a sitting position, his boots nearby, with a bullet hole in his skull.

DEAD NEGRO DRAW (Roosevelt; W of Elida). Locally this is called *Dead Nigger Draw,* the name a relic from a time when the term *nigger* didn't have quite the pejorative meaning it does today. The story behind the name is that sometime in the late 1880s an African-American servant of Dr. Caleb Winfrey, riding

with some cowboys, was caught in a storm here and perished. Dr. Winfrey buried him on his ranch, built a fence around the grave, and planted a willow to shade it. For many years it was the only marked grave in the county.

DEAD NEGRO HILL (Roosevelt; SE of Causey). Known locally as *Nigger Hill,* this feature owes its name to the tragic "Lost Nigger" expedition of 1877. In July of that year, Company A of the 10th Cavalry, commanded by Capt. Nicholas Nolan and composed of African-American troops, set out upon the waterless, sun-baked Llano Estacado in pursuit of Indians who had killed a buffalo hunter. They eventually came to this hill, where defeated, exhausted, and wracked by thirst they abandoned their search for the Indians and began a desperate quest for water. Several African-American soldiers died on the expedition, hence the name.

DEADMANS CANYON (Grant; W of Tyrone, runs N from the Big Burro Mountains to enter Mangas Creek). The body of a murdered man was found here.

DEAN CANYON (Colfax; runs E into Poñil Creek, 2 mi N of Cimarron). Robert Dean came to NM during the 1870s and acquired a ranch in this canyon. He managed H.M. Porter's cattle operations from 1883 until his death in 1892. *Dean Mountain,* 7,897 ft., is 1 mi S of Dean Canyon, 3 mi NW of Cimarron.

DECATUR (San Miguel; settlement; in W part of county, on the AT&SF RR). George Adlai Feather identified this as a lumber town active around 1913. It probably was named for Decatur, IL.

DEDMAN (Union). See *Capulin.*

DEEP TUNNEL (Colfax; settlement; on the side of Baldy Mountain, NE of Eagle Nest). Abandoned mining camp, named for a mine shaft.

DEER (general). GNIS shows 64 places in NM named for deer; the state has two deer species, mule deer and whitetails.

DEFIANCE (McKinley; trading point; on US 66, 9 mi SW of Gallup; PO 1881–87, 1889–90, mail to Gallup). With the coming of the A&P RR in 1882, the main shipping point for Fort Defiance in Arizona became *Defiance Station.* Later,

Defiance Station was superseded by Ferry Station, now Manuelito (see entry), and later still by Gallup, but the name and the locality of Defiance survive. The Navajo name for the locality means "gap in the rocks."

DEHAVEN (Harding; settlement; in N-central part of county, near Union County line; PO 1895–1900, 1901–18, mail to Bueyeros). Only a few people remain at this locality, which took the name of its first postmaster, George W. DeHaven.

DEL MEDIO (Guadalupe). See *Rancho del Medio.*

DELAWARE RIVER (Eddy; rises in Texas and flows into NM to join the Pecos River just N of Red Bluff Reservoir). Name origin unknown.

DELPHOS (Roosevelt; settlement; on US 70 12 mi SW of Portales; PO 1905–40). This name is said to have been transferred here from Delphos, OH, which in turn took it from the Greek isle of Delphos. The settlement, now abandoned, was one of many small towns that sprang up almost overnight with the arrival of the PV&NE RR.

DEMING (Luna; settlement, county seat; at junction of NM 11, NM 26, US 70-80, US 180, and I-10; PO 1881–present). Although Juan Bautista de Anza passed near here in 1780, the modern settlement of Deming dates from 1881 when the AT&SF and SP RRs met near here, giving NM its first rail access to both coasts. The settlement originally was called *New Chicago* and was located 10 mi E of the present site, but it was moved to have better access to water. *Mimbres Junction* also has been mentioned as an early name. Charles Crocker, a SP RR official, gave the fledging settlement his wife's family name.

DE-NA-ZIN WILDERNESS (San Juan; in the San Juan Basin, 26 mi SE of Farmington). The Navajo *de-na-zin* means "standing cranes," and in Navajo mythology, large flocks of cranes stopped in *De-na-zin Wash* on their migrations. The 22,454-acre BLM wilderness, created in 1984, combines rolling grasslands with rugged badlands interspersed with sandy washes and gently sloping mesas.

DENNIS CHAVEZ ESTATES (Bernalillo; settlement; 11 mi E of Albuquerque, 1.5 mi W of Sedillo, 1.5 mi N of I-40). Dennis Chávez was US Senator from NM for 18 years, beginning in 1935. This modern residential development honors him.

DENNISON (Santa Fe; settlement; near Stanley; PO 1912, mail to Stanley). Short-lived PO bearing the surname of early settlers, some of whose descendants still live in the area.

DERENO (De Baca; settlement; 12 mi S of Tolar, near the De Baca County line; 1907–33, mail to Taiban). Abandoned settlement, name origin unknown.

DERRAMADERO (Torrance; trading point; in E part of county, 15 mi NE of Encino). Spanish, "drain, sink," likely referring here to one of the area's many sinkholes.

DERRY (Sierra; settlement; on US 85, 11 mi N of Hatch; PO 1893–94, 1911–present). This name most likely was transferred from Derry, Ireland, and is said to have been suggested for the PO by a former US Army soldier; certainly many former Irishmen were among the troopers at nearby forts. But Derry coexists with an earlier Spanish name, *Loma Parda,* "gray hill," a name shared by this community and Garfield just to the S, though some old-timers have placed Loma Parda a few miles N of Derry. Hispanic settlers came here around 1869, to take advantage of free range and the Homestead Act of 1862; prominent early family names included Gonzáles, Apodaca, Torres, Martínez, and Encinas.

DES MOINES (Union; settlement; at junction of US 64-87 and NM 325, 38 mi SE of Raton; PO 1906–present). This village was born in 1887 when the C&S RR came through the county and put up a sign reading "Des Moines," for Des Moines, IA. The settlement was intended to be the junction of four RR lines, but only two were constructed. Locally the name is pronounced Dez Moynz. See *North Des Moines.*

DES MONTES (Taos; settlement; 2 mi E of Arroyo Seco). This has appeared on early maps as *Los Montes,* but as early as 1832 it appeared in records as Des Montes, and local people still know this inhabited community as Des Montes, an obscure name likely referring to the mountains nearby to the E. An 1844 record called the settlement *Sangre de Cristo de los Des Montes.*

DESEO (Lincoln; settlement; in the Paradise Valley, 12 mi N of Capitan; PO 1916–18, mail to Encinoso). *Deseo* is Spanish for "desire"; this former PO was given this name, for reasons unknown, by Miss Sarah Aguayo, a member of a prominent Hispanic pioneer family. The settlement has vanished.

DETROIT (Doña Ana; settlement; on SP RR, at the NW foot of San Diego Mountain, SE of Rincon; PO 1889–92, mail to Rincon). Abandoned settlement, named for the nearby Detroit Land and Cattle Co. headquarters.

DE VARGAS (Cibola; settlement; in W part of county, E of Cerro Alto; PO 1935–36, mail to Trechado). Little is known about this ephemeral community. The name possibly commemorates Don Diego de Vargas, governor and captain-general of NM, 1691–97, but more likely it refers to a local family name.

DEVIL (general). According to GNIS, 36 places in NM have Devil in their names, probably for the "devilish" nature of their terrain. The Spanish form, *Diablo*, occurs 13 times.

DEVILS BACKBONE (Socorro; at S end of the Magdalena Mountains, NW of Milligan Gulch). Descriptive metaphor for a distinctive ridge.

DEVILS CREEK, DEVILS PARK (Catron; creek heads N of Lost Lake Mountain and flows W of the San Francisco River N of Alma, park is to the N). Persons familiar with this area describe it as "devilish rough country." *Devils Park* is said to be haunted by the ghost of a woman who died here.

DEVILS LAKE (De Baca; in SW part of county). Large sinkhole, perhaps resembling the entrance to hell.

DEVILS PASS (McKinley). See *Satan Pass.*

DEVILS RACETRACK (Chaves; landform; 4 mi N and 25 mi E of Roswell, 3 mi N of US 380). Jagged igneous dike thought to resemble a racetrack. It extends E from *Mesa Diablo.* On some maps it is labelled *Camino del Diablo.*

DEVILS WELL (Chaves; near Lincoln County line, SW of Roswell). James

Cooney, a Chaves County historian, wrote: "The Devil's Well is an awe-inspiring sight, and the name fits the place exactly."

DEVOY (Union; settlement; 2.5 mi from the Colorado line, 10 mi NE of Folsom). Michael Devoy was an early pioneer on the Dry Cimarron River; he has been called "Father of the Cimarron." This abandoned settlement, as well as nearby *Devoy Peaks* and *Devoys Canyon,* bear his name.

DEWEY (McKinley). See *Coolidge.*

DEXTER (Chaves; settlement; 16 mi SE of Roswell, on NM 2; PO 1902–present). This community originally was located at Lake Van (see entry), but with the building of the RR and irrigation canal, a new town was needed. Three men—Theodore Burr, Milton H. Elford, and Albert Macey—selected the site, but as Macey was the only married man in the group, he was given the privilege of selecting the name. He chose Dexter, for his hometown in Iowa. *Dexter National Fish Hatchery,* 1 mi E of Dexter, is operated by the US F&WS especially to propagate endangered species.

DIABLO (general). See *Devil (general).*

DIABLO RANGE (Grant; in N-central part of county, N of the Gila River). Devilish rough mountain country. Highest elevation, Unnamed summit, 8,820 ft.

MESA DIABLO (Chaves). See *Devils Racetrack.*

SIERRA DIABLO (Sierra). See *Black Range.*

DIAMANTE (Rio Arriba). See *Ojo Sarco.*

DIAMOND CAVE (De Baca; in SW part of county, 12 mi W and 6 mi S of Dunlap). An early pioneer saw crystals shining like diamonds and sought investors for his treasure. Further investigations, however, revealed only gypsum crystals, and the cave was mockingly called Diamond Cave.

DIAMOND PEAK, 9,850 ft. (Sierra; on the Continental Divide, in the Black Range, N of Reeds Peak). *Diamond Creek,* along which were found crystals from whence came the name, heads at Diamond Peak and flows NW and then SW to join the East Fork of the Gila River. This is a major drainage, whose branches include *Dry Diamond Creek, Diamond Creek, Middle Diamond Creek, East Diamond Creek,* and *South Diamond Creek*—all heading W of Diamond Peak. The well-known *Diamond Bar Ranch* is located just to the S.

DIENER (Cibola; settlement; 9 mi S of Bluewater Lake; PO 1916–31, mail to Bluewater). Copper mining was responsible for Deiner, a small settlement of about 10 cabins housing 20 to 30 miners from California. But mining here never was very profitable, and the settlement died in the 1930s. *Diener Canyon* and *Post Office Flat* nearby recall its brief existence.

DILCO (McKinley). See *Mentmore*.

DILIA (Guadalupe; on US 84, at junction with NM 119, near San Miguel line; PO 1911–68, mail to La Loma). One of a cluster of settlements along the Pecos River, Dilia is said to have been named for the daughter of an early settler. An Hispanic writer recalls knowing the locality as *Vado de Juan Paiz*. Just to the W is a subvillage called *Upper Dilia*.

DILLMAN CREEK (Catron; runs S into the San Francisco River, 1 mi E of Luna). A man named Dillman, who taught school and ran a PO in Luna, attempted unsuccessfully to homestead here.

DILLON (Colfax; settlement; on AT&SF RR, 3 mi S of Raton). Abandoned RR settlement named for Richard C. Dillon, NM governor from 1928 to 1932. The settlement began around 1880 as a junction for RR branch-lines leading to nearby mining camps. *Dillon Canyon* heads near the Colorado line and runs SE toward Raton. The abandoned coal-mining community of Brilliant (see entry) is in Dillon Canyon.

DILLON MOUNTAIN, 8,710 ft. (Catron; 1 mi N of the San Francisco River and 9 mi NE of Luna). A man named Dillon attempted to homestead here, but he left for the Spanish-American War and never returned.

DIMMITT LAKE (Chaves; just SE of Bottomless Lakes State Park). Bears the name of a Roswell family.

DINETAH (San Juan, Rio Arriba; exact extent undetermined). The Dinetah is as much a concept as a place, one of great historical and cultural importance to the Navajos. As ethnologist J.P. Harrington explained in 1940: "It is well known to every Navajo that the tribe was anciently much smaller than it is now and that it developed in a region lying partly in the easternmost portion of the present Navajo Reservation. This old homeland is still known to all the Navajos as *Tinetzah*, literally, 'among the Navajo,' that is 'the home of the real old-time Navajo.' This Navajo expression would be more literally rendered by the French idiom 'chez les Navajos,' meaning 'in the homeland of the Navajos' or 'Navajo homeland place.'" As for the location of the Dinetah, the book about the Dinetah published by the Navajo Curriculum Center of the Rough Rock Demonstration School says, "In general terms, it is located S and E of Farmington, NM, and includes Blanco, Largo, Carrizo, and Gobernador Canyons. How far E and S it extends is not clearly known."

DIRTY DRAWERS CANYON (Otero; in the Sacramento Mountains, between Cloudcroft and Sunspot). A localism, said to be derived from a woman who lived here whose garments—and reputation—both were soiled.

DISMUKE (Socorro; settlement; 21 mi SW of Magdalena). In 1919 Dewey Dismuke arrived here to homestead, and his ranch headquarters were here; he died in 1979 at the age of 81.

DIXON (Rio Arriba; settlement; on NM 75, 20 mi NE of Española, 2 mi E of NM 68; PO 1900–present). This community is in an area settled by Spaniards in the 17th century and called *Embudo*. Two explanations exist for the name of this locality, once the site of an Indian pueblo. One is that the settlement received the name from 17th-century Spanish settlers because here the Rio Grande is funneled between the steep walls of a gorge; see *Embudo (general)*. The other is that the village was named for its proximity to Embudo Creek (see entry), a stream that flows through a gorge of its own to enter the Rio Grande just W of this community. In the will of Juan Francisco Martín, the village is called *San Antonio del Embudo*. When the D&RG RR built a station near the Rio Grande about 2 mi W of the village, the RR called the station Embudo, which caused great confusion and led to the renaming of the old Embudo settlement to Dixon, in honor of the area's first school teacher, Collin Dixon. See *Embudo.*

DOC LONG PICNIC AREA (Bernalillo; on the E side of the Sandia Mountains, on NM 536). This popular Cibola NF picnic area was named for William Henry "Doc" Long, a USFS forest pathologist– one of three forest pathologists in the country at the time–who worked here from 1910 to the mid-1930s. Long had an experimental station at the site of the picnic area, and he lived here in a cabin.

DODSON (Quay; settlement; 12 mi S of Tucumcari, in the Quay Valley; PO 1901–16, mail to Quay). The Dodson PO was first located about 2 mi E of Lovers Peak, in the home of Eliza L. Robertson, first postmistress. In 1904 it moved several miles to the E, to the home of William Briscoe. Dodson, the origin of whose name is unknown, was a lively community, but it long has been abandoned.

DOG (general). At least 61 places in NM have Dog in their names (GNIS), in-cluding several Dogtowns. History usu-ally has forgotten the specific incidents behind these names, and often the "dogs" referred to are not canines but prairie dogs; see *Tusas (general).*

DOG CANYON (Otero; on the W side of the Sacramento Mountains, 9 mi SE of Alamogordo). While Geronimo was im-prisoned at Fort Sill, OK, he lamented that the white invaders had occupied Dog Canyon. Of all their southern NM campsites, the Apaches were especially fond of this canyon, and it's easy to see why: perennial springs in the canyon's bottom provided Indians and edible plants with life-giving water, while the stark limestone cliffs flanking the can-yon made for effective defense against attackers. At least five battles between the Apaches and Army troops were fought in the canyon, and the canyon was named when troops, pursuing Apaches here, came upon a hastily aban-doned camp, finding only a little dog. See *Oliver Lee Memorial State Park.*

DOG HEAD, 4,916 ft. (Hidalgo; S of Lordsburg, just NE of Pyramid Peak).

Well-known locally for its resemblance to a dog's head.

DOG TOWN (Otero). See *Valmont.*

DOGTOWN (Eddy). See *Seven Rivers.*

DOLORES (general). Places in NM with this name usually commemorate *Nuestra Señora de Dolores,* "Our Lady of Sor-rows," one of the titles of the Virgin Mary.

DOLORES (Santa Fe; settlement; 4 mi SE of Madrid, on the NE side of the Ortiz Mountains; PO as Real de Dolores 1869–70, as Dolores 1887–90, 1894–1901, mail to Santa Fe). The origi-nal name for this site was *Real de Dolores;* in colonial NM *real* referred to a "campsite, headquarters," though it is also was legal title for a mining camp; it's unknown why this term was applied here. *Dolores* is one of the names of the Virgin Mary; see *Dolores (general).* In 1828 placer gold was discovered here, and before long a mining camp sprang up taking the old name, though it soon became simply Dolores or *Old Placers.* Lt. James W. Abert visited here in 1846 and described the place thus: "The houses were the most miserable we had yet seen, and the inhabitants the most abject picture of squalid poverty, and yet the streets of the village are indeed paved with gold." At one time almost 4,000 people lived in the camp, and in 1900 Thomas A. Edison erected a plant in Dolores where he attempted to ex-tract placer gold using static electricity. Numerous rock spoil piles mark the site today. *Dolores Gulch* heads in the Ortiz Mountains and runs NE.

DOLORES (Union; settlement; on Ute Creek, at the Harding County line; PO 1913–14, mail to Pasamonte). Ephemeral community; name origin unknown; see *Dolores (gen-eral).*

THE DOME, 11,336 ft. (Mora, San Miguel; in the Sangre de Cristo Mountains, on the Mora–San Miguel County line, 1.5 mi N of the Rio Medio).

DOME WILDERNESS (Sandoval; in the Jemez Mountains, adjoining Bandelier National Monument on the SW). This 5,200-acre wilderness, the smallest USFS wilderness in the Southwest, takes its name from 8,463-foot *Saint Peters Dome,* name origin unknown, which dominates the landscape here.

DOMINGO (Sandoval; settlement; 3 mi E of Santo Domingo Pueblo, on the AT&SF RR; PO 1909–42, mail to Algodones). Domingo, sometimes called *New Domingo,* began as a settlement on the AT&SF RR and was an important stop between Lamy and Albuquerque; its population in 1884 was 1,000. The locality first was called *Wallace,* to honor former Gov. Lew Wallace, but its PO was called *Annville,* a name chosen by postal officials without consulting local people, who persisted in using the name Wallace. Wallace, however, was too similar to Waldo to the E, so the name was changed to *Thornton,* to honor still another territorial governor. But this is said to have conflicted with the name of still another community, perhaps Thoreham in Roosevelt County. Finally, Domingo was settled upon as the name, for nearby Santo Domingo Pueblo, though by this time the settlement had dwindled to a trading post.

DOMINGUEZ (San Miguel; settlement; near Tecolote). Former community, bearing an Hispanic family name.

DOMINGUEZ (Sandoval; settlement; just N of Cabezon Peak). Locality bearing the name of a family whose members still live in this area.

DON CARLOS CREEK (Union; SW part of county, rises along the Colfax County line and flows S to join Holkeo Creek). According to legend, Don Carlos was a Spanish military officer stationed at Santa Fe charged with controlling the Apaches and Comanches. At an undetermined date he won a decisive battle along the creek now bearing his name.

Don Carlos Hills (Union; in SW part of county, 6 mi NE of Gladstone). These volcanic hills, named like the creek for the Spanish military officer, were popularized in Ernest Thompson Seton's stories "The Pacing Mustang" and "Lobo, King of the Currumpaw."

SIERRA DE DON FERNANDO, 10,365 ft. (Taos). See *Fernando Mountains.*

DOÑA ANA (Doña Ana; settlement; 5 mi N of Las Cruces, 2 mi E of NM 185; PO 1854–55, 1866–present). This is among the most difficult and controversial place names in NM, as persistent efforts have failed to identify definitively the respected woman for whom this community was named. One reason for the difficulty is the name's antiquity; it almost certainly dates from the late 17th century. One account attributes the name to the 80-year-old widow Ana Robledo, granddaughter of Pedro Robledo (see *Robledo*). Fleeing S after the Pueblo Revolt in 1680, she beheld Mount Robledo (see entry), where her grandfather had died. The anguish she experienced was too much for her after the siege of Santa Fe and the arduous journey; a few miles further S she too died, and the place of her burial acquired her name.

But a more likely eponymn was one Doña Ana María de Córdoba, whose ranch was located here. Adolph Bandelier, searching archives in Mexico City, found mention of this Doña Ana in a report dated 1693 by an army officer, Don Gabriel del Castillo, writing from Parral in Chihuahua to Mexico City: "I have just received report of Indian raids in the region of Los Organos where three Spaniards were killed, the raiders then going on to a place called Las Cruces, and stealing stock also at Mesilla, then raiding the ranch of Doña Ana María, Niña de Córdoba."

The locality of Doña Ana was visited by Governor Otermín during his unsuccessful attempt at reconquest in 1682. The area was abandoned throughout the 18th century. In 1839, the governor of Chihuahua, seeking to alleviate crowding in El Paso, granted *El Ancón de Doña Ana* ("the Doña Ana cove, or bend"; this became known as the Doña Ana Bend Colony Grant), but it was not settled until 1843 when Bernabé Montoya led 33 settlers to a site N of present Las Cruces. They named their settlement after the semi-legendary Doña Ana. Many residents moved to Mesilla after the treaty of Guadalupe Hidalgo in 1848. The community gave its name to *Doña Ana County* (see entry) and was the first county seat.

The *Doña Ana Mountains,* 5 mi N of the village of Doña Ana, are a small range running SE-NW; highest elevation *Doña Ana Mountain,* 5,835 ft.

DOÑA ANA COUNTY (S-central NM, bordering Texas and Mexico; county seat, Las Cruces). One of nine counties created by the territorial legislature in 1852. Its first county seat was the village of *Doña Ana* (see entry), hence the name, but in 1853 Las Cruces became the county seat.

DORA (Roosevelt; settlement; at junction of NM 206 and 114, 17 mi S of Portales; PO 1906–present). At least three explanations exist for this village's name. The least widely accepted is that it was named for one Dora Mitchell. More common is the version stating that this site was the homestead of two sisters, one named Dora, whose surname was Lee. But the most widely accepted is that Frederick Humphrey, the community's first postmaster, submitted the name of his daughter, Dora, to the postal authorities when asked for a name for the PO. The settlement was founded in 1905 and originally located 1 mi W and 0.75 mi S of the present site; it was relocated to be near the highway.

DORETTA (San Miguel; settlement; on AT&SF RR, 18 mi SW of Las Vegas; PO 1915–39, mail to Serafina). Former postal locality, name origin unknown.

DORIS (Quay; settlement; 9 mi NW of Quay; 1908–13, mail to Dodson). Abandoned homesteader settlement; name origin unknown.

DORSEY (Colfax; settlement; N of Maxwell, 1 mi W of the Canadian River, near Eagle Tail Mountain; PO 1889–1912, mail to Maxwell). Abandoned settlement, named for *Dorsey Lake* (see entry) to the W.

DORSEY LAKE (Colfax; 9 mi N of Maxwell, 0.5 mi W of NM 455). Named for US Sen. Stephen W. Dorsey of Arkansas, who also had ranching interests in NE NM. See also *Clayton, Chico,* and *Mount Dora.*

DOUGLAS (Quay). See *Tucumcari.*

DOUBTFUL CANYON (Hidalgo; in the Peloncillo Mountains, 19 mi W of Lordsburg, 9 mi N of I-10). In the 19th century, travelers to California taking the route through S NM passed through a canyon in the northern Peloncillo

Mountains that frequently was a site of Apache ambushes. So "doubtful" were the travelers' chances of making it through the canyon unattacked that the gap was called *Doubtful Canyon,* a name it still bears. When the Butterfield Overland Mail route came through here in 1858, the company built a station here called *Steins Peak Station,* for *Steins Peak,* 5,867 ft., at the SW end of the pass. The *East Garrison Relay Station* on the mail route at the E end of Doubtful Canyon was a garrison of soldiers who accompanied west-bound travelers. The station was used by later freighters into the 1870s, but eventually it was abandoned.

DOVER (Colfax). See *Uña de Gato.*

DOWA YALANNE, 7,235 ft. (Cibola; 3 mi SE of Zuni Pueblo). Dowa Yalanne, a Zuni Indian name meaning "corn mountain," is a dramatic 1,000-foot mesa with special significance for the Zunis. For example, it has been a formidable fortress; when Coronado attacked their ancestors in July 1540, the Zunis sought refuge here. They maintain shrines on Dowa Yalanne's flat top, and a Zuni myth associates the mountain with the House of the Gods and the making of rain, lightning, and thunder; this has inspired the name sometimes used by English-speakers, *Thunder Mountain.* The name Dowa Yalanne often has been written *Taaiyalone,* but in 1983 the USBGN established as the accepted form Dowa Yalanne, which closer approximates the Zuni pronunciation. The Navajos' name for the mesa means "rock house."

DOWLINS MILL (Lincoln). See *Ruidoso.*

DOWLINS MILL ROAD (Lincoln, Otero, Chaves, Eddy; extended from Dowlins Mill, now Ruidoso, down Elk Canyon to the Rio Penasco and eventually to Seven Rivers). A major Indian trail, later used by settlers. See *Ruidoso.*

DRAGON RIDGE (Luna; at NW end of the Florida Mountains, SE of Deming). Conspicuous jagged ridge.

DRIPPING SPRING (general). A common and obvious descriptive name, occurring on at least 12 NM springs. The Spanish equivalent, *gotera*, occurs four times.

DRIPPING SPRING (De Baca; 4 mi NW of Taiban and 2 mi N of US 60-84, flows into Red Lake). At one time called *Wilcox Springs* after a cattleman who made it his headquarters, Dripping Spring (the name often appears in the plural) and the lake it feeds were stops for travelers and cattledrivers. Billy the Kid and Charley Bowdre spent the night here after Tom O'Folliard was shot near Fort Sumner.

DRIPPING SPRING (Sierra; settlement; in the N San Andres Mountains, just W of Salinas Peak; PO 1892–93, mail to Lava). Nothing remains of this primitive settlement, once a site on the road connecting Fort Stanton with the Rio Grande Valley. Jack Crawford, a colorful local personality, had his ranch here.

DRIPPING SPRING (Socorro; settlement; at the W entrance to Abo Pass). Tiny inhabited settlement, named for the spring 0.25 mi to the W.

DRIPPING SPRINGS (Doña Ana; near Ice Canyon in the W Organ Mountains E of Las Cruces). Water from this spring flows in a scenic waterfall over a sheer rock face, making it a pleasant place to escape summer's heat, so much so that in the late 1870s Maj. Eugene B. Van Patten built a resort hotel here called the *Dripping Springs Hotel*. Van Patten was a colorful figure, an Indian fighter and former major in the Confederate army, and the site of his hotel often was referred to as *Van Pattens*. The hotel is in ruins now, but Dripping Springs is still a popular destination for local people. It's now administered by the BLM as part of the Organ Mountains Recreation Area.

DRIPPING SPRINGS (Union; in NE part of county, in a cave in Peacock Canyon). Named for water dripping from stalactites.

DROLET (San Juan). See *Naschitti.*

DRY (general). A common descriptive name element in NM, though not a very precise one, as it's not uncommong for many NM water bodies to be dry at least part of the year. GNIS lists 71 places named Dry. The Spanish equivalent is *Seco,* listed 50 times.

DRY CIMARRON RIVER (Colfax, Union; heads at the E base of Johnson Mesa, flows E across the N part of Union County into Oklahoma, then into Kansas, eventually to join the Arkansas River near Tulsa). Most US maps label this simply as the *Cimarron River,* the term Dry Cimarron being used only in NM, likely to describe it but also to distinguish it from the Cimarron River (see entry) that flows past Cimarron to join the Canadian River E of Springer. Other names have been *Cimarron Creek* and *Oak Creek,* but in 1969 the USBGN accepted Dry Cimarron.

DRY GULCH (Lincoln). See *Nogal.*

DUG SPRINGS (Lea; 20 mi S of Monument Springs, SW of Eunice). These were three springs, a few yards apart, that Indians had dug out into wells six feet deep and four feet across. Col. William R. Shafter saw the springs in 1875 and named them. They were important landmarks on the arid Llano Estacado.

DULCE (Rio Arriba; settlement; on US 64, 26 mi W of Chama; PO 1892–present). Spanish, "sweet." This settlement, headquarters and trading center of the Jicarilla Apache Reservation, takes its name from *Dulce Spring,* a spring of sweet water located 4 mi S of the town. The settlement was established in 1883 when the reservation headquarters were moved from Amargo (see entry), whose name, in contrast to Dulce, means "bitter." *Dulce Lake* is 4 mi S of Dulce, at Dulce Spring.

DUNKEN (Chaves; settlement; in SW part of county, on NM 24; PO 1908–19, mail to Hope). This isolated inhabited community takes its name from Oscar J. Dunken, founder and first postmaster.

DUNLAP (De Baca; settlement; on NM 20, 34 mi SW of Fort Sumner; PO 1907–61, mail to a Roswell rural station). Dunlap was born during the homesteading boom of the early 20th century, and like many similar communities it faded when homesteaders could not make a living on their claims and moved on. It took its name from W.O. Dunlap, the community's founder, who located homestead sites for many early settlers. Though the settlement is gone, an active church remains, and rural people here still identify themselves as residents of Dunlap.

DUNNAHOO HILLS (Chaves; NE of Roswell, just N of US 70). Though this name has appeared as *Donahue, Donahoo,* and *Dunahoo,* the correct form, as established by the USBGN in 1964, is Dunnahoo, for a local family with that surname.

DUNNS CROSSING (Taos; on the Rio Grande, W of Arroyo Hondo). This local landmark, among the few places to cross the Rio Grande in northern NM and now a popular put-in site for rafters, was named for "Long John" Dunn, who operated a toll bridge here around 1905 and built the first road.

DUORO (Guadalupe; RR depot and PO; on the AT&SF RR, 18 mi SE of Vaughn; PO 1922–44, mail to East Vaughn). Abandoned settlement, name origin unknown.

DURAN (general). As early as 1628 a Juan Durán is mentioned as being in NM, the husband of Catalina Bernal, daughter of Juan Griego. But this Durán probably arrived even earlier, with the 1598 Oñate expedition, then using the name Juan de la Cruz; he was nineteen then and described as tall, swarthy, and beardless. He very likely adopted the Durán surname to avoid confusion with another Juan de la Cruz. Persons with the Durán surname were among the Spaniards who fled NM during the Pueblo Revolt of 1680; some of them returned after the reconquest of 1692. GNIS lists 20 features named either Duran or Duranes.

DURAN (Torrance; settlement; at junction of NM 3 and US 54, 15 mi SW of Vaughn; PO 1902–present). Duran was named for two brothers, Blas and Espiridón Durán. They owned the *Moreno Wells* from whence the EP&SW RR obtained water for work crews. The RR activity spawned a little settlement, but when the RR moved its shops to Carrizozo, Duran began to wither, and little remains now beyond a few families and the PO.

LOS DURANES (Bernalillo; settlement; about 1 mi N of Old Town in Albuquer-que). This was one of several hamlets, most of them named for a dominant family, that surrounded early Albuquerque. Estevan Durán, a native of San Buenaventura, near the present city of Chihuahua, settled in the Rio Abajo after the reconquest of 1692 and may be associated with this community, but a Juan Bautista Durán, of European origin, was listed as living in the Albuquerque area in 1740. He was a merchant, and his descendants could have been the nucleus for the community.

DURAZNO (Rio Arriba). See *Rinconada.*

DURFEE (Socorro; settlement; in the N San Mateo Mountains, at the mouth of Durfee Canyon). A small settlement and store were here in 1897; name origin unknown.

DUSTY (Socorro; settlement; in SW corner of county, on NM 52; PO 1927–48, 1950–?). Socorro County has two communities whose names, one in Spanish and the other in English, both refer to "dust"—Polvadera (see entry) N of Socorro and this isolated ranching community.

DUTCH SPRING (Chaves). See *South Spring.*

DUTCHMAN LAKE (Curry). See *Greene Lake.*

DUTCHMANS CANYON (Colfax; heads 8 mi NW of Raton and runs SE into Dillon Canyon). This canyon takes its name from a man who lived in the canyon when mining operations started at Blossburg. Despite the name, the man's national origin is uncertain, as in the American West of the 1800s, any non-English northern European tended to be known as a "Dutchman."

DWYER (Grant; settlement; on NM 61 and the Mimbres River, SE of Silver City; PO 1895–1917, mail to Swarts). *San Jose* was this locality's original name—the church here still bears that name—but when the PO that had been at Faywood moved here it took the surname of G.W. Dwyer, who homesteaded here in 1883.

DZILNTSAHAH (San Juan; fronts San Juan River W of the mouth of Largo Canyon). Navajo, "big mountain," a landform sacred to the Navajos and important in their folklore.

E-TOWN (Colfax). See *Elizabethtown.*

EAGLE (general). NM's two species of eagles—the golden and the less common bald—are dramatic, conspicuous birds, and it's not surprising GNIS lists 69 places named Eagle, including 9 Eagle Nests. The Spanish *aguila* is less common but occurs in such names as Sierra Aguilada (see entry).

EAGLE CREEK (Lincoln; heads in the White Mountain Wilderness and flows SE through Alto into Little Creek). Named for the Eagle Mining and Milling Co. Eagle Creek has been mentioned as being the original name of Alto (see entry).

EAGLE HILL (Roosevelt; settlement; 8 mi NW of Milnesand; PO 1914–18, mail to Valley View). Abandoned settlement, named for a high chalk hill on the DZ Ranch, 0.5 mi S of the settlement, where many eagles roosted.

EAGLE NEST (Colfax; settlement; at junction of US 64 and NM 38; PO as Therma 1920–35, as Eagle Nest 1935–present). This community in the Moreno Valley owed its existence and eventually its name to *Eagle Nest Lake,* created in 1919. The town began when Talmadge D. Neal arrived from Oklahoma that year and saw an opportunity to open a store and PO at the newly relocated Cimarron, Taos, and Red River roads; before that, the nearest mail and shopping facilities were at Elizabethtown, a nearly deserted mining camp 5 mi away. The PO, established in Neal's store, was named *Therma,* for the daughter of the postal inspector who had helped Neal establish the PO. Soon fishermen and tourists began to arrive, attracted by the lake, and by 1922 a small but growing town had sprung up, along with an un- savory reputation as a wide-open gambling town. In 1935 gambling was outlawed, the PO got a new postmaster, and the town's name was changed to Eagle Nest, to conform to that of the lake and perhaps also to improve the town's image.

EAGLE NEST LAKE (Colfax; at the head of Cimarron Canyon, immediately S of the town of Eagle Nest). Sometime before 1919 Charles Springer, an influential rancher near Cimarron (see *Springer*), acquired land in the Moreno Valley and undertook to build a dam for irrigation. The project was completed in 1919, and the reservoir was named Eagle Nest Lake. The name is said to have been inspired by the region being where members of several Indian tribes came to collect eagle feathers for ceremonies. Springer stocked the reservoir with trout, and soon it became popular with fishermen and tourists, giving rise to the settlement of *Eagle Nest* (see entry) just to the N.

EAGLE TAIL MOUNTAIN, 7,761 ft. (Colfax; 13 mi S of Raton, just E of I-25). This name and that of nearby Tinaja Mountain (see entry) are said to have been bestowed by drivers on the Santa Fe Trail, which passed near here, and indeed it's not difficult, especially when viewing this broad mesa from the N and NW, to imagine the graceful fan of an eagle's tail. *Eagle Tail Creek* heads on the mountain's NE side. *Eagle Tail Mesa* also is nearby.

EARLHAM (Doña Ana). See *Vado.*

EAST CAMP (Grant; settlement; in NW part of county, near the Arizona line; PO 1940–42, mail to Duncan, AZ). Abandoned settlement, name origin unknown.

EAST GARRISON (Hidalgo). See *Steins Pass.*

EAST GRAND PLAINS (Chaves; settlement; 6 mi SE of Roswell, 2 mi E of NM 2 on NM 253). The name simply describes this active farming community. *West Grand Plains,* now abandoned, was about 4 mi to the W.

EAST LAS VEGAS (San Miguel). See *Las Vegas.*

EAST POTRILLO MOUNTAINS (Doña Ana). See *Potrillo Mountains.*

EAST VAUGHN (Guadalupe; settlement; 1 mi E of Vaughn; PO 1911–73, mail to Vaughn). This community has merged with *West Vaughn* to become simply *Vaughn* (see entry).

EASTERN NEW MEXICO STATE PARK (Roosevelt; on US 70, 9 mi S of Clovis). The only state park to be abandoned after its creation, this originally was part of a large federal relief project to reforest 9,600 acres in the Dust Bowl. The state legislature, however, reduced it to 400 acres. Though the park's facilities and attractions were many, it had financial problems, and finally in 1951 the state deeded the property to Eastern NM University, which built a sports stadium and the Blackwater Draw Museum (see *Blackwater Draw*).

EASTSIDE (eastern NM). This is the term widely used in NM to designate the eastern portion of the state, topographically and culturally distinct from other regions of the state.

EASTVIEW (Torrance; settlement; 10 mi NW of Mountainair; PO 1890–1919, mail to Torreon). This abandoned settlement in the foothills of the Manzano Mountains was settled by two families: B.B. Spencer arrived in 1879 and August Kayser in 1891. The inspiration of the name was the view eastward across the Estancia Valley.

ECHO AMPHITHEATER (Rio Arriba; on US 84, 17 mi NW of Abiquiu). Here a picturesque concavity in sandstone cliffs creates prolonged echoes. A USFS campground is nearby.

ECHO CANYON (Bernalillo; heads N from Tijeras Canyon into the SW Sandia Mountains, 2 mi E of Albuquerque). Small box canyon, with echogenic walls.

EDDY (Eddy). See *Carlsbad.*

EDDY COUNTY (SE NM; county seat, Carlsbad). Eddy County was created in 1889 from Lincoln County and like its county seat— Carlsbad, then named Eddy—it bore the surname of Charles B. Eddy, who along with his brother, J. Arthur Eddy, played a major role in the region's development. Charles was born in Milford, NY, in 1857 and moved west to Colorado and then to SE NM. He acquired cattle interests, but above all he was a promoter and has been described as a man who "lived dreams, fastened on ideas, promoted them, got men and capital interested, lived to see many of his dreams come true." One of his dreams was the Carlsbad Irrigation Project. Another was the RR that linked Carlsbad with Pecos, TX. He and his brother also were instrumental in the development of the Tularosa Valley, particularly the construction of the EP&NE RR northward from El Paso (see *Alamogordo*). In 1917, the eastern part of Eddy County became Lea County.

EDEN (Guadalupe; settlement; 8 mi N of Santa Rosa, on the E side of the Pecos River; PO 1885–94, mail to Santa Rosa). Eden never was much more than a RR section house with a PO, and now it's not even that. The name's origin is unknown, though where this name appears elsewhere in the US it often commemorates a family name and not necessarily the biblical garden.

EDEN VALLEY (Chaves; about 10 mi N of Roswell, just E of US 285). When this area was settled, it was green and fertile, soon planted with orchards and alfalfa. Robert Goddard conducted many pioneer rocket experiments here.

EDEN VALLEY (Lea; settlement; 8 mi W of Hobbs). Eden Valley, now abandoned, once was an active community that in 1909 had a Sunday school with an enrollment of 41. The name presumably was inspired by high hopes for the settlement's future.

EDGEWOOD (Santa Fe; settlement; at

junction of I-40 and NM 344, 20 mi E of Albuquerque; PO as Barton 1908–36, as Edgewood 1936–present). Edgewood has been known by many names: first *Venus,* then *Mountain View,* then *New Barton,* and finally its present name, which accurately describes its location, at the edge of the wooded hills where the grassy plains to the E meet the forested Sandia Mountains to the W.

EDITH (Rio Arriba; settlement; NE of Dulce, at the Colorado line, where the Navajo River enters NM; PO 1904–09, transferred to Colorado). Abandoned sawmill and lumber town, name origin unknown.

EICHEL (Lincoln; settlement; on the EP&RI RR, NE of Ancho; PO 1906–13, mail to Ancho). Former RR station and PO, name origin unknown.

EIGHTMILE DRAW (Chaves; 8 mi W of Roswell, emptying into South Berrendo Creek). Nearby are *Fourmile Draw, Fivemile Draw, Thirteenmile Draw, Fifteenmile Draw,* and *Sixmile Hill.* Map measurements indicate these names relate to the distances of these features from Roswell and not their lengths.

EIGHTEEN MILE HILL (De Baca; 25 mi S of Fort Sumner, 18 mi S of Old Fort Sumner). This was along an old stage route, named for its distance from Old Fort Sumner; stages would make a steep ascent here. Nearby are *Eighteenmile Draw* and, on the Pecos River, *Eighteenmile Bend.*

EIGHTY MOUNTAIN (Grant; 4 mi N of Silver City). Name is derived from the Eighty Ranch, just S of the mountain.

EILAND (Roosevelt; settlement; 5 mi SW of Arch; PO 1909–18, mail to Portales). Abandoned settlement, named for Thomas C. Eiland.

EL BARRANCO (Rio Arriba; 2 mi W of Abiquiu, S of NM 96). This inhabited Hispanic community's Spanish name— see *Barranca (general)*—aptly describes the hamlet's location abutting cliffs here. In 1735 a land grant known as the *Barranca Grant* was made to Gerónimo Martín and others.

EL BARRANCO (Rio Arriba; 1 mi N of Los Brazos, N of Tierra Amarilla). This van-

ished settlement was among several temporary, seasonal settlements in the early Tierra Amarilla, when Indian danger forbade permanent settlements. It was named for the *El Barranco* (see entry) near Abiquiu from which its settlers had come. The community was abandoned as early as 1859, for an American expedition then reported finding only ruins at "a charming spot at the forks of the Chama, where the Mexicans had formerly a settlement, now abandoned on account of the depredations of the Indians."

EL BOSQUE (Rio Arriba). See *Lyden.*

EL CURUCO (Rio Arriba; settlement; 0.25 mi W of Abiquiu). Tiny "suburb" of Abiquiu, whose name means "the tick," for reasons unknown. See also *Curuco Town.*

EL CUERVO (San Miguel; settlement; in E part of county, exact location unknown; PO 1888–92, mail to Bell Ranch). Spanish, "the crow." Abandoned settlement, name origin unknown, though it probably was derived from *Cuervo Creek,* an intermittent stream that flows into Conchas Lake from the S. The settlement of El Cuervo possibly was along this creek.

EL DADO MESA, CANYON, SPRING, PEAK, 6,915 ft. (McKinley; in SE part of county, 15 mi NE of San Mateo). These took their name from the *El Dado stage stop,* earlier called *Willow Springs,* located near *El Dado Spring* at the head of *El Dado Canyon,* S of *El Dado Mesa.* Local lore has it that the stage stop acquired the name El Dado (Spanish, "the die") because of a station keeper who would shake dice with passengers for drinks. The dice were loaded, the station keeper always won.

EL DUENDE (Rio Arriba; settlement; N of Hernandez, near the junction of US 84 and 285). Spanish, "the elf, the imp, the dwarf." But why this inhabited Hispanic community has this intriguing name is unknown. Its more formal name is *San Francisco el Duende.*

EL GUACHO (Rio Arriba; settlement; on the W bank of the Rio Grande, just E of US 285 and N of NM 584, about 1 mi

NW of Española). Tiny inhabited locality, whose name often appears as *El
Guache.* The settlement's original formal
name was *San Pedro del Guache. Guache*
sounds like a Tewa loan-word, but no
specific Tewa source has been found.
Tewas call the locality "owl dell." *Guacho*
is New World Spanish, "orphan, found-
ling," but it also can mean "furrow."
Which, if either, applies to this community is unknown.

EL GUIQUE (Rio Arriba; settlement; 2 mi
N of San Juan Pueblo, W of the Rio
Grande, opposite Alcalde; PO 1906–12,
mail to Chamita). This name likely is
derived from a Tewa name, not identi-
fied. Eighteenth-century records men-
tion a pueblo bearing this name or one
of several variants: *San Rafael del
Quiqui, San Antonio del Bequiu del
Guyqui, Guique,* and *Hique.* In 1765, one
Antonio Abeytie said in his will that he
lived at *San Antonio del Bequiu del
Guyqui.* The locality survives as El
Guique.

EL LLANO (Rio Arriba; settlement; on NM
291, 2 mi NE of Española). Small inhabited community. See *Llano (general).*

EL LLANO (San Miguel; settlement; on
NM 65, 0.5 mi SE of Montezuma). Tiny
inhabited residential cluster, located on
the edge of "the plain." See *Llano (general).*

EL MALPAIS NATIONAL MONUMENT
(Cibola; S and W of Grants). Created in
1987 and administered by the National
Park Service, this 115,000-acre area features geological and archaeological sites
associated with the dramatic lava formations created by 3 million years of volcanic activity in this valley. Adjoining the
national monument is *El Malpais National Conservation Area,* administered
by the BLM. For generations, this area
has been known as *El Malpais,* a term
that in NM refers to land overlain by
lava flows; see *Malpais (general).* See also
West Malpais Wilderness and *Cebolla
Wilderness.*

EL MORRO NATIONAL MONUMENT
(Cibola; on NM 53, 42 mi SW of
Grants). *El Morro* is Spanish and simply
means "the bluff, headland," but the

Zuni name for the ruined village atop
this 200-foot sandstone butte is more
descriptive of the feature's significance.
The Zunis call the ruins *Atsinna,* "writing upon the rocks," not far removed
from the butte's English name, *Inscription Rock,* as is the butte's Navajo name,
which means "rock upon which there is
writing."

As a landmark on the ancient Zuni-
Acoma trail El Morro and its deep pool
of fresh water were well-known to prehistoric Indians, who carved
petroglpyhs, likely religious symbols,
into the rock faces. The Indians were
succeeded by early Spanish explorers,
who incised into the soft sandstone me-
mentoes of their visits. The first Spanish
inscription reads: *Paso por aquí el
adelantado Don Juan de Oñate al
descubrimiento de la mar del sur a 16 de
Abril de 1605,* "There passed by here the
Governor Don Juan de Oñate from the
discovery of the sea of the south [Gulf of
California] on the 16th of April, 1605."
Subsequently, hundreds of other inscrip-
tions commemorated visits by missionaries, soldiers, traders, emigrants, and
tourists.

EL MORRO (Cibola; settlement; immediately E of El Morro National Monument;
PO 1927–63, mail to Ramah). Settlement associated with and named for the
famous butte.

EL MORRO MESA (De Baca; 10 mi SW of
Yeso). Spanish, "the butte, headland."

EL PASO GAP (Eddy; trading point; in SW
corner of county, on NM 137, 6 mi N of
the Texas line). This locality, which once
included a school, was settled by Sam
Hughes, who came to the Guadalupe
Mountains from Texas in 1941 and
staked claims. The gap, 5,494 ft., is a
natural break in *El Paso Ridge,* 5,874 ft.,
which runs N-S.

EL PORVENIR (San Miguel; settlement; on
NM 65, 17 mi NW of Las Vegas; PO as
Porvenir 1896–99, 1907–22, as El
Porvenir 1928–66, mail to Montezuma).
Around 1890 Margarito Romero, a Las
Vegas merchant, admired the beauty of
this site on Beaver Creek, and with ro-
mantic enthusiasm he gave the place a

Spanish name meaning "the future." He built a resort hotel here that was very popular. The community that grew up around the resort still enjoys the site's beauty. A monolith near the village also has taken the name, as has *Porvenir Canyon* to the NW.

EL PRADO (Taos; settlement; on US 64, 2 mi NW of Taos; PO 1936–present). Spanish, "the meadow." The name reflects the agricultural origins of this community, now closely associated with Taos.

EL RANCHO DE LAS GOLONDRINAS (Santa Fe; settlement, historic site; E of I-25, 9 mi SW of Santa Fe). During the 18th and 19th centuries, El Rancho de las Golondrinas, "the ranch of the swallows," was either the first or last stop from Santa Fe for travelers on the Camino Real. The site was acquired in 1710 by Miguel Vega y Coca. Today, the ranch buildings have been restored, and El Rancho de las Golondrinas is operated as a living museum depicting early Hispanic culture in NM.

EL RINCON DE LOS TRUJILLOS (Rio Arriba; settlement; 1 mi E of Chimayo). Inhabited settlement, "the corner, or homestead, of the Trujillos."

EL RITO (Cibola; settlement; on the Laguna Indian Reservation, about 2 mi SE of Mesita). This tiny community, now abandoned, was located on the N bank of the Rio San Jose, "the creek" for which it was named; see *Rio, Rito (general)*. The community endured throughout much of the 19th century and was mentioned by American travelers then.

EL RITO (Rio Arriba; settlement; on NM 554, 14 mi NW of Ojo Caliente; PO 1870–present). This old Hispanic community, now home to many artists, originally was named *El Rito Colorado,* "the red creek," taking its name from the creek that passes through the village; see *Rio, Rito (general)*. Tewas call the El Rito region "pink below place," for the *El Rito Mountains,* known to them as the "pink mountains."

EL RITO (Sandoval). See *Bandelier National Monument.*

EL TURQUILLO (Mora; settlement; on NM 434, 11 mi NE of Mora; PO 1910–13, mail to Guadalupita). Spanish, "little Turk," tiny inhabited community, name origin unknown.

EL VADO (Rio Arriba; settlement; 14 mi SW of Tierra Amarilla, beneath El Vado Lake; PO 1904–08, 1916–28, mail to Tierra Amarilla). *El Vado* is Spanish for "the crossing," and in the late 19th century a community sprouted at a ford here on the Rio Chama wide and shallow enough for horses, wagons, and narrow-gauge trains to cross easily. El Vado, as the settlement was called, grew rapidly and soon was a bustling RR and lumber center, served by several narrow-gauge RR lines, but it later faded in importance; it was doomed with the creation of *El Vado Lake.* Today, a tiny resort community on the lake has the name El Vado, but it's a shadow of the former settlement.

EL VADO LAKE STATE PARK (Rio Arriba; off NM 112, 14 mi SW of Tierra Amarilla). In 1935 the impoundment of the Rio Chama by the new *El Vado Dam* created *El Vado Lake,* drowning the site of what had been northern Rio Arriba County's largest town, El Vado (see entry). But though the town and the ford for which it had been named vanished, the name remained. In 1962 the state park was established, including all of the lake and 1,729 acres of land along the NE shoreline.

EL VALLE (Taos; settlement; in SE part of county, 3 mi SE of Trampas). Spanish, "the valley." Inhabited community in the valley of the Rio de las Trampas.

ELDORADO (Lea; settlement; 6 mi N of Jal). This was a new townsite, promoted in 1934 and named optimistically for the mythical city of gold. The town's reality proved as elusive as that of its eponymn, and the development failed.

ELDORADO AT SANTA FE (Santa Fe; settlement; 5 mi SSE of Santa Fe, 2 mi SW of the junction of US 285 and I-25). This modern residential development, located on lands included in the Cañada de los Alamos Grant (see *Cañada de los Alamos*) bears a name that the Spanish in the New World used to refer to any region rich in gold or opportunity.

ELENA GALLEGOS PICNIC AREA
(Bernalillo; in the W foothills of the
Sandia Mountains, fronting Pino Canyon). Eleña Gallegos was a member of a
family that returned to NM in 1692 with
the reconquest, and in 1699 she married
one Santiago Gurulé. A dozen years later
Governor Peñuela granted to Capt. Diego Montoya lands between Sandia
Pueblo's S boundary and the N boundary of the Villa de Alburquerque, including the hamlet known as Ranchos de
Albuquerque; the grant extended E to
the crest of the Sandia Mountains. In the
meantime, Gurulé died, and soon afterward Montoya conveyed his lands to
Gurulé's widow, who according to custom had returned to using her maiden
name. Subsequently, the lands became
known as the *Eleña Gallegos Grant* and
included 70,000 acres. Eleña Gallegos
died in 1731, after asking in her will that
she be interred in Albuquerque's parish
church and transferring her lands to her
son, Antonio Gurulé. Eventually, much
of the land was acquired by Albert
Simms and given to Albuquerque Academy. In the 1980s, acting under the possibility that the mountainous portion of
the grant might be sold to developers,
Albuquerque voters approved a quarter-
cent sales tax to purchase the land. That
part of the grant now is administered by
the USFS and the City of Albuquerque.

ELEPHANT BUTTE (Sierra; toward the S
end of Elephant Butte Reservoir). It
takes only a little imagination, especially
when viewing from the S, to see an elephant in this gray, humpbacked mass
rising from the waters of Elephant Butte
Reservoir (see entry). The butte's name
has been applied as well to a settlement,
the reservoir, and the state park, as well
as to numerous commercial establish-
ments.

Several other features in NM also are
named for their supposed resemblances
to an elephant:

Elephant Mountain, 8,020 ft. (Socorro; 3 mi
S of Magdalena);

Elephant Mountain, 4,675 ft. (Otero; 3 mi
NW of Orogrande);

Elephant Rock, (Union; in E part of county,
near Corrumpa Creek);

Elephant Rock, (Taos; 7 mi E of Questa).

ELEPHANT BUTTE (Sierra; settlement; on
NM 51, at the S end of Elephant Butte
Reservoir; PO 1910–20, mail to Engle,
1935–present). This inhabited settlement, like the reservoir, was named for
the prominent butte (see entry).

ELEPHANT BUTTE ESTATES (Sierra;
settlement; 2 mi NE of Truth or Consequences). Modern inhabited residential
area, named for the butte (see entry).

ELEPHANT BUTTE LAKE STATE PARK
(Sierra; on the SW side of Elephant
Butte Reservoir). Created in 1965 and
named for the reservoir that is its main
feature, this state park is the most
heavily used in NM, receiving more than
a million visitors a year for boating, fishing, swimming, picnicking, and camping.

ELEPHANT BUTTE RESERVOIR (Sierra;
on the Rio Grande, at its junction with
Alamosa Creek). Plans to build a large
dam on the Rio Grande here began as
early as 1896 but were stalled because of
legal challenges by Texas, which feared
loss of water. Construction finally com-
menced in 1911; the dam was completed
in 1916 and named for the prominent
butte (see entry) just upstream. At the
time the dam was the largest in the
world, and the reservoir was the largest
water impoundment in the US. The impact of this water storage project has
been enormous. Not only did the dam
create a lake 40 mi long, with 200 miles
of shoreline, but also it transformed the
economy and culture of the Mesilla Valley to the S, where repeated floods had
impeded settlement and farming of the
rich Rio Grande floodplain.

ELIDA (Roosevelt; settlement; in SW part
of county, at the junction of US 70 and
NM 330 and 114, 24 mi SW of Portales;
PO 1902–present). At least three explanations exist for this name. One is that
John H. Gee, who platted and sold lots
in the town in 1902, named it by combining the first names of two daughters,
Ella and Ida. (Early settlers deny these
daughters ever existed.) Another version

reports Gee as saying he found a stake in the ground with a name "Elida" on it and for reasons he couldn't explain he adopted the name for the settlement. Still another version is that a construction engineer named the place for his hometown in Ohio, and indeed an Elida exists in Allen County there.

ELIZABETH PEAK (Colfax). See *Baldy Mountain.*

ELIZABETHTOWN (Colfax; settlement; at the N end of the Moreno Valley, on Moreno Creek, on NM 38, 4 mi N of Eagle Nest; PO 1868–1931, mail to Therma, now Eagle Nest). Prospectors swarming over Baldy Mountain in the 1860s soon congregated into a tent camp here, called *Virginia City* for the Nevada boom town. By 1868 John W. Moore and others had established a townsite; Moore built the first house and store, and the new town was named for Moore's daughter, Elizabeth. Elizabethtown became the first incorporated town in NM, and also was Colfax County's first seat, but people in the area familiarly referred to the settlement as *E-town.* Eventually the mining that created Elizabethtown dwindled, and lacking other resources Elizabethtown became a ghost town.

ELK (general). Throughout their range in the West, elk have inspired place names. GNIS lists 19 Elk names in NM; curiously, the Spanish form, *alce,* does not appear in any.

ELK (Chaves; settlement; in SW part of county, on US 82, 29 mi E of Cloudcroft; PO 1894–1958, mail to Artesia). Elk was established in the mid-1870s by Billy Matthews (see *Matthews Canyon*), William Walker Paul, Thomas C. Tillotson, and Frank, Al, and Austin Coe. The community received its name when Angie Hendrix Cleve chose it for the new PO. At that time, large herds of elk traveled down *Elk Canyon* (see entry) to water on the Rio Peñasco. Since then, the elk population has shrunk, and so has the human population of Elk.

ELK CANYON (Chaves, Lincoln; heads in the Sacramento Mountains SE of Mescalero and runs SE, paralleling NM 244 through Elk to join the Rio Peñasco). Named for large elk herds here.

ELK MOUNTAIN, 11,661 ft. (San Miguel; in the Las Vegas Range, on the E side of the Pecos Valley). A bare-topped summit, sometimes called *Rincon Peak*—see *Rincon (general)*—on older maps.

ELK MOUNTAINS (Catron; part of the Mogollon Plateau complex, S of the Plains of San Agustin, on the Continental Divide). Highest elevation, *Elk Mountain,* 9,799 ft.

ELK SPRINGS (Otero; settlement; in the N Sacramento Mountains, in Elk Canyon, on NM 244). Small cluster of houses in the Mescalero Apache Indian Reservation, in what would be good elk habitat.

ELKINS (Chaves; settlement; 37 mi NE of Roswell on US 70; PO 1907–43, 1945–72, mail to Clovis). Though a few government buildings are here, little else would suggest that this was once an active community. Its name, like that of the Elkins in Colfax County (see entry), may be commemorative of Stephen B. Elkins, territorial delegate to Congress, 1873–77, ardent advocate of statehood, and later chairman of the Republican National Committee and holder of other political posts.

ELKINS (Colfax; settlement; in NW part of the county, in the valley of the Vermejo River; PO 1876–1900, mail to Catskill). Abandoned community, once the center for stockmen in the valley. Name probably honors Stephen B. Elkins; see *Elkins (Chaves).*

ELLIS CREEK (Bernalillo). See *Las Huertas Creek.*

ELMENDORF (Socorro; settlement; 1 mi E of US 85, on AT&SF RR, 20 mi S of Socorro; PO 1906–18, mail to San Antonio). The Elmendorf brothers once managed a large general store and PO here; Charles H. Elmendorf served as first postmaster. But the flood of 1929 destroyed most of the buildings, and today Elmendorf is but an isolated RR siding.

ELOTA (Sandoval; locality; on the AT&SF

RR N of Algodones). This was a RR station that connected with the line eventually contructed to Hagan. The name's meaning is unknown.

ELVA (Chaves; settlement; NE of Roswell, on the E side of the Pecos River; PO 1910–16, mail to Acme). Abandoned settlement, name origin unknown.

ELVIRA (Guadalupe; settlement; on De Baca County line and Salado Creek, 10 mi W of the Pecos River; PO 1908–24, mail to Puerto de Luna). Abandoned community, once the site of a rural school. Named for the daughter of Jésus María Casaus, a representative in the second state legislature.

EMBERSON (Union; settlement; in SE part of county, S of Amistad; PO 1908–09, mail to Centerville). Little is known of this ephemeral community, including the origin of its name.

EMBUDO (general). Spanish, "funnel," a fairly common metaphor for canyons passing through a narrow defile, as through the neck of a funnel. The diminutive is *embudito*. Albuquerque examples include *Embudo Canyon* on the W side of the Sandia Mountains, S of *Embudito Canyon*. GNIS lists 9 *embudo* names; curiously, the English form is absent.

EMBUDO (Rio Arriba; settlement; between Taos and Española, at the junction of NM 68 and 75; PO 1881–1902, 1905–09, 1914–present). The present settlement of Embudo is not the original one; that older settlement was renamed Dixon (see entry), to end confusion that resulted when the D&RG RR named its "Chili Line" station here Embudo and a settlement sprang up around it; the complex of RR structures on the W bank of the Rio Grande now is known as the *Embudo Historic District*. Also a part of the district is the *Embudo Gaging Station*. In 1889 John Wesley Powell, the famous explorer, established the original station, the first of its kind anywhere, for the USGS. The present station still measures the flow of the Rio Grande here. The locality now known as Embudo appears on some maps as *La Cienaga*—

see *Cienaga, Cienega (general)*—with Embudo simply the PO, though on other maps La Cienaga appears as a "suburb" of Embudo, just N of NM 68. See *Dixon*.

EMBUDO CREEK (Rio Arriba, Taos; formed near the W end of the Peñasco Valley by the flowing together of the Rio Pueblo and the Rio Santa Barbara; the combined stream then flows NW and W to join the Rio Grande above Embudo). This creek is believed to take its name from a narrow, funnel-like gap about a mile W of Picuris Pueblo; see *Embudo (general)*. The stream also has been labeled the *Embudo River, Río de Peñasco*, and *Río Peñasco*, but in 1959 the USBGN established Embudo Creek as the accepted form.

EMERY (Bernalillo; settlement; in N part of county, exact location unknown; PO 1891–92, mail to Bernalillo). Ephemeral postal locality, name origin unknown.

EMERY GAP (Union; extends from Colorado through mountains into the Dry Cimarron country, 7.5 mi E of the Colfax County line, on NM 551). In 1862 Madison Emery, with his wife, Susanne, and two step-children, Sarah Jane and Bud Sumpter, attempted freighting produce from their home along the Dry Cimarron River to Denver. The gap where they entered Colorado now bears their name, as does Emery Peak (see entry), as well as the settlement of Emery Gap (see entry), associated with the pass and named for it. The pass formerly had been known as *Cimarron Pass*. See also *Madison*.

EMERY GAP (Union; settlement; at Emery Gap; PO 1906–08, 1909, 1925, mail to Branson, CO). Abandoned settlement, named for the pass (see entry).

EMERY PEAK, 7,322 ft. (Union; on the S bank of the Dry Cimarron River, 4 mi NE of Folsom, 8 mi S of Emery Gap). Like the abandoned settlement of Madison at its base, this was named for Madison Emery. See *Madison* and *Emery Gap*.

EMORY PASS (Sierra; in the southern Black Range, on NM 152). In 1846 Lt. William H. Emory of the Topographical Engineers, guided by Kit Carson, crossed the Black Range with the Army of the West at the pass now bearing his name. Emory wrote *Notes of a Military Reconnaissance from Fort Leavenworth in Missouri to San Diego in California.* The pass has been known by several names, including *Black Range Divide, Iron Creek Divide, Kingston Pass, Whitetail Pass,* and *Wrights Cabin Pass,* but in 1939 the USBGN approved the name Emory Pass.

EMZY (Roosevelt; settlement; 25 mi SE of Portales and 3 mi W of the Texas border; PO as Redland 1907–17, as Emzy 1917–33, mail to Causey). This abandoned homesteader village originally was called *Redland,* for the color of the soil here. The name was changed when Emzy Roberts opened a store and became postmaster.

MESA ENCANTADA (Cibola; 2.3 mi NE of Acoma Pueblo). This Spanish name and its English equivalent, *Enchanted Mesa,* are translations of the Acoma name, *Katzimo.* The people of Acoma believe nature gods live on its summit, which is inaccessible by normal means. The Acoma Indians also have a tradition that long ago they lived atop the mesa, but a fierce storm destroyed the trail up the cliffs, forcing them to relocate to their present mesa site.

ENCIERRE (Mora; settlement; on Ocate Creek, E of Naranjos; PO 1887–90, mail to Wagon Mound). From the Spanish, *encerrar,* "enclose." Little is known about this abandoned community, including the origin of its name, though it could refer to a corral or holding pen.

ENCINADA MESA (Rio Arriba; 18 mi N of Counselor, 3 mi NE of Cañon Largo). Spanish, "group of oaks." Not *Ensenada Mesa,* as appears on some maps (USBGN decision).

ENCINAL (Cibola; settlement; on the Laguna Indian Reservation, 6 mi NW of New Laguna). In 1744 Franciscans established a mission for the Navajos at this location, but it failed after two years. The present village, inhabited by Laguna Indians, was a farming community that did not become a permanent village until 1870, when it was settled by refugees from bitter factionalism at Laguna. See *Encino (general).*

ENCINO (general). Spanish, "evergreen oak." Though *encina* is the term used in Spain, in the New World *encino* is much more common. Place name variants in NM include *encinal, encinoso, encinosa,* and *encinada. Encino* and its variants appear 37 times in GNIS.

ENCINO (Torrance; settlement; on US 60 17 mi W of Vaughn; PO 1904–present). Encino was named for the scrub oak that once was common in the area; see *Encino (general).* Intensive sheep ranching later destroyed this growth. Early travelers to and from the territorial capital of Santa Fe often stopped at Encino, especially as a spring 1.5 mi SE of town supplied water. The economy has been based on the three R's of ranching, RRs, and roads, but the first two have declined in recent years, though US 60 continues to keep Encino alive.

ENCINOSO (Lincoln; settlement; on NM 246, on the N side of the Capitan Mountains; PO 1915–20, mail to Capitan). In 1915 R.A. Durn and Sam Farmer settled here, opening a general store and establishing a PO, which they named for a stand of oak trees. The community thrived briefly, but today only a single residence remains. See *Encino (general).*

ENDEE (Quay; settlement; on NM 93, 2.5 mi S of I-40, 5 mi SW of Glenrio; PO 1886–1955, mail to Bard). Endee began about 1885 and was named for the brand of the ND Ranch, established by the Day brothers, John and George, in 1882. Endee was a community of picket houses, with upright poles forming the walls and sod-covered poles forming the roofs. The settlement, still inhabited, has moved several times from its original location farther S.

ENGLAND (Colfax; settlement; location unknown; PO 1881). Ephemeral locality, name origin unknown.

ENGLE (Sierra; settlement; on NM 51 and AT&SF RR, 11 mi E of Elephant Butte; PO 1881–1956, mail to Elephant Butte). Engle was born when the AT&SF RR built a station here around 1880–81; it was named for R.I. Engle, an engineer supervising RR construction. The name mistakenly was registered as *Angle* with the postal department and not corrected for six months. During the early 1880s Engle was known locally as *Rogers Ranch,* for Alex Rogers who opened a store here. At the time Engle was an important supply center for miners and ranchers in the Black Range. In 1923–24 an attempt was made to change the name to *Engel,* to honor Edward J. Engel, RR vice-president, but US Sen. Bronson Cutting, at the urging of cowboy novelist Eugene Manlove Rhodes, blocked the move. Engle grew rapidly with the construction of Elephant Butte Dam in 1911–16 but dwindled thereafter. The creation of the White Sands Missile Range to the E, restricting travel in that direction, limited Engle's future further. Today only a few residences remain.

LOS ENLAMES (Socorro). See *Adelino.*

ENSENADA (Rio Arriba; settlement; on NM 573, 2 mi NE of Tierra Amarilla; PO 1906–58, mail to Tierra Amarilla). Though this tiny settlement appears by this name on many maps, Ensenada likely is a corruption of the community's original Spanish name, *Encinada,* meaning "the oaks" and referring to the many oak trees lining the Rio Brazos nearby and in the surrounding forest. The village was settled about 1864 and in 1880 consisted of 35 families. It is still inhabited.

ENTERPRISE (Lea; settlement; 12 mi E of Lovington). Enterprise began as a rural school and was given this optimistic name by its first teacher. A community including a grocery store began to form around the school, but the school was consolidated with the Prairieview School in 1927, and the settlement died.

EPRIS (Guadalupe; settlement; on US 54 and SP RR, 20 mi SW of Vaughn; PO 1905–07, mail to Duran). Epris was little more than a RR station with a PO; now it's not even that. The name's origin is unknown.

ESCABOSA (Bernalillo; settlement; on NM 337, 16 mi S of Tijeras, in the foothills of the Manzano Mountains; PO 1900–04, mail to Chilili, 1921–33, mail to Zamora). This name is a corruption of the Spanish *escobosa,* referring to a grass used to make brooms (Spanish, *escobas*). A small lake is near this inhabited village around which grow reeds once used for the making of *escobas.*

ESCAVADA WASH (San Juan; heads S of Nageezi and runs SW into the Chaco River.). Though *Escabada* and *Escarbada* appear on many maps, Escavada, derived from the Spanish *escavar,* "to dig, excavate," is the correct form, as established by the USBGN in 1968. The name here is derived from early people digging in this usually dry wash to obtain water. See also *Tohatchi Wash.*

SIERRA LA ESCOBA (Cibola). See *Broom Mountain.*

CERRO DE ESCOBAS, 8,212 ft. (San Miguel; 4 mi SW of Pecos, S of I-25). Spanish, referring to grass used to make brooms (Spanish, *escobas*).

ESCONDIDA, ESCONDIDO (general). Spanish, "hidden," a common name element throughout the Southwest, occurring on 32 places in NM (GNIS).

ESCONDIDA (Otero; settlement; on US 54 and SP RR, 20 mi S of Alamogordo). Former settlement and RR siding, named for *Escondido Canyon,* which enters the Tularosa Valley to the E.

ESCONDIDA (Socorro; settlement; S of Socorro, near Luis Lopez). This vanished community has lived up to its name— see *Escondida, Escondido (general)*—as little information about it has been found. The community appeared in the 1860 US Census as *La Escondida,* then was not mentioned for 25 years only to reappear in the 1885 US Census under its present name. It also appeared on the Wheeler map of 1873–76 and the General Land Office map of 1882, but since then it has returned to obscurity.

ESCONDIDA (Socorro; settlement; on US 85, 2 mi N of Socorro; PO 1903–05, February to July 1931, mail to Socorro). Inhabited settlement, the inspiration of whose name is unknown. Also unknown is what connection, if any, this had with the Escondida (see entry) farther S.

ESCONDIDO (Lincoln; settlement; 2.5 mi W of NM 368, 9 mi N of Tinnie, on the SE side of the Capitan Mountains). Tiny Hispanic settlement, now abandoned, possibly named for *Escondido Creek,* which runs E through here, or for *Escondido Canyon* also nearby.

ESCONDIDO MOUNTAIN, 9,869 ft. (Catron; S of Quemado, N of Quemado Lake). A large, conspicuous mass, likely named for a spring that would be "hidden," unlike the mountain.

ESMERALDA (Valencia; settlement; exact location unknown; PO 1894–96, mail to Belen). Ephemeral community, name origin unknown. *Esmeralda* is Spanish and means "emerald," but it also is a feminine given name. The community is said to have gone by the name *Azul* as well.

ESPAÑOLA (Rio Arriba, Santa Fe; settlement; in SE part of Rio Arriba County but including a corner of Santa Fe County, on the Rio Grande, at the junction of US 84-285 and NM 68; PO 1881–present). The present community of Española did not come into being until after the middle of the 19th century, though several of its component settlements doubtless are much older. What appears to outsiders as Española actually is an agglomeration of communities—*Quartelez, Sombrillo, Santa Cruz, San Pedro, Santo Niño, Riverside, Fairview* (see entries), and perhaps others. As one native put it, "No one's really from Española." Española was not listed in Escudero's *Noticias* of 1849, and to this day Tewas know Española by a name meaning "new town." An 1882 business directory of NM listed Española's population as 150 persons, and as late as the 1950s Española was officially only the small part of the present community that was on the W side of the Rio Grande, while Riverside and the other communities were separate settlements on the E side. Now all have come within the city limits of Española.

The site originally was known as *La Vega de los Vigiles,* "the Vigils' meadow." The present name has been thought to mean "Spanish woman," and local tradition is that it was given by RR workers for a woman who worked in a restaurant here. The name also has been linked to *Hispaniola,* "New Spain." But in fact, the name is a shortened form of the original *Plaza Española,* "Spanish town." And further, Plaza Española might have reflected a distinction between Spaniards and Indians that the *conquistadores* of NM made three centuries earlier with the term *San Gabriel de los Españoles,* "St. Gabriel of the Spaniards," a name given in 1598 to Oñate's colony located nearby; see *San Gabriel.*

CERRO DE ESPIA, 7,595 ft. (Mora; in central part of county, just N of the Santa Fe Trail). Spanish, "lookout hill," appropriate for this distinctive landform.

LA ESPIA PEAK, 4,048 ft. (De Baca; S of Fort Sumner, 3 mi N of the Chaves County line). Though this sometimes appears on maps as *La Espeja Peak,* Spanish, "the mirror," La Espia, "the lookout," probably is correct; de Sosa is said to have named it in 1591, because it was a natural lookout point.

LA ESPIAITA, 3,877 ft. ((Chaves; just E of the Pecos, 3.5 mi S of the De Baca County line). Spanish, "the little spy." Sometimes appearing in English as *Spy Mountain,* this name indicates that this small conical hill would have been a good lookout point.

ESPINOSA (general). Spanish, "thorny," usually describing brushy country, though this also can be a personal name. Nicolás Espinosa was among the original Spanish settlers of Santa Cruz, and Pedro Espinosa was listed in as being in Santa Fe and Albuquerque after the reconquest.

ESPUELA (Eddy; settlement and RR siding; on AT&SF RR, 5 mi N of Artesia). Spanish, "RR spur, siding." Once known as the site of the Espuela cotton gin, Espuela now is the focus of a residential cluster.

ESTACA (Rio Arriba; settlement; on the W side of the Rio Grande, on NM 582, 1.5 mi NW of Alcalde). Spanish, "stake," the name referring here to a stockade where a detachment of soldiers once was stationed. The Tewa name for the locality means "the place below, where holes are in the ground."

ESTALINE CANYON (Socorro; heads 17 mi SW of Magdalena, runs SE into Milligan Gulch.) May be a corruption of Spanish, *estalino,* "stopping place."

ESTANCIA (general). Spanish homesteads, especially along the Rio Grande, were called *estancias* in the 17th century and *haciendas* in the 18th, though they were hardly the luxurious estates that those terms came to mean elsewhere in the Spanish New World. As livestock herds increased, *estancia* owners often established smaller residences for herdsmen and their families; these were called *ranchos,* from the term used in the 17th century for encampments during military campaigns. See *Hacienda (general).*

ESTANCIA (Torrance; settlement, county seat; at the junction of NM 41 and 55; PO 1903–present). Though the Spanish word *estancia* usually refers to a homestead—see *Estancia (general)*—here it carries a meaning of "resting place" and is identified with *Estancia Spring,* which still flows here. In the early days, before the settlement was established, travelers and herders would stop at the spring and the lake it fed, and the place came to be known as Estancia, as it was a "resting place." The surrounding area was primarily ranching country until the coming of the NMC RR early in the 20th century opened it to homesteaders and farmers; the present settlement began then, between 1901 and 1904. Until the 1950s, pinto beans were the dominant crop.

ESTANCIA VALLEY (Torrance; E of the Manzano Mountains). This large basin, named for *Estancia* (see entry), the largest settlement in the valley, once held *Lake Estancia,* which during the Pleistocene was a vast inland lake; ancient shorelines and a few salt lakes are its remnants. In the early days of American settlement, this was called a plain, but John W. Corbett, a prominent settler, is said to have proposed the name Estancia

Valley, now widely used. The valley also has been called the *Salinas Basin,* because of salt deposits associated with the shallow lakes; the Tiwa name for the basin means "salt-getting place."

ESTERO LARGO (Doña Ana). See *Las Cruces.*

ESTERO REDONDO (Doña Ana; exact location unknown.) This, like Estero Largo (see entry), was a campground on the Camino Real that ran N from El Paso to Santa Fe. The Spanish *estero redondo* means "round pond, estuary, marsh."

ESTEROS CREEK (Guadalupe; tributary of the Pecos River, entering it 8 mi N of Santa Rosa). Spanish, "marshes." See *Plaza de los Esteros.*

ESTEY CITY (Lincoln; settlement; 37 mi SW of Carrizozo; PO 1901–03, 1904–10, mail to Oscuro). Around 1900 a little copper-mining camp sprang up on the SE edge of the Oscura Mountains. It took the surname of David M. Estey, of Owasso, MI, the promoter behind the Estey Mining and Milling Co. By 1901 Estey City—often called simply *Estey*—had 250 residents, but in 1902 David Estey filed for bankruptcy, and he died a year later; by 1910 the village, its water source having failed, had died also. The site today is within the White Sands Missile Range.

ESTRADA (San Miguel; settlement; in E part of county, SW of Trementina, 8 mi N of Variadero on Conchas Creek; PO 1900–21, mail to Trementina). Though this Spanish word means "lane," Estrada here probably originated with a family name associated with this abandoned community.

ESTRELLA (McKinley). See *Star Lake.*

EUNICE (Lea; settlement; 18 mi S of Hobbs, at the junction of NM 8, 207, and 234; PO 1909–present). About 1909 J.N. Carson was running a country store in Shafter Lake, TX, when he circulated a petition seeking a PO at where Eunice now is located. He obtained the necessary signatures, but he lacked a name, so patrons at his store made suggestions. A cowboy suggested naming the PO for

Carson's oldest daughter, Eunice, and though this was last on a list of names submitted to the US postal authorities, it was accepted. Carson's son, E.O. Carson, became the first postmaster. The oil boom gave a much-needed boost to the local farming and ranching economy, and the town has adopted the motto, "Where oil flows a city grows."

EUREKA (Grant; settlement; in the Little Hatchet Mountains, 12 mi SW of Hachita). Eureka, using as its name the traditonal exclamation used by miners upon discovering pay dirt, was a small mining camp; by the 1870s a small smelter was here. (It's said a counterfeit-ing operation was here also, with the bogus dollars used in Mexico to buy cattle.) But the gold deposits here were small, and the camp died.

EVANS (Mora). See *Levy.*

EWING (Torrance; settlement; between Estancia and Mountainair). The name Ewing designates a diffuse cluster of farms and ranches. The community received its name in 1923 with the construction of the *Ewing Consolidated School,* on land donated by the prominent Estancia dentist, Charles E. Ewing. The district served by the school came to be known as Ewing.

EXTER (Union). See *Valley.*

F

FAIRACRES (Doña Ana; settlement; on US 70, on the W bank of the Rio Grande, opposite Las Cruces; PO 1926–present). An inhabited suburb of Las Cruces, with a flattering name..

FAIRFIELD (Curry; settlement; in SE part of county, near the Roosevelt County line). This could be a personal name but more likely is a commendatory name chosen for its pleasant connotations. There's no village here, but the area still is called *Fairfield Community.*

FAIRPOINT (San Juan; settlement; slightly S of the San Juan River, between Bloomfield and Blanco; PO 1894–98, mail to Largo). Abandoned settlement, name origin unknown.

FAIRVIEW (Rio Arriba; settlement; 2 mi NE of Española, on NM 68; PO 1952–present). This began as a Mormon colony in the 1890s, but the Mormons departed after 1900. The community survives, like many others in the area, as a satellite of Española.

FAIRVIEW (Sierra). See *Winston.*

FAJADA BUTTE, 6,625 ft. (San Juan; in Chaco Culture National Historical Park, just S of the junction of Chaco Wash and Fajada Wash, 4 mi SE of Pueblo Bonito). The Spanish name of this prominent landform, also known as *Mesa Fajada,* means "belted, cinch for a saddle," and likely refers to a sedimentary layer in the butte, appearing to encircle it like a belt. The name, however, could also be a corruption of *fachada,* "facade." Lt. James H. Simpson used this latter name when he described the butte in his journal of 1849: "The chief object in the landscape was Mesa Fachada, a circular mound with tableau top, rising abruptly midway in the canyon to a height of from 300 to 400 feet." "Holy rock" is the meaning of

the name used by Navajos for the butte, an important place in the Male Shooting Chant. The butte apparently was of religious significance as well to the ancient Anasazi of Chaco Canyon, for they inscribed petroglyphs here, including the famous spiral design through which a "dagger" of sunlight passes at the summer solstice. The name often is spelled *Fahada,* but the form approved by the USBGN is Fajada. *Fajada Wash,* formerly *Vicente Wash* but now named for the butte, heads SW of it and runs NW to join the Chaco River just NW of the butte.

FANNING DRAW (Eddy; heads NW of Carlsbad and runs E into Rocky Arroyo). Martin Fanning, born in Illinois, came to NM from Texas with the Peter Corn wagon train and settled in this area.

FANNY HILL, SPRING (Catron; hill immediately N of Mogollon; spring 2 mi E of Mogollon on Silver Creek). The Fanny Mill at Mogollon likely gave its name to these two features.

FARLEY (Colfax; settlement; in SE part of county, on NM 193, 3 mi N of US 56; PO 1932–66, mail to a rural branch of Springer). Farley began in 1931 with construction of the SF RR's Colmor Cut-off line, intended to bypass Raton Pass and shorten the transcontinental route by 70 mi. The project was aborted at Farley, however, just 35 mi from Colmor. The settlement, still inhabited, was named for D.S. Farley, who became assistant general manager of the SF RR's eastern division. The Farley PO was established by relocating the one at Pittsburg (see entry), which earlier had been moved from Hatod. Farley was poised to become a major town in NE

NM, with a high school, restaurants, an electric plant, a veterinary, and two newspapers, but with the failure of the RR and the general depopulation of the area, the name now designates a diffuse ranching area more than an actual village.

FARMINGTON (San Juan; settlement; at the junction of US 64 and NM 550; PO 1879–present). Long before European settlers came to this valley, Navajos had recognized the unique character of the confluence of the Animas, La Plata, and San Juan Rivers; they gave the area a descriptive name meaning "three waters," or "between the waters." When English-speaking settlers arrived, the confluence was a natural site for a settlement, and in 1879 one sprang up. It was named in that year by Milt Virden, one of the first white settlers, as he and others were laying out the townsite. Stockmen had been coming to this rich farming area to buy vegetables and forage, and they called the locality the "farming town." Virden suggested dropping the w and combining the two words. All agreed, and submitted the name for the new PO. Farmington was not the first settlement in the area; it was preceded on the S side of the rivers by Junction City (see entry), which for a time rivalled Farmington in importance, but as settlement shifted to the N Junction City faded. With the discovery in the late 1940s of oil and gas in the region, Farmington's economy shifted from agricultural to industrial.

FAULKNER (Sierra; settlement; 7 mi NE of Hillsboro; PO 1893–98, mail to Hillsboro). This abandoned mining settlement likely takes its name from a local settler. Faulkners homesteaded in the area, though their relation to this settlement is unclear.

FAULKNER CANYON (Doña Ana; heads 5 mi SW of Radium Springs and runs NE). Named for an early rancher here.

FAYWOOD (Grant; settlement; at Faywood Hot Springs, on NM 61, 3 mi NE of US 180; PO 1901–present). This name, like that of the springs (see Faywood Hot Springs), combined the surnames of two of the three partners who developed the site around 1900. Later the PO was moved to the village of Dwyer (see entry), to the NE, though the PO has retained the name Faywood.

FAYWOOD HOT SPRINGS (Grant; 0.5 mi W of NM 61, 2 mi NE of its junction with US 180). In 1785 a Capt. Martinez stopped here and observed wild bulls watering here; he called the site Ojo Toro, "bull spring." In 1851 John Bartlett with the US Boundary Commission referred to the springs as Ojo Caliente, "hot spring." In 1859, A. Kuhne and William "Billy" Watts, former El Paso sheriffs, filed a homestead claim and built a bath house and hotel, which they called Hotel of Accommodation. In 1868, Grant County was created, with Col. Richard Hudson its first sheriff and later first judge. Hudson, believing the mineral springs had cured his gout, acquired the property, which then was called Mimbres Hot Springs in 1878; in 1879 he changed the name to Hudson Hot Springs and in 1881 began constructing a hotel that was completed in 1884. The hotel burned in 1890, and in 1894 Andrew Graham acquired the property. In 1895–96 he erected what was at the time the fanciest hotel in NM Territory; he called it Casa del Consuelo, "house of delight." But Graham's tenure was brief, and by 1900 T. C. McDermott and two partners, J. C. Fay and William Lockwood, acquired the property and gave it a new name, Faywood, an amalgam of the two partners' surnames. Fay and Lockwood soon departed, but McDermott lived at the site until his death in 1947 at age 97. The hotel had been in steady decline since its heyday during World War I, deriving much business from the Army base near Deming. Casa del Consuelo was razed in 1952, and eventually Chino Mines acquired the property. It currently is owned and being developed by husband and wife, Wanda Fuselier and Elon Yurwit.

FELIX (Chaves; settlement; 40 mi E of Alamogordo; PO 1903–1918, mail to Elk). This name probably refers not to a settlement but rather to a rural PO serving ranchers along the *Río Felix* (see entry), hence the name. Originally the name was spelled *Feliz,* and some oldtimers still use this spelling.

FELIZ (Chaves). See *Hagerman.*

FENCE LAKE (Cibola; settlement; in SW part of county, on NM 36; PO 1936–present). Sometime around 1925, Sylvester Mirabel put a fence around his lake here to prevent free-ranging cattle from getting mired down. In 1936, after the area was more densely settled by refugees from the Dust Bowl in Texas and Oklahoma and a settlement had developed, a meeting was held to choose a name for the new PO. Because the "fenced lake" was a major local landmark, it was decided to drop the *d* and call it Fence Lake. The fence has since disappeared, and the lake has been dry for many years, but the community named for it survives.

FENTON LAKE STATE PARK (Sandoval; in western Jemez Mountains, on NM 126, 9 mi W of its junction with NM 4). The state park, the lake it features, and the old ranch surrounding it were all named for Elijah McClean Fenton Sr., a Presbyterian minister and civil engineer who came to NM in 1881 and was stationed at Jemez Pueblo in 1892. Discovering land available for homesteading along Cebolla Creek, he began filing claims, retired from the ministry, and took up ranching and real estate development. He built ponds near the present lake. He died in 1945 and is buried in the family plot overlooking the lake. In 1940, the State Game and Fish Commission purchased 80 acres from Fenton as wildlife habitat and in 1946 constructed the present dam. The area became a state park in 1984.

FERGUSON MOUNTAIN, 7,970 ft. (Grant; in the Big Burro Mountains, W of Burro Peak). This, the third highest summit of the range, recalls Lord Ferguson of England, who established the original Burro Mountain Homestead.

FERNANDEZ CREEK (Taos). See *Río Fernando de Taos.*

FERNANDEZ DE TAOS (Taos). See *Taos.*

FERNANDO MOUNTAINS (Taos; a ridge running SE-NW immediately SE of Taos, S of US 64). Like many other features in the area, this bears the name of Don Fernando de Chávez, an important landowner before 1680. Its two main summits are *Cerrito Colorado,* 10,246 ft., and *Sierra del Don Fernando,* 10,365 ft.

DON FERNANDO DE TAOS (Taos). See *Taos.*

FERNDALE (San Miguel; settlement; in W part of county, 0.5 mi N of Mineral Hill; PO 1914–19, mail to San Geronimo). Abandoned community, name origin unknown.

FERRY (Valencia; settlement; exact location unknown; PO 1881). Ephemeral PO associated with a ferry across the Rio Grande.

FIELD (Curry; settlement; 18 mi NE of Melrose, at the junction of NM 224 and NM 288; PO 1907–24, mail to Melrose). Field was created with the consolidation of three rural schools; Field's original site was 1.5 mi N of the present inhabited community. Name origin unknown.

FIELD (Socorro). See *Puertecito.*

FIERRO (Grant; settlement; on NM 356, 3 mi NE of Hanover; PO 1899–1969, mail to Hanover). *Fierro* is an archaic form of the modern Spanish *hierro,* "iron," though *fierro* still is widely used in rural NM, where it sometimes also means "branding iron, brand." This inhabited settlement bears the name because of local iron deposits; 6 million tons have been shipped from mines here, though most mining has ceased.

FIGUEREDO WASH (McKinley; heads near Nakaibito and runs NE E of Tohatchi). Bears a Spanish surname.

FIVE DOLLAR CANYON, CREEK (Colfax; 7 mi N of Dawson). Local lore says this small tributary of the Vermejo River was named for a settler who always wanted to bet five dollars—but never had it.

FIVE POINTS (Bernalillo; settlement; in the Albuquerque area, W of the Rio Grande and NE of Armijo). Former suburb, now within the largely urbanized South Valley of Albuquerque, named because Bridge Street, Sunset Road, and Five Points Road converge here at a five way intersection.

FIVEMILE DRAW (Chaves; heads in NW corner of county and runs SE to join the Pecos River, its upper portion divided into East, Middle, and West Forks). See *Eightmile Draw.*

FLAG MOUNTAIN, 11,946 ft. (Taos; in the Sangre de Cristo Mountains; 5 mi SE of Questa and S of Red River). Name origin unknown.

FLAGGIE MOUNTAIN, 9,292 ft. (Taos; just N of the village of Red River). When Red River was a booming mining town, its residents proudly put a flag atop this small mountain, where it flew 24 hours a day. But when the town began to decline just before WW I, the flag was abandoned.

FLAT LAKE (Doña Ana; 12 mi NE of Rincon). Early settlers, not being certain whether this was a lake, as it was following rains, or a flat, as it was at other times, opted for both and called it Flat Lake.

FLEMING (Grant; settlement; 9 mi NW of Silver City; PO 1883–87, mail to Silver City). According to local tradition, the silver- mining camp of Fleming was born when John W. "Jack" Fleming grubstaked a prospector who subsequently found rich ore that in 1882 led to the development of the Old Man Mine. The camp that sprang up around the mine briefly was called *Bonanza City,* but soon was named for Fleming, one of the mine's owners and a prominent local citizen; he was postmaster for two months in 1883. The Old Man Mine was worked steadily until 1888 and then intermittently until 1893, when Fleming became a ghost town. See also *Penrose.*

FLORA VISTA (San Juan; settlement; on US 550, 5 mi SW of Aztec; 1878–80, 1884–present). By 1877 settlers from Colorado already had built cabins along the Animas River where the community of Flora Vista would be located. The Spanish name means "flower view" and probably was inspired by wildflowers in meadows near the river.

FLORENCE (Eddy). See *Loving.*

FLORIDA (Luna; trading point; on NM 26, 14 mi NE of Deming; PO 1928–40, mail to Deming). This former trading site and still-active RR loading point originally was called *Porter Station,* for reasons unknown, then *Cummings,* for *Fort Cummings* nearby (see entry). Its present name was inspired by the Florida Mountains (see entry), visible from here to the S.

FLORIDA (Socorro; settlement; N of Socorro; PO 1950–55, mail to Socorro). This settlement, status unknown, was named for local wildflowers, though in some Hispanic communities the name is associated with *Pascua Florida,* the customary term for Easter.

FLORIDA MOUNTAINS (Luna; SE of Deming). Local people say that in the spring, following a wet winter, the slopes of these desert mountains are golden with the blossoms of poppies—and the origin of the name is obvious. The name was given by Spanish explorers; on Juan Nentwig's map of 1762 appears "S. [Sierra] Florida" and "Valle de Florida." Highest elevation, *Florida Peak,* 7,448 ft.

LITTLE FLORIDA MOUNTAINS (Luna; approx. 2 mi NE of the Florida Mountains). A low hogback, named for its proximity to the larger Florida Mountains. Rock Hound State Park (see entry) is on the SW side of the Little Florida Mountains.

FLOYD (Roosevelt; settlement; on NM 267, 16 mi W of Portales; PO 1903–present). Inhabited farming and ranching community, named for Floyd Wharton, pioneer settler.

FLUORINE (Sierra; settlement; in SE corner of county, on the E side of the Black Range, N of Winston; PO 1910–18, mail to Chloride). This abandoned mining camp was named for the chemical element fluorine, found in the mineral fluorite, which would have been familiar to miners here.

FLYING H (Chaves; settlement; on NM 13 NW of Artesia and SW of Roswell; PO 1938–present). This rural PO, at the site of the former Tunstall Ranch, was named for the Flying H Ranch on the Rio Felix, served 100 people as recently as 1975.

FLYING V CANYON (Catron, Grant; on

the Middle Fork of the Gila River).
Named for a ranch brand.

FLYING W MOUNTAIN, 6,215 ft. (Luna;
highest point in the Cedar Mountains,
NE of Hachita). Named for the Flying W
Ranch in the mountains.

FOLSOM (Union; settlement; on the Dry
Cimarron River, at the junction of NM
72, 325, and 456; PO as Capulien
1883–88, as Folsom 1888–present). Early
maps show a settlement labeled *Mexican
Town* where Folsom is now. The
community's first PO was called
Capulien, doubtless for Capulin Mountain to the W. But with the coming of
the C&S RR in 1887–88 the little settlement was transformed. A RR construction camp sprang up that was called
Ragtown, because saloons, restaurants,
and dwellings were all in tents. Then
with the coming of the first trains the
town was renamed Folsom, to honor
Frances Folsom, who in 1886, at age 22,
became wife of President Grover Cleveland at a White House ceremony.
Folsom soon grew into a thriving stockyard and shipping point, but its fortunes
declined after a disastrous flood in 1908.
In 1926 George McJunkin, a cowboy,
found some chipped stone darts amid
very large fossil bones in Dead Horse
Gulch near Folsom, and eventually his
"Folsom points" became accepted as
evidence that a paleo-Indian culture had
existed here more than 10,000 years ago,
hunting mammals now extinct.

FORD (Quay; settlement; N of House, 3 mi
N and 3 mi W of McAlister; PO
1907–10, mail to House). This abandoned Caprock settlement likely bears a
family name, as no perennial streams
exist in the area requiring fords to cross.

FORREST (Quay; settlement; in S part of
county, on NM 210, 2 mi S of NM 209;
PO 1908–19, mail to Melrose, 1933–67,
mail to rural Tucumcari branch). This
inhabited Caprock village originally was
located 1 mi S, at a site where homesteaders had drilled a well and where
Watt Farr kept a general store. Two stories explain the village's name, both re-
lating to Farr, who moved here from
Missouri in 1907 to homestead with his
family. The most widely accepted and
most plausible version is that Farr
named the PO for his son, Forrest. But
another story, likely apocryphal, says
that Farr's store and the well were a
popular resting place, and Farr submitted the name Farr's Rest to the PO Department, which altered it to Forrest
instead.

FORT BASCOM (San Miguel; military installation; in a horseshoe bend on the S
side of the Canadian River, 12 mi N of
Tucumcari; PO as Fort Bascom 1874–92,
as Johnson 1892–95, mail to Liberty). In
1863 Brig. Gen. James H. Carleton, acting commander of the Military Department of NM, ordered a military post
built here to protect settlers and control
the *comanchero* trade; he named it
Bascom to honor Capt. George N.
Bascom, 16th US Infantry, who fell at
the Battle of Valverde the previous year.
But Fort Bascom, sometimes called simply *Bascom Camp,* with a garrison of
only 88 men, proved ineffective, and in
1870 the post was closed, the troops
transfered to Fort Union. Shortly after
the post was established, an Albuquerque newspaper wrote: "We suggest that
the town that will probably spring up in
that neighborhood before long also be
called *Bascom.* The name is euphonic,
and we know of no better way of honoring those who have died in our defense
than by giving their names to counties
and towns." A civilian settlement and a
PO did spring up, and they took the
newspaper's suggestion, as both were
called *Bascom,* though after the fort was
closed the PO changed its name to
Johnson before it, too, was abandoned.
Little now remains at the site.

FORT BASSETT (Quay; military installation; N of Tucumcari, S of Fort
Bascom). This wasn't really a fort; soldiers camped here for one winter only.
The name's origin is unknown.

FORT BAYARD (Grant; military installation; 10 mi E of Silver City; PO 1867–70,
name changed to Central City). The
discovery of gold at Pinos Altos in 1859
brought miners and prospectors to this
area, which provoked the wrath of the

Warm Springs Apaches, who regarded the land as theirs. To protect the settlers, a fort was established in 1866 and named for Brig. Gen. George D. Bayard, who fought on the frontier with the First Cavalry and died at Fredericksburg, VA, in the Civil War. At first the fort was but a cluster of log and adobe huts and offered little protection, but it grew over the years and was an important base during campaigns against Mangas Coloradas, Victorio, and Geronimo. The post remained active until 1900, when it became an Army hospital. It is now used by the NM Dept. of Public Welfare. The nearby community of Bayard (see entry) was named for the fort.

FORT CONRAD (Socorro; military installation; 35 mi S of Socorro, on the W bank of the Rio Grande, near the present Tiffany RR siding). Fort Conrad was established in 1851 by Col. Edmond Vose Sumner to protect the lower Rio Grande Valley, but it was poorly situated, consisted primarily of cottonwood logs, pole huts, and tents, and has been described as a "useless, hard-luck post." Its principal function was as a hay camp for Fort Craig, built later. The fort was named to honor Charles M. Conrad (1804–78), who at the time of the fort's founding was Secretary of War under President Fillmore. Fort Conrad was abandoned in 1854 and its troops moved to Fort Craig (see entry), 9 mi farther S.

FORT CRAIG (Socorro; military installation; on the W side of the Rio Grande, 44 mi S of Socorro; PO 1855–79). Established in 1853 and garrisoned in 1854 by troops from Fort Conrad (see entry), 9 mi N, Fort Craig was named for Capt. Louis S. Craig, murdered by deserters in California in 1852. In February 1862 troops from Fort Craig were defeated by Confederate forces during the Battle of Valverde, 7 mi away; the fort itself was not attacked. Between 1863 and 1865, Fort Craig was headquarters for campaigns against the Gila and Mimbres Apaches, but as Indian threats declined the fort's importance diminished, and it was deactivated in 1885. It is now being preserved as a historic site.

FORT CUMMINGS (Luna; military installation; near the mouth of Cookes Canyon, near Cookes Spring; PO 1866–91, mail to Hadley). In 1863 Gen. James H. Carleton ordered a fort built at Cookes Spring, a vital water hole along a stage route in Cookes Canyon (see entry) vulnerable to Apache attacks. He named the fort for Maj. Joseph Cummings, 1st NM Cavalry, killed that summer by Navajos in the Four Corners area. The fort was abandoned in 1873, when the Indian threat was believed to be over, but renewed attacks led to the fort's reopening in 1880. Fort Cummings was abandoned finally in 1886.

FORT FAUNTLEROY (McKinley). See *Fort Wingate*.

FORT FILLMORE (Doña Ana; military installation; 6 mi S of Las Cruces on US 85 and 1 mi E of Brazito; PO 1852–61.) Fort Fillmore, named for President Millard Fillmore (1850–52), was established in 1851 by Col. Edmond Vose Sumner, military commander in NM, to protect travelers from Indian attacks. At the onset of the Civil War, loyalties in southern NM were divided, and many soldiers took up the Confederate cause. In 1861 Union troops from Fort Fillmore marched on Mesilla to demand the capitulation of Confederates, but they were repulsed and retreated to the fort, which they surrendered the next day. Union troops reoccupied the fort when the Confederates left, but it was abandoned permanently later in 1861, and today nothing remains to mark the site.

FORT FLOYD (Grant). See *Fort McLane*.

FORT HATCH (San Miguel). See *Chapman*.

FORT LOS LUNAS (Valencia; military installation; at Los Lunas). In 1851 Col. Edmond Vose Sumner ordered Capt. Richard S. Ewell, First Dragoons, to establish a post at either Sabinal or Los Lunas, on the basis of which site had "good winter quarters and sufficient forage at reasonable prices." Ewell chose Los Lunas. In January 1852 he arrived, renting quarters and land and beginning farming. The post, never an actual fort, was garrisoned until 1860.

FORT LOWELL (Rio Arriba). See *Camp Plummer.*

FORT LYON (McKinley). See *Fort Wingate.*

FORT MARCY (Santa Fe; military installation; NE of the Plaza in Santa Fe). In August 1846, immediately after his occupation of Santa Fe, Gen. Stephen W. Kearny began constructing Fort Marcy to overlook the city; he named the fort for William L. Marcy, at the time serving as Secretary of War under President Polk. The fort, large enough to accommodate 1,000 soldiers, never was used or needed. It was abandoned in 1868, but the Fort Marcy Military Reservation, created downtown at the site of present McKenzie and West Marcy streets, lasted until 1894. Only earthen mounds remain at the fort's site, upon which townhouses have been built. The *Garita* (Spanish, "guardhouse") was a diamond-shaped prison somewhat lower on the slope from Fort Marcy.

FORT MCLANE (Grant; military installation; 4 mi S of present Hurley). In 1860 Maj. Isaac Lynde of the 7th US Infantry established a small post on the bank of a small stream flowing from Apache Springs. He named the post *Fort Floyd,* after John B. Floyd, then Secretary of War under President Buchanan. But soon thereafter Buchanan requested Floyd's resignation, and Floyd joined the Confederacy, so in 1861 the fort was renamed to honor Capt. George McLanc, killed by the Navajos that year. The site has been associated with *Apache Tejo,* a small settlement and watering place on the old Santa Rita–Janos Trail. The name is of obscure origin but has been thought to have been derived from an individual Indian, *Pachiteju,* though a contemporary account called it *Apache de Ho,* perhaps meaning "Apache water." By whatever name, the fort was never more than a few log buildings, and it was abandoned later in 1861, its troops moved to Fort Fillmore. It is remembered primarily for Mangas Coloradas, the Apache chief, being killed here.

FORT MCRAE (Sierra; military installation; on the E side of what is now Elephant Butte Reservoir). The adobe post of Fort McRae was built in 1863 to protect travelers on the Jornada del Muerto and to oversee the ford over the Rio Grande leading to Palomas hot springs. The post was named for Capt. Alexander McRae, 3rd US Cavalry, killed in 1862 at the Battle of Valderde; McRae had commanded an artillery battery that was seized by the Confederates but not before every defender was killed, including McRae. The post was decommissioned in 1876 but kept open until 1884 for use by travelers. Its ruins now are at the bottom of the reservoir.

FORT SELDEN (Doña Ana; military installation, state monument; just E of NM 185, 1 mi SE of Radium Springs, on E bank of Rio Grande; PO 1866–77, 1881–91, as Leasburg 1891–98, as Selden 1911–13, as Fort Selden 1913–23). This fort, established in 1865 to protect settlers in the Mesilla Valley and travelers on the Jornada del Muerto, was named for Col. Henry R. Selden, 1st NM Infantry and one-time captain of the 5th US Infantry. Troops at Fort Selden saw little action, and it was temporarily abandoned, then regarrisoned during Geronimo's raids, only to be abandoned for good in 1890. Capt. Arthur MacArthur served here in 1884, and his son Douglas A. MacArthur learned to ride and shoot here. The state monument was established in 1972.

The *Selden Hills* are low hills 2 mi N of Radium Springs.

FORT SELDEN SPRING (Doña Ana). See *Radium Springs.*

FORT STANTON (Lincoln; military installation; SE of Capitan, on NM 214, 3 mi S of US 380; PO 1857–63, 1868–present). In January 1855, Capt. Henry W. Stanton led 12 men up a deep ravine in the Sacramento Mountains in pursuit of Indians. The Indians fired from ambush, and Captain Stanton fell, a bullet through his forehead. Two months later, on March 19, a detachment of soldiers arrived in the northern Sacramento Mountains, and as James A. Bennett recorded in his diary, "They are here for the purpose of building a fort to be called Fort Stanton in commemoration of the captain who was killed.... Gen. John Garland selected the site for the fort today. The officers all got drunk." The fort was built to encourage settlement and to control the Mescalero Apaches, but it really succeeded only in the former. The fort was deactivated in 1896, and in 1899 it became a military hospital; in 1939 it was an internment camp for captured German seamen; and in 1953 it was turned over to the state for a public hospital and school. *Fort Stanton Cave* is 1 mi SE of the fort.

FORT SUMNER (De Baca; military installation; 4 mi SE of the town of Fort Sumner, on NM 212). In 1862 Gen. James H. Carleton, determined to end Navajo and Apache raiding, ordered a fort built in the Bosque Redondo to supervise Navajos and Apaches who were to be brought to a reservation there, where they would be taught agriculture. Carleton named the fort for Col. Edmond Vose Sumner, commander of the 9th Military District, who was responsible for the establishment of Forts Craig, Fillmore, Union, and Thorn. Approximately 8,000 Navajos and 400 Mescalero Apaches were brought to the reservation, but the internment was a failure. The Apaches decamped, and the Navajos, desperate and demoralized, pleaded successfully to be allowed to return to their homeland in return for a promise to foreswear raiding. Its purpose gone, the fort was deactivated in 1868. The fort often is called *Old Fort Sumner,* to distinguish it from the modern settlement. Navajos call the ordeal of their exodus from their homeland to the fort the Long Walk. See *Fort Sumner (settlement).*

FORT SUMNER (De Baca; settlement, county seat; on the Pecos River, at the junction of US 60 and 84 and NM 20; PO 1866–70, 1873–78, 1879, 1907, mail to Sunnyside, 1910–present). The name Fort Sumner has had four manifestations. First came the military fort (see entry), 1862–68. Then in 1875 the fort and buildings were purchased by Lucien

Maxwell, around whose home and operations a small settlement developed, also called Fort Sumner. (Pat Garrett killed Billy the Kid in Maxwell's bedroom.) These holdings later were purchased by the New England Cattle Co., and when the properties deteriorated, residents moved slightly farther S and started another settlement, again called Fort Sumner, the third manifestation. Then finally, when construction for the AT&SF RR began around 1905, a settlement grew up around the holdings of the Fort Sumner Land and Development Co., near the present town. This settlement was immediately S of the RR camp known as Sunnyside (see entry), but when Sunnyside was devastated by a storm in 1908, its residents met on April 17, 1909, and asked to join Fort Sumner, thus creating the present town, which again was named Fort Sumner.

FORT THORN (Doña Ana; military installation; at upper end of the Mesilla Valley, on the W bank of the Rio Grande, N of Hatch and W of Salem; 1855–59). Fort Thorn was established in 1853 by Col. Edmond Vose Sumner and named by Lt. William H. Emory of the Topographical Engineers for Capt. Herman Thorn, who in 1849 drowned while escorting wagons to El Paso, TX. The site previously had been known as *Santa Barbara.* Fort Thorn was intended to protect settlers and travelers against Apaches and outlaws, but its troops battled sickness more often than enemies. Today, almost nothing remains of Fort Thorn, as the site has been ravaged by flooding of the Rio Grande.

FORT TULAROSA (Catron; military installation; at the site of what is now Aragon, on NM 12). This fort was established in 1872 and named for *Tularosa Creek* on whose E bank it was located. Fort Tularosa was built to protect the agency of the newly created Apache reservation, intended for about 1,600 Apaches then living at the Warm Springs Apache Reservations. But the Apaches did not want to move—about half of them fled into the hills—and before Fort Tularosa was completed the agency was moved to

Horse Springs, about 18 mi E of the present site, and then in 1874 back to the Warm Springs Reservation, when Fort Tularosa was abandoned. It was never more than a collection of log huts, with a few frame buildings, and no trace of it has survived.

FORT UNION (Mora; military installation, national monument; on NM 161, 8 mi N of Watrous; PO 1851–91, mail to Tiptonville). In 1851, after deciding not to purchase Alexander Barclay's fort (see *Barclays Fort*), the US Army decided to build Fort Union at the foot of the mesa opposite the Turkey Mountains. The fort gradually grew in size and importance until it was the largest military post in the Southwest, with a peak population of 3,000. Capturing Fort Union was a major objective of the Confederate incursion into the state during the Civil War. But by the 1880s, Indian action had shifted to southern NM and the coming of the AT&SF RR made protection of the Santa Fe Trail unnecessary, so Fort Union finally was abandoned in 1891. The property deteriorated over the years until it became a national monument in 1954.

FORT WEBSTER (Grant; military installation; on NM 152, near San Lorenzo). Fort Webster was established in 1851 to control the Apaches and also to protect the US–Mexican Boundary Commission. The commission arrived from El Paso in April 1851 and occupied the old private Mexican fort that Francisco Elguea built in 1834 to protect the Santa Rita copper mines. The commission called the post *Cantonment Dawson.* In October it was occupied by the Army and renamed Fort Webster, in honor of Daniel Webster, then US Secretary of State under President Fillmore. In 1852 the post was moved to the Mimbres River, but it retained its name. It was abandoned in 1853, when its troops were transferred to Fort Thorn on the Rio Grande. Only rubble marks the site today.

FORT WEST (Grant; military installation; on the E side of the Gila River, at the confluence of Bear Creek and the Gila River, SE of Cliff). Named for Brig. Gen. Joseph Rodman West, this post was established in 1863 to protect miners at Pinos Altos from Apaches. It lasted only a year, and as the troops marched away to Pinos Altos, the Indians burned it.

FORT WINGATE (McKinley; military installation, settlement; just S of I-40, 12 E of Gallup; PO 1874–present). The first site of this former US Army outpost, established around 1849, was at Seboyeta. From there it was moved S and W to a site near Ojo del Gallo (see entry), where Hispanic settlers had created a small community, now San Rafael (see entry), around the spring of that name. The site of the fort appeared as *Hay Camp* on an 1850 map, and many people at El Gallo earned money selling hay to the fort. In 1862 the fort was named Fort Wingate, for Capt. Benjamin Wingate, who had died that year at the Battle of Valverde.

In 1868, Fort Wingate was moved again, to its present location, occupying what had previously been *Fort Fauntleroy* and then *Fort Lyon.* Fort Fauntleroy had been established in 1860 by Col. Thomas T. ("Little Lord") Fauntleroy, who named it for himself. But in 1862 Fauntleroy resigned from the US Army to join the Confederacy, and the fort was quickly renamed Fort Lyon, for Brig. Gen. Nathaniel Lyon, who had recently died fighting for the Union. It remained Fort Lyon until 1868, when it became Fort Wingate.

Fort Fauntleroy/Lyon/Wingate was located at *Ojo del Oso,* (Spanish, "spring of the bear"), a translation of its Navajo name. Navajos tell that a bear once frequented the spring, and a warrior on a war party, hoping to gain success, cast offerings into the spring for the bear. The raid was successful, and in gratitude the warrior named the spring.

Fort Wingate was an active military installation for a much longer time than most frontier forts. As *Fort Wingate Army Depot,* it was used for munitions storage from 1918 until its closing in 1992.

The village named *Fort Wingate,* on

NM 400 just E of the former Army depot, survives as the location of schools and other facilities serving a wide rural area.

FOUR CORNERS (San Juan; at the junction of NM, Utah, Arizona, and Colorado). The only place in the US where four states meet. Navajos call the site by a name meaning "rocks standing out."

FOUR HILLS (Bernalillo; settlement; SE Albuquerque, at the mouth of Tijeras Canyon, S of Tijeras Arroyo). Around 1950 Wiley Johnson of Moriarty ran the Four Hills Riding Academy, a dude ranch that took its name from four steep linked hills ranged along the front of the Manzanita Mountains to the SE. In 1957 he sold his land to the developers of the Four Hills Village and Country Club, which became the nucleus for the present residential area. The Four Hills themselves came to be within Kirtland Air Force Base and were used during the Cold War (1947–91) for underground storage of the US's stock of nuclear weapons.

FOUR LAKES (Lea; NW of Tatum). Americans discovered these lakes during the 1879–80 expedition against the Indians led by Capt. G.W. Arrington and his Texas Rangers. The lakes were well-known to early hunters on the Llano Estacado, who sometimes called them the *Lost Lakes.* Their individual names are *North, East, Middle,* and *House.* The lakes originally were seep springs surrounded by rich grazing land, but they have since been diminished by pumping of the Ogalalla Aquifer. The name Four Lakes denotes the region as well as the lakes themselves.

FOURMILE DRAW (Eddy; heads W of US 285 and runs E to join the Pecos River, S of Artesia). The draw crosses the highway approximately 4 mi N of Lakewood, which probably accounts for the name as the draw is more than than 4 miles long.

FOURTH OF JULY CANYON (Taos; on Colfax County border, 5 mi SE of Red River). This canyon is said to have been named by early travelers between Elizabethtown and Red River because the snow here often was so deep travelers couldn't get through until the Fourth of July.

FOURTH OF JULY SPRINGS (Torrance; in the Manzano Mountains, 6 mi NW of Tajique). This pleasant spot was where early settlers would gather for a picnic each Fourth of July—hence the name. A USFS picnic area still is here, and the site remains very popular, especially in the fall when the uncommonly numerous red maples here turn scarlet.

FOX MOUNTAIN, 9,200 ft. (Catron; 3 mi W of Jewett Gap on NM 32). A homesteader named Fox and not the animal is responsible for the name of this mountain, which has a USFS lookout on its summit.

FRA CRISTOBAL RANGE (Sierra; between the Rio Grande and Elephant Butte Reservoir to the W and the Jornada del Muerto to the E). This stark N-S desert range, highest elevation 6,834 ft., is said to take its name from Fray Cristóbal de Salazar, a pioneer Franciscan and Oñate's cousin and *sargento mayor.* The name Cristóbal is a common NM spelling of Cristóval, Spanish, "Christopher." (Fray Cristóbal is believed to have died near here in 1599 while returning to Mexico following Oñate's successful *entrada* in 1598. Vargas in his campaign journal of 1692 mentioned that from the *Paraje de Fra Cristóbal* (see entry) he could see the *sierras* of El Muerto and Peñuelas to the E. *El Muerto,* "the dead man," has been identified as the Fra Cristobal Range. Attempts have been made to link the name with a supposed resemblance between the range's outline on its N end and the profile of the friar, but these attempts smack of folk-etymology. Though *fray* is the more proper Spanish title for a friar, *fra* seems to have been chosen by many cartographers.

LA FRAGUA CANYON (Rio Arriba; flows SW into La Jara Creek, 8 mi N of Gobernador). Though Fragua is a personal name, the Spanish equivalent of Smith, the use of the article suggests this canyon was named for a forge or blacksmith's shop here.

FRALEY (Socorro; settlement; 8 mi E of San Antonio, at the NW edge of the Carthage coal fields; PO 1893–96, mail to San Antonio). This settlement, now abandoned, grew up around some kilns that exploited high-quality lime deposits here. When a branch line of the AT&SF RR was removed about 1900, kiln operations ceased, and the settlement died.

FRAMPTON (Union; settlement; in central part of county, exact location unknown; PO 1892, mail to Clapham). Ephemeral postal locality, name origin unknown.

FRANCES CANYON (San Juan; now mostly submerged on the S side of Navajo Reservoir). A Frenchman once lived here, and his Hispanic neighbors called him el Francés, "the Frenchman." *Frances Creek*, a tributary of the San Juan River, drains into Navajo Reservoir through this canyon from the SE. *Frances Canyon Ruin*, an archaeological site on a mesa near Frances Canyon, was a prehistoric village of 40 surface rooms, presumably built by Navajos influenced by Pueblo Indians who lived among the Navajos in the 1700s.

FRANKLIN (Colfax; settlement; 9 mi SW of Springer; PO 1876–79). An 1870 map shows Franklin as a major trail junction. Name origin unknown.

FRANKLIN CITY (Taos; settlement; on the Red River, 4 mi S of village of Red River). This abandoned mining camp began in 1897 in connection with the Franklin Placer Co.'s operations, but competition from nearby camps stunted its growth, and at its height it had only a few cabins, one store, and two saloons.

FRANKLIN MOUNTAINS (Doña Ana; in S part of county, E of the Rio Grande, extending into Texas S to El Paso). A common explanation for this name is that a portion of the mountains' ridgeline resembles the profile of Benjamin Franklin. But far more likely is that the range bears the given name of Franklin Coons, who also gave the city of El Paso an earlier name, Franklin. Most of this small N-S range is in Texas; the NM section has one major summit, *North*

Anthonys Nose, 5,388 ft.

FRASER MOUNTAIN, 12,163 ft. (Taos; in the Sangre de Cristo Mountains, 1 mi S of the Taos Ski Valley). William Fraser was a mining man who, along with Al Helphenstine, discovered the strikes that led to the establishment of the mining camp of Amizette (see entry). When Amizette declined in 1895, William Fraser found copper and gold farther E in the canyon of the Rio Hondo, and he organized the Fraser Mountain Copper Mines. Fraser was involved in numerous other mining ventures; he was a controversial figure, and many accused him of luring capitalists to their ruin with exaggerated claims. He died in 1914, shot in the forehead in a gun battle with a former partner. The name sometimes is spelled *Frazer Mountain*, but the USBGN ruled that Fraser, as William Fraser spelled it, is the correct form.

FRAZIER (Chaves; settlement; on US 70, 20 mi NE of Roswell; PO 1937–54, mail to Roswell). The stone ruins of the *Frazier School* still stand at this site, but nothing else. Name origin unknown.

FREEMAN MOUNTAIN, 8,700 ft. (Catron; 12 mi NE of Luna). A man named Freeman was killed on this mountain, where he also was buried.

FRENCH (Colfax; settlement; on E bank of the Canadian River, at the junction of the AT&SF RR and the PD Dawson RR line along the Vermejo River, 7 mi NE of Springer; PO 1908–45, mail to Springer). This former settlement was named for Capt. William French, who came to the US from French Park, Ireland, in 1883. He settled first in Grant County, then moved to Colfax County, where he became a prominent landowner. French was the author of *Recollections of a Western Ranchman 1883–1889*. He organized the *French Tract*, a group of farms with French as its center, but litigation over water rights doomed the enterprise. This lack of irrigation water, the community of French being overshadowed by nearby Springer and Maxwell, and the decline of rail transportation combined to doom the settlement, which never had more than 250 residents. Captain French eventually moved to England, where he died. Today the community of French survives only as a RR siding.

FRENCH CORNERS (Colfax; settlement; at junction of US 85 and NM 58, 6 mi N of Springer). Small, diffuse, inhabited community, named for the former village of French 3 mi NE (see entry).

FRENCH HENRY RIDGE (Colfax; NE of the Baldy Mountain summit). In 1870 a group of Frenchmen were among the many prospectors working in the Baldy Mountain area; they were led by Henry Buruel, known locally as "French Henry." He opened the French Henry Mine. *French Henry Camp* is located near the headwaters of South Poñil Creek, NE of Baldy Peak.

FRENCH LAKE (Colfax; 7 mi E of Cimarron). Like the settlement, this lake likely was named for Capt. William French, prominent local rancher and landowner (see *French*). The lake appears on some maps as *No. 2 Lake*.

FRESNAL (Otero). See *High Rolls*.

FRESNAL CANYON (Otero; on W side of the Sacramento Mountains, paralleling US 82 near High Rolls). This canyon takes its name from ash trees (Spanish, *fresno*), some of which are still found at the canyon's head. The first gristmill in the county was built on *Fresnal Creek* in 1887. The old Box Canyon Road from the crest of the Sacramento Mountains to Alamogordo passed through Fresnal Canyon. Fred Griffin, an early freighter, pronounced this road a "real team killer." See also *High Rolls*.

FRIJOLES CANYON, CREEK (Taos; 3.5 mi NE of Taos Pueblo). Named for bean fields irrigated by the stream.

FRIJOLES FALLS (Sandoval). See *Rito de los Frijoles*.

FRIO (general). Spanish, "cold," the 13 GNIS listings applied mostly to springs and streams.

FRIO (Quay; settlement; 3 mi NW of Forrest; PO 1918–22, mail to Jordan). This abandoned settlement was named for its proximity to the head of *Frio Draw* (see entry), which runs SE from here.

FRIO DRAW (Curry, Quay; heads about 3 mi NW of Forrest and runs SE into Texas). This is one of the few surface drainages in this portion of the Caprock. The origin of its name (Spanish, "cold") is unknown, though possibly it was inspired here by cold air collecting in the shallow valley.

FRISCO (Catron). See *San Francisco Plaza*.

FROG ROCK (McKinley; in NW corner of county, just E of Red Lake). A 1915 USBGN decision called this rough red-rock formation *The Beast*, but in 1959 the board approved Frog Rock as the accepted name.

FRONTERA (Doña Ana; settlement; 8 mi N of El Paso, W of the present NM–Texas boundary). Ephemeral settlement, named for its location near the Mexican border (Spanish, *frontera*, "border"). In 1851 a PO was operated here by T.F. White at Whites Rancho, but there was some question as to whether it was in NM or Texas; 1851 postmarks show NM, but 1852 ones show Texas.

FROST (Bernalillo; settlement; in the E foothills of the Sandia Mountains, E of San Antonio). Though this community and the early settler for whom it was named have vanished, *Frost Road* and *Frost Arroyo* preserve their memory.

FROST (Quay; settlement; 20 mi SE of Logan; PO 1909–10, mail to Porter). This ephemeral homesteader settlement has vanished; the origin of its name is unknown.

FRUITLAND (San Juan; settlement; on US 550, 11 mi W of Farmington; PO 1891–present). Mormons settled here about 1877–78, and they originally called this community *Burnham* to honor the Mormon bishop Luther C. Burnham, who was among the settlers. But soon afterward, in 1886, the Fruitland Trading Co. was established and named for extensive fruit growing in the area; when postmaster James R. Young in 1891 submitted a name for the PO, he chose Fruitland, presumably to promote local agriculture. Fruitland still is a rich farming area. Navajos call the locality by a name meaning "burned bread," from an incident in which a Navajo once observed a man burning a batch of bread here. Another Navajo name exists, meaning "cottonwood planted in place."

FRUITVALE (Bernalillo; settlement; NE of the junction of I-40 and the Rio Puerco). Ephemeral community that appeared on some maps. The name perhaps is derived from orchards associated with irrrigation projects here around 1920.

FRYING PAN CANYON (Catron; rises in the Kelly Mountains and runs S and W into San Francisco River). One story is that a frying pan was found here, another is that one was left hanging on a tree. SW NM also includes another *Frying Pan Canyon,* as well as a *Frying Pan Creek,* both in Luna County NW of Deming.

FULLERTON (Catron; settlement; on S side of the Plains of San Agustin). Former ranch trading point, named for John F. Fullerton, proprietor. Fullerton sold the store and ranch when his wife and one of two children died here. *Fullerton Canyon* is just SW.

FULLERTON (Luna). See *Chance City.*

FULTON (San Miguel; settlement; on AT&SF RR, NW of San Jose; PO 1888–1911, mail to Ribera). Fulton, now abandoned, was a RR station and PO. Origin of name unknown.

FUNDERBURG DRAW, SPRING (Catron; 6 mi NE of Luna). Named for a homesteader.

FUZZY MOUNTAIN, 8,573 ft. (McKinley). See *Zilditloi Mountain.*

GABALDON (San Miguel; settlement; SW
of Romeroville at Ojitos Frios; PO
1941–76). This was the name of the PO
at *Ojitos Frios* (see entry). Juan Manuel
Gabaldon came from Puebla, Mexico,
in 1731 and settled in Santa Fe. His descendants likely settled in this area, as
the settlement often is called *Los Gabaldones.*

GAGE (Luna; settlement, RR stop; on I-10,
20 mi W of Deming; PO 1882–1965,
mail to rural station of Deming). This
former settlement, now devolved to a
RR stop and highway interchange, was
settled in 1880 and named William
Gage, who with two other men was instrumental in developing mining in the
Victorio Mountains 3 mi to the SW, and
the settlement of Gage was an important
shipping point for the mines. A construction engineer on the SP RR also has
been mentioned as an eponymn. Gage's
first school, established 1916, was in a
boxcar, with children coming from the
RR, nearby ranches, and the Gage
mines.

GALENA (Lincoln). See *Nogal.*

GALISTEO (Santa Fe; settlement; on NM
41, 22 mi S of Santa Fe; PO 1893–1959,
mail to Lamy). Long before Europeans
settled here, this site on *Galisteo Creek*
was occupied by Indians. When
Coronado passed through in 1541, he
visited their pueblo, located 1.5 mi N of
the present village; he recorded its name
as *Ximena.* The pueblo was still here
when the Fray Rodríguez expedition
came in 1581, as it was when Castaño de
Sosa visited in 1591; he named the
pueblo *San Lucas.* In 1598, Oñate renamed the pueblo *Santa Ana,* and it was
known by that name until the Pueblo
Revolt of 1680, when the Indians killed
the priests and drove out the Spaniards.

In 1692 Vargas retook the pueblo from
the Indians, but in 1706 Gov. Cuervo y
Valdes re-established the pueblo with 90
Tano Indians, this time naming it
*Nuestra Señora de los Remedios de
Galisteo,* "Our Lady of the Remedies of
Galisteo," though it also was called Santa
Maria. By 1749 the pueblo had 350 in-
habitants, but smallpox and repeated
Comanche raids reduced their number
so that in 1794 the few survivors moved
to Santo Domingo Pueblo, where their
descendants still live.

Modern settlement of the site appears to have occurred after 1850,
though Hispanic ranchers and sheepherders had been in the area earlier. The
name Galisteo is an old term for a native
of Galicia in Spain, but it could also have
been transferred from a town in
Estremadura, Spain. To the Tewas, the
ancient pueblo and the modern town
are called by a name meaning "down-
country place," which also refers to the
whole region S of Santa Fe.

Galisteo Creek, also known as the
Galisteo River, heads near Lamy and
flows W to join the Rio Grande, 2 mi N
of Santo Domingo Pueblo. *Galisteo Lake*
is 1.5 mi S of Galisteo.

GALLEGO, GALLEGOS (general). Spanish,
"native of Galicia." The first persons in
NM with the Gallegos surname were the
brothers, José and Antonio Gallegos,
who had arrived sometime before the
Pueblo Revolt of 1680. They fled to El
Paso, where they died before the reconquest of 1692, but their children returned, and their descendants have given
their names to places throughout NM;
GNIS lists 45 places bearing the Gallegos
name.

GALLEGOS (Harding; settlement; in S part
of county, on Ute Creek, on NM 39; PO

1884–97, 1892–94, 1896–1955, mail to Logan). This community was settled in 1840 by Don Jesús María Gallegos, whose descendants still live and ranch here.

GALLEGOS (Torrance; settlement; in NW part of county, 9 mi W of Moriarty). A tiny community, located in *Cañon de Gallegos.*

GALLEGOS (San Juan; settlement; SE of Farmington, on ridge overlooking Gallegos Canyon). In 1896 Richard Thomas Findell Simpson, born in England, sold his farm at Kirtland (then Olio) and established a trading post and stage stop here; the tiny settlement took its name from nearby *Gallegos Canyon* (see entry). The settlement lasted through 1927, when Simpson sold the Gallegos complex to the Progressive Mercantile Co. and moved to Farmington.

GALLEGOS CANYON (San Juan; runs N to enter the San Juan River 3 mi E of Farmington). Also called *Gallegos Wash.* A family named Gallegos once grazed sheep here but did not homestead. Gallegos Spring in this canyon also bears their name.

GALLEGOS PEAK, 10,528 ft. (Taos; in the Sangre de Cristo Mountains, 3 mi N of Tres Ritos and the Rio Pueblo). See *Gallegos (general).*

GALLINA (general). This Spanish word can mean "chicken, hen," but in NM place names it usually refers to the *gallina de la tierra*, the wild turkey. GNIS lists 45 places in NM with this in their names; the English name Turkey appears 81 times. See *Gallo (general).*

GALLINA (Doña Ana). See Salem.

GALLINA (Rio Arriba; settlement; in the NW foothills of the Jemez Mountains, on NM 96; PO as Jacquez 1888–90, as Gallina 1890–present). Settled in 1818 by Antonio Ortiz, this community was called Jacquez when a PO was established, but two years later it reverted to Gallina. About 2 mi W of the main settlement is a tiny "suburb" called Gallina Plaza, named because *Gallina Creek* (see entry) is just to the W.

GALLINA CREEK, RIO GALLINA (Rio Arriba; creek heads in the NW Jemez Mountains, in the San Pedro Mountains,

and flows N past the hamlet of Gallina Plaza, north of which the stream becomes the Rio Gallina, which flows N and then swings SE S of Dead Man Peak eventually to join the Rio Chama). The Navajo name for this stream, "white water," is similar to the Tewa name. See *Gallina (general).*

GALLINA PEAK, 10,887 ft. (Taos; in Taos Range, N of Rio Hondo and S of Lobo Mountain). See Gallina (general).

GALLINAS (Lincoln). See *Holloway.*

GALLINAS (San Miguel; settlement; on NM 65, 12 mi NW of Las Vegas). Also known as *Las Gallinas*, this tiny inhabited community was named for its location on *Gallinas Creek,* as was the neighboring community of *Las Gallinas* approximately 2 mi W; 5 mi SE is the settlement of *Lower Gallinas.*

GALLINAS CREEK, GALLINAS RIVER (San Miguel, Guadalupe; creek heads in the Sangre de Cristo Mountains, SE of Elk Mountain, and flows SE to Las Vegas, where it becomes the Gallinas River, continues flowing SE to join the Pecos River 6 mi NW of Colonias). Early Hispanic settlers called this by its full name, *Río de las Gallinas*; see *Gallina (general).* A folktale says the stream originated as a teardrop from the "eye" on the rock race of Big Mike, a peak in the San Miguel Mountains.

GALLINAS MOUNTAINS (Lincoln; in NW part of county, immediately W of Corona, in Cibola NF). A domal uplift, with *Gallinas Peak,* 8,615 ft., its highest summit; the name appears in English on *West Turkey Cone,* a secondary summit immediately to the W of Gallinas Peak. See *Gallina (general).*

GALLINAS MOUNTAINS (Socorro; NW of Magdalena, in Cibola NF). The highest summit of this volcanic group is *Gallinas Peak,* 8,442 ft. The peak's Tewa name also means "turkey mountain"; see *Gallina (general).*

GALLINAS SPRING (San Miguel; settlement; in S part of county, 7 mi S of Chaperito; PO 1874–1906, mail to Chaperito). Former community, named for its association with *Ojo de las Gallinas.*

GALLO (general). Spanish, "rooster," but in NM place names it more often means "wild turkey." See *Gallina (general)*.

GALLO MOUNTAINS (Catron; in Apache NF, in W-central part of county, N of Aragon). This name likely refers to wild turkeys in this forested range; highest summit, *Gallo Peak*, 9,215 ft. *Gallo Lake* is in the S foothills of the Gallo Mountains; *Gallo Spring* is in the SE part of the mountains.

OJO DEL GALLO (Cibola; 3 mi SW of Grants, immediately N of San Rafael, on the W side of NM 53). This spring, an important historical site, likely was named for wild turkeys that frequented it; see *Gallo (general)*. It appeared as Ojo del Gallo on Bernardo Miera y Pacheco's map of the 1776 Domínguez-Escalante Expedition. It also was an important watering place for Navajos, and Col. John Washington's troops camped here during their expedition against the Navajos in 1849. Fort Wingate (see entry) was established here, before being moved farther W. And the village of San Rafael (see entry) owes its existence to this spring, which still feeds a pond ringed with reeds.

GALLO PEAK, 8,664 ft. (Cibola; in the E Zuni Mountains, SW of San Rafael). This summit, likely named for wild turkeys—see *Gallo (general)*—marked the western boundary of Laguna Pueblo tribal lands. Acoma Indians call it Ram Peak, probably for bighorn sheep that once lived here.

GALLO PEAK, 10,003 ft. (Torrance; in the central Manzano Mountains, 2.5 mi S of Osha Peak). See *Gallo (general)*.

GALLUP (McKinley; settlement, county seat; in W part of county, at the junction of I-40 and US 666 and NM 602; PO 1882–present). David L. Gallup in 1880 was auditor and paymaster for the A&P RR (later acquired by the AT&SF), and on payday RR workers would announce they were "going to Gallup's" to collect their money. David Gallup later became comptroller in the RR's New York office, but his name remained on the former RR camp. Before the RR arrived, the site was a stage stop, and the combined sta-tion, saloon, and store were called the *Blue Goose*. Navajos, for whom Gallup is an important trading center, call the town by a name meaning "spanned across," referring to a former foot-bridge over the Rio Puerco adjacent to the RR depot.

GAMERCO (McKinley; settlement; on US 666, 3 mi N of Gallup; PO 1923–64, mail to rural station of Gallup). In 1920 the Gallup American Coal Co. began sinking shafts into coal deposits here, but even before mining was underway the new company town had been platted and named by combining syllables in the company's name. The company moved abandoned houses from Heaton (see entry), another nearby coal camp, as well as building new ones. Heaton has not survived, but Gamerco has. Navajos call the coal camp by a name meaning "white smokestack."

GARCIA (general). Marcos García and Alvaro García Holgado, probably not related, arrived in NM with Oñate, and between 1598 and 1692 other Garcías came from Zacatecas, Puebla, and Mexico City. The name García comes from a village in Spain, which in turn comes from a Basque word, *artza*, meaning "crown prince." García is the most common and widespread Spanish surname in the Spanish-speaking world; GNIS shows it on 53 places in NM.

GARCIA (Union; settlement; in S-central part of county, NE of Bueyeros; PO 1892–98, 1904–09, mail to Barney). This settlement took the surname of its first postmistress, Placida R. García, and members of the García family still live in the area, though only a cemetery re-mains at the settlement.

GARCIA (Valencia; settlement; NW of Belen). A cluster of García families gave the name *Los Garcias* to this inhabited settlement. The community once was divided into *North Garcia* and *South Garcia*, though these now are primarily road names.

GARCIA PEAK, 10,925 ft. (Colfax; in the Cimarron Range, W of the headwaters of Rayado Creek). The connection be-tween this summit and a specific individual or family named García is unknown.

GARCIA PLAZA (Union). See *Louis*.

GARDEN OF THE GODS (Santa Fe; landform; on NM 14, N of Cerrillos). Vertical beds of polychrome sandstone and mudstone, a miniature version of the better-known Garden of the Gods near Colorado Springs, CO.

GARDINER (Colfax; settlement; 3 mi W of Raton, in Dillon Canyon; PO 1897–1940, mail to Raton). About 1881 James T. Gardiner, geologist for the SF RR, discovered coal in Dillon Canyon, and in 1882 the Old Gardiner Mine, or Blossburg No. 4, as it was called, began production. By 1896 a battery of coke ovens had been built here, and the town of Gardiner was growing. But after the Depression the mines closed. The machine shop closed in 1954, the coke ovens were abandoned, and Gardiner now is a ghost town.

Gardiner Canyon heads NW of Raton and runs E into Dillon Canyon.

GARFIELD (Doña Ana; settlement; on NM 187, 9 mi NW of Hatch; PO1896–present). The farming community now known as Garfield originally had been on a rise W of the present site; it moved after Elephant Butte Dam, completed in 1916, eliminated periodic flooding of the Rio Grande floodplain and permanent settlement became possible Like many towns in the Upper Mesilla Valley, this one originally had a Spanish name, *Loma Parda*, "gray hill," for a nearby hill, a name said to have been shared by both Garfield and Derry (see entry). The name Garfield likely somes from President James A. Garfield, assassinated in 1881, 15 years before the PO was established.

GARRAPATA CANYON, RIDGE (Taos; 3 mi N of San Cristobal, W of NM 522). Spanish, "sheep and cattle tick," which would have accompanied early ranching in the area.

GARRISON (Roosevelt; settlement; 29 mi S of Portales, 5 mi W of Causey; PO as Leach 1909–11, as Garrison 1911–19, mail to Longs). This homesteader settlement first was called *Leach*, for reasons unknown, but when Joel J. Garrison became postmaster he changed the name to his own. Nothing remains of Garrison but the name, which local people still recognize and use.

GASCON (Mora; settlement; in E foothills of Sangre de Cristo Mountains, on NM 105, NW of Rociada; PO 1898–1901, 1905–29, mail to Rociada). Gascon was named by early settler Jean Pendaries (see *Pendaries*) for the French province where he was born, Gascony. The *Rito de Gascon* heads NW of this inhabited village and flows into the Rito de San Jose here. Local people pronounce the name GAS-con.

GATLIN LAKE (Catron; in W part of county, 6 mi NW of Fox Mountain). Named for a locally prominent ranching family.

GAVAEDON (San Miguel; settlement; near Las Vegas, exact location unknown; PO 1917–19, mail to East Las Vegas). Ephemeral postal locality, name origin unknown.

GAVILAN (general). Spanish, "sparrow hawk," though the term is applied in NM to all sorts of raptors, except eagles.

GAVILAN (Rio Arriba; settlement; on NM 595, 6 mi N of Lindrith; PO 1915, rescinded, 1929–47, changed to Tapacitoes, 1947–1963, mail to Lindrith). This is a tiny farming and ranching community, mostly abandoned. Tapicitoes (see entry) is 5 mi to the N. *Gavilan Lake* is 3 mi SW.

GEM COMMUNITY (Union; settlement; NW of Clayton). Shortly after 1914 Gem was a diffuse but densely settled dry-farming community that took its name from the initials of George E. Merrilatt, one of the area's first homesteaders. Now large cattle ranches are in the area, and the name is all but forgotten.

GEMMERVILLE (Torrance; settlement; at the S side of Exit 203 on I-40 E of Moriarty). When members of the Gemmer family arrived here in 1981 to operate a service stop, the site was called *Longhorn Ranch*, but by 1986 truckers and other regulars were calling the place Gemmerville. Soon a sign was painted labelling the place "Gemmerville, pop.

20, elev. 7,000 ft." In 1995, 10 Gemmers resided at the locality, which included a restaurant, motel, gas station, CB radio shop, and night club.

GENOVA (Harding; settlement; in SE part of county; PO 1884–98, 1904–05, mail to Logan). Abandoned settlement, name origin unknown.

GEORGETOWN (Grant; settlement; NE of Silver City, 3 mi W of Mimbres; 1875–1903, mail to Mimbres). As early as 1866 prospectors had found silver in the hills just W of the Mimbres River, and by the early 1870s a small settlement had taken root around the Mimbres Mining and Reduction Co.'s operations. The camp was named Georgetown, for a multitude of reasons: the brothers, George and John R. Magruder, founders of the Mimbres Mining and Reduction Co., in 1872 had moved to Grant County from their hometown, Georgetown, D.C.; Georgetown, WI, was the hometown of Stanton Brannin, one of the first prospectors to locate claims in the area; and many of the miners had come from Colorado, where Georgetown was the site of the first important silver discovery in that state. It also has been suggested that John R. Magruder named the community to honor his brother. At the community's peak around 1888 Georgetown had 1,200 people, but smallpox drove away many residents, and when the price of silver fell in 1893 the camp was doomed. It has since vanished.

GERHARDT VALLEY (De Baca; in NE part of county). John and Frederick Gerhardt arrived as immigrants from Germany in 1854 and moved to NM. One brother settled here and the other at Cedar Springs, N of Alamogordo Creek. Their descendants still live in the valley named for them.

GERONIMO (general). In the Spanish Southwest this name usually refers to San Gerónimo, "St. Jerome," (ca. AD 340–420) a father of the Catholic Church and translator of the Vulgate Bible. But in NM and Arizona the name Geronimo also can refer to the name given by Hispanic people to the

Chiricahua Apache leader they so greatly feared. Among his own people, however, Geronimo was known by his Apache name, Goyathleh, "one who yawns."

GERONIMO (San Miguel). See *Mineral Hill.*

GERONIMO SPRINGS (Sierra; on Main St. in Truth of Consequences). These springs, with their reputed healing waters, were a favorite resting place of the Apaches, and Geronimo certainly would have known them well.

GHOST RANCH (Rio Arriba; conference center; 13 mi NW of Abiquiu). When Arthur Newton Pack, founder of the conference center, arrived in 1933, his guide to the property told him it had been called *Rancho de los Brujos,* "ranch of the witches," because it was supposed to have been haunted by evil sprits. "The name came to be freely translated as Ghost Ranch," said Pack. Some cottonwoods on the property were reputed to have served as gallows for local cattle thieves. The canyon was settled near the end of the 19th century by the Archuleta family, who built a stockade of cedar poles that came to be known as the Ghost House. A girl brought up in this house said she always believed the canyon was inhabited by evil spirits, or *brujos,* including "Earth Babies," six feet tall with red hair.

GIBSON (McKinley; settlement; 3 mi NE of Gallup; PO 1890–1945, mail to Gallup). Soon after coal was discovered here in 1882, the Crescent Coal Co. was organized, with John Gibson as mine superintendent. He was a popular local figure, and his name was given to the new camp. Despite fires in the mines and other problems, the town prospered and in 1919 had 1,200 inhabitants. But newer mines and a dwindling demand for coal in the 1940s doomed the town; today nothing remains, though *Gibson Canyon* N of Gallup preserves the name.

MESA GIGANTE, 6,657 ft. (Cibola; 8 mi E and NE of Laguna). "Giant Mesa" is a good descriptive name for this sprawling landform, 8 mi long and 5 mi wide, but the name may also be derived from Indian beliefs that a giant lived here.

GILA (general). The origin of this name is problematic. It almost certainly is a Spanish corruption of an Indian word, and the tribe most likely is Apache, for they are the Indians who in historic times inhabited the Gila region. The name has been linked to the Apache word for "spider," but some authorities on the Apache language have challenged this, and the most plausible explanation is that it is linked to the Apache word for "mountain," often transliterated as *tsihl* or *dzil*; the Apaches were a mountain people, and this is a very mountainous region. The name first appears in the Benavides journal of 1634, when he refers to the *Apaches de Xila*. The earliest map reference is the Nicolás de Fer map, produced in Paris in 1700, based upon the explorations and writings of Fray Eusebio Kino; this shows a *R. di Hila* flowing into the *R. de Sonaca*. *Río Xila* appears on Juan Nentwig's map of 1762, located W of *S. d. Mogollon Nacimiento de Xila*. These make clear that most early references were to the Gila River and not to the mountains, but the name, like the river, likely has a mountain origin.

GILA (Grant; settlement; on NM 211, about 27 mi NW of Silver City, 2 mi E of Cliff, on the E side of the Gila River, near its confluence with Duck Creek; PO 1875–present). This inhabited community takes its name from the Gila River. Locally, Gila often is linked with the nearby village of Cliff (see entry), their names often joined.

GILA CLIFF DWELLINGS NATIONAL MONUMENT (Catron; national monument, archaeological site; on the West Fork of the Gila River, 44 mi N of Silver City). Ancient Indians of the Mogollon culture lived in this area for an undetermined period, but sometime after A.D. 1000 they began constructing masonry dwellings in natural grottoes in the cliffs here. The dwellings were large and sophisticated, and the Indians practiced agriculture in the valley below. But by the early 1300s they had abandoned their homes; why they left is not known. The ruins were mentioned by Adolph Bandelier in 1884, and in 1907 they were designated a national monument.

GILA HOT SPRINGS (Grant; settlement; just S of Catron County line, on NM 15; PO 1903–04 in Catron County, rescinded, as Gila Hotsprings 1966–69, as Gila Hot Springs 1969–71, converted to rural branch). The locality here was first developed in 1898 by the cattle baron Tom Lyon, who established a hunting logdge called Lyons Lodge on the East Fork of the Gila River about a 1 mi E of the present resort, which was named for the hot springs and for the Gila River, which flows by here.

GILA NATIONAL FOREST (Grant, Hidalgo; SW NM). The vast Gila NF is comprised of areas originally established as the Datil and Gila Forests in 1899 and the Big Burros Forest in 1907; these units were combined in 1931 to form the Gila NF, named for the Gila River.

GILA RIVER (Grant; East, Middle, and West Forks rise in the Gila NF, come together near Gila Hot Springs and flow SW, crossing into Arizona to enter the Colorado River at Yuma). When Coronado passed through what is now SE Arizona in 1540, he christened as the *San Juan*—"as we reached it on St. John's day"—a river that since has been identified as the *Gila Bonita*. But when Fray Eusebio Kino explored the Southwest, the map he produced in 1695–96 mentioned this river, and Nicolás de Fer's map of 1700, based upon the Kino map, shows a *R. de Hila* flowing into a *R. de Sonaca*; the river has been known as the Gila ever since, though it has borne other names and variants as well: *Xila River, Río Gila, Jila River, Hela River, Río de los Apostles,* and *Río de Nombre Jesús*; a 1969 USBGN decision established Gila River as the accepted form. The three forks at the headwaters of the Gila have been referred to as "prongs." See *Gila (general)*.

GILA WILDERNESS (Catron, Grant; W of the Continental Divide, including the headwaters and drainage of the Gila River and nearby mountains). Mounting concern over loss of animal species and habitat here after 1900 led to the creation in 1924 of the Gila Wilderness, the first such wild area in the world to be preserved. The wilderness, named for the river, originally contained 755,000 acres, but portions later were excised to create the Aldo Leopold Wilderness (see entry), so the Gila Wilderness now contains 558,065 acres.

GILITA CREEK (Catron; at the headwaters of the Middle Fork of the Gila River). The name Gilita Creek combines elements of three languages—Apache, Spanish, and English; see *Gila (general)*.

GILLESPIE (De Baca; settlement; on the AT&SF RR, SW of Fort Sumner, E of Yeso). This abandoned locality was named for Powers Gillespie, a local resident.

GILLESPIE (Hidalgo; settlement; on the NE slopes of the Animas Mountains). George Adlai Feather reported this to be a small mining camp active in the late 1800s, as well as a hangout for the Curly Bill Brocius and Clanton gang of Tombstone, AZ. The camp sometimes was called *Gillespieville*. Name origin unknown.

GILMAN (Sandoval; in Guadalupe Canyon, on NM 485, 0.75 mi N of Cañones). The name Gilman was created in 1931 at the death of William H. Gilman, who came to the area in 1929 after the stock market crash and became vice president of operations for the SFNW RR. The former Gilman Sawmill here also was named for him.

GISE (San Miguel; RR locality; SE of Rowe, at the foot of Glorieta Mesa). Now just a RR sign, if that, this locality took the name of C.C. Gise, a local merchant.

GIVENS (Roosevelt; settlement; in E part of county, SE of Portales; PO 1908–13, mail to Arch). Abandoned homesteader settlement, named for its first postmaster, Joel E. Givens.

GLADIOLA (Lea; settlement; on US 380, 24 mi NE of Lovington, 8 mi E of Tatum; PO 1919–56, mail to Tatum). Originally called *Warren*, for a local family, this pioneer community at one time had a school, store, service station, and PO. Today little remains, though the the Gladiola oil pool here and the Warren Petroleum Co. plant preserve the community's two names. The origin of Gladiola is unknown.

GLADSTONE (Union; settlement; in SW part of county, near Colfax County line, on US 56, 36 mi E of Springer; PO 1888–present). About 1880 William H. Harris, an Englishman, immigrated here from Des Moines, IA. He had dreams of founding a religious colony, to be called the *Gladstone Colony*, named for the English statesman William E. Gladstone, whom Harris is said to have known. Settlers came to Harris's community from Texas, Oklahoma, and Kansas, but many soon became disillusioned and left. A service station-store and a PO still survive here.

GLASSCOCK (Eddy; settlement; in the Guadalupe Mountains, 20 mi S of Hope). Former ranch community, named for Lee Glasscock, owner of a sheep ranch here.

GLEASONS CANYON (Union; in NW part of county, NE of the junction of NM 456 and 551, a tributary of the Dry Cimarron River). Named for cattle rancher Fritz Gleason, who arrived in the late 1860s.

GLEN (De Baca; settlement; in S part of county, on W bank of the Pecos River; PO 1899–1908, mail to Sunnyside). Abandoned community, name origin unknown.

GLEN-WOODY (Taos; settlement; 14 mi SW of Taos, on the W bank of the Rio Grande, about 1 mi S of Pilar). In the late 1890s W.M. "Glen" Woody discovered low-grade gold deposits on the E bank of the Rio Grande about 1 mi below Pilar, and in 1902 Woody returned from the Klondike to develop them. A small mining camp, called Glen-Woody, with impressive milling facilities, developed, but the results were disappointing, and Woody turned to operating a flour mill and a stage coach line. The advent of the automobile doomed Woody's operations, and the settlement bearing his name has vanished.

GLENCOE (Lincoln; settlement; in the Ruidoso Valley, on US 70, 10 mi NE of Ruidoso Downs; PO 1901–present). This hamlet combines a synonymn for "valley" with the Coe family name. Coes settled here in 1880; Jasper N. Coe was the first postmaster. The Coes were among the early pioneers of Lincoln and Otero Counties (see *Mayhill*). Originally from Missouri, several brothers worked the Santa Fe Trail and homesteaded near Las Vegas, but in the mid-1870s they moved south. They got caught up in the Lincoln County War, backed the losing McSween faction, and moved away but soon returned; their descendants still live in the area. See also *Old Coe Lake*.

GLENRIO (Quay; settlement; on the CRI&P RR just S of I-40, at the Texas line; PO as Rock Island 1909–15, as Glenrio 1915–present). This small community was founded around 1901 when the CRI&P RR pushed W through here; it initially was named *Rock Island* for the RR. The name later was changed to Glenrio to avoid confusion between mail intended for the CRI&P depot here and mail meant for the town's PO, as well as to avoid confusion with Rock Island, TX. The inspiration of Glenrio, a rare blend of English (*glen*) and Spanish (*río*) name elements, is unknown, particularly as the village is neither in a valley nor on a river.

GLENWOOD (Catron; settlement; in SW part of county, 4 mi N of Pleasanton on US 180; PO as Graham 1895–1904, as Clear Creek 1904–06, as Glenwood 1906–12, 1917–present). The community later known as Glenwood had its beginnings in 1878, with a house built about 5 mi NE of the present village by two men, Fauster and Diming. When Allen Bush settled at the site, the locality became known as *Bush Ranch*, then as *Whitewater*, for being on Whitewater Creek. Still later, when it was a stage stop, it was called *Glenwood Springs*. About 1889, gold and silver discoveries in the nearby mountains led to a mining boom, and the community known as Graham sprang up, named for John T. Graham, superintendent of the Confidence Mine in Mogollon and builder of the mill here in 1893. In 1904, the name was changed to Clear Creek, then in 1906 when the PO moved to its present

location it took the name Glenwood, a name chosen by Mrs. Sarah Kitt. Graham remained behind and persisted until the mill, always a disappointment, closed in 1913; the town died soon after. The main reminder of Graham's existence is the steel walkway through the gorge of Whitewater Creek, where once pipes brought water to the mill; the walkway was nicknamed the *Catwalk* by miners who had to maintain it. Today Glenwood is a pleasant resort community and the site of a fish hatchery.

GLOBE (Eddy; settlement; 12 mi NW of Carlsbad, on the AT&SF RR, NW of Avalon Reservoir). Cattle-loading pens are all that remain of the tiny settlement that grew up around the Globe Mills and Mining Co. The company mined gypsum here and made it into plasterboard.

GLORIETA (Santa Fe; settlement; 18 mi SE of Santa Fe on I-25; PO as La Glorieta 1875–80, as Glorieta 1880–present). Several explanations have been offered for this Spanish name, meaning "bower, arbor." One is that early Spanish settlers named the site for its dense vegetation. But in Mexico the term also refers to a small square or gathering place surrounded by trees, as well as to a traffic circle and a street or road intersection, so the meaning "forested crossroads" possibly is behind the name here. *La Glorieta Pass* was a landmark for wagons on the Santa Fe Trail, and before the Civil War Pigeon's Ranch (see entry) near the summit was a hostelry and stage stop between Las Vegas and Santa Fe. Near the ranch, 1 mi E of the village of Glorieta, on March 26–28, 1862, a Union force commanded by Maj. John M. Chivington decisively defeated Confederate troops, dooming the Southern cause in NM. The modern village dates from 1879, with the construction of the AT&SF RR. The Glorieta Baptist Conference Center is here.

GLORIETA BALDY, 10,199 ft. (Santa Fe; in the Santa Fe Range of the Sangre de Cristo Mountains, E of Santa Fe and N of the village of Glorieta). Bare-summit peak, named for the nearby village.

GOAT (general). Since the earliest days of

European settlement, goats have been an important domestic animal in NM, and they have contributed 59 place names (GNIS) to the NM landscape, by getting lost, being found, getting killed, being rescued, or just being present. The Spanish form, *cabra*, is less common, occurring in only 13 names.

GOBERNADOR (Rio Arriba; settlement; in NW part of county, on US 64, near the heads of Gobernador and Frances Canyons; PO 1916–42, mail to Blanco). Established as a mining camp in 1875, this tiny settlement was named for *Gobernador Canyon* (see entry). Postal records show the PO briefly was known as *Smithburg*, but the name reverted to Gobernador; only a few abandoned buildings remain. *Gobernador Camp*, 2 mi W of NM 527, is a company town for workers in the the surrounding oil and gas fields.

GOBERNADOR CANYON (Rio Arriba; heads about 2 mi S of the site of the village of Gobernador, S of US 64, and runs NW into San Juan County to join the San Juan River at Archuleta). Two explanations exist as to why this name, Spanish for "governor," appears on this major watercourse. One is that as the major drainage in the area, the canyon "governs" all the nearby canyons. But more likely the name was transferred from El Gobernador Knob (see entry), or perhaps the name commemorates some early Spanish governor of NM or perhaps a Navajo elder.

EL GOBERNADOR KNOB, 7,600 ft. (Rio Arriba; mountain; 5 mi S of Gobernador). Spanish, "the governor." Prominent cone-shaped peak, whose name refers either to its dominance on the landscape or its location at the head of Gobernador Canyon (see entry). Gobernador Knob is one of several mountains sacred to the Navajos, and the peak goes by several names in the Navajo language. One name means "spruce, looking out," a simple descriptive name, but its other Navajo names refer to its importance in Navajo mythology; their meanings have been rendered as "hard goods mountain," "entrance mountain," and "male hogan mountain." Whiteshell Woman, a Navajo mythological figure, was born here.

GODFREY HILLS (Lincoln; in SW part of county, SE of Oscura). Said to have been named for an agent to the Mescalaro Apaches in the 1870s.

GOLD (general). Gold has been important in NM since the first Europeans arrived here in 1540 searching for it. GNIS lists 20 places with gold in their names, including Gold Dust, Golden Link, Golden Eagle, Gold Pan, Golden Cross, Golden Nugget, Golden Gate, and Fools Gold. The Spanish form, oro, is less common, appearing 11 times. See *Silver* (general).

GOLD CAMP (Doña Ana; settlement; on the E side of the San Andres Mountains, 12 mi N of Organ). Now within the White Sands Missile Range, Gold Camp was a mining camp.

GOLD DUST (Sierra; settlement; on NM 152, 4 mi NE of Hillsboro). Around 1880 a gold-mining boom brought miners to this area, and by 1881 the little tent camp of Gold Dust had developed. In the same valley, 2 mi NW, was the little camp of *Placeres*, and George Adlai Feather reported that during the boom here the valley was "almost a continuous line of tents and stone houses for a great distance." But when gold fever subsided, both camps died, and today little remains of either.

GOLD GRADE (Torrance; settlement; on the RR between Mountainair and Willard; PO 1907, mail to Willard). Little is known about this emphemeral community, including the inspiration of its name.

GOLD GULCH (Grant; SW of Silver City, in the Big Burro Mountains). Long known for its placer gold deposits. See also *Rattlesnake City*.

GOLD HILL (Grant; settlement; 13 mi NE of Lordsburg, just E of the Hidalgo County line, S of NM 90; PO 1886–96, mail to Lordsburg). In September 1884 David Egelston, a Forty-niner prospector, and two partners, Robert Black and Tom Parke, located the Gold Chief Mine here, and as other prospectors arrived a small camp developed, taking the name Gold Hill. The camp remained active for more than 20 years, with 125 residents in 1897, but eventually the deposits played out, the miners moved on, and today only the cemetery remains.

GOLD HILL, 12,711 ft. (Taos; in the Taos Range, N of the Taos Ski Valley). Extensive gold-mining operations were here in the 1890s and later. *Placer Fork*, a tributary of Columbine Creek, heads on the W side of this mountain; its name also refers to gold deposits here.

GOLDEN (Santa Fe; settlement; in SW part of county, on NM 14, 12 mi NE of San Antonito; PO 1880–1913, 1915–28 mail to Madrid). In 1839 placer gold was discovered on Tuerto Creek on the SW side of the Ortiz Mountains, and soon two small mining camps developed—Tuerto (see *New Placers*), on the creek, and *Real de San Francisco*, a short distance to the S, where Golden is now. The settlements were small, a few hundred Hispanics and Indians living in adobe dwellings and using burros to carry ore. But around 1880 several large mining companies moved in, and Real de San Francisco changed its name to Golden, reflecting high expectations of mineral wealth. The hopes were disappointed, however, and after 1884 Golden's population dwindled. Mining now is all but gone from the area; Tuerto has vanished, but Golden survives.

GOLDENBURG CANYON (Doña Ana; in SW San Andres Mountains). This canyon, near a military road that once crossed the mountains, was named for two brothers who built a trading post and saloon here about 1880. The canyon runs into *Goldenburg Draw*.

GOLONDRINA (general). Spanish, "swallow." The name, like the bird, is usually plural.

GOLONDRINAS (Mora; settlement; 21 mi N of Las Vegas, on NM 161). Tiny and tidy inhabited community on the Mora River.

GOLONDRINAS (Santa Fe). See *El Rancho de las Golondrinas*.

GOMEZ (general). A Francisco Gómez came to NM in 1598, but his descendants fled during the Pueblo Revolt of 1680 and apparently did not return until much later, as the name is not common in NM; GNIS lists only 5 Gomez place names.

GONZALES (general). The date of the first arrival of persons with this surname in NM is unknown, but Domíngo González, a lieutenant among the Spanish military, probably arrived as early as 1600. Sebastian González in 1642 was one of four regents of NM. And in 1664 another Domíngo González was living in Santa Fe with his wife, Francisca Martín; numerous other Gonzálezes are mentioned as being in NM before the Pueblo Revolt of 1680. Many of them and their descendants were among those who returned to NM with Vargas in 1692, and their name appears on 35 places in the state (GNIS).

GONZALES (McKinley; trading point; on NM 122, 3 mi W of Thoreau). *Gonzales Lake*, usually dry and just to the W of this active trading area, also bears the Gonzáles family name, though no Gonzáles's currently live here.

GONZALES (San Miguel). See *Maes*.

GONZALES RANCH (San Miguel; settlement; in W part of county, 6 mi SW of Villanueva; PO 1953–present). This is the name of the PO serving the community of *Los Diegos* (see entry).

GOOD HOPE (Rio Arriba). See *Hopewell*.

GOOSE CREEK, LAKE (Taos; creek heads at Goose Lake, just SE of Gold Hill, and flows NE to join the Red River 2 mi SE of the village). The creek and lake were named for waterfowl abundant in the area.

GOTERA (general). Spanish, "leak, drip, gutter, sprinkling"—all terms that in NM have been applied to various springs. See *Dripping Springs (general)*.

GOULD (Harding; settlement; near Mosquero; PO 1906–08, mail to Mosquero). Name origin unknown. Around 1906 land-hungry immigrants swarmed here, and from his makeshift office at Gould, Benjamin Brown, lawyer and real estate agent, did a brisk trade helping settlers locate 160-acre tracts. But Gould never was more than Brown and his office; with the burgeoning of Mosquero, Gould died and vanished.

GOULD PASS (Rio Arriba; 15 mi S of Navajo Reservoir, 1 mi E of the San Juan County line). Named for Harlan Gould, heavy equipment superintendent for the El Paso Natural Gas Co. in the San Juan Basin.

GRADY (Curry; settlement; in N part of county, at the junction of NM 209 and 469; PO 1907–present). This tidy farming and ranching community was named for Mrs. Pearl B. Grady, owner of much of the townsite and its first postmistress, though another account credits an Elizabeth Grady, also an early landowner, with the naming. Grady was intended to be a hub for the AT&SF RR; surveying began in 1906, with development soon thereafter, but the RR never arrived. Still, Grady has survived; in 1990 it had 110 residents, a school, a PO, and a grocery store.

GRAFTON (Sierra; settlement; in NW corner of county, 7 mi NW of Chloride; PO 1881–1904, mail to Phillipsburg). One of several Black Range mining camps, Grafton was born in the early 1880s and by 1883, with 75 houses, was one of the most important camps in the area. It had a school in 1884 and at its peak had over 300 residents. But its prominence was short-lived; by 1892 the camp had only 15 houses and 20 residents. A few abandoned buildings are all that remain today. The origin of its name is unknown, though D.F. Graft and Col. B. Grafton have been mentioned as eponymns.

GRAHAM (Catron). See Glenwood.

GRAMA (Sierra; RR locality; on the AT&SF RR, N of Rincon). This locality, now little more than a name, probably took the NM Spanish name for a pasture grass (genus Boutelona), though as George Adlai Feather observed after visiting here, this "may have been grama country once, but now the surrounding country has been denuded of grass."

GRAMA RIDGE (Lea; in SW part of county, S of NM 176). Grama is NM Spanish for a pasture grass (genus Boutelona).

GRAMMA VALLEY (De Baca; in SW part of county). This name comes from the grama grass growing here. In the early 1900s a man named White was killed here in a range quarrel, and the flat also became known as White Flat. A rural school named White Flat once was here.

GRAN QUIVIRA (general). Both as a name and as a place bearing the name, Gran Quivira is as elusive today as it was for the Spanish explorers who sought its fabled wealth more than four centuries ago. They associated Quivira with a fabulous realm always just beyond the horizon, and it was in search of Quivira that Coronado in 1541 journeyed from today's NM onto the Great Plains. In 1599, Oñate trekked eastward on a similar expedition—with similar fruitless results. At one time the name Quivira referred to all the unknown land in what is now the western US. Michael Lok's 1582 map shows Quivira at the western tip of the continent, with Culiacan, Galicia, and Florida covering the rest of the area between what are now Canada and Mexico. Fray Alonso de Benavides, head of early mission friars in NM, in 1634 referred to "the kingdom of Quivira" in the W and to another of the same name in the E. On a 1700 map based upon the 1695–96 explorations of Fray Eusebio Kino, the area W of NM is called Gran Quivira; the Gran means "great."

Then in the late 1800s, the name became associated with the extensive pueblo ruins SE of modern Mountainair. Probably some confusion arose between Quivira and Tabira, the name of one of the ruined pueblos. Indeed, when in 1909 another of the ruins, Pueblo de los Jumanos, was set aside for preservation, the name used was Gran Quivira National Monument; see Gran Guivira. Nor has the quest for Gran Quivira's legendary wealth abated; even in recent years treasure hunters have dug in the ruins by night searching for Spanish gold believed buried there.

As to the origins of the alluring

name, some scholars have attempted to trace it to the French *cuivre*, "copper," saying Indians got the term from Jacques Cartier. The name also has been said to be a Spanish corruption of the Wichita tribal name *Kirikurus*. More likely is an association with the Arabic *quivir*, "big," which appears in such Spanish place names as Guadalquivir. But like the place it names, Quivira remains essentially a mystery.

GRAN QUIVIRA (Torrance; settlement; adjacent to the former Gran Quivira National Monument; PO as Gran Quivera 1904–09, 1920–29, as Gran Quivira 1929–63). Small community, named for the ruins.

GRAN QUIVIRA (Socorro, Torrance; archaeological/historic site; on NM 55, 25 mi SE of Mountainair). Before a Spanish mission was established here, the mesa was the site of a Tompiro Indian pueblo, one of the Salinas group. The first Spaniards came with Oñate in 1598, when the pueblo was still inhabited; the Spaniards called it *Pueblo de los Jumanos*, "town of the striped ones," because the Indians decorated themselves with a stripe painted across the nose. (Another version of the Spanish name was *Pueblo de las Humanas*.) This name survives in *Mesa de los Jumanos* to the NE. The pueblo's inhabitants are said to have called it *Cueloze*, a name that appears related to the Tiwa name for the pueblo, *Queloo-she-aye*, "shield spring."

After the Spaniards arrived, Franciscan missionaries were assigned to convert the Indians; Fray Alonso de Benavides toured the Salinas Pueblos in 1627, and the first church was built in 1629. In 1659 Father Diego de Santander supervised construction of the massive church of *San Buenaventura*, whose ruins still stand. But by 1670, the pueblo and the mission had been abandoned, as had been those at Abo and Quarai (see entries), because of famine and Apache attacks.

As for how the site came to be called Gran Quivira, as Territorial Governor and NM scholar L. Bradford Prince explained: "It is not at all unlikely that when some party from the Rio Grande Valley, in search of game or gold, crossed the mountains and the wilderness lying to the E, and was suddenly amazed by the apparition of a dead city, silent and tenantless, but bearing the evidences of large population..., they should have associated with it the stories heard from childhood of the mythical center of riches and power, and called the new-found wonder the Gran Quivira." It also has been suggested the name is a corruption of *Tabira*, the name of one of the pueblos in the area. See *Gran Quivira* (general).

Since 1909, the ruins have been preserved, first as *Gran Quivira National Monument*, now as part of *Salinas Pueblo Missions National Monument*.

GRANADA (Cibola). See *Hawikuh*.

GRANADA (Doña Ana; settlement; 6 mi S of Mesilla Park and 7 mi E of La Mesa; PO 1896–98, mail to Mesilla Park). This name probably referred to a PO associated with Brazito (see entry); the name's origin is unknown, though it possibly was transferred here from the Granada of Spain.

GRANDE (general). Spanish, "big." A common name element, as in *Río Grande, Valle Grande*, and *Sierra Grande* (see entries).

GRANDE (Union; settlement; on US 64-87 and C&S RR, 11 mi NW of Grenville; PO 1908–11, mail to Des Moines). Abandoned homesteader community, likely named for nearby *Sierra Grande* (see entry).

GRANITE (general). GNIS lists 16 places in NM named for this common, durable rock, usually a complex admixture of quartz, feldspar, and biotite.

GRANT (Hidalgo). See *Shakespeare*.

GRANT CITY (Grant; settlement; 1 mi N of the confluence of Mangas Creek and the Gila River, NW of Silver City). A town by this name was laid out in 1868 near Fort West (see entry), but little or nothing came of it.

GRANT COUNTY (SW NM; county seat, Silver City). This county came into being in January 1868 when Gen. Ulysses S. Grant, credited with winning the Civil

War for the Union, was cresting in popularity. The following November he was elected US President.

GRANTS (Cibola; settlement, county seat; on the Rio San Jose, on I-40; PO as Grant 1882–1935, as Grants 1935–present). Prior to the Civil War, one Antonio Chávez is said to have settled on the S side of the Rio San Jose here. Later, in 1872, Don Jesús Blea homesteaded here, and because of cottonwoods—said to have been planted by Chávez—growing near the river, Blea called the place *Los Alamitos*, "the little cottonwoods." In 1881 the A&P RR pushed W through here, and with the RR came the Grant brothers: Angus A., John R., and Lewis A. They had been born in Ontario, Canada, but in the 1860s they had gone to Kansas to become RR contractors. At Los Alamitos they established a construction site that became known as *Grants Camp*. Later a coaling station was added, because it was halfway between Albuquerque and Gallup, and then a depot and a station that was called *Grants Station*. When the locality acquired a PO, it took the name *Grant*. But over the years, local Spanish-speaking people used the brothers' name in its plural form, calling the place *Grantes*, and in 1935 the PO name was changed to recognize this usage. Though the Grant brothers forever will be associated with the town bearing their name, most of their efforts were spent in Albuquerque, where they started a newspaper and a water works, owned the local electric utility, and built the Grant Opera. Another Albuquerque man important to the development of Grants was the lumberman George E. Breece (see *Breece*). In the 1920s he shifted his lumbering operations eastward from the Zuni Mountains and on the west side of Grants built a RR roundhouse and company housing that came to be known as *Breecetown*. The population of Grants mushroomed, resulting in Grants getting electricity and running water in 1929.

To Navajos, the site of Grants is important because the Comanche Massacre occurred here. At a spring near here a group of Navajos ambushed and massacred a Comanche raiding party that had stolen some Navajo horses. Two Navajo names have been reported for Grants: one meaning "white smoke," likely referring to a fumarole, the other meaning "legs spread apart," a reference to a prostitute who once plied her trade here.

GRAPEVINE CANYON (Otero; on the W slope of the Sacramento Mountains, about 35 mi SE of Alamogordo). Named for wild grapes growing at water sources here.

GRAPEVINE CANYON (Quay, Curry; S of NM 278, between Tucumcari and Grady). This was named for *Grapevine Springs*, just S of the Norton PO. Three brothers are said to have used the spring to irrigate vineyards here, nurturing a tiny community, but the vineyards and the community are gone, and only the name remains.

GRASS MOUNTAIN, 9,841 ft. (San Miguel; 1 mi NE of Cowles and SE of Pecos Baldy). Low mountain, with good pasture.

GRASSHOPPER (general). Insect names are rare in NM place names. Two canyons and one spring in NM are named for grasshoppers:

Grasshopper Canyon (McKinley; heads N of North Nutria, runs S).

Grasshopper Canyon (Santa Fe; heads S of Glorieta Baldy and runs S into Galisteo Creek, 3 mi W of Glorieta). Associated with *Grasshopper Spring*.

GRAY (Lincoln). See *Capitan*.

GRAY RANCH (Hidalgo; nature preserve; in S part of county, along the Continental Divide, E of NM 338). In the early 1950s the Kern County Land and Cattle Co. sold a 321,000-acre parcel of the historic Diamond A Ranch to a private investor, and this property became known as the Gray Ranch, honoring one of the earliest pioneer ranchers in NM's Bootheel. When the Nature Conservancy purchased the property in 1990, it became perhaps the world's largest private nature conservation project; the 500-square-mile tract is considered to have a remarkable array of plant and animal species. Since then, ownership of the Gray Ranch has passed to the Animas Foundation.

GREATHOUSES TAVERN (Lincoln; stage stop; in the Gallinas Mountains, in Red Cloud Canyon, W of Corona). Greathouses Tavern, operated by James "Whiskey Jim" Greathouse, was a stage stop on the White Oaks–Las Vegas road. It also was an outlaw hangout, and in 1880, following the killing here, possibly by Billy the Kid, of a deputy of Sheriff Pat Garrett, a posse burned the place to the ground. See *Corona*.

GREEN TREE (Lincoln). See *Ruidoso Downs*.

GREENE LAKE (Curry; in the center of Clovis). Old-timers still refer to this as *Dutchman Lake*, named for the Liebelt brothers who homesteaded in the area; in the American West of the 1800s, any non-English northern European tended to be known as a "Dutchman." But in the 1970s the name was formally changed to Greene Lake, to honor the man who owned the lake and gave it to the city.

GREENFIELD (Chaves; settlement; 4 mi NW of Hagerman on NM 2; PO 1911–25, mail to Dexter). This community was named for the Green Ranch, 1 mi S, developed by J.J. Hagerman and named by him for a friend. Though a few houses remain, the community's identity and name are fading.

GREENHORN (San Juan; settlement; in NW part of county, E of the La Plata River and W of McDermott Wash). Only the cemetery and an abandoned adobe building mark the site of this abandoned Hispanic community, among the earliest in the county. The origin of the name Greenhorn, clearly non-Hispanic, is unknown. The name survives on the *Greenhorn Ditch*, W of the former settlement.

GREENS GAP (Catron; settlement; 18 mi SW of Datil on NM 12; PO 1918–42, mail to Mangas). Only the cemetery remains at this former community, named for the M.M. and G.C. Green families, pioneer homesteaders.

GREGORIO LAKE (Rio Arriba; in the Si-
erra Nacimiento, 6 mi E of Cuba, at the entrance to the San Pedro Parks Wilderness). This scenic lake was created about 1900 when the Cuba Water Users Assoc. dammed *Cienega Gregorio* for irrigation. Though the name often appears as San *Gregorio Lake*, the correct form is simply Gregorio and comes not from St. Gregory but from a sheepherder who worked in the area before 1900.

GRENVILLE (Union; settlement; on US 64-87 and NM 453, 27 mi NW of Clayton; PO 1888–present). Grenville is located about 4 mi NW of the Santa Fe Trail, but this tiny settlement really owes its existence to the arrival in 1880 of the C&S RR, bringing land-hungry sodbusters eager to settle. They named the town for Grenville M. Dodge, soldier, politician, and RR official instrumental in the completion of the line through this part of the state. By 1921 the town's population had reached 700. But it has declined steadily ever since, and in 1988 only 27 people—in nine families—remained. *Grenville Caves* are 8 mi W.

GRIEGO (general). In the Italo-Spanish of the 16th century, *Griego* meant "Greek," and when Juan Griego answered Oñate's muster-roll in 1597 in Mexico, he stated he was a native of the city of Candia in Greece. (The great painter, El Greco, "the Greek," would have been a contemporary and also came from Candia.) Juan Griego married Pascuala Bernal, who died in 1626, and their descendants have spread throughout NM. The name Griego appears on 9 NM places (GNIS).

GRIEGOS, LOS GRIEGOS (Bernalillo; settlement; NW suburb of Albuquerque; PO 1903–13, mail to Old Albuquerque). One of Albuquerque's many satellite communities, established about 1708 when land was granted to Juan Griego; his family name meant "Greek." Scattered along Griegos Road, the community was absorbed into the city of Albuquerque in the 1950s. See *Griego (general)*.

LOS GRIEGOS, 10,117 ft. (Sandoval; mountain; in central Jemez Mountains, 1.5 mi S of NM 4, 1 mi N of Cerro Pelado). "The Griego folks," for reasons unknown. See *Griego (general)*.

GRIER (Curry; settlement; on US 60-84, 11 mi W of Clovis; PO as Havener 1910–21, as Grier 1921–56, mail to Clovis). This was one of the farming communities that sprang up almost overnight during construction of the SF RR's Belen Cutoff (1903–07). The settlement originally was called *Havener*, said to commemorate a town founder, a lawyer from Clovis, who eventually relocated to Amarillo, TX, while its RR station was called Grier. The origin of this name is obscure; some say Grier was an early mountain man and trapper, like Bent and St. Vrain, whose names the RR placed on nearby communties. Others say Grier was a RR official. Still other accounts say Grier was the maiden name of an official's wife. A few houses and a grain elevator remain, but little else.

GRINGO LAKE, PEAK, 7,305 ft. (Colfax; in E part of county, S of Johnson Mesa). Though the term since has acquired pejorative overtones, *gringo* originally was used by NM Hispanics simply to refer to non-Hispanic and non-Indian foreigners who spoke Spanish poorly, particularly English-speaking immigrants after 1848. The term originally came from Spain, where perhaps it was a corruption of *griego*, "Greek." The specific origin of these NM names is unknown.

GROUSE MESA, 11,403 ft. (Rio Arriba; in the Brazos region, SE of Chama, 1.5 mi NW of Brazos Peak). Named for the bird.

GROUSE MOUNTAIN, 10,135 ft. (Catron; in the Mogollon Mountains, S of Whitewater Creek and W of Whitewater Baldy). Without doubt, grouse are found here.

GRULLA NATIONAL WILDLIFE REFUGE (Roosevelt; 3 mi S of Arch, SE of Portales). This 3,236-acre refuge, including grasslands and a shallow saline lake, is a winter roosting area for large numbers of lesser sandhill cranes, hence the name; *grulla* is Spanish and means "crane."

LA GRULLA RIDGE, 10,032 ft. (Colfax; in S part of county, SE of Agua Fria Peak). Spanish, "the crane."

GRUMBLE GULCH, GRUMBLE DRAW (Socorro; N of Bingham and W of Claunch, on Chupadera Mesa). Said to have been named for an early homesteader.

GUACHUPANGUE (Rio Arriba; settlement; on NM 30, just SW of Española, on the W bank of the Rio Grande). Likes its neighbor, *El Guache* (see entry), this tiny inhabited settlement has a name that appears to have a Tewa origin, though no specific Tewa source words have been discovered. The current Tewa name means "mud string place," perhaps meaning "string of mud puddles."

GUADALUPE (general). Most of the 44 Guadalupe names in NM (GNIS) honor *Nuestra Señora de Guadalupe*, Jesus's mother who appeared as a vision to the Indian Juan Diego at the Indian village of Tepeyac near Mexico City in 1531. The vision was extremely important for the spread of Catholicism in the New World, for the appearance of the "Dark Virgin" was taken by the Indians as a sign that Christianity was not just for light-skinned Europeans but was meant for them also.

GUADALUPE (De Baca; settlement; in NW part of county, 0.5 miles W of the Pecos River; PO 1900–29). When the Casaus family settled here in the 1860s, they named the locality for the Virgin of Guadalupe—see *Guadalupe (general)*— and a church dedicated to *Nuestra Señora de Guadalupe* still stands here. The community thrived, but its future was truncated when the AT&SF RR bypassed it around 1905, though Guadalupe retained enough population and status that the community in 1917 was considered a possible seat for newly created De Baca County. The Trujillo family had an *hacienda* at Guadalupe— Trujillos still live in the area—and they called the locality *Las Tortolas*, "the turtledoves," for the doves in the cottonwoods surrounding a spring. Though the community is all but gone, the name Guadalupe still is recognized and used in the area.

GUADALUPE (Doña Ana). See *Tortugas*.

GUADALUPE (Guadalupe; settlement; on
SP RR, 15 mi W of Santa Rosa; PO
1900–41). This was never much more
than a RR siding with a PO; now it's not
even that. The locality's name, like that
of the county, commemorates the Virgin
of Guadalupe; see *Guadalupe (general)*.
Nearby is the *Mesita de Guadalupe.*
GUADALUPE (Sandoval; settlement; on the
Rio Puerco, 5 mi SW of Cabezon Peak;
PO as Miller 1898–1905, as Ojo del Padre 1940–58, mail to Cuba). At one time
four communities existed in the Rio
Puerco area: Casa Salazar, Cabezon, San
Luis (see entries), and this hamlet,
named for the Virgin of Guadalupe; see
Guadalupe (general). Guadalupe once
was known as *Ojo del Padre*, "spring of
the Father," for a spring by that name at
the community. The PO also has been
known as *Miller*, for reasons unknown,
though Miller is a common family name
in the county. A short distance up *Cañon
Guadalupe* is *Guadalupe Spring. Cañon
Guadalupe* heads in the Cebolleta
Mountains and runs E to join the Rio
Puerco just S of the village of Guadalupe. The canyon's Navajo name means
"little rock canyon." *Cerro Guadalupe*,
6,844 ft., a volcanic plug, is 2 mi NE of
village of Guadalupe.
GUADALUPE COUNTY (E-central NM;
county seat, Santa Rosa). This county
was created by the territorial legislature
in 1891 and named for Our Lady of
Guadalupe; see *Guadalupe (general)*. In
this area, however, the name predates
the county, for earlier documents show
an old road running by the *Mesita de
Guadalupe*, 16 mi SW of Santa Rosa, to
the *Llano de Guadalupe* (Guadalupe
Plain). When the county was created, its
first seat was Puerto de Luna, 10 mi SE
of Santa Rosa, but as Santa Rosa grew
the seat was moved N. In 1903, following the creation of Roosevelt County,
which honored the "Rough Rider" President, Theodore Roosevelt, the territorial
legislature renamed this county *Leonard
Wood*, for a colonel in the First NM Volunteer Cavalry (the "Rough Riders"),
but people disliked the name change,
and Guadalupe became possibly the

nation's only county to lose its name
and then regain it.
MESA DE GUADALUPE, 6,968 ft.
(Sandoval; steep-sided mesa, just N of
the confluence of the Jemez River and
the Rio Guadalupe). In his journal entry
of Aug. 20, 1849, Lt. James Simpson recorded that Francisco Hosta, his Jemez
Indian informant, had told him that
while the Indians were living on this
mesa, many years earlier, they had killed
a priest. Then, ignoring warnings that
armed Spaniards were in the valley below, the Indians went to sleep. During
the night, the Spaniards attacked the
Indians, and during the ensuing battle
there appeared from the direction of
Cañon de Guadalupe a vision of *Nuestra
Señora de Guadalupe*—see *Guadalupe
(general)*—while from *Cañon de San
Diego* came a vision of the saint for
whom that canyon was named. The Indians fled in terror. *Virgin Mesa* (see
entry), the much larger mesa just to the
N of which Mesa de Guadalupe is an
outlier, also likely takes its name from
the Guadalupe association. The legend
may be just that, but the pueblo on the
mesa was real, as its ruins atop the mesa
attest. Its name in the Towa language is
Astialakwa (see entry).
MESITA DE GUADALUPE (Guadalupe).
See *Guadalupe County.*
GUADALUPE MOUNTAINS (Chaves,
Eddy, Otero; in SE NM, W of Carlsbad,
extending into Texas). The most likely
explanation for the name being on this
major range is that it was transfered
from the Franciscan mission of *Nuestra
Señora de Guadalupe*—see *Guadalupe
(general)*—established in 1668 at El
Paso, the southernmost of the
Franciscan missions of NM. A western
spur of the range has been named the
Brokeoff Mountains (see entry).
Guadalupe Pass, in Texas, was on an important stage route, and *Guadalupe Peak*
and *El Capitan*, also in Texas, were important landmarks for pioneers.
GUADALUPITA (Mora; settlement; on NM
434, 14 mi NE of Mora; PO
1879–present). Small community, whose
formal name is *Nuestra Señora de*

Guadalupita, "Our Lady of Little Guadalupe."

GUAJE CANYON (Santa Fe; heads in extreme NW part of county and runs SE to join the Rio Grande 2 mi SW of San Ildefonso Pueblo at Otowi). American Spanish, "gourd." Tewas at San Ildefonso call it "great canyon." *Guaje Mountain,* 7,636 ft., is just S of Guaje Canyon, 1 mi NE of Los Alamos.

GUAJOLOTE (general). In NM Spanish this means "turkey."

GUAM (McKinley). See *Coolidge.*

GUIQUE (Rio Arriba). See *El Guique.*

GUILLOU (San Miguel; settlement; on the Rio Tecolote, SE of Geronimo; PO 1899–1904, mail to Las Vegas). This name appears on some early maps as *Guillott,* but in fact, the village, now abandoned, took the name of its postmaster, H.C. Guillou.

GUNSIGHT CANYON (Eddy; heads at Guadalupe Ridge, 36 mi SW of Carlsbad). Someone looking out from the head of this canyon sees a small hill between the mountains, resembling a gunsight.

GURULE (Bernalillo; settlement; N of Albuquerque, exact location unknown; PO 1892, mail to Albuquerque). Persons with this Spanish surname were living in the Albuquerque area as early as 1699, when Eleña Gallegos married Santiago Gurulé (see *Elena Gallegos Picnic Area*). Felipe J. Gurulé was postmaster during the three months a PO existed here.

GUSDORF (Taos; settlement; on US 64 E of Taos, W of Agua Fria). Alexander Gusdorf, locally known as Don Alejandro, and his brother, Gerson, were pioneer businessmen in Taos. They were involved in the mining ventures of the 1890s and operated a mercantile store in Twining.

GUSANO (San Miguel; settlement; SE of Rowe, exact location unknown). Spanish, "worm." George Adlai Feather reported this as the site of an ancient pueblo near Pecos Pueblo, with a settlement here in 1820; it was an *alcaldía* in 1844. Gusano Mesa is on the SW bank of the Pecos River, SW of San Ysidro.

GUT ACHE MESA (Catron; N of Alma, near Saliz Pass on US 180). As T.M. Pearce related, "This grazing area was named *Belly-ache* or *Gut-ache Mesa,* because a cowboy cook warmed over some soured *frijoles,* thus upsetting the stomaches of all the cowhands on a roundup. Another version blames bad son-of-a-gun stew for the upset." USFS officials complain about signs with this name repeatedly being stolen as curiosities.

GUTIERREZVILLE (Catron; settlement; on NM 12, 7 mi SW of Datil). Tiny residential cluster, named for a Gutiérrez family that once lived here. The first Gutiérrez mentioned as being in NM was Alonso Gutiérrez, who in 1626 was a 40-year-old married soldier living in Santa Fe.

GUY (Union; settlement; on NM 370, 37 mi NW of Clayton; PO 1910–45, mail to Des Moines). This abandoned community was once an important ranching headquarters. The name, whose origin is unknown, is still recognized in the area.

GUZMANS LOOKOUT MOUNTAIN, 4,762 ft. (Doña Ana; SW of Las Cruces, 3 mi N of the Mexican boundary, 9 mi W of Mount Riley). Name origin unknown. *Guzmans Mine* is here, and a *Guzman Lake* is farther S in Mexico. The peak was an observation point during the Apache wars.

GYSIN CITY (Taos; settlement; in the Sangre de Cristo Mountains, NE of Red River). In spring 1895, as mining fever swept the Keystone Mining District, miner John A. Gysin promoted a new town 1,300 yards W of Anchor (see entry). But despite a favorable location and initial enthusiasm, by summer the miners—including Gysin—had lost interest and drifted elsewhere.

HAAG (Curry; settlement; 6 mi N of Ranchvale, 12 mi NW of Clovis; PO 1900–13, mail to Clovis). This abandoned homesteader community took the name of its first postmaster, George F. Haag.

HACHITA (Grant; settlement; in S extremity of county, at the junction of NM 9 and 81; PO 1882–present). About 1875 a mining camp developed in the Little Hatchet Mountains. The mountains supplied the camp not only with silver, lead, copper, and turquoise but also its name, "little hatchet." Hachita grew to 300 residents by 1884, but it began to decline in the 1890s. Soon after 1900, the EP&SW RR laid tracks 9 mi E of Hachita, and a RR settlement sprang up, siphoning off still more residents and dividing the community into *Old Hachita* and *New Hachita*. Today the RR has gone, but Hachita—New Hachita, that is—remains. The *Hachita Valley* is S of Hachita.

HACIENDA (general). Spanish homesteads, especially along the Rio Grande, were called *estancias* in the 17th century and *haciendas* in the 18th, though they were hardly the luxurious estates designated by the term elsewhere in the Spanish New World. An example of the few wealthy *haciendas* in NM was the *Hacienda de los Luceros,* situated on the Sebastian Martín land grant of 1703. The main house was used in 1846–54 as the Rio Arriba County courthouse.

HACIENDA ACRES (Doña Ana; settlement; 9 mi NE of Las Cruces, on US 70-82). Modern inhabited rural residential development, with a fanciful name lacking association with an historical *hacienda* here.

HACKBERRY (general). At least two species of hackberry (genus *Celtis*) are found in NM: the Texas hackberry and the more common netleaf hackberry. T.M. Pearce described it as "a small tree with veiny thick leaves that seems very much a stranger in the arid NM environment." GNIS lists at least 30 places in NM with Hackberry in their names.

HADLEY (Luna; settlement; on the NE side of Cookes Peak; PO 1890–95, mail to Cookes). Walter C. Hadley was a miner with projects and interests throughout SW NM. He managed mines in Lake Valley, and he probably was involved with this mining camp. Originally from Las Vegas, NM, he died in 1896. Of the settlement likely named for him, only foundations and a cemetery remain. See also *Hadley (San Miguel).*

HADLEY (San Miguel; settlement; in NW part of county, exact location unknown; PO 1904–05, mail to Rociada). Ephemeral postal locality, name origin unknown, though an association with Walter C. Hadley is possible; see also *Hadley (Luna).*

HAGAN (Sandoval; settlement; 10 mi SE of Algodones, on Uña de Gato Arroyo; PO 1903–09, 1929–31, mail to Bernalillo). Hagan was born in 1902 with the discovery of coal here and the establishment of the NM Fuel and Iron Co; two years later Hagan's sister community of Coyote (see entry) was born 3 mi to the NE. Hagan had abundant coal but lacked a means of getting it to markets, and repeated promises and plans to built a RR ultimately proved barren. Finally, in 1924, the RGE RR laid tracks to Hagan—Coyote already had died—and Hagan enjoyed a six-year boom. But when the coal mines failed, the town died also, and by 1950 no residents remained. The origin of its name has been lost. *Hagan Junction*, NW of Hagan, NE of Algodones, near the Rio Grande, was a station on the short-lived RR line to Hagan; see also *Elota.*

HAGARSTOWN (Sierra; settlement; in the Black Range, on Carbonate Creek, 5 mi N of Kingston). This was one of numerous ephemeral mining camps in the Black Range in the late 1800s; in 1895 it had a dozen houses. George Adlai Feather reported that it was named for H.J. Hagar, a lumberman.

HAGERMAN (Chaves; settlement; on NM 2, 17 mi SE of Roswell; PO as Feliz 1894–95, as Hagerman 1895–present). In 1894 a town was laid out on the new PV&NE RR and named *Feliz,* for the Rio Felix (see entry), which enters the Pecos just N of the town, but the name was soon changed to honor J.J. Hagerman, builder of the RR. Hagerman's RR later was acquired by the AT&SF, but his name remains on the town.

HAHN (Bernalillo; settlement; on NM 313, 4 mi N of Albuquerque). Hahn appears on early maps as an AT&SF RR stop and trading point. It was established about 1910 and named for W.H. Hahn, an early Albuquerque merchant. The name survives on *Hahn Arroyo,* which runs from the Sandia Mountains to the Rio Grande.

HAILE (Guadalupe; settlement; S of Cuervo; PO 1907–18, mail to Cuervo). Abandoned community; first postmaster, James W. Haile.

HALF WAY HOUSE (Doña Ana). See *Anthony.*

HALFMOON PARK (Catron; just E of Mogollon Baldy Peak). Grassy area, shaped like a half-moon.

HALFWAY (Lea; settlement; on US 62-180). Service locality, located "halfway" between Hobbs and Carlsbad.

HALLS PEAK (Mora; settlement; on Ocate Creek, 5 mi NW of Ocate; PO as Vandoritos, 1886–87, as Halls Peak 1887–1912, mail to Ocate). In 1878 a young Presbyterian missionary couple, Robert H. and Sadie H. Hall, arrived in NM to established a school at Ocate, as few public schools existed in NM at that time. They established a school in a canyon, at the foot of the 8,756-foot peak

later named for them; two years later they established another school two miles farther up the canyon and built a house. A PO was established in 1886 and originally called *Vandoritos,* a misspelling of the Spanish *vanderitos,* meaning obscure, but the name was changed to Halls Peak when the PO was moved to the site of the school in 1887. For 20 years the Halls lived and labored near Ocate, until Robert's health failed, and in 1898 the couple returned to Ohio, where Robert soon died. An Ocate resident later wrote of him, "Heroic is not too strong a word to characterize this couple of great workers in NM missions." The school closed in 1899. Today the Halls' residence is a ranch house.

HALONA (Cibola). See *Zuni.*

HAMILTON (San Miguel). See *Copper City.*

HAMILTON MESA, 10,483 ft. (Mora, San Miguel; runs NE from Cowles). Long, high mesa; name origin unknown but likely related to the abandoned locality of Hamilton (see entry).

HANLEY (Quay; settlement; 10 mi W of Tucumcari; PO 1907–18, mail to Tucumcari). Hanley, now abandoned, was a homesteader community, with a general store, a school, and a PO. The name originally proposed for the PO was *Palomas,* because that was the name of the nearest RR station, but a Palomas already existed in NM, in Sierra County, so the name Hanley was given instead, for reasons unknown.

HAMMONDSVILLE (Grant; settlement; on the Gila River, exact location unknown). An 1874 issue of the *Mesilla News* mentioned that 7 families from California located at this site, which seems soon thereafter to have vanished from history.

HANNA MOUNTAIN, 6,268 ft. (Grant; in NW corner of county, 5 mi E of Arizona line, 4 mi N of Mule Creek). The story told around Glenwood is that a wagon train was ambushed by Indians here, and an entire family named Hanna was killed.

HANOVER (Grant; settlement; on NM 152, 4 mi NE of Central; PO 1892–present). This mining camp was named for the

Hanover Mines, named by prospectors, at least one of whom, Sofio Henkel, had come to the US from Hanover, Germany. Henkel mined here from 1841 to 1843, when he was driven away by Apaches. When the SC&N RR was built here in 1891 the camp's future looked bright; it sometimes was called *Hanover Junction.* But Hanover's hopes were dashed by the depression of 1893, and today slag heaps, rusty machinery, and a few aging Victorian houses are grim reminders of the fickleness of mining fortunes.

HANSBURG (Grant; settlement; on the Mimbres River, near Dwyer; PO 1892–94). This postal locality, long defunct, took the name of its first postmistress, Emma J. Hansburg. Another postmaster, H.H. Hansburg, was jailed for embezzlement of postal funds.

HANSONBURG (Socorro; settlement; in E part of county, NW of Oscura Peak; PO 1906–10, mail to San Antonio). Abandoned mining community, said to be named for an old prospector named Hanson.

HAPPY VALLEY (Eddy; settlement; western suburb of Carlsbad). Happy Valley, located indeed in a valley, began as a farming community. Later, potash miners settled here. One person has explained the name by saying the absence of land-use restrictions "made a lot of people happy."

HARD CASH (Santa Fe; settlement; 5 mi N of Cerrillos). Tiny, short-living mining locality associated with the Hard Cash Mine.

HARDCASTLE CANYON (Catron; runs SE into Apache Creek). Capt. E.L. Hardcastle served on the US-Mexican Boundary Commission in 1849.

HARDING COUNTY (NE NM; county seat, Mosquero). Created by the state legislature in 1921, this county was named to honor Warren G. Harding, who had just been inaugurated 29th President of the US.

HARENCE (Sandoval; settlement; near Cuba, exact location unknown; PO 1911, mail to Señorito). Ephemeral locality, name origin unknown.

HARLAN (Colfax; locality; just W of Cimarron). This locality was named for T.B. Harlan of St. Louis, MO, who was chief counsel of the Maxwell Land Grant Co. Little remains but the name.

HARRINGTON (Union; settlement; in SW corner of county; PO 1910–17, mail to Gladstone). Ephemeral homesteader community, name origin unknown.

HARRIS (Quay; settlement; in SW corner of county; PO 1908–18, mail to Lucille). This abandoned community took the surname of its first postmaster, Otto W. Harris.

HARRIS MESA (San Juan; NE of Angel Peak, SE of Bloomfield). Named for R.W. "Lazy" Harris, first superintendent for the El Paso Natural Gas Co. in the San Juan Basin. His nickname came from his large size and slow movement rather than from sloth.

HARRY MCADAMS STATE PARK (Lea; at the Hobbs Industrial-Air Park, 4 mi NW of the city on NM 18). Harry McAdams was born in Lorena, TX, in 1916. After a distinguished military career he settled in Hobbs in 1946 and soon became a prominent civic leader. He became a state senator in 1977 and worked in the legislature for the creation of a state park near Hobbs. The park originally was called *Lea County State Park,* but in 1982 the name was changed to honor the man so instrumental in the park's creation.

HART CITY (Cibola; settlement; 22 mi SE of Gallup, in the Zuni Mountains). By 1899 the lumbermen Henry Hart and W.S. Bliss had sawmills operating in the Zuni Mountains, and the following year *The Elk,* a Gallup newspaper, described Hart City as having a well-stocked merchandise store and "one of the best sawmills in the Zuni range." Like other Zuni Mountains lumber camps, Hart City vanished with the stands of virgin forest that had created it.

HARTFORD (Quay; settlement; 12 mi NW of House; PO 1907–10, mail to Looney). Nothing remains of this abandoned homesteader community, including information about its name.

HARTSBURG (Otero; settlement; in the Jarilla Mountains, exact location unknown). This was never more than a short-lived restaurant and inn, established by a man named Hart.

HASPEROS CANYON (Lincoln; heads in the Jicarilla Mountains 3 mi E of Ancho and runs N). *Hasperos* is a local Spanish word for a gypsum-like rock, used for making plaster for adobes, found within the canyon. The name has been spelled *Asparos* and *Hasparos,* but the USBGN in 1981 established Hasperos as the accepted form. *Little Hasperos Canyon* is nearby.

HASSELL (Quay; settlement; in SW corner of county, 20 mi NE of Fort Sumner; PO 1907–48). Like many other homesteader communities on the eastern plains, Hassell took the surname of its first postmaster, John W. Hassell. The village is gone, but the cemetery is maintained, and people in the area still recognize the name.

HASSLER VALLEY (McKinley; settlement; 2 mi N of Gallup). Red Hassler subdivided his property here and created this inhabited settlement.

HATCH (Doña Ana; settlement; at the junction of NM 185, 187, 26, and 154, 33 mi NW of Las Cruces; PO 1887–present). Hatch originally was settled as *Santa Barbara* in 1851, but Apache raids drove the settlers away until the establishment of Fort Thorn (see entry) in 1853. When the fort closed in 1860, the settlement was again abandoned and not reoccupied until 1875, when it was called Hatch, in honor of Gen. Edward Hatch, who had been commander of Fort Thorn, a few miles NW of the present site. In the 1880s the settlement became a stop on the AT&SF RR's diagonal line between Rincon and Deming, the RR calling it *Hatchs Station.* In addition to the old village of Santa Barbara, Hatch has been associated closely with two other nearby villages: Colorado, now Rodey (see entry), to the SE, and Santa Teresa, or Placitas (see entry), to the W.

HATCHET MOUNTAINS, BIG AND LITTLE (Grant, Hidalgo; in SW corner

of NM, S and E of the Continental Divide, the Little Hatchets to the N, the Big Hatchets to the SE). This name's origin is obscure. The mountains' English name clearly is a corruption of the Spanish *hacheta,* "little ax." Some scholars have attempted to link the name to "little torch," or "signal hill," but it appears as *S. de la Hacha,* "mountains of the ax," on Juan Nentwig's 1762 map. The mountains are separated by *Hatchet Gap.* The highest summit is *Big Hatchet Peak,* 8,366 ft.

HATCHS RANCH (San Miguel). See *Chapman.*

HATOD (Colfax). See *Pittsburg.*

HAVENER (Curry). See *Grier.*

HAWIKUH (Cibola; Indian pueblo, archaeological site; a few miles SW of Zuni Pueblo, near the Zuni village of Ojo Caliente). This pueblo in the 16th century was the westernmost—and likely the most important—of the Zuni villages; as such it likely was the one seen by Fray Marcos de Niza during his 1539 reconaissance of what is now NM. His fulsome description sent Coronado here in 1540, and on July 7 Coronado took the pueblo by storm, renaming it *Granada* after the city in Spain; it was the first non-Indian place name in NM. Later Spanish explorers approximated the Zuni name; the Rodríguez-Chamuscado party of 1581–82 called it *Aconcagua,* while the Espejo expedition a year later called it *Aguico* and *Acinco.* The Franciscans established a mission here in 1629, but in 1673 nomadic Indians raided the settlement, killing the priest, Father Pedro de Ávila, and burning the church. The pueblo was abandoned and today is in ruins. The meaning of its name, sometimes spelled *Hawikku,* is not known. Pronounced HAH-wee-koo.

HAYDEN (Union; settlement; in S part of county, 4 mi W of NM 402, 2 mi S of NM 102; PO 1908–74). In 1907 George L. Cook, a surveyor locating land for homesteaders, took out a homestead himself and marked out a townsite here. The name he submitted to the postal authorities was *Central City,* but soon it became apparent that the name was being confused with Silver City, so a new name was proposed, Hayden, for Miss Tessie Hayden, the postmistress. Hayden grew little, and eventually most residents moved away, though a few inhabitants remain.

HAYNES (Rio Arriba; settlement; in SW part of county, exact location unknown; PO 1908–29, mail to Cuba). This former community took the surname of its first postmaster, Samuel H. Haynes. *Haynes Canyon*, which heads 1 mi W of Counselors and runs N into Largo Canyon, was associated with the *Haynes Ranch* and trading post.

HAYNES (San Juan; settlement; in SE part of county, exact location unknown; PO 1930–32, mail to Chijuilla). This community and the Haynes (see entry) in Rio Arriba County clearly had some connection, and possibly were the same, with the PO in different locations.

HAYSTACK (general). A common metaphor for conical hills and mountains. GNIS lists 6 in NM: one each in Catron, Grant, and McKinley Counties and 3 in Chaves County.

HAYSTACK MOUNTAIN, 7,833 ft. (McKinley; 15 mi NW of Grants, 3 mi E of I-40). Paddy Martínez, a Navajo, made the first important uranium discovery in NM here in 1950.

HAYTON (Cibola; settlement; in the Zuni Mountains at the head of Bluewater Creek). Abandoned community, named for the parents of Vern and Stan Hayton of Grants, who settled in that area.

HEAD (general). Throughout the US rock formations often are named for a fancied resemblance to a human head, usually in profile. In NM are *Indian Head* (Colfax; 5 mi W of Cimarron); *Preachers Head* (Grant; 16 mi NE of Silver City); and *Queens Head* (Catron; 10 mi NW of Aragon), among possibly many others known locally.

HEART LAKE (Taos; 9 mi NE of Questa, in the Latir Peak Wilderness). Conspicuously heart-shaped. Sometimes called *Lost Lake*, though not to be confused with the Lost Lake in the Wheeler Peak Wilderness.

HEATON (McKinley; settlement; in Heaton Canyon, 3 mi NE of Gallup; PO 1909–22, mail to Gibson). Abandoned settlement, probably associated with the Heaton Mine of the Gallup American Coal Co.

HEBRON (Colfax; settlement; on AT&SF RR, 11 mi S of Raton; PO 1902–10, mail to Dorsey). Former settlement, today just a RR siding, at the site of *Hebron Dam* on the Canadian River. More than 25 cities, towns, and villages in the US bear the name of this ancient Palestinian city, home of Abraham, one of four holy cities of the Talmud.

HECK CANYON (Colfax; canyon, settlement; SW of Springer, on Sweetwater Creek; PO 1927–43, mail to Miami). The Heck family owned property in the canyon. Mathias Heck came to NM in 1864 and was among the discoverers of gold in the Moreno Valley. *Heck Springs* is nearby.

HEIFERS DELIGHT CANYON (Catron; in SW part of county, 6 mi SW of Glenwood). Name origin unknown, but it's worth mentioning that the canyon just to the N is named *Bull Run.*

HELL (general). Hardscrabble places, rough country, places of ill chance and disappointed dreams throughout the US were given the opprobrious transfer name Hell. GNIS lists 27 NM places with Hell in their names, including *Howinahell Canyon* (Torrance), *Hellion Canyon* (Torrance), *Hells Half Acre* (Grant), and *Hell Roaring Mesa* (Catron).

HELL CANYON (Bernalillo; on the W side of the Manzano Mountains, E of Isleta Pueblo). Discovery of mineral traces here in the 1870s raised hopes that this could be an important mining district for Albuquerque, but the prospects never fulfilled their initial promise.

HELLS HALF ACRE (Grant; 10 mi NW of Silver City). An area of caves, canyons, and pinnacles, described as "rougher 'n hell."

HELLROARING MESA (Catron; 4 mi NW of Luna). In the early days, the brook that heads near here was called *Roaring Creek* by local cowboys because during flood it really roared, so much so that the intensifier Hell was added. The creek's name eventually was changed to *Trout Creek,* but Hellroaring remained on the mesa.

HELWEG (Bernalillo; settlement; NE of Albuquerque, in the E foothills of the Sandia Mountains, 3 mi from Santa Fe County line, on Frost Road; PO 1922–34, mail to Sandia Park). About 1913 Benjamin N. Helweg filed on government land here. He started a store, and his ranch home became a PO. Little remains, except the name.

HEMATITE (Colfax; settlement; 5 mi NW of Elizabethtown; PO 1897–99, mail to Elizabethtown). The discovery of rich ore veins on W Moreno Creek near Red River Pass, about 3 mi from Elizabethtown, stimulated the short-lived mining camp of Hematite, named for a form of iron ore. By 1896 the camp had 200 residents, but the strikes were not rich enough to keep the camp alive, and today all traces of it have vanished, though the name survives on *Hematite Creek.*

HEMBRILLO CANYON, PASS (Doña Ana; in the San Andres Mountains, E of Hatch). Spanish, "seed, or nut, of the live oak."

HENDRICKS (San Juan). See *Riverside.*

HENPECK (Eddy). See *Seven Rivers.*

HENRY (Lea; settlement; 6 mi S of Eunice; PO 1909–12, mail to Eunice). Henry, named for its first postmaster, Henry B. May, was one of many communities in this region that came briefly into existence during the homesteader era and then faded back into the prairie.

HEREFORD (Otero). See *Newman.*

HERMANAS (Luna; settlement; on NM 9 and SP RR, 32 mi SW of Deming; PO 1903–25, mail to Columbus). Hermanas was founded in 1879 and named for the *Tres Hermanas Mountains* (see entry) to the E. The settlement was sustained for several years by the SP RR, supplemented by farming, ranching, and mining. But the population probably never exceeded 150, and today it has no inhabitants at all.

HERMIT PEAK, 10,260 ft. (San Miguel; 20 mi NW of Las Vegas, in the E Sangre de Cristo Mountains). In 1863 a remarkable man arrived in the Las Vegas area, having walked the Santa Fe Trail from Council Grove, KS. Juan María de Agostini was a native of Italy, well-educated, from a family of means, and intensely religious. He took up residence in a cave near Romeroville, ministering to the poor and sick, and soon became revered as a holy man. Later he moved to a cave 250 feet below the rim of this huge granite monolith, at that time known locally as *Cerro del Tecolote,* "owl peak." He lived here, carving crucifixes and religious emblems, which he traded for food, and receiving the many supplicants who climbed the mountain seeking his blessing and healing. In 1867 he left his hermitage here to live in another cave in the Organ Mountains near Las Cruces. There, in 1869, he was murdered, stabbed in the back at the age of 68. His murder was never solved.

But he was not forgotten in San Miguel County. As late as 1965 annual pilgrimages were made to his cave by the *Sociedad del Eremitano,* and after 1863 the mountain was called *Mount Solitario* in his honor, later Hermit Peak.

HERMITS PEAK (Colfax; SW of Raton, near the abandoned mining camp of Gardner). Local lore tells that in the 1880s a ranch laborer named Juan became demented upon losing his wife to another man. Around 1892 he built a lean-to and became a hermit at the peak previously known as *Red River Peak.* "Crazy Juan" was well-known in the area until his death in 1918 of the flu.

HERMOSA (Sierra; settlement; on the S fork of the Palomas River, 28 mi W of Truth or Consequences; 1884–1929, mail to Cuchillo). Soon after mineral discoveries here in 1883, J.C. Plemmons brought a herd of cattle to graze, and before long he built a house and a store. The settlement was called Hermosa, Spanish, "beautiful," likely for its scenic setting. By the late 1880s Hermosa was thriving; it even could boast the Hermosa Literary Society. But within 10 years Hermosa was declining; today only ruins remain.

HERNANDEZ (general). Several persons with the Hernández surname were among the Oñate expeditions of 1598 and 1600. No Hernández males were among the refugees from the 1680 Pueblo Revolt, but a widow, María Hernández, was mentioned as being with her four children, and possibly some of them returned to NM with the reconquest of 1692.

HERNANDEZ (Rio Arriba; settlement; on US 84-285, 6 mi N of Española; PO 1920–65, mail to a rural branch of Española). This inhabited settlement originally was known as *San José de Chama,* for the Rio Chama flowing just to the W. When a PO was established, the name proposed was *Alabam,* for a local saloon with that name, but Benigno C. Hernández, US Congressman from NM, disapproved, so the PO adopted the congressman's name instead. (Had the congressman not intervened, Ansel Adams's famous photo might have been titled "Moon over Alabam"!) Some maps label the S section of the community *Capilla de San José,* "Chapel of St. Joseph."

HERNANDEZ (Chaves; settlement; in N part of county, on Hernandez Draw, 2 mi E of the Pecos River). This tiny community, now ruins, was named for the Hernández brothers, who came from California. It is said one of the brothers drowned in *Hernandez Lake. Hernandez Draw,* named for them, drains San Juan Mesa and has been known as *San Juan Draw.*

HERON LAKE STATE PARK (Rio Arriba; 13 mi SE of Chama). Although the reservoir is habitat for several species of herons, it was not named for them but rather for K.A. Heron, local landowner and surveyor who promoted the building of the dam that created *Heron Reservoir.* Heron died in 1974. The nearby PO of Rutheron (see entry) was named for his wife, Ruth.

HERRERA (general). Juan de Herrera's descendants claimed he was among the first colonists to arrive in NM with Oñate in 1598, but several persons with that name also appear in the records.

The Spanish surname Herrera was derived from the blacksmith profession and is the Spanish equivalent of the French Ferrer and the English Smith.

HERRERA (Bernalillo; settlement; location unknown; PO 1900, mail to Albuquerque). Ephemeral PO locality, named for its first and only postmaster, Nicholas Herrera.

HERRERAVILLE (Bernalillo; settlement; location unknown; PO 1920–21, mail to Armijo). Like Herrera, an ephemeral postal locality that took the surname of its only postmaster, Bernardo Herrera.

HERRON (Doña Ana). See *Vado.*

HICKEY CITY (Grant; settlement; location unknown). This was a stillborn townsite, conceived by a local mining discovery, laid out in 1882, said to have been named for Maurice Hickey.

HICKMAN (Catron; settlement; 14 mi N of US 60, 10 mi E of NM 36; PO 1937–55, mail to Pie Town). Abandoned locality, once a PO and store, on property of James. L. Hickman, who homesteaded here.

HIDALGO COUNTY (SW NM; county seat, Lordsburg). Created in 1919, Hidalgo County is said to have been named for the patriot priest, Miguel Hidalgo y Costilla, who in 1810 led the revolt that resulted in Mexico's independence. He has been called Mexico's George Washington. When the county was created, some local citizens proposed that it be called *Pyramid,* for the Pyramid Mountains (see entry).

HIDDEN CAVE, LAKE (Guadalupe; on NM 91, 2 mi SE of Santa Rosa). Surrounded on all sides by low, rocky hills and completely hidden from view.

HIGGINS FLAT, MOUNTAINS (Catron; mountains 2 mi NE of Reserve, flat 4 mi NE of Reserve). Pat Higgins was a homesteader here.

HIGH LONESOME (general). One must be familiar with the seemingly endless expanse of the High Plains of NM to feel the compelling poetry in this name. It appears on 22 features in NM, many of them windmills, in 14 of the state's 33 counties (GNIS).

HIGH LONESOME (Chaves; trading point; NE of Roswell, overlooking the Pecos River on US 70). Only foundations are left here, but the site remains conspicuously high and lonesome.

HIGH LONESOME (Lea; ranch settlement; 10 mi E of Lovington). This ranch settlement, now decaying, was perhaps the original High Lonesome in NM. It was one of the Mallet chain of ranches, and at the time of its establishment late in the 19th century, the nearest settlement to the E was Lubbock, TX, several days' ride away, while the nearest to the W was even farther, on the Pecos River. The ranch was situated on a slight rise on the otherwise flat plains. A rural school once was here.

HIGH LONESOME (Lincoln; settlement; on US 380 SE of Lincoln). Abandoned resort community.

HIGH LONESOME PEAK, 5,397 ft. (Grant; in SW part of county, 7 mi N of Red Rock).

HIGH PLAINS (eastern NM). The grassy plains of W-central North America rise steadily as they approach the Continental Divide, but they undergo an especially abrupt rise along a N-S axis approximately paralleling the 100th meridian, with the vegetation and climate—and hence the human culture and economy—different on the High Plains from those of the lower plains to the E.

HIGH ROLLS (Otero; settlement; in the Sacramento Mountains, on US 82, 11 mi NE of Alamogordo; PO 1913–56, transferred to High Rolls-Mountain Park, 1956–present). This community's original name, *Fresnal*, is easy to explain: it's derived from being on *Fresnal Creek*, named in turn for the ash trees (Spanish, *fresno*) that still are here. But the current name, High Rolls, is an enigma and has evoked several etymologies, none completely convincing. One is that "rolls" is a local term for "rapids" on Fresnal Creek tumbling down here. But actually the creek has a rather gentle gradient near the village. Another explanation is that the name comes from the "high, rolling hills" near the village. A

fanciful explanation is that the name refers to the steep ascent up Fresnal Canyon to here: "If you ever lie down and start rolling, you won't stop until you reach the next county." But most likely none of these explanations is correct, and the true origin lies unrevealed in time. See *Mountain Park*.

HIGHWAY (Roosevelt; trading point; on NM 206, 26 mi S of Portales, 2 mi S of Pep). Inhabited locality, located on a state highway; sometimes spelled *Hiway*.

HIGHTOWER MOUNTAIN, 7,341 ft. (LIncoln; 8 mi NE of Ruidoso). Bears the name of a prominent local family.

HILARIO (San Miguel). See *San Hilario*.

HILL (Doña Ana; settlement; on NM 158, 10 mi NW of Las Cruces; PO 1913–37, mail to Las Cruces). In 1904 a retired dentist named Charles Lee Hill, his wife, Anna, and their two daughters, Mary and Hanna, came from West Virginia and settled here. Their large home became a focus for community social and political life, and soon the community took their name; originally the locality was called *Hill Station* but later became simply Hill. Though the Hills no longer reside here, and the PO and school are gone, the community and their name remain.

HILLBURN CITY (Lea; settlement; on NM 206, 10 mi N of Lovington). A recent tiny but inhabited settlement, name origin unknown.

HILLCREST (Rio Arriba; settlement; 16 mi SE of Dulce). Abandoned trading point, name likely referring to its location.

HILLSBORO (Sierra; settlement; on NM 152, 17 mi W of Caballo, in the Black Range foothills; PO 1879–present). In 1877 prospectors found gold float in this area, and a particularly significant find is said to have been made by Joe Yankie. Knowing that a mining camp would soon follow the strike, the prospectors gave to Yankie the honor of naming it. He chose *Hillsborough*, for his hometown of Hillsborough (original spelling), OH. Another story says that when a PO was applied for, the settlers put names in a hat, and the one drawn was Hillsborough, later shortened to

Hillsboro. A mining camp did indeed develop, one that was the center of intense mining activity. Even persistent Apache raids could not dampen the mining fervor; $6 million in gold and silver was produced; and in 1884 Hillsboro was named Sierra County seat, with a handsome brick courthouse built in 1892. But the mining faded, the town lost the county seat to Hot Springs (now Truth or Consequences), and the town today survives mainly on tourism and its past. *Hillsboro Peak,* 10,011 ft., is in the Black Range, 6 mi NW of Kingston, on the Grant County line.

HILTON (Otero; settlement; on the Agua Chiquita, in the E foothills of the Sacramento Mountains; PO 1887–94, mail to Weed). Abandoned locality that took the name of the Hilton family, who ranched here. C.F. Hilton was shot and killed in 1894 in a dispute with a nearby property owner.

HILTON LODGE (San Miguel; settlement; 2 mi W of Lower Rociada; PO 1935–46, mail to Rociada). Tiny settlement, associated with Ivan J. Hilton, prominent banker in Las Vegas and mayor of East Las Vegas, 1950–54. *Hilton Canyon* adjoins this settlement.

HOBART (Santa Fe; settlement; on the Rio Grande, 5 mi SW of Española; 1894–1912, mail to Española). This former locality on the now abandoned D&RG RR was named for E.F. Hobart, merchant and postmaster here.

HOBBS (Lea; settlement; at the junction of NM 18 and US 62-180, 2 mi from the Texas line; PO 1910–present). In 1907 James Isaac Hobbs and his wife, Fannie, sold their family farm in Brown County, TX, and with children Winnie, Minnie, Ella, and James Berry, moved to SE NM, for Fannie's health. At the site of the city that would bear their name, near present First and Texas Streets, they constructed a dugout. Berry Hobbs, who opened a store in 1909 and later served as postmaster, is credited with being the founder of Hobbs. When he applied for a PO, he submitted *Taft* and *Prairieview* as names, but when the permit was granted the postal officials had put Hobbs's name on the PO. For about 15 years, Hobbs remained a tiny agricultural community, but in 1928 the Midwest Oil Co. (now Amoco) discovered oil here, and an oil boom ensued. The old village became three towns—*Hobbs, New Hobbs,* and *All Hobbs*—together with about 12,000 people. Eventually the three merged.

HODGES (Taos; settlement; in SE part of county, SE of Picuris, exact location unknown; PO 1909–13, mail to Peñasco). Little is known about this former locality; name origin unknown.

HOGADERO (Quay; settlement; location unknown; PO as Red River Springs 1878–84, as Hogadero 1884–85, mail to Fort Bascom). The meaning of this settlement's original name, *Red River Springs,* is easy to understand, though the location of the springs has been difficult to determine, but the meaning of Hogadero is obscure. The most plausible translation of the name is "drowned man," derived from NM–Spanish, *ahogarse,* "to drown," though possibly a connection exists between the name and the Spanish noun *hogar,* meaning either "fireplace, hearth" or "home."

HOGBACK MOUNTAIN (San Juan, McKinley; trends generally N and S, especially conspicuous where intersected by US 64, between Waterflow and Shiprock; a portion also is visible where intersected by I-40 E of Gallup). *Hogback* is a widely used descriptive metaphor for a ridge of upwardly tilted sedimentary rocks. The Navajo name for this formation means "rock going into the water," because of the formation descending toward a water body.

HOGBACK OIL FIELD (San Juan; S of where Hogback Mountain intersects US 64). The first oil in the San Juan Basin was produced here.

HOGBACK TRADING POST (San Juan; trading point; S and E of the intersection of Hogback Mountain and US 64). Named for the conspicuous rock formation nearby, this trading post sometimes is labeled *Wheeler,* for the Wheeler family that has owned and operated this for four generations.

HOLDEN PRONG (Sierra; heads N of Hillsboro Peak in the Black Range and flows N into Las Animas Creek). In the southern Appalachian Mountains, *prong* refers to a branch of a stream or inlet. Possibly Holden was a miner from that region. A tributary of Holden Prong is *Side Prong.*

HOLE IN THE WALL (Cibola; in the Malpais, 22 mi S of Grants). This and *Little Hole in the Wall* 2 mi NW are islands of grassland surrounded by lava, called *steptoes* by geologists.

HOLIDAY MESA (Sandoval; in the Jemez Mountains, between Jemez Springs and the Rio Guadalupe). During the lumbering era, a man named Holiday maintained a logging camp here. Previously, the mesa had been called *Pueblo Chise* (chi-SEH), an Indian name; old-timers in the Cañon area still refer to the mesa by this name.

HOLLAND (Union; settlement; in S-central part of county, S of NM 562, NE of Bueyeros; PO 1905–17, mail to Clapham). Abandoned community, name origin unknown.

HOLLENE (Curry; settlement; 32 mi NE of Clovis, 3 mi SE of Bellview; PO 1907–53, mail to Clovis). This was named for Hollene Thompson, infant daughter of a Texico man who sold townsite lots here in 1906–07. Though only a single ruined building remains, the name is still recognized and used in the area, and in the Hollene Cemetery fresh graves still are dug.

HOLLOMAN AIR FORCE BASE (Otero; military installation; on US 70-82, 7 mi SW of Alamogordo; PO as Monista 1944–49, as Holloman 1949–56, as Holloman Air Force Base 1956–present). This was called *Alamogordo Army Air Field* when construction began in 1942, but in 1948 it was renamed Holloman Air Force Base to honor the late Col. George V. Holloman, a pioneer in guided missile research. Associated with the base was a civilian housing project; the name proposed for its PO was *Monte Vista,* but postal authorites chose *Monista* instead; the PO lasted from 1944 to 1949, when Monista was re-named *Holloman,* later expanded to Hollowman Air Force Base.

HOLLOWAY (Lincoln; settlement; in N part of county, just W of the SP RR; PO 1908–15, mail to Corona). Abandoned community. Though the settlement was called *Gallinas,* for the nearby *Gallinas Mountains,* the PO took the name of its first postmaster, James M. Holloway.

HOLLYWOOD (Lincoln; settlement; on US 70, between Ruidoso and Ruidoso Downs; PO 1926–70, mail to Ruidoso branch). When George A. Friedenbloom established a PO here in 1926, he named it for his previous residence, Hollywood, FL. Unfortunately, at least 14 other places in the US have the same name, and misplaced mail was common.

HOLMAN (Mora; settlement; 6 mi NW of Mora on NM 518; PO 1894–present). When this area was settled in 1816, the area now known as Holman was part of what was called *San Antonio lo de Mora,* or *El Valle de San Antonio.* Later, the settlement here was called *Agua Negra,* "black water." But when the community received a PO, it took the surname of its first postmaster, Charles W. Holman, though the earlier name of *San Antonio* still is recognized and used.

HOLMES MINES (Otero; settlement; S of High Rolls, on the W side of US 82, at the head of Dry Canyon). Ephemeral settlement and school, associated with a copper mine.

HOLY CROSS (Luna). See *Camp Cody.*

HOLY GHOST CREEK (Santa Fe, San Miguel; heads at Spirit Lake and runs SE into the Pecos River at Terrero). One legend says this was named by a priest who was concealed from hostile Indians by a mist that had collected here, but Elliott Barker is almost certainly correct when he says the name originated with its source at *Spirit Lake* (see entry), known to the early Spanish-speakers as *Laguna del Espíritu Santo,* or "Lake of the Holy Ghost." The creek issuing from the lake took the same name, while the lake's name became simply Spirit Lake.

HOLY GHOST SPRING (Sandoval). See *Ojo del Espíritu Santo.*

HONDALE (Luna; settlement; about 12 mi

SW of Deming, on the EP&SW spur leading from Deming to Hermanas; PO 1908–34, mail to Deming). Around 1900 LeRoy Hon settled here, among the area's first homesteaders, and in 1907 he and his brothers formed a real estate corporation to sell lots to easterners. The resulting settlement, which incorporated Hon's surname, was described by a former resident as having "a train that came through every day, a PO, a club house owned by the ladies of the Hondale Club and a tomato cannery...and a lumber yard." In the latter were held political rallies and dances. "Oh, those dances, sometimes just a boot heel and fiddle made the music.... The building literally rocked. There is nothing left now that indicates such a place existed, but for us who remember, happy memories."

HONDO (general). Spanish, "deep."

HONDO (Lincoln; settlement; in SW part of county, at the junction of US 70 and 380; PO 1900–present). The Rio Bonito and Rio Ruidoso join here to form the *Rio Hondo* (see entry), hence the present name of this inhabited community and also its earlier name *La Junta,* Spanish, "the junction." *Chihuahua* also has been reported as an early epithet for the site.

HONDO (Taos). See *Arroyo Hondo.*

RIO HONDO (Chaves; settlement). See *Roswell.*

HONEA (Roosevelt; settlement; NE of Portales). Abandoned community, named for a local family.

HOOD (San Juan; settlement; on US 550, 3 mi NE of Farmington; PO 1898–1906, mail to Farmington). George T. Hood was first postmaster of this former community. Just to the N is *Hood Mesa,* also named for the family, whose members still live in the area.

HOOVERVILLE (San Miguel; settlement; at the S end of Conchas Lake, 0.5 mi W of Conchas Lake State Park). Tiny inhabited residential development probably named for Herbert Hoover, whose presidency had preceded construction of the dam here.

HOPE (Eddy; settlement; on US 82, 21 mi W of Artesia; PO 1890–present). When this community was settled around 1884, its residents called the place *Badgerville,* or simply *Badger,* because they lived in dugouts, like badgers. This name would not serve, however, when the growing community needed a PO. The most popular and widely accepted explanation of the present name is that two early settlers, Elder Miller and Joe Richards, discussing who should give the name, tossed a dime in the air and shot at it with pistols to settle the issue. "I hope you lose," exclaimed Richards. Miller did, and Richards chose the name Hope. Richards's brother, J. Allen Richards, later wrote, "I remember the story as being told many times and that Joe did name the town Hope as a result of the shooting match." But one researcher has said that store owner Jasper Gerald hoped for a PO at Badgerville and mail carrier Tom Tillotson hoped to expand his stops and increase his income, and the name resulted from both their "hopes" being fulfilled.

HOPE (Union; settlement; in W part of county, exact location unknown; PO 1888–89, mail to Grenville). Ephemeral postal locality, name origin unknown.

HOPEWELL (Rio Arriba; settlement; W of Tres Piedras, 2 mi S of US 64; PO 1894–1906, 1913–15). This abandoned mining camp possibly was named for its association with the Good Hope mining claim, but a far more likely association is with Willard S. Hopewell, a promoter engaged in cattle and mining enterprises around 1878. The town of *Willard (Torrance)* (see entry) also was named for him. *Hopewell Lake,* 2 mi N of Hopewell, was named for the mining camp nearby.

HORSE (general). Horses, introduced to the Southwest by Spanish explorers, rapidly spread throughout the region. Soon herds of wild horses were found in mountains and canyons and at springs and water bodies, such places often being named for them. These names often appear in their Spanish form *caballo,* which appears 14 times in NM (GNIS); *potrillo,* "colt," also is common, appearing 10 times. Horses, like the automobile today, were an essential and ubiquitous part of the frontier culture and economy. This is evidenced by at least 174 places in NM having Horse in their names in some form (GNIS). These include *Horse Camps, Horse Pastures, Wild Horses, Horseshoes, Horseheads, Horsethiefs,* and even a *Horse Heaven.*

HORSE CAMP (general). In the early days of cattle ranching, horse camps were established to care for crippled cow horses, as well as to maintain breeding stock.

HORSE LAKE (Rio Arriba; 20 mi NW of Tierra Amarilla). Local tradition says this was named because in the winter horses would wander onto its frozen surface, fall through the ice, and drown, as well as become mired in the mud around its banks. Also called *Northern Lake.*

HORSE SPRINGS, OLD HORSE SPRINGS (Catron; settlement, springs; on NM 12, 28 mi SW of Datil; PO 1879–82 mail to Socorro, 1922–present). These springs received their name when some soldiers traveling from Fort Tularosa to Socorro lost a horse and found it on their way back. The original community of Horse Springs, now labeled *Old Horse Springs,* is 2 mi W of *New Horse Springs.*

HORSESHOE LAKE (Colfax; just below timberline, at the head of the main East Fork of the Red River, NE of Wheeler Peak). Named for its shape.

HORSETHIEF MEADOWS, HORSETHIEF CREEK (San Miguel; creek heads in the Sangre de Cristo Mountains NW of Cowles and flows SE to join Panchuela Creek; meadow is 3 mi long on Panchuela Creek, just below its junction with Horsethief Creek). As Elliott Barker tells the story, an organized band of horse thieves, possibly part of the notorious Vincente Silva gang of Las Vegas, active in the 1880s, used this area to pasture stolen horses. It is said that after a particularly valuable stallion was stolen, the owner and the sheriff of Las Vegas trailed the stolen horses to the meadows, where they found animals newly rebranded; the thieves had fled.

HOSPAH (McKinley; settlement; on NM 509, 26 mi N of Ambrosia Lake). An active oil settlement, with a Navajo name meaning "treeless bluffs." Pronounced HAHS-pah.

HOSTA BUTTE (McKinley; 6 mi S of Crownpoint, 3 mi W of NM 371). Hosta, also known as Francisco, was civil governor of Jemez Pueblo who served as guide for the 1849 expedition against the Navajos and also for William Henry Jackson's Chaco Canyon expedition of 1877. His full name, in the Towa language of Jemez Pueblo was *Waash e hoste,* "the lighting." This prominent butte recalls his journeys here.

HOT SPRINGS (general). Vulcanism, often recent (geologically speaking), has shaped much of NM's landscape, and place names such as Hot Springs and its Spanish equivalent *Ojo Caliente* are frequent reminders. See *Caliente (general).*

HOT SPRINGS (San Miguel; settlement; on US 65, 1 mi W of Montezuma, 5 mi NW of Las Vegas; PO as Las Vegas Hot Springs 1882–93, 1895–1902, as Hot Springs 1902–04, 1905–07, mail to Las Vegas). Originally known as *Las Vegas Hot Springs,* this small inhabited community takes its names from the hot springs here on Gallinas Creek. The AT&SF RR operated a series of luxury hotels here from 1880 to 1903.

HOT SPRINGS (Sierra; settlement; at Truth or Consequences; PO 1914–51, changed to Truth or Consequences). This name has had a hard time of it. Hot Springs was the original name of Truth or Consequences, for the thermal springs in the center of town. After the name Hot Springs was displaced by *Truth or Consequences* (see entry), the community of Williamsburg just to the S adopted the orphan name, but in 1959 its citizens voted to return to Williamsburg, orphaning Hot Springs once again. Today, the name survives on the residential development of *Hot Springs Landing,* near Elephant Butte State Park, and on the high school in TorC. See *Truth or Consequences, Williamsburg.*

HOUSE (Quay; settlement; at the junction

of NM 89 and 252, NE of Fort Sumner; PO 1906–present). In 1902 the House family settled on the Caprock here. John L. House built the first store in 1904, and when a PO was established in the store two years later, Lucie Jordan House was the first postmistress. Though the Houses have since left the area, the community bearing their name survives.

HOXIE (Colfax; trading point; S of Raton, at the junction of US 85 and 64). Old-timers in Raton still remember fondly dances held at the crossroads business owned by William Hoxie in 1925, but memories are all that remain. Earlier, from the 1820s, the locality had been called *Santa Fe Forks,* because the Santa Fe Trail forked here.

HUDSON, HUDSON HOT SPRINGS (Grant). See *Faywood Hot Springs.*

HUDSON (Quay; settlement; on US 54, 11 mi SW of Logan; PO 1908–26, mail to Logan). Hudson began in 1901, when the CRI&P RR built a line between Dahlhart, TX, and Santa Rosa, NM. Soon a PO was needed for the new settlement; the RR proposed the name *Eureka,* but when postal authorities rejected this the PO took the name *Rice* instead. Clara Rice not only owned a large store near the depot, but also she had the only water well in the area, from which she sold water for 25 cents a barrel—and she operated the PO. Later, the community changed its name to Hudson, to honor a Civil War veteran who lived here. The settlement has since been abandoned.

HUDSON SPRING (Catron; 3 mi NW of Reserve). Named for the Hudson family, whose members still live in the area.

HUECO MOUNTAINS (Otero; in S part of county, straddling the Texas line). The Spanish *hueco* means "hole, hollow," but in Southwest Spanish it also means "water hole," and several features in the southern Tularosa Valley, including this small range, have this name. Highest elevation in NM 6,057 ft. A RR siding named *Hueco,* N of Newman and W of the Hueco Mountains, is said to have been named for a water-retaining tank

worn in rocks.

HUERFANA, HUERFANO (general). Spanish, "orphan," diminutive *huerfanito,* a common descriptive metaphor for isolated mountains and mesas. GNIS lists it 13 times, yet curiously, it rarely appears in English.

LAGUNA HUERFANA, MESA HUERFANA, CAÑON HUERFANA (San Miguel; near Trujillo). Several features, likely named for *Mesa Huerfana,* conspicuously isolated from other mesas in the vicinity.

HUERFANO MOUNTAIN, 7,474 ft. (San Juan; 2 mi NE of Huerfano Trading Post, 30 mi SE of Bloomfield, 0.75 mi NW of NM 44). This prominent, vertical-sided mesa, visible for up to 50 miles, was named "orphan" by early Spanish explorers because of its isolation. Often called *El Huerfano,* the mesa is among the mountains sacred to the Navajos, and they say it is suspended from the sky with sunbeams. Their name can be translated as "turning or rotating mountain," a reference to the mesa appearing similarly from all sides; in Navajo mythology, the gods tested the Navajos by having them recognize their sacred mountains from above, turned from their normal positions. Changing Woman is said to have dwelt here, and the mesa also is called "female hogan," because the sedimentary layers resemble the wattled logs in women's hogans. 8 mi NE is *El Huerfanito Peak,* a small sandstone mesa resembling the larger mesa; *Huerfanito Canyon* is 2 mi N.

EL HUERFANO TRADING POST (San Juan; trading point; on NM 44, 30 mi SE of Bloomfield). Named for El Huerfano Mountain (see entry), 1 mi to the NE.

HULSEY CIENAGA (Catron; 4 mi NE of Luna). The Hulseys were early settlers; their descendants still live in the area.

HUMANOS MESA (Torrance). See *Mesa de los Jumanos.*

HUMBLE CITY (Lea; settlement; on NM 18, just NW of Hobbs; PO 1930–76).

This inhabited community was named for the Humble Oil Co., which had oil interests in the area; pumping rigs and other equipment still dominate the landscape.

HUMBOLDT CAMP (Sierra; settlement; in the Caballo Mountains, exact location unknown). An ephemeral mining camp, name origin unknown.

HUMMER (Colfax; settlement; location unknown; PO 1919–20, mail to Raton). Ephemeral postal locality, name origin unknown.

HUNGO PAVIE (San Juan; archaeological site; in Chaco Culture National Historic Park, 1.5 mi E of Chettro Ketl). On August 20, 1849, Lt. James Simpson and his New Mexican guide, Carravahal, came to this ruin, which Carravahal said was named Hungo Pavie, a name he interpreted to mean "crooked nose." Hungo Pavie, however, is likely derived from the Hopi language, and why it was applied here remains a mystery. Spelled variously as *Hungo Pavi, Hungo Pavia,* and *Hungo Payi,* Hungo Pavie is the form accepted by the USBGN in 1931.

HUNTER (Rio Arriba; settlement; exact location unknown; PO 1893–94, mail to Abiquiu). Ephemeral postal locality; name origin unknown.

HURLBURT (Lincoln; postal locality; 12 mi N of Carrizozo; PO 1908–15). In 1900 the RR pumping station known as *Coy-* *ote* took on a new identity when a PO was established here; it took the name of F. Hurlburt, the pumper who became the first postmaster. The Hurlburt PO later was succeeded by one named *Bogle* (see entry).

HURLEY (Grant; settlement; on US 180, 6 mi S of Central; PO 1910–present). Hurley is a mining town. It was born as *Hurley Siding* when the Chino Copper Co. purchased the Santa Rita Mining Co. around 1910 and put in a rail link with the Santa Rita copper mines. The name honored J.E. Hurley, general manager of the AT&SF RR.

HURSCHBURGER PEAK (Otero). See *Alamo Peak.*

HYDE MEMORIAL STATE PARK (Santa Fe; on NM 475, 8 mi NE of Santa Fe). One of NM's oldest state parks, and at 8,000 ft. one of the highest, Hyde Memorial State Park was established in 1938 on land donated by the widow of Talbot Babbit Hyde, a well-known Santa Fe educator and naturalist.

HYER (Santa Fe; settlement; in SW corner of county, near the junction of NM 344 and 472; PO 1908–26, mail to Stanley). During the homesteader era this area was densely settled, and Hyer, named for its first postmaster, Charles O. Hyer, was one of several farming communities in the area. Now Hyer has vanished, and only old-timers recall that *Simmons Road* once was called *Hyer Road.*

I

ICE CAVES (Cibola; on the W side of El Malpais National Monument, 27 mi SW of Grants). Sunlight never penetrates these caves and lava tubes, so ice formed in the winter is slow to melt.

IDLEWILD (Colfax; settlement; on NM 127, 1.5 mi W of Eagle Nest). Modern residential development, name origin unknown.

ILDEFONSO (Santa Fe; settlement; on NM 4, 10 mi SW of Española; PO 1901–15, mail to Buckman). Former settlement, named for *San Ildefonso Pueblo.*

ILFELD (San Miguel; settlement; on US 84 and AT&SF RR, SW of Las Vegas, between San Juan and Rowe; PO 1929–64, mail to rural branch of Santa Fe). In 1867 a German Jew named Charles Ilfeld joined other European settlers and merchants in coming over the Santa Fe Trail to the Las Vegas area. He developed a prosperous mercantile business and became a prominent civic, business, and political leader. His son, Louis C. Ilfeld, an attorney, was a member of the first NM senate. This inhabited community, originally known as *June,* for reasons unknown, and also called *Ilfeld Station,* bears the Ilfeld family name.

ILLINOIS CAMP (Eddy; settlement; 17 mi SE of Artesia). The first oil discovery E of the Pecos River was at this locality. The strike was made by Van Welch and Tom Flynn, both from Robinson, IL; they named their wells and the oil company they founded for their home state. A refinery and associated settlement still are here.

IMA (Quay; settlement; on NM 156, 26 mi SW of Tucumcari; PO 1908–55, mail to Cuervo). In October 1902 I.W. Moncus left Texas with his family; they were headed for Arizona, but winter overtook them, and they stayed instead in eastern NM. Living in their wagon, they built two picket houses in a canyon near the Caprock (see *Moncus Canyon*), then later a frame house on the Caprock itself. In 1903 their first daughter was born; they named her Ima. Soon other settlers joined them, and in 1908 the community received a PO; in 1909 Moncus opened a store. He named the PO for his daughter. The store, PO, and any semblance of a village are long gone, but the Ima Quilters still meet at the Ima Community Center, and the name of Moncus's daughter still is recognized and used as a place name in this part of NM.

INCA (San Juan). See *Aztec, Rosing.*

INDIAN (general). GNIS lists 138 places in NM with Indian in their names. The 138 do not include places named for specific Native American tribes (see entries); the Apaches are the group for which the most features have been named. Usually, the specific incident or association behind the name has been lost.

INDIAN PETROGLYPH STATE PARK (Bernalillo). See *Petroglyph National Monument.*

INDIAN POINT, 10,241 ft. (Sandoval; in Baca Location No. 1, N of Valle San Antonio, 1 mi W of Cerro Toledo). Name origin unknown.

INDIAN SPRINGS CANYON (Doña Ana; 6 mi SW of Radium Springs). Apaches camped here while observing soldiers at Fort Selden.

INDIAN VILLAGE, WINGATE INDIAN VILLAGE (McKinley). See *Navajo Wingate Village.*

INEZ (Roosevelt; settlement; 20 mi SE of Portales, 5 mi from the Texas line; 1908–30, mail to Arch). Evin P. Williams, first postmaster in this homesteader community, is said to have named the PO for Inez Mullins, daughter of Jess Mullins, an early settler. Only a church and a cemetery remain at the community named for her.

INGLEVILLE (De Baca; settlement; in SW part of county; PO 1908–23, mail to Dunlap). James L. Ingle was the first postmaster at this abandoned homesteader community. Only old-timers would recognize the name today.

INGRAM (Roosevelt; settlement; 12 mi NW of Elida; PO 1907–15, mail to Benson). Abandoned homesteader community, name origin unknown.

INSCRIPTION ROCK (Cibola). See *El Morro*.

IOLA (Luna; settlement; 16 mi SW of Deming; PO 1911–17, mail to Hondale). For reasons unknown, Iola was the name requested for the PO here by George T. Taylor, the first postmaster. The site has long been abandoned.

IONE (Union; settlement; in SE corner of county, 3 mi S of NM 420; PO 1908–62, mail to Nara Visa). Ione was settled in 1908 by Iowa farmers; C.F. Snyder was the first postmaster. He is said to have named the place for a girl he left behind in Iowa. Ione, or at least its PO, has moved three times, but now nothing remains to move.

IRON CREEK (Catron; small tributary of the Middle Fork of the Gila River, SE of Reserve). Thomas J. Wood, prospecting on this creek, discovered a dike of ferrous rock crossing the stream. Hoping for other minerals he dug a tunnel in the hill, but he found only more iron, so he named the place Iron Creek. *Iron Creek Mesa* is just to the S.

IRVINS (San Miguel; settlement; on the Pecos River, 3 mi S of Terrero). Vanished settlement that flourished when mining was active at Terrero; name origin unknown.

ISAACK LAKE (Doña Ana; E of the Doña Ana Mountains). Shallow lake, named for the Isaack family, pioneer ranchers.

ISIDORE (Guadalupe; settlement; in NE part of county, N of Newkirk; PO 1906–29, mail to Montoya). This abandoned community bears an Anglicized Spanish given name honoring San Ysidro (St. Isidore), patron saint of farmers. The Isidore PO was located first W of NM 129 and then E.

ISLETA PUEBLO (Bernalillo; straddling the Rio Grande, on NM 314, 147, 47, 13 mi S of Albuquerque; PO 1882–83, 1887–present). When the Spaniards first saw this Tiwa pueblo in 1540, it was situated on an *isleta*, "little island," in the Rio Grande, hence the present name. Governor Otermín, in his report on the Pueblo Revolt of 1680, refers to this as *La Isleta*, while it is labeled *San Agustín de la Isleta* on L'Atlas Curieux of 1700. Local Tiwa tradition says the pueblo originally was located at the base of the Manzano Mountains to the E. According to a Tiwa account, "The people there got crazy talking about how the yellow- and red-faced people with red hair were coming; then they ran away and crossed the river and made Isleta." The Tiwa name for the present village means "flint kicking place," a reference to a contest once popular among Pueblo Indians in which pieces of flint are kicked along in a race. Navajos call Isleta Pueblo by a name meaning, appropriately, "tribe by the water."

ITALIAN CANYON, PARK (Taos; SE of the village of Red River, on the Old Red River Road, E of Red River Pass). In the early mining days, numerous Italians staked claims here.

IVANHOE (Grant; settlement; near Central; PO 1894–97, mail to Hanover). Abandoned settlement associated with a mill and likely named for it.

IYANBITO (McKinley; settlement; 15 mi E of Gallup, 1.5 mi N of I-40). Inhabited community whose name is Navajo and means "buffalo springs." Another Navajo community with the same name but in English is on US 666 just S of the San Juan County line.

J

JA Volcano (Bernalillo). See *Vulcan*.

JACKS PEAK, 7,553 ft. (Lincoln; in the N part of the Jicarilla Mountains). Named for a prospector, whose last name has been forgotten.

JACKSON (Grant; settlement; in NW corner of county, at the junction of US 180 and NM 78; PO 1912–16, mail to Buckhorn). After 1900 R.W. Jackson and his family had a ranch on what then was known as the Mogollon Road. They began offering lodging to travelers, and they opened a PO bearing their surname. Nothing now remains.

JACKSON (San Juan; settlement; 7 mi N of Farmington, on the La Plata River). Jackson, named for a local family and still inhabited, was one of the first Mormon communities in the region. *Jackson Lake*, just to the N, was built by residents of Jackson.

JACONA (Santa Fe; settlement; on NM 502, 1 mi W of Pojoaque). The sprawling, diffuse communities of Jacona and *Jaconita* occupy the site of an ancient Tewa pueblo, and their names are corruptions of a Tewa word meaning "a place for drying tobacco." The pueblo was occupied when the Spanish arrived, and until 1680 it was a *visita* of the Nambe mission. But its inhabitants fled during the reconquest of 1692, and those who later returned to the Pojoaque Valley joined Santa Clara and other Tewa pueblos. In 1702, Governor Cubero gave the abandoned pueblo grant to Ignacio de Roybal and his wife, Francesca Gomez.

JACONITA (Santa Fe). See *Jacona*.

JACQUEZ CANYON (San Juan; heads S of Angel Peak, 3 mi E of NM 44, runs NE to join Blanco Canyon). Sometimes and more accurately spelled *Jaques Canyon*, this feature's name recalls Candelero

Jaques, Navajo patriarch who owned grazing allotments here. Nearby is *Candaleros Spring*, also named for him. The canyon's Navajo name means simply "lesser rock canyon."

JAKES (Lincoln; stage stop; 6 mi NE of Oscuro). This vanished locality was a stage stop that drew water from nearby *Jakes Spring*; with the arrival of the SP RR, it became known as *Jakes Section House.*

JAL (Lea; settlement; in SE corner of county, at the junction of NM 18 and 128; PO 1910–present). Around 1885 four Cowden brothers—W.H., George, John W., and Buck—arrived in southeastern NM from Texas with a herd of cattle bearing the brand JAL. Tradition has it that this brand originated with an East Texas cattleman named John A. Lynch, though contemporaries of the Cowdens say the brothers purchased the brand from "Uncle" Alonzo Edwards, who created it in 1872; other sources have said the cattleman's name was John A. Lawrence or J.A. Lee; one person suggested the name referred to the first initials of three Cowdens—James, Amos, and Liddon. Regardless of the origin of the brand, the Cowdens established the JAL Ranch in Monument Draw, about 6 mi E of the present settlement of Jal, and when Charles W. Justice applied for a PO in 1910, he named it for the ranch where the PO was to be located. The Jal PO remained at the ranch site until 1916, when it moved to its present location, taking the name Jal with it. It moved to a site formerly known as *Muleshoe*, for C. Cochran's Mule Shoe Ranch. Jal remained primarily a ranching community until 1927 when oil was discovered. Ranching still continues around Jal, but the JAL ranch, which once ran 40,000 cattle, has gone.

JALAROSO (Cibola; settlement; in W part of county, NE of Fence Lake; PO 1898–99, mail to Zuni). Little is known about this ephemeral community. Its name, sometimes spelled *Jalarozo*, likely is a corruption of the Spanish *jaralosa*, "filled with willows"; see *Jara (general)*.

JAMES CANYON (Otero; heads in the Sacramento Mountains just E of Cloudcroft and runs SE paralleling US 82 to join the Rio Peñasco E of Mayhill). This canyon originally was called *Tillotson Canyon*, for Thomas S. Tillotson, who in 1876 became the first permanent settler to establish a farm in the area. In 1878, Tillotson moved to the Lower Peñasco, where *Tillotson Canyon*, a tributary of the Rio Peñasco, still bears his name. He sold his earlier claim to John James of Texas, who moved onto the land with his wife and five children. Local legend tells that James, during his stay in the canyon, killed two men in gunfights, and in 1888 he and his family, now including seven children, returned to Texas. The James Canyon cemetery and school are just E of Wimsatt.

JAMES DAM (Union). See *Wetherly Lake*.

JAQUEZ (Rio Arriba). See *Gallina*.

JARA (general). In Spain, *jara* refers to the European rock rose shrub (*Cistus* genus), but in NM the term refers to the water-loving scrub willow. Here it's a very common place-name element, especially when referring to creeks and canyons, appearing most often as *La Jara*, with 86 listings in GNIS. Variants include *Jaralosa, Jarosa, Jarilla,* and *Jarita*. Other Spanish terms for willow are *mimbres* and *sauz*. See *Willow (general)*.

JARAL LARGO (Socorro; settlement; on the E bank of the Rio Grande, S of Socorro, S of Arroyo de las Cañas). This tiny settlement, whose name refers to a long stretch of willows—see *Jara (general)*—was better known in the 19th century than today, though the ford across the river with which the village was associated still is used occasionally, and a few houses remain here.

JARALES (Valencia; settlement; on the W bank of the Rio Grande, 3 mi SE of Belen, on NM 109; PO 1895–98, 1900–present). The most plausible explanation for this community's name is that it refers to the willow thickets along the Rio Grande just to the E, especially as the village also has been called *Jaralosa*; see *Jara (general)*. But at least some old-timers say the name comes from a family here named Jarales, and *Los Jarales*, reported as a variant name, would support this. It was called simply *Ranchos* when Fray Francisco Domínguez visited here in 1776. The community of *Jarales Station* was located 1 mi SW of Jarales.

JARAMILLO (general). When Governor Otermín in 1680 led NM Spaniards southward in their flight from the Pueblo Revolt, one Pedro Varela Jaramillo was listed among the refugees, thus becoming the first person with that surname in NM records. Pedro died at what is now Juarez, but his sons, Cristóbal and Juan, returned with the reconquest of 1692. Nine NM places bear their family name (GNIS).

JARAMILLO (San Miguel; settlement; in central part of county, exact location unknown; PO 1892–93, mail to East Las Vegas). Ephemeral postal locality that took the surname of postmaster Benigno Jaramillo.

JARDIN (San Miguel; settlement; on upper Manuelitas Creek, just S of the Mora County line; PO 1902–04, mail to Rociada). The origin of this name is unknown, but the village's proximity to Gascon and other places named by the Frenchman Jean Pendaries (see *Pendaries*) leads one to suspect that he also gave this village its name, using the French word—and Spanish word—for "garden."

JARILLA (Otero). See *Brice*.

JARILLA JUNCTION (Otero). See *Orogrande*.

JARILLA MOUNTAINS (Otero; in S part of Tularosa Valley, NW of Orogrande). A small, low range, whose name refers to "willows"; see *Jara (general)*. The range, once the site of extensive mining, is divided by a low pass, *Monte Carlo Gap*, 4,232 ft. The highest point is 5,301 ft.

JARITAS CREEK (Colfax; flows into Canadian River just N of Harding County line). See *Jara (general)*. Appears incorrectly on some maps as *Jacetas Creek*.

JAROSA (general). See *Jara (general)*.

JAROSA (Mora; 6 mi W of Wagon Mound, on the slopes of Turkey Mountain). Cowboys in this area speak of going to "The Jarosa," an area characterized by willows; see *Jara (general)*.

JAROSA CANYON (Rio Arriba; heads in N Jemez Mountains and runs N into the Rio Puerco). A tiny settlement named *Jarosa* is at this canyon's head; see *Jara (general)*.

JAVALINA BASIN (Lea; W of Jal). Spanish, "peccary."

JAWBONE MOUNTAIN, 10,680 ft. (Rio Arriba; in E Brazos Mountains, 1 mi N of US 64). Shaped like a jawbone.

JELLISON CITY (Taos; settlement; NE of village of Red River). In 1895, during the prospecting boom in the Keystone Mining District, S.B. Jellison tried to found "Jellison City" near his claims, but the plan died when only a few miners showed interest in the plan.

JEMEZ MOUNTAINS (Los Alamos, Rio Arriba, Sandoval, Santa Fe; N-central NM, W of the Rio Grande). These mountains, like all features named Jemez, take their name from the Towa Indian pueblo in the SW part of the range. The mountains—and their many hot springs—are remnants of the great volcanic upheavals of the late Neogene era, which began 11 million years ago; the Valle Grande (see entry), 16 miles across, at the center of the Jemez Mountains, is among the world's largest calderas. The highest Jemez summit is Chicoma Mountain (see entry), 11,561 ft., on the E. The Jemez Mountains include many peaks and areas sacred to several Indian groups, but their common names for the range usually are simply descriptive. To the Navajos, the Jemez Mountains are the "black mountains," while to the Tewas of the Rio Grande they are the "western mountains." See also *Jemez Pueblo*.

JEMEZ PUEBLO (Sandoval; in SW foothills of Jemez Mountains, on the Jemez River, on NM 4, 5 mi NW of San Ysidro; PO as Jemes 1879–1907, as Putney 1907–08, as Jemes 1908–50, as Jemez 1950, as Jemez Pueblo 1950–present). The name Jemez comes from the Towa language of the people living at the pueblo; it usually is transliterated as *hay mish;* its elements are of obscure meaning, but it has come to mean to the Towas and most other groups "Jemez Indian." The Jemez Indians are the sole surviving members of the Towa-speaking group, which once also included Pecos Pueblo, and their name for their pueblo is *Walatowa,* "the people in the canyon." They say their ancestors originally came from the N, from a lagoon called *Aubunatota,* but they traveled S and settled along the Jemez River and its tributaries. When Coronado arrived in 1541, the Jemez Indians were living in seven pueblos in the Jemez valley area, including *Anyukwinu, Guisewa* (see *Jemez Springs*), and *Hanakwa*. The name Jemez—or something like that—was in use when Espejo visited here in 1583, for he called the region *Ameyes* or *Amies;* it also appears as *Xemes* on several early maps. About 1622 all the people moved to two main villages, *Astialakwa* (see entry) and Guisewa. But while the Jemez Indians have contracted from several villages to just one, their name has spread and now includes the entire region.

JEMEZ RIVER (Sandoval; heads in the Jemez Mountains and flows SW through Jemez Pueblo, then SE to join the Rio Grande N of Bernalillo). Earlier also known as the *San Diego River,* as well as *Jemez Creek* and *Río de Jemez,* the present name was accepted by the USBGN in 1987. In its upper stretches the river consists of the *East Fork,* heading in the Valle Grande and joining San Antonio Creek at Battleship Rock to become the Jemez River proper. *Jemez Falls,* approximately 70 ft. high, are on the Jemez River, S of NM 4, between La

Cueva and the Valle Grande. *Jemez Reservoir* is on the Jemez River, S of Santa Ana Pueblo.

JEMEZ SPRINGS (Sandoval; settlement; on the Jemez River and NM 4, 12 mi NE of Jemez Pueblo; PO as Archuleta 1888–94, as Perea 1894–1907, as Jemez Springs 1907–present). When the Spanish arrived here in 1541, they found ancestors of the present Jemez Indians living here at a pueblo the Indians called *Guisewa,* "pueblo of the hot place," a reference to the natural hot springs here. Around 1622, Franciscan missionaries built the mission of *San José de Guisewa,* whose ruins, along with those of the pueblo, are the focus of *Jemez State Monument* (see entry). When Lt. James Simpson visited here in 1849, he recorded the locality's name as *Ojo Caliente,* "hot springs." The first PO here bore the name *Archuleta;* in 1894 it changed its name to *Perea,* likely for a prominent family in Bernalillo whose members may have operated the PO here; then in 1907 it took its present name, which combines the locality's Indian and natural elements.

JEMEZ STATE MONUMENT (Sandoval; in village of Jemez Springs, on NM 4). This features the ruins of the Spanish mission of *San José de Guisewa,* built in 1622 by Franciscans at the site of the Jemez Indian pueblo of *Guisewa.* See *Jemez Springs.*

JENKINS (Lea; settlement; in N part of county, 5 mi W of Crossroads; PO 1910–26, mail to Crossroads). Abandoned homesteader community, named for its founder and first postmaster, William L. Jenkins, a Methodist minister.

JERKY MOUNTAINS, CANYON, SPRING (Catron; in the Gila Wilderness, 15 mi NW of Gila Cliff Dwellings and N of the West Fork of the Gila River). In the late 19th century, the Grudging brothers had a cabin at a spring on the S side of these mountains, and there they made "jerky," dried meat that they sold in Mogollon.

JEWETT, JEWETT VALLEY (San Juan; settlement; 17 mi W of Farmington, W of Waterflow, S of the San Juan River; PO 1884–1907, mail to Fruitland).

Along with Liberty and Waterflow, this was an early English-speaking community. Name origin unknown.

JEWETT GAP, 8,200 ft. (Catron; a pass through the Gallo Mountains, on NM 32). The person for whom this pass was named is unknown. An Apache NF station is here.

JICARILLA (general). This Spanish name means "little cup, or little gourd for drinking," and as such has served as a descriptive metaphor for cup-shaped landforms; see *Jicarilla Peak* and *Jicarita Peak.* But in NM *jicarilla* also was the name the Spanish applied to a group of nomadic Apache Indians Spanish explorers encountered on the state's northern and eastern plains. These Apaches were skilled at basketmaking, particularly little woven cups, and soon they were called Jicarillas. Soon after contact with the Spanish in the 17th century, the Jicarillas adopted agriculture and later moved closer to the Rio Grande. Until 1700, the Spanish usually did not differentiate the Jicarillas from Apaches in general; in that year NM Governor Cubero ordered a condemned criminal's head to be impaled on a pole in Taos to warn the *Apaches de la Xicarilla* against harboring Spanish fugitives. Confrontations with settlers and soldiers continued until 1855, when the Jicarillas sued for peace. During the next 30 years they were shunted from reservation to reservation until 1887, when they were given the almost 750,000 acres they now occupy within the Jicarilla Apache Indian Reservation (see entry), whose administrative center is Dulce. See *Apache (general).*

JICARILLA (Lincoln; settlement; in the Jicarilla Mountains, 27 mi NE of Carrizozo; PO 1892–1942, mail to Ancho). Though Hispanics had done placer mining in this area since the 1850s, the mining camp of Jicarilla, named for the mountains, wasn't really born until Anglo prospectors became active in the 1880s. The camp peaked during the Depression, when a few dollars could be made mining, but when better opportunities opened up elsewhere, Jicarilla began to decline. Today, only a handful of residents remain.

JICARILLA APACHE INDIAN RESERVA-
TION (Rio Arriba, Sandoval; Indian
reservation; NW NM). This 750,000-
acre tract was created in 1887 as a permanent home of the Jicarilla Apaches.
The tribal headquarters are at Dulce (see
entry). See *Jicarilla (general).*

JICARILLA MOUNTAINS (Lincoln; in central part of county, NE of Carrizozo).
Named for the Jicarilla Apaches, whose
nomadic journeys would have brought
them here and who once shared a reservation with the Mescalero Apaches at
nearby Fort Stanton. Highest elevation,
Ancho Peak, 7,825 ft. A 1982 USBGN
decision established this group as distinct from the Sacramento Mountains to
the S.

JICARILLA PEAK (Rio Arriba–Mora). See
Chimayosos Peak.

JICARITA PEAK, 12,835 ft. (Taos; in SE
part of county, in the Sangre de Cristo
Mountains, 1.5 mi N of the Rio Santa
Barbara). This was called *Jicarilla* by the
Wheeler Survey, but that name and the
present name have the same meaning,
"little cup"; see *Jicarilla (general).* The
peak is said to have been named because
on its W slope is a cup-shaped depression from which a strong air current
continually blows. The mountain is sacred to the Indians of Picuris Pueblo.

JIM SMITH PEAK, 9,278 ft. (Catron; 12 mi
N of Luna). This peak was named for an
incident, the details of which have been
lost, involving Jim Smith, who worked
as a cowboy in the 1890s for Montague
Stevens (see *Rancho Grande Estates*).
Smith has been described as "a real
boomer, cowpuncher, and gunfighter."
He married a maid named Annie that
Stevens had brought from England, and
they moved to Kansas City, where Smith
became prominent in construction and
business.

JOHN MILLS LAKE (Rio Arriba; on US 64,
on the Jicarilla Apache Reservation, SW
of Dulce). The name of this small lake
recalls the chairman of the Jicarilla
Tribal Council from 1941 to 1950.

JOHNSON (San Miguel). See *Fort Bascom.*

JOHNSON (Sandoval; trading point; on
NM 197, SW of Cuba and NE of
Torreon). Active trading center, bearing
the name of a local family.

JOHNSON (Union; settlement; in NE corner of county, just S of the Colorado
line; PO 1906–11, mail to Kenton, OK).
Abandoned homesteader community,
named for its first postmaster, David C.
Johnson.

JOHNSON CANYON (Catron; tributary of
White Creek, in the Mogollon Mountains). As Jack Stockbridge told the
story, in the 1880s lawman "Keecheye"
Johnson was sent to White Creek to ar-
rest one Ralph Jenks, suspected of rus-
tling, but when he got to this canyon
Johnson was killed—hence the name.
Jenks reported the killing in Mogollon,
and as he was the prime suspect he in
turn was shot.

JOHNSON MESA (Colfax; 16 mi E of
Raton and N of US 64-87). Johnson
Mesa, rising 2,000 feet above the surrounding terrain, its level grassland extending 7 by 14 miles, has been
described as an island in the sky. It bears
the surname of Elijah "Lige" Johnson,
who settled just S of the mesa at a place
that came to be called *Johnson Park.*
Johnson let his cattle graze on the mesa,
and soon it too was called Johnson. By
the early 1880s, farmers had begun to
settle on the mesa, then a PO was established under the name of *Bell* (see entry), and eventually a family lived on
every 160 acres, with four schools for
the mesa children. But conditions on the
mesa often were harsh, and by World
War I residents had begun to leave; even
Lige Johnson, after 25 years, moved to
Raton. Today a few families still live on
the mesa, but none in the winter.

JONES (McKinley; settlement; NE of
Thoreau, just E of Smith Lake). Abandoned trading point bearing the surname of Homer Jones, a trader active in
Thoreau circa 1925–55.

JONES CITY (Lea; settlement; 3 mi NE of
Eunice). Tiny locality, origin of name
unknown, a creation of the nearby oil
fields.

JONES RANCH (McKinley). See *Chi Chil
Tah.*

JONESVILLE (Curry; settlement; 6 mi SW of Grady; PO 1908–11, mail to Pleano). Ephemeral homesteader community, now vanished, named for its first postmaster, Joseph C. Jones.

JONETA (Lincoln). See *Lon*.

JORDAN (Quay; settlement; in SW part of county, on NM 156; PO 1902–55, mail to McAlister). Jordan began as a ranching community and took the family name of W.O. Jordan and his wife, Jennie. When the settlement got a PO, the Jordans' son, James, was postmaster while Jennie, or "Grandma" Jordan as she was known, was his assistant. Between 1902 and 1909 the area saw frequent disputes between sheepmen and cattlemen, but these subsided as homesteaders moved in. Jordan once had its own school and its own baseball team, and though the settlement has vanished, a sense of community remains; the name still is recognized and used.

JORNADA (Sierra; settlement; on AT&SF RR, 3 mi S of Engle; PO 1903–04, mail to San Marcial). This locality, primarily a mail stop, was named like many other features in the area for the *Jornada del Muerto* (see entry).

JORNADA DEL MUERTO (Doña Ana, Sierra, Socorro; between the Rio Grande and the Fra Cristobal Range on the W and the San Andres and Oscura Mountains on the E). "Journey of death" is how many people translate the Spanish name of this 90-mile route on the Camino Real, and it's easy to see why this translation has become popular. For while travelers' journeys over the Jornada del Muerto were shorter by at least a day than the difficult route along the Rio Grande, the Jornada del Muerto was waterless, sandy, desolate, and vulnerable to frequent Indian attacks; scores of people died along the route, and their graves and bones would have been grim reminders of its terrors.

But the name Jornada del Muerto actually translates to mean not "journey of death" but "journey of the dead man," specifically one Bernardo Gruber, a German trader who in 1670 had escaped

two years of imprisonment at the Ortega *estancia* in the Sandia Pueblo jurisdiction, where he had been accused by the Inquisition of witchcraft. He was fleeing S over the route later named for him when he perished. From the discovery of his sun-dried corpse at a place later called *El Alemán* (see entry), "the German," the name Jornada del Muerto is believed to have evolved. *Jornada Lakes* (Sierra; 5 mi S of Engle).

JOSE (Luna; settlement; on Cookes Peak, just SW of Cookes; PO 1902–05, mail to Cookes). This was one of the camps associated with mining on Cookes Peak. The postal application signed by Samuel Eamon Wood asked that the PO be called either *Alma* or *Jose*, for reasons unknown; the postal authorities crossed out Alma, probably because a PO by that name existed elsewhere in NM, and the PO became Jose.

JOSE BUTTE, 8,185 ft. (Colfax; 6 mi NW of Capulin). Named for José Griego, who homesteaded nearby.

JOSE PINO (Valencia; settlement; in S part of county, exact location unknown.) Territorial legislation in 1852 regarding Valencia County referred to the town of Jose Pino as a boundary marker. Little else has been reported about the locality.

JOSEPH (Catron). See *Aragon*.

JOSEPH (Rio Arriba). See *Abiquiu*.

JOYA (general). Although the Spanish *joya* means "ornament, jewel," it also can be translated "valley, basin, hole," and in NM La Joya place names usually refer to a feature's location in a basin or valley.

LA JOYA FLATS (Santa Fe; 9 mi SE of Madrid). Spanish, "valley, basin"; see *La Joya (general)*.

JUAN DE DIOS (Guadalupe; settlement; about 10 mi SE of Santa Rosa, on Juan de Dios Creek; PO 1912–19, mail to Santa Rosa). Former postal locality, name origin unknown.

JUAN LA CRUZ CANYON (Colfax; at the head of the Vermejo River). Juan La Cruz had a home here around 1875.

JUAN TABO CANYON (Bernalillo; on the W face of the Sandia Mountains, N of Domingo Baca Canyon). The identity of the man whose name is on this canyon—and numerous features in Albuquerque—remains a mystery. The name first appears in a 1778 petition using *Cañada de Juan Taboso* as a landmark. It's been suggested this person was a Taboso Indian, a tribe akin to the Lipan Apaches, and though the Tabosos' traditional territory was far to the SE, it's not impossible that one of their members settled here; at least one legend attributes the name to an Indian sheepherder who grazed his flocks in the canyon. Another legend is that Juan Tabo was a priest who lived here, though the name is absent from church records. But these are just conjecture, and Juan Tabo is likely to remain the stuff of legends. The *Juan Tabo Picnic Area,* at the head of Juan Tabo Canyon, was established by the USFS in 1936.

JUAN TAFOYA (Cibola). See *Marquez.*

JUAN TOMAS (Bernalillo; settlement; in the foothills of the Manzano Mountains, E of NM 337 SE of Tijeras). Today only a hamlet, this former bean-growing communty bears the Spanish version of the name of John Thomas, who owned a ranch here about 1870.

JUANA LOPEZ (Santa Fe; settlement; location unknown; PO 1866–70). Abandoned settlement, likely associated with the *Juana López Grant* W of Cerrillos.

JUDSON (Roosevelt; settlement; 8 mi SE of Elida; PO 1907–18, mail to Elida). Abandoned homesteader community, named for its first postmaster, Judson Hunter.

MESA DE LOS JUMANOS (Torrance; in SW part of county, NE of Gran Quivira). This large, prominent mesa takes its name from the Indians Oñate found living at the pueblo now known as Gran Quivira (see entry); he called the Indians *Jumanos,* "the striped ones," because they painted a stripe across their nose. The name has been spelled *Humanos, Juamanes,* or *Jumanes,* but Jumanos is the form recognized by the USBGN in 1975.

JUNCTION, JUNCTION CITY (San Juan; settlement; between the Animas and San Juan Rivers, E of their junction at Farmington; PO as Junction City 1891–95, as Junction 1895–96, mail to Farmington). When San Juan County was created in 1887, a group of landowners and promoters created a town they hoped would become the county seat. The site formerly had been called *Mesa City,* but the promoters renamed it Junction City, for its proximity to the junction of the Animas and San Juan Rivers. Aztec, which had temporarily been given the county seat, vigorously opposed Junction City as county seat, but in a countywide election in 1890 to settle the issue Junction City got 255 votes, Aztec 246, and Farmington one. In a recount, however, many Junction City voters were disqualified, and Aztec won. Soon afterward, Junction City faded and eventually was permanently eclipsed by Farmington.

JUNE (San Miguel). See *Ilfeld.*

JUNIPER (general). Along with its almost constant companion the piñon pine, the one-seed juniper (*Juniperus monosperma*) all but defines the Upper Sonoran life zone, covering vast portions of the state; hills and mesas dotted with these shrubby trees provide a picturesque transition between grasslands and forested mountains. Though often called a "cedar," the tree technically is a juniper—no true cedars grow in NM; its dense reddish wood, with a cedar-like fragrance, makes the cedar identification inevitable. The berries were an important food for Native Americans, the bark produces a green dye, and the wood still heats numerous New Mexicans' homes. *Cedar* also is common as a name element in NM; it appears 90 times in GNIS, along with its Spanish form, *cedro.* The Spanish terms *sabino, sabinal, sabinoso* also refer to this plant; though *sabina* is the correct Spanish term for a certain species of dwarf juniper (*Juniperus sabina*), in NM colonists gave the name a masculine ending and applied the name to the common scrub cedar. All these names are derived from the Latin *Sabina herba,* and even in English *savin* is a common name for *J.*

sabina. Sabino names occur 23 times; *Cedro* occurs 10 times (GNIS).

Another species of juniper, the Rocky Mountain juniper (*J. scopulorum*) also is commonly called "cedar," *cedro,* and *sabino;* it grows at higher elevations than the one-seed juniper. But neither of the two "cedars" is to be confused with the tamarisk, often called "salt cedar" (*Tamarix pentandra*), which was introduced to NM just in the 20th century, though it is now common throughout the state.

LA JUNTA (general). Spanish, "the junction," usually applied to the confluence of streams or rivers.

LA JUNTA (Lincoln). See *Hondo.*

LA JUNTA, RIO LA JUNTA (Mora). See *Watrous.*

LA JUNTA CREEK (Taos; main tributary of the Rio Pueblo, joining it at Tres Ritos). Appears on many maps as *Río La Junta;* see *La Junta (general).*

KAISER LAKE (Eddy; on the Pecos River, 10 mi SE of Artesia). This lake, now dry, was formed after 1917 after the US Reclamation Service planted tamarisks to prevent siltation of Lake McMillan. It took the family name of three Kaiser brothers, who homesteaded here from 1906 to 1910.

KAPPUS (Quay; settlement; 10 mi S of Nara Visa; PO 1910–13, mail to Nara Visa). Abandoned homesteader settlement, that took the name of its first postmaster, Anthony Kappus.

KARR CANYON (Otero; in the Sacramento Mountains, 6 mi SW of Cloudcroft). Will Karr homesteaded here in 1886.

LAKE KATHERINE (Santa Fe; in the Sangre de Cristo Mountains, 1 mi NE of Santa Fe Baldy). This timberline tarn commemorates Katherine Chávez Page Kavanaugh, owner of the Los Pinos Guest Range on the Pecos River.

KEARNYS GAP (San Miguel; passes through a small group of hills, about 5 mi SW of Las Vegas). Originally called *El Puertocito*, "the little door," this gap later was named for Gen. Stephen Watts Kearny who passed through here on August 17, 1846, with his army. Although the gap through which I-25 now passes is generally accepted as Kearnys Gap, some local historians say Kearny actually took his troops through another, smaller gap 2 miles to the N. See also *The Creston*.

KELLS (Otero; settlement; 10 mi NW of Mayhill, in Sixteen Springs Canyon; PO 1916–17, mail to Cloudcroft). When residents of this community, now abandoned, petitioned for a PO, they wanted to call it *Sixteen*, for Sixteen Springs Canyon, but postal authorities rejected this name and called it Kells instead, for reasons unknown.

KELLY (Socorro; settlement; 3 mi SE of Magdalena; PO 1883–1945, mail to Magdalena). Around 1866 Col. J.S. "Old Hutch" Hutchason was prospecting in this area when he found a promising lead, which he turned over to a friend, Andy Kelly, who operated a local sawmill. Kelly gave his name to the mine and worked it for a time; when other prospectors came to the area around 1879 and laid out a townsite, they named it for Kelly. The camp boomed, first with silver mining and then with zinc mining, and at one time 3,000 people lived here; a strong rivalry developed between Kelly and the growing town of Magdalena. But when the zinc ores played out in the 1930s, Kelly began to die, and today only ruins remain.

KELLY MOUNTAINS (Catron; 13 mi SW of Reserve). Small group, named for the Kelly family of Alma, whose members still live in the area. Highest point, 7,667 ft.

KEMP (Bernalillo; settlement; on the E side of the Sandia Mountains; PO 1907–08, mail to Albuquerque). Former community, origin of name unknown.

KENNA (Roosevelt; settlement; on US 70, 11 mi SW of Elida; PO as Kenna 1902–06, as Urton 1906–07, as Kenna 1907–present). This locality originally was called *Urton*, for two brothers, W.G. and George Urton, who came to the region from Missouri in 1884 to become ranchers; see *Urton Lake*. It was still primarily a ranching community when William and Euphemia Littlefield arrived from Texas around 1897 and became prominent in the community. Reportedly, two settlements, Urton and Kenna, existed adjacent to each other, but when the people applied for a PO, they requested the name Kenna. One explanation is that a RR contractor named Kenna camped here during construction of the AT&SF RR roadbed, and the place became known as *Kennas Camp*. But the vice-president of the AT&SF RR at the time was E.D. Kenna, and this also could account for the name. Kenna briefly changed its name back to Urton, but then returned to Kenna, the name it still bears.

KENNEDY (Lincoln; settlement; location unknown; PO 1888–91, mail to Lower Peñasco). Short-lived PO that took the name of its first postmaster, Silas A. Kennedy.

KENNEDY (Santa Fe; settlement; on AT&SF RR, 20 mi S of Santa Fe, 2 mi W of Galisteo; PO 1906–18, mail to Galisteo). The abandoned settlement of Kennedy, located where the old NMC RR crossed the AT&SF RR, was named for Arthur Kennedy, a RR official.

KENT (Doña Ana; settlement; at the NE end of the Organ Mountains, E of Organ; PO 1904–11, mail to Organ). This abandoned mining camp likely took the name of its first postmaster, Garard W. Kent, though F.H. Kent was general manager of the Doña Ana mines about 1909.

KENTUCKY MESA (San Juan). See *Waterflow.*

KEPHART (Union; trading point; 20 mi SE of Abbott; PO 1915–23, mail to Gladstone). In 1914 Grace L. Kephart filed on 320 acres here, but as the nearest PO was at Pasamonte 25 mi E she and her neighbors petitioned for a PO, which was named for her. In 1916 Kephart married rancher Harry V. Lammon, and they kept the PO until 1923, when they sold out to a man who discontinued mail delivery, though the name Kephart remained on a voting district.

KERES (northern NM, along the Rio Grande). Today this term denotes a linguistic group among Pueblo Indians; modern pueblos speaking Keresan dialects include Laguna, Acoma, Zia, Santa Ana, San Felipe, Santo Domingo, and Cochiti. To the early Spanish explorers, however, Keres also denoted the region where the Keresan-speaking Indians lived. Coronado (1541) called it *Quirix,* Espejo (1581) *Quires,* and Castaño de Sosa (1590) *Quereses.*

KERMIT (Roosevelt; settlement; on AT&SF RR, 15 mi SW of Portales; PO 1910–18, mail to Elida). The most likely explanation for the name of this abandoned community, previously called *Plateau,* is that it recalls D. Kermit Fitzhugh, one of two brothers from Clovis who laid out a townsite here.

KETTNER (Cibola; settlement; in the Zuni Mountains, 32 mi W of Grants; PO 1904–09, moved to Sawyer). One of several logging camps in the Zuni Mountains, Kettner was headquarters of the American Lumber Co. The camp, also called *Spud Ranch,* took its name from a local homesteader (a Palmer Kettner came to Gallup in 1888 as bookkeeper for the Aztec Coal Co.). Kettner at one time had a two-story hotel and cookhouse that could feed 700 workers. In 1910 the headquarters and the PO were transferred to Sawyer (see entry) a few miles away. In 1913 the American Lumber Co. went bankrupt, and both Kettner and Sawyer were abandoned.

KIDNEY WATER SPRING (Sandoval). See *Sulphur Springs.*

KIMBALL (Hidalgo; settlement; in the Steins Pass area). A little mining camp, long abandoned; see *Steins Pass, Beck,* and *Pocahontas.*

KIMBALL (Union). See *Spring Hill.*

KIMBETO (San Juan; trading point; 8 mi SW of Nageezi, on Kimbeto Wash). Navajo trading post and settlement whose name is Navajo and means "hawk's nest." The name sometimes is spelled *Kinbeto.*

Kimbeto Wash heads S of Nageezi and flows SW into Chaco Canyon.

KIN KLETSO (San Juan; archaeological site; in Chaco Culture National Historical Park, in Chaco Canyon, on Chaco Wash, NW of Pueblo Bonito). As with many other Anasazi sites in the Chaco Canyon complex, this ruin bears a Navajo name, here meaning "yellow house."

KIN KLIZHIN (San Juan; archaeological site; on Kin Klizhin Wash, S of the Chaco River, W of the main Chaco Culture National Historical Park). This ruincd village, now administered as part of Chaco Culture National Historical Park, consists of a tower dominating a small cluster of rooms. Its name is Navajo and means "black house."

KING (Lea; settlement; 10 mi SE of Tatum, E of McDonald; PO 1909–18, mail to McDonald). This former settlement took the name of the family who established the PO. At one time King had stores, a school, and a weekly newspaper, *The King of Progress.*

KINGSBURY CAMP (Sierra; settlement; in the Black Range, 3 mi N of Grafton). One of numerous ephemeral mining camps in the Black Range in the late 1800s; named for brothers named Kingsbury.

KINGSTON (Sierra; settlement; in the E foothills of the Black Range, on NM 152, 9 mi W of Hillsboro; PO 1882–1957, mail to Hillsboro). Kingston was born soon after silver was discovered in the area in 1880; a man named Barnaby pitched a tent under a cottonwood tree and opened a store. As the center of a rich silver-producing district the camp grew rapidly. A town was laid out by the Kingston Townsite Co. and named for the Iron King Mine. Eventually Kingston had 7,000 people, 22 saloons, three hotels, and three newspapers. But when the deposits played out and the price of silver dropped, Kingston became a shadow of its former self, though it continues to survive.

KIOWA (Colfax; settlement; 15 mi SW of Capulin; PO 1877–80, 1890–92, 1901–04, mail to Folsom). The Kiowa Indians often camped here, and the locality came to be known as *Kiowa Camp,* later as *Kiowa District.* The settlement was at the NW base of *Kiowa Mesa; Kiowa Springs* are on the mesa's NE side; and to the NE are the extensive *Kiowa Flats.* The Fort Union Road passed just NW of Kiowa. Of the former settlement, only a schoolhouse remains.

KIOWA MOUNTAIN, 9,735 ft. (Rio Arriba; 4 mi NE of Cañon Plaza). This and *Kiowa Lake* and *Kiowa Canyon* just to the S were named for some forgotten assoction with the Kiowa Indians.

KIRK (Quay; settlement; S of Tucumcari, 5.5 mi W of Forrest; PO 1908–21, mail to Jordan). Abandoned settlement, name origin unknown.

KIRKWELL (Eddy). See *Malaga.*

KIRTLAND (San Juan; settlement; on US 64, 8 mi W of Farmington; PO as Olio 1884–1903, as Kirtland 1903–present). Kirtland's first identity was as *Olio,* a name said to have been pulled from the dictionary by first postmaster, Columbus John Moss; it's meaning is "a stew of mixed meat and vegetables, hence a mixture, a hodgepodge," and that, said Moss, described the community made up of Navajos, Hispanics, Mormons, and Anglo-Gentiles. Veterans of the Mormon Battalion were among the settlers here. In 1903 the community changed its name from Olio to Kirtland, for reasons unknown, the name it bears today.

KIRTLAND AIR FORCE BASE (Bernalillo; military installation; at the SE edge of Albuquerque's city limits). Roy G. Kirtland was born at Fort Benton, MT, in 1874. In 1913, following earlier military service, he commanded the First Aero Squadron when military aviation was in its infancy, and during World War I he commanded the Third Regiment in France and was inspector of all aviation activities in England. In 1919 he commanded the US Military Aviation School at College Park, MD, and later held other aviation commands. He retired in 1936 but returned to active service in 1941; he died of a heart attack the same year. When the Air Corps Advanced Flying School was established here in 1941, it was named to honor this pioneer Air Corps officer, and the air base has continued to bear his name.

KIT CARSON (general). In 1826 a 16-year-old boy in Franklin, MO, abruptly left his apprenticeship as a saddlemaker, said goodbye to no one, and caught a wagon train headed west. Thus began the career of the West's most famous scout and mountain man, Christopher "Kit" Carson. From his arrival in Taos in 1826 until his death 42 years later, Carson was a trapper, scout, rancher, trader, and Indian agent, but it was his knowledge of the West—its land and peoples—that made him a legend in his own lifetime. Though he rarely stayed in one place for long, he considered Taos his home, and it was there he died in 1868. Since then, scores of places throughout the West have been named for him, including Carson City, the Nevada state capitol. In NM 12 features bear his name, the largest being the Carson National Forest (see entry). Almost every county in the West, it seems, has at least one cave, knoll, butte, peak, etc. named because Carson was believed to have fought Indians there; to have actually visited all these places, he would have had to have been much older than 58 when he died. See *Carson.*

KIT CARSON MEMORIAL STATE PARK (Taos; N of the plaza in Taos, on US 64). This small but popular state park features Kit Carson's grave. In 1973, a group of Taoseños, mostly Pueblo Indians, sought to change the park's name to *Santiago "Jimmy" Lujan Park* to honor a member of Taos Pueblo killed in the Bataan Death March. Many Native Americans, now as when he was alive, see Carson as their enemy, but Carson is too firmly embedded in NM history to be removed, and the name-change was not adopted.

KIT CARSONS CAVE (McKinley; 7 mi E of Gallup, 3 mi N of Navajo Wingate Village). Local folklore says Kit Carson took shelter here during his 1864 campaign against the Navajos, but no official record corroborates this.

KIT CARSON MESA (Colfax; 1.5 mi S of Rayado). Kit Carson was the first English-speaking settler at Rayado (see entry.)

KIT CARSONS MOUND (Quay; NW of Grady). Old-timers say Kit Carson stood off an Indian attack here, but again, documentation is lacking.

KLONDIKE (Colfax; settlement; 2 mi W of Eagle Nest). George Adlai Feather reported this to be a mining camp, doubtless named for the Klondike in Alaska, also the scene of mining.

KNEELING NUN (Grant; at the end of Ben Moore Mountain, near Santa Rita). Ac-

cording to a legend at least 200 years old, this conspicuous rock formation represents Raquel Mendoza de Alarcón, daughter of a Mexican miner and an Apache woman. Raquel was sent to a Chihuahua convent and returned a nun, but she fell in love with Capt. Fernando Alarcón; she renounced her holy vows and married the dashing captain, but he soon deserted her. Distraught and destitute, she climbed Ben Moore Mountain (see entry), where she prayed for forgiveness even as a snowstorm overtook her. When the weather cleared, her kneeling figure had been turned to stone. Other versions of the legend say the nun was a Sister Teresa, who fell in love with a soldier named Diego. Becoming a stone pillar was her fate too.

KNICKERBOCKER PEAKS, 6,788 ft. (San Juan; 6 mi E of Aztec). Peter Knickerbocker was a local rancher whose lands included these low mountains. He was a tall, striking figure, and dressed as Uncle Sam—in red, white, and blue costume and tall stovepipe hat—he was a popular feature of local Fourth of July celebrations. *Knickerbocker Canyon* heads at the peaks and runs NW to the Animas River.

THE KNOB, 10,625 ft. (Taos; in S part of county, 2.5 mi S of Tres Ritos). Simple descriptive name. *Knob Creek* flows N from The Knob into the Rio Pueblo.

KNOWLES (Lea; settlement; on NM 132, 13 mi SE of Lovington, 7 mi N of Hobbs; PO 1903–44, mail to Hobbs). In 1903, Ben L. Knowles staked out a homestead on the featureless Llano Estacado NE of Monument Springs; he set up a store and a PO in his home and thus created the second settlement in what was to become Lea County. The community briefly called itself *Oasis,* because it was the first civilization one reached traveling W from Texas, but in 1908 the town moved 0.5 mi to the E, Knowles resigned as postmaster, and a new community was formed that was named for him. At its height, Knowles had 500 residents and was the largest settlement in the county, but with the discovery of oil at Hobbs and the creation of the county seat at Lovington, Knowles was eclipsed by these two settlements, though the name and vestiges of the community survive today.

KOEHLER (Colfax; settlement; 16 mi SW of Raton, 6 mi NW of US 64, in Prairie Crow Canyon; PO 1907–32, 1943–57, mail to Raton). Koehler (pronounced KAY-lor) was a coal-mining town that began in 1906 and was named for Henry Koehler, president of the board of the American Brewing Co. of St. Louis and of the St. Louis, Rocky Mountain and Pacific Co., which mined coal here and owned the town; Henry's brother, Hugo A. Koehler, was vice-president of the company. The demand for coal by railroads was high, and by 1907 Koehler had 1,000 residents. But like so many other coal towns, its existence was precarious. In 1955 the Kaiser Steel Corp. purchased the town and razed almost all its buildings. *Koehler Junction* was a settlement, now vanished, on the Ute Division of the AT&SF RR where the line to Koehler began, 2 mi E of Koehler.

KOOGLER (San Miguel). See *San Ignacio.*

KUAUA (Sandoval; archaeological site; in Coronado State Monument, 0.5 mi NW of Bernalillo, on the W bank of the Rio Grande). Pronounced Koo-WA-wa. This southern Tiwa pueblo, situated on a bluff overlooking the Rio Grande, is believed by some people to be where Coronado and his *conquistadores* wintered in 1540–1541, the place they called *Alcanfor,* Spanish, "camphor." Contemporary Tiwas know this pueblo as *Ghowye,* "evergreen." But while Coronado doubtless would have visited this pueblo, many historians and Indian scholars believe the explorer actually wintered at a less exposed site, at a pueblo known to Tiwas today as *Stolen Town,* located at the present site of *Bernalillo* (see entry).

L

LA AGUITA (Mora; settlement; between Carmen and Mora). Spanish, "the little water," likely a reference to a freshet or a spring at this tiny inhabited neighborhood in the Mora area.

LA BELLE (Taos; settlement; 8 mi NE of Red River; PO 1895–1901, mail to Elizabethtown). La Belle, sometimes spelled *Labelle,* was a gold-mining camp. Valuable minerals had been discovered here as early as 1866, but the locality didn't really take off until much later, with the general mining enthusiasm of the 1890s in the Red River area. The camp was named on August 28, 1894, for Belle Dixon, wife of a prospector who was one of the original investors in the mining area. Within a year of its naming, La Belle had 80 buildings and 600 residents—only about 12 of them women, wives of miners—but the gold strikes ultimately were disappointing, and today even the ruins of La Belle are difficult to find.

LA BOLSA (Rio Arriba; settlement; just N of NM 68, on the S side of the Rio Grande, 0.5 mi NE of the junction of the Rio Grande and Embudo Creek). Spanish, "purse, bag," but the name here likely refers to the hamlet's location in a small, enclosed space.

LA BOCA (San Juan; postal locality; in NE part of county, just S of the Colorado line; PO 1902–09, moved to La Plata, CO). It's unknown why this rural PO had a Spanish name meaning "the mouth." The PO after being moved from NM to Colorado remained in La Plata County until being discontinued in 1937.

LA CANOVA (Rio Arriba; settlement; NE of Española, on the W side of the Rio Grande, opposite Velarde). Tiny inhabited community whose Spanish name means "water trough, sluice," doubtless a reference to the extensive irrigation in the area.

LA CAÑADA (Sandoval). See *Cañada.*

LA CEBOLLETA (Mora; settlement; between Buena Vista and the San Miguel County line). Only ruins remain of this village located on an old road to Fort Union. The name probably was derived from the *Rito Cebolla* nearby. See *Cebolla (general).*

LA CIENAGA (Rio Arriba). See *Embudo.*

LA CIENEGA (Santa Fe; settlement; on NM 22, 9 mi SW of Santa Fe, on Cieneguilla Creek). Spanish, "the marsh." Inhabited settlement located on the site of a Keres pueblo that participated in the Pueblo Revolt of 1680. The name *La Cinega* appears on the map prepared by Peñalosa in 1686–88 and also on the 1700 L'Atlas Curieux. In 1776 Fray Francisco Atanasio Domínguez referred to the locality as *Ciénega Grande,* as opposed to *Cieneguilla* (see entry), the "little Cienega." The community of Cienega actually has two divisions, *Upper La Cienega* and *Lower La Cienega.* Just 2 miles to the N is the tiny settlement of *Cieneguilla; Cieneguilla Creek* crosses I-25, 9 mi SW of Santa Fe.

LA CONCEPCION (San Miguel; settlement; 13 mi SE of Romeroville, on the N bank of the Gallinas River; PO 1882–85, mail to Las Vegas). Little remains of this isolated Hispanic community, whose name honors The Immaculate Conception.

LA CONSTANCIA (Valencia; settlement; on the E side of the Rio Grande, on NM 47 3 mi S of Adelino). Manuel A. Otero operated a gristmill at the site of this inhabited community and is said to have named the place La Constancia because the mill was running constantly.

LA CORDILLERA (Taos; settlement; near Ranchos de Taos). Spanish, "the mountain range," inhabited suburb of Taos, whose name likely refers to the Sangre de Cristo Mountains to the E.

LA CUCHILLA (Rio Arriba; settlement; W of US 84, 1 mi S of Chili). This tiny inhabited settlement sometimes is labeled *La Chuachia,* but this likely is a corruption of La Cuchilla, "the ridge," from a nearby landform. See *Cuchilla, Cuchillo (general).*

LA CUESTA (San Miguel). See *Villanueva.*

LA CUESTECITA (Rio Arriba; settlement; on Cañada de Ojo Sarco, 3.5 mi SE of Dixon). Inhabited residential cluster whose name means "the little ridge."

LA CUEVA (Bernalillo; settlement; along the Río Puerco, exact location unknown). George Adlai Feather reported that a settlement by this name was mentioned in 1855 and again in 1877.

LA CUEVA (Mora; settlement; on the Mora River, at the junction of NM 518 and 442, 5 mi SE of Mora; PO 1868–1961, mail to Buena Vista). Shortly after the establishment of Fort Union in 1851, Vicente Romero established what was to be the new fort's chief supply ranch. He named it La Cueva, Spanish for "the cave"; he is said to have slept in nearby caves while he built his ranch. During the 1860s *La Cueva Valley* became famous for its harvests, and Romero for his skill as an irrigation engineer and businessman; his mill supplied grain to military outposts throughout the West. Much of the ranch complex still remains and has been preserved as a National Historic District. *La Cueva Lake* is 1 mi E of settlement of La Cueva.

LA CUEVA (Rio Arriba; settlement; on the Rio Ojo Caliente and NM 111, N of Ojo Caliente). This locality takes its name from *Cañada de la Cueva,* which enters the Rio Ojo Caliente from the W and was named for caves in the cliffs.

LA CUEVA (Sandoval; settlement; in the Jemez Mountains, at the junction of NM 4 and 126). Just S of this active trading center is a cave high in the volcanic formations overlooking the Jemez River. *La Cueva Spring* nearby also was named for this cave.

LA CUEVA (Santa Fe; settlement; 3 mi W of Pecos, 1.5 mi N of I-25). Diffuse residential area, likely named for its location in *La Cueva Canyon.*

LA CUEVA PEAK, 10,669 ft. (Taos; in the Sangre de Cristo Mountains, N of NM 518, N of Tres Ritos). *La Cueva Lake* is S of La Cueva Peak and N of Tres Ritos.

LA FRAGUA (San Miguel; settlement; on the E bank of the Pecos River, on NM 3, just SE of Pueblo). This inhabited hamlet has a Spanish name meaning "the forge, blacksmith's shop," likely because a blacksmith's forge was here. The use of the definite article implies this origin rather than the common Spanish surname Fragua.

LA GARITA (San Miguel). See *Variadero.*

LA HUERTA (Eddy; settlement; in N part of Carlsbad). This neighborhood, formerly a separate community, was named for the gardens and orchards (Spanish, *huertas*) that once provided food for Carlsbad.

LA JARA (general). See *Jara (general).*

LA JARA (Mora; settlement; 3 mi N of Rainsville, 0.5 mi N of NM 442). While Fort Union was active, this settlement was too. A few families still live here, and the name remains alive, but the village is now entirely within a private ranch. It likely took its name from *La Jara Creek,* which flows S to enter Coyote Creek near here. See *Jara (general).*

LA JARA (Sandoval; settlement; on NM 96, 2 mi N of NM 44, 4 mi NW of Cuba; PO 1911–17, 1926–present). This diffuse community was named for being strung out along *La Jara Creek.* The area in the upper end of the valley is called *Upper La Jara.* Navajos know this area by a name meaning "willows coming out braided," referring, like the Spanish name, to willows along the creek. See *Jara (general).*

LA JOLLA (Rio Arriba). See *Velarde.*

LA JOYA (Socorro; settlement; on the E side of the Rio Grande, on NM 304, 20 mi N of Socorro; PO as La Joya 1871–73, 1883–95, as Lajoya 1895–present). For most of its long history, this inhabited settlement was known as *Sevilleta,* or more fully, *La Joya de Sevilleta. Nueva Sevilleta* was the name Oñate's expedition in 1598 gave a Piro Indian pueblo here, because its location on a bluff overlooking the Rio Guadalquivir—an early name for the Rio Grande—reminded them of Seville in Spain. The Benavides Memorial of 1630 mentions that the Piro name for the pueblo was *Seelocú,* meaning unknown. By the end of the 17th century, repeated Apache attacks had forced the pueblo to be all but abandoned, and it remained uninhabited until 1800 when a Spanish *estancia* was established, by the Robledos and Romeros, that took the name La Joya de Sevilleta. Although the Spanish *joya* means "ornament, jewel," it also can be translated "basin, hole," and the name here most likely refers to the settlement's location in a basin of the Rio Grande. Following its abandonment in the 18th century, the village was resettled around 1800, under orders of Gov. Fernando Chacón; it was listed in Escudero's 1833 *Noticias* as *Plaza Sevilleta* and elsewhere as *La Joya de Sevilleta* and *Pueblo de la Joya.* US Census records showed it as *El Jollal,* then as *Ranchitos de la Holla,* then as *La Jolla,* essentially the name it bears today.

LA JOYITA (Socorro; settlement; on E bank of the Rio Grande, opposite San Acacia). This abandoned community could have been named either for being located in a little valley—see *Joya (general)*—or more likely from its association with the village of *La Joya* (see entry) to the N. The earliest references to this settlement are in the 1846 maps and records of Lt. James W. Abert. In subsequent US Census records it appeared variously as *La Hollita de Valencia, La Jollita,* and *La Joyita.* But later census records contain no mention of the village, and it possibly was destroyed in the flood of 1884.

LA JUNTA (general). Spanish, "the junction," in NM usually applied to the confluence of streams or rivers.

LA JUNTA (Guadalupe; settlement; at the confluence of the Pecos and Gallinas Rivers). Spanish, "the junction." Shown on an 1890 map.

LA JUNTA (Lincoln). See *Hondo.*

LA JUNTA, RIO LA JUNTA (Mora). See *Watrous.*

LA JUNTA (Rio Arriba; settlement; just N of NM 68, on the S bank of the Rio Grande, at the junction of the Rio Grande and Embudo Creek). Hamlet, whose name—see *La Junta (general)*—refers to its location.

LA LADERA (Valencia; settlement; S of Isleta Indian Reservation, SE of Peralta). Spanish, "the slope," diffuse residential settlement, at the foot of the hills rising from the floodplain.

LA LADERA (Valencia; settlement; 1 mi SE of Adelino). Spanish, "the slope," like the community of the same name to the N, a diffuse residential settlement, at the foot of the hills rising from the floodplain.

LA LANDE (De Baca; settlement; on US 60, 7 mi E of Fort Sumner; PO 1906–55, mail to Fort Sumner). Two explanations, both plausible and neither conclusive, exist for the name, pronounced La LAN-dee, of this tiny inhabited settlement. The first is that La Lande is the name of a French trapper and explorer, Bautista La Lande, who came to NM as early as 1804 and spent most of the rest of his life as a guide in the state. Zebulon Pike mentioned a Baptiste La Lande in his 1810 account of his expedition. When the RR came through after 1900, its officials tended to name stations along the line for early mountain men—St. Vrain (see entry) is nearby—and La Lande possibly was named similarly. The second explanation is that La Lande was named for a long-time RR employee who died during RR construction around 1905. But this, too, is unconfirmed. One local historian who researched the name concluded, "Nobody knows."

LA LIENDRE (San Miguel; settlement; SE of Las Vegas at the end of NM 67; PO 1878–80, 1882–84, 1906–42, mail to Las Vegas). Now essentially a ghost town, La Liendre was settled around 1845 by people named Durán and Maes; it soon became the center of an Hispanic stock-raising community, appearing in the 1850 US Census as *Los Valles de San Antonio*. Its present Spanish name means "nit, louse." One explanation for the name is that it described the community, where houses were strung along the roadside, "like nits." But residents of La Liendre were told that it referred to a local family with conspicuously small children, "like nits."

LA LOMA (Guadalupe; settlement; on NM 119, part of Anton Chico; PO 1942–present). Spanish, "the hill." Inhabited community, named for its location on the slope of a hill.

LA LOMA (Taos; settlement; suburb of Taos, 2 mi W of Taos Plaza). Spanish, "the hill," the name descriptive of its location.

LA LUZ (Otero; settlement; 2 mi E of US 54, 5 m N of Alamogordo; PO 1886–present). This name likely dates from 1719, when Spanish Franciscan missionaries built a chapel here dedicated to *Nuestra Señora de la Luz*, "Our Lady of the Light," one of many names for the Virgin Mary. Actual settlement, however, did not begin until around 1860, when Spanish-speaking settlers arrived from villages devastated by floods on the Rio Grande; one of the leaders was José Manuel Gutiérrez. A folk tale gives another etymology for the name dating from this period. It says male pioneers, leaving the women behind while they pushed ahead seeking the best spot to settle, lit a signal fire. Seeing it the women exclaimed, "La luz! Allá está la luz! Está bien." "The light. There's the light. All's well." Other explanations include the name referring to a will-o'-the-wisp light in the canyon and a lamp kept perpetually burning in an elderly woman's home. *La Luz Canyon* heads on the W slope of the Sacramento Mountains and runs W past the village of La Luz.

LA MADERA (Bernalillo; settlement; NE foothills of the Sandia Mountains). Spanish, "the wood." This name and that of nearby *La Madera Canyon* recall logging operations that existed here as late as the 1960s.

LA MADERA (Rio Arriba; settlement; at the junction of NM 111 and 519, 7 mi N of Ojo Caliente; PO 1906–08, 1911–present). Spanish, "the wood." Although settlement dates from 1820, when founded by Juan de Dios Chacón, the name likely came later, with sawmill operations here by the Halleck and Howard Lumber Co. of Denver, harvesting ponderosa pines from nearby forests.

LA MANGA (San Miguel; settlement; just W of US 84, 6 mi SW of Las Vegas). The Spanish *manga* means "sleeve," but it also can mean "fringe of land," and that doubtless is its meaning as the name of this tiny inhabited community.

LA MESA (Socorro). See *San Marcial*.

LA MESA (Doña Ana; settlement; on NM 28, 12 mi S of Las Cruces; PO as Victoria 1880–1908, as La Mesa 1908–present). Settled after 1854 and said to have been named for a nearby lava flow called *Black Mesa*. Just N of La Mesa was the little community of *Victoria*, name origin unknown, and when a PO was established it was called Victoria. But the community of Victoria faded, and in 1908 the PO's name was changed to that of the more prominent village.

LA MESA DE SAN MARCIAL (Socorro). See *San Marcial*.

LA MESILLA (Doña Ana). See *Mesilla*.

LA MESILLA (Rio Arriba; settlement; in SE part of county, in Santa Clara Pueblo Grant, on E bank of the Rio Grande, 2.5 mi S of Española on NM 399). Spanish, "the little mesa." Inhabited community, located at the mouth of *La Mesilla Arroyo*.

LA PARIDA (Socorro; settlement; on the E bank of the Rio Grande, opposite Socorro). The village of La Parida probably was established during the early Mexican period; Escudero mentioned it in 1833 as *Rancho de la Partida*, a stop along the fortnightly mail route between Santa Fe and Chihuahua. James J. Webb, in his *Adventures in the Santa Fe Trade, 1844–1847*, refers to *Parida Hill* as "the worst piece of road between Santa Fe and Chihuahua." The village appears in the historical records several times after that, including the 1850 and 1860 US Census records, but by 1860 it was being depopulated, likely because of flooding. Later the La Parida area was known as *Bosque de los Pinos,* likely for the Pino family. Though the village has gone, the name survives in *Arroyo de la Parida,* which heads at *Ojo de la Parida.*

The name's origin is unknown. The Spanish adjective *parida* means "having just given birth." Possibly someone gave birth at this place, but quite possibly the name is a corruption of *paridera,* "a sheltered place where shepherds bring sheep for lambing." George Adlai Feather suggested the name could be a corruption of the *parada,* "stop, end, stay, shutdown," as teamsters were forced to stop here.

LA PLACITA DE LOS GARCIAS (Bernalillo; settlement; N of Albuquerque, 1 mi S of Alameda). Little is known about this community, which is listed in the 1860 US Census as being between Ranchitos and El Pueblo.

LA PLACITA (Sandoval; settlement; 0.5 mi N of Cuba, 0.5 mi E of NM 44). Tiny inhabited residential cluster. See *Plaza, Placita (general).*

LA PLATA (San Juan; settlement; at the junction of NM 170 and 173, 15 mi N of Farmington; PO 1881 intermittently to present). In 1877 Edward Williams founded this community and named it for the *La Plata River* on which it's located. The lands originally were part of the Jicarilla Apache Reservation. Then the US government attempted to settle Ute Indians on it, but they refused, and it was then thrown open to settlement by non-Indians.

LA PLATA RIVER (San Juan; rises in the Colorado mountains and flows S to empty into the San Juan River below Farmington). Spanish, "the silver." Likely named for the *La Plata Mountains* in Colorado. In 1765 Juan Rivera led an expedition to these mountains investigating rumors of gold and silver, and he may have named the river then.

LA PLAZA (Rio Arriba; settlement; 0.5 mi E of US 84-285, 2 mi N of Española). Tiny inhabited community. See *Plaza, Placita (general).*

LA POSADA, UPPER AND LOWER (San Miguel; settlement; on the Pecos River, 5 mi N of Pecos, on NM 63). Spanish, "the inn." Two tiny inhabited settlements about 0.5 mi apart.

LA PUEBLA (Santa Fe; settlement; 2 mi E of Española). Inhabited Hispanic community whose Spanish name means "the town." The name more commonly appears as masculine; why it is feminine here is unknown; see *Pueblo (general).*

LA PUENTE (Rio Arriba; settlement; about 3 mi W of Tierra Amarilla, on NM 531; PO 1920–44, mail to Tierra Amarilla). Spanish, "the bridge," but though this is located on the Rio Chama, the settlement is said to have been named for a village near Abiquiu of the same name, from whence the settlers here had come. La Puente was one of the Tierra Amarilla's three original settlements, along with Los Ojos and Los Brazos (see entries); it is still inhabited.

LA PUENTE (Rio Arriba). See *Mariana.*

LA RINCONADA (Bernalillo; settlement; 1 mi N of Alameda, on the E side of the Rio Grande). Though elsewhere in NM *rincón* means "corner, box canyon"—see *Rincon (general)*—here it likely refers to a bend in the river. Little is known about this settlement, beyond its occasional appearance on some early maps.

LA TUNA (Doña Ana). See *Anthony.*

LA UNION (Doña Ana; settlement; on NM 28 and 182, 4 mi SW of Anthony; PO 1909–13, 1927–57, mail to Anthony). La Union is said to have been created and named with the combining of two earlier settlements—*Los Ojitos* and *Los Amoles*—that had been ravaged by floods, though in 1884 La Union itself suffered flooding. La Union itself has evolved into two closely related communities, "new" and "old": *La Union Nueva* and *La Union Vieja,* 1 mi W.

LA VEGA (Socorro; settlement; 2 mi NE of Socorro). This tiny community, whose Spanish name means "the meadow," has become a surburb of Socorro.

LA VEGA DE SAN JOSE (Cibola). See *San Fidel.*

LA VENTANA (Cibola; on NM 117, 17.6 mi S of its junction with I-40, in El Malpais National Monument). This dramatic natural arch created a brief controversy in the late 1980s when national monument officials discovered the USBGN, believing the feature to be unnamed, had earlier approved the name *Alta Arch,* "high arch," proposed by a single individual. Monument officials said local people had always known the arch by no other name than La Ventana, and an investigation by the NM Geographic Names Committee confirmed this, so the USBGN rescinded its earlier decision and approved the name La Ventana instead. For years this was thought to be NM's largest natural arch, until Snake Bridge (see entry) in western NM proved to be bigger, but with an opening 125 feet high and 165 feet long La Ventana still is very impressive.

LA VENTANA (San Miguel). See *Trujillo.*

LA VENTANA (Sandoval; settlement; on NM 44, 14 mi S of Cuba; PO 1925–31, mail to Cuba). Spanish, "the window," and here as elsewhere in NM the place name refers to a natural stone arch. *Ventana* appears on Miera y Pacheco's 1778 map, and Spanish-speakers made several attempts to settle here, near the fertile lands of the Rio Puerco but were driven off by frequent Indian raids. In the 1920s and early 1930s, La Ventana bloomed briefly as a coal-mining camp—coal miners dynamited the natural arch that had given the settlement its name—but the Depression and fires eventually killed the town, though a single residence—and the name—remain.

LA VILLITA (Taos; settlement; 2 mi N of Alcalde on NM 389, W of NM 68, E of the Rio Grande). As its Spanish name says, this is a "little village."

LABORCITA (general). As T.M. Pearce explained, the Latin word for "work," *labor,* came to mean in Spanish the plowing and tilling of land, and in NM and elsewhere *labor* was extended to mean the very land tilled; thus *laborcita* means a small patch of tilled land. The name has been spelled *Lavorcita* and *La Borcita,* but the USBGN in 1980 determined Laborcita to be the correct form.

LABORCITA (Socorro; settlement; 2 mi N of San Antonio, on the W side of the Rio Grande). A loose community of small farms, also called *River View,* because of its clear view of the Rio Grande. See *Laborcita (general).*

LABORCITA CANYON (Otero; on the W slope of the Sacramento Mountains, a tributary of La Luz Creek). Settled in 1885 by Frank and Jesús Borunda, who used its numerous springs to irrigate their small farms, hence the name; see *Laborcita (general).*

LACY (Roosevelt; settlement; 4 mi NW of Floyd; PO 1907–17, mail to Floyd). Abandoned homesteader settlement, named for Lacy Crabtree, who, with his father, had a store here.

LADD (Colfax; settlement; location unknown; PO 1886–89, mail to Springer). Shortlived postal locality named for postmaster Charles B. Ladd.

LADRON, LADRONES (general). Spanish, "thieves," which in NM can mean rustlers, raiders, bank robbers, highwaymen, and perhaps some other species of thieves; GNIS lists 5 places with this in their names. Usually the specific incident or association behind the name has been lost.

SIERRA LADRONES (Socorro; W of Bernardo, N of the Rio Salado). Spanish, "thieves mountains," named because Navajo and Apache raiders of the settlements along the Rio Abajo would take stolen stock here, safe from pursuit in the mountains' steep and treacherous canyons. Later, non-Indian rustlers and highwaymen used these rugged mountains as a hideout, and legends abound of treasure still hidden here. Often called simply *Los Ladrones.* Highest elevation, 9,210; *Ladron Peak* is 9,143 ft.

LADYBUG PEAK, 7,490 ft. (Sierra; in the N part of the San Andres Mountains). In the fall, ladybugs swarm during mating, and this small summit may have been named for this.

LAGARTIJA CREEK (San Miguel; in NE part of county). Spanish, "wall lizard, rock lizard."

LAGUNA, LAGUNITA (general). Spanish, "lake," "little lake."

LAGUNA PUEBLO(Cibola; settlement; on NM 124, 43 mi W of Albuquerque; PO 1879–present). As the Keresan-speaking Pueblo Indians who live here tell it, this area has been occupied by them since the 1300s, when it was settled by people migrating from the Mesa Verde area. Searching for a suitable location, they came to a place where a natural dam on the Rio San Jose had made a lake, and that is what the Keresan name, *Kawaik,* and the Spanish name, *Laguna,* both mean, "lake." The lake was noticed by Coronado when he passed by in the summer of 1540, and it existed into the 19th century, but today a meadow marks its location. Though earlier villages had existed in the area since before the Spaniards, the modern pueblo dates from around 1698; in 1699, the traditional date of the pueblo's founding, the Spanish governor, Pedro Rodríguez Cubero, while on an expedition to Zuni, visited the pueblo and named it Laguna. The present pueblo, formally called *Laguna de San José,* has spawned numerous satellite settlements, including *New Laguna,* 2 mi to the W. Others include Mesita, Casa Blanca, Seama, Santa Ana, Paraje, and Encinal (see entries). Laguna Indians who went to school in the East humorously named "suburbs" of the pueblo New York, Philadelphia, and Harrisburg.

New Laguna (Cibola; settlement; 2 mi W of Laguna, on NM 124; PO 1900–present).

LAGUNA (Sandoval). See *Cuba.*

LAGUNA DEL MUERTO (Sierra; E of the Fra Cristobal Range, on the Jornada del Muerto). Spanish, "lake of the dead man." More a puddle than a lake, this was the site of a campground on the Jornada del Muerto mentioned by Otermín in 1682. In 1692 Vargas referred to the location as *Aguaje del Muerto,* "watering place of dead man." It

also has been called *El Muerto Lagoon* and *Gallego Spring.* The specific dead man that inspired the name is unknown.

LAGUNA DEL PERRO (Torrance; 3 mi NE of Willard). Spanish, "dog lake," for reasons unknown. This is the largest of the salt lakes that are all that remain of Lake Estancia (see entry). Tiwa Indians once called them the "accursed lakes," believing correctly that they once held fresh water; a curse placed on an unfaithful wife who dwelt here turned them salty. But the lakes also were identified with the Salt Mother, and the lakes were an important source of this essential mineral.

LAGUNA GATUÑA (Lea; in W part of county, just N of US 62-180). Large intermittent salt lake whose Spanish name refers to the cloverlike plant, *Ononis spinosa.*

LAGUNA SALADA (Catron). See *Zuni Salt Lake.*

LAGUNITA (San Miguel; settlement; S of Las Vegas, on Hermanos Creek, 3 mi E of Chapelle). Tiny inhabited locality, named for a "little lake." *Lagunita Spring* is just to the W. A PO was established here in 1908 but never operated.

LAGUNITAS (Sandoval; settlement; 3 mi S of Cuba, just E of NM 44). Doubtless named for ponds here, but also perhaps referring to its status as a "suburb" of *Laguna,* an early name for Cuba (see entry).

LAKE (Hidalgo; settlement; in SE part of county, exact location unknown; PO 1913–15, mail to Hachita). Short-lived postal locality, name origin unknown.

LAKE ALICE (Colfax; in Sugarite Canyon State Park, about 2 mi S of Lake Maloya). Named for Alice Jelfs, daughter of John Jelfs, a Raton Banker prominent when the lake was created by the AT&SF RR.

LAKE ARTHUR (Chaves; settlement; on NM 2, 8 mi N of Artesia; PO 1904–present). In 1885 Arthur V. Russell was a sheep rancher who homesteaded 3 mi NE of what is now this community *in 1895.* His daughter later described the evolution of the community's name: "He raised a lot of sheep and ran a lot of them up around Capitan. But come shearing time, Daddy always sheared his sheep at the lake S of Lake Arthur. Somehow his name and the lake just got connected. There wasn't anything else here then. Lake Arthur and Hagerman were both just stopping off places." The locality earlier had been called *Tar Lake,* but by the time the village was surveyed and platted in 1904 it had assumed the name Lake Arthur. Though Lake Arthur has lost population to Artesia, it remains a living community.

LAKE AVALON (Eddy; just N of Carlsbad). This reservoir, created in 1893 along with Lake McMillan (see entry), was named by a Mr. Kidder, a retired sea captain who built a clubhouse on the lake's shore, where he kept sailboats. The name he gave the lake, Avalon, is Celtic and means "island of the apples," applied in Celtic mythology to the Island of Blessed Souls, an earthly paradise in the seas W of Britain; in the Arthurian legends, Avalon was the abode, and in some versions the burial place, of King Arthur. Near the NM lake are the *Avalon Hills.* See *Lake McMillan.*

LAKE FORK PEAK, 12,881 ft. (Taos; in the Sangre de Cristo Mountains, 2 mi W of Wheeler Peak). Named for *Lake Fork Creek,* which heads N of here and runs N into the Taos Ski Valley.

LAKE LUCERO (Doña Ana; at the SW end of White Sands National Monument). Lake Lucero is all that remains of *Lake Otero,* which 30,000 years ago covered most of the present Tularosa Valley. Because it's at the low point in the basin, Lake Lucero is where gypsum-laden water from the San Andres Mountains settles, and gypsum particles from the bed of this intermittently dry lake are blown NE by prevailing winds and provide the white sands for White Sands National Monument (see entry). In 1897 José and Felipe Lucero obtained title to 160 acres on the lake's S shore and gradually acquired more land until the Lucero Ranch eventually included 20,000 acres. The Luceros abandoned ranching during WW II, but their ranch sites remain, and so does their name on Lake Lucero.

LAKE MCALLISTER WATERFOWL AREA (San Miguel). See *Las Vegas National Wildlife Refuge.*

LAKE MCMILLAN (Eddy; on the Pecos River, between Carlsbad and Artesia). McMillan Dam and Avalon Dam (see *Lake Avalon*) were completed in 1893; McMillan Dam and the reservoir it impounded were named for W.H. McMillan, an industrialist who came to Eddy County from St. Louis,MO. He was prominent in the organization of the Pecos Valley Land and Ditch Co. in 1887. The dam proved ineffective against major floods, however, as well as being subject to siltation, and in 1972 Congress approved construction of Brantley Dam—see *Brantley Lake*—to replace McMillan; McMillan Dam was breached—portions of the dam still remain—and Lake McMillan's water flowed down to the new reservoir.

LAKE PEAK, 12,409 ft. (Santa Fe; in the Sangre de Cristo Mountains, S of Santa Fe Baldy, NE of Santa Fe Ski Area). Santa Fe Lake is on this mountain's SW flank, Nambe Lake on the NW side. The Tewa Indians regard Lake Peak as their sacred mountain of the E.

LAKE OTERO (Otero; in the Tularosa Valley). This is the name geologists have given to the huge prehistoric lake that once filled most of the Tularosa Valley. It reached its greatest extent 30,000 years ago, but about 20,000 years ago it began to dry up, and today only the intermittent Lake Lucero (see entry) remains.

LAKE ROBERTS (Grant; on NM 35, on Sapillo Creek). Austin Roberts was a well-known pilot for the NM Game and Fish Dept. who died in the early 1960s when his plane crashed as he was feeding antelope trapped by a blizzard. This lake was named to honor him.

LAKE VALLEY (San Juan; settlement; 20 mi N of Crownpoint, 2 mi E of NM 371). Inhabited Navajo community, whose name describes its location. The Navajo name for the lake means "white lake."

LAKE VALLEY (Sierra; settlement; on NM 27, 18 mi S of Hillsboro; PO 1880–81, 1882–1955, mail to Deming). In August 1878 the prospector George W. Lufkin discovered rich silver ore here, and a mining boom ensued. Lufkin sold his claim to George Daly and returned to the East. It was in this mine that was discovered the Bridal Chamber, one of the richest silver ore bodies ever found, but on the day of its discovery Daly was killed by Apaches. By this time, Lufkin had returned to NM; he settled near the site of the future Lake Valley and went into real estate. He named the locality *Daly,* after the man who had bought his claim. Another townsite sprang up near Daly in 1882, and the short-lived settlement of Daly was relocated and named Lake Valley, for a small lake, now dry. Between 1882 and 1888, silver production exceeded $4 million, but eventually the deposits played out, and today Lake Valley is essentially a ghost town.

LAKE VAN (Chaves; 1 mi E of Dexter, on NM 190, W of the Pecos River). Before the development of artesian wells, this spring-fed lake was an important surface water source in the area, and the settlement of *Lake Van* (see entry) was here. The lake originally was called *Horseshoe Lake,* but later it was named Lake Van, likely for Van C. Smith, founder of Roswell. Today Lake Van is a pleasant recreation area ringed with housing developments.

LAKE VAN (Chaves; settlement; 1 mi E of Dexter, at Lake Van; PO 1897–98, mail to Hagerman). This community grew up at the important water source of *Lake Van* (see entry), but when the RR was created 1 mi W the town moved there and assumed the new identity of *Dexter* (see entry).

LAKE VIEW PINES (Colfax; settlement; 1 mi W of US 64, W of Eagle Nest Lake). Modern inhabited residential development, located in pines overlooking Eagle Nest Lake.

LAKEWOOD (Eddy; settlement; 10 mi S of Artesia and 2 mi E of US 285, on the W side of Lake McMillan; PO as McMillan 1894–1904, as Lakewood 1904–present). This inhabited community originally had been called *McMillan Siding,* or simply *McMillan,* after the Lake McMillan (see entry), and also *White Town.* In

1904, it moved 4 mi to its present location and assumed its present name. The site had been the headquarters for the Turkey Track Cattle Co. Residential development resulted from readily available artesian water and extensive real estate promotions.

LAMA (Taos; settlement; 5 mi N of San Cristobal, just E of NM 522). The Spanish *lama* means "mud, ooze, slime," and residents confirm the mud here is formidable, especially in the spring. But in fact, *lama* is not the term local people use for mud—they use the colloquial *zoquete* or *lodo* instead—so the origin of the name Lama here is a mystery. The diffuse settlement is divided into *Upper* and *Lower Lama. Lama Canyon,* just N of the settlement of Lama, runs NW into the Red River.

LAMANCE (Cibola; settlement; on the W edge of the Malpais, NE of Fence Lake) Like many other localities in this area, this former community was settled in the 1930s. It took the name of a settler.

LAMY (Santa Fe; settlement; on AT&SF RR, 14 mi SSE of Santa Fe and 1 mi E of US 285; PO 1881, 1884–1963, mail to rural Santa Fe branch). Jean Baptiste Lamy, a native of France, was sent to NM by the Catholic Church in 1851, one year after NM had become a US Territory; two years later, NM, which had been part of the Mexican Diocese of Durango, became a diocese in its own right, and. Lamy became the diocese's first bishop. He lived for a time at what is called *Bishops Lodge,* built in 1854, located just N of Santa Fe, E of NM 590. As bishop, Lamy was a vigorous, controversial figure and is credited with reforming a religious establishment that had grown stagnant and corrupt. Willa Cather immortalized him in her novel, *Death Comes for the Archbishop.* In 1875, NM became an archdiocese, and Lamy became archbishop. When the AT&SF RR in 1880 built a spur line into Santa Fe, the rail junction was at a village in the center of the *Lamy Land Grant,* 16,547 acres that Lamy had taken in trust for the church, and the junction was named to honor Lamy. After passenger service on the spur line was abandoned in 1926, rail travelers reached Santa Fe by bus from Lamy. Tourists still arrive at Lamy by train, but Lamy, with its historic buildings and popular restaurants, has become a tourist attraction in its own right.

The archbishop's French surname is properly pronounced lah-MEE, but in NM it more frequently is pronounced LAME-ee.

LAMY PEAK, 9,328 ft. (Rio Arriba; in NE part of county, N of US 64, E of Tusas Ridge). Likely named for Archbishop Lamy (see *Lamy*).

LANARK (Dona Ana; settlement; on SP RR, 25 mi NW of El Paso; PO 1905–23, mail to Strauss). This vanished settlement was primarily a postal locality and a stop on the rail line between El Paso and Deming. The origin of its name is unknown.

LAND OF ENCHANTMENT. This popular phrase has become synonymous with NM, appearing on license plates, official publications, and scores of promotional materials. Yet earlier boosters had other slogans: *Sunshine State, Land of Opportunity,* and so forth. The present sobriquet first appeared in 1906 in Lilian Whiting's book *The Land of Enchantment: From Pikes Peak to the Pacific.* This widely read travelogue included two chapters on what was then the Territory of NM. When statehood was achieved in 1912, the state's official slogan was *The Sunshine State.* Then, in October 1934, *New Mexico Magazine* used The Sunshine State on its cover for the last time—no reason was given for the disappearance—and a year later Gov. Clyde Tingley launched his new administration with the slogan *Greater New Mexico.* In September 1935, Joseph A. Bursey, director of the State Tourist Bureau, designed a brochure entitled *Two Weeks in New Mexico: Land of Enchantment.* This was widely distributed, and the slogan quickly caught on. In 1937 the NM Highway Dept. distributed 350,000 copies of a pamphlet, *Welcome to the Land of Enchantment.* The slogan appeared on license plates in 1941, and it was adopted officially by the state in 1947.

LANEY SPRING (Catron; 6 mi SE of Luna). The Laney family—three brothers, two with families—came to Catron County in 1883 from St. George, UT, bringing with them 100 head of cattle, the first commercial herd in the area. Will and Bert Laney would camp at this spring while working cattle, and their descendants still are among the area's ranchers.

LANGTON (Curry; settlement; near the Roosevelt County line, NW of Floyd). This abandoned settlement was named for Joe Lang, first sheriff of Roosevelt County, who had a ranch near here. Often spelled *Langston.*

LARGO (general). Spanish, "long," a common name element, especially associated with canyons.

LARGO (San Juan; settlement; on the S bank of the San Juan River, on US 64, E of Blanco; PO 1883–1927, mail to Blanco). Originally on the N side of the San Juan River, this abandoned community was the earliest non-Indian settlement in the area, but later it moved across the river. It was named for its association with *Cañon Largo* (see entry), which enters the San Juan River here.

LARGO CANYON (San Juan). See *Cañon Largo.*

LARKSPUR PEAK, 11,992 ft. (Taos; in the Sangre de Cristo Mountains, N of Taos Pueblo). Blue larkspurs (genus *Delphinium*) are common high-elevation plants of the Rockies.

LAS BOCAS (Santa Fe; heads at springs below Cieneguilla and runs W to the Rio Grande above Santo Domingo Pueblo). Spanish, "the mouths." In 1776 Fray Francisco Atanasio Domínguez mentioned this watercourse, often dry, as a being route to the Rio Abajo. The name also designated a small settlement in colonial times situated at the stream's mouth; the full name for the locality has been given as *Las Bocas de los Cerritos,* "the mouths of the little hills."

LAS CAÑAS (Socorro; settlement; on the E bank of the Rio Grande, S of Socorro, S of Arroyo de las Cañas). This tiny Hispanic settlement, named either for the "canes" or "reeds" along the Rio Grande here or, more likely, for the village's proximity to *Arroyo de las Cañas,* was mentioned by 19th-century travelers but since has vanished. *Arroyo de las Cañas* heads at Ojo de las Cañas and flows W to the Rio Grande 3 mi S of Socorro; it likely named for "canes" or "reeds" at *Ojo de las Cañas,* "spring of the canes."

LAS CRUCES (Doña Ana; settlement, county seat; at the junction of I-25 and I-10, on the Rio Grande; PO 1854–present). Numerous stories attempt to explain why this city is named "the crosses." Some attribute the name to crosses marking the graves of unfortunates massacred by Apaches. Indeed, Susan Shelby Magoffin, wife of Santa Fe trader Sam Magoffin, in January 1847 wrote in her diary: "Yesterday we passed over the spot where a few years since a party of Apaches attacked General Armijo as he returned from the Pass with a party of troops, and killed some 14 of his men, the graves of whom, marked by rude crosses, are now to be seen...." Adolph Bandelier, searching archives in Mexico City, found a report from a Spanish army officer, Don Gabriel, who in 1693 wrote: "I have just received report of Indian raids in the region of Los Organos where three Spaniards were killed, the raiders then going on to a place called Las Cruces...."

Present-day Las Cruces has been identified with the site known as *Estero Largo,* "long swamp, estuary," mentioned in numerous 17th-century accounts of travel along the Camino Real, but the region sparsely populated during the 18th century. The present community dates from 1848, when local leader, Don Pablo Melendres, first justice of the peace in Doña Ana County, asked Lieutenant Sackett of the First US Dragoons to lay out a town several miles S of Doña Ana, to alleviate overcrowding in the village of Doña Ana resulting from Americans flocking to the newly acquired territory. The survey party chose a site 6 mi S of Doña Ana, near an old burial ground, with crosses likely the ones seen earlier by Magoffin; the new community took the name Las Cruces.

LAS CUEVAS (Doña Ana; on the W side of the Organ Mountains, just N of Ice Canyon). Rock formation containing several caves, including the one in which Juan María de Agostini, the hermit, lived and eventually was murdered in 1869 (see *Hermit Peak*).

LAS DISPENSAS (San Miguel; settlement; 12 mi NW of Las Vegas, 9 mi W of NM 518, on the E side of Hermit Peak). Tiny inhabited Hispanic settlement whose Spanish name means "storerooms for food."

LAS HUERTAS (Sandoval; settlement; in Las Huertas Canyon, 1 mi NE of Placitas). Early on the morning of April 13, 1541, Coronado and his men began exploring the N side of the Sandia Mountains, and that evening they camped in the valley where 200 years later this settlement would be located. In 1765 nine families petitioned for a grant here, but the *San Antonio de las Huertas Grant* was not approved until almost three years later. The well-watered valley is ideally suited for the vegetable or fruit gardens (Spanish, *huertas*), some still here, for which the locality was named. See also *Ojo de la Casa.*

Las Huertas Canyon and Las Huertas Creek head in the N Sandia Mountains and run N. The upper sections of the creek once were known as *Ellis Creek,* for the Ellis family that homesteaded here.

LAS MANUELAS (Mora; settlement; 4 mi NW of Ocate on NM 120, on Manuelas Creek). Small inhabited settlement, name origin unknown but probably commemorating a local family.

LAS NORIAS (Cibola; settlement; on the route between Zuni and Grants). Tiny abandoned Hispanic village, whose Spanish name in NM referred to dug wells.

LAS NUTRIAS (McKinley). See *Nutria.*

LAS NUTRIAS (Rio Arriba). See *Tierra Amarilla.*

LAS NUTRIAS (Socorro; settlement; on the E side of the Rio Grande, on NM 304, 14 mi SE of Belen). Spanish, "the beavers"; see *Nutria (general).* This locality, still inhabited, was called Las Nutrias as early as 1682, because Governor Otermín reported that he and his forces were here during their second withrawal from NM. In 1765 30 families settled at a place they called *San Gabriel de las Nutrias,* but the site they'd selected for a plaza was unsuitable, so they moved closer to the river. Like many Rio Abajo settlements, however, this new settlement was subject to Apache raids, and later it was abandoned, only to be resettled in the 19th century.

LAS PALAS (Lincoln; settlement; on the NE side of the Capitan Mountains, in the vicinity of Arabela). Only a few local people recall this tiny Hispanic community, whose name means "the shovels," for reasons unknown.

LAS PALOMAS (Sierra; settlement; 7 mi S of Truth or Consequences, on NM 187; PO 1881–1964, mail to Williamsburg). Las Palomas, Spanish, "the doves," like several other features nearby was named for flocks of doves in the cottonwoods near the Rio Grande. The village was settled around 1856 on *Palomas Creek* by the García and Tafoya families; they brought in numerous peons, who after fulfilling their obligations also settled here. The site was attractive not only because of the river and creek but also because of *Palomas Hot Springs* and *Palomas Gap* in the Caballo Mountains to the E, an important transportation route. The original settlement was closer to the Rio Grande; the 1870 Census labelled the locality *Río Palomas* and put its population at 200. But the completion of Caballo Dam in 1938 forced relocation farther W.

LAS PEÑUELAS (Doña Ana, Sierra; in the S part of the Jornada del Muerto, N of Aleman). Spanish, "the big rocks." This conspicuous cluster of rock outcrops was an important landmark and campground on the Jornada del Muerto. Vargas in his journal of 1692 wrote, "I reached Las Penuelas and in the nearby canyon the marsh had an abundance of water for the entire camp." The formation's name often appears in English as *Point of Rocks.* The individual outcrops aren't named; highest elevation, 5,172 ft.

LAS PLACITAS (Rio Arriba; settlement; 2 mi SE of El Rito, on NM 215, on El Rito). This inhabited settlement has a common descriptive name meaning simply "little plazas." The full name of the village here is *Las Placitas del Río;* see *Plaza, Placitas (general).*

LAS PLACITAS (Sierra). See *Placita.*

LAS TABLAS (Lincoln; settlement; on the N side of the Capitan Mountains). Spanish, "the boards, planks." Tiny Hispanic community, named for sawmills here. The community has vanished, but the name survives on *Las Tablas Canyon,* which heads in the mountains and runs N.

LAS TABLAS (Rio Arriba; settlement; 8 mi SW of Tres Piedras, on NM 519; PO 1911–present). Tiny inhabited ranching and lumbering community, whose Spanish name means "the boards, planks," doubtless for local sawmill operations.

LAS TRAMPAS (Taos; settlement; on NM 76, 6 mi SW of Peñasco, on the Rio de las Trampas; PO as Trampas 1898–1931, 1938–present). Often called simply *Trampas,* this settlement was established in 1751 by 12 families from Santa Fe, led by Juan de Arguello, who had received a land grant from Gov. Tomás Vélez Cachupin. The resulting settlement, officially christened *Santo Tomás Apostol del Río de las Trampas,* "St. Thomas the Apostle of the River of Traps," took its name from the *Río de las Trampas* (see entry) that flows through it.

TRAMPAS PEAK, 12,170 ft. (Rio Arriba; 7 mi SE of Las Trampas, in the Sangre de Cristo Mountains). Named for the *Rio de las Trampas* (see entry), which heads S of the peak.

LAS TRUCHAS CREEK (De Baca; heads in Quay County and flows SW into the Pecos River immediately N of Fort Sumner). Though the Spanish *truchas* means "trout," this usually dry watercourse likely was named for minnows instead.

TUSAS (general). Spanish, "prairie dogs."

LAS TUSAS (San Miguel; settlement; 2 mi W of Sapello on NM 266). Tiny inhabited community; see *Tusas (general)*

LAS TUSAS (Socorro; on the Jornada del Muerto, S of Fra Cristobal). Extensive prairie dog towns here inspired the name—see *Tusas (general)*—of this *paraje,* or stopping place, on the Jornada del Muerto. Otermín mentioned this place in 1682, and the name, if not the *paraje,* is still used.

LAS VEGAS (San Miguel; settlement, county seat; at the junction of I-25, US 85, and NM 518, 65, and 104; PO 1850–present). Not long after *San Miguel del Bado* (see entry) was founded in 1794, settlers and officials saw the plains near the Rio Gallina to the N as an outlet for expansion, and in 1821 Luis María C. de Baca petitioned for a land grant at *Las Vegas Grandes,* "the big meadows"; his petition was granted two years later. The formal name of the community that resulted from settlement was *Nuestra Señora de las Vegas,* "Our Lady of the Meadows." An 1829 military report referred to the area as *Begas de las Gallinas,* and sometimes residents referred to the area simply as *Las Gallinas,* but the name that has survived is Las Vegas. The settlement became an important stop on the Santa Fe Trail and later on the AT&SF RR. With the arrival of the RR in 1879, Las Vegas quickly evolved into not one town but three: *West Las Vegas,* or *Old Town,* located W of the Rio Gallinas; *East Las Vegas,* engendered by the RR, E of the river; and *Upper Town,* a suburb that peaked in 1870 with 796 residents and then declined. Cultural differences created strong rivalries between the new and predominantly Anglo East Las Vegas and the older and prominantly Hispanic West Las Vegas—the two communities once had separate POs—and though those tensions seem subsiding the distinction between the two survives today.

LAS VEGAS HOT SPRINGS (San Miguel). See *Hot Springs.*

LAS VEGAS NATIONAL WILDLIFE REFUGE (San Miguel; 5 mi SE of Las Vegas). This 8,750-acre refuge is a feeding and resting area for migrating and wintering waterfowl. The *Lake McAllister Waterfowl Area* is surrounded by the refuge but is owned by the NM Dept. of Game and Fish.

MESA DE LAS VIEJAS (Rio Arriba; SW of Canjilon, W of US 84, bordering the Rio Chama on the E). The Spanish name, "mesa of the old women," appears to be a translation of a Tewa Indian name. It's said to be derived from three aged Indian women left to live out their lives on the large mesa when their people moved to reservations.

LAST CHANCE CANYON (Eddy, Otero; heads in the Guadalupe Mountains, S of Coats Lake, and runs NE, crossing NM 137). According to local tradition, several ranchers—the Jones boys, Pete Corn, Marion Turner, Mart Fanning, Joe Woods, and Charlie Slaughter—set out to retrieve cattle stolen by Indians. When they reached this canyon they found a tributary stream fed by Sitting Bull Falls (see entry), and Slaughter said, "Well, boys, this is our last chance to get water."

CAÑADA DE LAS LATAS (Los Alamos, Rio Arriba; runs E, 4 mi NE of Los Alamos). Spanish, "tin cans." Several families homesteaded in his canyon, and its name probably was derived from their debris.

LATEAR (Socorro). See *Los Balen Buelas.*

LATIR (general). This name-cluster in the Sangre de Cristo Mountains NE of Questa is a mystery. *Latir* has been reported to be a French surname, but it also could be related to the Spanish verb, *latir,* "to howl, bark," which could have associations with wolf or coyote calls.

Latir Creek (Taos; heads at Latir Lakes and runs NE).

Latir Lakes (Taos; at the head of Latir Creek). Also called *Nine Lakes.*

Latir Mesa, 12,692 ft. (Taos; SW of the Latir Lakes).

Latir Peak, 12,708 ft. (Taos; in the Taos Range, NE of Questa).

Latir Peak Wilderness (Taos; in the Taos Range, NE of Questa). This 20,000-acre wilderness, designated in 1980 and administered by the Carson NF, includes three peaks exceeding 12,000 feet: *Venado,* 12,734 ft.; *Virsylvia,* 12,529 ft.; and *Latir Peak,* 12,708 ft., for which it is named. The *Latir Lakes* are just N of the wilderness.

MESA LAURIANO (San Miguel; in E-central part of county). A personal name, specific origin unknown.

LAVA (Rio Arriba; on C&TS RR, just S of the Colorado border). Active rail stop, named for the volcanic rock.

LAVA (Socorro; settlement; on AT&SF RR, 16 mi S of San Marcial, 22 mi N of Engle; PO 1886–98, 1900–03, mail to San Marcial). The senior RR surveyor on the Jornada route was named Morley (later father of Agnes Morley Cleaveland), and he named the sidetrack he laid out here for its location on the edge of the *malpais* S of Socorro. Now abandoned, it once was an important crossroads, rail station, PO on the route to White Oaks, and shipping point for guano mining.

LAVA BEDS (general). Several areas in NM are known by this name, synonymous with the Spanish *malpais;* see *Malpais (general).*

LE FEBRES (Mora; settlement; 3 mi NW of Ocate and 2 mi W of NM 120). Inhabited community that along with nearby *Le Febres Canyon* and *Le Febres Mesa* bears a French surname. Around 1850, a carpenter named Manuel La Favre worked for Lucien B. Maxwell and lived at Rayado, 15 mi NE, and it's possible this settlement bears a variation of his surname. A French family named Febre is said to arrived in NM in the 18th century.

LEA (Lea; settlement; on NM 176, NW of Eunice; PO 1929–31, mail to Carlsbad). This abandoned oil community, which once had several hundred residents, was named for the county.

LEA COUNTY (SE corner of NM; county seat, Lovington). The political struggle that led to Lea County's creation in 1917 was long, complex, and often bitter. In 1912 Robert Florence Love (see *Lovington*) proposed creating a new county from the eastern portions of Eddy and Chaves Counties, to be called *Heard County,* to honor Allen C. Heard, one of the founders of the High Lonesome Ranch and a founder of Knowles. This proposal was defeated. Then in 1917 a bill proposed creating *Llano*

County, named for the Llano Estacado dominating the landscape in SE NM. (In committee, House Speaker William H.H. Llewelyn argued against that name, saying nobody would be able to pronounce it correctly, much less spell it.) Chaves County representatives, seeing the inevitable, finally acquiesced but insisted the new county be named to honor Capt. Joseph Calloway Lea. Lea, born in 1841, had come to NM from Cleveland, OH, in 1876; in 1877 he arrived in Roswell, where he founded the NM Military Academy; he has been called the "father of Roswell." He was largely responsible for the creation of Chaves County and insisted that it be named for his friend, Col. J. Francisco Cháves, so Chaves County, by insisting the new county be named for Lea, was only reciprocating.

LEA COUNTY STATE PARK (Lea). See *Harry McAdams State Park.*

LEACH (Roosevelt). See *Garrison.*

LEASBURG (Doña Ana; settlement; on NM 185 and AT&SF RR, 5 mi SE of Radium Springs; PO as Leasburgh 1866–73, as Leasburg 1891–98, mail to Doña Ana). George Adlai Feather wrote that the community originally was in the river valley. (The valley, prior to 1868, had been called *Trinidad,* "trinity.") It burned in 1883, and most of the inhabitants moved to nearby Fort Selden (see entry), where Adolph Lea had become post trader. Flooding the next year completed the destruction of the village. When the AT&SF RR came through here, it put its tracks on higher ground, and the new station took the name, Leasburg; Adolph Lea became the first postmaster. The Leasburg Mercantile and a few other buildings remain in this tiny locality.

LEASBURG DAM STATE PARK (Doña Ana; off NM 185, at Radium Springs). Constructed in 1908, this dam is among the oldest diversion dams in NM. The dam and later the park, created in 1971, were named for the community of *Leasburg* (see entry).

LECHUGUILLA CANYON (Eddy; in the Guadalupe Mountains, heads at

Lechuguilla Spring, NW of Carlsbad Caverns, and runs NE). Named for the *Agave lechuguilla,* a characteristic plant of the Chihuahuan life zone. *Lechuguilla Cave* located here is among the world's most extensive cave systems, portions of it still unexplored.

LEDOUX (Mora; settlement; on NM 94, 4 mi SW of Mora; PO 1902–present). The original name of this settlement was *San Jose,* but when the PO was established the name was changed to recall Antoine Ledoux, a French trapper and guide who settled here in 1844–45. Although the French pronunciation of the name would be la-DOO, local people tend to pronounce the X, La-DOOX.

LEE ACRES (San Juan; settlement; just S of US 64 between Bloomfield and Farmington; PO 1966–present). Franklin Lafayette Lee moved here in 1937 from Tiffany, CO. He farmed here until 1957, when he subdivided his property to meet the demand for housing during the oil and gas boom. His descendants still live in the community.

LEGANSVILLE (Curry; 7 mi NE of Broadview; PO 1907–14, mail to Bellview). Abandoned homesteader community, named for its first postmaster, John W. Legan.

LEGGETT PEAK, 7,939 ft. (Catron; 8 mi W of Reserve, just S of US 180). This mountain, and nearby *Leggett Spring* and *Wet Leggett Spring,* were once on property owned by a man named Leggett. The spring furnishes water for the community of Rancho Grande Estates.

LEIGHTON (Union; settlement; in W part of county, exact location unknown; PO 1890–94, mail to Folsom). Short-lived postal locality, named for postmaster Hampton W. Leighton.

LEIGHTON GROVE (Union; 3 mi S of Clayton, where NM 402 crosses Perico Creek). Extensive cottonwood grove once owned by the Leighton family, whose members still live in Clayton, where the grove is remembered as a popular site for community picnics.

LEITENDORF (Hidalgo). See *Pyramid.*

LEMITAR (Socorro; settlement; on US 85, 6 mi N of Socorro; PO 1866 intermittently to present). Lemitar dates from 1831; it appeared as *Limitar* on the Emory, Abert, and Peck map of 1846; as *Limetar* on an 1870 map; and as *Plaza Limitar* on the General Land Office map of 1882. In 1905 the USBGN ruled Lemitar to be the accepted form. The name's origin is a mystery. It has been said to be a corruption of a Spanish family name, but it also has been attributed to a local plant, *lemita,* whose berries are used to make a beverage. Some maps include a related village, *Lemitarcito,* 1.5 mi to the S, and *Cañoncito del Puertocito de Lemitar,* "little canyon of the little gap of Lemitar," is to the W.

LEON (Harding; settlement; NE of Mosquero, W of Ute Creek; PO as Vaur 1889–92, as Leon 1892–95, 1898–1911, mail to Bueyeros). Abandoned settlement, originally called *Vaur,* for reasons unknown, later called Leon, for reasons also unknown.

MESA DE LEON (Guadalupe; 6 mi N of Vaughn). Named for a rock formation resembling a lion. The former RR stop *Leoncito,* "little lion," took its name from this formation.

LEOPOLD (Grant; settlement; 11 mi SW of Silver City, in the Little Burro Mountains; PO 1904–14, mail to Tyrone). Copper was first discovered in the Little Burro Mountains in 1871, and by 1902 mining had given birth to the sister mining camps of Tyrone (see entry) and Leopold, named for Asa F. Leopold, an important local figure. In 1907 the camp of Leopold had 1,200 residents, but when Phelps Dodge Corp. purchased the Burro Mountain Copper Co. and consolidated everything at Tyrone, Leopold died.

LEROUX (Taos; settlement; E of the Rio Grande, NW of Taos). In 1742 a land grant was made to Antoine Leroux, and a Joaquin Leroux appears in 1840s records. Only the grant's name surives on contemporary maps.

LESBIA (Quay; settlement; on CRI&P RR, 9 mi E of Tucumcari; PO as Rudulph 1908–10, as Castleberry 1910–13, as Lesbia 1913–18, mail to Tucumcari).

This locality began as a RR switch when the CRI&P line was put in between Amarillo and Tucumcari. It first was called *Rudulph,* for Carolina Rudulph, first postmistress, then *Castleberry,* for another postmistress. The RR likely bestowed its present name, for reasons unknown.

LESPERANCE (San Miguel). See *Mineral Hill.*

LEVY (Mora; settlement; on I-25 and AT&SF RR, 5 mi N of Wagon Mound; PO 1908–64, mail to Wagon Mound). This locality, formerly called *Evans,* was named in 1883 to honor the manager of the RR commissary; the origin of the name Levy is unknown. Today, Levy is just a siding. Local people pronounce it LEE-vie.

LEVY (San Miguel). See *Pecos.*

LEW WALLACE PEAK, 12,449 ft. (Taos; in the Taos Range, 7 mi W of Eagle Nest Lake and S of Wheeler Peak). Most of Gov. Lew Wallace's long and colorful life took place outside NM, in Indiana. He was born there in 1827, fought in the Mexican War and the Civil War, became a general, served in the court martial of the assassins of President Lincoln, ran unsuccessfully for Congress, and from 1878 to 1881 was territorial governor of NM. Here he is remembered for his role in the Lincoln County War and his dealings with Billy the Kid. Also, it was while Wallace was in NM that he wrote and published his novel, *Ben Hur,* about the life of Christ, a work immensely popular at the time and still read today. He died in 1905, in Indiana.

LEWIS (Curry; settlement; 8 mi S and 8 mi W of Grady; PO 1907–10, mail to Jonesville). This abandoned homesteader community was located on the Jack Lewis Ranch; its first postmaster was John H. Lewis.

LEWISTON (Roosevelt; settlement; in SW part of county, N of Elida; PO 1907–11, mail to Elida). Nettie Lewis was the first postmistress in this abandoned homesteader settlement. *Lewiston Lake,* 11 mi SE of Floyd, is an intermittent lake, named for the community.

LEYBA (San Miguel; settlement; 13 mi E of US 285, 28 mi SW of Las Vegas; PO 1908–present). This postal locality, now serving ranches, took the surname of its first postmaster, Francisco S. Leyba. The family name first appeared in NM with Pedro de Layva, mentioned in Spanish archives as early as 1661. He was lieutenant governor of the Salinas Pueblo district.

LFD (Chaves; settlement; S of Roswell). An appealing explanation for the ranch name around which this diffuse community grew is that LFD stood for "left for dead," the weak or injured cattle left behind on cattle drives. These cattle, rescued and revived, became the nucleus for the ranches here. But in fact LFD is derived from Littlefield, a rancher who used LFD as his brand.

LIBERTY (Quay; settlement; 3 mi from Tucumcari, on Pajarito Creek, 5 mi S of Fort Bascom; PO 1880–1902). Liberty began as *Tierra Blanca,* a tiny Hispanic community, but by the 1860s it was a rip-roaring cowtown named Liberty, a name some people have attributed to Fort Bascom soldiers being at liberty to drink whiskey here, alcoholic beverages being prohibited within 5 miles of a fort; Liberty was just beyond the five-mile point. Liberty was the first settlement in what is now Quay County, but it went into decline when Fort Bascom closed in 1870, and it died when Tucumcari boomed with the coming of the RR. Today, even its location is difficult to find.

LIBERTY (San Juan; settlement; 17 mi W of Farmington, W of Waterflow, on the N bank of the San Juan River; PO 1907–20, mail to Waterflow). Former community, name origin unknown.

LILLEY MOUNTAIN, 8,949 ft. (Catron; in the Jerky Mountains, N of the West Fork of the Gila River). John Lilley was an Englishman who settled in *Lilley Park,* near *Lilley Park Spring.* He and his neighbor, Thomas C. Prior, were killed by Apaches near Lilley's cabin in December 1885 and buried near there; see *Prior Creek.* His name sometimes was spelled Lilly, resulting in confusion with Ben Lilly, the professional hunter.

LINCOLN (Lincoln; settlement; on US 380, S of the Capitan Mountains, on the Rio Bonito; PO 1873–present). When Spanish-speaking settlers arrived here in 1855, they named their settlement *La Placita del Río Bonito,* "the village by the pretty river;" it also was referred to simply as *La Placita* and *Bonito.* The village consisted of a few adobe buildings around a plaza, fortified by a stout stone-walled tower. Twenty years later, in 1869, Saturnino Baca, with the support of Lawrence G. Murphy, post trader at Fort Stanton, Maj. William Brady, and Dr. J. H. Blazer, successfully proposed to the territorial legislature that a new county be created and named for President Lincoln, who had been assassinated four years earlier. La Placita, among the largest villages in the new county, changed its name to Lincoln also and was the county seat until the county offices were moved to Carrizozo in 1909. From 1878 to 1881, Lincoln figured prominently in the infamous feud known as the Lincoln County War. Today, Lincoln lives on memories—and tourists.

LINCOLN COUNTY (S-Central NM; county seat, Carrizozo). Created in 1869 and named for President Abraham Lincoln, assassinated just four years earlier. The county originally included a much larger area, but in 1889 Chaves and Eddy Counties were taken from its E side, and 10 years later Otero County was created from its SW corner.

LINCOLN NATIONAL FOREST (Eddy, Chaves, Lincoln, Otero; extends from the Jicarilla Mountains in the N through the Sacramento Mountains to the Guadalupe Mountains in the S). The *Lincoln Forest Reserve,* named for the town and county, was created in 1902 and later expanded; it was renamed Lincoln National Forest in 1918.

LINDA VISTA (Sandoval; settlement; location unknown; PO 1922–23, mail to Cuba). Spanish, "pretty view." Short-lived postal locality.

LINDRITH (Rio Arriba; settlement; on NM 595, NW of Cuba; PO 1919–present). This ranching and oil-gas community was named by Mr. and Mrs. C. C. Hill when they established a store and PO on their homestead. They named it to honor their son and stepson, Lindrith Cordell.

LINGO (Roosevelt; settlement; on NM 114 7 mi S of Causey and 5 mi from the Texas border; PO as Need 1916–18, as Lingo 1918–84). Lingo originally was called *Need,* for reasons unknown, but postal authorities said it sounded too much like Weed in Otero County, so the name was changed to Lingo and the PO moved 3 mi N of the former location, to where the community is now. T.M. Pearce concluded that despite reports that the name refers to the Southwest colloquial term "lingo," referring to speech, the name of Lingo here more likely resulted from a family name.

LISTON (Chaves; settlement; W of San Juan Mesa, in NE part of county; PO 1907–14, mail to Elida). Abandoned homesteader community, named for its first postmaster, Henry G. Liston.

LITTLE BLACK PEAK, 5,679 ft. (Lincoln; 10 mi NW of Carrizozo). This inconspicuous rise is the source of the extensive lava beds in Valley of Fires State Park (see entry).

LITTLE BURRO MOUNTAINS (Socorro; in SE corner of county, SW of the Oscura Mountains, NE of San Andres Mountains, N of Mockingbird Gap). Minor group; highest elevation 6,505 ft. Name origin unknown.

LITTLE COSTILLA PEAK, 12,580 ft. (Colfax; in the Cimarron Range, on the ridge between the Costilla and Vermejo drainages). The Spanish *costilla* means "rib," the term often used as a metaphor for ridges, though its application here probably refers to the mountain's proximity to *Little Costilla Creek; see Costilla Creek.* This was called *Costilla Peak* by the Hayden surveyors, and it was a triangulation point during the Wheeler survey. See *Big Costilla Peak.*

LITTLE JICARITA PEAK, 12,328 ft. (Rio Arriba; in E corner of county, in the Sangre de Cristo Mountains, 3 mi SE of Jicarita Peak). It's hard to call a 12,000-foot mountain "little," but this is indeed about 500 feet shorter than its eponymn, *Jicarita Peak,* 12,835 ft.

LITTLE SAN PASQUAL MOUNTAINS (Socorro; in SE part of Bosque del Apache National Wildlife Refuge). Tiny mountain group focussed on a single summit, *Little San Pascual Mountain,* 5,525 ft. The mountains comprise the *Little San Pascual Wilderness.* Name origin unknown. See *San Pascual (general).*

LITTLE WATER (McKinley; settlement; due E of Crownpoint, SE of Heart Butte). Active Navajo chapter house and school located in an arid area and named because very little water is here.

LITTLE WATER (San Juan; settlement; 11 mi N of Newcomb on NM 666; PO 1960–67). This inhabited community is the site of the *Little Water Trading Post,* whose English name probably translates a Navajo name referring to a small spring or creek.

LITTLE WHITE CONE, 8,396 ft. (San Juan; 7 mi NW of Crystal). Descriptive name. *Little White Cone Lake* is at the peak's base.

LIVING DESERT STATE PARK (Eddy; on the NW side of Carlsbad, between US 285 and NM 524). An ever-changing display of plants and animals of the Southwest.

LLANO (general). Spanish, "plain."

LLANO (Taos; settlement; on NM 73, 3 mi E of Peñasco, on the W side of the Rio Santa Barbara; PO 1898–1914, 1925–present). Along with *Llano Largo* and *Santa Barbara* (see entries), this small farming and lumbering community was founded soon after 1796, when Gov. Fernando Chacón gave permission for settlement in the valley. The inspiration for its name is obscure. See *Peñasco.*

LLANO DE SAN AGUSTIN (Catron, Socorro). See *Plains of San Agustin.*

LLANO DEL COYOTE (Mora). See *Rainsville.*

LLANO DEL MEDIO (Guadalupe). See *Rancho del Medio.*

LLANO ESTACADO (E NM). Early explorers compared its featureless vastness to the sea. Stretching from the Canadian River in NM, Texas, and Oklahoma S for 400 mi and encompassing 30,000 sq mi,

the expanse known as the Llano Estacado is among NM's greatest landforms. Yet the origin of its name remains obscure. It has been translated from the Spanish as "staked plain," a term said to come from yucca spikes or from the belief that early travelers used stakes to mark routes. The name *Staked Plains* continues to appear in many references, even though the USBGN in 1897 rejected it in favor of Llano Estacado. A more literal translation of *estacado* is not "staked" but "stockaded, palisaded," and this description is believed to have been inspired by the edge of the caprock marking the Llano Estacado's N and W rims; viewed from afar, these escarpments do indeed resemble stockade walls. But all these explanations, while plausible, lack documentation, and the name likely will remain a mystery.

LLANO LARGO (Taos; settlement; 3 mi E of Peñasco). Like Llano (see entry) just across the valley, the active farming community of Llano Largo (Spanish, "long plain") was created soon after 1796 when Gov. Fernando Chacón opened the valley for settlement. See also *Peñasco.*

LLANO QUEMADO (Taos; settlement; on NM 68, 0.5 mi S of Ranchos de Taos). Spanish, "burned plain." This inhabited area is located on a broad plain that at one time was burned.

LLANO VIEJO (Guadalupe; settlement; S of NM 119, W of Dilia). Spanish, "old plain," but perhaps distinguishing this inhabited community from a later one named Llano. One of several Pecos River communities here.

LLAVES (Rio Arriba; settlement; on NM 112 N of Gallina; PO 1942–present). Earlier called *Maestas,* doubtless for a local family, this locality's present Spanish name means "keys," but it also can mean "entrance, opening," possibly referring here to the site's location at the mouth of a canyon.

LOBO (general). Spanish, "wolf." Wolves, now extinct in NM, once were common here, and encounters with them often inspired place names. GNIS lists 25 Lobo names and 14 Wolf names.

LOBO (Taos; settlement; 4 mi NE of Arroyo Hondo; PO as Agua del Lobo 1888–1905, as Lobo 1905–11, mail to Arroyo Seco). Abandoned settlement, the origin of whose name is unknown; most likely it has some connection with *Lobo Creek* and *Lobo Peak* (see entry) to the E.

LOBO PEAK, 12,115 ft. (Taos; in the Sangre de Cristo Mountains, 4 mi E of San Cristobal). The ranch where D.H. Lawrence lived, and where his ashes are interred, is on the W side of this mountain. *Lobo Creek* heads here and flows W. Like most Lobo names, the specific incident or association behind the name has been forgotten.

LOCKNEY (Quay; settlement; 15 mi W of Nara Visa, near the Harding County line; PO 1909–35, mail to Nara Visa). In 1907 William John Rinestine, his wife, Sarah, and their only son, Martin, and his wife, Liz, and their two sons, Lester and Bill, homesteaded here. They soon were joined by other homesteaders, and a community formed, at first called *Ahmego,* sometimes *Panama,* for reasons unknown. But when a PO was established by Rinestine, he named it for his relative, Henry Lockney, who taught the first school here, in the Rinestine General Store.

LOCO ARROYO (Colfax; heads SE of Eagle Tail Mountain, S of Raton, and runs W into the Canadian River). Spanish, "crazy wash," named because of water flowing erratically in it.

LOCO HILLS (Eddy; settlement; on US 82, 14 mi W of Maljamar; PO as Smith 1938–41, as Loco Hills 1941–present). Loco Hills began as an oil camp in the late 1920s about 10 mi W of the present location of Loco Hills, near the old Illinois Oil Camp. At the time, the community consisted of shacks, a supply store, and a cafeteria that doubled as a school; it was called simply *Old Loco.* But with the development of the Loco Hills oil field, the community shifted to its present location. In the 1930s a man named Smith established a PO and a store; postal authorities called the PO *Smith,* but when Keith "Ropey" Miller bought out Smith in 1938, it was discovered there had been two towns in NM named *Smith* (the other in Union County), so the name was changed to Loco Hills, for the nearby hills.

LOCO HILLS (Eddy; 4 mi SE of the village of Loco Hills). At least five explanations exist for the name of these low sand hills—and all are plausible. One is that the hills were named by oil geologists for the "crazy" formations beneath the surface. Another is that Indians called them "crazy" because they looked deceptively like mountains after snow storms. Some people say the hills seem "crazy" when mirages appear on their tops during the summer. Still others say "crazy" describes the people who live among these barren sandhills. And some people say the name comes from abundant locoweed here.

LOCO MOUNTAIN, 8,015 ft. (Grant; 9 mi SE of Gila Hot Springs). A sheepherder is said to have gone "crazy" here, but more likely the name is derived from locoweed.

LOGAN (Quay; settlement; 24 mi NE of Tucumcari, on US 54 and NM 39, E of Ute Lake State Park; PO 1901–present). Logan sprang up around 1900 when the CRI&P RR began constructing a bridge over the Canadian River. William Kirkpatrick and his wife filed on land here, then sold it to M. Bishop and Eugene Logan, a well-known Texas Ranger who had come here to work on the bridge. Bishop sold his interest to J.E. Johnson, who subdivided his property, started a town, and named it for Logan. When the dam creating Ute Lake was built, the community of Logan took to calling itself "the best little town by a dam site."

LOGVILLE (Socorro; settlement; on US 60, 30 mi W of Magdalena on the Plains of San Agustin). The name describes the buildings in this settlement, now vanished.

LOHMAN CANYON (Doña Ana; heads in the San Agustin Mountains, 5 mi N of Organ and runs W). Named for early settlers, whose family name also is on a major street in Las Cruces.

LOMA (general). Spanish, "hill," diminutive

lomita. Lomas in NM typically are significantly smaller, with less relief, than hills denoted by the Spanish term *cerro;* see *Cerro (general).*

LOMA (Guadalupe). See *La Loma.*

LOMA PARDA (Doña Ana). See *Garfield* and *Derry.*

LOMA PARDA (Mora; settlement; on the N bank of the Rio Mora, 6 mi NW of Watrous; PO 1872–1900, mail to Watrous). Only silent ruins remain of this village, once infamous on E plains as the "Sodom on the Mora." Its name means "gray hill," but with the opening in 1851 of Fort Union nearby this tiny Hispanic community, formerly a gathering point for sheepherders and *comancheros,* acquired a reputation that was anything but drab. Soldiers came here to drink, gamble, and raise hell, and attempts by various fort commanders to place the village off-limits were unsuccessful. But when Fort Union closed in 1891, Loma Parda died also. Just 2 mi upstream on the Rio Mora from Loma Parda was an even smaller community called *La Pardita* and also *Parda Chiquita,* both meaning "little Parda."

LON (Lincoln; settlement; on NM 247, 30 mi SE of Corona; PO 1934–43, mail to Ramon). When this community, now abandoned, was established in 1924, it was called *Joneta,* for Mrs. Joneta Bagley, but when Ben Mosely opened a general store and was appointed postmaster, he changed the name to Lon, for his son, Lonnie. It also has been said the name honors Lon Merchant, a cattleman who lived here.

LONE (general). A common name element describing isolated features; the Spanish equivalent often is *Huerfano,* "orphan"; see *Huerfano (general).* GNIS lists 32 features with Lone in their names, and the variant *High Lonesome* also is popular, occurring 29 times; see *High Lonesome (general).*

LONE MOUNTAIN (Grant). See *Newton.*

LONE PINE (Catron; settlement; on the San Francisco River, at the site of present Glenwood; PO 1882–83, mail to Gila). Abandoned settlement; name origin unknown.

LONE TREE LAKE (Mora). See *Truchas Lakes.*

LONE WOLF (Eddy). See *Carlsbad.*

LONG CANYON MOUNTAINS (Catron; at the SW end of the Plains of San Agustin, E of the Continental Divide). Small range, named for a canyon.

LONGS (Roosevelt; settlement; 8 mi NW of Causey; PO 1907–20, mail to Rogers). Abandoned homesteader settlement, bearing the family name of its two postmasters, Thomas H. and Robert F. Long.

LONGWELL (Otero; settlement; 12 mi S of Cloudcroft; PO 1919–20, mail to Cloudcroft). Thomas B. Longwell was the postmaster of this abandoned settlement, which was centered around a sawmill of the Peñasco Lumber Co.

LOOKOUT (general). Throughout the US, natural observation points often are named Lookout. NM has 41 features with this name (GNIS).

Lookout Canyon (Catron; heads against Mogollon Peak, runs S to become a fork of Mogollon Creek). Mogollon Peak (see entry) would have been a natural lookout, and this creek heads there.

Lookout Mountain, 8,425 ft. (Catron; in the Mogollon Mountains, N of Mogollon Creek, just N of the Grant County line). Said to have been used as a lookout by Apaches.

Lookout Mountain, 9,112 ft. (Cibola; in the Zuni Mountains, SW of Bluewater Lake). The USFS used this peak as a fire lookout in the early 1900s.

Lookout Peak, 5,648 ft. (Doña Ana; in the Robledo Mountains, 3.5 mi S of Radium Springs). Used by Apaches to observe Fort Selden.

Lookout Peak, 11,400 ft. (Lincoln; in the Sierra Blanca complex, just N of Sierra Blanca).

LOOKOUT (Eddy; settlement; NW of Malaga, N of the Black River; PO 1883–92, moved to Malaga). When Lookout was founded in 1883, it was one of the area's first settlements. By 1885 Lookout had 350 residents and five saloons. But the elevation that gave Lookout its name also caused its demise; the RR bypassed Lookout because of the steep approach grade, and Lookout died. Little or nothing now remains of the settlement.

LOONEY (Quay). See *Woodrow.*

LOPEZ (general). Members of this family were in NM early in the colony's history, for in 1626 the family of Francisco López, then dead, was mentioned as being in Santa Fe. Juan López arrived in NM in 1633 and the next year married in Santa Fe. Many other Lópezes were mentioned in the early records. A Nicolás López was killed at Santo Domingo Pueblo during the Pueblo Revolt of 1680. His widow and three sons returned to NM in 1693, and a Pedro Lópes del Castillo also returned. The descendants of these families now are found throughout NM; GNIS lists 24 Lopez names.

LOPEZ (San Miguel; settlement; 5 mi W of San Miguel). The Lópezes were among the earliest prominent families in San Miguel County, and this former community bore their name.

LOPEZVILLE (San Miguel; settlement; in SE part of county, on upper Cuervo Creek; PO 1881–86, mail to Cabra Springs). Like Lopez (see entry) to the W, the name of this abandoned settlement is that of a prominent family in San Miguel County.

LORDSBURG (Hidalgo; settlement, county seat; on I-10 and NM 464; PO 1881–present). Lordsburg was born on October 18, 1880, when the SP RR reached here from the W, and the fledging camp soon had a population of RR workers, freighters, cowboys, gamblers, and merchants. Several explanations exist for the name. One version is that the town took the surname of a man who had a chain of eating places along the RR. Another is that it was the name of the engineer in charge of the construction crew here. The version most widely accepted is that it recalls Dr. Charles H. Lord, New York native, who came west during the Civil War and stayed to become one of Tucson's leading citizens. He and a partner started a banking and wholesale distributing business, Lord and Williams. When RR freight handlers at the new southern NM camp, still unnamed, came to a piece of the company's merchandise, they simply called out "Lords," a code name everyone knew, and in time the camp took the name Lordsburg. But the most likely explanation is that the town was named for Delbert Lord, SP RR chief engineer during construction of the main line. *Lordsburg Mesa* is about 10 mi NW of Lordsburg.

LORETTA (Colfax; settlement; 2 mi N of Dawson). Abandoned coal camp, named for the Loretta Coal Mine.

LOS ABEYTAS. See *Abeytas.*

LOS ALAMITOS (Taos; settlement; S of Taos Plaza, W of Los Cordovas). Inhabited suburb of Taos whose Spanish name means "the little cottonwoods."

LOS ALAMOS (San Miguel; settlement; 13 mi NE of Las Vegas; PO 1878–1914, mail to Las Vegas). Early records sometimes called this *El Montón de los Álamos,* "the clump of the cottonwoods," but now this tiny hamlet, still inhabited, is usually called simply Los Alamos. See *Alamo (general).*

LOS ALAMOS (Los Alamos; settlement, county seat; in E Jemez Mountains, on NM 502; PO as Otowi 1920–41, as Los Alamos 1941–43, 1947–present). An Hispanic settlement was located here as early as 1880, and the name *Los Álamos,* "the cottonwoods," likely dates from then. In 1918 Ashley Pond, a wealthy Detroit businessman, established the *Los Alamos Ranch School* for boys, which continued until 1942 when the locality was selected by the US government as the site to develop the atomic bomb. Under strict security, the laboratory and the community grew rapidly together. Today *Los Alamos National Laboratory,* a major research institution, continues to dominate this community on the Pajarito Plateau. For several years the PO here was called *Otowi* (see *Otowi Crossing*), but in 1941 it took the same name as the community it served. See *Alamo (general).*

LOS ALAMOS COUNTY (in the E Jemez

Mountains, NW of Santa Fe; county seat, Los Alamos). NM's smallest county, this was created in 1949 from portions of Sandoval and Santa Fe Counties and named for its main settlement.

LOS ANCONES (Rio Arriba; settlement; on NM 111, 9 mi N of Ojo Caliente, on the Rio Vallecitos). NM Spanish, "coves," likely referring here to coves where the Rio Vallecitos bends at this tiny inhabited community.

LOS BRAZOS (Rio Arriba; settlement; on the N bank of the Rio Brazos, 4 mi N of Tierra Amarilla, at the junction of NM 573 and US 84; PO 1898–1900, mail to Chama, 1912–17, mail to Park View). La Puente, Los Ojos (see entries), and this tiny inhabited community were the first three permanent settlements in the area known as the Tierra Amarilla. Its name comes from its location near the junction of the two main "arms," or *brazos,* of the Rio Chama.

LOS CHÁVEZ (Valencia; settlement; on NM 314, 4 mi N of Belen; PO 1929–34, mail to Los Lunas). In 1738 Don Nicolás Durán y Chávez applied to the Spanish crown for a land grant in the area now known as Los Chavez, saying in his petition that he was a descendant of the original Chávez family and son of Fernando Durán y Chávez, who was a captain with Vargas during the reconquest in 1692. A year later, his request was granted. This inhabited community still bears his family's name.

LOS CHULOS (Doña Ana; settlement; near Picacho Peak, NW of Las Cruces). This was an Hispanic village whose name appears in records of the 1870s. Its Mexican-Spanish name has the unflattering meaning, "the mutts, the mongrels."

LOS CHUPADEROS (Mora; settlement; 6 mi NE of Mora on old wagon road between Guadalupita and Ocate). Inhabited hamlet, origin of name unknown, though *chupadero* can mean either "sinkhole, seep," or "sucking insect, such as a tick."

LOS CISNEROS (Mora; settlement; on Coyote Creek, 9 mi N of Mora, 1 mi E of

NM 434). Inhabited hamlet bearing the Cisneros family name.

LOS COCAS (Mora; settlement; near Rainsville). Inhabited hamlet, named for the Coca family, whose members no longer live here.

LOS CORDOVAS (Taos; settlement; W of NM 240, 2.5 mi NW of Ranchos de Taos). Small inhabited settlement, bearing the name of the Córdova family, whose members still live here.

LOS CORRALES (Sandoval). See *Corrales.*

LOS DIEGOS (San Miguel; settlement; 9 mi SW of San Miguel del Bado). Like many settlements in this area, this inhabited community bears a Spanish family name; its English equivalent would be James. The PO here is named *Gonzales Ranch.*

LOS ESTERITOS (Guadalupe; settlement; on the E bank of the Pecos River, NE of Dilia). Abandoned locality that appears on some maps. The Spanish name, "little estuaries, swamps," survives on *Esteritos Creek* and *Esteritos Spring* here.

LOS FUERTES (San Miguel; settlement; 9 mi SE of Romeroville, on the E bank of the Gallinas River). Abandoned Hispanic community, whose Spanish name means "the forts."

LOS GABALDONES (Valencia; settlement; N of Belen). Like many communities in this area, this bears the name of a local family, Gabaldon, whose members still live here.

LOS HORNILLOS (Doña Ana). See *Rough and Ready.*

LOS HUERROS (Mora; settlement; 3 mi W of Ocate, on Los Huerros Creek). Spanish, "the fair-haired folks." Specific origin of the name unknown. A few families live here.

LOS LENTES (Valencia; settlement; W of the Rio Grande, between Isleta and Los Lunas). When Coronado visited here in 1540–41, he found a sizable Tiwa village closely allied with Isleta Pueblo, just to the N, and many residents of this community still have close ties with Isleta. The pueblo's name has been recorded as *Piquiratengo,* which the Spaniards later renamed *San Clemente,* probably for a mission here. The community's present name name comes from one Matías el Ente of Isleta marrying a woman from this village and then raising a family here, the name Los Lentes meaning "the Lente folks," just as Los Lunas means "the Lunas." Los Lentes was annexed to the village of Los Lunas in the 1970s.

LOS LUCEROS (Rio Arriba; settlement; on the E side of the Rio Grande, 7 mi N of Española W of NM 68; PO as Los Luceros, 1855–70, as Plaza de Alcalde, 1877–82, as Alcalde, 1890–92, 1894–present). Named for a prominent local family—see *Lucero (general)*—this inhabited village once was the capital of the *departamento* of Rio Arriba, established by the Mexican government in 1836; from 1855 to 1860 Los Luceros was the Rio Arriba County seat. See *Alcalde.*

LOS LUNAS (Valencia; settlement, county seat; on NM 6 and 314, 13 mi N of Belen; PO 1855–57, 1865–present). Many of the Lunas in NM are descended from one Diego de Luna, born in 1635. In 1716 the *San Clemente Land Grant,* which encompassed the present village of Los Lunas, was given to Felix Candelaria. Around 1750, Domíngo Luna purchased land here from Baltazar Baca, who had purchased land from Candelaria. Antonio José Luna, born 1808, has been called "the father of Los Lunas." A sheep rancher, he married Isabella Baca, from a prominent Belen family, and became a civic and political leader. Their son, Solomon Luna, married into the Otero family of Valencia, thus uniting two powerful and rich Republican families that dominated regional politics for almost a century; Luna played a major role in drafting the NM consititution. Luna County and the village of Luna (see entries) in Catron County also commemorate this family. Through the influence of the Lunas, the seat of Valencia County was moved from Tome to Los Lunas in 1876.

LOS MONTOYAS (San Miguel; settlement; on US 84, 12 mi S of Las Vegas). The name of this inhabited community recalls the family name of Bartolomé de Montoya, a Spaniard who married María de Zamora in Mexico City in 1600; they came with their family to Santa Fe that year.

LOS OJITOS (Doña Ana). See *La Union.*

LOS OJITOS (Guadalupe; settlement; on the Pecos River, at the head of Sumner Lake; PO 1878–81). This Hispanic settlement, named for "the little springs," was a companion community to Bess (see entry), but both died with the damming of the Pecos River and the filling of Sumner Lake.

LOS OJOS (Rio Arriba; settlement; 2 mi N of Tierra Amarilla, just W of US 84; PO as Parkview 1877–1972, as Los Ojos 1972–present). Los Ojos, named for natural springs in the area, was settled in 1860 and along with Los Brazos and La Puente (see entries) was one of the Tierra Amarilla's first three permanent settlements. Later, Hispanic settlers here were joined by Scandinavians who worked on the RR. For much of its history, Los Ojos has also been known as *Parkview.* Tradition has it that when the PO at the separate community of Parkview burned, developers, wishing to preserve the name, had the PO—and the name—re-established at Los Ojos. There it became known as *Parkview at Los Ojos,* and eventually Los Ojos itself began to be called Parkview, but in 1972 the community and the PO officially returned to the original name.

LOS ORGANOS (Doña Ana). See *Organ Mountains.*

LOS PACHECOS (Rio Arriba; settlement; N of Española, on NM 389, on the E bank of the Rio Grande, just S of Villita). This inhabited community was settled in the early 1700s by members of the Pacheco family. A soldier named Gerónimo Pacheco was recorded as being in NM in 1628, and Luis Pacheco and Vicente Pacheco, also soldiers, were recorded here in the 1630s.

LOS PACHECOS (Rio Arriba; settlement; 1 mi E of Chimayo). Inhabited community, named for the Pacheco family, whose members still live here.

LOS PADILLAS (Bernalillo; settlement; 4 mi N of Isleta Pueblo, on the W side of the Rio Grande, on NM 314). An 1803 account mentions this inhabited community; like many other early Hispanic communities in this area, its name identifies the predominant family. The village occasinally was called *San Andres de los Padillas,* and sometimes simply as *San Andres.*

LOS PECOS (Valencia; settlement; between Los Lunas and Los Chaves). Early Spanish documents mention this tiny community, which like Los Lunas and Los Chaves likely bore a family name. *Plaza de Arriba* (Spanish, "upper town") has been mentioned as an early name for the site, but by 1887 it was called Los Pecos.

LOS PINITOS (Cibola; settlement; 10 NW of Fence Lake, W of Atarque). Spanish, "little pines." Abandoned community, named for pine groves nearby. *Pinitos Draw* is here.

LOS PINOS (Rio Arriba; settlement; in NE corner of county, 3 mi W of the Taos County line and 1 mi S of the Colorado border). Though Pino is a common Spanish surname, this active trading center was named for its location on the *Río de los Pinos,* "river of the pines," which rises in Colorado and flows E at San Miguel, returning to Colorado, 1 mi N of settlement of Los Pinos.

LOS PINOS (Valencia). See *Peralta.*

LOS PINOS MOUNTAINS (Socorro; small range running NE-SW S of US 60 at Abo Pass). Spanish, "the pines," a curious name as forests of any tree species are rather scarce on these barren mountains. Highest elevation, *Whiteface Mountain,* 7,530 ft.

LOS PINOS RIVER (San Juan; heads in Colorado and and flows S to enter NM in the NE corner of county, just E of NM 511, where after less than a mile its waters are backed up by Navajo Reservoir). An 1897 USBGN decision established Los Pinos River as the accepted form and not *Pine River, Pinos River, Río de los Pinos,* or *Río los Pinos.*

LOS POBLANOS (Bernalillo; settlement; in SW part of Los Ranchos de Albuquerque, N of Montaño Rd. along Rio Grande Blvd.). Once a cluster of rural homes and farms but now indistinguishable from the surrounding conurbation, Los Poblanos, Spanish, "the Pueblans," was named for settlers coming here from Puebla, Mexico, led by Juan Cristóbal Ortega. In modern times the name was adopted for Albert Simms's estate-like home, just W of Rio Grande Blvd.

LOS PUEBLITOS DE BELEN (Valencia; settlement, SW of Belen). An 1856 map used in litigation labels a settlement here; it was, as its name implies, "the little towns of Belen," a satellite community of Belen.

LOS RANCHITOS (Bernalillo). See *El Ranchito.*

LOS RANCHITOS (Rio Arriba). See *Ranchitos.*

LOS RANCHOS DE ALBUQUERQUE (Bernalillo; settlement; N of Montaño Rd. and S of Alameda). After the reconquest of 1692 and the founding of Albuquerque in 1706, Spanish colonists quickly began settling available lands around the new *villa.* One cluster of farms to the N came to be known as *San José de los Ranchos,* the settlement of the Gurulés, who were descendants of Eleña Gallegos (see *Elena Gallegos Picnic Area*) and her husband, Santiago Gurulé. On maps made some 200 years after its founding, the placed appeared as *El Rancho Plaza* and was even confused with *Los Ranchitos* to the E. It was incorporated as the *Village of Los Ranchos de Albuquerque* in 1958; the municipal building is at the old center of the settlement.

LOS RANCHOS DE TOME (Valencia). See *Tome.*

LOS TANOS (Guadalupe; settlement; 15 mi NE of Santa Rosa, on SP RR; PO 1907–25, mail to Cuervo). This abandoned settlement, now just a RR siding, once was an active community, with a section house and a saloon (before a school was built, classes were held there). Local people say the name is Spanish and means "the swales," and indeed the community was located in an area of shallow valleys. An abandoned schoolhouse and a cemetery remain at the site of this village, but all residents have left.

LOS TANOS CREEK (Guadalupe; rises E of the Pecos River N of the former village of Los Tanos and flows SW to enter it just N of Santa Rosa). This creek is within the former territory of the Towa group of the Tano Indians and might have been named for them, but far more likely it was named, like the community (see *Los Tanos*), for the valley. It is an important tributary of the Pecos River.

LOS TOMASES (Bernalillo; settlement; in NW Albuquerque, N of Menaul Blvd. along Los Tomases Drive). One of several former hamlets now absorbed into Albuquerque, this place was settled in 1848 by Polinario Santillanes, whose descendants still live hereabout. The identity of the persons named Tomás is unknown.

LOS TORREONES (Socorro; settlement; on the E bank of the Rio Grande, S of Socorro, about 2 mi S of Bosquecito). Spanish, "the towers." Little is known about this vanished settlement, including its exact location and the inspiration for its name.

LOS TORRES (San Miguel; settlement 19 mi SE of Las Vegas, on the N bank of the Gallinas River). This former settlement, now abandoned and part of a large ranch, recalls a family name in the area. See *Torres. Torrez (general)*.

LOS TRUJILLOS (San Miguel). See *Trujillo*.

LOS TRUJILLOS (Valencia). See *Belen*.

LOS VALLES DE SAN AGUSTIN (San Miguel). See *San Agustin*.

LOS VALLES DE SAN GERONIMO (San Miguel). See *Mineral Hill*.

LOS VIGILES (San Miguel; settlement; NW of Las Vegas, just E of Montezuma; PO 1917–24, mail to Las Vegas). Tiny inhabited community, named for the Vigil family. See *Vigil (general)*.

LOST BEAR LAKE (Mora; 2 mi above Pecos Falls, 11 mi W of Mora). As Elliott Barker tells the story, a large grizzly bear he was trailing in June 1908 led him by this little lake. Later, Barker tried unsuccessfully several times to locate the lake. Finally, in 1934, forest ranger J.W. Johnson, acting upon Barker's directions, saw a depression from Santa Barbara Divide, and when he rode his horse

to it, he found the lake just as Barker had described. "He named it Lost Bear Lake," wrote Barker, "appropriate because I lost both the bear and the lake."

LOST MAN CANYON (Doña Ana; in the San Andres Mountains, 4 mi SE of Victorio Peak). This canyon, like *Dead Man Canyon* just to the S, was at the S end of the *Jornada del Muerto*, which in earlier times often was the scene of mishaps and sometimes tragedies. The specific incident behind this name has been forgotten.

LOST MULE CANYON (Catron; in the Gila Wilderness, in the Sign Camp area). A man named Rusty Richardson was building a road for the USFS near here when he lost a mule in this canyon, hence the name.

LOST RIVER (Chaves; heads S of US 70 NE of Roswell and runs generally SE into Bitter Lake). During dry periods this small stream doubtless becomes "lost."

LOST RIVER (Otero; heads on Holloman Air Force Base SW of Alamogordo and runs SW to become "lost" in the sands of White Sands National Monument).

LOUIS (Union; settlement; in SE part of county, on Tramperos Creek; PO as Tramperas 1879–92, as Louis 1892–96, mail to Clapham). Not long after the Mieras came to the Tramperos Creek country in 1874, other settlers joined them, including Luis F. García. He started a store, and the community it served was known as *Garcia Plaza*, sometimes also known as *Tramperos Plaza*. He also started a PO, which was called *Tramperas*, for Tramperos Creek (see entry), though in 1892 the PO changed its name to Louis, the English version of García's given name. The settlement long has been abandoned.

LOURDES (San Miguel). See *San Agustin*.

LOVERS PEAK (Quay; W of Quay). Two star-crossed lovers are said to have committed suicide by leaping from this peak, but local people are skeptical, saying easier ways exist to end it all.

LOVING (Eddy; settlement; on US 285, 10 mi SE of Carlsbad; PO as Florence 1894–1908, as Loving 1908–present). In 1891 a group of 54 Swiss immigrants settled here seeking irrigated farmland; they called their new home *Vaud* (pronounced Voh), after their native canton in Switzerland. The Swiss imported numerous laborers from Italy to work their farms. Many of these Italians settled in the nearby community of Malaga (see entry), and many later bought land from the Swiss. Because of their influence, Vaud in 1904 became *Florence,* for the town in Italy. Then finally, in 1908, the name was changed again, this time to honor Oliver Loving, who with Charles Goodnight had established the Goodnight-Loving cattle trail and who in 1866 was mortally wounded at nearby Loving Bend (see entry).

LOVING BEND (Eddy; on the Pecos River). Though local authorities differ as to exactly where this is located, there's agreement as to what happened here. In 1866, on his fourth cattle drive into NM, Oliver Loving and his companion, Billy Wilson, were ambushed by Indians. Wilson went for help, while Loving remained and was eventually able to escape, but he later died of his wounds at Fort Sumner. He was buried at his home in Weatherford, TX, as he requested before he died.

LOVINGTON (Lea; settlement, county seat; at the junction of NM 83 and 206 and US 82, 13 mi NW of Hobbs; PO 1908–present). Robert Florence Love arrived in SE NM from Texas around 1903, and in 1907 he was joined by his brother, James B. Love. An active promoter, Florence Love (as he preferred to be called) organized a town in 1908, and US Land Commissioner Wesley McAllister suggested naming it *Love,* for its founder, but Love felt the name *Loving* was more euphonious, so that was the name he submitted to the postal authorities. They, however, noted that a community named Loving already existed, so after some discussion McAllister and Love added a *ton* to Loving to create Lovington. James Love, Florence's brother, became the community's first postmaster.

LOWER COLONIAS (San Miguel). See *Colonias.*

LOWER PEÑASCO (Chaves; settlement; in SW corner of county, on US 82, on the Rio Peñasco; 1884–1917, mail to Dunken). Lower Peñasco, named for its location on the *Río Peñasco* (see entry), had the second PO in Chaves County (Roswell had the first), with Billy Matthews the first postmaster (see *Matthews Canyon*). This inhabited farming community once shared the narrow river valley with Upper Peñasco (see *Mayhill*) and several sawmills.

LOWER ROCIADA (San Miguel; settlement; on NM 276, 1.5 mi S of Rociada). Inhabited settlement. See *Rociada.*

LOWER SAN FRANCISCO PLAZA (Catron; settlement; 4 mi S of Reserve on NM 435, on the San Francisco River). This old inhabited community is the southernmost of three closely related San Francisco Plazas: see *San Francisco Plaza.*

LOWER VALLECITOS (Sandoval). See *Ponderosa.*

LOYD (Quay; settlement; in central part of county, SW of Tucumcari; PO 1906–14, mail to Norton). Abandoned homesteader community, origin of name unknown.

LUCAS (Harding; settlement; in NW part of county, NE of Roy; PO 1908–11, mail to Roy). Abandoned homesteader community, bearing the family name of its first postmistress, Anna Lucas.

LUCERO (general). Pedro Lucero de Godoy was a native of Mexico City who came to NM early in the 17th century; he was married in Santa Fe in 1628. Lucero de Godoy prospered in NM; Fray Angélico Chávez summarizes his career thus: "Pedro was involved in most of the church and political intrigues of his time, although he managed to steer clear of unpleasant consquences experienced by others." By 1663, when he was 63, Lucero de Godoy was the *maese de campo* in NM, second in command to the governor. His sons and grandsons were prominent in the reconquest of 1692. Their descendants—and the Lucero name—are found throughout NM; GNIS lists 29 Lucero place names.

LUCERO (Mora; settlement; 1 mi W of NM 442, 4 mi N of La Cueva; PO 1886–1936, mail to Mora). A few people still live in this old settlement, though most buildings have been abandoned. The locale once was a stop for *ciboleros* journeying onto the plains to hunt buffalo and was known as *La Placita de los Ciboleros*. See *Lucero (general)*.

LUCERO PEAK, 10,831 ft. (Taos; in Sangre de Cristo Mountains, 2.5 mi NE of village of Arroyo Seco). See *Lucero (general)*.

LUCIA (Torrance). See *Lucy*.

LUCIANO MESA (Quay; 20 mi SW of Tucumcari). At one time an Hispanic settler named Luciano, or Luisiano, lived here. The name has appeared as *Luciana Mesa,* and this in turn sometimes has been corrupted to *Louisiana Mesa.*

LUCILLE (Quay; settlement; in SW part of county, NW of House, 10 mi S of Ima, 7 mi NW of Hassell; PO as Orton 1908–11, as Lucille 1911–34, mail to Hassell). This abandoned homesteader settlement originally was called *Orton,* for reasons unknown, but in 1911 the name was changed to Lucille. This name was suggested by Elijah A. Mauzy, postmaster here, to honor his wife, Lucille Mauzy.

LUCY (Torrance; settlement; on US 60 and AT&SF RR, 12 mi NE of Willard; PO as Lucia 1908–14, as Lucy 1914–42, mail to Willard). As T.M. Pearce discovered, at least three explanations—all plausible—exist for the name of this former community, settled by homesteaders about 1905. The first is that the name recalls the wife of James Dunn, chief engineer of the AT&SF RR. The second is that Lucy was the name of an AT&SF RR attorney's mother. And the third is that Lucy was named for Lucy Myers, daughter of Frank Myers, construction engineer for the RR. It also is possible that none of these explanations is the true one, for the PO here was called *Lucia,* the Spanish form of Lucy, for six years before the name was changed to the English form. Lucy at one time was a thriving community, with a high school, church, stores, and a PO, but the Dust Bowl and the Depression began a decline from which Lucy never recovered.

NORTH LUCY (Torrance; settlement; 12 mi SE of Clines Corners, 2 mi E of US 285). Tiny inhabited community, named for *Lucy* (see entry) to the S.

LUERA MOUNTAINS (Catron; in E part of county, S of the Plains of San Agustin, E of the Continental Divide). These mountains, and their highest point, *Luera Peak,* 9,420 ft., as well as *Luera Spring* 2 mi NE, were named for the Luera family, whose members still live in the area.

LUIS LOPEZ (Socorro; settlement; 5 mi N of San Antonio). In 1667 the *alcalde mayor* of the Piro Indians at Senecu was one Luis López, a Spanish captain, and he established his *estancia* near the inhabited community that now bears his name. Governor Otermín, during his unsuccessful attempt in 1681 to reconquer NM, mentioned Luis Lopez as one of four deserted *estancias* in this area. As late as 1667, Bishop Tamarón was informed that the site owed its name, Luis Lopez, to its owner before 1680. By the 19th century the locality had been resettled and has appeared intermittently in US Census records from 1850 to the present.

LUMBERTON (Rio Arriba; settlement; 22 mi W of Chama on US 64; PO as Amargo 1881–94, as Lumberton 1894–present). Lumberton has been described as a relic left by the lumbering industry that sprang up in the Chama Valley following the RR's arrival in 1880. E.M. Biggs, the largest sawmill operator of the period, in 1884 bought a 40-acre ranch from Francisco Lobato, laid out streets, and sold lots. The community originally was called *Amargo,* "bitter," for the taste of the water in *Amargo Creek,* on whose banks the settlement was located, but in 1894 it was renamed Lumberton because of the area's many sawmills. Eventually, however, the demand for timber waned, and by the end of WW I the best timber had been harvested, and Lumberton declined as well.

LUMBRE (Rio Arriba; settlement; exact location unknown; PO 1907–10, mail to

Abiquiu). Abandoned settlement, likely named for its association with the *Piedra Lumbre Land Grant* here, which spanned the Rio Chama 10 mi W of Abiquiu. It was granted to Pedro Martín Serrano, lieutenant of the Militia Company of Chama, in 1766. *Piedra lumbre* can be translated from the Spanish as "fire rock," or "flint," abundant in the area.

LUMMIS CANYON (Sandoval; in Bandelier National Monument, just SW of Cañon de los Frijoles). Charles F. Lummis was born in Massachusetts in 1859 and first saw NM as a young man. He was enchanted with the state and returned often, his numerous books among the first to popularize the allure of NM. A close friend of Adolph Bandelier (see *Bandelier National Monument*), Lummis had a special fondness for the Pajarito Plateau—a chapter in his book, *Land of Poco Tiempo,* was set here—and he certainly would have been familiar with the canyon named for him in the plateau.

LUNA (general). See *Los Lunas.*

LUNA (Catron; settlement; on the San Francisco River, on US 180, 8 mi from Arizona; PO 1886–present). In the 19th century, this area was within the vast sheep-ranching domain of Don Solomon Luna, a powerful economic and political force in NM at the time, and this community took the Luna family name (see *Los Lunas*). Later, the area was settled by Mormon ranchers from Utah.

LUNA COUNTY (SW NM; county seat, Deming). During the late 19th century, rivalry between Silver City and Deming was intense, and agitation for division of Grant County began as early as 1888. Between 1881 and 1901, bills were introduced into the territorial legislature for the creation of a new county, to be called *Logan* or *Florida,* probably for the *Florida Mountains* (see entry), but when the county finally was created on March 16, 1901, it was called Luna, for Solomon Luna, the era's dominant political figure; see *Los Lunas.*

LYBROOK (Rio Arriba; settlement; on NM 44, between Farmington and Cuba, NW of Counselor). Rancher Will Lybrook came here from North Carolina in 1918 and soon was joined by his brother, Sam, and other family members who also homesteaded and set up cattle and sheep ranches. He built a three-story stone and log house here that was the center of the Lybrook Ranch. Today, most residents are associated with the gas refinery here. The locality's Navajo name means "water running down," probably for a local spring.

LYDEN (Rio Arriba; settlement; on NM 582, 18 mi NE of Española, on the W side of the Rio Grande; PO 1902 intermittently to 1957, mail to Velarde). Inhabited community, formerly known as *El Bosque,* "the forest, the thicket," for its location on the brushy Rio Grande floodplain. Origin of current name unknown.

LYKINS (Roosevelt; settlement; 13 mi W of Floyd; PO 1909–13, mail to Benson). Abandoned homesteader community, named for its first postmaster, Richard N. Lykins.

LYNCH (Lea; settlement; in W part of county, NW of Eunice). Abandoned settlement, once an oil pipeline station, said to be named for an early ranch.

LYNDON (Doña Ana). See *Brunswick.*

LYNN (Colfax; settlement; on AT&SF RR, 6 mi N of Raton, at S entrance to Raton Pass tunnel; PO 1891–1910, mail to Wooten, CO). Abandoned RR settlement, origin of name unknown.

LYONS CITY (Colfax; settlement; below the South and Middle Forks of the Poñil River). This was but a short-lived prospectors' camp in 1896. Harry Lyons was among the first prospectors here.

MACHO SPRINGS (Sierra; settlement; in SW corner of county, 12 mi NW of Nutt). George Adlai Feather related that a mineral discovery here triggered the laying out of a town, with more than 100 lots sold within a few days. But before a community really could develop, people abandoned the place because of legal disputes and disappointing ore.

MACY (Roosevelt; settlement; 12 mi W of Portales; PO 1907–13, mail to Dillard). Local people say the name of this abandoned homesteader community is an Anglo corruption of the Spanish *mesa,* and indeed a small mesa is near the settlement's site.

MADISON (Union; settlement; 8 mi NE of Folsom, in Dry Cimarron Canyon; PO 1874–88, mail to Capulien). In 1862 Madison Emery, exploring for routes N, came upon the beautiful valley of the Dry Cimarron, and in 1865 he and some friends created a tiny settlement here, the first in what is now Union County. The settlement was named for Emery, as was Emery Peak behind the town and Emery Gap (see entries). Madison soon boasted a store, saloon, blacksmith shop, grist mill, PO, and a few houses, but when the C&S RR put its tracks through Folsom 8 mi away, Folsom prospered and Madison withered. Today only ruins remain.

MADRID (Santa Fe; settlement; on NM 14, 24 mi SW of Santa Fe; PO 1896–1906, 1906–66, mail to Cerrillos). A Spaniard named Francisco de Madrid arrived in NM in 1603, and his descendants and other persons with the Madrid surname returned with Vargas's reconquest; Roque Madrid, one of Vargas's captains, was interested in lead mines in this area. Members of the family may have been this area when coal mining began here

in 1835, and it's likely the community that had evolved by 1869 took the family name, though it's also possible the name recalls the capital city of Spain. Coal production in Madrid peaked in 1920, and from 1920 to 1940 Madrid was a company-owned town of the Albuquerque and Cerrillos Coal Co. But after WW II, demand for coal dwindled, and in 1954 the entire town was offered for sale for $250,000; there were no takers. Today Madrid is undergoing a renaissance as a tourist center, ambiance replacing anthracite as a resource. Pronunciation of the town's name is controversial. Spanish speakers accent the second syllable, whereas English speakers move the accent to the first syllable and flatten the vowels. The English version seems to be predominating.

MAES (San Miguel; settlement; in central part of county, 9 mi E of Trujillo; PO as Gonzales 1904–13, as Maes 1913–57, mail to Trujillo). The earliest recorded member of this family in NM was Juan Maese, who was here in 1632. Later, after returning with the reconquest in 1692, the family spread E from Santa Fe to settle in San Miguel and Mora counties; Juan de Dios Maese was the first mayor of Las Vegas. His descendants later dropped the final *e* from their name. This community was settled in the 1870s and originally was known as *Gonzales,* for a local family. Later it changed its name to Maes, and while no village exists here, persons named Maes still live on ranches in the area.

MAESTAS (general). It's not known when the first person by this name entered NM, but in 1693 one Juan de Mestas Peralta was living with his wife in Santa Fe; in 1710 he was living in Pojoaque. Sometime during the 19th century the name Mestas came to be spelled Maestas. GNIS lists 11 places with this name.

MAGDALENA (Socorro; settlement; on US 60, 27 mi W of Socorro; PO as Socorro Mines, 1875–78, as Magdalena Mines, 1878, as Magdelena 1880–83, mail to Kelly, as Magdalena 1884–present). Magdalena began in the late 1800s when lead and zinc were found in the area (see *Kelly*). The mining community is said to have first gone by the name *Socorro Mines*, then later as *Magdalena Mines*, and finally simply as Magdalena, for *Magdalena Peak* just to the SW; see *Magdalena Mountains*. The town really took off in 1884 when a RR spur was built from Socorro to haul out ore, and soon the village became one of the largest cattle-shipping centers in the Southwest; the route over which livestock were driven to Magdalena from the W was formally known as the *Magdalena Livestock Driveway*, and informally as the *Beefsteak Trail* and the *Hoof Highway*; in 1919 21,677 cattle and 150,000 sheep were driven over the trail. But eventually lead-zinc mining died, and the RR spur and the cattle drives were abandoned, though Magdalena survives as an active trading and population center.

MAGDALENA MOUNTAINS (Socorro; S of the village of Magdalena). These take their name from *Magdalena Peak*, 8,152 ft., on the W side of the range; on the E slope of this mountain are rocks and shrubbery supposedly resembling the profile of Mary Magdalene; the face is said to have become less distinct when the drought of 1950–52 killed many of the shrubs outlining the face. A popular but apocryphal legend is that a group of Mexicans were besieged by Apaches on the mountain, when the face of Mary Magdalene miraculously appeared, frighting the Indians away, while another tradition says an early Spanish priest named the mountains in her honor. And equally apocryphal legends says no murder can be committed in the presence of Mary Magdalene's countenance. See also *Magdalena Peak (Doña Ana)*. The highest summit of the range

is *South Baldy*, 10,783 ft.; *North Baldy*, 9,858 ft., is 4 mi N.

MAGDALENA PEAK, 6,623 ft. (Doña Ana; 12 mi S of Hatch). As with the mountains in Socorro County, rock formations here supposedly resemble the profile of Mary Magdalene.

MAIZE (Curry). See *Portair*.

MAJOR LONGS CREEK (Union). See *Tramperos Creek*.

MALAGA (Eddy; settlement; on US 285, 15 mi SE of Carlsbad; PO 1892–present). Malaga, like Loving to the N, began in the early 1890s when Swiss immigrants arrived in the area to farm. They imported laborers from Italy, and many of the Italians settled here. When the community was a station on the PV RR it was known as *Kirkwell*, for reasons also unknown, but in 1892 it changed its name to that of a sweet Spanish wine, made from a variety of grape that flourished here. Today, the vineyards are gone, but the community named for their wine remains. See also *Lookout* and *Loving*.

MALDONADO (Mora; settlement; in E part of county, exact location unknown; PO 1896–97, mail to Wagon Mound). Little is known about this ephemeral community, though Maldonado is a common Hispanic surname.

MALJAMAR (Lea; settlement; on NM 82, 26 mi SW of Lovington; PO 1943–present). On July 26, 1926, the Maljamar Oil & Gas Co. successfully brought in its first oil well, the first in SE NM, thus triggering an oil boom and ending forever the region's rural isolation. The town that sprang up near the well was named for the company, founded in 1926 by William Mitchell. He wanted to honor his three children: MAlcolm, JAnet, and MARgaret— Maljamar. (In some accounts, the children's names were slightly different, such as Marjorie instead of Margaret, but the result was the same.) Today, Maljamar no longer is a boom town, but oil still dominates its life and economy.

MALLETTE CREEK (Taos; flows SW to the Red River, joining just above the town of Red River). In 1892 Sylvester M.

Mallette, from Fort Garland, CO, prospected in the Red River Valley, and the next year he returned with his brothers, Orrin D. and Jerome. They became the first homesteaders in the valley and remained active in prospecting and mining.

MALONE (Grant; settlement; 15 mi NE of Lordsburg, N of NM 90; PO 1884–88, mail to Gold Hill). In 1884 John B. Malone discovered gold deposits here, and soon a little mining camp sprang up bearing his name. But the camp was never large, and it has long since been abandoned.

LAKE MALOYA (Colfax; 6 mi NE of Raton, near head of Sugarite Canyon). Origin of name unknown.

MALPAIS (general). Though literally translated "bad land" from the Spanish, in NM the term usually refers more specifically to land overlain by lava flows, which for commercial purposes is very bad indeed. Numerous lava flows in NM have this name; it occurs 17 times in GNIS. See *Lava Beds;* see also *El Malpais National Monument* and *Valley of Fires State Park.*

MALPAIS (Doña Ana; 2 mi N of the Mexican border, on SP RR, 22 mi E of Columbus). A settlement, now abandoned, located near a lava flow; see *Malpais (general).*

MALPAIS HILL (Harding; 1 mi W of Ute Creek and S of the Sierra Negra). Rugged remnant of a volcano; see *Malpais (general).*

THE MALPAIS (Lincoln). See *Valley of Fires State Park.*

MALPIE (Colfax; settlement; 12 mi S of Capulin, near Union County line; PO as Malpais 1909–11, mail to Des Moines, as Malpie 1916–39, mail to Des Moines). As T. M. Pearce pointed out, the spelling Malpie is a clue to the widespread pronunciation of *malpais* in the West; see *Malpais (general).* This abandoned settlement, located on an old US Army route to Fort Union, was named for nearby volcanic rocks.

MANBY HOT SPRINGS (Taos; on the Rio Grande, W of Taos). Arthur R. Manby was an English mining engineer who came to Taos in 1894 and soon became a controversial figure. Among his many activities in the area was the purchase of these hot springs. In June 1929 he was reported missing, and in July his decapitated body was found in his Taos home; the exact cause or circumstances of his death have never been determined.

MANCHESTER (Lincoln; settlement; near White Oaks; PO 1881). The ephemeral community of Manchester began when a group of people settled here with the idea of competing with White Oaks, in anticipation of a RR line to the community. They opened a PO in June 1881, and they proposed opening a bank as well, but the bank was insolvent, and by October the PO had closed. The name's inspiration is unknown.

MANCO DE BURRO PASS (Colfax; NE of Raton). During Maxwell Land Grant litigation, Calvin Jones in 1883 testified: "I understand, from the old settlers, that there was a pack train going through to trade with the Indians. Up on the mountains this burro put his knee out of place and limped, and when anything limps they say it is *manco* [Spanish, 'maimed, crippled']."

MANCOS RIVER (San Juan; heads in La Plata Mountains of Colorado, flows SW to enter the San Juan River in extreme NW corner of state). Spanish, "maimed, crippled." The name is said to have originated from a soldier on the Domínguez-Escalante Expedition of 1776 falling from his horse while fording the river and injuring his hand. The river also has been called *El Río de San Lazaro,* "the river of Saint Lazarus."

MANGAS (Catron; settlement; 16 mi SE of Quemado, on Mangas Creek; PO as Pinoville 1905–09, as Mangas 1909–43, mail to Datil). Though the Spanish *manga* can mean "fringe of land," this tiny inhabited settlement, as well as *Mangas Creek* and *Mangas Mountain,* 7 mi to the S on the Continental Divide, more likely take their name from Mangas Coloradas, "red sleeves," head of the Warm Springs Apaches whose territory included this region and who were prominent in the history here. Before being called Mangas, this community was known as *Pinoville,* likely for a family named Pino. The first settlers are said to have been José María Baca (*Baca Spring* is 6 mi SE of the village), along with members of the Leyva family and an American named Thompson.

MANGAS, MANGUS, MANGAS SPRINGS (Grant; settlement; on US 180, 15 mi NW of Silver City; PO 1896–98, mail to Cliff). Beginning in 1873, the families of James Shackleford and James Metcalf were living at the springs known as *Mangas Springs,* and earlier as *Santa Lucia Springs.* The springs were an important water source, and certainly would have been familiar to the Warm Springs Apaches and their leader, Mangas Coloradas. "red sleeves." He had a son named Mangus. The settlement that grew up took its name from the springs and still is often called *Mangas Springs.* Otherwise, opinion is divided as to the name's spelling; it's often Mangas but almost as often Mangus.

MANGAS CREEK (Grant; rises at Tyrone on the Continental Divide and flows NW into the Gila River). Likely named for the leader of the Warm Springs Apaches, Mangas Coloradas, "red sleeves."

MANGAS MOUNTAINS (Catron; in center of county, N of the Plains of San Agustin). Highest point, *Mangas Mountain,* 9,500 ft. See *Mangas (Catron).*

MANN (Roosevelt; settlement; 10 mi S of Portales; PO 1907–17, mail to Portales). Abandoned homesteader settlement, named for its first postmaster, Jasper N. Mann.

MANUELITAS (San Miguel; settlement; 15 mi N of Las Vegas, 2 mi NW of Sapello). Spanish, "little Manuelas." Manuel is the Spanish form of the Hebrew, Emmanuel, "God is with us," and among Spanish-speaking peoples the name often is given in baptism to girls by simply adding a feminine ending. It is said that a farmer in this area had three daughters, each named Manuela, and that this inhabited hamlet took its name from them. *Manuelitas Creek* rises above Sapello and flows through Rociada.

MANUELITO (McKinley; settlement; on NM 118, 16 mi SW of Gallup, 2.5 mi E of the Arizona line; PO 1881–1974). Manuelito was a famous 19th-century Navajo leader. One American described him thus: "He was a man of magnificent physique, tall, well-proportioned, a strikingly intelligent countenance, every inch a warrior and a king.... He introduced himself as Manuelito, the war chief of the Navajos." (See also *Manuelito Spring.*) Ironically, however, the Navajos who live near the inhabited community call it by a name that means "ugly house" or "ruin, abandoned house, where death occurred," referring to a nearby Anasazi ruin. The settlement originally was called *Cooks Ranch.* It assumed importance with the coming of the RR in 1881 as a trading center and communication link for Fort Defiance to the W; the telegraph station was called *Ferry Station.* In 1882 Manuelito became the location of the successful trading station of S.E. Aldrich.

Manuelito Canyon runs NW to join the Puerco River at Manuelito. The old freighting trail through this canyon was once the main route between Ferry Station, the telegraph station at Manuelito, and Fort Defiance. The Navajo name for the canyon means "spring under a house."

MANUELITO SPRING (McKinley; in the Chuska Mountains, NW of Tohatchi). This was named for the great Navajo leader who died here in 1893. He was born around 1818, and his Navajo name meant "blackweeds." In 1879, with the death of Barboncito, Manuelito joined Ganado Mucho in being the two leading Navajo leaders. He went to Washington, DC, and he was the first Navajo chief to allow his children to be sent away from Navajo country to school, but when one son died at Carlisle, PA, in 1883 he demanded his childrens' return. His abiding interest was the return of traditional tribal lands to his people. See also *Manuelito.*

MANZANA (Torrance). See *Manzano.*

MANZANARES (general). This family name is an old one in NM, appearing in records before and after the Pueblo Revolt of 1680. GNIS lists 5 Manzanares names.

MANZANARES (San Juan; settlement; on the S bank of the San Juan River, E of Bloomfield). The first Hispanic settlers along the San Juan River here included the Archuleta, Pacheco, and Manzanares families, and this tiny former community, as well as *Manzanares Canyon,* which parallels US 64 to join the San Juan River near Blanco, bears the Manzanares family name, here sometimes spelled *Manzonares.* See also *Archuleta* and *Manzanares (general).*

MANZANITA MOUNTAINS (Bernalillo; at N part of Manzano Mountains, S of Tijeras Canyon). Low extension of the Manzano Mountains, defined by the USBGN as a separate subrange in 1982; see *Manzano Mountains.*

MANZANO (Torrance; settlement; in the E foothills of the Manzano Mountains, on NM 55, 13 mi NW of Mountainair; PO as Manzana 1871–72, as Manzano 1876–80, 1881–95, 1898–1918, mail to Torreon). Tradition says this small Hispanic village takes its name from apples (Spanish, *manzanas*) grown in two ancient orchards here. These are believed by some to have been planted by Franciscan friars in the 17th century, when one of the Salinas pueblos was here, but the current trees have been dated to no earlier than the early 1800s. The trees certainly are believed to have been here when the present settlement was established. The exact date for this is unknown, but certainly a settlement was here before 1829, for in that year petitioners received the *Manzano Land Grant,* though certainly the site had been occupied before that, by settlers from Tome. Remnants of the orchards still survive here, and the name they inspired has spread throughout the region. 3 mi SE of the village is the tiny satellite community of *East Manzano. Manzano Lake,* SE of the village of Manzano, was once the site of a grist mill.

MANZANO MOUNTAINS (Bernalillo, Torrance; N-S Range E of the Rio Grande, S of the Sandia Mountains). This wild range originally was considered part of the Sandia Mountains to the N and only later acquired its present name from the village on its eastern foothills. The Tiwa name for the range means "closed fist mountains." Highest elevation, *Manzano Peak,* 10,098 ft.

Manzano Mountains State Park (Torrance; in E foothills of Manzano Mountains, 3 mi SW of the village of Manzano). Pleasant mountain forest, at 7,500 ft.

Manzano Mountain Wilderness (Torrance, Valencia; in the central Manzano Mountains). The 36,970 acres of this wilderness, created in 1978 and administered by the Cibola NF, span piñon-juniper forest from 5,000 ft. upward to ponderosa stands at 10,000 ft. The terrain is steep and rugged, cut by deep canyons.

MARBLE CANYON (Otero; on the W side of the Sacramento Mountains, at the base of Alamo Peak). Named for extensive marble deposits here. Quarrying began in 1898 with the founding of Alamogordo.

MARCIA (Otero; settlement; in the Sacramento Mountains, 8 mi SE of Cloudcroft; PO 1923–42, mail to Cloudcroft). This lumbering community, now abandoned, was named for the Marcia Logging Co. Pronounced mar-SEE-yah.

MARGUERITA (San Miguel; settlement; location unknown; PO 1891–92, mail to Genova). Ephemeral postal locality, name origin unknown.

MARIANA (Rio Arriba; settlement; near Abiquiu, exact location unknown; PO 1891–92, 1901–06, mail to Abiquiu). This former community originally was known as *La Puente,* Spanish "the bridge," because of a bridge or crossing at the Rio Chama here, but the name was changed when Mormons settled here around 1889. The site was ravaged by floods, which hastened its abandonment. Origin of the name Mariana unknown.

MARIANO LAKE (McKinley; settlement; 11 mi SW of Crownpoint). The Navajo leader Mariano, whose name in his own language meant "slim yellow," was headman in the Fort Wingate vicinity from 1870 to 1890. He was responsible for damming a natural sink here to collect rainfall, creating the lake named for him around 1885; Navajos tell that Mariano and his men used cowhides to carry clay to construct the dam. Descendants of Mariano still live in this area. The Navajo name for the lake means "broad lake."

MARION (Sierra; settlement; on the E side of Caballo Reservoir; PO 1907–10, mail to Cutter). Abandoned locality, origin of name unknown.

MARKHAM SPRING (Doña Ana; 6 mi NE of Organ). Bears an early settler's name.

MARQUEZ (Sandoval; settlement; at the junction of McKinley, Cibola, and Sandoval Counties; PO as Juan Tafoya 1888–1895, as Juantafoya 1895–1899, as Marquez 1901–64, mail to Seboyeta). The isolated inhabited community of Marquez was settled in 1866 and was first called *Cañon de Juan Tafoya*. The name of the Marquez family, whose members still live in the area, appears not only on this community but also on *Mesa Marquez* and *Cañon de Marquez* nearby. The earliest Marquez in NM was Gerónimo Marquez, who arrived as *maese de campo* of Oñate's 1600 troops, bringing with him his wife and five grown sons. Marquez was described as swarthy, with a black beard; Fray Angélico Chávez says, "His name runs through all the Oñate annals as an adventurous leader."

MAROON CLIFFS (Eddy; in E part of county, 3 mi S of US 62-180). Named for their color.

MARTINEZ (general). This is a Spanish patronymic name, "son of Martin," common throughout the Spanish-speaking world. In NM the name is traceable to Herman Martín Serrano, who arrived with Oñate in 1598. His descendants and other persons bearing the Martínez name returned to NM with the reconquest. By the 19th century, many descendants had dropped the Serrano and adopted the form Martínez. GNIS lists 34 Martinez names.

MARTINEZ (Bernalillo; settlement; in the Los Ranchos de Albuquerque area; PO 1902–09, mail to Alameda). Little is known about this community, which appears on early 20th-century maps. It possibly is related to *Martineztown* (see entry), just to the S.

MARTINEZ (Colfax). See *Aurora*.

MARTINEZ (San Juan; settlement; in NE part of county, on the San Juan River). This community, now beneath the waters of Navajo Reservoir, was settled by members of the Martínez family. Only the church and the cemetery survived the inundation.

MARTINEZTOWN (Bernalillo; in Albuquerque, near the N end of Broadway). During the 18th century this area was common land where sheep and cattle were grazed by residents of the *villa* of Alburquerque (now Old Town), to the SW. In 1850, Don Manuel Martín moved his family permanently into the area, and a community sprang up. It colloquially was called *Dog Town*, because of its numerous dogs, but it eventually became known as Martineztown, for the Martín family, possibly because the Spanish plural of their surname was *Los Martínes*. Though Martineztown long since has been surrounded by Albuquerque, this neighborhood still retains its identity—and its name.

MASSACRE CANYON (Sierra; heads on the E side of the Black Range and runs S into Las Animas Creek). On September 18, 1879, Apaches led by Victorio (see *Victorio Park*) ambushed pursuing Army troops at the mouth of this canyon and inflicted heavy losses. At least 30 graves of soldiers, mostly African-American "buffalo soldiers," can still be seen nearby.

MASSACRE GAP, MASSACRE PEAK, 5,303 ft. (Doña Ana; NW of Las Cruces, peak is S of the Sierra de las Uvas, 2 mi from the Luna County line). Two explanations—at least—exist for this name, both recalling massacres. One is that in 1870 a Mexican family from La Mesilla was ambushed and killed here by Mexican enemies disguised as Indians. The victims were buried in a common grave. The other is that in 1879 a 14-wagon train of the Ochoa Company freighting between Juarez and Silver City was ambushed by Apaches and massacred, the victims also buried in a common grave. The gap earlier had been called *Magdalena Gap,* for *Magdalena Peak* (see entry) to the NE.

MASSACRE PEAK, 5,667 ft. (Luna; SE of Cookes Peak). Apaches are reported to have used this flat-topped mountain as a lookout from which they planned ambushes. Numerous Apache attacks occurred near here, but the specific one that inspired this name was the so-called Mills Massacre, on the peak's N side on July 21–23, 1861. The Secessionist Emmett Mills and six companions, fleeing California along the Butterfield Trail, were attacked by a large Apache force led by Cochise and Mangas Coloradas. The death toll, especially among the Apaches, was high. The ultimate outcome of the battle is unknown.

MASSEY (Curry; settlement; 15 mi N of Melrose; PO 1909–10, mail to Ard). Massey once had a grocery story, gas station, laundry, and PO. Now all have gone. Name origin unknown.

MATER (Quay; settlement; 17 mi NE of Tucumcari on US 54, 3 mi S of Logan). This locality, now uninhabited, was created in 1901 when the CRI&P RR put in its line between Dalhart, TX, and Santa Rosa. Mater is said to be a family name.

MASTODON (Doña Ana; RR locality; on SP RR, in SE part of county). Mastodon, never more than a RR siding, received its intriguing name from the discovery nearby of the bones of a mastodon, an extinct species of elephant.

MATHEWS CANYON (Chaves; in NW part of county, just S of Elk). Named for Jacob B. "Billy" Mathews, who had a claim at the mouth of this canyon. He sold his claim to John Tunstall, the rancher-merchant-banker who figured in the Lincoln County War. Mathews, who was aligned with the Dolan faction in that conflict, was the "deputized" sheriff who led the posse that was to impound the Tunstall cattle at the Tunstall headquarters on the Rio Felix. Mathews later served as a ranch manager in the area and also as postmaster in Roswell. The canyon has appeared as *Matthew Canyon* and as *Mathew Canyon;* Mathews Canyon is the form in GNIS.

MAVERICK (general). Sometime before the Civil War, Samuel A. Maverick of Decros Point, TX, received as payment for debt a herd of cattle. He placed them in the care of a hired hand, who failed to brand them, and soon unbranded cattle in the area were called "Mavericks." Since then, the term has spread throughout the West to mean any unbranded cow, especially a calf. In NM, where untended cattle were common, 19 places exist named Maverick (GNIS).

MAXWELL (Colfax; settlement; on I-25, 13 mi N of Springer; PO as Maxwell City 1890–1909, as Maxwell 1909–present). This community was established in the late 1880s as a project of the Maxwell Land and Irrigation Co., which was attempting to develop irrigation in the area. At first it was optimistically called *Maxwell City,* then simplified to Maxwell in 1909. See *Maxwell Land Grant.*

MAXWELL LAND GRANT (Colfax, Union, Taos, and parts of Colorado. The most well-known of the Mexican land grants, this once encompassed 1,714,765 acres and was the largest single landholding in the Western Hemisphere. It was granted in 1841 by Gov. Manuel Armijo to Carlos Beaubien, a French trapper, and Guadalupe Miranda of Taos. In 1849 Lucien Bonaparte Maxwell arrived in NM from Kansas and became a hunter and trapper. He married Beaubien's daughter, Luz, and after Beaubien's death in 1864 he bought out the other heirs for $3,000. Maxwell soon established himself as a land baron, supervising a vast array of enterprises that included sheep and cattle ranching, milling, and military procurement. Eventually he sold his vast holdings to foreign investors and moved to Fort Sumner, where he died in 1875.

MAXWELL NATIONAL WILDLIFE REFUGE (Colfax; just NW of village of Maxwell). Approximately 3,000 acres of lakes, marshes, and associated uplands provide habitat and feeding areas for wintering waterfowl and other wildlife.

MAYHILL (Otero; settlement; on US 82, 33 mi E of Peñasco; PO as Upper Peñasco 1884–1902, as Mayhill 1902–present). Albert Coe, among the first settlers in this area, arrived around 1873 and settled about 0.5 mi E of the present townsite. In 1875 he returned to Missouri to marry his childhood sweetheart, Mary L. "Molly" Mahill, and brought her to NM; in 1880 her parents came also, and in 1882 her father, John Mahill, bought the land where the present village is located. The settlement that grew up was known as *Upper Peñasco,* for the Rio Peñasco on which it's located (see also *Peñasco* and *Lower Peñasco*), but in 1902 the community decided to change its name to honor the Mahill family. Unfortunately, the person filling out the application mispelled the name, resulting in the name approved by the postal authorities being Mayhill, not Mahill, and subsequent efforts to change it to the correct spelling have been unsuccessful.

MCALISTER (Quay; settlement; on NM 252 and 312, 36 mi S of Tucumcari; PO 1907–present). A.I. McAlister and his wife were early settlers on the High Plains, and in 1907 they opened a grocery store and PO here, with Mrs. McAlister the first postmistress. Despite being in the midst of very rich farmland, the community began losing population in the 1940s, but an active church and PO have survived, as has the name.

MCCARTYS (Cibola; settlement; on the Acoma Indian Reservation, on NM 124, 13 mi SE of Grants; PO intermittently as both McCarty and McCartys 1887–1911, mail to Seama). Though most persons attribute the English name of this Indian community to a RR contractor whose camp was here, the journalist John H. Beadle mentioned staying at "McCarty's Ranche" in the early 1870s, several years before the RR's arrival. Records of the AT&SF RR records also say the name was derived from a ranch crossed by the original rail line. Beadle described McCarty as a "wandering Irishman," who drifted into these parts, settled, and married a local Hispanic woman.

McCartys and nearby Acomita are outlying villages of Acoma Pueblo; pueblo government offices are at McCartys.

MCDONALD (Lea; settlement; on NM 206, 13 mi N of Lovington; PO 1912–41, 1948–present). This agricultural and oil community, originally located 1 mi E, was named for William C. McDonald, NM's first state governor (1912–17).

MCDONALD LAKE, MCDONALD FLAT (Otero; 9 mi E of Weed). A.C. McDonald arrived in this area from Texas in 1884 and established his ranch headquarters on what is now called McDonald Flat. He ranched the open range with "waterings" scattered throughout the region.

MCGAFFEY (McKinley; settlement; 16 mi SE of Gallup, 8 mi S of Fort Wingate on NM 400; PO 1919–30, 1933–44, mail to Fort Wingate). Once described as the biggest and "most genteel" of the Zuni Mountains lumber camps, McGaffey owes its existence and its name to Amasa B. McGaffey, a trader at Thoreau who became a lumber baron. Starting in 1903 with a string of stores in local lumber camps, McGaffey rapidly expanded his operations to become a RR contractor, cutting ties and poles, eventually becoming a lumberman. In 1910 he organized the McGaffey Co., and the village of McGaffey became his headquarters; in 1912 he built a RR spur from Perea to the village. At one time the community had 200 families, a Catholic church, a five-room school, and a large hall called the Alhambra, for cultural events. Since the collapse of the lumbering boom, the village has shrunk considerably in size and importance, but it still is a scenic, tidy place. *McGaffey Lake* is at the village of McGaffey.

MCGREGOR CITY (Taos; settlement; on the Rio Hondo, several miles upstream from the village of Arroyo Hondo; PO 1882–83, mail to Ranchos de Taos). In May 1881 John McGregor, a prospector, struck a rich vein here that quickly attracted more than 100 other prospectors. Some erected houses and began building a wagon road to their camp, which they appropriately named

McGregor City. But like so many such camps, it was short-lived.

MCHALLIS CANYON (Lincoln; heads on East Capitan Peak and runs NE). Bears a homesteader's name.

MCINTOSH (Torrance; settlement; on NM 41 9 mi S of Moriarty; PO 1906–present). Among the early sheep ranchers in Torrance County was a man named McIntosh, a native of Scotland who settled near Cienega Spring, a good place for lambing, and this community bears his name. McIntosh was a partner in the McIntosh and McGillivray sheep company, and McIntosh held county offices during the early years of Torrance County.

MCKENNA PARK (Catron; 9 mi W of Gila Cliff Dwellings, S of the West Fork of the Gila River). The correct name of this woodland park is *McKinney Park,* for Joe McKinney who built a cabin here. McKinney was a Civil War veteran who scouted for the 8th Cavalry when they were pursuing Apaches. He died at age 70 and was buried at Mogollon. Unfortunately for McKinney's posterity, however, a James McKenna also lived in the area. He was a miner and author of *Black Range Tales,* and over time his name was confused with that of McKinney. *McKenna Creek,* in McKenna Park, originally was known as *McKinney Creek* but also has suffered from mistaken identity.

MCKINLEY COUNTY (western NM; county seat, Gallup). For 10 years prior to this county's creation in 1889, citizens in western Bernalillo and Valencia Counties had agitated for a new county, which they intended to be called *Summit County.* But the popularity of President William McKinley overrode the earlier sentiments, and the new county was named for him. In September 1901 President McKinley was assassinated.

MCKITTRICK (McKinley). See *Pinehaven.*

MCKNIGHT MOUNTAIN, 10,165 ft. (Grant-Sierra; on the crest of the Black Range, S of Reeds Peak). While the origin of this name is not certain, it's worth mentioning that Robert McKnight was a prominent figure in this region in the early 19th century. In 1828 he was hired by Kit Carson as a scout, and later he mined copper at Santa Rita until forced by Apaches in the late 1830s to abandon his mine. *McKnight Canyon* heads on McKnight Mountain and runs SW into the Rio Mimbres.

MCLEAN (Curry; settlement; N of Pleasant Hill, 1 mi from the Texas line, 18 mi N of Texico; PO 1907–09, mail to Hollene). George McLean was a homesteader who used to run sheep where Clovis is today, and he started a store and PO here. The resulting community, now abandoned, took his name.

MCMILLAN (Eddy). See *Lakewood.*

MCNEES CREEK, MCNEES CROSSING (Union). See *Corrumpa Creek.*

MCPHERSON (San Miguel). See *Sands.*

MCWILLIAMS CANYON (Colfax; heads 15 mi NW of Raton and runs NW into Colorado). Named for a Baptist minister who made his home here in the 1870s.

MEADOW LAKE (Valencia; settlement; E of Los Lunas, just S of the Isleta Indian Reservation, near the W foothills of the Manzano Mountains). In 1966 developer D.W. Falls purchased 814 acres from Don Pope and began planning a community. Using new and existing wells, he created a small lake, and in 1967 the first residents arrived, David and Eleanor Ross, at the village named for the lake. By 1981 109 families were living at Meadow Lake, and the community has continued to grow since then.

THE MEADOWS (San Juan; about 6 mi N of Fruitland). In the 1850s and 1860s cattlemen established residences here and used the thick, tall grass for grazing. Today the land has been fenced, and its owners live in nearby communities.

MEDANALES (Rio Arriba; settlement; on NM 233, 1 mi E of US 84, on the E side of the Rio Chama, 8 mi SE of Abiquiu; PO 1945–present). The Spanish *medanales* means " sand dunes, hills, banks," but it also is a Spanish family name. Which meaning inspired the name of this community is not known.

LOS MEDANOS (Eddy; in E part of county, NE of NM 128). NM Spanish, "the sand dunes, hills, banks."

MEDIO DIA CANYON (Sandoval; on the S side of the Jemez Mountains, heads W of Bandelier National Monument and runs SE toward the Rio Grande). Spanish, "noon"; origin unknown, though it possibly results from sunlight not reaching the bottom of this very deep canyon until noon. More likely, though, this name is derived from the Spanish *mediodia,* "south."

MEEK (Lincoln; settlement; on the NE side of the Capitan Mountains; PO 1904–22, mail to Tinnie). Few people recall this abandoned community, which took the surname of its first postmaster, Thomas B. Meek.

MEERSCHAUM (Grant; settlement; on the Sapillo River, about 1.5 mi E of NM 15). This was to be a company mining town of the American Meerschaum Co. working local deposits of meerschaum, a soft, light, claylike mineral used for carving into tobacco pipes. The town was short-lived, but the name *Meerschaum Canyon* recalls the enterprise.

MELOCHE (Colfax; settlement; 10 mi S of Raton). Abandoned settlement, named for Tony Meloche, owner of the TO Ranch.

MELROSE (Curry; settlement; on US 60-84 and NM 267 and 268, 25 mi W of Clovis; PO as Brownhorn 1905–06, as Melrose 1906–present). This area was settled around 1882, and when a community sprang up it was called *Brownhorn,* combining the surnames of Walter "Wildhorse" Brown and Lonny Horn, owner of the Pigpen Ranch; the two men maintained adjacent POs. But in 1906, when the SF RR selected Brownhorn as the site of a roundhouse and laid out a formal townsite, they called it Melrose, for Melrose, OH, and that's the name that's survived, though a Brownhorn Street in Melrose recalls the earlier name.

MELVIN (Mora; settlement; exact location unknown; PO 1895–99, mail to Wagon Mound). This was a short-lived farming and ranching community, that George Adlai Feather said was named for Melvin Mills, who also gave his name to the village of Mills (see entry) in Harding County.

MEMPHIS (Taos; settlement; on Bitter Creek, 5 mi NE of the village of Red River). This abandoned mining camp, located in the Keystone Mining District, took its name from the Memphis mining claim.

MENTMORE (McKinley; settlement; 1 mi N of I-40 and NM 118, 5 mi W of Gallup; PO 1916–present). This settlement was created with the opening of the Dilco coal mine in 1913, and originally the camp was called *Dilco,* but when a PO was established it took the name Mentmore, for reasons unknown. The mines closed here in 1952, but the settlement has managed to survive.

MESA, MESITA, MESILLA (general). Though the Spanish *mesa* means, literally, "table," in western North America it has become a generic term for flat-topped landforms, as well as for level areas abutting higher eminences. The diminutive is *mesita* or *mesilla.*

MESA (Chaves; settlement; on US 285, 39 mi NW of Roswell). This store and filling station was named for the small mesa to the E.

MESA CHIVATO (Cibola; in NE part of county, N of Cebolleta). Extensive mesa, known by several names, including *Banco del Cerro Chivato, Cebolleta Mountains, Mount Taylor Mesa, Sierra Chivato,* and *Sierra Chivoto,* but in 1963 the USBGN settled upon Mesa Chivato. See *Chivato (general).*

MESA MONTOSA (general). Spanish, "wooded mesa." The name appears three times in Rio Arriba County and once in San Miguel County.

MESA POLEO (Rio Arriba; settlement; in N foothills of the Jemez Mountains, SW of Coyote). The mesa and the diffuse inhabited settlement named for it bear the Spanish name of an herb probably known in English as "false pennyroyal," (genus *Hedeoma*).

MESA PRIETA (Rio Arriba). See *Black Mesa (Rio Arriba).*

MESA REDONDA (Quay; 12 mi S of Tucumcari). Mesa Redonda, Spanish "round mesa," is not round. Rather, say local residents, it's so deeply incised that it's actually two mesas; the larger, southern one is shaped like a horseshoe, its open end pointed NW; perhaps the rounded southern end inspired the name. An old stage road once passed through the gap between the two mesas, and the stage stop there took the name *Mesa Redonda.* In 1899 John Spikes and his family moved to this area and began ranching, but they became embroiled in one of the range disputes common at the time, and two Spikes brothers were killed; *Spikes Creek,* bearing their name, runs NW from Mesa Redonda.

MESA RICA (San Miguel; settlement; on NM 104, 5 mi S of Conchas Reservoir; PO 1938–41, mail to Newkirk). This tiny inhabited settlement took its name from nearby *Mesa Rica,* Spanish "rich mesa," a large landform said to have been named because a group of 49er's returning from the California goldfields were massacred here by Indians, who took the gold and hid it on the mesa. Another story says it was a gold-bearing burro train that was ambushed, and the gold was hidden by a few survivors.

MESCALERO (general). The term Mescalero, "mescal maker," was used by the Spanish to refer to one of NM's major Apache groups, because of their extensive use of the mescal plant. This plant, also called agave, provided the Indians not only with food in several forms but also with fibers and a fermented beverage. At least eight NM place names include Mescalero (GNIS). See *Mescalero* and *Mescalero Apache Indian Reservation.*

MESCALERO (Otero; settlement; 16 mi NE of Tularosa on US 70; PO as White Sulphur Springs 1875, as South Fork 1875–87, as Mescalero 1887–present). Sometime after the Civil War, ex-solders, particularly those from the California Column, began settling in this area. In 1875 a PO was established and called *White Sulphur Springs,* then *South Fork* (the modern community is located at the junction of South Fork and North Fork of Tularosa Canyon), but later the PO was moved to *Blazers Mill,* where Dr. Joseph H. Blazer served as postmaster. Around 1887 the PO moved again, this time to the home of the agent for the Mescalero Apaches, whose reservation had been established here four years earlier, and the PO was renamed Mescalero. The community is the headquarters for the tribe.

MESCALERO APACHE INDIAN RESERVATION (Otero; N and S of US 70 E of Tularosa, encompassing parts of both the White Mountains and the Sacramento Mountains). By the early 1850s, Territorial records showed the Mescalero Apaches as "claiming" all of SE NM, land that certainly coincides with much of their traditional tribal territory, and in 1857 this was designated the *Mescalero Reserve.* Two treaties, in 1852 and 1855, formalizing boundaries were not ratified by Congress, so the Mescaleros' first experience with a reservation was in the early 1860s, when they were interned with the Navajos at Fort Sumner; in 1865 they abruptly decamped. In 1869, a new reservation, encompassing most of the Mescaleros' traditional hunting grounds, was created, but presidential proclamations in 1873 and 1882 shrank these boundaries, opening new land for settlement and mineral development. Finally, in 1883, the Mescaleros were given their own reservation, and since then they have skillfully managed its natural resources to develop one of the nation's most prosperous Indian reservations. See also *Apache (general).*

MESCALERO RIDGE (Chaves, Lea; begins in E part of Chaves County and runs N, paralleling Lea County line, for almost 50 miles). Named for the Mescalero Apaches who hunted here. *Mescalero Spring* and *Mescalero Point* are located along this ridge, while *Mescalero Valley* is to the W.

MESCALERO SANDS (Eddy; 6 mi N of Loco Hills). Drifting sand dunes, named for the Mescalero Apaches who once were here.

MESILLA (Doña Ana; settlement; on NM 28, 2 mi SW of Las Cruces; PO 1858–present). Though this site may have been recognized and named by early Spanish explorers and settlers, the settlement's modern history began in 1850, following the Mexican War and the treaty of Guadalupe Hidalgo. A group of Mexicans living on the E side of the Rio Grande in what had suddenly become American territory wished to retain Mexican citizenship, so they moved W across the river to here, which was still part of Chihuahua. The settlement took the name Mesilla, often also referred to as *La Mesilla* or *Old Mesilla,* for its location on a small tableland rising above the Rio Grande floodplain; the parish was named *San Albino,* since it was founded on that saint's feast day, March 1. The residents petitioned the Mexican government for a land grant, and in 1853 the Mexican government approved what became known as the *Mesilla Civil Colony Grant.* The Mexicans' efforts to distance themselves from the Americans were in vain, however, for in 1854 the Gadsden Purchase realigned the international boundary again, and Mesilla became part of the US. The settlement thrived, but its fortunes declined when the AT&SF RR routed its line through Las Cruces, and Mesilla lost the county seat. Still, the settlement has survived, even prospered, and Mesilla has retained its historic character. Because of a shift in the Rio Grande's channel, the town now is on the river's E side.

MESILLA PARK (Doña Ana; settlement; adjoining University Park at Las Cruces on US 80; PO 1892–present). In 1887, after the village of Mesilla surrendered its status as county seat to nearby Las Cruces, a group of citizens formed two land companies, the second being called Mesilla Park, for the Mesilla Valley (see entry) in which it was located. When the state agricultural college was established in 1889, the new settlement prospered. Today, Mesilla Park is a neighborhood of Las Cruces, but it retains its PO—and its name.

MESILLA VALLEY (Doña Ana; extends along the Rio Grande from Radium Springs S to El Paso, TX). Cotton, chile, pecans, and other crops are grown in this fertile valley, which has NM's largest area of irrigated farmland. The Mesilla Valley is divided into *Upper* and *Lower,* with Las Cruces the approximate dividing line.

MESITA (Cibola; settlement; on the S bank of the Rio San Jose, on I-40, 5 mi SE of Laguna). This small inhabited settlement within the Laguna Indian Reservation was established in the late 1870s by members of a conservative faction of Laguna Indians who felt threatened by the faction then dominant in the pueblo. The village took its name from a small mesa nearby.

MESQUITE (general). Mesquite is the the English spelling of the Mexican-Spanish *mezquite,* derived in turn from the Nahuatl *mizquitl.* In NM mesquite refers to plants of the genus *Prosopis,* a member of the pea family. Here mesquite is a large shrub or small tree whose wood has fueled countless fires and whose beans are eaten by a wide variety of animals. GNIS lists 8 Mesquite names.

MESQUITE (Doña Ana; settlement; on NM 478, 12 mi SE of Las Cruces; PO 1913–present). This farming community was established in 1882 and named by RR executives for the many mesquite bushes here.

MEXICAN CREEK (Colfax; in the N part of the Moreno Valley, flows into Moreno Creek). Named for Mexican gold miners from Elizabethtown who made adobes here.

MEXICAN SPRINGS (Hidalgo). See *Shakespeare.*

MEXICAN SPRINGS (McKinley; settlement; 20 mi N of Gallup, 3 mi W of US 666; PO 1939–43, 1950–85). This translates the Navajo name for this settlement, *Nakaibito,* pronounced Na-KAI-bi-toh. The name results from the water hole here being frequented by early Spanish expeditions into the area.

MEXICO CITY (Lea; settlement; 15 mi SE of Hobbs). Mexico City was the name given, for reasons unknown, to a new oil town promoted in 1928 during the oil boom here, but its hopes were not realized.

MIAMI (Colfax; settlement; on NM 21 13 mi W of Springer; PO 1908–75, mail to rural branch of Springer). Around 1908, a group of promoters from Miami, OH, inspected land along Rayado Creek, along an old stage route between Springer and Elizabethtown, and decided it would be good farming country. After meetings with the Maxwell Land Grant Co., they interested German Dunkards and other religious groups in settling in the area, and the resulting community took the name of the town in Ohio, which in turn took its name from an Indian tribe in the Midwest. (The Arizona mining town of Miami also was named by settlers from Miami, OH.) *Miami Lake* is 6 mi W of Miami.

MICHO (Lea; settlement; 3 mi SE of Tatum; PO 1920–21, mail to Tatum). Ephemeral community, name origin unknown.

MIDDLE FORK LAKE (Taos; in the Sangre de Cristo Mountains, S of the village of Red River). Located at the head of the Middle Fork of the Red River.

MIDNIGHT (Taos; settlement; about 4 mi NE of the village of Red River; PO 1895–98, mail to Cerro). During its brief existence Midnight enjoyed a reputation as a rip-roaring mining camp, and folklore has it the camp was named because midnight was the liveliest time of day. In fact, however, the town was laid out by miners working the Midnight Mine here and named for it. The camp often was referred to as *Midnight City.*

MIDWAY (Chaves; settlement; 9 mi SE of Roswell on NM 2; PO 1907–33, mail to Dexter). This inhabited settlement now is known as Midway, because when the townsite was filed in 1903 it was midway between Roswell and Dexter. It was named *Cumberland* in 1907 by the Rev. Charles W. Lewis, first settler and president of the Cumberland Development Co. A church was built in 1908, followed soon by Cumberland College. But World War I ended the college and other development, and the settlement was all but a ghost town by the 1930s. It has since been resettled and has taken the name Midway. The local Cumberland Water Assoc. preserves the old name.

MIDWAY (Lea; settlement; NE of Lovington; PO 1909–17, mail to Plainview). This abandoned settlement was named because its school stood "midway" on the NM-Texas border. During the 1950s the community was called *Antioch,* for a nearby church.

MIDWAY (Luna; settlement; midway between Deming and Hermanas; PO 1909–18). The townsite here was mapped in 1909 and named for its location, but the small community vanished when EP&SW RR tracks later were taken up.

MIDWAY (Socorro; settlement; near San Marcial). On the roadway linking Old and New San Marcial was a cluster of houses known as Midway, and the name appeared on some maps and the 1920 and 1930 US Census records. It also was known as *Torres Junction.*

MIERA (general). The earliest Miera recorded in NM was Bernardo Miera y Pacheco, the military officer and mapmaker who was in Santa Fe as early as 1756, when he was *alcalde mayor* of Galisteo and Pecos.

MIERA (Bernalillo). See *Yrisarri.*

MIERA (Union; settlement; in S-central part of county, near the Harding County line, on Tramperos Creek; PO as Miera 1889–1904, 1905–10, as Reyes 1910–18, as Miera 1918–27, mail to Clapham). In the spring of 1873 Juan Miera was living in Watrous when he, his 21-year-old son, Francisco, and his 16-year-old son, Andres, journeyed E seeking a well-watered grazing area for their large flocks of sheep. They found such a place on Tramperos Creek, spent the summer here, returned the next year to establish a permanent camp that soon was known as Miera. In 1889, Francisco established a PO at the little settlement and became its first postmaster. Later, the PO was briefly called *Reyes,* doubtless for a local family, then Miera again. Eventually the original community, or *Old Miera,* gave way to *New Miera,* located several miles downstream at a ford. Both localities are abandoned now, though descendants of the Mieras still live in Union County.

MIESSE (Luna). See *Silton.*

MILAGRO (Guadalupe; settlement; 2.5 mi S of I-40, 35 mi W of Santa Rosa; PO intermittently 1916–35, mail to Palma).

Spanish, "miracle." Local people tell that the name was inspired by a group of early Hispanic travelers on the arid plains miraculously finding a spring here, and indeed a spring approximately 4 mi W of the original village still is called *Milagro Spring.* The village originally was 2.5 mi S of what is now I-40; it later moved to become a filling station and bus stop on US 66 between Albuquerque and Amarillo. Though a highway exit on I-40 still marks Milagro, only ranches are here now.

MILAGROS (Bernalillo; settlement; in the central Manzano Mountains; PO 1902–06, mail to Chilili). Spanish, "miracles." The locality, site of a health resort, took the name of the nearby Milagros Mine.

MILAN (Cibola; settlement; 3 mi W of Grants on I-40 and NM 122 and 605). When the 1950s uranium mining boom occurred near here, this town sprang up and was incorporated in 1957. It took the name of Salvador Milán, who with his wife, Veneranda Mirabal, had large land holdings here. When Milán died in 1979 at the age of 70, he had been Milan's only mayor. He had been born in Mexico, the 11th of 12 children; the family moved to Gallup in 1913 to work in the coal mines, and Milán moved to the Grants area in 1932. Local pronunciation accents the second syllable.

MILKHOUSE DRAW, MESA (Sierra; 27 mi SW of Truth or Consequences). A milkhouse at one time was here.

MILL (general). Throughout the US places were named Mill because a mill was located there. In NM the mill often was a sawmill. The Spanish form is *molino.*

MILLER (Cibola; settlement; 12 mi S of Acoma; PO 1911–12, mail to Acomita). Abandoned community, name origin unknown.

MILLER (Eddy). See *Artesia.*

MILLER (Sandoval). See *Guadalupe.*

MILLER FLAT (Otero; just E of Weed). Named for the J.B. Miller family. G.W. Holland and F.E. Goodman maintained a small general store in the area in the mid–1880s.

MILLIGAN, MILLIGANS PLAZA (Catron). See *Reserve.*

MILLIGAN GULCH (Socorro; rises in the Cat Mountains and runs SE into Elephant Butte Reservoir). Named for a ranching family whose members still live in the area. Earlier the gulch had been known as *La Cañada de la Cruz,* "canyon of the cross."

MILLIGAN RANCH (Socorro; on the W bank of the Rio Grande, S of Fort Craig, immediately S of Milligan Gulch). The 1880 US Census reported 83 residents here, making it a sizable settlement. This census also mentioned a William Milligan, 37, who was a retired soldier from Fort Craig who had established the ranch.

MILLIGAN (Socorro). See *San Marcial.*

MILLS (Harding; settlement; on NM 39 10 mi NW of Roy; PO 1898–1901, 1908–present). Melvin W. Mills was a rancher, lawyer, and entrepreneur. Among his many projects was an orchard, with 14,000 trees, along a 10-mile stretch of the floodplain of the Canadian River W of here, but a flood in 1904 destroyed all his work. He died in 1925, a broken man, in the mansion he had built in Springer, but it then belonged to his former law partner, Thomas B. Catron, and Mills was forced to beg to be allowed to die on a cot in his old home. The settlement named for Mills is now almost a ghost town, though a few inhabited residences remain.

MILNESAND (Roosevelt; settlement; at junction of NM 206, 258, and 262, 38 mi S of Portales; PO 1915–present). Milnesand was settled around 1913 by homesteaders from Texas and Oklahoma. A descendant of one of the original settlers explained the name: "Because of the deep sandy soil and the three windmills on the Jodie Ranch 1 mi from Milnesand it was called Mill-in-sand."

MIMBRES (general). Spanish, "willows." The Spanish applied the term *Mimbreños* to an Apache group who lived in SW NM, and Mimbres also designates a prehistoric Indian culture famous for its decorated pottery. Most NM Mimbres names are in SW NM and are derived for their association with the

Mimbres River (see entry), doubtless named in turn for willows growing along its banks.

MIMBRES (Grant; settlement; on NM 35, 6 mi NW of San Lorenzo, on the Mimbres River; PO 1886–present). Named for the river.

MIMBRES HOT SPRINGS (Grant; settlement; 6 mi SE of San Lorenzo, 2 mi E of NM 61; PO 1878–79). Like other features in the area, named for the river. A few inhabited residences remain here.

MIMBRES LAKE (Grant; on the crest of the Black Range, 2 mi NE of McKnight Mountain). Located at the headwaters of the Mimbres River (see entry).

MIMBRES MOUNTAINS (Grant, Sierra). See *Black Range.*

MIMBRES RIVER (Grant, Luna; heads in the Black Range NE of Mimbres and flows S toward the Mexican border past Deming). This appears as *Valle de las Mimbres* on Juan Nentwig's map of 1762. It probably was named for osiers along its banks; see *Mimbres (general).*

MINCO (Roosevelt; settlement; 6 mi NW of Causey; PO 1909–13, mail to Carter). Abandoned homesteader settlement, origin of name unknown.

MINEOSA (Quay; settlement; near Union County line, 9 mi NW of Nara Visa; PO 1908–13, mail to Nara Visa). This name is possibly a misspelling of *miniosa,* Spanish, "containing *minio,*" a lead compound. On the basis of rumors that the RR would be arriving here, a townsite was laid out, but the rumors proved false, and the townsite remained only that.

MINERAL CITY (San Miguel; settlement; about 25 mi W of Las Vegas, at the junction of Tecolote Creek and Blue Canyon; PO 1881–83, mail to Las Vegas). Mineral City was a mining camp that flowered in the early 1880s; it had stores, the elegant 20-room Fairview Hotel, and a weekly newspaper. But in the late 1890s the ore played out, and Mineral City went the way of so many other short-lived NM mining towns.

MINERAL CREEK (Catron; heads S of Silver Peak and runs SW into the San Francisco River near Alma). Named for extensive mineralization and mining in

the area. A flood here in 1911 destroyed much of the mining camp of Cooney, located here.

MINERAL CREEK (Sierra; heads in the Black Range just E of the Continental Divide and runs E to Chloride). Coincides with a heavily mineralized area.

MINERAL HILL (San Miguel; settlement; on NM 283, 9 mi W of Las Vegas; PO as Lesperance 1890–96, as Geronimo 1896–1902, as Mineral Hill 1902–36, mail to Las Vegas). Pedro Lesperance, a descendant of a French trapper, also named Pedro Lesperance, was the first postmaster here and gave the community its first official name, *Lesperance.* Later the name was changed to *Geronimo,* for the village of *Los Valles de San Gerónimo* 3 mi to the S. And finally it took the name Mineral Hill, for ore deposits in the area. Once much more populous, Mineral Hill still has a few residents.

MINERAL SPRINGS (Valencia; settlement; location unknown; PO 1877–78). Abandoned community, origin of name unknown.

MISHAWAKA (San Miguel; settlement; 18 mi SE of Las Vegas; PO 1910–11, mail to Casa Grande). About 1908 families from Mishawaka, IN, settled here and attempted dry-land farming. Despite a townsite plat, a settlement never developed; nonetheless, for years all locations in the vicinity were said to be in Mishawaka. By the 1930s, the failure of dry-land farming had become evident, and now even the name is dying.

MISSOURI PLAZA (Chaves; settlement; 13 mi W of Roswell, on the Rio Hondo). Around 1865 Spanish-speaking settlers from Manzano in Torrance County arrived here and established the first settlement in what is now Chaves County. The community originally was called *La Plaza de San José.* In 1867 the Hispanic pioneers were joined by two English-speaking families, who maintained a general store here. Many of the men were freighters to Kansas City and St. Joseph, MO, so they began calling their settlement *La Plaza de Missouri,* to give it distinction. But around 1870 upstream irrigation reduced the water flow in the Rio Hondo, and Missouri Plaza was abandoned. Today only foundations remain.

MISSOURI SETTLEMENT (Curry; settlement; about 12 mi N of Melrose). In 1906 14 men from Missouri came to NM to homestead here. Later other Missourians came, and the community came to be known as Missouri Settlement; its school and church were called *Prairie Valley*. Now the settlement has vanished, though the name Prairie Valley survives.

MITCHELL (Lea; settlement; near Maljamar). Abortive oil community, promoted in 1931, its main street to be called Wall Street, but the development fizzled.

MITCHELL (McKinley). See *Thoreau*.

MOCKINGBIRD GAP, 5,240 ft. (Socorro; passes between the San Andres Mountains and the Oscura Mountains to connect the Jornada del Muerto with the Tularosa Valley). This pass, now on the White Sands Missile Range, was named by soldiers pursuing Indians for mockingbirds here. The gap also named the *Mockingbird Mountains*, a minor group just SW of the gap; highest elevation 7,475 ft.

MODOC (Doña Ana; settlement; about 7 mi S of Organ, at the W foot of the Organ Mountains; PO 1901–03, mail to Las Cruces). This mining camp owed its existence—and its name—to the Modoc Mine. The mine was worked intermittently from 1879 to 1905, producing mostly lead but also some silver and copper. When the mine died, so did the settlement. Only ruins remain.

MOGOLLON (general). Found on numerous features throughout SW NM, this name, pronounced muggy-YOHN, likely commemorates Juan Ignacio de Flores Mogollón, governor of NM from 1712 to 1715. He may have been involved in the discovery and development of mineral deposits in SW NM. But given the obscure nature of the name and lack of documentation of the commemoration, it is possible the name has another origin. Stanley Crocchiola speculated thus:

"*Mogollón* may mean a parasite or a bore. Personally I doubt the name is Spanish. It seems to be Mexican. There is a word in Mexico, *mogollo*, which is the name for a thin cake or bread such as was made by the Indians. Again, *mogollón* in Mexico means a gawk, a *tonto*. Now the Spaniards called Indians of the region Tonto Apaches. The New Mexicans may have substituted Mogollon, which meant the same thing."

The first features named Mogollon in this region probably were the mountains, with other Mogollon features named for them. The name also appears on several features in Arizona, the most prominent and well-known being the *Mogollon Rim*, the huge linear escarpment that divides the topography of eastern Arizona; see *Mogollon Plateau*.

MOGOLLON (Catron; settlement; on NM 159, 9.2 mi E of junction US 180, 4 mi N of Glenwood; PO 1890–present). The first mining camp in this area was Clairmont (see entry), followed by Cooney (see entry). Then in 1889, when John Eberle's Last Chance Mine turned into a bonanza, he built a permanent residence at the mine, and when Henry Hermann moved his lumber mill from Cooney, the boom town of Mogollon was on its way, soon overshadowing the other two. The town took its name from the surrounding Mogollon Mountains (see entry). A PO opened in 1890, a school in 1892. The town survived a fire in 1894, and later a flood; by 1900, when the Fannie Mill was built, the town had 2,000 residents. Eventually, $2 million in gold and silver were taken from the area, mostly silver.

But with the decline in gold and silver prices during WWI Mogollon also began to decline, a trend that culminated during WWII, despite a brief revival 1931–42. The Little Fannie Mine survived until 1950. Today tourism keeps what remains of the town alive.

MOGOLLON BALDY PEAK, 10,770 ft. (Catron; at the S end of the Mogollon Mountains, just N of the Grant County line). Sometimes called *Mogollon Peak*. See *Mogollon (general)*.

MOGOLLON CREEK (Catron, Grant; heads S of Mogollon Baldy and flows S into the Gila River). Its major tributary is the *West Fork Mogollon Creek,* which heads NW of Mogollon Baldy. See *Mogollon (general).*

MOGOLLON MOUNTAINS (Catron, Grant; large complex, S of Reserve, N of Cliff, E of the San Francisco River). The name *S. de Mogollón Nacimiento de Xila,* "Mogollon Mountains, birthplace of the Gila," appears on Juan Nentwig's 1762 map of this region. See *Mogollon (general).*

MOGOLLON PLATEAU (Catron, Grant; includes much of these counties). As Herbert Ungnade explained, "This area, about 100 mi in diameter, was formed 25 to 40 million years ago during a period of greater volcanic activity in the S part of NM. It includes the Mogollon, San Francisco, Long Canyon, Tularosa, Elk, Saliz, Kelly, Jerky, Diablo, and Pinos Altos Mountains. All of these consist of lava flows, tufa, ashes, pumice, and other volcanic materials." See *Mogollon (general).*

MOGOTE (general). Mexican Spanish, meaning "isolated grove or clump of trees or scrub brush" as well as "hummock, hillock." *Mogote* also is said to be a Spanish word referring to the horns of a young animal but used metaphorically for a mountain.

MOLYBDENUM (Taos; settlement; on NM 38, between Questa and Red River). This is the site of the Molycorp plant, which processes molybdenum ore mined here.

MONCUS CANYON (Quay; in S part of county, near Ima). The Moncus family settled here in 1902; later they established a store and PO at Ima (see entry). Black Jack Ketchum and his outlaws used the canyon as a hideout.

MONERO (Rio Arriba; settlement; on US 64, 9 mi E of Dulce; PO 1884–1963, mail to Lumberton). *Monero* means "money" in Italian, and at the time of its settlement in 1884 as a small coal-mining community a number of Italians lived here. Now it is all but abandoned.

MONIA CREEK (Union; flows E across S tip of county into Texas). This doubtless is a corruption of the Spanish *monilla,* a shrub that grows here.

MONICA (Socorro; settlement; N of Mount Withington, on NM 168; PO 1881–83, mail to Socorro). The origin of the name of this short-lived settlement is unknown. *Monica Canyon* and *Monica Spring* are on the slopes of Mount Withington.

MONISTA (Otero). See *Holloman Air Force Base.*

MONJEAU MOUNTAIN, 9,641 ft. (Lincoln; in the Sacramento Mountains, NE of Sierra Blanca). It's said a Frenchman by this name once had mining claims in this area; George Adlai Feather told of a prominent preacher named Montjeau who had extensive mining interests near White Oaks. The mountain now is the site of a USFS fire lookout.

MONTE APLANADO (Mora; settlement; about 4 mi SW of Mora). Spanish, "flat mountain." Inhabited hamlet in the foothills of the Sangre de Cristo Mountains. Sometimes this appears on maps as *Pacheco Village,* for the Pacheco family here.

MONTE CRISTO (Catron; settlement; in the Mogollon Mountains, exact location unknown). Ephemeral mining camp that doubtless took its name from *The Count of Monte Cristo,* a popular romance by Alexander Dumas.

MONTECITO (Rio Arriba; settlement; on the S bank of Embudo Creek, 1 mi SE of Dixon). Spanish, "little mount, woods." Tiny inhabited locality.

MONTERREY (Otero). See *West Tularosa.*

MONTEZUMA (Sandoval; settlement; 0.5 mi E of Placitas; 1879–80). The former settlement was associated with the Montezuma Mine.

MONTEZUMA (San Miguel; settlement; NM 65, 6 mi NW of Las Vegas; PO 1924–present). In 1841, Julian and Antonio Donaldson, aware of the potential value of the hot springs here, obtained from the local *alcalde* a grant to the site, and in 1846 they had a small bathhouse here, which could be used for a fee. In 1879 the SF RR bought the site and the next year constructed a 75-room hotel named the Montezuma, for the Aztec ruler conquered by Cortes, a name likely inspired by a Pecos Indian legend that

Montezuma had journeyed here for the springs' healing waters. The hotel later became the Montezuma Seminary and most recently the site of United World College.

MONTEZUMA (Socorro; settlement; location unknown; PO 1896–1900, mail to Eastview). Abandoned community, name origin unknown.

MONTICELLO (Bernalillo; settlement; on the N side of Tijeras Canyon, 3 mi E of Albuquerque). Recent residential area located in the lower portion of Three Gun Spring Canyon, bearing a name likely chosen when the area underwent residental development shortly after WW II.

MONTICELLO (Sierra; settlement; on NM 142, 21 mi NW of Truth or Consequences; PO as Montecillo 1881–92, as Monticello 1892–present). This locality on Alamosa Creek was settled in 1856 and was originally called *Cañada Alamosa,* for its location in a cottonwood-lined canyon by that name. (The Cañada Alamosa that once gave its name to the the town now bears the town's present name and is called *Monticello Canyon.*) In 1874 two French brothers, Alphonse and Aristide Bourguet, immigrated to the US. Later, they followed their aunt, Sarah Bourguet, to New Mexico, where she'd been living in Socorro since 1850. The brothers settled in Cañada de Alamosa, where their descendants still live. In 1892 Aristide applied for a post office; the name he submitted was Monticello (Cañada de Alamosa would have been rejected as being too long and violating the policy current then of postal names being one word). The Bourguets say Aristide chose the name Monticello because Alphonse Bourguet had served as postmaster in Monticello, NY, after arriving in the US. *Monticello Canyon* heads at Monticello and runs SE to the Rio Grande, crossing I-25 12 mi N of Truth or Consequences.

MONTOSA (general). A common corruption of the Spanish *montuousa,* "hilly, mountainous, well-wooded."

MONTOYA (San Miguel). See *Los Montoyas.*

MONTOYA (Quay; settlement; on US 54, 21 mi W of Tucumcari; PO as Rountree 1901–02, as Montoya 1902—1972, mail to a rural Tucumcari branch). The coming of the CRI&P RR in 1902 stimulated the growth of a community here, which took the name *Rountree,* for its first postmaster, Henry K. Rountree, but the next year it changed its name to Montoya, likely at the suggestion of the RR. Many Montoya residents have departed, though a few inhabitants remain.

MONUMENT (Lea; settlement; on NM 8, 9 mi SW of Hobbs; PO 1900–present). Monument was the first permanent settlement in what is Lea County and was named for *Monument Spring* (see entry) about 3 mi W of the town. Jim Cook built a general store here and established a PO. Monument later was eclipsed by other settlements, but it was revitalized during the oil boom of the 1930s, and it remains primarily an oil-patch community. *Monument Draw,* S of Monument, runs NW-SE between NM 8 and NM 18.

MONUMENT CANYON (Otero; heads at Monument Spring and runs SE to the Sacramento River). Named for the spring, at which a monument had been constructed.

MONUMENT MOUNTAIN, 8,401 ft. (Catron; 3 mi S of San Francisco River, 6 mi NW of Reserve). A pile of rocks, presumed to have been heaped up by Indians, is at the summit of this.

MONUMENT PEAK, 5,682 ft. (Sierra; 2 mi E of Lake Valley). Named for a large, black formation at the steeper end of the mountain. The Army once flashed heliograph messages from this peak.

MONUMENT SPRING (Lea; about 12 mi SW of Hobbs, 3 mi W of the village of Monument). In 1875, on his expedition against the Plains Indians, Col. William Rufus Shafter came here and in his report wrote: "Monument Spring is so named from a monument I had built on a hill SW and 1.2 mi distant from the spring. This monument is of nearly white stone, about 8 ft in diameter at the base, four at the top, and 7.25 ft high. It can be seen for several miles in all directions." At the time, the spring was the only permanent natural water in any quantity in the entire southern Llano Estacado, and while the monument later was torn down by buffalo hunters to build a fort and corrals, the spring, the ranch associated with it, and the name still survive, as does the nearby village of Monument (see entry).

MOONSHINE CANYON (Catron; a tributary of the Middle Fork of the Gila River). Old-timers say the best grain in Catron County was grown near here, and to save shipping expenses farmers converted the grain into the more concentrated form of bootleg whiskey.

MOORAD (Socorro). See *Veguita.*

MOORE (Quay; settlement; 9 mi S of Tucumcari; PO 1903–12, mail to Tucumcari). Abandoned community, named for its first postmaster, John A. Moore.

MOQUINO (Cibola; settlement; 12 mi N of Laguna, between Paguate and Cebolleta, 1 mi E of Bibo). Inhabited hamlet likely named for Miguel Moquino, one of four individuals who claimed ownership of the area around Paguate (see entry) and Moquino prior to the Paguate Purchase. The short *Río Moquino* heads just W of here; *Arroyo Moquino* is just to the E.

MORA (Mora; settlement, county seat; at the junction of NM 518, 94, and 434, on the Mora River; PO 1864–present). Encouraged by Gov. Alberto Maynez's policy of encouraging new settlements, Hispanic settlers moved into the Mora Valley in 1816, but long before then the valley had been used as a thoroughfare for Indians, trappers, and traders traveling between the upper Rio Grande and the Plains, and from that the name Mora, referring to an entire region and not just a settlement, most likely is derived. The earliest documents and settlers never referred to the locality simply as Mora but rather as *Demora,* meaning a "camp, a stopover," from the Spanish noun, *demora,* "delay." For this reason, the place often was referred to as *Lo de Mora,* or "stopping place." Later, other etymologies were advanced. One is that the name was derived from persons surnamed Mora. This explanation is not to be discounted entirely, because persons such as Mora Pineda and García de la Mora came into NM with the reconquest in 1692, and persons with this surname lived at the frontier of what is now Mora County at the end of the 18th century. Another version is that the name comes from *moras,* or "mulberries," growing in the area, though persons in the county say mulberries aren't common here. Josiah Gregg, in *Commerce of the Prairies* (1844), wrote of the Mora River: "As mora means mulberry, and this fruit is to be found at the mouth of this stream [at the Canadian River], one would suppose that it had acquired its name from that fact, did not the Mexicans always call it *Río de lo de Mora,* thus leaving it to be inferred that the name had originated from some individual who had settled upon it." Most fanciful of all is the story that the French trapper Ceran St. Vrain in 1823 found a dead man on the banks of the Rio la Casa and called the place *L'Eau de Mort,* "the water of the dead."

The first settlement here was called *San Antonio de lo de Mora,* and it lasted until 1833, when Plains Indians drove the settlers out. Two years later, however, Gov. Albino Pérez gave the *Mora Land Grant,* extending from present Mora to Wagon Mound, to 76 individuals who recolonized the area. The valley then consisted of two parts: *El Valle de San Antonio,* or *El Valle de Arriba,* "the Upper Valley," including what is now Chacon, Cleveland, and Holman; and *El Valle de Santa Gertrudis,* the lower part of the valley, including present Mora.

The town of Mora, named for the grant tends to be organized into a number of named neighborhoods: *El Alto,* "the Heights"; *Juarez,* because it's across the river; *Tramperos,* "trappers"; and *China Block,* for reasons unknown.

MORA COUNTY (N-central NM; county seat, Mora). Created in 1860, with Mora as its county seat.

MORA FLATS (San Miguel; along the Rio Mora in the Pecos Wilderness, 3 mi NE of Iron Gate Campground). Broad meadows along the stream, also known as *Vega Mora,* "Mora Meadow."

MORA RIVER (Mora, San Miguel; heads in the Sangre de Cristo Mountains near Chacon, flows S through Mora then E through La Cueva and Watrous, eventually to join the Canadian River N of Sabinoso). Though early maps label the river as *Río de lo de Mora,* or simply *Río Mora,* the name usually is now anglicized as Mora River. The stream is not to be confused with the *Río Mora* (see entry) to the SW in the Pecos Wilderness.

MORAGA CANYON (Catron; S of Long Canyon Mountains, 3 mi E of the Continental Divide). Members of the Moraga family were in NM both before and after 1680.

MORENO RIVER (Colfax; heads in the Sangre de Cristo Mountains and flows S to Eagle Nest Lake). Spanish, "brown." Formed by the confluence of *North* and *South Moreno Creeks.* The river's water once washed placer gravel in the Elizabethtown Mining District. The river gave its name to the *Moreno Valley* and also to *Moreno,* a residential cluster 2 mi N of Elizabethtown.

MORIARTY (Torrance; settlement; on I-40 and NM 41, 25 mi E of Albuquerque; PO 1902–present). In the spring of 1887, young Michael Moriarty left his home in southeastern Iowa and headed by train for California, seeking relief in the milder climate for his sciatic rheumatism. But soon after arriving in NM he was received cordially by the son of Gov. Edmond Ross, who persuaded him to consider staying here, and the matter was decided after young Moriarty noticed he felt considerably better after his stay in the Estancia Valley. He returned to Iowa and relocated his family to NM; he died in 1932 on his sheep ranch. Locally, Moriarty is often pronounced Mor-YAHR-ty. In the settlement's early days, the townsite E of the RR was owned by H. Crossley, and from 1903 to 1933 that section was known as *Buford,* for Crossley's son, but the two sections have merged, and the name Buford no longer is used.

MORNINGSTAR (Taos; settlement; N of Taos). This was among several communes that flourished briefly in the Taos area in the late 1960s and early 1970s. This sometimes was called *Morning Star East.*

MORPHY LAKE STATE PARK (Mora; on the E side of the Sangre de Cristo Mountains, about 4 mi SW of Mora). The appeal of this state park is obvious—an alpine tarn at the edge of the Pecos Wilderness—but the origin of its name is less clear. It appears as *Murphy Lake* on some maps, and as John V. Young explained, "There was an Irish settlement in the vicinity long ago, but if one of its members named Murphy gave his name to the lake, nobody now seems to know who he was. In any event, the name Morphy seems to be nothing more than an orthographic error which has been perpetuated in officialdom."

MOSCA PEAK, 9,509 ft. (Torrance; in the Manzano Mountains, N of Bosque Peak). Spanish, "fly," inspiration for the name here unknown.

LA MOSCA PEAK, 11,053 ft. (Cibola; subsidiary summit of Mount Taylor, 1 mi NE). Spanish, "the fly," specific reason for name unknown. *La Mosca Canyon* runs NW of La Mosca Peak.

SIERRA MOSCA, 11,801 ft. (Santa Fe; in the Sangre de Cristo Mountains, 12 mi E of Nambe). Spanish, "fly mountain."

MOSES (Union; settlement; on NM 406, 3 mi W of the Oklahoma line, N of Corrumpa Creek; PO 1909–55, mail to Seneca). The first settlement by this name was located near Corrumpa Creek, near McNees Crossing, and took the name of its first postmaster, Frank Moses. Later, one Delphín Espinosa owned the Moses store, but when the Espinosa Ranch was sold, a new store and PO were started at a curve on the highway; the two settlements were called *Old Moses* and *New Moses.*

MOSQUERO (Harding; settlement, county seat; on NM 39, 18 mi SE of Roy; PO 1908–present). Around 1906 the EP&NE RR designated Mosquero as a siding and water stop (see *Mosquero Creek*), and with the RR came land-hungry immigrants. At the locality called Gould (see entry), lawyer and real estate agent Benjamin Brown organized the Mosquero Land Co., named for nearby Mosquero Creek, and began selling tracts. He was so successful that in July 1908 he laid out a townsite, and in September that year he constructed a hotel near the siding. Mosquero, as the new town was called, soon eclipsed Gould and became the largest settlement in Harding County.

MOSQUERO CREEK (Harding; rises E of settlement of Mosquero and flows SE to join Ute Creek). The Spanish *mosquero* means "flytrap, flypaper," but in NM the meaning has been "swarm of flies or mosquitoes," such as would have existed near a creek. An early EP&NE RR siding sign, however, spelled the name *Moquero*, and one source says a still earlier map also labeled the creek Moquero, suggesting this might have been the original name; *moquero* is a Spanish word meaning "handkerchief."

MOUNT DORA, 6,290 ft. (Union; 18 mi NW of Clayton). This important landmark often appears on recent maps as *Cieneguilla del Burro Mountain,* for its proximity to Cieneguilla del Burro Creek, now called Seneca Creek (see entry). It was named Mount Dora by US Senator Stephen W. Dorsey of Arkansas to commemorate his sister-in-law. See *Clayton.*

MOUNT DORA (Union; settlement; on US 64-87 18 mi NW of Clayon; PO 1908–present). An important immigrant route ran through here, and as ranchers replaced Indians on the Plains, this became a shipping point for cattle, sheep, and grain on the C&S RR. At one time Mount Dora had three hotels. The settlement was named for *Mount Dora* (see entry), the prominent 6,290-foot landmark is immediately E

MOUNT RILEY (Doña Ana; settlement; in SW part of county, on old SP RR, 2 mi N of Mexican border). Abandoned community, named for *Mount Riley,* the 5,905-foot summit 8 mi to the N, the origin of whose name is unknown.

MOUNT VERNON (Roosevelt; settlement; 11 mi NE of Causey; PO 1910–13, mail to Givens). Abandoned homesteader community, likely named for George Washington's home.

MOUNTAIN PARK (Otero; settlement; NE of Alamogordo, on US 82, 1 mi E of High Rolls; PO 1904–55, mail to High Rolls). Like High Rolls (see entry), its neighbor community in Fresnal Canyon, Mountain Park was founded in the 1880s by the Button Nelson, Bill Karr, and Jack Tucker families. It takes its name from its location in a pleasant valley of the Sacramento Mountains.

MOUNTAINAIR (Torrance; settlement; on NM 60 and NM 337, 36 mi E of Bernardo; PO 1903–present). When the AT&SF RR was considering the Belen Cut-off around 1900, John W. Corbett, a newspaper man from Winfield, KS, learned of the proposed route and that it would go through Abo Pass. He and a friend, Col. E.C. Manning, came here in 1901 and located a townsite at the summit of the pass, the highest point on the AT&SF's southern transcontinental route. Noting the delightful summer breezes from the Manzano Mountains nearby to the N, they named their new community Mountainair.

MOUNTAINVIEW (Bernalillo; settlement; S of Albuquerque, E of the Rio Grande, across the river from Pajarito, W of NM 47). Inhabited residential community, named for its view of the Sandia and Manzano Mountains to the E.

MOUNTAINVIEW (Luna; postal locality; 13 mi S of Deming; PO 1911–14, mail to Deming). Ephemeral postal locality; the view would have been of the Florida Mountains.

MOUNTVIEW (Colfax). See *Dawson.*

MOWRY CITY (Luna; settlement; 25 mi N of Deming). This locality began as a stop on the San Antonio and San Diego stage line. About 1857 retired US Army Lt. Sylvester Mowry, who was active in the territorial affairs of Arizona, saw potential in the site, and eventually went on to promote it as Mowry City. In 1858 the site became a stop on the Butterfield

Overland Mail route, but neither the stage line nor Mowry City lasted long, though the locality had a brief existence as *Camp Mimbres* (see entry). Today Mowry City is little more than a historical footnote.

MUD SPRING (general). A common descriptive name, occurring 29 times in NM (GNIS); see *Puerco (general).*

DEL MUERTO CREEK (Harding; heads E of Bueyeros and flows W into Ute Creek). Spanish, "of the dead man." The name's specific origin is unknown.

LAGUNA DEL MUERTO, OJO DEL MUERTO (Sierra; in the E foothills of the Caballo Mountains). Josiah Gregg, writing in *Commerce of the Prairies* (1844) about his journey on the *Jornada del Muerto* (see entry), said: "Early the next morning we found ourselves at Laguna del Muerto, or 'Dead Man's Lake,' where there was not even a vestige of water. This lake is but a sink in the plain of a few rods in diameter, and only filled with water during the rainy season.... To procure water for our thirsty animals, it is often necessary to make a halt here [at Laguna del Muerto, usually dry] and drive them to the Ojo del Muerto (Dead Man's Spring), 5 or 6 miles to the westward, in the very heart of the mountain ridge that lay between us and the river. This region is one of the favorite resorts of the Apaches, where many a poor *arriero* ['muleteer'] has met an untimely end." The identity of the dead man, or men, that inspired the names is unknown.

MUIR (Hidalgo; locale; at the junction of I-10 and NM 113). Interstate Exit 34 took its name from the SP RR flag stop named for John T. Muir, a pioneer rancher.

MULE (general). Mules were common beasts of burden before automobiles; 26 places are named for them or incidents involving them (GNIS).

MULE CANYON (Otero; in the Sacramento Mountains, SE of Alamogordo). Sometime prior to the Civil War, settlers from the Rio Grande trailed some Indians who had stolen some mules, and here they found one of the mules. From this, the canyon and nearby *Mule Peak,* 8,097 ft., received their names.

MULE CREEK (Grant; settlement; in NW part of county, on NM 78, 6 mi E of the Arizona border; PO 1916–present). Dan McMillen founded this tiny settlement in 1877 and is said to have named it because he found a mule track at *Mule Creek,* which heads near the Arizona border and flows NE through settlement of Mule Creek to the San Francisco River. Nearby, 10 mi S of Pleasanton, are the *Mule Mountains.*

MULESHOE (Lea). See *Jal.*

MUÑOZ (general). This name, sometimes appearing as *Muñiz,* occurs several times in 18th-century documents.

MUÑOZ CANYON (San Juan; heads S of Blanco and runs N to the San Juan River). A rancher named Muñoz grazed sheep here.

MURDOCK (Quay; settlement; 12 mi NW of Melrose; PO 1907–17, mail to Forrest). This abandoned homesteader community began as a land office, where homesteaders could file their claims. When a PO was established, the name originally proposed was *Victor,* but Murdock was chosen instead, for an early family in the area.

MURRAY (Socorro; settlement; in SE part of county, on the W side of Mockingbird Gap; PO 1909–13, mail to Oscuro). Murray, which took the name of its postmaster, John P. Murray, was a small mining camp and water stop on the route between Oscuro and the Rio Grande.

MUSTANG CREEK (San Miguel; joins Arroyo de la Cinta, 5 mi S of the Bell Ranch). Anglicized from NM Spanish *mesteño, mesteña* "a wild, unbranded horse."

MYNDUS (Luna; settlement; on SP RR, 18 mi E of Deming; PO 1912–21, mail to Silton). The PO was named for the RR station here. The PO application stated, "The town has not been laid out yet but will soon, the surrounding country is settling fast." By 1913 Myndus had a school with 19 students, but now the community is but a memory. The name's origin is unknown.

N

NACIMIENTO (Sandoval). See *Cuba.*
SIERRA NACIMIENTO (Rio Arriba,
Sandoval; in the N-central part of
Sandoval County, extending N into Rio
Arriba County, on the W edge of the
Jemez Mountains complex). Spanish,
"birth, scene depicting the Nativity" but
also "source of a river or spring," and
that likely is its meaning here because in
18th-century land grant documents
mention is made of the *Pueblo de Señor
Sn Joaquin del Nacimento del Río Puerco,*
the implication being that the moun-
tains were named for their being where
the river heads. On Bernardo Miera y
Pacheco's 1778 map of the 1776—1777
Domínguez-Escalante expedition, this
range is labeled "*Nacimto.*" In the N part
of the range is *Nacimiento Peak* 9,801 ft.
NADINE (Lea; settlement; on NM 18 5 mi
S of Hobbs; PO 1910–34, mail to
Hobbs). This inhabited settlement was
once called *Roberts,* but when James H.
Hughes became the first postmaster, he
renamed it for his daughter, Nadine.
NAGEEZI (San Juan; settlement; on NM
44, 44 mi SE of Bloomfield; PO
1941–present). This active trading point
bears a Navajo name meaning "squash."
NAKAIBITO (McKinley). See *Mexican
Springs.*
NAMBE PUEBLO (Santa Fe; 16 mi N of
Santa Fe, 4 mi E of Pojoaque; PO
1901–22, mail to Santa Fe). As the Tewa-
speaking inhabitants of the pueblo tell
it, "Our Tewa name is *Nambay-ongwee,*
which means 'people of the roundish
earth.' From our oral history we know
that our ancestors inhabited at least
eight villages prior to contact with Europeans." The ruins of one of these villages
is believed to have been on a mound,
hence the "roundish earth."
Río Nambe, Nambe Creek (Santa Fe; heads

near Puerto Nambe, N of Lake Peak, and
flows NW past Nambe Pueblo). This
starts out as *Nambe Creek,* then becomes
the *Río Nambe,* then changes its name to
Pojoaque Creek, for the pueblo downstream, just E of Nambe Pueblo.
Nambe Falls (Santa Fe; on the Rio Nambe, 5
mi E of the pueblo). Three waterfalls,
wedged into a narrow canyon, the tallest
falling from 100 ft. The falls gave their
name to nearby *Nambe Falls Reservoir.*
Nambe Lake (Santa Fe; in the Sangre de
Cristo Mountains, at the NW base of
Lake Peak, near the headwaters of
Nambe Creek).
Puerto Nambe (Santa Fe; in the Sangre de
Cristo Mountains, in the Pecos Wilderness, between Lake Peak and Santa Fe
Baldy). This broad meadow is at the
height-of-land between the Pecos River
drainage and that of the Rio Grande.
The Spanish *puerto* here means "pass,
gap," while Nambe refers to the broad
divide being near the headwaters of
Nambe Creek (see entry).
NARA VISA (Quay; settlement; on NM 54
and NM 402, 24 mi NE of Logan; PO
1902–present). Nara Visa was founded
in 1901 with the construction of the
CRI&P RR line to Tucumcari, becoming
a water station and shipping point for
cattle. The village took the name of *Nara
Visa Creek* (see entry), on which it's located. The first settlers lived in a boxcar,
but by 1902 Nara Visa boasted two
buildings.
NARA VISA CREEK (Quay; flows through
the village of Nara Visa). In the 1880s,
an Hispanic sheepherder named
Narvaez lived here. English-speaking
settlers pronounced his name "Narvis,"
which in turn was corrupted further to
Nara Visa.
NARANJOS (Mora; settlement; on NM

120, 3 mi SE of Ocate; PO 1886–88, 1913–17, mail to Ocate). Almost all the buildings here have been abandoned, but owners still visit their properties and regard the settlement as still alive. Alonso Naranjo, perhaps an ancestor of the Naranjos for whom this village was named, came to NM with Oñate's troops in 1600.

NARBONA PASS (San Juan; in SW part of county, in the Chuska Mountains, on NM 134, 12 mi W of Sheep Springs). On December 10, 1992, in the final days of the 500th anniversary of Columbus's arrival in the New World, an anniversary Native Americans have said signified a renewed commitment to the preservation of their cultures, the USBGN voted 4-0 to approve a proposal by students of Navajo Community College (NCC) in Shiprock to change the name of *Washington Pass* to Narbona Pass.

The renaming had its roots in the discovery by some NCC students and their teacher, Herbert Benally, that the name Washington Pass honored not George Washington or Washington, D.C., as most Navajos had assumed, but rather Col. John Washington, leader of a US military expedition against the Navajos in 1849. In a skirmish at the pass, Col. Washington's troops, during a failed parley with the Navajos, killed the Navajo leader Narbona, who lived at the pass and who, with tragic irony, had been a leading Navajo proponent for peace. Narbona was scalped, and Lt. James Simpson, the expedition's chronicler, named the site Washington Pass for his commander.

Navajos deeply resented this name on a feature in the Navajo homeland. Benally and NCC student Freda Garnanez organized support among Navajos for changing the name to Narbona Pass. The proposed name change received widespread support from non-Navajos in NM. The NM Geographic Names Committee also played an important role; its chairman, Bob Julyan, spoke to Navajos about the formal procedures for changing a name and arranged for Navajos to meet personally with USBGN members.

Indeed, the only obstacle was minor confusion as to what new name the pass should have. Most Navajos preferred Narabona Pass, but some in the Tohatchi area preferred a translation of the Navajo name, which meant *Copper Pass*. But finally consensus was reached; the pass was to bear the name of the Navajo leader who had lived and died there.

Soon after the USBGN decision approving the NCC proposal, Roger Payne, USBGN executive secretary, said: "This is a precedent-setting move. We know of no other instance anywhere in the country of a Native American commemorative name initiated by Native Americans."

NASCHITTI (San Juan; settlement; on US 666 42 mi N of Gallup). This Navajo community was born in 1886 when Tom Bryan established one of the first trading posts on the E side of the Chuska Mountains. Its name is Navajo and means "badger springs." The name *Drolet* has been associated with this community, likely because of a trader here by that name.

NAT STRAW CANYON (Catron; a tributary of the W Fork of the Gila River, W of Gila Cliff Dwellings). Robert Nelson Straw—better known as Nat Straw—had been a RR engineer out of Springfield, MO, but he wound up in the Gila country where he was a well-known figure around 1900. Jack Stockbridge described him thus: "I guess Nat Straw was about 40 or 45 years old when I was first in the wilderness area around 1900. He was a good-sized man, right close to six feet, light-complected, and generally wore a moustache. He was just about like any old trapper and prospector."

NAVA (San Juan). See *Newcomb*.

NAVAJO (general). Navajos are the largest Native American group in the US. Their language is included in the Athabascan family of languages, and Navajos refer to themselves by the Navajo word *Diné*, "the people." (Apaches, a closely related Athabascan group, call themselves *N'de*, also meaning "the people.") But to the outside world these Indians are known as Navajos, most likely from a Tewa word meaning "wide valley fields," a reference to the Navajos' practice of farming in Cañon Largo and other canyons of early-day Navajoland, an area that Navajos call the *Dinetah* (see entry). Fray Alonso de Benavides in his *Memorial* of 1634 wrote, "But these [Apaches] of Navajo are very great farmers, for that is what Navajo signifies, 'great planted fields.'" Some persons have mentioned the similarity between the name Navajo and the Spanish *navaja*, "razor, or clasped knife," suggesting that the name might have been derived from Navajo men carrying stone knives, but the agricultural origin is more likely. 39 NM places have Navajo in their names (GNIS).

NAVAJO (McKinley; settlement; just E of the Arizona line, 18 mi NE of Window Rock). Site of a large sawmill owned by the Navajo tribe and named by an offical act of the Navajo Tribal Council in 1959; the Navajo name for the locality means simply "sawmill."

NAVAJO (McKinley; settlement; 3 mi NE of Gallup). As T.M. Pearce explained, "The opening of the Navajo coal mine by the American Fuel Co. produced the camp of Navajo." In the mid–1930s Navajo had 600 residents, but mining shifted elsewhere, the houses eventually were moved, and the settlement was abandoned.

NAVAJO (Rio Arriba; on the D&RGW RR, 8 mi NW of Lumberton; PO 1880–81). Abandoned settlement, once called *El Navajo,* because Navajos lived here.

NAVAJO CANYON (Rio Arriba). See *Cañon del Navajo.*

NAVAJO DAM (San Juan; settlement; at the lower end of Navajo Reservoir; PO 1959–present). Settlement associated with the dam and state park.

NAVAJO INDIAN RESERVATION (McKinley, San Juan; the Four Corners area, including Arizona and Utah). The treaty of 1868 created what is now the largest Indian reservation in the US, about 14,000,000 acres, equal to the combined area of Vermont, New Hampshire, and Massachusetts. The *Navajo Nation,* as it is called, includes approximately 120,000 members. Creation of the reservation here, in the Navajo homeland—see *Dinetah*—followed an unsuccessful and tragic attempt to establish a Navajo reservation on the Pecos River; see *Fort Sumner.*

NAVAJO RESERVOIR (Rio Arriba, San Juan; on the San Juan River, near the Colorado border). This 15,000-acre reservoir is appropriately named, for it is within the *Dinetah* (see entry), the traditional Navajo homeland. The US Bureau of Reclamation dam creating the lake is the second largest of its kind in the US. The project was begun in 1958 and completed in 1963. The name *Navajo Reservoir,* as listed in GNIS, distinguishes the impoundment from a "lake," a natural water body, but most maps and common usage ignore the distinction in favor of *Navajo Lake. Navajo Lake State Park,* created in 1964, surrounds the reservoir and includes 17,959 acres of land and 13,351 acres of water, including 3.5 miles of the San Juan River below the dam.

NAVAJO RIVER (Rio Arriba; heads in Colorado NE of Dulce and returns NW of Dulce to Colorado, where it is a tributary of the San Juan River). See also *San Juan River.*

OJO DE NAVAJO (Rio Arriba; in Cañon del Navajo, NW of Abiquiu). According to oral tradition, this small spring in Cañon del Navajo was a stopping place for travelers to and from the Tierra Amarilla. One evening, Navajo raiders rushed down an embankment here to ambush some campers, but one of the travelers shouted an oath, and at that instant one of the attackers slipped off the embankment to his death. Fearing strong magic, the other Navajos broke off the attack, and from this incident the spring was named.

NAVATA (McKinley). See *Tohlakai.*

NED HOUK MEMORIAL PARK (Curry). See *Running Water Draw State Park.*

NEED (Roosevelt). See *Lingo.*

NEGRA, NEGRO (general). See *Black (general).*

NEGRA (Torrance; settlement; on US 60, 5 mi W of Encino; PO 1909–18, mail to

Encino). This community began when the AT&SF RR built the Belen Cut-off about 1905–06 and is said to have been named because of the soil here, though a black water tank is here now. Only foundations and a single residence remain.

NEGRITO CREEK (Catron; two forks, North and South, head in the Tularosa Mountains and flow W to join the San Francisco River 2 mi S of Reserve). Spanish, "little black," because the canyon through which it flows is deep and dark.

NESTOR CANYON (Rio Arriba; trends NNW to Cañones Creek, 6.2 mi NE of Brazos). Sometimes incorrectly labeled *Nester Canyon,* this was named for Nestor Sari, a Finnish immigrant who lived in the canyon in the 1920s and 1930s.

NEW BUFFALO (Taos; settlement; near Arroyo Hondo). This ephemeral community was among several "hippie" settlements that sprang up in N NM in the 1970s. Their names often expressed their respect for Indian cultures. The main commune building in 1993 became a bed-and-breakfast.

NEW CAVE (Eddy). See *Slaughter Canyon Cave.*

NEW DOMINGO (Sandoval). See *Domingo.*

NEW HOBBS (Lea; settlement; 1 mi S of Hobbs; PO 1930–31, consolidated with Hobbs). See *Hobbs.*

NEW LAGUNA (Cibola). See *Laguna.*

NEW MEXICO. A blend of Native American, Spanish, and Anglo-American elements, the name New Mexico is an appropriate paradigm for the state itself. The name's roots extend into Mexico; the Nahuatl Indians who created the Aztec empire were called *Aztecas,* from *Aztlán,* their traditional place of origin, but also *Mexicas,* from *Mexi,* their traditional leader, and an alternative name for Tenochtitlan, the Aztec capital, was *Mexitli. Mexico* was the term the Spanish used to refer to the former Aztec empire. The first Spaniard to give a name to the region that is now New Mexico was Fray Marcos de Niza, in 1539. Beholding the Zuni pueblos from a distance and be-

lieving them the fabled cities of Cibola, he formally bestowed the name *Kingdom of St. Francis.* Coronado explored the region in 1540–42, and the region was labeled *Nova Hispania,* "New Spain," on Gaspaldi's 1546 map and the Mercator map of 1569. The first documented use of the name New Mexico came in 1563 when Don Francisco de Ibarra, after his appointment as governor of the Mexican province of Nueva Vizcaya, referred to the region to the N as *un otro* or *Nuevo Méjico,* "another" or a "New Mexico." Ibarra had led an expedition to an Indian village, whose inhabitants reminded him of the Aztecs of Mexico. The idea of a new Mexico was an appealing possibility, for the Aztec empire had been fabulously wealthy, and the thought of another Mexico to conquer and plunder was tantalizing indeed, despite Coronado having demonstrated 20 years earlier that the dream did not match the reality. In 1581, Captain Chamuscado explored the northern regions, and on August 21 he and his men took possession of the land for the king. They named the pueblo where this occurred *San Felipe* and also gave that name to the entire province. Obregón in his *Historia,* written in 1584, almost invariably wrote *San Felipe de Nuevo Méjico.* In 1582–83 Antonio de Espejo explored portions of what is now New Mexico and reported "visiting and exploring the provinces of New Mexico, which I gave the name *Nueva Andalucía,* as I was born in the district of Cordoba." Lujan, the chronicler of Espejo's expedition, used the name *Nuevo Méjico* on the title page of his journal, and that is the name by which it has been called ever since. When Oñate took permanent possession in 1598, he called himself "governor, captain general, and *adelantado* of New Mexico and its kingdoms and provinces."

That was not the end of the story, however, for while the name New Mexico was secure for more than 250 years, when the American territory of New Mexico desired statehood, objections were raised that the name would suggest the region still was part of Mexico and not the US. (Perennial gaffs by persons and institutions that should know better prove those fears weren't entirely unfounded.) Other names were proposed: *Lincoln, Hamilton, Montezuma,* and *Acoma* (the latter proposed in part because it would dislodge Alabama at the head of the alphabetical list). In 1873 a traveler wryly suggested that the territory be called *Pobrita,* "little poverty." But territorial representatives made clear that people here would have no other name than New Mexico. See also *Land of Enchantment.*

NEW PLACERS (Santa Fe; settlement; about 1 mi NE of Golden). About 1839 gold was discovered in the tributaries of Tuerto Creek in the San Pedro Mountains, and soon miners flocked from *Old Placers* (see *Dolores*) to New Placers, also called *Tuerto.* By 1845 New Placers, or Tuerto, was the active center of the district, with 22 stores, and so much mining had been done that when Lt. James W. Abert passed through he remarked that the area appeared to be inhabited by giant prairie dogs. But eventually the placer deposits played out, other strikes were made elsewhere, and today New Placers is but a memory and a name.

NEW YORK (Cibola). See *Laguna.*

NEWCOMB (San Juan; settlement; on US 666, 52 mi N of Gallup; PO as Nava 1924–29, as Newcomb 1929–44, mail to Tohatchi). This inhabited settlement on the Navajo Indian Reservation originally was called *Nava,* using the first syllables of Navajo. In 1914 Arthur J. Newcomb and his wife, Frances L. Newcomb, established a trading post here. The Navajo name for the locality means "adobe or earthen bank pointing out."

NEWHOPE (Roosevelt; settlement; 1 mi W of NM 206, 29 mi S of Portales; PO 1910–21, mail to Elida). This vanished community was named about 1902 when a homesteader finally found water after digging several wells.

NEWKIRK (Guadalupe; settlement; at the junction of I-40 and NM 129, 27 mi E of Santa Rosa; PO 1910–present). *Conant* was the first name of this communnity;

it was settled in 1901 when the CRI&P RR came through and named for James P. Conant, an early rancher (see *Casa Colorada*). Later, the name was changed to Newkirk by a settler from Newkirk, OK.

NEWMAN (Otero; settlement; on US 54, 20 mi NE of El Paso, on the NM–Texas line; PO as Hereford 1904–06, as Newman 1906–92, site moved to El Paso County, TX). This active trading point was named for L. E. Newman, an early El Paso real estate promoter who sold building sites here. The first postmaster was Henry L. Newman. The site originally was called *Longhorn,* a name that later was changed to *Hereford,* doubtless reflecting a change in the predominant cattle breed in the area.

NEWTON (Grant; settlement; in central part of county, 2 mi NW of Hurley; PO 1883, mail to Silver City). Newton began in the 1870s as a gold-mining camp. It originally was called *Lone Mountain,* for a nearby peak, but the name chosen by postal officials when the community applied for a PO was Newton, for reasons unknown; local people are said to have refused to accept the name Newton. The camp has long since been abandoned.

NIGGER (general). In the 19th century, this term was used throughout the American frontier to refer to African-Americans. Because of the strong racist overtones of this term, place names using it are being eliminated or changed by cartographers, and for many years official USBGN policy has been to make these changes, but Nigger names on earlier maps nonetheless are reminders of the African-American presence in the West.

NIGGER CREEK (Colfax; drains into the Moreno River, at N end of the Moreno Valley). This recalls a young African-American who came to Elizabethtown during the boom years of 1865–90 and lived apart from whites on this creek.

NIGGER ED CANYON (Otero; on the W side of the Sacramento Mountains, SE of Alamogordo). Oliver M. Lee, whose ranch was nearby, had an African-American servant who proudly bore the nickname "Nigger Ed."

NIGGER HILL (Roosevelt). See *Dead Negro Hill.*

NIGGER MESA (Union; on the Colorado line, between Branson and Folsom). Named by cowboys in the early 1880s after a fight staged here involving an African-American.

NINE-MILE HILL (Bernalillo; parallels I-40 W of Albuquerque). This ascent of the West Mesa is 9 mi long.

NINEMILE CREEK (Colfax; at the S end of the Moreno Valley, flows into Cieneguilla Creek). This and *Sixmile Creek* 3 mi N were named for their distance from Elizabethtown, which in the late 1800s was the primary reference point in the area.

NO AGUA (Taos; settlement; just E of US 285, N of Tres Piedras). This abandoned settlement was born as a stop on the D&RG RR, the old "Chili Line," and named for *No Agua Peaks,* 8,868 ft., nearby to the E. In the 1890s No Agua had several frame buildings, and around WW I several homesteaders moved to the area. Trains still stopped here in the 1930s, but after WW II almost all the residents departed, and in 1955 No Agua's church, long unused, was moved to Tres Piedras.

NO NAME CANYON (Catron; heads in Little Park in the Gila Wilderness and runs NE into the Middle Fork of the Gila River). A paradoxical name, as clearly this canyon *does* have a name. While this is the only innominate name in NM, the temptation to be clever in naming is universal, and No Name names are fairly common throughout the world.

NOBE (Roosevelt; settlement; 16 mi W of Causey; PO 1907–14, mail to Judson). Abandoned homesteader settlement, name origin unknown.

NOBLE ACRES (McKinley; settlement; 8 mi S of Gallup). Inhabited subdivision and trading post, likely bearing a personal name.

NOGAL (general). This Spanish term is used throughout the American Southwest for various species of walnut, usually the Arizona walnut (*Juglans major*), and is a common place-name element,

appearing 21 times in NM (GNIS); see *Walnut (general).*

NOGAL (Lincoln; settlement; on NM 37, 12 mi SW of Carrizozo, in the foothills of the Sacramento Mountains, at the mouth of Nogal Canyon; PO as Galena 1880–82, as Nogal 1882–present). *Dry Gulch* was the original name of this locality, likely given by prospectors for the drainage running through the village. Free gold had been discovered here about 1879, and when a PO was established it was called *Galena,* for a native lead sulfide found in mining operations in the vicinity. Only two years later the community took the name Nogal, for walnut trees growing here and in nearby *Nogal Canyon.* In 1899 the EP&NE RR established a water station N of here that it called *Walnut,* also for the trees. *Nogal Lake* is 1.5 mi SE of the village of Nogal.

Nogal Peak, 9,957 ft. (Lincoln; in SW part of county, 6 mi SW of village of Nogal). Named for the village, Nogal Peak was the site of gold-mining in the early 1880s, the Nogal Peak Mine producing $500,000 in ore in 24 years.

NOISY BROOK (Mora; in SW part of county, heads on the NE side of Round Mountain and flows SE into the Pecos River). Named for its tumultuous descent off the steep side of Round Mountain. Nearby another stream was given the same name but in Spanish, *Rito Ruidoso.*

NOLAN (Mora; settlement; on AT&SF RR, 11 mi N of Wagon Mound; PO 1908–44, mail to Levy). Most of the people who lived here were RR employees; they're gone, and so is the community, though the Nolan RR siding preserves the name. George Adlai Feather said the community of Nolan took its name from a land grant made to Gervaseo (Gervais) Nolan, a French-Canadian who came to NM in 1824 and became a naturalized New Mexican in 1829.

NOMBRE DE DIOS (Doña Ana; settlement; 21 mi S of Las Cruces). This tiny agricultural community was founded by Spanish-speaking farmers after the 1848 Treaty of Guadalupe Hidalgo, but its Spanish religious title "Name of God" failed to shield it from being ravaged by a flood in 1884 and again in 1892, when it was re-established further W. As late as 1916 two families continued living at the new site; the old one had vanished completely.

NOONDAY CANYON (Grant; heads 3 mi E of Mimbres and runs into the Mimbres River at San Lorenzo). As T.M. Pearce told it, in the days when Kingston and Pinos Altos were booming mining camps, persons traveling between the two always tried to arrive at this canyon and its reliable water at noon, hence the name.

Noonday Peak 7,340 ft. (Grant; 9 mi SE of San Lorenzo). Though *Noonday Canyon* is 9 mi away, the likelihood is great the peak was named for the canyon in some way.

NORIA (Doña Ana; settlement; 1.5 mi N of the Texas border, on the SP RR). This word comes from Arabic, and in North Africa and southern Spain it denotes a kind of water wheel used to raise water for irrigation. In NM the word was used as early as the mid-17th century to refer to a dug well, and that likely explains the name of this abandoned settlement.

NORTH CANADIAN RIVER (Union). See *Corrumpa Creek.*

NORTH DES MOINES (Union; settlement; N of Des Moines; PO 1909–15, mail to Des Moines). Little is known about this abandoned settlement. See *Des Moines.*

NORTH GUAM (McKinley). See *Coolidge.*

NORTH SEVEN RIVERS (Eddy; 6 mi N of village of Seven Rivers). This stream, one of three branches of Seven Rivers, also sometimes has been known as *Branch Seven Rivers.* See *Seven Rivers.*

NORTH SPRING RIVER (Chaves; heads W of Roswell and flows E through the city to join the Rio Hondo). Originally the spring creating this short stream was called *Old Man Spring,* the old man being Robert Casey. Later, however, Van Smith, who named Roswell, renamed the spring *North Spring,* to be the counterpart to *South Spring* (see entry) S of town. The pumping of artesian water has lowered the water level in this river.

NORTH STAR MESA (Grant; on the W side of Mimbres River, 6 mi N of Mimbres). Named for the North Star Mine.

NORTHERN LAKE (Rio Arriba). See *Horse Lake.*

NORTON (Quay; settlement; on NM 278, 20 mi SE of Tucumcari; PO 1907–42, mail to Tucumcari). In 1907 Michael J. Norton, originally from Michigan, established a store and PO here and became the first postmaster. Though the village named for him no longer exists, its name is still recognized and used by people in the area.

NUESTRA SEÑORA DE GUADALUPE (Doña Ana). See *Tortugas.*

NUESTRA SEÑORA DE LA LUZ SAN FERNANDO Y SAN BLAS (settlement; on the Rio Puerco, exact location unknown). A long-abandoned 18th-century settlement.

NUESTRA SEÑORA DE SOCORRO DE PILABO (Socorro). See *Socorro.*

NUTRIA (general). In Spain this means "otter," but when Spanish colonists saw the North American beaver, an otter-like animal, they gave it the same name, and that is what it usually means in NM place names.

NUTRIA, LOWER AND UPPER (McKinley; settlement; on the Zuni Indian Reservation, 21 mi NE of Zuni Pueblo). *Lower Nutria* and its sister community, *Upper Nutria,* 1.5 mi NE, both inhabited, were named for being on *Río Nutria* (see entry), Upper Nutria also being located near *Nutria Spring.* Their Zuni name means "seed place," or "planting place," while Navajos living just to the N call the locality "rock which starts to get black."

Nutria Lake (McKinley; 12 mi NE of Zuni Pueblo). Actually, there are two Nutria Lakes, *No. 1* and 3 mi NE *No. 2,* both on the Rio Nutria.

NUTRIAS (Rio Arriba; settlement; 9 mi S of Tierra Amarilla, 2 mi E of US 84). Tiny inhabited community, named for being on the *Río Nutrias* (see entry), which heads to the E and flows W through the village to the Rio Grande.

NUTT (Luna; settlement; at junction of NM 26 and NM 27, 18 mi SW of Hatch; PO 1881–84, 1899–1939, mail to Lake Valley). Nutt began as an AT&SF RR terminal serving the mining communities of the Black Range; it was named for Colonel Nutt, one of the RR's directors. Nutt was an important point for shipping ore, but when the RR in 1884 was extended to Lake Valley, Nutt lost much of its importance and population. Still, Nutt, unlike Lake Valley, has survived as a trading point and has retained a sense of humor; a sign in Nutt proclaims it "The Middle of Nowhere." *Nutt Mountain*, 5,940 ft. (Sierra; 3 mi N of Nutt). Also sometimes labelled *Sunday Cone,* for reasons unknown, though perhaps it's a misspelling of *Sundae Cone,* which with a little imagination it resembles.

OAK (general). Numerous species of oaks (genus *Quercus*) exist in NM, and GNIS lists 47 Oak names. Curiously, the Spanish form, *roble*, is rare, though the Mexicanism, *encino*, referring to the evergreen oak, is common, appearing in 37 place names. See *Encino (general)*.

OAK GROVE (Grant; settlement; in the Burro Mountains, 10 mi SW of Silver City). In the early 1880s the Queen City Copper Co. erected its smelter here, and the resulting community, mostly miners and woodcutters, named it for its being in an oak grove. In December 1882 Oak Grove had 300 residents, but later it died and has since vanished.

OAK SPRING (Sierra; stage stop; between Hillsboro and Lake Valley). Until 1899 this was where stages changed horses while passengers had a meal at the cafe.

OAKWOOD SPRINGS (San Miguel; settlement; in W part of county, exact location unknown; PO 1891–93, mail to Lesperance). Short-lived postal locality, name origin unknown.

OASIS (Chaves; settlement; on the W bank of the Pecos River, 9 mi SE of Roswell). This community was organized around the Oasis Ranch, which in turn owed its existence to the artesian well drilled in 1931 that with a flow of 9,225 gallons per minute was the world's largest at the time. The ranch still exists as a farm and hunting preserve; the name also is recognized and used.

OASIS (Lea). See *Knowles*.

OASIS STATE PARK (Roosevelt; 4 mi N of Portales, 2 mi W of NM 467). This state park is well-named, for the small lake and surrounding vegetation are indeed an oasis in the harsh, arid environment of the *Llano Estacado*. Once the lake was artesian, but lowering of water tables by irrigation has meant the lake must be

fed by well water. The park opened in 1962.

OBAR (Quay; settlement; on US 54, 8 mi SW of Nara Visa; PO as Perry 1907–08, as Obar 1908–53, mail to Nara Visa). About 1906–07, a community sprang up around a switch on the N side of the CRI&P RR tracks. At the time the little settlement was called *Perry*, for a man by that name, but when in 1908 the rapidly growing community moved to the S side of the tracks, it changed its name to Obar, for the Circle Bar Ranch, whose brand was a circle with a bar under it. The NM Land and Immigration Co. promoted Obar heavily; one advertisement read, "The Coming City of the Famous Circle Bar Country.... Nothing can keep Obar down any more than it could hold back Chicago, Seattle, Oklahoma City or San Francisco. KEEP YOUR EYE ON OBAR." But Obar at its height never had more than about two dozen buildings, and today only abandoned structures remain.

O BAR O MOUNTAIN, 9,410 ft. (Catron; E of the Elk Mountains, just S of the Continental Divide). Named for a ranch brand.

OCATE (Mora; settlement; at the junction of NM 442 and 120, 23 mi NW of Wagon Mound; PO 1866–67, 1870–present). Two explanations, both plausible, exist for this name. The more commonly accepted one is that it comes from the Mexican Spanish, *ocote*, "pitch pine." The other is that it's from Jicarilla Apache and means "valley of the winds." Certainly the Jicarillas were in the valley of *Ocate Creek* around the time Hispanics settled here about 150 years ago, moving SE from Taos with their flocks of sheep, but hard evidence for either origin of the name is lacking. Ocate has been depopulated, and many buildings are abandoned, but it still has a PO and a few residents. The name is pronounced oh-cah-TAY locally. *Ocate Mesa,* 10,379 ft., is NW of the village of Ocate; *Ocate Peak,* 7,788 ft., is immediately S of the village.

Ocate Creek (Colfax, Mora; rises in Colfax County, flows SE through Ocate, below which it is diverted into Charette Lake, entering the Canadian River at Colmor).

OCHOA (Lea; settlement; 14 mi W of Jal; PO 1917–40, mail to Jal). This abandoned settlement is said to have been named for Ochoa, TX, but more likely the name comes from that of a Spanish family who settled here in relatively recent times. The name Ochoa also designates a prehistoric Indian culture that once existed here, as well as rocks of the late Permian geologic period.

ODEN (Grant; settlement; on the W side of the Mimbres River, S of San Lorenzo; PO 1912–17, mail to Sherman). Little is known of this abandoned community, including the origin of its name, sometimes spelled *Odon.*

OGLE (Quay; settlement; 15 mi SW of Tucumcari, between Circle S Mesa and Montoya; PO 1906–13, mail to Montoya). In May 1896, David Ogle, accompanied by five of his six sons and three sons-in-law, drove their cattle and horses from Oklahoma onto what came to be known as *Ogle Flat.* In 1901 the CRI&P RR came to what was to be Tucumcari, and with it came Ogle's wife, Mary, and their daughters. In 1906 a man named Adamson established a store and PO, naming it for the pioneer Ogle family. But when hard times struck, most residents left the area, and today Ogle is abandoned.

OHAYSI (Otero; settlement; in the Jarilla Mountains, NW of Orogrande; PO 1916–21, mail to Orogrande). This abandoned locality took its name from a PO at a mine in the nearby Jarilla Mountains. There the PO name proposed was OIC, for the Occidental Iron and Coal Company, but when the postal department rejected that, a phonetic rendering was submitted instead,

Oh-aye-si, which became Ohaysi, now often spelled *Ohayse.*

OIL CENTER (Lea; settlement; on NM 8, 16 mi SW of Hobbs; PO 1937–present). Since the oil-boom era of the 1930s, this aptly named inhabited community has been a center of oil activity, including being the site of Phillips Petroleum Co. and El Paso Natural Gas Co. plants.

OIL CITY (Eddy; settlement; 14 mi SE of Artesia). Mentioned in records as a developing community associated with the oil boom, but while the area is dotted with oil wells, no city is here.

OJITO (Rio Arriba; settlement; 9 mi NW of Lindrith; PO 1941–67, mail to Lindrith). This postal locality likely was named for its location in *Cañon de los Ojitos,* "canyon of the little springs," which heads just W of the Continental Divide. See *Ojo, Ojito (general).*

OJITOS FRIOS (San Miguel; settlement; 12 mi SW of Las Vegas). Spanish, "cold springs." Tiny inhabited Hispanic community; its PO was named *Gabaldon* (see entry).

OJO, OJITO (general). As T.M. Pearce explained, the word used in Spain for a spring is *fuente,* but this typically refers to a full-flowing upwelling of water from the ground, which is rare in NM, so the term used here is *ojo,* a Spanish archaism referring to a small, slow flow of water. The diminutive is *ojito.*

OJO CALIENTE (general). Spanish, "hot spring." GNIS lists 9 in NM.

OJO CALIENTE (Cibola; settlement; in NW part of county, on the Zuni River). The Spanish name of this small farming community on the Zuni Indian Reservation merely approximates its Zuni name, which means "place from whence flow hot waters."

OJO CALIENTE (Rio Arriba, Taos; settlement; on NM 285, 26 mi N of Española; PO 1871–present). Spanish, "hot spring," and the present settlement is only the most recent to have been centered on the geothermal waters here; on the mesa above the present village are the ruins of three ancient Tewa pueblos. The Tewas call the springs by a name that means "emerald green," because of the blue-green algae that grows in the hot water. During the late 1600s the Spanish established a settlement here, but in 1748 it was abandoned because of Ute and Comanche attacks. The site was resettled later in the 18th century. Lt. Zebulon Pike, brought here as a prisoner in 1807, estimated that 500 people lived here. The *Río Ojo Caliente* flows S from La Madera through Ojo Caliente, paralleling US 285, to join the Rio Chama N of Hernandez.

OJO CALIENTE (Socorro; military installation, Indian reservation; in SW corner of county, on the Alamosa River). Ojo Caliente, an adobe military installation that was never quite a fort, was established in 1874 as headquarters for the *Warm Springs Apache Reservation*, and in 1875–76 1,500–2,000 Apaches were here, but by 1877 most of them had departed. In 1877 Geronimo, who had escaped from the San Carlos Reservation, was recaptured here, and in 1879 Apaches led by Victorio attacked the garrison here. But in 1880 Victorio was killed in Mexico, and in 1882 Ojo Caliente was abandoned.

OJO DE LA CASA (Sandoval; settlement; in Las Huertas Canyon E of Placitas). This area was settled perhaps as early as 1661 when mines near here were opened by the Spanish. The locality originally was called *Cañon las Huertas,* "gardens, or orchards, canyon," (see *Las Huertas*), but the spring here was uncovered and being polluted by livestock, so as a result of a community meeting an adobe house was built to cover the spring, and soon the name Ojo de la Casa, "spring of the house," began to be used.

OJO DE LA VACA (Santa Fe; trading point; 20 mi SE of Santa Fe, on a county road 10 mi SE of Cañoncito; PO as Cow Spring 1899–1906). Only the cemetery remains at this locality, named for the spring, *Ojo de la Vaca,* 2 mi to the SW. The locality's name sometimes appears in English as *Cow Spring. Las Vegas de las Vacas,* "the meadows of the cows," is just to the SE.

OJO DE LAS VACAS (Luna; stage station; W of the Mimbres River). Spanish, "spring of the cows." According to George Adlai Feather, this was a stop on the Butterfield Overland Mail route that earlier had been a watering stop on the road from Santa Rita to Janos in Mexico. Metcalf, an 1849 American traveler, said the spring was named for cows that watered here. In 1870, Feather said, a hotel, probably small, was operated here.

OJO DE LOS ALAMOS (Otero; stage station; W of the Cornudas Mountains, 2.5 mi N of the Texas line). Spanish, "spring of the cottonwoods." George Adlai Feather reported this to be an old station on the Butterfield Overland Mail route, located at the base of *Alamo Mountain,* 6,670 ft. The station, which featured a large stone corral, was watered by seven seep springs

OJO DEL ESPIRITU SANTO (Sandoval; on the Jemez Indian Reservation, on NM 44, 18 mi NW of San Ysidro). Legend says these thermal springs were named when a member of an expedition one night saw two wraithlike spirals rising from the ground and rushed to his camp crying, "*El Spíritu Santo!*", "the Holy Spirit!" Other members of the expedition followed him back to the place and discovered columns of steam rising from the hot springs. The name *Espíritu Sto* appears on Miera y Pacheco's map of 1779, and in 1815 the *Ojo del Espíritu Santo Land Grant* was made to Luis María Cabeza de Baca. The name often appears in English as *Holy Ghost Spring.*

OJO DEL LLANO (Quay; settlement; E of Tucumcari, between US 54 and I-40). Ojo del Llano, "spring of the plain," was a well-known water source on the plains E of Tucumcari, and it was here that Don Higinio Esquibel, one of the early Hispanic settlers of this area, established his ranch, which soon attracted other families. Esquibel in 1880 built a chapel here dedicated to *El Santo Niño de Atocha.* The settlement has since been abandoned.

OJO DEL PADRE (Sandoval). See *Guadalupe.*

OJO DEL PERRILLO (Doña Ana; on the Jornada del Muerto, exact location unknown). In May 1598 the Oñate expedition was crossing the arid route later known as the Jornada del Muerto, and on the evening of May 23, after having traveled a day and a night without finding water, they made a dry camp. That evening, a small dog that had wandered from camp returned with muddy paws, and using this clue two of Oñate's men were able to locate two water holes, which they named "spring of the little dog." Later, the Apaches here became known as the Apaches del Perrillo, and Benavides in 1630 referred to the Jornada del Muerto district as the *Provincia de los Apaches del Perrillo*—all perhaps because of a little dog with muddy feet.

OJO ENCINO (McKinley; settlement; 6 mi NE of Star Lake). Spanish, "oak spring," but the Navajos who live here call the spring by a name meaning "rough rock water," referring to a number of fallen pinnacles.

OJO FELIZ (Mora; settlement; 1 mi E of NM 442, 9 mi SW of Ocate; PO 1922–77, mail to Wagon Mound). Spanish, "pleasant spring," though persons familiar with this inhabited settlement say the name was derived not because of the spring's appearance but rather because early settlers simply were happy for the spring's existence, as no other water is nearby.

OJO SARCO (Rio Arriba; settlement; in SE part of county, on NM 76, 1 mi S of Las Trampas; PO as Diamante 1909–12, as Ojo Sarco 1912–present). This small Hispanic community takes its name from being located on the *Cañada del Ojo Sarco,* named for a nearby "blue spring." The name sometimes is spelled *Ojo Zarco.* When a PO was established, it originally was called *Diamante,* for reasons unknown, but perhaps in deference to the postal department's reluctance to approve two-word names.

OLD COE LAKE (Doña Ana; in SE corner of county, just W of Otero County line). Albert and Mary Coe began ranching here in 1903. Albert had been born in Virginia in 1844, and his family had been involved in the infamous Lincoln County War, but Albert has been de-

scribed as "steady and quiet." See also *Glencoe.*

OLD HACHITA (Hidalgo). See *Hachita.*

OLD HORSE SPRINGS (Catron). See *Horse Springs.*

OLD BALDY (Otero). See *Sierra Blanca.*

OLD MAN HILL (Chaves). See *Sixmile Hill.*

OLD MAN SPRING (Chaves). See *North Spring River.*

OLD MIKE, 13,113 ft. (Taos; 2 mi SE of Wheeler Peak, at the head of Blue Lake Valley). This probably is an Anglo nickname for a summit previously known by the Spanish name, *Miguel.*

OLD PLACERS (Santa Fe). See *Dolores.*

OLD SAN JOSE (Cibola). See *San Fidel.*

OLGUIN (general). A Juan López Holguin came to NM with his wife, Catalina de Villanueva, with Oñate's troops in 1600, and other Olguins are mentioned as being in NM before 1680.

OLGUIN (San Miguel; settlement; in S part of county, exact location unknown; PO as Olquin 1905–11, mail to Anton Chico). The postal name clearly is a misspelling of the surname of the first postmaster, Juan B. Olguin. The community has long been abandoned. See *Olguin (general).*

OLGUIN MESA, 10,436 ft. (Rio Arriba; in the Tusas Mounains, 3 mi NW of Broke Off Mountain). Bears the Olguin family name, specific reason unknown. See *Olguin (general).*

OLIO (San Juan). See *Kirtland.*

OLIVE (Chaves; settlement; in NE part of county, 16 mi NW of Kenna; PO 1909–55, mail to Elida). The accepted local explanation for the name of this abandoned community in the San Juan Mesa area is that it recalls a rancher's wife.

OLIVER LEE MEMORIAL STATE PARK (Otero; 5 mi E of US 54, 8 mi S of Alamogordo). This state park, created in 1979, centers on scenic *Dog Canyon* and the ranch site of Oliver Milton Lee, one of NM's most powerful and controversial figures around the turn of the century. Lee, originally from Texas, settled here in 1892 when he joined Francois-Jean "Frenchy" Rochas in developing an irrigation system. After Rochas's unsolved murder in 1894, Lee's ranch became the headquarters of an extensive ranching empire. As his influence and holdings expanded, Lee became embroiled in the often-violent political and personal feuds of the time. He was a suspect in the murder of Col. Albert J. Fountain, a bitter rival, but was acquitted for lack of evidence. Along with other businessmen, he formed the Circle Cross Cattle Co., which at one time controlled a million acres of range land. Active in state and local politics, Lee served in the state legislature from 1918 until 1931. He died in 1941 at the age of 76. His descendants still live in the area. See *Dog Canyon*. See also *Omlee*.

OLLA (general). Spanish, "jar." Often a descriptive metaphor for landforms. See *Cerro de la Olla*.

OMEGA (Catron; settlement; on US 60, 8 mi E of Quemado; PO as Sweazeville 1928–30, as Omega 1938–66, mail to Quemado). When Felipe Padilla settled here in 1870, he called the community *Rito*, "creek"; *Rito Spring* is 1 mi W of Omega. Later the village was called *Sweazeville* by a filling station owner named Sweaze, whose name is still preserved on *Sweazea Lake*, 1 mi W of the village. Finally, in 1938, the name was changed to Omega, the last letter in the Greek alphabet, for reasons unknown.

OMLEE (Otero; settlement; on US 54 and SP RR, 5 mi S of Alamogordo). Originally a RR switch and now a loose inhabited community, Omlee combiness the initial letters and surname of Oliver M. Lee, whose ranch was nearby. Many persons in the area pronounce this name ah-ma-LEE. See *Oliver Lee Memorial State Park*.

OÑATE MOUNTAIN, 7,257 ft. (Doña Ana; in the San Andres Mountains, N of San Andreas Canyon, S of San Andrecito Canyon). It's ironic that probably the only place-name honoring the great colonizer of NM, Don Juan de Oñate, from whose 1598 expedition permanent European settlement here is dated, is on an obscure ridge Oñate himself likely never noticed nor would have cared to.

ONAVA (San Miguel; settlement; on US 85, 10 mi NE of Las Vegas; PO 1902–06,

1908–24, mail to East Las Vegas). Abandoned settlement. George Adlai Feather reported that a man named Wright in 1904 prepared "Onava Alterative Water," apparently some kind of curative water, and used it to treat ailing guests at his ranch; from this came the name Onava for the locality. Feather also observed that the Onavas form the population of an Indian town in Sonora, Mexico.

ONE BUTTE (Otero). See *Tres Hermanos*.

OPAL (Otero; settlement; in the Sacramento Mountains, 25 mi W of Weed; PO 1904, mail to Cloudcroft). Abandoned settlement, name origin unknown.

OPTIMO (Mora; settlement; 1 mi E of US 85, 9 mi SW of Wagon Mound; PO 1909–47, mail to Wagon Mound). According to T.M. Pearce, this area was settled by Pennsylvania Dunkards, a German-American religious sect, who attempted farming E of the RR. Local residents remember Optimo as a lively place, and while the settlement is gone, local people still refer to "the Optimo country." Name origin unknown.

ORAN (Otero; settlement; in E part of county, between Timberon and Piñon; PO 1904–07, mail to Avis). Abandoned postal locality and trading point, name origin unknown.

ORANGE (Doña Ana; settlement; 5 mi NW of Sunland Park, on NM 273). Small settlement, also known by the Spanish version of its name, *Naranjo*, "orange tree."

ORANGE (Otero; settlement; in SE part of county, just N of the Texas border; PO 1904–25, mail to Ables, TX). Rural PO that George Adlai Feather said took its name from attempts, all unsuccessful, to grow citrus fruit here.

ORCHARD PARK (Chaves; settlement; 13 mi SE of Roswell, between NM 2 and US 285; PO as Alellen 1904–07, as Orchard Park 1907–26). *Alellen*, likely a combination of two given names, Al plus Ellen, was the first name of this community. Later it was called Orchard Park, for the orchards planted by early settlers, among them the Christmans and Hortenstines. A WW II POW camp was located at Orchard Park, but it ended with the war, and eventually the orchards failed for lack of water. Now little remains of the community but the name, which is still recognized and used in the area.

OREJAS MOUNTAIN (Taos). See *Tres Orejas.*

ORGAN MOUNTAINS (Doña Ana; N-S range 10 mi E of Las Cruces, S of US 70-82). As Joseph P. Sánchez, director of the Spanish Colonial Research Center, NPS, tells it, when Don Juan de Oñate in 1598 saw these mountains, he jokingly called them the *Sierra de Olvido,* "Mountains of Forgetfullness," because some members in his party who previously had been in the area couldn't offer any recollections about the peaks, but less than a hundred years later, when Governor Otermín passed by in 1682 he referred to them by the descriptive metaphor, *Los Organos,* "the pipe organs." Later, in 1766–68, Nicolás Lafora called them *La Sierra Grande de los Mansos,* "the Big Range of the Fingers," though *Mansos* also referred to an Indian group; he also referred to them as the *Sierra de la otra Banda,* "mountains of the other side, or border," though Lafora also was aware of the name Los Organos. Other Spanish sources labeled them *La Sierra de Soledad,* "the Mountains of Solitude." But Organ Mountains is the name that has stuck, perhaps because organ pipes is such an appropriate metaphor for the 20-mile succession of stark, vertiginous peaks making up the range. The highest elevation is *Organ Needle,* 9,012 ft., at the S end of the range. The *Organ Mountains Recreation Area,* administered by the BLM, includes much of the W side of the mountains, while much of the E side is within Fort Bliss Military Reservation. On the W side is the *A.B. Cox Visiter Center,* preserving the historic Cox Ranch House, located 9.5 mi E of Las Cruces at the end of the Dripping Springs Road.

ORGAN, OLD AND NEW (Doña Ana; settlement; on US 70-82, 11 mi NE of Las Cruces; PO 1881–95, 1896–present). Organ began as a mining camp in the N foothills of the Organ Mountains, from which it took its name. Millions of dollars worth of lead, copper, and silver were mined here, and as many as 1,800 people once resided at Organ, but eventually the mines filled with water, and *Old Organ* all but died, only to be encompassed later by *New Organ,* which is a living community, many of whose residents work at the White Sands Missile Range or in Las Cruces.

ORIENTAL (Eddy; settlement; on the AT&SF RR, N of Carlsbad; PO 1910–16, mail to Lakewood). Little is known about this abandoned community, including the origin of its name.

ORO (general). See *Gold (general).*

OROGRANDE (Otero; settlement; on US 54 35 mi SW of Alamogordo; PO as Jarilla Junction 1905–06, as Orogrande 1906–present). As early as 1879 prospectors were exploring the Jarilla Mountains W of here, and in 1897 the EP&NE RR built a station here, calling it *Jarilla Junction.* By 1906 a gold rush was underway, and in that year the bustling mining camp changed its name to Orogrande, "big gold." The camp had 2,000 residents and a weekly newspaper; Oliver M. Lee piped water to the town all the way from the Sacramento Mountains. But as happened so often, the ore deposits soon were depleted, and the town today survives on its memories and on providing highway services.

ORTIZ MOUNTAINS (Santa Fe; between Madrid and Golden, E of NM 14). Early records and maps refer to this small mountain cluster as the *Sierra de San Lazaro,* "Mountains of St. Lazarus," most likely by association with the nearby 17th-century Tano mission named San Lazaro. Legend says that before 1680 the Spanish used Indian slaves to work gold mines here, sealed and hidden by the Indians after the Pueblo Revolt. The present name possibly recalls Nicolás Ortiz, a native of Mexico City who with his wife, Doña Mariana Coronado, in 1693 arrived in NM, and their descendants were active in the affairs of colonial NM. But the Ortiz most directly connected with the mountains' history was a sheepherder named José Francisco

Ortiz who in 1828 discovered gold in these mountains; in 1833 he and Ygnacio Cano petitioned for and were given the *Ortiz Mine Grant.* Several gold-mining camps sprang up, including Dolores (see entry), or Old Placers, and sporadic mining continues in the Ortiz Mountains to this day. The highest summit is the appropriately named *Placer Mountain,* 8,897 ft., also known as *Ortiz Peak.* Another summit is named *Sierra de Oro,* "mountain of gold."

ORTIZ PEAK, 11,209 ft. (Taos; in the Taos Range, NE of village of Red River, at head of Cabresto Creek). Specific origin of name unknown.

ORTON (Quay). See *Lucille.*

OSCURA (Lincoln; settlement; on US 54 17 mi SW of Carrizozo; PO as Oscuro 1901–43, as Oscura 1947–51, mail to Carrizozo). Though the name here, derived from the *Oscura Mountains* to the W, dates from when the community was in Socorro County prior to 1869, the present community received its impetus when the EP&NE RR came through in 1899; prior to that the locality had been a stop on the route, passing through Lava Gap in the San Andres Mountains, from Fort Stanton to the Jornada del Muerto. In 1906 E. G. Rafferty of Chicago purchased the land and laid out a townsite. Today a few residences keep the locality alive.

OSCURA (Socorro). See *Oscura (Lincoln).*

OSCURA MOUNTAINS (Lincoln, Socorro; N of the San Andres Mountains, separating the Jornada del Muerto on the W from the Tularosa Valley on the E). Spanish, "dark," the range said to bear this name because vegetation and volcanic rock formations make the mountains appear dark. This is especially conspicuous when the range is viewed from the Tularosa Valley to the E; from there forests near the top of the range give the mountains a distinct dark appearance in stark contrast to the barren gray summits of the San Andres Mountains just to the S. Highest elevation, *Oscura Peak,* 8,732 ft. The mountains often are labeled *Sierra Oscura* or *Oscura*

Range, but in 1975 the USBGN established Oscura Mountains as the accepted form.

OSHA (general). This is the NM Spanish name for the plant, *Ligusticum porteri,* known in English as lovage. Its stem is said to taste like celery, while its root is used medicinally. (Note: the parsley-like leaves of this plant resemble those of poison hemlock, *Conium maculatum,* also a member of the Umbelliferae family but potentially fatal if eaten, so extreme caution should be used when gathering *osha.*)

OSHA (Colfax). See *Black Lake.*

CAÑON OSHA (Sandoval; in the N Sandia Mountains, heads at Osha Spring and runs NW to Las Huertas Canyon). See *Osha (general).*

OSHA MOUNTAIN, 10,885 ft. (Colfax-Taos; in Sangre de Cristo Mountains, SE of Taos, on Colfax-Taos border). Also known by its Spanish name, *Cuesta del Osha. Osha Pass* is 2 mi N. See *Osha (general).*

OSHA PEAK, 9,313 ft. (Torrance; at the head of Trigo Canyon, on the crest of the Manzano Mountains, 2.5 mi N of Gallo Peak). See *Osha (general).*

OSO (general). Spanish, "bear." See *Bear (general).*

RITO DEL OSO (Mora; in SW part of county, a tributary of the Mora Pecos). The naturalist L. L. Dyche visited the Upper Pecos region in 1881–82 to collect animal specimens, and seeing numerous grizzlies near here he established his "bear trail" camp on this creek, which later became known as the Rito del Oso, "bear creek."

OTERO (general). The name Otero first appears in NM in 1759, when Pedro Otero was recorded as marrying Maria Juliana Alari; their descendants' names appear in 18th-century records in Albuquerque and Tome. The Oteros were especially prominent in the Los Lunas area. GNIS lists 8 Otero names.

OTERO (Colfax; settlement; at the foot of Raton Pass; PO 1879–80). In 1879, when the AT&SF RR reached the foot of Raton Pass, a lively little end-of-the-line construction camp sprang up, and in a festive ceremony it was named to honor Miguel A. Otero, NM Territorial delegate to Congress. The camp of Otero bustled for a few months, but when the line moved on to what is now Raton, Otero's residents moved with it, and Otero has vanished. See also *Otero County.*

OTERO (Valencia; settlement; near what is now Bosque Farms; PO 1905–06, mail to Los Lunas). This community, now absorbed into Bosque Farms, bears the name of the Otero family, long prominent in the Rio Abajo, whose members still live in the area. See *Otero (general).*

OTERO COUNTY (SE NM; county seat, Alamogordo). Otero County was created January 30, 1899, from southern Lincoln County and eastern Doña Ana County, in response to general population growth in the area, though political machinations of rival factions also may have been a factor; it resolved the embarrassing standoff between Oliver M. Lee and Sheriff Pat Garrett by removing Lee from Garrett's jurisdiction. The county originally was to have been named *Sacramento,* for the prominent mountain range dominating the county, but the name was changed to Otero to gain the support of Miguel A. Otero, who at the time was Territorial Governor of NM. Otero had been appointed by President McKinley in 1897 and served until 1906, the first Hispanic to hold that office.

OTIS (Eddy; settlement; on US 285, 5 mi SE of Carlsbad; PO 1893–1910, mail to Carlsbad). This inhabited farming community bears the name of T.E. Otis, a director of the AT&SF RR.

OTOWI CROSSING (Santa Fe; on the W bank of the Rio Grande, where NM 502 crosses the River, 7 mi W of Pojoaque). The name of this site on the Rio Grande comes from a Tewa word meaning "gap where water sinks," referring to a place where the water of nearby Pueblo Creek often sinks into the sand. Near this sandy spot, some 5 mi W of Otowi Crossing, are the ruins of *Otowi Pueblo;* the Indians of San Ildefonso Pueblo say their ancestors once lived there and at Tsankawi (see entry).

In modern times, *Otowi Bridge,* was the only crossing of the Rio Grande for many miles. The swinging roadway bridge, now restored near the current bridge, had a well-known stream-gauging station, and nearby was a freight stop on the "Chili Line," the D&RG RR line that ran until the 1940s between Santa Fe and San Antonito, CO. Otowi Crossing was made famous through books about Edith Warner, a remarkable woman who once was stationmaster at Otowi Crossing and who kept a tea room in her home here for about 20 years, until her death in 1951. The best-known of these books was *The House at Otowi Bridge,* in which Peggy Pond Church used Edith Warner's life story to write about the conjunction of the ancient Indian world and the modern nuclear age. Church says the name should be accented on the second syllable.

The name Otowi also appeared for a while on the PO in Los Alamos. In 1920, a PO was requested for Los Alamos Ranch, using the ranch name, but other names also were submitted, and the postal officials chose Otowi; in 1941, however, the PO name was changed to that of the community it served, Los Alamos.

OTTEN (Socorro; settlement; location unknown; PO 1922–32, mail to Abeytas). Abandoned postal locality, name origin unknown.

OTTO (Santa Fe; settlement; 5 mi N of Moriarty, on NM 41; PO 1907–23, mail to Stanley). Otto was one of several homesteader communities in this area. It took the given name of its first postmaster, Otto H. Goetz. Though the village has long since vanished, the name survives on the Otto Airport Beacon at the site.

OTTO (Union; settlement; N of US 56, SW of Clayton). Otto took the name of local rancher Christian Otto. Nearby was the related community of *Willow,* said to be an amalgam of the names of Will Otto.

Though Willow and Otto have vanished, the names still are recognized in the area, and the Otto cemetery still is maintained.

OUTLAW CANYON (McKinley; in the Zuni Mountains, near Nutria). As Gary L. Tietjen told it, Ramah in the early days was surrounded by outlaws, and in this steep, deep box canyon horse thieves built wooden ramps so that stolen horses could be driven to its bottom, otherwise inaccessible.

OVERTON (De Baca; settlement; 10 mi SW of Yeso). A ranch settlement, still inhabited by the Overton family.

OWL (general). See *Tecolote (general).*

OZANNE (Socorro; settlement; between Carrizozo and San Antonio; PO 1906–09, mail to San Antonio). This locality, sometimes called *Ozanne Springs,* was a stopping place for stages traveling between Carrizozo and San Antonio. It was named for Urbane Ozanne, born in Chateaubriand, France, who in 1880s opened a stage line between Carthage and White Oaks. The locality also was called the *Coane Stage Station.* The building of the RR line between El Paso and Vaughn ended the usefulness of the stage station, and while an inn operated here as late as the 1930s, only ruins remain today.

PAAKO (Bernalillo; archaeological site; in San Pedro Valley, just N of NM NM 14, 3 mi NE of San Antonito). This pueblo was first inhabited in prehistoric times, around A.D. 1300, to take advantage of the nearby spring, now called *San Pedro Spring,* but the pueblo continued to be inhabited into the early Spanish colonial period. The Franciscan mission *San Pedro del Cuchillo,* "St. Peter of the Ridge," was founded here in 1661 but abandoned before 1670. Paako is said to be an Indian word, probably Tiwa, meaning "root of the cottonwood."

PACHECO VILLAGE (Mora). See *Monte Aplanado.*

PAGE (McKinley; settlement; in the Zuni Mountains, 25 mi SE of Gallup; PO 1912–15, mail to Perea). Abandoned logging settlement named for Gregory Page, Gallup businessman, who along with his brother, James, operated a sawmill in Foster Canyon in the 1880s. *Page Valley* in the Zuni Mountains, renowned for good farmland, was named for the Page brothers.

PAGUATE (Cibola; settlement; on NM 279, 8 mi N of Laguna; PO as Paquate 1905–08, 1922–28, as Paguate 1928–present). In the 18th century, Antonio Paguat (spelling uncertain) was given a grant of land here, later purchased by the Laguna Indians who established seasonal farming communities. The site now known as Paguate was settled permanently around 1870 by refugees from the factional disputes at Laguna. The *Río Paguate* heads near here and flows S into *Paguate Reservoir* NE of Laguna. *Paguate Mesa* also is nearby.

PAINTED CAVE (Sandoval; in lower Capulin Canyon, in SW part of Bandelier National Monument). The shallow cave here contains early Indian and Spanish polychrome paintings.

PAINTER (Roosevelt; settlement; 6 mi W of Floyd; PO 1908–12, mail to Floyd). Abandoned homesteader settlement, named for its first postmaster, William A. Painter.

PAJARITO (general). Spanish, "little bird." This name occurs throughout NM, though its origins vary. Sometimes it is derived from birds nesting in trees, sometimes from a person's surname, and sometimes from other circumstances (see *Pajarito Plateau*). Occasionally the name *Pajarita* occurs; this means "paper kite or bow tie," but whether these meanings are intended or Pajarito has been incorrectly transcribed usually is unknown.

PAJARITO (Bernalillo; settlement; on the W bank of the Rio Grande, S of Rio Bravo Blvd. on Isleta Blvd.; PO 1868 intermittently to 1929, mail to Albuquerque). This community, now a southern suburb of Albuquerque, was first mentioned in the 17th century, and a tract of land called the *Sitio de San Ysidro del Pajarito Grant* once extended from here S to the Rio Puerco. The origin of the name here is obscure; it may refer to birds in the cottonwood groves along the Rio Grande, though Pajarito also is an Indian surname in the area. After Mexican Independence in 1821, Pajarito and Alameda gained municipal councils, and Pajarito maintained its PO into the 20th century. Today, several street names and an elementary school preserve the community's identity and name.

PAJARITO (San Miguel; settlement; on US 84, 3 mi SE of Rowe). Tiny inhabited settlement, settled after Pecos and San Miguel. See *Pajarito (general).*

PAJARITO (Santa Fe; settlement; on NM 30, 2 mi NE of its junction with NM 4, on the W bank of the Rio Grande). Tiny residential cluster, within San Ildefonso Pueblo Grant, likely named for the *Pajarito Plateau* (see entry) to the W.

PAJARITO ACRES (Los Alamos; settlment; immediately S of White Rock). Modern residential development, located on the *Pajarito Plateau* (see entry).

PAJARITO CREEK (Guadalupe, Quay, San Miguel; rises in NE Guadalupe County and flows NE to the Canadian River). Likely named for birds in trees along its course; see *Pajarito (general).*

PAJARITO PLATEAU (Sandoval, Santa Fe, Los Alamos; on the E flank of the Jemez Mountains, encompassing Los Alamos and Bandelier National Monument). The early archaeologist Edgar L. Hewett gave the name Pajarito to this sprawling high plateau of tufaceous volcanic rock, incised by deep canyons and arroyos. Hewett said the inspiration for the name came from the ruined pueblo whose Tewa name, *Tshirege,* means "place of the bird people." Tshirege ruin, near the modern town of White Rock, was described by Hewett as "the largest pueblo in the Pajarito district, and with the extensive cliff-village clustered about it, the largest aboriginal settlement, ancient or modern, in the Pueblo region of which the writer has personal knowledge, with the exception of Zuni." *Pajarito Mountain,* 10,441 ft., W of Los Alamos, is at the head of *Pajarito Canyon,* which runs W to E, 3 mi S of Los Alamos.

PAJARITO PEAK, 9,042 ft. (Sandoval; 10 mi NW of Jemez Pueblo). Origin of name unknown; see *Pajarito (general).* The peak's Navajo name means "grinding snakes," and the mountain is an important site in Navajo Wind Chant stories. It also has been known as *Bird Peak* and *Jemez Peak,* but the USBGN in 1909 accepted Pajarito Peak as the formal name.

PALISADES SILL (Colfax; landform; in Cimarron Canyon). Spectacular cliffs cut by the Cimarron River through igneous rock known as a *sill.* The gray pillars

of monzonite are reminiscent of a palisade, or fence, of lodgepole pine logs.

PALIZA CANYON (Sandoval; in the Jemez Mountains, heads S of Cerro Pelado and runs SW towards Ponderosa). Spanish, "sticks, wooden debris," likely referring to the dense stand of ponderosas and other trees here. A USFS campground named Paliza is here.

PALMA (Torrance; settlement; on US 60, 32 mi NW of Vaughn; PO 1903–35, mail to Encino). In NM, this term refers to the soapweed plant, or yucca. This abandoned community probably was named for an association with this plant.

PALMER RANCH (McKinley; western part of county; settlement; PO 1922–23). Short-lived postal locality that took its name from the ranch where it was located.

PALMILLA (Taos; settlement; 10 mi S of Antonito, CO). *Palmilla Station* was the first stop on the D&RG RR "Chili Line" out of Antonito, CO, and included numerous service facilities. It was named for a local abundance of yucca plants (*palmilla,* diminutive of the Spanish *palma,* "soapweed, yucca").

PALO (general). Though in Spain *palo* means "pole, stick," in the New World *palo* has come to be a generic term for "tree."

PALO BLANCO (Colfax; settlement; in SE corner of county). Some early maps show a settlement by this name SE of Abbott, likely named for the creek to the N.

PALO BLANCO CREEK (Colfax; heads in SE part of county and flows SE into Ute Creek). Spanish, "white tree." Named for *Palo Blanco Mountain* to the N, origin of that name unknown.

PALO ENCEBADO PEAK, 10,115 ft. (Taos; in the Sangre de Cristo Mountains E of Taos, 3 mi N of Shadybrook and US 64). Meaning obscure but likely Spanish, "burned tree." *Palo Encebado Canyon* heads on the NW side of this peak and runs NW into the Rio Pueblo de Taos.

PALO FLECHADO PASS, 9,101 ft. (Taos; on US 64, 3.5 mi W of Agua Fria). This was an important pass used by Indians, Hispanics, and Anglos traveling from the plains to Taos by way of the Cimarron River. The name is Spanish and means "tree pierced with arrows," and two explanations exist for it. One is that many arrows were found sticking in trees after an Indian fight here, but a more likely explanation is that it comes from an old Taos Indian custom; following a buffalo hunt on the plains, the Indians would shoot their remaining arrows into a large tree at the summit of a mountain near the pass. The pass was called simply *La Flecha,* "the arrow," and in 1706 mention was made of the *Flecha de Palo* Apache band inhabiting the plains E of the mountains. The pass also has been called *Taos Pass.* Nearby is *Palo Flechado Creek,* a tributary of Agua Fria Creek.

PALO VERDE (Lincoln). See *Ruidoso Downs.*

PALOMAS (general). Spanish, "doves."

PALOMAS (Quay; trading point; on CRI&P RR, 15 mi W of Tucumcari). Palomas began as a RR switch when the CRI&P built its line between Dalhart, TX, and Santa Rosa in 1901–02. A truck stop is here now. The name likely is derived from the *Palomas Hills* and *Palomas Mesa,* immediately to the SW.

PALOMAS CREEK (Sierra; heads SW of Cuchillo and flows SE to empty into Caballo Reservoir at Las Palomas). Likely named for doves nesting in the cottonwoods along its course.

PALOMAS GAP (Sierra; in the Caballo Mountains, S of Truth or Consequences). Soon after 1900 a toll road was built through this pass to connect the settlements on the W side of the Caballos, such as *Las Palomas,* for which the pass likely was named, with those on the E side, such as Cutter and Engle.

PALOMAS SPRINGS (Sierra; settlement; exact location unknown but likely near the mouth of Palomas Creek; PO 1911–14, mail to Hot Springs). Short-lived postal locality, likely named for springs near Palomas Creek (see entry).

PANCHO VILLA STATE PARK (Luna; immediately SW of Columbus, on NM 11). Shortly before dawn on March 9, 1916, the Mexican revolutionary—some say

brigand—Pancho Villa led his band of 400–500 soldiers on a raid of the US border town of Columbus. The purpose of the attack remains a mystery, and ultimately it failed; a week later, Gen. John J. "Blackjack" Pershing led 10,000–15,000 American troops in an equally futile pursuit of Villa. When the state park was created in 1959, it became the only public park in the US named for a foreign invader and was intended as a gesture of goodwill between the US and Mexico; the tree-lined lane in the park, planted with sycamores donated by the Governor of Chihuahua, is named *Avenida de Amistad,* "Avenue of Friendship." Pancho Villa was not the Mexican's leader's real name; he was christened Doroteo Arango, but he took the name Francisco "Pancho" Villa when he became a revolutionary at age 17.

PANCHUELA CREEK (Mora, San Miguel; heads W of Pecos Baldy and flows S to join the Pecos River at Cowles). This is a feminine form of Pancho, a Spanish nickname for Francisco, other feminine forms being Pancha and Panchita, but Elliott Barker said that locally *panchuela* seems to mean a piece of flat, open country fanning out from a timbered area—possibly derived from the word *poncho,* meaning a military coat—and this describes the mouth of Panchuela Creek. Some years ago the USFS renamed the Panchuela Ranger Station "Overton W. Price," for the great early organizer of the USFS under Gifford Pinchot, but the name didn't stick; Panchuela was too well established.

PANCHUELA CREEK (Santa Fe; flows N from Nambe Pueblo into Cundiyo Creek). Feminine form of Pancho, a Spanish nickname for Francisco, but possibly also a descriptive term for a creek's mouth. See *Panchuela Creek (Mora, San Miguel).*

PANKEY CANYON (Sierra). See *San Jose Arroyo.*

PANTHER HILL (Chaves; 0.5 mile W of US 285, 15 mi N of Roswell). A panther was killed here.

PARADISE HILLS (Bernalillo; settlement; NW of Albuquerque, near the Sandoval County line). This subdivision most likely bears a promotional name given by a developer.

PARADISE PLAINS (Guadalupe; settlement; exact location unknown; PO 1909–10, mail to Potrillo). Ephemeral settlement, name origin unknown.

PARAJE (general). Spanish, "place, residence," but in NM the term has also become a place name, referring usually to a "stopping place" or "campground" for travelers. Many old settlements originally were *parajes,* such as *Paraje de Belen* and *Paraje de Bernalillo.* Josiah Gregg, in *Commerce of the Prairies* (1844), described the *Paraje of Fra Cristobal* as "like many others on the route, neither town nor village, but a simple isolated point on the river bank—a mere *paraje,* or camping ground."

PARAJE (Cibola; settlement; on NM 124, between New Laguna and Casa Blanca). This inhabited community on the Laguna Indian Reservation had been just a seasonal farming settlement until it was settled permanently in the 1870s by refugees from the factionalism at Laguna. See *Paraje (general).*

PARAJE (Socorro; settlement; on the E bank of the Rio Grande, S of Socorro and Fort Craig; PO 1867–1910, mail to Milligan). The village of Paraje likely was established in the approximate location of the earlier *Paraje de Fra Cristóbal* (see entry); see also *Paraje (general).* In 1854 W.W.H. Davis passed by here and noted that this was only a campground, with no residences, but by 1860 195 persons lived here; William B. Rufsel had a hotel and Celso Medino a store. The village appeared in the 1860 Census records as *Fra Cristobal* but in later records simply as Paraje. It had 527 residents in 1870 and 315 in 1880. But Paraje declined with the deactivation of Fort Craig, and in 1915 the village was condemned during construction of Elephant Butte Dam and later flooded. N of Paraje was the hamlet of *Placita,* "small village," the site of festivities such as rodeos; in the foot-hills of the Fra Cristobal Range was *Los Parades,* "the stops, the ends, the shutdowns," labelling ruins of a large adobe structure there.

PARAJE DE FRA CRISTOBAL (Socorro; campground; on the Rio Grande, near San Marcial). For travelers setting out upon the Jornada del Muerto from the N, this was the last watering point. For most of its history Paraje de Fra Cristóbal was never a settlement, just a campground, a *paraje;* see *Paraje (general).* Vargas mentioned it in his campaign journal of 1692, as did Josiah Gregg in his *Commerce of the Prairies* (1844): "Our next camping place deserving of mention was Fray Cristobal, which, like many others on the route, is neither town nor village, but a simple isolated point on the river-bank—a mere paraje, or camping-ground." It was still just a paraje when W.W.H. Davis visited here in 1857, but the US Census of 1860 recorded 195 residents living at a village here. Now even its exact location is unknown, likely beneath the waters of Elephant Butte Reservoir. Like the mountain range to the E, it was named for Fra Cristóbal de Salazar, who may have died here; see *Fra Cristobal Range;* see also *Paraje (Socorro).*

PARK (general). As T.M. Pearce explained, "In certain areas of NM, chiefly the N and W, *park* is used, as it is in Colorado, to describe a valley shut in by high hills or mountains. This is an old English usage, but it also was common to early French trappers who came to the Rocky Mountains. They spelled the word *parc,* applying it to a cleared, grassy basin that served as a kind of enormous pen or corral for deer, buffalo, and other animals."

PARK CITY (Socorro; settlement; W part of Socorro; PO 1892–94, mail to Socorro). In 1881 Gustav Billing, a German immigrant, built a smelter just SW of Socorro, and the smelter and associated dwellings took the name Park City. In the early 1900s, the smelter was dismantled, and the "city" faded with it. This area also sometimes went by the name *La Smelta,* an Hispanicized version of "the smelter."

PARK SPRINGS (San Miguel; settlement; 5 mi E of US 84, 30 mi SE of Las Vegas; PO 1913–19, mail to Chaperito). A ranch now occupies the site of this former community, likely named for nearby geographical features.

PARKS (Grant; settlement; near Lordsburg; PO 1882–83, mail to Lordsburg). Ephemeral settlement, sometimes called *Park City,* named for its postmaster, William J. Parks.

PARKVIEW (Rio Arriba). See *Los Ojos.*

PARSONS (Lincoln; settlement; on the South Fork of the Rio Bonito, 5 mi above Bonito Dam, at the foot of Nogal Peak; 1888–1926, mail to Nogal). In 1886 R.C. Parsons made a gold strike here that quickly resulted in a bustling mining camp bearing his name. Only ruins remain today.

PARTON (Colfax; settlement; S of US 64-87, between Raton and Capulin; PO as Troyburgh 1878–84, as Parton 1884–86, mail to Raton). In 1849, Daniel Troy Sr. left his native Midwest for California to search for gold. Failing there he turned to farming and ranching, and in 1872 he established the Troy Ranch in Colfax County, NM, where he was joined in 1875 by his three sons: Daniel Jr., Oscar, and Jerome. Daniel Troy Sr. returned to California in 1877, where he died in 1879, but his sons remained on the NM ranch, and in 1878 the *Troyburg* PO was established as a ranch PO on the Raton-to-Tequesquite government mail route. Postal records spell the name *Troyburgh,* but locally it was Troyburg. In 1884 the PO was moved from the Troy Ranch to that of Alfred P. Rogers, 20 mi S, and the name was changed to Parton, for reasons unknown. Two years later the Parton PO was discontinued.

PASAMONTE (Union; settlement; on US 56, 33 mi W of Clayton; PO 1899–1947, mail to Gladstone). Before a community was established here, this site was visited by buffalo hunters and Indian traders traveling the Taos-Tascosa Trail. The name Pasamonte was manufactured from Spanish, and at least two explanations exist for its meaning. One is that it means "pass through or to the moun-tains," yet the terrain here hardly is mountainous but rather is rolling hills. The other is that it means "having traveled past the mountains," as one would do traveling eastward. Neither explanation is convincing. The Carl Gilg and Theodore Bangerter families were among the first homesteaders in the area; Carl Gilg started a store and became first postmaster. The PO was a mile S of the present Pasamonte Ranch headquarters.

PASCHAL (Grant; settlement; in the Burro Mountains, about 15 mi SW of Silver City; PO 1882–83, mail to Silver City). In 1879, Col. J.W. Fleming (see *Fleming*), John Swisshelm, and James Bullard (see *Bullard*) opened the St. Louis copper mine, the first in the Burro Mountains. A year later, Paschal R. Smith of Deming and Gen. Frank Marshall of Denver purchased the property. They organized the Valverde Copper Co. and built a smelter; the burgeoning mining camp took Smith's first name. By mid–1882 the town of Paschal had approximately 1,000 residents and was one of the nation's leading copper camps. But after 1883, when copper prices fell and labor costs rose, the town began to die. Eventually the smelter was dismantled, the buildings were torn down, and Paschal vanished.

PASTURA (Guadalupe; settlement; on US 54, 18 mi SW of Santa Rosa; PO 1903–60, mail to Santa Rosa rural branch). Spanish, "pasture"; in the American West *pasture* refers to any area used for grazing. This inhabited community was founded in 1901 by employees of the SP RR and the Pastura Trading Co., owned by the Charles Ilfeld Co. of Las Vegas.

PATOS (Lincoln; settlement; on Patos Creek, 9 mi E of White Oaks). Spanish, "ducks." Freighters between Socorro and Lincoln often camped overnight here, at *Patos Lake,* now usually dry but formerly with abundant water and many wild ducks. The lake is on *Patos Creek,* which heads on *Patos Mountain,* 8,508 ft., to the W and flows N and E into Cienega del Macho. The locality at one time had a school.

PATTERSON (Catron; settlement; 6 mi W of Horse Springs; PO 1884–87, as Whitfield 1890–92, as Patterson 1892–1906, mail to Joseph). George Patterson was a soldier who retired as a rancher at *Patterson Spring.* Richard Chase Patterson served as postmaster at Patterson; he had homesteaded in Catron County in 1875, fought Apaches, and dug *Patterson Lake* with just a wheelbarrow and a shovel. The PO here briefly was called *Whitfield,* for reasons unknown, but soon reverted to Patterson. A ranch is at the locality now.

PATTERSON (Union; settlement; location unknown; PO 1910–18, mail to Grenville). Abandoned community that took the surname of its first postmistress, Gertie Patterson.

PAXTON SPRINGS (Cibola; settlement; on NM 53, 15 mi SW of Grants; PO 1929–30, mail to Grants). Paxton Springs was a logging camp and in 1928 became the terminus of the Breece Co. RR (see *Breece*). At one time the community of Paxton Springs had a store, a school, a PO, and 100–300 residents. The site is said to have taken its name from an elderly homesteader woman known only as Mrs. Paxton, who lived here in the 1880s.

PEACH CANYON, SPRING (De Baca; N of Taiban). Old-timers say these names are corruptions of *Petes Canyon* and *Petes Spring,* Pete being Pete Maxwell, the rancher who owned the land.

PEACOCK CANYON (Union; a tributary of Cimarron Canyon, 35 mi NE of Folsom). A family named Peacock settled here in the early 1870s.

PEARL (Lea; settlement; 20 mi W of Hobbs; PO 1908–29, mail to Monument). Pearl was a PO in a residence—both now gone—that took the given name of its postmistress, Mrs. Pearl Roberts.

PEARSON (Roosevelt). See *Benson.*

PECOS (general). This widespread name is likely a Spanish approximation of the Keresan *payakona,* possibly derived in turn from a Towa Indian word *pa-kyoo-la,* meaning "place where there is water," doubtless referring to a spring at Pecos Pueblo. The reason a Keresan-derived

name might appear on a Towa-speaking pueblo—and hence on all the features named for the pueblo—is that when Oñate arrived here in 1598, he was accompanied by Keres guides and naturally adopted the name they used. See *Pecos Pueblo.*

PECOS (San Miguel; settlement; on NM 50, 63, and 223, just E of Santa Fe County line; PO 1883–88, 1893–present). Founded about 1700, this Hispanic community at one time was known as *Levy,* for reasons unknown. When a PO was created in 1883, the name was changed to that of the river on which the town is located. During the 1920s and 1930s, mining supplemented tourism in the local economy, but today tourism predominates.

PECOS BALDY, EAST, 12,529 ft., and WEST, 12,500 ft. (Mora; in SW tip of county, in the Truchas region of the Sangre de Cristo Mountains). Streams heading on these peaks are among the headwaters of the Pecos River. East Pecos Baldy formerly was called *Cone Peak*—it appears thus on an 1889 USGS map—or simply *The Cone. Pecos Baldy Lake* is at the E base of East Pecos Baldy.

PECOS PUEBLO (San Miguel; just N of I-25, 23 mi E of Santa Fe). When Coronado visited the Towa Indian pueblo now known as Pecos more than 400 years ago, he beheld what likely was the largest inhabited settlement in North America north of Mexico. The pueblo housed 500 warriors, had buildings four stories tall, and dominated the other pueblos of the area. The name Coronado recorded was *Cicuyé,* derived from a Towa word transliterated as *Acuyé* or *Pakora* and reported to mean "place down where the stone is on top." The pueblo was first called Pecos when Oñate arrived here in 1598; he had come from Keres country, accompanied by Keres guides, and naturally adopted the name they used; see *Pecos (general).* Franciscan missionaries to the pueblo bestowed upon it the title *Nuestra Señora de los Angeles,* "Our Lady of the Angles." But the pueblo began to decline with the arrival of the Spanish. Though the Spanish established a mission here, the population dwindled, reduced by sickness and Plains Indians raids, until finally, in 1838, the last inhabitants of Pecos moved to Jemez Pueblo, the only surviving Towa-speaking settlement. In 1935 *Pecos National Monument* was created to preserve the ruins and their history; this has since become *Pecos National Historical Park.*

PECOS RIVER (E-central NM). The Pecos River rises on the E side of the Sangre de Cristo Mountains and flows S, eventually to leave NM SE of Carlsbad and enter Texas, where it joins the Rio Grande NW of Del Rio. The first Europeans to see the river likely were Álvar Nuñez Cabeza de Vaca, Alonzo de Castillo Maldonado, Andrés Dorantes, and the Moorish slave, Esteban, who after being shipwrecked near Galveston in 1528 made their way across the Southwest to arrive at Mexico City eight years later. When Coronado and his men explored the Plains, they encountered a great river that was likely the Pecos; they called it the *Río Cicuyé,* because of its association with Cicuye Pueblo, now called Pecos Pueblo (see entry); this river also could have been the Canadian. But certainly it was the Pecos that Antonio de Espejo followed returning to Mexico from his expedition in 1583; he called it the "river of cows," for the great herds of bufflo he encountered along it. When Gaspar Castaño de Sosa passed by in 1590, he referred to it as the *Río Salado,* "salt river." But eventually the river again took the name of the famous pueblo it flowed near, though now the pueblo was called Pecos, not Cicuye. Tewas call the Pecos River by names meaning "down country river."

Pecos Falls, near the headwaters of the Pecos River, 1 mi N of its junction with Jarosa Creek, descends tumultuously some 50 ft. over steps of Precambrian quartzite.

PECOS WILDERNESS (Santa Fe, San Miguel, Mora; in the Santa Fe National Forest, in the Sangre de Cristo Mountains, both E and W of the Pecos River). Designated in 1933 and containing 223,333 acres, the Pecos Wilderness lies at the S end of the Sangre de Cristo Mountains, at the headwaters of the Pecos River, for which the wilderness is named. It includes numerous high summits and more than 150 miles of streams. It is administered jointly by the Santa Fe and Carson NFs.

PEDERNAL (general). Spanish, "flint."

PEDERNAL (Torrance; settlement; 3 mi S of US 60, 9 mi SW of Encino; PO 1917–55, mail to Encino). This former community sprang up around 1902 with the construction of the AT&SF RR and then survived on the agricultural economy of the Estancia Valley. It was named for the *Pedernal Hills* (see entry) to the N. When local agriculture declined, Pedernal faded as well.

PEDERNAL HILLS (Torrance; 12 mi SE of Clines Corners, 3 mi W of US 285). Low hills named for their flint by the Spaniards. Springs at the hills made them a stopping point for travelers. The highest point is *Pedernal Mountain,* 7,576 ft.; its Tewa name also means "flaking stone mountain."

PEDRO DE ARMENDARIS GRANT (Sierra, Socorro; E of Elephant Butte Reservoir and on both sides of the Rio Grande immediately N of the reservoir). This sprawling tract was granted to Pedro de Armendaris in 1820. Armendaris, a lieutenant stationed in Santa Fe since 1808, was forced by Indian raids to abandon his grant before leaving NM for Chihuahua. In 1993 the grant was purchased by media magnate Ted Turner and his wife, the film celebrity Jane Fonda, to complement other property they own in S-central NM. The name sometimes is spelled *Armendariz.*

PELADO (general). Spanish, "bald," referring in place names to barren, treeless summits.

PELON (general). When applied to hills or mountains in the Southwest, this Spanish term usually means bald, lacking vegetation. The diminutive is *peloncillo* or *peloncilla.*

PELONA MOUNTAIN, 9,204 ft. (Catron; in SE part of county, on the Continental Divide). Spanish, "baldy."

PELONCILLO MOUNTAINS (Hidalgo; in SW corner of county, running N and S along the Arizona border). Two equally plausible explanations exist for this name. *Peloncillo* in Spanish means "little baldy," and that accurately describes the range's barren summits, particularly in contrast to the higher, forested Chiricahua Mountains to the W in Arizona. But *peloncillo* also could be a misspelling of *piloncillo,* which in the Southwest referred to conical pieces of brown, unrefined sugar—a "sugarloaf"— and numerous peaks in the range do indeed resemble this; see *Sugarloaf (general).* The mountains also have been called the *Black Hills* and the *Guadalupe Mountains,* as well as the *Peloncillo Range,* but in 1985 the USBGN approved Peloncillo Mountains. The highest elevation is 6,928 ft., on *Gray Mountain.*

PEÑA (general). Spanish, "stone, rock." Also a common Spanish surname.

PEÑA BLANCA (Sandoval; settlement; on NM 22, 3 mi S of Cochiti Lake; PO 1867 intermittently to present). As T.M. Pearce explained, the Spanish name "white rock" could have come from the alkali-saturated knoll between this village and Santo Domingo Pueblo or else from the whitish cliffs prominent against the dark Jemez Mountains. And farther up the Rio Grande the town of White Rock was named for white deposits on rocks in the Rio Grande. But as Pearce said, "It should be noted, however, that the first, or at least one of the first, to establish himself in this territory was a José Miguel de la Peña, and the settlement was known as *El Rancho de José Miguel de la Peña* up to the time it was first referred to *El Rancho de la Peña Blanca.*" The area was originally part of the Montes Vigil Grant, awarded in 1745, but in 1758 José Miguel de la Peña bought 500 acres here; he founded his ranch in 1770, a date generally accepted for the establishment of Peña Blanca and also, most likely, the name.

PEÑA FLOR (Colfax; settlement; 4 mi S of the Colorado line, on the upper Vermejo River; PO 1888–1901, mail to Catskill).

Former rural PO, origin and meaning of name obscure.

PEÑASCO (general). Though this Spanish term often is translated as "rocky," in place names it usually means "rocky outcrop, bluff."

PEÑASCO (Taos; settlement; on Embudo Creek, on NM 75, 2 mi SE of Picuris Pueblo; PO 1874–present). This village, actually comprised of several smaller settlements, was founded in 1796 by three families from San Jose who petitioned Gov. Fernando Chacón to establish settlements in the area. Peñasco is said to have taken its name from being in a denuded valley, whose rocks were exposed, though in NM the Spanish *peñasco* more often refers to a rocky outcrop, or bluff. *Peñasco Creek,* now called Embudo Creek (see entry), flows through Picuris Pueblo to join the Rio Grande at Embudo.

PEÑASCO AMARILLO, 10,712 ft. (Rio Arriba; E of Tierra Amarilla, 2 mi S of the Rio Brazos). Spanish, "yellow outcrop."

PEÑASCO BLANCO (San Juan; archaeological site; in Chaco Culture National Historic Park, at the junction of Chaco and Escavada Washes, 3 mi NW of Pueblo Bonito). When Lt. James Simpson in 1849 saw this Anasazi ruin—in exterior dimensions second only to Pueblo Bonito—his New Mexican guide, Carravahal, told him its name was *Pueblo de Peñasco Blanco,* likely a reference to its location on a light-colored bluff—and that's the name that has stuck. The Navajo name for the ruin means "house on a point."

PEÑASCO BLANCO (San Miguel; settlement; on NM 94, less than 1 mi from Mora County line). Not really a settlement, this locality likely was named for a conspicuous "white bluff" in the Sangre de Cristo foothills to the W.

PEÑASCOSO MOUNTAIN, 10,979 ft. (Taos; in the Sangre de Cristo Mountains, in S part of county, S of NM 518). This name clearly is related to the Spanish, *peñasco,* "bluff, rocky," and indeed the peak also has been known as *Peñasco Mountain.* Several tributaries eventually entering the *Río Peñasco* (now Embudo Creek) head here.

PENDARIES (San Miguel; settlement; S of NM 105, 10 mi NW of Sapello; PO 1917–1926, mail to Rociada). Jean Pendaries (pronounced pan-da-RAYS) was a Frenchman who in the 19th century settled on a ranch here and founded the nearby community of Rociada (see entry). Later he moved up the valley to what is now Gascon (see entry), on the Rito de Gascon, naming both for his native Gascony. Pendaries now is not so much a settlement as a resort development, and golfers now stroll where once sheep grazed.

PENDLETON (San Juan; settlement; on NM 170, just S of the Colorado border; PO 1903–22, mail to La Plata). Former community, name origin unknown, though it could have some connection with Granville Pendleton, prominent rancher, farmer, jurist, and legislator from San Juan County at the time this community was active.

PENISTAJA (Sandoval; settlement; in NW part of county, N of NM 197, 18 mi W of Cuba; PO 1930–43). Former farming and stock-raising community that grew up around *Penistaja Spring; Penistaja Arroyo* is 1 mi W, while *Penistaja Mesa* is 1.5 mi N. While this curious name has been said to be derived from the Spanish *peña*, "boulder," more likely it's a corruption of the Navajo name for the place, transliterated as *binishdaahi'*, "I forced him to sit."

PENITENTE PEAK, 12,249 ft. (Santa Fe; in the Sangre de Cristo Mountains NE of Santa Fe, 2 mi S of Santa Fe Baldy). This bears the name of the Catholic sect calling themselves *Los Hermanos de la Luz*, "the Brothers of the Light," and popularly known as *Los Hermanos Pentitentes*, "the Penitent Brothers," or simply *Penitentes*. The sect, which functioned also as a fraternal society in isolated rural northern NM, was active throughout the 19th century and into the 20th. The group likely maintained a shrine on this summit, hence the name. See also *Sangre de Cristo Mountains*.

PENNINGTON (Union; settlement; 1 mi S of US 56, 6 mi E of Pasamonte; PO 1914–21, mail to Barney). Abandoned community, named for a local family.

PENROSE (Grant; settlement; 11 mi W of Silver City, 0.5 mi from Fleming). As the mining camp of Fleming (see entry) boomed in the 1880s, three Silver City men—M.B. Mikesell, Thomas Kendall, and a Mr. Ross—laid out a second townsite half a mile away and began sinking wells and selling lots. They selected the name Penrose, likely for the prospector whose strike had launched Fleming. According to local legend, Penrose chanced one day to sit on a ledge of what proved to be rich ore. He had been grubstaked by John W. Fleming and named the mining camp after him. By mid-1883, the village of Penrose had a butcher shop, bakery, store, blacksmith shop, and two saloons. But it has long since been abandoned.

PEP (Roosevelt; settlement; on NM 206, 24 mi S of Portales; PO 1936–present). Numerous explanations exist for this intriguing place name. Among the most popular is that it was inspired by the breakfast cereal, Pep, sold around 1950, but many local historians regard this theory as "baloney." Still another explanation is that the name was transferred here from Pep, TX, located to the E of the NM community. But T.M. Pearce, after much research, finally concluded that Pep was "named in the fall of 1925 by Edward Cox, when he established residence and a store here, choosing the name for a lively and energetic place." And that is the version subscribed to by at least some of the present residents of Pep.

PERALTA (Valencia; settlement; on NM 47, 4 mi NE of Los Lunas; PO 1861 intermittently to present). This community's name recalls Andrés and Manuel de Peralta, who came to NM before 1680, and also Pedro de Peralta, a native of Valladolid in New Spain, who was among those returning to NM after the reconquest of 1692. Their descendants still live in the area. Locally, the community has been known as *Los Placeres*, "the placers," for reasons unknown. In 1862, a battle between Confederate and Union troops occurred near here. In 1863 Col. Kit Carson mobilized his forces here prior to their campaign against the Navajos. In 1865, the PO's name was changed to *Los Pinos,* "the pines," or perhaps a family name, but in 1866 it reverted to Peralta.

PERALTA CANYON (Sandoval; heads on the S side of the Jemez Mountains and runs SE to join the Rio Grande at Cochiti Pueblo). This major canyon bears an Hispanic surname—see *Peralta* (*Valencia*)—but the canyon has not been associated with any particular individual or family.

PERCHA (Sierra; settlement; in the Black Range, 4 mi N of Kingston, on North Percha Creek; PO 1882–83, mail to Kingston). Percha, sometimes called *Percha City,* was one of many short-lived mining camps in this area and for most of its brief history consisted mostly of tents. The camp was named named for *North Percha Creek* (see *Percha Creek*) on which it was located. In 1893, when the price of silver began to drop, Percha began to die, and today only ruins remain.

PERCHA CREEK (Sierra; heads on the E side of Hillsboro Peak in the Black Range, flows E through Hillsboro to join Rio Grande at Percha Dam). The origin of the Spanish name *Percha* here is obscure. It means "coat rack, or hanger," though in the SW it also means "chicken roost, clothesline, robin," and it's possible the creek was named for birds roosting in trees here. George Adlai Feather reported that in 1887 the place also was known as *Findlays Camp.*

PERCHA DAM STATE PARK (Sierra; on the Rio Grande, immediately below Caballo Reservoir). Percha Dam was built in 1917 for irrigation and named for *Percha Creek* (see entry), which enters the Rio Grande here. The state park was established in 1970.

PEREA (general). History records members of the Perea family in Juarez in 1681. They joined the refugees of the Pueblo Revolt in returning to NM following the reconquest of 1692.

PEREA (McKinley). See *Coolidge.*

PEREA (Sandoval). See *Jemez Springs.*

PERICO (Union). See *Clayton.*

PERICO CREEK (Union; rises in central part of county, flows E and S, S of Clayton, into Texas). The Spanish *perico* means "parrot," but it also can be a family name. In Mexican Spanish *perico* refers to a plant, specifically *Canna,* a genus of reedlike tropical plants not found naturally in NM. The specific inspiration for the name here is unknown.

PERRY (Quay). See *Obar.*

PERRYVILLE (Colfax; settlement; in Cimarron Canyon, 3 mi SE of Eagle Nest; PO 1894–95, mail to Elizabethtown). Perryville, established in 1877, was a small community at the head of Cimarron Canyon that had a hotel, store, school, and several log cabins. It was named for a Mr. Perry, who had a blacksmith shop and worked as a machinist at the Moreno Valley placer mines. The village has long been abandoned.

PESCADO (McKinley; settlement; on NM 53 and the Rio Pescado, 5 mi SW of Ramah). The Zuni name for this place means "place of glyphs," referring to petroglyphs on the walls of an ancient village here; the Navajo name means "looming horizontal rock point." *Ojo Pescado,* Spanish, "fish spring," for which the settlement of Pescado was named, was an important watering point on old Indian, Spanish, and American trails, as well as a stopping place on the route laid out by Captain Willis in 1863 for the opening of Arizona Territory. See *Río Pescado.*

PETACA (Rio Arriba; settlement; on NM 519 11 mi SW of Tres Piedras; PO 1900–present). Spanish, "trunk for clothes," an old word for a hamper made of hide but now also used for modern American trunks and lockers. This inhabited settlement possibly was named for its proximity to *Mesa Petaca,* just to the NE, which may resemble a trunk. Petaca was settled around 1836 after Julian Martínez, his father, Antonio, and Francisco Antonio Atencio were granted land here that 12 years earlier had been granted to others who failed to occupy it.

PETROGLYPH NATIONAL MONUMENT (Bernalillo; on Albuquerque's West Mesa, from N of I-40 to Paradise Blvd.). Created in 1990 and absorbing the former *Indian Petroglyph State Park,* Petroglyph National Monument includes the five extinct volcanoes along Albuquerque's western horizon and the 17-mile-long volcanic escarpment among whose black boulders is a spectacular gallery of Indian rock art. Between 15,000 and 17,000 individual petroglyphs are estimated to exist in the monument. Most were created from A.D. 1300 to 1700, though a few are much earlier. While the purposes of the ancient artists still are obscure, many of the pictures have been linked to religious symbols still used by contemporary Pueblo Indians living along the Rio Grande.

PHANTOM BANKS (Eddy; in SE corner of county, near the Texas line, N of Red Bluff Reservoir). These hills, when viewed from Texas on foggy mornings, are magnified by the mist, like phantoms, to appear as huge cliffs, whereas in reality they are only 100 to 150 ft. high.

PHENIX (Eddy; settlement; early suburb of Carlsbad). This along with *Lone Wolf* were where saloons, gambling houses, and brothels were clustered during Carlsbad's early days, Lone Wolf on the N end of town, Phenix on the S. The reason for the unconventional spelling of Phoenix is unknown, but it appeared thus on the town's original plat. Phenix, often called *Jagtown* by the Eddy press, thrived as an alternative to Eddy, a dry community; Eddy County's first sheriff was part-owner of one of Phenix's largest saloons. But in October 1895, during a paroxysm of righteousness, the "undesirables" of Phenix were driven out, and Phenix became only a colorful memory.

PHILADELPHIA (Cibola). See *Laguna.*

PHILLIPS HILLS, SPRING (Lincoln; in SW part of county, the spring 3 mi W of Oscuro, the hills 5 mi SW). These bear the name of a family who homesteaded here.

PHILLIPS HOLE (Doña Ana; landform; 17 mi E of the Luna County line, 10 mi N of the Mexican border). Large volcanic depression, named for the Phillips family, with ranch holdings in this area.

PHILLIPSBURG (Sierra; settlement; on NM 52, about 6 mi NW of Chloride; PO 1904–06, mail to Fairview). About 6 mi N of Fairview (now Winston) a man named Phillips built a mill, to which ore was hauled in wagons, but the mill ran only a few days before being destroyed by fire, and soon the little community of Phillipsburg was abandoned.

PHILMONT SCOUT RANCH (Colfax; S of Cimarron). Once part of the sprawling Maxwell Land Grant, Philmont Scout Ranch was the creation of Waite Phillips, the Oklahoma oil magnate and philanthropist (see *Waite Phillips Mountain*). When Phillips first acquired the ranch, he intended to call it the *Hawkeye,* in honor of his native Ohio, but he soon changed this to Philmont, combining his name and a synonym for mountain. When Phillips in 1938 gave the ranch to the Boy Scouts of America, he suggested the name *Philturn,* combining his name with the word "turn," symbolic of every Scout's obligation to do a daily good deed, but the name Philmont is the one that has remained. Phillips was very fond of creating names that incorporated his surname; in addition to Philturn and Philmont he also manufactured Philbrook (his mansion) and Philtower and Philcade, the names of two buildings he owned.

PICACHO (general). Spanish, "a peak or pointed summit."

PICACHO (Doña Ana; settlement; 6 mi NW of Las Cruces). Located at the base of *Picacho Mountain* (see entry) and named for it, this inhabited settlement once was a stop on the Butterfield Overland Mail route. George Adlai Feather reported that *Picacho de los Nevárez,* "peak of the Nevarez family," was the original name of the locality, which he said was settled in 1855 by Candelario Chávez and some people from Socorro.

PICACHO (Lincoln; settlement; on US 70-380, 46 mi SE of Carrizozo; PO 1891–92,

1894–present). One of several small Hispanic communities along the Rio Hondo, this village is said to have been named for 5,853-foot *Picacho,* 3 mi NNW of town, although it is nearer *Picacho Hill* to the E, named for its steep and dangerous grade.

PICACHO (Socorro). See *Bernardo.*

PICACHO MOUNTAIN, 4,959 ft. (Doña Ana; 3 mi NW of Las Cruces). A major street in Las Cruces is named for this conspicuous cone-shaped peak, whose name is a Spanish-English double-generic, like Rio River or Laguna Lake.

PICK HANDLE FLAT (Lea; near Eunice). Said to have been named for weapons used in a fight between two feuding homesteading groups.

PICKETT SPRING CANYON (Sierra; trends SE to Middle Percha Creek, 1.3 mi NE of Kingston, on the E slopes of the Black Range). Sam Pickett was an outlaw and horsethief in this area in the late 1880s.

PICURIS (Taos; settlement; 17 mi E of Embudo N of NM 75, on the Rio Pueblo). On July 13, 1598, Oñate visited "the great pueblo of Picuries," likely applying to the Tiwa pueblo a Spanish corruption of its Keres name, *Pee-koo-ree-a,* "those who paint." In 1732 the pueblo was called *San Lorenzo de Picurís.* The Tiwa-speaking inhabitants of Picuris say, "Our native name is *Piwetha,* which means 'pass in the mountains,' probably from a gap about a mile downstream from the pueblo. When the Spaniards first entered NM our pueblo was quite large, some of the buildings were six stories high and our population was about 2,000." But by 1900, after centuries of disease and appropriation of the tribal lands, the pueblo was poor and underpopulated, with only about 200 persons. Today, Picuris is recovering, its population active and growing. *Picuris Creek* rises in the mountains E of the pueblo. *Picuris Peak,* 10,801 ft., 5 mi NE of Picuris Pueblo, is the main summit of the *Picuris Mountains,* a small subrange of the Sangre de Cristo Mountains; in the late 19th and early 20 centuries,

Picuris Peak was called *United States Peak. La Sierrita Picuris* is a small landform 3 mi NW.

PIE TOWN (Catron; settlement; on US 60, 14 mi E of Quemado; PO 1927–present). Here's the story, as researched by Kathryn McKee-Roberts: In October 1922 Clyde Norman (some local residents say his name was Herman L. Norman) filed a mining claim in the middle of the stock-drive route here. Mining wasn't profitable, so he opened a gas station that he called "Norman's Place," but he liked to bake, and when he began offering homemade apple pies as well as gas, he changed his sign to read "Pie Town." Early in 1924, Norman Craig arrived from Texas and went into partnership with Norman, but mining still wasn't profitable, and in November that year Craig bought out Norman. Craig continued the pie-making enterprise, however, and soon his new wife and her two daughters also were involved. The pies were very popular, not only with road travelers but also with local ranchers and cowboys. In 1927 the citizens of "Pie Town" asked for a PO; local lore tells that when a postal inspector suggested a more conventional name, Craig told him, "It'll either be named Pie Town, or you can take your PO and go to hell." Craig knew best; Pie Town remains among NM's most intriguing place names.

PIEDRA LUMBRE (general). Spanish, from either *piedra de alumbre,* "alum rock," or *piedra de lumbre,* "rock of light, fire," i.e., flint.

PIEDRA LUMBRE (Cibola; settlement; in NE part of county, on the Laguna Indian Reservation). Abandoned community, located on *Arroyo de Piedra Lumbre.* See *Piedra Lumbre (general).*

PIERCE CANYON (Eddy; runs W into the Pecos River 8 mi SE of Loving). Named for M.L. Pierce, wounded in a shootout here. A shot fired by Bob Ollinger passed through the body of John Jones, killing him and striking Pierce. *Pierces Camp,* the oldest cow camp in the area, used as early as 1874, was here.

PIGEONS RANCH (Santa Fe; historic site; near the summit of Glorieta Pass, E of Santa Fe). This was the largest and best-equipped hostelry on the Santa Fe Trail between the capital and Las Vegas. It was named for its owner, Alexander Valle, a French-American whose peculiar "pigeon-wing" style of dancing at *fandangos* earned him the nickname "Pigeon." Much of the action during the March 26–28, 1862, Civil War battle at Glorieta Pass swirled around Pigeons Ranch.

PILAR (Taos; settlement; on the Rio Grande, at the junction of NM 68 and 570, 17 mi SW of Taos; PO as Cieneguilla 1903–04, as Pilar 1918–21, mail to Embudo). Originally a Jicarilla Apache farming village was here; it was sacked and burned by Spaniards in 1694. In 1795, 25 Spanish families were granted land along the Rio Grande here, and the locality then was known as *Cieneguilla*, "little marsh." Relations between Europeans and the Jicarillas deteriorated until in 1854 at the Battle of Cieneguilla, fought at Embudo Mountain near here, Jicarillas and Utes inflicted heavy losses on 60 dragoons from Cantonment Burgwin near Taos. The community was known as Cieneguilla into the 20th century, but when a PO was re-established in 1918 it took the name Pilar. The Spanish *pilar* means "pillar," but the name possibly could be derived from the feminine name Pilar; Hispanic women in early NM often were given the name Pilar to honor the shrine of Nuestra Señora del Pilar ("Our Lady of the Pillar") in Zaragoza, Spain, one of the country's chief religious sites. The village's name also has been reported to have come from a male Indian named Pilar Vigil. Today Pilar is a popular site for persons running the rapids in the Rio Grande Gorge. The *Rito de Cieneguilla* enters the Rio Grande here from the NE.

PILAR (Valencia). See *Pueblitos*.

PILOTS KNOB (Mora). See *Santa Clara*.

PINA (Taos). See *Amalia*.

PINABETE (general). Rubén Cobos, in his *Dictionary of NM and southern Colorado Spanish*, says this refers to pine trees in general. The adjective form is *pinabetal*. GNIS lists it 9 times.

PINABETE PEAK, 11,948 ft. (Taos; in Taos Range, NE of Questa and N of Cabresto Creek). See *Pinatebe (general)*.

PINABETITOS (Union; in S-central part of county, near Barney). Abandoned Hispanic community, likely taking its name from *Pinabetitos Creek*, now called *Pinabete Creek*. See *Pinabete (general)*.

PINE, PINO (general). Several species of pines exist in NM—limber pine, Apache pine, Mexican white pine, Chihuahua pine, bristlecone pine, lodgepole pine, ponderosa pine, and piñon—but the one that most often has inspired "pine" place names is the towering ponderosa pine, as the limber pine is uncommon, and piñon usually appears under its own name. It should be noted, however, that with names such as Pino and Los Pinos, it's difficult to decide whether they're derived from association with pine trees or from the Spanish family name. Settlements are more likely to be the former, natural features the latter. GNIS lists 49 Pino names and 109 Pine names. See *Piñon (general)*.

PINE (San Miguel; settlement; 28 mi SW of Las Vegas; PO 1943–67, mail to Pecos). Former trading point, named for the tree.

PINEDALE (McKinley; settlement; 18 mi NE of Gallup). Trading point, its name likely describing its setting. The locality's Navajo name means "dried up bank around the water."

PINE FOREST (Grant; settlement; likely at site of Pinos Altos; PO 1860–61). This short-lived post office was likely associated with the village of Pinos Altos, as its postmaster, Isaac Langston, was living there at the time.

PINE HILL (Cibola; settlement; 4 mi S of NM 53, SW of El Morro National Monument). Inhabited community, on the Ramah Navajo Indian Reservation.

PINE LODGE (Lincoln; settlement; on the NE side of the Capitan Mountains, 3 mi SW of NM 246). Site of a summer resort constructed in 1909. The lodge burned before 1980, but cabins remain, now used by the USFS.

PINEHAVEN (McKinley; settlement; 12 mi SE of Gallup, 6 mi E of NM 602; PO as Danoffville 1923–24, as Pinehaven 1939–43, mail to Gallup). Active trading center located on the forested slopes of the Zuni Mountains. Hans Neuman operated a trading post here around 1900. Then Charley McKittrick operated a trading post from the Box S Ranch near here, and the locality was called *McKittrick*. Next the Danoff brothers, Russian-Jewish immigrants, operated a store and PO here in the 1920s, calling the PO *Danoffville*. Finally the community became known as Pinehaven, describing its setting. The Navajo name for the locality means "hard nose," for reasons unknown.

PINES (Sandoval; settlement; 2 mi W of Bandelier National Monument, in Cochiti Canyon; PO 1907–13, mail to Bland). Abandoned settlement.

PINESPRING (Otero; settlement; 9 mi SE of Cloudcroft, on US 82 in James Canyon; PO as Pine Spring 1890–95, as Pinespring 1895–1902, mail to Cloudcroft). Former community, named for a spring situated among pines in a side canyon to James Canyon.

PINKERTON (Mora). See *Wagon Mound*.

PINO MOUNTAINS (Socorro). See *Los Pinos Mountains*.

PIÑON (general). As early as 1542 Cabeza de Vaca was among the Spanish explorers who had noticed a resemblance between *Pinus edulis*, a species of pine producing edible nuts, and a similar plant in Spain and was using the same term for both—*piñon*. Because of the importance of these edible nuts to the diets and economies of the early NM settlers, place names incorporating *Piñon* are very common, occuring 27 times (GNIS). The name often appears with an English spelling, *pinyon*.

PIÑON (Otero; settlement; on NM 24, 44 mi SE of Cloudcroft; PO 1907–present). When a PO was established here and needed a name, John W. Nations, a schoolteacher, chose Piñon, because of nearby piñon trees. *Piñon Creek* is just N

of town.

PINOS ALTOS (Grant; settlement; 7 mi NE of Silver City on NM 15; PO 1867–1964, mail to rural branch of Silver City). In 1860 three prospectors, including Thomas "Three-fingered" Birch, found gold on Bear Creek. Soon other prospectors and miners flocked to the area, and the fledgling mining camp was called *Birchville*, for Birch. But Apache raids in 1861 and 1864 drove away many settlers, and when the town was resettled it took the name that earlier had been used by local Spanish-speakers, *Pinos Altos*, "tall pines," for the towering ponderosas that grew here (the variant *Pino Alto* was sometimes used). Mining no longer is important in the area, but the scenic town still nestles among the pines that gave it its name.

PINOS WELLS (Torrance; settlement; 6 mi NE of Cedarvale; PO as Pinos Wells 1884–94, as Pinoswells 1894–1913, 1914–1918, mail to Cedarvale). The first settlers here were Isidoro Lucero, José Rufindo Chávez, and Antonio Salas. Salas had two wells W of the settlement near two pine trees, so Pinos Wells was chosen as the name for the community. The route from White Oaks to Santa Fe passed through here, as Pinos Wells was among few reliable water sources, and the settlement boasted two stores, two saloons, a rooming house, and the area's first PO. (The two words later were combined into one, *Pinoswells*, in keeping with a postal policy, since rescinded, discouraging two-word postal names.) By 1914 Pinos Wells had 400 residents, but the population dwindled with the drought of 1917–20, and today only a few residents remain.

PINOVILLE (Catron). See *Mangas*.

PINTADA (Guadalupe; settlement; 8 mi S of I-40, 24 mi W of Santa Rosa; PO 1899–1947, mail to Santa Rosa). Spanish, "painted." Inhabited settlement, named for vividly colored soil in *Pintada Arroyo*, which heads in NE Torrance County and runs E through the community of Pintada. The Charles Ilfeld Co. of Las Vegas was active in developing sheep-ranching here in the late 19th century.

PIONEER (Lea; settlement; exact location unknown; PO 1910–11, mail to Bronco, TX). Ephemeral community, specific origin of name unknown.

PIPELINE CANYON (Otero; in the W Sacramento Mountains, 22 mi S of Alamogordo). Named for an ambitious project by Oliver M. Lee (See *Oliver Lee Memorial State Park*) to lay a water line from the mountains across the valley to support the RR at Orogrande.

PITA (Harding; settlement; location unknown; PO 1912–14, mail to Roy). *Pita* is a Spanish term for "century plant," but it's unknown whether that has anything to do with the name of this short-lived postal locality.

PITCHFORK (Lea; settlement; 25 mi NE of Tatum). Abandoned settlement and rural school, named for the pitchfork brand used by the ranch where the school was located. The community briefly was called *Slaton,* for reasons unknown, but the name reverted to Pitchfork. The locality's first location was 6 mi W.

PITTSBURG (Colfax; settlement; in SE corner of county, 6 mi W of Farley; PO as Hatod 1916–24, as Pittsburg 1924–32). Pittsburg was a High Plains farming community. Its name likely was derived from the Pittman family here; Mrs. Bernice Pittman was the first postmistress. The PO was established with the relocation to here of the *Hatod* PO, located about a mile W of Pittsburg. The Hatod PO had been established in 1916 by Harvey A. Todd, who named the PO for himself using his first two initials and the first three letters of his surname. In 1932 the PO moved once again, this time to Farley.

PITTSBURG (Sierra; settlement; on the SE side of Caballo Reservoir, where Apache Canyon entered the Rio Grande prior to the establishment of the lake; PO as Shandon 1904–06, mail to Garfield). Pittsburg was the little mining camp that sprang up almost overnight in 1903 when Bernardo Silva, intoxicated one night in Hillsboro, revealed the location of a rich placer gold deposit. On December 8, 1903, a meeting was held to determine a name for the camp, and it was decided to name it for the local mining district. By 1905 the camp had 150 persons, but the gold deposits soon were depleted, the miners left, and the camp vanished. Its PO was called *Shandon*, a name said to be that of the wash having the greatest placer gold deposits.

PLACER (general). *Placer* is a Spanish word referring to washing alluvial sediments, primarily from stream deposits, to obtain minerals, usually gold. Because of the intense interest in prospecting in NM throughout the years, Placer appears often in place names, especially along creeks and in mining areas.

PLACER FORK (Taos). See *Gold Hill.*

PLACER MOUNTAIN (Santa Fe). See *Ortiz Mountains.*

PLACERES (Sierra). See *Gold Dust.*

PLACERS (Bernalillo; settlement; on the Rio Grande, S of Albuquerque). This ephemeral community was named for gold-panning here; it vanished in a flood late in the 19th century.

PLACITA (general). See *Plaza, Placita (general).*

PLACITA (Sierra; settlement; 3 mi S of Monticello). Tiny inhabited community; its first settlers included the Sedillos, whose descendants still live in the area. Locally the village often is called *Las Placitas.* See *Plaza, Placita (general).*

PLACITA (Taos). See *Río Pueblo.*

PLACITA DE GARCIA. S of Canjilon.

PLACITAS (Doña Ana; settlement; NW suburb of Hatch). Also known as *Santa Teresa,* this little settlement still exists as a distinct adjunct of Hatch. See *Plaza, Placita (general).*

PLACITAS (Rio Arriba; settlement; on Canjilon Creek, 2.5 mi S of Canjilon). Small inhabited community. See *Plaza, Placita (general).*

PLACITAS (Sandoval; settlement; on NM 44, 7 mi E of Bernalillo; PO 1901–intermittently to present). The site of what is now Placitas originally was where Indian pueblos were located near water sources at the N end of the Sandia Mountains. Spanish settlement occurred in the 1760s, when the locality became part of the *San Antonio de las Huertas Grant,* but the main community, a walled town, was abandoned in the 1820s because of Apache raids. The inhabitants moved to Algodones; when they returned in 1840 they established three closely related villages: *Ojo de la Casa, Tejon* (see entries), and *Placitas.* Tejon has all but vanished, Ojo de la Casa survives as a few houses, but Placitas has flourished; during the 1960s and 1970s it was popular among the counter-culture movement in New Mexico, and now it thrives with more upscale residents seeking a scenic non-urban setting yet close to Albuquerque. See *Plaza, Placita (general).*

PLAIN (Quay; settlement; 3 mi S of Forrest; PO 1907–32). Located on the High Plains and likely named for this, Plain once had several stores and a school offering two years of high school. The settlement now is abandoned.

PLAINS OF SAN AGUSTIN (Catron, Socorro; runs NE-SW E and SE of Datil, E of NM 12). The basin of a vanished lake, 45 miles long and 12 wide, this is one of NM's most interesting landforms. The reason for the name being here is unknown. The name often appears, with the same meaning, as *Llano de San Agustin* and *San Agustin Plains,* but the USBGN in 1965 settled upon the form Plains of San Agustin. See *San Agustin (general).*

PLAINVIEW (Lea; settlement; 15 mi NE of Lovington; PO 1907–29, mail to McDonald). Plainview, an early homesteading settlement named for being on the High Plains, originally was called *Rat,* for the Rat Mill, an old watering place, whose name was derived from Bud Ratcliff, whose ranch brand was RAT. During its heyday, Plainview had three stores, a school, dance hall, hotel, skating rink, cotton gin, and a weekly newspaper, the *Plainview Herald.* Like many other homesteading communities, Plainview is now abandoned.

PLATA (general). See *Silver (general).*

PLATEAU (Roosevelt). See *Kermit.*

PLATERO (Bernalillo; settlement; on the Cañoncito Navajo Reservation, 6 mi N of I-40, 4 mi W of the Rio Puerco; PO 1916–18, mail to Seboyeta). The locality was once a PO operated by the Platero family, whose members still live in the area.

PLAYA (general). Spanish, "beach," but in the Southwest this term more often refers to depressed, sandy areas that are dry except after rains; see *Bolson (general).*

PLAYAS (Hidalgo; settlement; 4 mi S of NM 9, E of the Playas Valley; PO 1912–17, mail to Animas). The original Playas townsite, now vanished, was N of this settlement, along the SP RR. The present community is owned by Phelps Dodge Corp. and maintained for its workers. Both settlements were named for the conspicuous *playas* in the valley to the W; see *Playa (general).*

PLAYAS LAKE (Hidalgo; in the Playas Valley, S of NM 9, W of the Little Hatchet Mountains). 14 mi long and less than a mile wide, this is a lake in wet times, a *playa* in dry; see *Playa (general).* The *Playas Valley* was named for this. *Playas Peak,* 5,863 ft., is at the NW end of the Little Hatchet Mountains, overlooking the Playas Valley.

PLAZA, PLACITA (general). Though in Spain *plaza* means "courtyard, square," in NM, as in much of the Spanish-speaking world, the word very early became a synonym for "town," as the typical Hispanic communities here were organized around a *plaza;* the square, ringed by houses, not only was protection against Indian attacks but also was a focus for community activities. The diminutive, *placita,* has come to signify any small cluster of houses. Thus rural people in NM speak of a trip to town as a trip to *la plaza.* Fray Angélico Chávez points out that Spanish priests visiting NM in 1798 noticed the people here used *plaza* and the diminutive *placita* for "town" instead of other Spanish terms such as *aldea, poblacion,* or *pueblo,* the latter term here usually used for Indian villages. Plaza occurs 29 times in NM; Placita 10 times (GNIS).

PLAZA (Doña Ana). See *Salem.*

PLAZA, PLAZA LARGA (Quay; settlement; 10 mi S of Tucumcari; PO as Plaza 1908–11, mail to Tucumcari). Abandoned community, also known as *Plaza Larga*, "long town." This name is said to be derived from several long house-like buttes in the area having the appearance of a linear town. See *Plaza, Placita (general)*. *Plaza Larga Creek*, named for its association with the settlement of *Plaza Larga*, heads SW of Tucumcari and flows NE.

PLAZA BLANCA (Rio Arriba; settlement; 3 mi W of Tierra Amarilla, near NM 95, across the Rio Chama W of La Puente). Tiny inhabited community whose Spanish name means "white town," origin obscure but probably transplanted here by settlers from *Plaza Blanca* (see entry) near Abiquiu.

PLAZA BLANCA (Rio Arriba; settlement; 4 mi NE of Abiquiu). Inhabited hamlet, inspiration for of name, "white town," unknown. The *Plaza Blanca Land Grant* was made to Manuel Bustos in 1739 by Gov. Gaspar Domíngez de Mendoza. See *Plaza Blanca (Río Arriba)*.

PLAZA COLORADA (Rio Arriba; settlement; just S of Abiquiu). Spanish, "red village." Hamlet, mostly in ruins, associated with the *Plaza Colorada Grant*, made in 1739 by Governor Mendoza to Rosalia, Ignacio, and Juan Lorenzo de Valdéz, brothers and sisters, of Villa Nueva de Santa Cruz.

PLAZA DE ALCALDE (Rio Arriba). See *Alcalde*.

PLAZA DE ARRIBA (Valencia; settlement; N of Belen). Spanish, "upper village." An 1856 map used in litigation labels a settlement here, between Los Chaves and Los Gabaldones, opposite Tome on the W side of the Rio Grande. It's unclear what community this settlement was upper in relation to.

PLAZA DE LOS ESTEROS (Guadalupe; settlement; 8 mi N of Santa Rosa on the Pecos River). Here at Horseshoe Bend was a river crossing and campsite used frequently by prehistoric Indians and later by Jicarilla Apaches. Hispanic *comancheros* and herders established themselves here also, in a cluster of adobe buildings on the river's E bank— and probably following the signing of the Comanche Peace Treaty of 1786.

Foremost among the village occupants was Pedro José Perea, an Albuquerque *rico* whose herders grazed large flocks of sheep and goats on the vast grasslands extending eastward. Lt. Charles G. Morrison, US Army Corps of Engineers, visited the small hamlet in the fall of 1875, recording it then as the 'deserted plaza of esteros." Later, a Capt. William P. Calloway, formerly of Fort Sumner, built a three-room rock home on the ruins of the settlement, and he attempted damming the river for irrigation. Still later, an Hispanic family ran a trading post in the rock house. The site was abandoned in 1903, and the ruins were inundated by Santa Rosa Lake in the 1980s. *Esteros Creek* joins the Pecos River here; the Spanish *esteros* has been taken locally to mean "badlands" and "marshes," although the word more properly means "estuaries."

This community is not to be confused with the settlement of Los Esteritos (see entry), also in Guadalupe County on the Pecos River but further N.

PLAZA DE LOS LUCEROS (Rio Arriba). See *Alcalde*.

PLAZA LARGA (Rio Arriba; settlement; W of the Rio Chama, NW of Española and S of Hernandez). Spanish, "long town."

PLEANO (Quay; settlement; 8 mi W of Grady; PO 1907–14, mail to Plain). Abandoned homesteader community, name origin unknown.

PLEASANT (Union; settlement; 10 mi E of Des Moines; PO 1913–14, mail to Des Moines). Abandoned homesteader community, also called *Pleasant Valley*.

PLEASANT HILL (Curry; on NM 77 NE of Clovis, 1 mi from the Texas border). This tiny inhabited community originally was part of the Brown Ranch and the Shenault Ranch. It was organized as a community around 1910, and Lee Barnes is credited with naming the town at a meeting of "nesters" to decide a school location and a town name. After Barnes's death, his widow said he got the name from Pleasant Hill, TX, a town he was fond of.

PLEASANT VALLEY (general). Valleys are natural watercourses, and in arid NM this would enhance their appeal greatly; in the enthusiasm and optimism of settlement, a name such as Pleasant Valley would come readily to mind. The name occurs in at least 6 NM counties (GNIS).

PLEASANT VALLEY (Otero). See *Sixteen Springs Canyon.*

PLEASANT VALLEY (Roosevelt; settlement; SW of Dora). Abandoned settlement, its name describing its setting.

PLEASANTON (Catron; settlement; on US 180, 3 mi S of Glenwood; PO 1882–86, mail to Alma). This inhabited Mormon community—George C. Williams is said to have been the first settler, arriving in 1879—was named not for its pleasant location on the San Francisco River, surrounded by fields and orchards, but for an Army officer named Pleasanton.

PLOMO (Doña Ana; settlement; 46 mi NE of Las Cruces; PO 1902, mail to Las Cruces). Spanish, "lead." This abandoned mining camp owed its existence and its name to a lead mine. A large mill and smelter were built here but were abandoned when the lead deposits played out.

POCAHONTAS (Hidalgo; settlement; in the Steins Pass area). A little mining camp, long abandoned, served by the PO in Doubtful Canyon; see *Steins Pass, Beck,* and *Kimball.* The circumstances behind the name are unknown.

POE (Chaves; settlement; on AT&SF RR, 5 mi NE of Roswell). This locality, now just a RR siding, was named for the Poe family, pioneer settlers in the region. John W. Poe, born in Kentucky in 1850, was Sheriff Pat Garrett's deputy the night Garrett killed Billy the Kid; Poe later succeeded Garrett as Lincoln County Sheriff and still later became a prominent banker in Roswell.

POINT OF ROCKS (Colfax; landform; at eastern county line, near Ute Creek). This name describes a mound of syenite rocks rising from the prairie. The mound and the spring nearby were important landmarks on the Santa Fe Trail. It was near Point of Rocks that J.M.

White was killed by Indians and his wife and daughter kidnapped; they were killed six months later during the unsuccessful rescue attempt led by Kit Carson.

POINT OF ROCKS (Doña Ana). See *Las Peñuelas.*

CERROS DE LOS POSOS, 10,449 ft., 9,342 ft., and 9,555 ft. (Sandoval; in the Jemez Mountains, just E of the Valle Grande). Each of these three volcanic hills has a crater in its summit resembling a post hole, hence the Spanish name, "mountains of the post holes." *Valle de los Posos* is immediately to the S.

POISON (general). Six places in NM, including three springs, have this in their names, most likely because of toxic minerals in the water.

POJOAQUE (Santa Fe; Indian pueblo; on US 84-285, 16 mi NW of Santa Fe; PO 1870–1919, mail to Santa Fe). As the Tewa-speaking residents of this pueblo explain, "*P'o-suwa-geh,* 'a place where you drink water,' is the name of our village, the non-Indians pronounced it Pojoaque. Our village was occupied long before the period of the Spanish expeditions in the 15th century. We abandoned our pueblo after the Pueblo Revolt of 1680, and many of our people went to live with other Indian groups. The Spaniards settled in our village and farm lands in 1706; it was not until 1934 that 14 Pojoaque people reclaimed our land and established residence at the present location. Between AD 1200 and AD 1500 Pojoaque was one of the largest Tewa pueblos; today it is the smallest of the Eight Northern Pueblos." To the E of the settlement of Pojoaque, on the height above the village, is a residential cluster that both Indians and Hispanics called *Pojoaquito,* "little Pojoaque."

POJOAQUE CREEK (Santa Fe; heads in the Sangre de Cristo Mountains and flows W to the Rio Grande). This flows through two Indian pueblos—Nambe and Pojoaque—and is named for both of them. It's *Río Nambe* (see entry) from its headwaters to just E of Nambe Pueblo, when it becomes Pojoaque Creek, for the pueblo downstream.

POLVADERA (general). Spanish, "dusty, or more specifically, a dust storm or cloud of dust raised by any agent, such as horses, wagons."

POLVADERA (Socorro; settlement; just E of I-25, 10 mi N of Socorro; PO 1881–83, 1895–present). In 1846 Lt. William H. Emory, sent here to respond to an Indian attack on the village, wrote in his report: "Arrived at the town of Pulvidera, which we found, as its name implies, covered with dust." According to a local folktale, God told the residents here during a drought that if rain didn't come by August 10, the place would be a desert. Rain didn't come, hence the name, yet August 10, the feast day of the village's patron saint, San Lorenzo, is said always to bring rain. George Adlai Feather offered the explanation that the name came from a road detour over a dusty hill here. In the 1870 census, the village appeared as *San Lorenzo de Polvadera*. Socorro County has two places with this name, one in Spanish, the other in English; see *Dusty*. 4 mi W of Polvadera, in the Lemitar Range, is a small summit called *Polvadera Mountain*.

POLVADERA PEAK, 11,232 ft. (Rio Arriba; in the NE Jemez Mountains, SW of Abiquiu and NW of Chicoma Mountain). Hikers describe this mountain as being indeed dry and dusty. On Miera y Pacheco's 1778 map, based on the 1776–77 Escalante-Domínguez expedition, this mountain appears and is labeled *Polbadera*. The peak also has been called *Abiquiu Mountain*. Its Tewa name means "cicada mountain." *Polvadera Creek* rises S of Polvadera Peak and joins Cañones Creek. In 1776, Juan Pablo Martín was given the *Polvadera Land Grant*, extending N from Polvadera peak to Cañones.

PONCE DE LEON HOT SPRINGS (Taos; 7 mi SE of Taos). Reputed to have healing properties, these springs were named for the Spanish *conquistador* who in Florida sought the "Fountain of Youth."

PONDEROSA (Sandoval; settlement; on NM 290, 3 mi SE of Jemez Pueblo; PO 1933–43, 1949–present). This community originally had been known as *Vallecitos,* because of its location in a small valley, on *Vallecitos Creek*. Paulin Montoya and five other family heads arrived here in 1768. Other settlers followed, and soon two plazas had evolved, *Upper Vallecitos,* with San Antonio as its patron, and *Lower Vallecitos,* with San Toribio as its patron; St. Turibius was a 16th-century archbishop of Lima. When the sawmill at Vallecitos de los Indios, farther N in the Jemez Mounains, moved here because of the milder climate, local people referred to the two communities as *Upper Vallecitos* and *Lower Vallecitos,* but when this community applied for a PO, a new name was needed because Vallecito was duplicated on a PO elsewhere in the state, so the name Ponderosa was chosen instead, for tall ponderosa pines in the area. The old name, Vallecitos, still appears on some maps and still is used by a few old-timers, but it is being replaced by Ponderosa.

POÑIL (Colfax; settlement; on Poñil Creek, N and W of Cimarron; PO 1879–80, 1888–1913, mail to Cimarron). Abandoned community, named for its location on *Poñil Creek* (see entry). Usually referred to as *Poñil Park,* this settlement was a lively place, and miners from the Red River camps came here for dances.

POÑIL CREEK (Colfax; North, Middle, and South branches head in the Sangre de Cristo Mountains NW of Cimarron and flow SE to join the Cimarron River SW of Cimarron). This significant drainage takes its name from the Spanish word for the Apache plume shrub, *Fallugia paradoxa*.

POPE (Socorro; settlement; on AT&SF RR, 7 mi S of San Marcial). Three explanations—all plausible—exist for the name of this abandoned RR stop. One is that it was named for William Hayes Pope, first district judge in 1917. More likely is that it recalls Brevet Capt. John Pope who in 1855–56 identified locations for possible artesian well locations on the Jornada del Muerto. And the third is that it was named for one of the surveyors along the RR line. See also *Morley, Crocker, Engle, Cutter, Upham,* and *Grama*.

PORTAIR (Curry; settlement; on US 60, 7 mi W of Clovis; PO as Blacktower, 1905–12, mail to Havener). What is now the inhabited community of Portair began as a locality on the AT&SF RR and was named *Blacktower* by the RR because of a black water tank visible for miles on the flat countryside. Later the name was changed to *Maize,* for the sorghum grain grown in the area. Still later the name was changed to Portair, in recognition of Cannon Air Force Base located here.

PORTALES (Roosevelt; settlement, county seat; on US 70 and NM 206, 19 mi SW of Clovis; PO 1899—present). About 1881 Doak Good, a cattleman, became the first permanent resident of what is now Roosevelt County when he settled at *Portales Spring,* 6 mi SE of the present town. The springs, issuing from seven caves and among the few reliable water sources on the Llano Estacado, had long been known to travelers; Albert Pike visited them in 1832, and they were a regular water stop on the Fort Sumner Trail. Spanish-speaking travelers had called them *Los Portales,* because the overhanging cliff formations, offering welcome shade, resembled the porches, or *portales,* of Spanish adobe houses. Pumping for water in the area has lowered the water table, and the springs no longer flow.

The city of Portales began with "Uncle" Josh Morrison, who opened a store in a one-room building at Portales Springs. With the establishment of the construction camp for the PV&NE RR—known locally as the "Pea Vine"—Morrison put his store on skids and moved it to the camp, taking the name Portales with it. RR promoters promised irrigation water, but the project failed, and many homesteaders attracted here soon moved on, but the community survived and thrived. Eastern New Mexico University was established here in 1934, and today the university and agriculture support the community.

PORTER (Quay; settlement; on NM 392, 8 mi N of San Jon; PO 1908–15, mail to Revuelto). Porter began in 1907 when Jim and Mary Porter arrived from Virginia to homestead. They built a half-dugout that served as a PO, school, church, and community center. Eventually, the Porters moved to Arkansas, but the community they started—and their name—survive here, though only barely.

PORTER (San Juan). See *Bloomfield.*

PORTER (Sandoval; settlement; in the western Jemez Mountains, NW of Jemez Springs, on the Rio de las Vacas; PO 1933–37, mail to Bernalillo). Porter, also known as *Porter Landing,* was a logging camp operated by Lyman Porter, Bernalillo businessman who owned Lyman Porter Mercantile that in the 1920s and 1930s was a very important business there. Though the settlement has all but vanished, the names Porter and Porter Landing still are used.

PORTER STATION (Luna). See *Florida.*

PORTERIA (Sandoval; settlement; at the base of Cabezon Peak). A 1779 map shows a village named Porteria, Spanish, "gatekeeper's place," here, along with Mestas and Montoya *ranchos.*

PORVENIR (San Miguel). See *El Porvenir.*

POST OFFICE FLAT (Cibola). See *Diener.*

POTATO CANYON (Colfax; heads W of Raton and flows E, paralleling NM 555, to join the Canadian River). An farmer from the East settled here and raised potatoes, selling them to the miners at the nearby mining camp of Blossburg.

POTRERO (general). Gov. L. Bradford Prince and Adolph Bandelier both said this term was used in the Jemez Mountains along the Rio Grande to refer to long, finger-like mesas, separated by deep canyons.

POTRILLO (general). See *Horse (general).*

POTRILLO (Doña Ana; settlement; 3 mi N of the Texas border, 36 mi W of El Paso on the SP RR). Abandoned RR site, named for the *Potrillo Mountains* (see entry) nearby.

POTRILLO (Guadalupe; settlement; exact location unknown; PO 1908–14, mail to Riddle). Abandoned locality, though the school building still remains on a ranch here, likely named for its proximity to either *Potrillo Draw* or *Potrillo Hill,* in the NW part of county. See *Horse (general).*

EAST POTRILLO MOUNTAINS (Doña Ana; 3 mi N of Mexican border, SW of Las Cruces). Small, low limestone range; highest elevation 5,185 ft.

WEST POTRILLO MOUNTAINS (Doña Ana; in SW part of county, from S of I-10 to the Mexican border). Much more extensive than the *East Potrillo Mountains*, these mountains also are volcanic rather than sedimentary. The highest summit is 5,297 ft.; *Potrillo Peak* is 5,397 ft. The name is Spanish meaning "colt," possibly for wild horses that once ran in the mountains. See *Horse (general)*.

POWDER HORN CANYON (Grant; heads W of Mimbres Lake and runs W and SW into the North Fork of the Mimbres River). Two explanations exist for this name: one is that the canyon is shaped like a powder horn, which it is, and the other is that a powder horn was found here.

MOUNT POWELL, 8,748 ft. (McKinley; 4 mi NE of Thoreau). Bears the name of traders who once operated around Smith Lake.

PRAIRIE (general). As T.M. Pearce explained, this term, French not Spanish and referring to a broad tract of grassland, is not common in NM, where the Spanish term *llano* often is used instead, referring to a treeless plain. Nine NM places have Prairie in their names (GNIS).

PRAIRIE DOG (general). See *Tusas (general)*.

PRAIRIE VALLEY (Curry). See *Missouri Settlement*.

PRAIRIE VIEW (Lea; settlement; 15 mi NE of Lovington and 4 mi N of US 82). This pioneer settlement on the Llano Estacado, hence the name, once had a store and a three-teacher school that survived until 1948. Located in a rich farming area, a diffuse community remains here.

PRAIRIE VIEW (Quay; settlement; 35 mi SE of Tucumcari, NW of Grady; PO 1908–15, mail to Puerto). Abandoned homesteader community whose location on the Caprock would indeed have given a good view of the surrounding prairie.

PRATT (Hidalgo; RR locality on NM 9 W of Animas; PO 1905–13, mail to Animas). Former siding on the old SP RR; name origin unknown.

PREACHERS HEAD (Grant; 16 mi NE of Silver City). This rock formation, also called *Preachers Point*, is said to resemble the head of a man in prayer.

PRESIDIO (Otero; settlement; on La Luz Creek, near its confluence with Fresnal Creek). Spanish, "garrison, fortress." George Adlai Feather reported this to be an old settlement, inhabited in the early 1860s and destroyed by a flood around 1900.

PRESTON (Curry; settlement; in NE part of county, 1 mi N of Bellview; PO 1907–10, mail to Legansville). In 1907 a PO was established in the small grocery store 1 mi W of Liberty Bell School and named for Preston B. Trower, a homesteader. The community of Preston, now abandoned, was closely associated with *Bellview* and *Legansville* (see entries), their POs serving the same population but in different locations at different times.

PREWITT (McKinley; settlement; on NM 122 and 412, 19 mi NW of Grants; PO 1928–present). This community originally was called *Baca*, for a local family, but in 1916 two brothers, Bob and Harold Prewitt, arrived here from Gunnison, CO. Harold worked briefly in Grants, then set up a trading post in a tent here, and gradually the Prewitt name replaced that of Baca, though the Baca name survives on a Navajo chapter house here. The Navajo name for the locality is "white house."

PRIETA, PRIETO (general). Spanish, "dark, black." Descriptive name element, especially common on volcanic landforms.

PRIMERA AGUA (Bernalillo; settlement; just E of Tijeras). Now a residential adjunct of Tijeras, this community was named for a reliable spring whose name means "first water." *Primera Agua Canyon* enters from the SW.

PRIOR CREEK, SPRING (Catron; 8 mi NW of Gila Cliff Dwellings). Thomas C. Prior was an Englishman who settled between the Middle and West Forks of the Gila River, at the spring named for him. In December 1885, while visiting John Lilley, another Englishman and a neighbor, both were killed by Apaches. His name sometimes was spelled *Pryor.* See *Lilly Mountain.*

PRITCHARD (Curry; settlement; 2 mi N and 1 mi W of Pleasant Hill; PO 1907–08, mail to Texico). This was less a settlement than simply a rural school accompanied by a PO; name origin unknown.

PROGRESSO (Torrance; settlement; 13 mi SE of Willard on NM 42; PO 1894–1901, 1904, mail to Torrance). Originally spelled *Progreso,* Spanish, "progress," Progresso was a stop on the NMC RR. A box-car station and water tank stood beside the tracks, a country store and PO were run by a Mr. Boone, a one-room schoolhouse and Catholic chapel were here, and several ranches were at the foot of the nearby Rattlesnake Hills. Col. J. Francisco Cháves, a powerful political force in NM at the time (see *Chaves County),* owned a large sheep ranch near here when Torrance County was created, and through his influence Progresso was made the county seat; on January 1, 1905, the RR sent a special train with a passenger car to serve as a "courthouse on wheels." But the RR has gone, the county seat has moved elsewhere, and Progresso, never much, has become even less.

PROVIDENCIA (Luna; settlement; about 12 mi E of Deming, exact location unknown). Little is known about this long-abandoned locality, including what inspired its Spanish name meaning "providence."

PUARAY (Sandoval; Indian pueblo; SE of Coronado State Monument, exact location unknown). Also spelled *Puarai,* this name was applied to one of the Tiguex pueblos encountered by Coronado in 1540 and later by other Spanish explorers. It was at Puaray that Fray Agustín Rodríguez and Fray Francisco López were killed in 1581. The location of Puaray has been the subject of much controversy. Adolph Bandelier thought it was on the W side of the Rio Grande, opposite Bernalillo, whereas others have put it on the E side, N of Sandia Pueblo, perhaps at Bernalillo itself; fragments of pottery have been found at Las Cocinitas there. The name's meaning is unknown.

PUEBLITO (Rio Arriba; settlement; just across the Rio Grande from San Juan Pueblo). Spanish, "little pueblo." Suburb of the pueblo. Its Tewa name means "turquoise pueblo."

PUEBLITO (Socorro; settlement; 4 mi N of Socorro, on the E bank of the Rio Grande). Pueblito was most likely settled in the 1850s, probably by former residents of *La Parida,* whose village was being lost to the Rio Grande; it was called *Pueblito de la Parida* in the 1860 US Census. But Pueblito was not mentioned after that and has disappeared, though the area is still inhabited.

PUEBLITOS (Valencia; settlement; between Belen and Jarales; PO 1902–06, mail to Jarales). Tiny inhabited farming community, said to have briefly gone by the name of *Pilar,* for reasons unknown.

PUEBLO (general). The Spanish *pueblo* means "town, people," and as early as 1540 Castañeda, chronicler of the Coronado expedition, was calling the adobe Indian villages in NM *pueblos;* the Indians of these pueblos, being highly social and living communally in compact villages, fit the double meaning of the word perfectly. Eventually, *pueblo* was adopted into American English, and the Indians became known as Pueblo Indians, to distinguish them from nomadic Indian peoples, a meaning that has persisted to this day. Early Spanish-speaking New Mexicans tended to reserve the term *pueblo* for Indian villages, using *plaza* for non-Indian settlements, though a few Hispanic communities have been called Pueblo, and many more by the diminutive *Pueblito.* See *Plaza, Placita (general).*

PUEBLO (San Miguel; settlement; on NM 3, 3 mi S of San Miguel, on the E bank of the Pecos River; PO as El Pueblo 1876–98, mail to San Miguel). Also called *El Pueblo,* "the town," this inhabited community is one of several Hispanic agricultural settlements along the Pecos.

PUEBLO ALTO (McKinley; trading point; on NM 197, 7 mi E of Pueblo Pintado). Spanish, "high town." This active trading post, opened in 1916 by Charles Tucker, originally was near the junction of Chaco and Pueblo Alto washes, adjacent to Tanner Lake. The present location is at a place long known as *Raton Spring*. The Navajo name for Pueblo Alto means "spring on the edge of the rock."

PUEBLO ALTO (San Juan; archaeological site; in Chaco Culture National Historical Park, on the mesa N of Chaco Canyon). This Spanish name means "high town," derived from the site's commanding position overlooking Chaco Canyon. This location also has resulted in the ruin figuring prominently in the traditions of the Navajos, to whom it has been known by a term meaning "house of the great chief," or "house of the gambler."

PUEBLO BONITO (San Juan; archaeological site; in SW part of county, on the Chaco River). The largest of the ruins in Chaco Culture National Historical Park, Pueblo Bonito, "pretty town," has been called this since at least the early 19th century. Lt. James Simpson, visiting here in 1849, wrote: "We met another old pueblo in ruins, called Pueblo Bonito. This pueblo, though not so beautiful in the arrangement of the details of its masonry as Pueblo Pintado, is yet superior to it in point of preservation. The circuit of its walls is about 1,300 ft." When it was inhabited, circa A.D. 900–1300, Pueblo Bonito contained more than 800 rooms and housed perhaps 1,500 inhabitants. Its Navajo name means "propped rock," for an overhanging monolith known in English as *Threatening Rock* that finally fell in 1941, damaging some of the ruins.

PUEBLO CREEK (Taos; heads at Blue Lake in the Taos Mountains and flows through Taos Pueblo into Taos Creek). Named for *Taos Pueblo*.

PUEBLO DEL ARROYO (San Juan; archaeological site; in SW part of county, on the Chaco River). In his journal of the 1849 expedition here, Lt. James Simpson wrote: "A few hundred yards farther down the cañon [from Pueblo Bonito] we fell in with another pueblo in ruins, called by the guide Pueblo del Arroyo." It was aptly named, because it's located on the verge of the deep arroyo running up the middle of the canyon. The Navajo name for the ruins means "house beside the wash."

PUEBLO PEAK, 12,305 ft. (Taos; 7 mi NE of Taos Pueblo). A mountain sacred to the Taos Indians for whose pueblo it was named.

PUEBLO PINTADO (McKinley; settlement; on NM 197, 38 mi NE of Crownpoint). Active Navajo center, with school, stores, government buildings, etc. Named for the ruins 3 mi W (see entry). Near the center is the closely related but separate settlement of *Pintado*.

PUEBLO PINTADO (McKinley; archaeological site, 3 mi W of the settlement of Pueblo Pintado). When Lt. James Simpson visited here in 1849, he described this Anasazi site as "a conspicuous ruin called, according to some of the Pueblo Indians with us, *Pueblo de Montezuma*, and according to the Mexicans, *Pueblo Colorado*. Hosta [of Jemez Pueblo] calls it *Pueblo de Ratones* ['town of the rodents']; Sandoval, the friendly Navajo chief with us, *Pueblo Grande*; and Carravahal, our Mexican guide, who probably knows more about it than anyone else, *Pueblo Pintado* ['painted town']." One hopes Carravahal's authority was indeed superior, for his is the name that has stuck. The Navajo name in common usage for this ruin, which rises to three stories, means "wide house."

PUEBLO UNA VIDA (San Juan; archaeological site; in SW part of county, on the Chaco River). As with the names of many Anasazi ruins in this region, Lt. James Simpson's guide during the 1849 expedition, Carravahal, is credited with establishing the name of this Anasazi ruin; he called it Pueblo Una Vida, Spanish, "one life town," a name later authorities believe referred to the living stump of a tree once growing in the ruin.

PUERCO (general). Spanish, "dirty,"

though when applied to rivers it is synonymous with "muddy." Three NM rivers—the *Puerco River* in McKinley County, the *Río Puerco* in Rio Arriba County, and the *Río Puerco* in central NM (see entries)—have this in their names; GNIS lists 12 Puerco names.

PUERCO RIVER (McKinley; heads S of Crownpoint and flows SW through Gallup into Arizona). This often is known as the *Río Puerco of the West*, to distinguish it from the Rio Puerco flowing S and SE in Sandoval, Bernalillo, and Socorro Counties, which has been called the *Río Puerco of the East*. The Puerco River has appeared on maps as *Río Puerco del Orinte, Río Puerco del Ouest, Río Puerco of the West*, and even simply *The Perky*, but the USBGN in 1974 settled upon the name Puerco River.

PUERTO, PUERTECITO (general). Spanish, "door, gateway," but in place names it means "pass, gap."

PUERTECITO (Socorro; settlement; 35 mi NW of Magdalena, on Alamocito Creek, 2 mi W of its junction with the Rio Salado; PO as Puertecito 1903–30, as Field 1930–43, mail to Magdalena). Abandoned community whose Spanish name means "little gap," because the village was near a gap through which passes the Rio Salado. The PO here originally was Puertecito, but in 1930 it took the name *Field,* for Nelson Field, cattleman and former land commissioner in whose home the PO then was located. The first settler is said to have been José Angel Chávez, who ran sheep here in 1872.

PUERTO (Quay; settlement; 18 mi SE of Tucumcari; PO 1901–18, mail to Plain). This community, now abandoned, was settled by people from Borden, TX, and named for *Puerto Canyon,* through which an old trail crossed from the valley to the plains. Local English speakers often pronounce the name PURR-toh.

PUERTO DE LUNA (Guadalupe; settlement; on NM 91, 10 mi SE of Santa Rosa; PO 1873–1966, mail to a rural Santa Rosa branch). A fanciful folktale continues to be told about Coronado camping here and, seeing the moon rise

through a gap to the E, exclaiming *"Puerto de luna!"*—"gateway of the moon!" But in fact, the name's real origin is more prosaic. Members of the Luna family (see *Los Lunas*), settled here in the 1860s, at the mouth of *Puerto Creek,* later moving to the community's present location—indeed their descendants still live here—so the name really means simply "Lunas' gap." (Stanley Crocchiola advanced the theory that because *puerto* in colonial NM meant a firewood area, the name referred to where sheepherders employed by the Luna family gathered their firewood.) In the 1880s, Puerto de Luna was the Guadalupe County seat, with 1,500 residents, but the community later was overshadowed by Santa Rosa, and the seat was moved there. Now only 200 persons remain in Puerto de Luna, and local people often refer to the village simply by its initials—PDL.

PUNTA DE AGUA (Torrance; settlement; on NM 55, 7 mi N of Mountainair; PO as Punta de Agua 1890–93, as Punta 1894–1913, mail to Eastview). This inhabited community was settled after 1850 and took its name, "point of water," from a spring. Punta de Agua is its full original name, but in recent years it often has been abbreviated to *Punta.*

PUTNAM (San Juan; trading point; at Pueblo Bonito in Chaco Canyon; PO 1901–14, mail to Crownpoint). When the pioneer rancher-archaeologist Richard Wetherill and his family established a trading post at Pueblo Bonito in what is now Chaco Culture National Historical Park, the post came to be called by the name of the famous Anasazi ruin, Pueblo Bonito. But when the Wetherills applied for a PO at the post also to be called *Pueblo Bonito,* their proposed name was rejected by postal officials as being too long. So Mrs. Wetherill proposed the name Putnam for the PO, to honor the Wetherills' benefactor, Dr. Frederick Ward Putnam of Harvard University, who prepared the first plans for the study of archaeology here. Richard Wetherill was the first postmaster.

PUTNEY (Sandoval). Ephemeral name for the PO at Jemez Pueblo; origin unknown.

PUTNEY MESA (Cibola; 5 mi SW of Acoma Pueblo). The Putney family were 19th-century traders and wholesalers in Albuquerque.

PUYE RUINS (Rio Arriba; on the Santa Clara Indian Reservation, 10 mi W of Santa Clara Pueblo, on the N side of Santa Clara Canyon). These cliff dwellings are said by the Santa Clara Indians to have been the homes of their ancestors before drought drove them to the Rio Grande. The name is Tewa: *pu,* "cottontail rabbits," and *ye,* "to assemble," likely a place for hunting rabbits.

PYRAMID (Hidalgo; settlement; 9 mi S of Lordsburg; PO 1882–84, 1891–97, mail to Lordsburg). Abandoned mining camp, named for the *Pyramid Mountains* (see entry), in which it is located. Previously the site had been a water station on the southern overland route to California, the water coming from *Leitendorfs Wells;* the associated settlement was referred to as *Leitendorf.* Eugene Leitendorf dug wells here in 1852 when he drove cattle from Illinois to California. The camp of Pyramid, sometimes called *Pyramid City,* was born in the early 1880s and died in the late 1890s.

PYRAMID MOUNTAINS (Hidalgo; S of Lordsburg). Named for pyramid-shaped *Pyramid Peak,* 6,008 ft., the range's highest summit; the second highest is *South Pyramid Peak,* 5,910 ft.

PYRAMID PEAK, 10,597 ft. (Mora; in the Sangre de Cristo Mountains, W of LeDoux, SW of the Rio de la Casa). Forested summit, named for its shape.

PYRAMID PEAK, 4,990 ft. (Quay; 16 mi S of Tucumcari). This descriptive name was applied by geologist Jules Marcou during the Whipple Pacific RR Expedition along the 35th parallel in 1853. Locally, the summit also has been known as *Lovers Peak, Crazy Peak,* and *Crazy Woman Butte,* the last two names said to have come from an incident in pioneer days. As T.M. Pearce told the story, "A pioneer and his wife came from the East and settled in the valley near the peak. The woman, unaccustomed to the vast country, with its overpowering silences and its harsh extremes in weather, became demented. One day her husband missed her from their home, and after long searching finally found her body lying at the base of a high bluff on the N side of the peak from which she had jumped. From that time the peak has been known as Crazy Peak."

QUAHADA RIDGE (Eddy; 14 mi E of Carlsbad, S of US 62-180). This name is said to be a corruption of the Spanish *quijada,* "jaw," because the ridge's outline resembles a jaw.

QUALACU (Socorro; Indian pueblo; on E bank of the Rio Grande, 24 mi S of Socorro). In 1598 Oñate mentioned this, the most southerly pueblo of the Piro Indians, but in 1692 Qualacu was described as abandoned, and after that it faded into obscurity. *Qualacú* is how the Spanish transliterated a Piro word; its meaning is unknown.

QUARAI (Torrance; archaeological site, national monument; 10 mi NW of Mountainair, 3 mi W of Punta de Agua off NM 55; PO 1916–18, mail to Mountainair). The Tiwa Indians had a pueblo here long before the arrival of the Spanish, and all the many subsequent variations of the name are derived from the Tiwas' name for the place, *Kuah-aye,* "bear place." (*Acolocu* has been reported as an earlier name for the pueblo.) The Spanish established a mission here in 1629—the 1686–88 Peñalosa map identified the site as *Nra Señora de Querac, ou La Concepción*—but drought, failure of the springs, sickness, and raids by nomadic Indians caused the mission and the pueblo to be abandoned by 1674. In 1935 a national monument was established to preserve and display the mission's ruins, which now are part of *Salinas Pueblo Missions National Monument;* see also *Abo* and *Gran Quivira.*

QUARTELES (Rio Arriba; settlement; on NM 76, 3 mi E of Española). From the Spanish *cuarteles,* "district, or barracks for quartering soldiers." One of several Española suburbs, Quarteles was named

for a detachment of troops that once was quartered here.

QUAY (Quay; settlement; on NM 209 15 mi S of Tucumcari; PO 1904–present). Settled around 1902, Quay received its name in 1904 with the establishment of the PO. The name Quay, honoring US Sen. Matthew S. Quay (see *Quay County*), was chosen by postal officials from among several names submitted by the first postmaster, Simon J. Adamson. By 1906 a sizable tent city was at Quay. Sometime before 1926 the settlement was moved to its present location from 1.5 mi NW to be near the new highway. The broad valley surrounding the settlement is called the *Quay Valley.*

QUAY COUNTY (eastern NM; county seat, Tucumcari). Matthew S. Quay, born in 1833, built upon a distinguished Civil War record and other achievements to become US Senator from Pennsylvania in 1887. For reasons not entirely clear, he became a proponent of statehood for the Territory of NM and championed the issue valiantly. Enthusiasm for Quay ran high in NM, and when a new county was created here in February 1903, a resolution to name it for him was drawn up by its residents and sent to Governor Otero. Quay was invited to a special ceremony in Santa Fe later in 1903, but he never responded, possibly because he was ill; he died the following year.

QUEBRADA (general). Spanish, "break, ravine," in NM often referring in plural to the eroded escarpment of a plain or mesa.

QUEEN (Eddy; settlement; on NM 137, 30 mi SW of Carlsbad, in the Quadalupe Mountains; PO 1905–20, mail to Carlsbad). In 1898 Elias Gilkon Queen and his family settled in the Guadalupe Mountains. In 1891 he donated part of his ranch as a site for a general store and PO on the condition that it be called Queen. Hillsman Queen, Elias's son, and his bride, Abby Tulk, operated the store and PO. The village of Queen eventually declined and was abandoned, a lone chimney being an important landmark in the Guadalupe Moutains, but the area now is being resettled.

QUEENS HEAD, 8,184 ft. (Catron; 10 mi NW of Aragon). Conspicuous conical peak, but any resemblance to the head of a female monarch is not obvious.

QUELITES (Valencia; settlement; in NW part of county, at the junction of the Rio San Jose and the Rio Puerco). In 1761 Governor del Valle approved a land grant here called the *San Francisco del Valle Grant,* also called *Los Quelites Grant.* He stipulated that the village to be established be built in "one or two squares, and that they shall be joined, the walls of the houses of the settlers serving for each other, and the plazas they may establish must each be garrisoned by the round towers opposite each other for the defense from enemies." It's not known whether the settlers met those conditions, but an 1870 map of NM shows a *Los Quelites* settlement; nothing remains today. The name in NM refers to an herb, *Chenopodium album* known in English as "lamb's quarters."

QUEMADO (general). Spanish, "burned." Common descriptive term, appearing 16 times in GNIS.

QUEMADO (Catron; settlement; on US 60 and NM 36, 43 mi W of Datil; PO 1886–96, 1901–present). The meaning of this Spanish name is clear— "burned"—but numerous explanations exist for it being applied here. One is that when José Antonio Padilla and his family moved from Belen to a small stream near here, they found that the vegetation on its banks had been burned by Indians. They called the stream *Rito Quemado,* "burned stream," and the little settlement also took that name. An Hispanic settlement called *Rito* did indeed exist in the canyon 5 mi NE of the present village, but some persons say the name came from the village itself having been burned by Indians; the village then became known as *Rito Quemado,* later shortened to Quemado. Other local residents say the name came from ancient volcanic activity in the area having given the land a scorched appearance. Still other residents say it came from a burning underground coal deposit. And still another version says the name recalls an Apache chief here whose hand had been burned in a campfire. The first explanation, that of the burned stream banks, appears most plausible, but *quien sabe?*

QUEMADO (Santa Fe). See *Agua Fria.*

QUEMAZON CANYON (Los Alamos; runs NW from Los Alamos). Spanish, "conflagration," and this area does indeed seem to be in the path of electrical storms that would ignite fires. *Burnt Mesa* in nearby Bandelier National Monument was named for the same reason. The Tewa name for this canyon means "tufa-strewn arroyo."

QUERECHO PLAINS (Eddy, Lea; a high, flat plain rising to Mescalero Ridge midway between Carlsbad and Lovington). Early Spanish explorers mention encountering Indians here, probably Apaches, whose name the Spaniards recorded as *Querecho.*

QUESTA (Taos; settlement; on NM 522 and 38, 22 mi N of Taos; PO 1883–present). In 1829, Don Francisco Laforet came to this area and attempted to settle along the Red River, but Indian attacks eventually forced him onto a more protected site up on a ridge—and that is what *cuesta* means, "slope, ridge." (Why the name here is spelled with a *q* is unknown.) The community's formal name throughout much of its history, however, was *San Antonio del Río Colorado.* The name Questa, which likely had long been in common use, was adopted when a PO was established in 1883. The village had been a farming and trading center, but since the early part of the 20th century molybdenum mining has dominated its economy.

QUIEN SABE (general). Spanish, "who knows?" And as for the reason for these intriguing names, ¿quien sabe?

Quien Sabe Creek (Taos; E of US 64, between Taos and Ranchos de Taos).

Quien Sabe Canyon (Grant; SE of San Lorenzo).

QUIGUI, QUIQUI (Sandoval; Indian pueblo; near Santo Domingo Pueblo). According to Adolph Bandelier, the Santo Domingo Indians once lived at two pueblos, each of which was called Quigui. The earlier Quigui was on the Arroyo de Galisteo, more than 1 mi E of present Santo Domingo; the subsequent village was built farther W. The name's meaning is unknown. The mission here was called *San Rafael del Quiqui*. See also *Guique.*

QUINCY (Luna; locale; on I-10, W of Deming). Now simply Exit 55 on the Interstate, Quincy was the site of an SP RR station.

QUIQUI (Rio Arriba). See *El Guique.*

QUIVIRA. See *Gran Quivira (general).*

RABBIT (general). Rabbits, ubiquitous in NM, gave their name to 15 NM places, including 3 Rabbit Ears; the Spanish form *conejo* appears 11 times (GNIS).

RABBIT BRUSH (McKinley; settlement; in NW part of county). Inhabited Navajo community, whose English name likely translates its Navajo name.

RABBIT EAR MOUNTAIN, 6,058 ft. (Union; 6 mi N of Clayton, E of NM 370). While the numerous stories behind the name of this small mountain conflict in their details, they all agree on one thing: the mountain was named for an Indian by this name. Some accounts say he was a Cheyenne chief, others say he was Comanche. Some say he preyed on wagon trains here. Others say he was killed in a battle here and buried on the mountain. Most accounts say the chief's ears had been frozen, but why this resulted in the rabbit-ear sobriquet is unknown. It's likely the name existed in Spanish as *Orejas de Conejo* before the opening of the Santa Fe Trail; certainly the mountain has been an important landmark for a long time. Local people call the feature the *Rabbit Ears,* for there are actually two summits, even though the name was not derived from the landform itself. About 4 mi to the E is *Rabbit Ear Butte.* Both are on *Rabbit Ear Mesa. Rabbit Ear Creek,* listed as *Apache Creek* in GNIS, heads on the S side of Rabbit Ear Mountain and flows E into Texas.

RABENTON (Lincoln). See *Reventon.*

RACETRACK MESA (Catron; 1.5 mi W of Alma). Each Fourth of July for many years, local people would gather for horse races and a large picnic here.

RADIUM SPRINGS (Doña Ana; settlement; on NM 185, 15 mi N of Las Cruces; PO 1926–present). This community owes its name to free-flowing mineral hot springs here. When the springs were frequented by soldiers from nearby Fort Selden (see entry), they were known as *Fort Selden Springs.* The name *Randall Station* also has been reported for the locality. Later, when a PO was established, a mineral analysis of the spring water showed 2.57 millimicrocuries of radium per liter of water, which was enough to permit the use of *radium* in the town's name, a privilege not accorded any other town in the nation. Though the springs ceased flowing, wells continued to tap the mineral-laden hot water, and a resort spa was built. Recently Radium Springs has been a women's prison and an art center.

RAEL (Colfax; settlement; in SW part of county, exact location unknown; PO 1901–02, mail to Springer). Short-lived postal locality, name origin unknown.

RAGLAND (Quay; settlement; on NM 209 and 156, 23 mi S of Tucumcari; PO 1908–17, mail to Tucumcari). About 1906 Tom Ragland and his family filed on a claim that had been known as *Caprock,* because it's located on the Caprock, near the escarpment. They opened a small store and PO, with Maud Ragland the first postmistress. Later, the community moved 0.25 mi E to its present location. The store and the PO have closed, and most residents have moved away, but a few remain, and so does the name.

RAILROAD CANYON (Catron; enters Beaver Creek just N of Beaverhead). Around 1912 the USFS considered running a RR line from Magdalena to the N end of the Gila country to bring out timber, and this canyon was considered a likely route. Ultimately, however, the Gila was deemed to have too little timber, so the project was dropped.

RAILROAD CANYON (Colfax; parallels I-25 N of Raton). The AT&SF RR tracks follow this canyon to the highest point on the system, 7,622 ft., at Raton Pass.

RAILROAD MOUNTAIN (Chaves; begins 25 mi NE of Roswell and runs E about 35 mi, intersecting US 70). Not really a mountain but rather an elevated, narrow, linear igneous dike that viewed from some perspectives strongly resembles a RR bed.

RAINSVILLE (Mora; settlement; 2 mi E of NM 442, 8 mi NE of Mora; PO 1920–present). Originally, this settlement was called *Llano del Coyote,* "plain of the coyote," for reasons unknown, a name still recognized and used in the area, but when a PO was established it took the surname, Rains, of its first postmaster.

RAINY MESA (Catron; 12 mi SE of Reserve). Two explanations exist locally for this name: one is that a settler named Rainy lived here, and the second is that abundant rain has produced lush grass on the mesa.

RALSTON (Hidalgo). See *Shakespeare.*

RAMAH (McKinley; settlement; on NM 53 SE of Grants, 16 mi E of Zuni Pueblo; PO 1884–present). In 1874, Mormon missionaries moved into this area, settling a few miles N of the present village at a place variously called *Cebolla, Seboyeta, Savoia,* and *Savoya.* These names were derived from the Spanish *cebolla,* meaning "onion," which duplicates the meaning of the Navajo name for the site. A smallpox epidemic drove the settlers away in 1880, but other Mormon families came in 1882 from Sunset, AZ, settling at the present village. They originally called the site *Navajo,* for the Indians living nearby, but this name duplicated a postal name already used elsewhere in the state, so the name Ramah, taken from the Bible (Joshua 18.15), was chosen instead. The Hebrew word means "high place."

Ramah Lake (McKinley; 1 mi N of Ramah). When Ramah was settled, its residents built a dam across Cebolla Creek, creating this lake, which sometimes has been called *Timber Lake.*

RAMAH NAVAJO INDIAN RESERVATION (Cibola, McKinley; in the Zuni Mountains, SE of Ramah). This reservation is home to the largest of several Navajo groups living apart from the main reservation, governing themselves but keeping social and cultural ties with the main group. Navajos had lived in this area before the Long March (see *Fort Sumner*), and many returned here.

RAMON (Harding). See *David.*

RAMON (Lincoln; settlement; on US 285, 30 mi SE of Vaughn, on the De Baca County line; PO 1925–45, mail to Yeso). This name, a Spanish form of Raymond, was chosen by postal authorities from a list submitted for a PO; the submission is unexplained. Only a single residence, intermittently inhabited, remains at the site.

RANA (Quay; settlement; 28 mi NE of Tucumcari; PO 1908–25, mail to Logan). Rana was among many homesteader communities in this area, and at one time as many as 50 families lived at Rana, which had a school, church, and PO. Like many other such homesteader communities, however, it is now abandoned. It took its name from *Rana Creek,* which flows N past here into the Canadian River. *Rana* is Spanish and means "frog."

RANCHITO (Taos; settlement; on NM 240, 1.5 mi W of Taos). Spanish, "little ranch"; just 0.5 mi W is *Lower Ranchito,* also an inhabited satellite of Taos. Both names often appear in the plural, *Ranchitos,* and *Lower Ranchitos.* See *Rancho (general).*

RANCHITOS (Bernalillo; settlement; N of Albuquerque, between Los Ranchos de Albuquerque and Alameda). Sometimes called *El Ranchito,* sometimes *Los Ranchitos,* this community was closely associated with *Los Ranchos de Albuquerque,* and their names were almost synonymous. See *Rancho (general).*

RANCHITOS (Rio Arriba; settlement; on NM 68, at the N end of Española; PO 1905–07, mail to Española). Inhabited community, also called *Ranchitos de San Juan* but more commonly called simply

Los Ranchitos. See *Rancho (general).* Arroyo de Ranchitos enters from the E.

RANCHO (general). In Spain this term refers to encampments during military campaigns, but in Spanish North America, as livestock herds around *estancias* increased, the term *rancho* came to refer to smaller residences established for herdsmen and their families by estancia owners. From there the term *rancho*, and its Anglicized form *ranch*, came to refer to dwellings associated with any livestock operation. *Ranchito*, of course, is a smaller settlement than a rancho, and *ranchos de* has come to be synonymous with the English "suburb," as in *Los Ranchos de Albuquerque.* See also *Estancia (general).*

RANCHO (Roosevelt; settlement; in NW part of county, 14 mi NW of Melrose; PO 1913–25, mail to Melrose). Abandoned homesteader community, though its sole remaining building, the *Rock Lake School,* still functions as a community center, site of family reunions.

RANCHO COLORADO (Cibola; settlement; on the Rio San Jose, exact location unknown). An American traveler in 1853 reported this to be an abandoned sheep-ranching settlement on a cliff overlooking the stream.

RANCHO DEL MEDIO (Guadalupe; settlement; N of the Pecos River, 2 mi W of Dilia). Inhabited settlement, also called *Llano del Medio* or simply *Del Medio,* "the middle," possibly derived from the community's location between Anton Chico and Dilia.

RANCHO DE LA POSTA (Sandoval). See *Cabezon.*

RANCHO GRANDE ESTATES (Catron; settlement; on US 180, 1 mi S of its junction with NM 12, 8 mi SW of Reserve). This modern community was built on the site of a sawmill owned by Montague Stevens, who came to NM from Cambridge, England, in 1881 and was a direct descendant of Mary Queen of Scots. He had a sawmill and other operations here, sometimes called *Stevens Sawmill Plaza,* now the site of a housing development called *Rancho*

Grande Estates, whose name was the creation of a developer, having no historical basis.

RANCHOS DE ALBUQUERQUE (Bernalillo). See *Los Ranchos de Albuquerque.*

RANCHOS DE ATRISCO (Bernalillo). See *Atrisco.*

RANCHOS DE HIDALGO (Hidalgo; settlement; N of NM 9 E of Animas, S and W of the Continental Divide). This is a modern trailer park built and owned by Phelps Dodge Corp. for its employees.

RANCHOS DE LA JOYA (Socorro). See *La Joya.*

RANCHOS DE TAOS (Taos; settlement; 5 mi S of Taos on NM 68; PO as Ranches of Taos 1875–1982, as Ranchos de Taos, 1982–present). Before the Spanish settled here in 1716, this was the site of a Taos Indian farming settlement, hence the name. Apache raids led to the site's abandonment at least once, but it was resettled by the end of the 18th century. At that time it was called *Río de las Trampas de Taos,* "river of the traps of Taos"; its parish name is *San Francisco de Ranchos de Taos.* Later the name was changed to *Ranchos de Don Fernando de Taos*—see *Taos*—subsequently shortened to *Ranchos de Taos,* its present name.

RANCHVALE (Curry; settlement; 8 mi NW of Clovis on NM 311, 6 mi N of Cannon Air Force Base; PO 1916–17, mail to Clovis). Ranchvale was named by Vernon Tate, one of its first settlers and its first postmaster. The Ranchvale School, completed in 1919, was the first consolidated school in NM. A school and a few residents are still here.

RANDALL STATION (Doña Ana). See *Radium Springs.*

RANGER LAKE (Lea; settlement; 12 mi NE of Tatum; PO 1908–20, mail to Tatum). In the winter of 1879–80, Capt. G.W. Arrington led a contingent of Texas Rangers into this area in pursuit of Indians. Here they found a large spring-fed lake, which Arrington christened *Ranger Lake.* The Indians who had been camping at the lake had fled. The lake still exists 9 mi NE of Tatum, but the homesteader community 2 mi to the NE named for the lake has been abandoned.

RAT (Lea). See *Plainview*.

RATON (Colfax; settlement, county seat; on US 64-87 and I-25, 8.5 mi S of Raton Pass; PO as Willow Springs 1877–79, as Otero 1879–80, as Raton 1880–present). When the SF RR laid its tracks over Raton Pass in the spring of 1879, the only habitation near what is now the town of Raton was the *Willow Springs Ranch,* located on the W bank of Willow Creek opposite Soldier Hill in North Raton and named for two large willow trees watered by springs. The ranch, which included a PO, a tavern, and soon a general store, long had been a stopping and trading point for ranchers and travelers. When the RR pushed S in the fall of 1880, the residents of *Otero* (see entry) at the foot of the pass moved with it. The Willow Springs site had better water access than Otero, so A.A. Robinson, chief engineer for the RR, chose it as the permanent site for the division headquarters. The name Raton soon replaced Willow Springs as the name of the burgeoning settlement, most likely because of other features named Raton in the area and also because Raton was a daily utterance by RR men coming over the pass. The earlier settlement of Willow Springs often was called *Boggstown,* for the manager of the Willow Springs Ranch. Spanish-speaking settlers nicknamed their barrio E of the RR tracks *Buena Vista,* but Anglos used the epithet *Chihuahua.* Flushed with success as a burgeoning RR community, Raton called itself "the Pittsburg of the West."

The name Willow Springs was not forgotten, however. In 1986 a local sign-painter proposed changing the town's name back to Willow Springs, saying it would give the town a better image than the Spanish Raton, which means "mouse." But the citizens of Raton overwhelmingly opposed the change, and the Chamber of Commerce voted unanimously to drop the issue.

RATON MOUNTAINS (Colfax; part of the long range dividing NE NM from Colorado). Though the Spanish *raton* means "mouse," in NM the name has been thought also to refer variously to rock squirrels and chipmunks. *Barela Mesa* (see entry), 8,868 ft., directly N of Raton on the Colorado border, is the highest point in the range.

RATON CREEK (Colfax; heads in the Raton Mountains N of Raton and flows S through Railroad Canyon through Raton). Formerly called *Willow Arroyo,* then *Willow Creek.* See *Raton.*

RATON PASS (Colfax; in the Raton Mountains, on the boundary between NM and Colorado, 8.5 mi N of Raton, crossed by I-25). Since prehistoric times travelers have used this route connecting SE Colorado and NE NM. William Becknell crossed it in 1821 when he explored the Santa Fe Trail, and when subsequent travelers also chose the trail's N route from Bent's Fort, they had to confront Raton Pass; heavily laden wagons took up to 5 days to make the tortuous journey. (Now a car traveling I-25 over the pass between Raton and Trinidad, CO, makes the trip in less than half an hour.) After the American occupation of NM, Richens Lacy "Uncle Dick" Wootton received permission to put in a toll road over the pass; he blasted out 27 mi of wagon road. In 1879 the SF RR laid tracks over the pass, at 7,622 ft. the highest point on the line; trains now travel through a tunnel through the mountains beneath the pass.

RATTLESNAKE (general). Several species of rattlesnakes exist in NM, and places named for them also are ubiquitous; GNIS lists 51 throughout the state. The Spanish word, *culebra,* means "snake" but in NM usually is a synonym for "rattlesnake." The name *Punta Culebra de Cascabel* in Chaves county leaves no doubt as to which species is meant. Culebra appears only 4 times in GNIS.

RATTLESNAKE (San Juan; settlement; 6 mi SW of Shiprock). This oil-patch settlement is part of a name-cluster than includes *Rattlesnake Wash* 5 mi SW of Shiprock and the *Rattlesnake Oil Field,* 9 mi SW of Shiprock.

RATTLESNAKE CITY (Grant; settlement; in Gold Gulch, at the SW end of the Big Burro Mountains). This short-living mining camp received its name when 14 rattlesnakes were killed by miners making the first location; miners doing assessment work in the area had to be very careful where they sat down. The camp died with the establishment of Gold Hill (see entry).

RAVENTON (Lincoln). See *Reventon.*

RAW MEAT CREEK (Catron; flows into the West Fork of the Gila River, N of the Diablo Range). Though their details differ, all accounts agree this creek was named for an incident in which a hunter was forced to eat meat raw because he had no matches with which to make a fire for cooking.

RAYADO (Colfax; settlement; on NM 21 12 mi S of Cimarron; PO as Ryado 1873–81, as Rayado 1881–83, 1900–07, 1915–17, mail to Springer). Spanish, "streaked, as with lines drawn across a surface," but why this community bears this name is obscure. Certain tribes of Plains Indians were called Rayados by early Spaniards because of painted lines marking their faces. It's said the name was inspired by an Indian chief, possibly of this tribe, lived here in a hut until he died; he had lines on his face over which he streaked paint. And possibily a cliff marked with mineral veins or faults or water stains would be described thus. Kit Carson was the first Anglo settler here, and it was here that Lucien Maxwell married Luz Beaubien; they lived here before moving to Cimarron. The settlement now is administered by Philmont Scout Ranch as an historic site. *Rayado Creek* heads in the Cimarron Range and flows E through Rayado to join Urraca Creek W of Springer. *Rayado Mesa* is a large mesa SE of Rayado, S of Rayado Creek. *Rayado Peak,* 9,805 ft., is in the Cimarron Range, W of Rayado.

RAYO (Socorro; settlement; 32 mi NE of Socorro, on the W side of Chupadera Mesa; PO 1916–40, mail to Scholle). Spanish, "ray of light, thunderbolt." Abandoned community, circumstances of naming unknown.

REAL DE DOLORES (Santa Fe). See *Dolores (Santa Fe).*

REAL DE SAN FRANCISCO (Santa Fe). See *Golden.*

RECHUELOS (Rio Arriba; settlement; on the Rio del Oso, 15 mi NW of Española). This tiny community likely derived its name from the nearby creek, *El Rechuelos,* which heads on the W side of Polvadera Peak and flows NW into Polvadera Creek; the Spanish *rechuelos* means "freshet, small creek."

RECORD (Lea; settlement; W of Monument). During the 1930s oil boom, promoters hoped to launch a new town here, which they named for pioneer rancher, Henry Record, but the venture failed.

RED BLUFF RESERVOIR (Eddy; on the Pecos River, S of Carlsbad, E of US 285, spanning the NM-Texas border). Named for a nearby landform. To the NE is *Red Bluff Draw.*

RED CAÑON (Socorro; settlement; on the route between Carthage and White Oaks, about halfway between the two; PO 1886–88, mail to White Oaks). R.H. Hills, the postmaster here, also had a ranch here and furnished overnight lodging for travelers.

RED CLOUD (Lincoln; settlement; in the Gallinas Mountains, 9 mi SW of Corona; PO 1882–90, 1904–06, mail to Mountainair). Abandoned mining camp associated with and named for the Red Cloud Mine. A USFS campground is now at the site. The PO is said to have been first discontinued when the mail carrier was killed by outlaws before he could reach the stage stop where the PO was located.

RED DOME, 12,681 ft. (Taos; in the Sangre de Cristo Mountains, SE of Wheeler Peak, between Old Mike and Taos Cone). Appropriate descriptive name.

RED HILL (Catron; settlement; on US 60, 23 mi W of Quemado; PO 1935–57, mail to Quemado). Small, inhabited community, named for a nearby landform.

RED LAKE (De Baca; 4 mi W of Taiban, 1 mi N of US 60). This lake's waters have a reddish hue from the red-clay soil here.

Fed by Dripping Springs, this was a watering hole for early travelers and cattle drivers across the plains to Fort Sumner. It formerly was known as *Wilcox Lake;* see *Dripping Springs.*

RED LAKE (McKinley; just W of NM 134, on the AZ border). This name translates the lake's Navajo name, derived from red dust coloring the water in the spring here. Just to the N is *Red Valley.*

RED LAKE (Roosevelt; settlement; 9 mi W of Dora; PO 1907–17, mail to Portales). The lake for which homesteaders named this community is still here, but the settlement has gone.

RED MOUNTAIN (San Miguel; settlement; in E part of county, 12.5 mi NW of Trementina, 9 mi SE of Sabinoso; PO 1916–17, mail to Trementina). Short-lived postal locality, name origin unknown.

RED RIVER (Taos; heads N and E of Wheeler Peak in the Sangre de Cristo Mountains and flows N and then W into the Rio Grande). The Taos Indian name for this river means "red river"; the Spanish name is *Río Colorado;* and the English name is Red River—all because mineralized sediments turn the water reddish after heavy rains.

RED RIVER (Taos; settlement; on NM 38, 12 mi E of Questa, on the Red River; PO 1895–present). Prospectors had prowled the Red River Valley as early as 1869, and certainly local Hispanic ranchers had grazed livestock here, but settlement didn't actually begin until 1892 when Sylvester Mallette and later his brothers, Orrin and Jerome, arrived from Fort Garland, CO, and became the first homesteaders. Soon, however, other settlers, most of them prospectors, followed, and in 1894 E.I. Jones, a promoter from Colorado Springs, arrived at what is now Red River, bought the Mallette's claims, and organized a townsite. It was named for the river, and like most mining camps in the area it was euphemistically called a "city"; as late as 1930, the name *Red River City* still appeared on the front of T.D. Neal's Mercantile Co. building, though the "city" at that time consisted of little

more than two dozen decaying shacks. Eventually, recreation provided a more solid base for the local economy than mining ever had, and snow became a more valuable resource than gold.

RED RIVER PASS, 9,854 ft. (Colfax, Taos; on the county line, connecting the N end of the Moreno Valley with the Red River country).

RED RIVER SPRINGS (Quay). See *Hogadero.*

RED RIVER TOWN (Taos; settlement; on the Red River, about 3 mi from where it enters the Rio Grande from the E). In 1882, the Aztec Placer Co. and the California Placer Co. erected sawmills on the lower Red River, and an ephemeral mining-lumbering community sprang up called Red River Town.

RED ROCK (McKinley; settlement; on NM 602, 4 mi S of Gallup). Inhabited community named for reddish rock formations in the area; *Red Rock Hill* is just to the S.

RED ROCK STATE PARK (McKinley; just N of I-40, 6 mi E of Gallup). The park centers on huge red-orange sandstone formations, often called *Red Cliffs* and mentioned frequently in early expedition reports. E.F. Beale in 1857 wrote: "On our right runs, bounding the valley, a curious range of red sandstone bluffs, some hundred feet perpendicular in height, and stone abutments extending into the plain like capes at sea." A Navajo legend says the bluffs originally were gray but were stained red by the blood of a great stag fatally wounded by an evil demon.

REDLAND (Roosevelt). See *Emzy.*

REDONDO, REDONDA (general). Spanish, "round."

REDONDO PEAK, 11,254 ft. (Sandoval; in the Jemez Mountains 5 mi E of La Cueva). Named because of its conspicuous rounded shape. On some old maps this was labeled *Mount Pelado,* causing some confusing with Cerro Pelado (see entry) to the S. Other names for this conspicuous summit include *Cerro de la Jara,* "willow mountain," and *Sierra de Jemez,* "Jemez Mountains," because the Jemez region lies at its western base. The

Tewa name for the summit is of obscure etymology but could be translated as "flower mountain."

REDONDO PEAK, 12,200 ft. (Santa Fe). See *Capulin Peak.*

REDROCK (Grant; settlement; at end of NM 464, 22 mi N of Lordsburg; PO 1896–1968, mail to Lordsburg rural branch). This hamlet on the Gila River, now just a PO, was named for local geology and now associated with a wildlife area here. On most maps, the name is spelled as two words, *Red Rock,* but it's one word in GNIS.

REDSTONE (Grant; settlement; 15 mi N of Pinos Altos). A long-abandoned lumbering camp.

REED CANYON (Colfax; settlement; near the head of the Vermejo River, entering from the N). In 1875 "Cump" Reed from Missouri settled here. This abandoned community and the canyon where it was located bear his name.

REEDS PEAK, 10,015 ft. (Grant, Sierra; on the Grant-Sierra County line, S of Diamond Peak). Likely named for the family whose ranch was located 3 mi to the N.

REEDS RANCH (Doña Ana; settlement; N of Radium Springs; PO 1879). Owned by J.D. Reed, this was a ranch and settlement that served as a way station for travelers.

REGINA (Sandoval; settlement; on NM 96 13 mi N of Cuba). When J.H. Haleri, W.F. Fish, and a Mr. Collier in 1911 founded this settlement, still inhabited, they transferred the name of Regina, Saskatchewan, Canada.

REHOBOTH (McKinley; settlement; just S of I-40, 4 mi E of Gallup; PO 1910–present). In 1903 the Christian Reformed Church established a mission, boarding school, and hospital here, giving it the name Isaac in *Genesis* (26:22) gave to a well, declaring, "For now the Lord hath made room for us, and we shall be fruitful in the land."

RENCONA (San Miguel; settlement; on NM 34, 13 mi S of Rowe; PO 1916–75). The most likely explanation for this name is that it's a corruption of the Spanish *rinconada,* which can mean

"crossroads," describing the location of this locality.

RENDEZVOUS (Sierra; settlement; up Mineral Creek, NW of Chloride). The origins and correct form of the name of this abandoned mining camp are hopelessly confused. The camp has been called *Rendezvous, Rendezville, Roundyville,* and *Roundville*—all for reasons unknown.

RENDIJA CANYON (Los Alamos; heads NW of Los Alamos and runs E N of the village). Spanish, "fissure, cleft," describing this deep, steep-sided canyon.

RESERVE (Catron; settlement, county seat; on NM 12, in the SW part of the county; PO 1901–present). Settled in the late 1870s, Reserve originally was known as *Upper San Francisco Plaza,* or simply *Upper Frisco Plaza,* one of three closely related settlements along the San Francisco River; see *San Francisco Plaza.* The locality also was known locally as *Milligans Plaza,* or simply *Milligan,* for a prominent merchant and saloon keeper; perhaps he was related to one of two Fort Tularosa soldiers, Milligan and Patterson, who are said to have taken their discharge to search for the Lost Adams Diggings (see entry) and later established ranches in the area. The name Reserve was chosen for the PO to commemorate the US National Forest reserves and the USFS ranger headquarters here.

REVENTON (Lincoln; settlement; 20 mi NE of Carrizozo; PO as Raventon 1896–1900, mail to White Oaks; as Rabenton 1910–28, mail to White Oaks). This abandoned farming and ranching community flourished during the heyday of White Oaks. The name Reventon is believed to have been an Americanization of an earlier Spanish spelling, and the name also is often spelled *Raventon* and *Rabenton,* though Reventon is the form accepted by the USBGN in 1939. Its origin and meaning are unknown.

REVUELTO (Quay; settlement; on SP RR and US 54, 11 mi SW of Logan; PO 1897–1916, mail to Lesbia). Named for nearby *Revuelto Creek* (see entry), this community likely began as the *Revuelto*

Ranch in the late 1800s; George Adlai Feather said it was founded by 1875 by Cruz Gallegos. Later a store and PO were here. Today only a few abandoned buildings remain.

REVUELTO CREEK (Quay; heads E of Tucumcari and flows NE into the Canadian River W of Logan). Spanish, "muddy, turbid." Sometimes called *Revuelto River.*

REYES (Union). See *Miera.*

RHODES PASS (Socorro; in the San Andres Mountains, between Tularosa and Truth or Consequences). Until the land was withdrawn for the White Sands Missile Range, the highway connecting Tularosa and Truth or Consequences (then Hot Springs) passed through here. At the pass was the ranch of Eugene Manlove Rhodes, the cowboy-novelist whose fiction was well-known around 1900. *Rhodes Canyon* and *Rhodes Spring* also bear his name. Rhodes was a working cowboy throughout S-central NM, but most of his fiction was written at his wife's home in upstate New York. Finally, shortly before his death, he was able to return to his beloved NM, and he is buried here. His grave is marked by a stone table bearing the dates 1869—1934 and the inscription *Paso Por Aqui,* "he passed by here," the title of one of his more memorable works.

RIBERA (San Miguel; settlement; on NM 3 near San Miguel, on the Pecos River; PO 1894–present). Although the Spanish meaning of this name, "shore, banks," accurately describes this community's location on the Pecos River, the name in fact is derived from the Ribera family, whose members were among the pioneer settlers of nearby San Miguel and whose descendants still live here. Many NM Riberas are descendants of Salvador Matías de Ribera or Juan de Ribera, both of whom arrived in NM soon after the reconquest of 1692. The family name often is spelled Rivera.

RICARDO (De Baca; settlement; 5 mi S of US 60, on the AT&SF RR, 10 mi SW of Fort Sumner; PO 1908–56, mail to Fort Sumner). When the AT&SF RR built the Belen Cut-off, this was among many towns that sprang up almost overnight along the tracks. Said to have been named for a RR official with this given name, Ricardo was a RR water station and section house that also had a hotel and PO. Nothing remains here now.

RICE (Quay). See *Hudson.*

RICHARDSON (Lincoln; settlement; on NM 246, on the N side of the Capitan Mountains; PO 1895–1912, mail to Capitan). Abandoned settlement named for its first postmaster, Andy Richardson, who also managed the Capitan Land and Cattle Co. He was a brother of Judge Richardson of Roswell. As late as 1952, the descendants of him and his wife still lived in the area.

RICHEY (Guadalupe; trading point; on the route from Tucumcari to Santa Fe; PO 1912–20). Former store and PO, likely named for its owner and postmaster.

RICHLAND (Roosevelt; settlement; 5 mi E of NM 206, 30 mi S of Portales; PO 1908–36, mail to Pep). Abandoned homesteader community, name origin unknown.

RICHMOND (Hidalgo). See *Virden.*

RICOLITE (Grant; settlement; NE of Virden, exact location unknown; PO 1890–91, mail to Lordsburg). An abandoned mining camp based on a stone quarry, Ricolite was named for a banded variety of serpentine called ricolite unique to this area.

RIDDLE (Guadalupe; settlement; 10 mi SE of Puerto de Luna; PO 1909–20, mail to Santa Rosa). The Riddles were merchants in this community, now abandoned, and likely operated the PO. Old-timers remember going to dances in the Riddles' Model T, one of the first automobiles in the area.

RILEY (Socorro; settlement; 20 mi N of Magdalena, on the Rio Salado; PO 1892–98, 1899–1902, mail to Magdalena). This began as an Hispanic farming and ranching settlement called *Santa Rita,* and on May 22, the feast day of Santa Rita, a priest still comes to celebrate mass at the church here. Lorenzo Padilla, who came here in 1880, was

among the first settlers. The name Riley
is that of a local sheep rancher and likely
was formalized with the establishment
of a PO. Riley enjoyed a brief period of
mining activity, but now it's a ghost
town.

RINCON (general). Spanish, "corner," but
in NM Spanish this also means "small,
secluded place, box canyon," and it can
also mean "crossroads, junction, corner."
Sometimes the term appears descrip-
tively as *Rinconada*.

RINCON (Bernalillo; settlement; on NM
333, E of Tijeras). Housing development,
located in a *rincón*; see *Rincon (general)*.

RINCON (Doña Ana; settlement; 2 mi N of
NM 185, 5 mi E of Hatch; PO as Thorne
1881–83, as Rincon 1883–present). This
village originally was called *El Rincón de
Fray Diego*, for a 17th-century Franciscan
who died here. When a PO was established, it briefly was called *Thorne*,
doubtless either for Fort Thorne (see entry) N of Hatch or for the fort's
eponymn, Capt. Herman Thorn. With
the coming of the SF RR, Rincon became
the area's main business and trading center; the line forked here, one branch going S to El Paso, the other W to Deming.
Rincon also became a haven for outlaws,
including the Kinney Gang, and the town
sometimes was referred to as *Kinneyville*.
Rincon thrived for many years, but eventually it was eclipsed by Hatch, and now
it leads a much quieter existence than
formerly. *Rincon Arroyo* runs through the
village of Rincon, while the floodplain of
the Rio Grande SE of Hatch and SW of
Rincon is called the *Rincon Valley*. See
Rincon (general).

RINCON (Mora). See *Rociada*.

RINCON BONITO (San Miguel; in NE part
of Pecos Wilderness, just S of the S Fork
of the Rio de la Casa). As Elliott Barker
said, "If you doubt that it lives up to its
name ('pretty cove') a glimpse of it from
the Rio La Casa–Pecos Divide will con-
vince you."

RINCON MOUNTAINS (Mora; extend N
and S in W Mora County, W of Coyote
Creek and E of the Mora River). See
Rincon (general).

RINCONADA (Cibola). See *San Fidel*.

RINCONADA (Rio Arriba; settlement; on
NM 68, 25 mi NE of Española, near Taos
County line; as Durazno 1887–89, as
Rinconada 1880–81, 1889–1918, mail to
Dixon). Tiny inhabited community
named for its location at the junction of
three creeks; see *Rincon (general)*. The
settlement also has been called *Durazno*,
"peach, peach tree," doubtless for orchards along the Rio Grande valley here.

RING (Colfax; settlement; in Poñil Park on
N Poñil Creek, 2 mi S of the Valle Vidal).
About 1880 Timothy and Catherine
Ring purchased 320 acres from the Maxwell Land Grant Co., and soon the *Ring
Ranch* became the nucleus and eponymn
for a small but vigorous mining, ranching, and railroading community. Today
the Ring Ranch is on the National Register of Historic Places, but the community had died by the 1920s.

RIO, RITO (general). Spanish, "river," diminutive, *rito*, "little river, or creek." As
T.M. Pearce explained, in place names
using *de*, academic Spanish would require the definite article with names of
topographic features, families, and
plants or animals, e.g., *El Río de la
Arena, El Río de las Vacas, El Río de las
Luceros*. But in NM, where several languages have interacted, the standard
academic forms often have been lost,
and *rio* names may appear in several
forms: *Río de las Perchas, Río las Perchas,
Río Perchas*, and finally *Perchas River*.
These factors, among others, explain
some of the irregularities in *rio* and *rito*
names. Furthermore, this intermingling
of languages, along with the arid character of NM, have blurred the distinctions
between *rio* and *rito* as to stream dimensions and quantity of water.

RIO AGUA NEGRA (Guadalupe; heads at
Agua Negra Spring and flows E to enter
the Pecos River 3 mi S of Santa Rosa).
This along with the Los Tanos are tributaries of the middle Pecos River. The
water issuing from the spring is clear but
with a dark hue, hence the name, "black
water." A smaller stream also named
Agua Negra Creek is 8 mi S.

RIO ARRIBA, RIO ABAJO. Almost from their beginning, Hispanic settlements along the Rio Grande were grouped into two geographic regions: the *Río Arriba* ("upper river") and the *Río Abajo* ("lower river"). In 1610, soon after the capital of NM was moved to Santa Fe, *alcaldías* were established to administer the province, and the *Alcaldía de Río Abajo* encompassed the Middle Rio Grande Valley, with the *alcalde* usually residing in Albuquerque. The Rio Abajo's northern boundary has been reported being as far N as Santa Fe and as far south as Bernalillo, but La Bajada Mesa 19 mi S of Santa Fe, with its dramatic declivity from the Santa Fe Plateau, is the dividing line now generally accepted. Most sources accept Sabinal, S of Belen, as the southern boundary; Fray Francisco Atanasio Domínguez, Father Visitor of New Mexico, writing in 1776 put the Rio Arriba as extending from San Ildefonso Pueblo N to Taos and the Rio Abajo as running from Cochiti Pueblo to below Isleta Pueblo. Persistent Indian raids left settlements farther S depopulated during the 17th and 18th centuries. In his *Commerce of the Prairies* (1844), Josiah Gregg recognized the existence of the two regions and said: "The latter [Rio Abajo] comprises over a third of the population, and the principal wealth of NM." While the term Rio Abajo has never crystallized into a formal civil designation, as Rio Arriba did with Rio Arriba County (see entry), the term still is recognized and used.

RIO ARRIBA COUNTY (N-central NM, abutting the Colorado border; county seat, Tierra Amarilla). Rio Arriba County preserves the name the early Spaniards used when referring to this region. (See *Río Abajo, Río Arriba*.) The county, formalized in 1852, was created from the Mexican *departamento* of Rio Arriba, created by the Mexican government in 1836; its capital was Los Luceros, which was the Rio Arriba County seat from 1855 to 1860, when the county seat was moved to Alcalde; in 1880 the seat moved to Tierra Amarilla, where it has remained. The county was enlarged in 1880 to include lands W to the Arizona border, but it assumed its present boundaries in 1897 with the creation of *San Juan County*, though a SW section later was added to *Sandoval County*.

RIO BONITO (Lincoln; rises in the northern Sacramento Mountains, flows into Bonito Lake, then E through Fort Stanton and Lincoln to join the Rio Ruidoso at Hondo, where the two rivers form the Rio Hondo.). Spanish, "pretty river." And so it must have appeared to the Hispanic settlers who, traveling with their belongings in ox carts from the Rio Grande and the *ranchos* and *placitas* near the Manzano Mountains, arrived in the fertile Hondo Valley around 1855. They called their new home *La Placita del Río Bonito*, "the village of the pretty river," later renamed *Lincoln*.

RIO BRAVO STATE PARK (Bernalillo; between Isleta Blvd. and the Rio Grande, S of Rio Bravo the street). *Río Bravo*, Spanish, "wild, rapid river," was an early name for the Rio Grande, and still is used in Mexico for the Rio Grande. In NM the name is preserved in this 22-acre state park, dedicated in 1982.

RIO BRAZOS (Rio Arriba; East Fork and West Fork rise in the Brazos Mountains E of Chama, flow S to the Rio Chama at Brazos). Named for its many tributaries, or *brazos* (Spanish, "arms"), the Rio Brazos has engendered numerous other place names in the area.

Brazos Box (Rio Arriba; canyon; on the Rio Brazos, S of Brazos Peak).

Brazos Cliffs (Rio Arriba; N of the Brazos Box and the Rio Brazos). Sheer cliffs of Precambrian quartzite marking the abrupt boundary between the 7,500-foot agricultural lands of the Rio Chama Valley and the 10,000-foot Brazos high country. Very popular with rock climbers; site of *Brazos Falls,* highest waterfall in NM.

Brazos Meadows (Rio Arriba; high, open parkland, near the confluence of the East and West Forks of the Rio Brazos, W of Brazos Ridge).

Brazos Mountain Range (Rio Arriba). See *Tusas Mountains.*

Brazos Peak, 11,294 ft. (Rio Arriba; 13 mi NE of Tierra Amarilla).

Brazos Ridge (Rio Arriba; high N-S ridge E of the East Fork of the Rio Brazos).

Los Brazos (Rio Arriba; settlement). See entry.

RIO CAPULIN (Rio Arriba; heads in the NW Jemez Mountains, just N of the San Pedro Peaks, then flows generally N and then W through the village of Gallina to join Gallina Creek just W of Gallina Plaza). See Capulin (general).

RIO CAPULIN (Santa Fe; heads 3 mi N of Santa Fe Baldy, W of Capulin Peak, and flows SW into Nambe Creek). Spanish, "chokecherry river." See Capulin (general).

RIO CEBOLLA (Rio Arriba; heads W of Red Mountain, NE of the village of Cebolla, flows SW through the village and the Cebolla Valley, eventually to join the Rio Chama). Like the village of Cebolla (see entry), the river takes its name from the valley, whose Spanish name El Valle de Cebolla means "onion valley." See Cebolla (general).

RIO CEBOLLA (Rio Arriba, Sandoval; heads S of Cerro Pelon in the central Jemez Mountains, flows SW through Fenton Lake to join the Rio de las Vacas at Porter). Spanish, "onion river." See Cebolla (general).

RIO CHAMA (Rio Arriba; rises in Colorado and flows S past the village of Chama to join the Rio Grande just N of Española). See Chama (general). The Peñalosa map of NM of 1686–88 shows a Zama Ria in this approximate location, though farther to the E. The Río Chamita, also known by its English translation, Little Chama River, is a tributary of the Rio Chama, rising W of the Rio Chama and flowing SE and then S to enter it at the S end of the town of Chama.

RIO CHAMA WILD AND SCENIC RIVER (Rio Arriba; extends 25 mi downstream from El Vado Dam). Designated in 1988 and administered jointly by the USFS and the BLM, this is dominated by the Río Chama (see entry) and its steep canyon walls, sometimes towering 1,500-feet above the river. See also Chama River Canyon Wilderness.

RIO CHIQUITO (Santa Fe; settlement; on the Rio Quemado, 2 mi SE of Chimayo). Inhabited community, whose Spanish name, "very small river," is an apt description of the Rio Quemado.

RIO CHIQUITO (Taos; heads in the Sangre de Cristo Mountains and flows W to join the Rio Grande del Rancho at Talpa, S of Taos). This Spanish name, "very small river," likely translates the stream's Tewa name, meaning "little water creek."

RIO CHIQUITO (Taos; heads on the NW side of Trampas Peak and flows NW to join the Rio Santa Barbara at Peñasco). Spanish, "very small river."

RIO CHUPADERO (Santa Fe; heads in the Sangre de Cristo Mountains NE of the village of Tesuque and flows W and then NW to join the Rio Pojoaque). Spanish, "sinkhole river." See Chupadera, Chupadero (general).

RIO COLORADO (Taos; settlement; location unknown; PO 1871–72, 1877–78). Though this Spanish name means the same as the English name of the community later known as Red River, it's not known whether any connection existed between the two.

RIO DE ARENAS (Grant; flows S from Pinos Altos through the settlement of Arenas Valley to join San Vicente Arroyo 7 mi SE of Silver City). This watercourse usually is dry, hence its Spanish name, "river of sands." But that's only one of two names the stream has had, and their history is as shifting and unpredictable as the stream itself. During the mining boom of the late 1800s Pete Nest, an enterprising Pinos Altos miner, returned from El Paso with a barrel of whiskey in his wagon. His wagon broke down in the dry stream bed; when thirsty miners heard about the incident, they hiked en mass to the site and drank the whiskey on the spot. This led to the creek being called Whiskey Creek. Later, however, some local residents were embarrassed by this name, so at their urging the local state senator sponsored legislation officially changing the name back to its original Spanish name, Rio de Arenas, sometimes appearing as Arenas Creek, from which the community of Arenas

Valley (see entry) took its name. In 1989 a USGS mapping team urged changing the name back to Whiskey Creek, saying this was the name local people preferred and used, but when the NM Geographic Names Committee sought public opinion, they found the community still divided, though a slight majority favored Whiskey Creek. But the issue was moot: because of its earlier action, only the state legislature now can make further changes in the name.

RIO DE CHAMA (Rio Arriba; settlement; near Medanales, between Española and Abiquiu). Tiny inhabited Hispanic settlement, named for its location on the Rio Chama.

RIO DE LA CEBOLLA (Rio Arriba; heads in the Sangre de Cristo Mountains E of the village of Truchas and flows NW to join the Rio de Truchas). Spanish, "river of the onion;" see *Cebolla (general).*

RIO DE LAS TRAMPAS (Taos; heads at San Leonardo Lakes, N of the Truchas Peaks, and flows N and W through the village of Las Trampas to Embudo Creek). Spanish, "river of the traps," likely for beaver traps placed along it. Sometimes the name appears as *Las Trampas Creek* or *Las Trampas River,* but Rio de las Trampas is the name accepted by the USBGN in 1966.

RIO DE LAS VACAS (Sandoval; flows S from the San Pedro Mountains to join the Rio Cebolla and other streams to become the Rio Guadalupe). Spanish, "river of the cows."

RIO DE LOS PINOS (Rio Arriba; rises in Colorado and flows SE into NM, then E at San Miguel, then NE to return to Colorado 1 mi N of the settlement of Los Pinos). Spanish, "river of the pines."

EL RIO DE SAN LAZARO (San Juan). See *Mancos River.*

RIO DE TRUCHAS (Rio Arriba; heads in the Sangre de Cristo Mountains, W of the Truchas Peaks, and flows NW to join the Rio Grande S of Velarde). Spanish, "trout river." Sometimes labeled *Truchas Creek* or *Truchas River,* the USBGN in 1966 accepted the name Rio de Truchas. The Tewa name for the creek means "crooked chin place arroyo," for reasons unknown. The community of Truchas and the Truchas Peaks (see entries) owe their names to this stream.

RIO DEL OSO (Rio Arriba; heads in the NE Jemez Mountains and flows generally NE to join the Rio Chama at Chili). Spanish, "river of the bear," doubtless because of a long-forgotten incident.

RIO DEL PLANO (Colfax; flows SW to enter the Canadian Red River NE of Springer). As T.M. Pearce explained, this name may be an Anglicism in Spanish; *Río del Llano* would be standard Spanish for "river of the plain," though here perhaps the Spanish *plano,* "level, smooth," was intended, to describe the terrain through which the river flows.

RIO EN MEDIO (Mora, Santa Fe; heads on the NW side of Pecos Baldy and flows W to Santa Cruz Reservoir through the village of Rio en Medio). Spanish, "middle river," likely named for the stream being between the Rio Nambe to the N and the Rio Chupadero to the S. Also sometimes called *Río del Medio, Río Medio,* and *Medio Creek.*

RIO EN MEDIO (Santa Fe; settlement; NE of Tesuque, at the end of NM 592). Inhabited village, named for its location on the *Río en Medio* (see entry).

RIO FELIX (Otero, Chaves; rises in eastern Mescalero Indian Reservation and flows E to the Pecos River above Hagerman). Spanish, "happy," and indeed any flowing water would have been welcome in this arid region. The specific origins of this very old name have been lost. The name usually is pronounced feh-LEEZ, corresponding with the more standard spelling, *feliz.*

RIO FERNANDO DE TAOS (Taos; heads in the Sangre de Cristo Mountains and flows W, paralleling US 64, past Taos, to join the Rio Grande). Also called *Fernandez Creek,* this stream takes its name from Don Fernando de Chávez, an important landowner in the Taos area before 1680.

RIO FRIJOLES (Santa Fe; heads N of Santa Fe Baldy and flows NW to join the Santa Cruz River near Cundiyo). Spanish, "beans river," the name likely referring to beans grown near the stream.

RIO GRANDE (rises on the E slope of the Continental Divide, in the San Juan Mountains of Colorado, flows S to enter NM near Ute Mountain and flows S approximately 470 mi to enter Texas near Anthony, from whence it flows SE, forming the boundary between Texas and Mexico, eventually to enter the Gulf of Mexico at Brownsville-Matamoros). The Rio Grande, with its multiplicity of names from many languages and cultures, symbolizes the history of NM. The oldest extant names, those of the Pueblo Indians, usually mean the same as the present Spanish name, "big river," though some Pueblo Indians refer to it simply "the river." Navajos know the river as "female river," for reasons related to Navajo mythology, or as "Mexicans' river"; the river also is mentioned in the Shootingway Ceremony by an untranslatable ceremonial name.

Europeans first saw the river at its mouth at the Gulf of Mexico, where in 1519 Alonso Álvarez de Piñeda named it *El Río de las Palmas*, "the river of the palms," but this name never extended farther N than the palm region near the coast. When Coronado's expedition arrived in NM in 1540, his captain, Hernando de Alvarado, on September 7 encountered a great river near the site of modern Isleta Pueblo; his party named it the *Río de Nuestra Señora*, "River of Our Lady," because they discovered it on the eve of the Virgin Mary's feast day. When the cartographer Abraham Ortelius in 1577 drew his map of the New World, he labeled a river *Río Grande*—but showed it flowing into the Pacific. The Rodríguez-Chamuscado expedition of 1581–82 formally named the river *Guadalquivir,* in honor of the largest river of southern Spain. None of these names took, however, and when Oñate formally claimed NM in 1598, he called the river by the name by which it would primarily be known for the next 250 years—*Río del Norte:* "It springs and flows from the N, and thus it takes its name, and it turns to the E, and there is called *Río Bravo.*" In 1776, Fray Francisco Atanasio Domínguez corroborated

that the river took its name from rising far in the N, but he add the river sometimes was called *La Junta de los Ríos,* because of the many tributaries joining it during its course through New Mexico. In his *Commerce of the Prairies* (1844), Josiah Gregg wrote: "This river is only known to the inhabitants of NM as Rio del Norte, or North River, because it descends from that direction; yet in its passage southward, it is in some places called Rio Grande, on account of its extent; but the name Rio Bravo (Bold or Rapid River), so often given to it on maps, is seldom if ever heard among the people." The name Rio del Norte persisted even after the American occupation in 1846 and routinely appeared on American-made maps. But by the end of the 19th century, the present name had begun to supplant the older name and now is firmly established, at least in the US; the river still is called the Rio Bravo in Mexico.

Paul Horgan, in his monumental history *Great River,* listed the names for the Rio Grande he encountered in his research:
Grand River (General Wilkinson, 1806)
P'osoge (modern Tewa, "big river")
Río Bravo (Castaño de Sosa, 1590, and Oñate, 1598)
Río Bravo del Norte (Escudero, 1849)
Río Caudaloso ("carrying much water")
Río de la Concepción (Rodríguez expedition, 1581)
Río de las Palmas (Piñeda, 1519)
Río de Nuestra Señora (Alvarado, 1540)
Río de San Buenaventura del Norte (Fernando del Bosque, 1675)
Río del Norte (Perez de Luxan, 1582)
Río del Norte y de Nuevo México (Map, in Sigüenza y Góngora's *Mercurio Volante,* 1693)
Río Grande del Norte
Río Guadalquivir (Rodríguez, 1581)
Río Turbio (Pérez de Luxán, 1581)
River of May (David Ingram, 1568)
Tiguex River (Jaramillo, 1540).
RIO GRANDE DEL RANCHO (Taos; heads in the Sangre de Cristo Mountains SE of Taos near Cerro Olla, flows W then N through Ranchos de Taos to enter the

Rio Pueblo de Taos at Los Cordovas). This stream likely takes its name from the village of *Ranchos de Taos* (see entry). Also known as the *Little Río Grande, Little Río Ranchos de Taos,* and *Río Grande del Ranchos,* the stream's present name's was established by a 1966 USBGN decision. The river sometimes is divided into the *Upper Little Río Grande,* from its head to Rito de la Olla, and the *Lower Little Río Grande.* The large land grant, *Rancho del Río Grande,* S and E of Talpa takes its name from this drainage.

RIO GRANDE GORGE STATE PARK (Taos; SW of Taos, on NM 570, on the Rio Grande). Established in 1959, this state park was named for its location in the scenic gorge of the Rio Grande.

RIO GRANDE WILD AND SCENIC RIVER (Taos; along the Rio Grande, from the Colorado border to Rio Grande Gorge State Park). Designated in 1968, the Rio Grande Wild and Scenic River includes 48 mi of the Rio Grande, including the spectacular Rio Grande Gorge, and the lower 4 mi of the Red River Canyon in Colorado. The area is valuable wildlife habitat, as well as offering outstanding whitewater rafting.

RIO GUADALUPE, CAÑON GUADALUPE (Sandoval; heads in the W Jemez Mountains and runs S to join the Jemez River, just N of Cañon). The name doubtless was given in the area by early Franciscan missionaries; see *Mesa de Guadalupe.*

RIO GYPSUM (Cibola; heads in the Laguna Indian Reservation and flows N to join the Rio San Jose at Laguna Pueblo). Likely named for gypsum deposits along its course.

RIO HONDO (Chaves, Lincoln; formed by confluence of the Rio Ruidoso and the Rio Bonito at Hondo, flows E through Roswell to join the Pecos River E of the city). Spanish, "deep river."

EL RIO HONDO (Chaves). See *Roswell.*

RIO HONDO (Taos; heads at timberline above the Taos Ski Valley, leaves the mountains 12 mi N of Taos to join the Rio Grande). Spanish, "deep river." Consists of *Upper, Lower,* and *South Forks.* See *Arroyo Hondo.*

RIO HONDO (Taos; settlement; 3 mi NE of Pilar). Abandoned community, named for its proximity to *Hondo Canyon.*

RIO LA CASA (Mora; rises in the Sangre de Cristo Mountains, in the W-central part of county, and flows E to join the Mora River near Mora). Local people call this mountain stream *Río de la Caza,* "river of the hunt." But because the Spanish *caza* and *casa,* "house," are pronounced similarly, a long-standing uncertainty has existed among map-makers as to the correct name. A folk-etymology offered by T.M. Pearce is that "river of the house" had to do with numerous beaver lodges along the stream. The river often is labeled *Río de la Casa* or *Las Casas Creek,* but a 1965 USBGN decision accepted Rio la Casa, as Jerold G. Widdison observed, "a modest corruption of both tradition and grammar."

RIO LA JUNTA (Mora). See *Watrous.*

RIO LA JUNTA (Taos). See *La Junta Creek.*

RIO LUCERO (Taos; heads in the Sangre de Cristo Mountains S of Wheeler Peak and flows S then W and then S to join the Rio Pueblo de Taos NW of the town of Taos). See *Lucero (general).* In 1836 a small community named *Río Lucero,* mostly irrigated farms, existed where the Rio Lucero emerges from the mountains N of Taos.

RIO LUCIO (Taos; settlement; just S of Picuris Pueblo, on NM 75; PO 1921–23, mail to Peñasco). Spanish, "shiny river," yet curiously no creek near this inhabited community is named Rio Lucio.

RIO MEDIO (Mora, Santa Fe; heads in the Sangre de Cristo Mountains SW of Truchas Peak and flows generally W to join the Rio Frijoles at Santa Cruz Reservoir). Spanish, "middle river," likely because it is between the Rio Frijoles to the S and the Rio Quemado to the N.

RIO MIMBRES (Grant, Luna). See *Mimbres River.*

RIO MIMBRES (Luna). See *Mowry City.*

RIO MOQUINO (Cibola; rises N of the village of Moquino, S of Cebolleta, and flows S into the Rio Paguate, N of Laguna). Flows through the village of *Moquino* (see entry), for which it was named.

RIO MOLINO (Santa Fe; heads in the Sangre de Cristo Mountains NE of Santa Fe and flows NW to join the Rio Medio). Spanish, "mill river," possibly because a mill was located along it, though Molino also is a common Spanish surname.

RIO MORA (Mora, San Miguel; heads in the E Pecos Wilderness and flows SW to join the Pecos River S of Cowles). This stream is not to be confused with the Mora River (see entry), and that is why this drainage sometimes is called the *Mora Pecos.* The origin of the name *Mora* here is obscure; see *Mora.*

RIO MORA (Mora, San Miguel). See *Mora River.*

RIO NAMBE (Santa Fe). See *Nambe Pueblo.*

RIO NUTRIA (McKinley; heads in the Zuni Mountains N of Ramah and flows SW to join the Zuni River near Zuni). Spanish, "beaver river." Likely named for beavers living along its course; see *Nutria (general),* also *Nutria, Upper and Lower.*

RIO NUTRIAS (Rio Arriba; heads E of the village of Nutrias, flows W through the village to the Rio Chama.) This stream is excellent habitat for beavers; see *Nutria (general)*

RIO NUTRIAS (Rio Arriba; heads in the Tusas Mountains and flows NE to join the Rio San Antonio). Spanish, "beavers river"; see *Nutria (general).*

RIO OJO CALIENTE (Rio Arriba). See *Ojo Caliente.*

RIO PAGUATE (Cibola). See *Paguate.*

RIO PEÑASCO (Otero, Chaves, Eddy; heads in the Sacramento Mountains E of Cloudcroft and flows generally SE to the Pecos River). Spanish, "bluff, or outcrop, river." Although this name traditionally has been explained as having been inspired by the travertine bluff forming the waterfall at Bluff Springs, other authorities say Peñasco here is a corruption of what originally was an Apache phrase meaning "place of plenty." Because the Apache word sounded like the Spanish word, the "bluff" explanation naturally evolved.

RIO PEÑASCO (Taos, Rio Arriba). See *Embudo Creek.*

RIO PESCADO (McKinley; rises in the Zuni Mountains W of Ramah and flows W into Black Rock Reservoir). Spanish, "fish river." The stream and the small Zuni farming village of Pescado (see entry) both were named for small fish in *Ojo Pescado,* located on the stream 5 mi SW of Ramah.

RIO PUEBLO (Taos; heads in the Sangre de Cristo Mountains SE of Tres Ritos and runs NW to join Embudo Creek). A 1959 USBGN decision established this as the accepted name and not *Río Picuris* or *Río del Pueblo.* All these names originated from the river running by Picuris Pueblo.

RIO PUEBLO (Taos; settlement; on NM 75, 20 mi S of Taos; PO 1910–14, mail to Peñasco). This village's name is borrowed from a nearby mountain stream, the *Río Pueblo* (see entry). On some maps the village has appeared as *Placita* or *Placitas,* and indeed residents of the village usually speak of it as Placita. The name recalls the central square, or "little plaza," that the community's homes are clustered around, but it also denotes a small village; see *Plaza, Placita (general).*

RIO PUEBLO DE TAOS (Taos; rises in the Sangre de Cristo Mountains near the Colfax County line and flows S and then W through Taos Pueblo to the Rio Grande). This stream has had several names, including *Pueblo Creek, Río Taos,* and *Taos Creek,* but in 1966 the USBGN settled upon Rio Pueblo de Taos.

RIO PUERCO (Bernalillo; settlement; on I-40 16 mi W of Albuquerque). Highway service stop, named for its location on the *Río Puerco* (see entry).

RIO PUERCO (McKinley). See *Puerco River.*

RIO PUERCO (Rio Arriba; rises in the Jemez Mountains SW of Coyote and flows NE to join the Rio Chama just W of Abiquiu Reservoir). See *Puerco (general).*

RIO PUERCO (Sandoval, Bernalillo, Socorro; heads in the Sierra Nacimiento E of Cuba and flows S to join the Rio Grande just S of Bernardo). Josiah Gregg wrote in *Commerce of the Prairies* (1844), "so called from the extreme muddiness of its waters"; see *Puerco (general)*. The Spanish name parallels the Jemez Indian name for the stream, which means "dry mud with creek," and in 1776 Fray Francisco Domínguez wrote, "It is called the Rio Puerco because its water is as dirty as the gutters of the streets." This Rio Puerco sometimes has been called the *Río Puerco of the East*, to distinguish it from the Rio Puerco River of the West, more properly called the *Puerco River* (see entry). W of Albuquerque, where I-40 crosses the Rio Puerco, is the service center named *Río Puerco*.

RIO QUEMADO (Rio Arriba, Santa Fe; heads on the Truchas Peaks and flows NW and W to Cordova and the Santa Cruz River). Spanish, "burned river," likely because vegetation along its banks was burned at one time. *Río Quemado Falls* are located on the N Fork of the Rio Quemado, near its headwaters; they are more than 100 ft. high and have been called among the most scenic in NM. Truchas residents call them simply *El Caido*, "the falls."

RIO RANCHO (Sandoval; settlement; 9 mi N of Albuquerque, on the W side of the Rio Grande; PO 1988–present). Prior to the late 1950s, what is now Rio Rancho was open grazing land, part of the Thompson Ranch that had been carved out of the 18th-century Alameda Land Grant. But in 1962 Rio Ranch Estates, Inc., a subsidiary of what would become AMREP Southwest, Inc., began developing the area for lot sales and housing, and by the 1980s Rio Rancho had become one of NM's largest and fastest growing communities; from 1970 to 1995 its population increased from less than 2,000 to 42,000. Originally called *Río Rancho Estates*, the community became incorporated as the City of Rio Rancho in 1981. The name Rio Rancho certainly refers to the Rio Grande and perhaps to the old Thompson Ranch, but more likely it's just a fanciful name coined by developers to appeal to potential lot buyers from outside NM.

RIO RUIDOSO (Lincoln, Otero; rises on the E side of Sierra Blanca in Otero County and flows E through Ruidoso and Lincoln County to the Rio Hondo). Spanish, "noisy river," from its water rushing down the rocky slopes of Sierra Blanca. Its headwaters are divided into *North, Middle,* and *South Forks*. (In the Pecos Wilderness are *Rito Ruidoso* and *Noisy Brook*.) See *Ruidoso*.

RIO SALADO (Sandoval; rises in Salado Canyon in the W Jemez Mountains and flows SE to join Jemez Creek near San Ysidro). Spanish, "salty river." The Indians of Jemez Pueblo call this by a name meaning "white earth," and they gather whitish earth here for whitewashing the interior of buildings. The bed and banks of this shallow and intermittent stream in places are white with mineral salts, hence the name.

RIO SALADO (Catron, Socorro; rises in NE Catron County and flows E and then SE to join the Rio Grande N of Polvadera). Spanish, "salty river."

RIO SAN ANTONIO (Rio Arriba; heads in the Tusas Mountains in N part of county and flows E through the former village of San Antonio, W of San Antonio Mountain, and then N to the Rio de los Pinos N of Los Pinos). One of several features with this name in the area; see *San Antonio (Río Arriba)* and *San Antonio Mountain (Río Arriba)*.

RIO SAN JOSE (Bernalillo, Cibola, Valencia; begins at the confluence of Bluewater Creek and Mitchell Draw, 2 mi N of Bluewater, then flows E and S paralleling I-40, eventually to join the Rio Puerco in SW Bernalillo County). In early Spanish times, this stream was called the *Río Cubero*, for the settlement of Cubero past which it flows; *Arroyo del Rito*, "gully of the little stream," also has been reported as an early name. The present name is one of many San Jose names in this area, perhaps associated with nearby Acoma and Laguna Pueblos. In 1629 King Carlos II of Spain presented to Acoma Pueblo a painting of St. Joseph, while St. Joseph is the patron saint of Laguna Pueblo; the village of San Fidel in the San Jose valley was shown on early maps as *San Jose*.

RIO SAN LEONARDO (Rio Arriba; heads at San Leonardo Lakes, NW of North Truchas Peak, and flows NW into the Rio de las Truchas). St. Leonard was a Frank at the 6th-century court of Clovis. He founded the monastery of Noblac and is the patron of prisoners.

RIO SANTA BARBARA (Rio Arriba, Taos; East, Middle, and West Forks head on the W slopes of Santa Barbara and flow NW to come together just over Taos County line, then flow as the Rio Santa Barbara into Embudo Creek near Picuris Pueblo). A community named *Santa Barbara* once existed along this drainage, and the *Santa Barbara Land Grant* was made to Valentín Martín in 1796. See *Santa Barbara (Taos)*.

RIO TESUQUE (Santa Fe; formed by Tesuque Creek and Little Tesuque Creek about 1 mi S of the village of Tesuque Pueblo and runs NW to join Pojoaque Creek just W of the village of Pojoaque, where the two streams become the Pojoaque River). This stream takes its name from *Tesuque Pueblo*, past which it flows.

RIO TUSAS (Rio Arriba; heads in the Tusas Mountains and flows SE to enter the Rio Vallecitos at La Madera). The name sometimes appears as *Tusas Creek* or *Tusas River,* but Rio Tusas is the form accepted by the USBGN in 1933; see *Tusas (general).*

RIO VALDEZ (Mora, San Miguel; heads in the SW corner of Mora County and flows SW to join the Rio Mora at N end of Mora Flats). Bears an Hispanic surname.

RIO VALLECITOS, UPPER AND LOWER (Rio Arriba; heads in the Tusas Mountains S of Hopewell Lake and flows SE paralleling NM 111 through Cañon Plaza and Vallecitos to join the Rio Ojo Caliente at La Madera). Spanish, "little valleys river." *Upper Vallecitos* refers to the river from its source to Ancones.

RIPLEY POINT, 11,799 ft. (Taos; in S corner of county, near Jicarita Peak). Name origin unknown.

RITCHEY (De Baca; settlement; N of Fort Sumner, 1 mi from Guadalupe County line; PO 1913–19, mail to Riddle). Noth-ing remains of this former trading point and rural school, said to have been named for the owners of a store here.

RITO (general). See *Rio, Rito (general).*

RITO (Catron). See *Omega, Quemado.*

RITO (Cibola; settlement; NE of Acoma on the Rio San Jose). George Adlai Feather reported this community to have been abandoned when Lt. James W. Abert visited here in 1846, having had its irrigation water depleted by upstream users of the Rio San Jose, which Feather said once was called the *Arroyo del Rito,* "wash of the little stream." Abert saw several stone houses and a chapel.

RITO CHAPERITO (San Miguel). See *Chaperito Knob.*

RITO DE LOS ESTEROS (Mora; small fork of the Rio Mora, entering from the E at the lower end of Mora Flats, 5 mi NE of Cowles.) As Elliott Barker explained: "Rito de los Esteros (Creek of the Marshes) is rightly named because of the boggy marshes at its source W of Spring Mountain, many of which used to be difficult to cross on horseback before trails were cut through the deadfalls around them."

RITO DE LOS FRIJOLES (Sandoval; heads in the Jemez Mountains and flows SE through Bandelier National Monument to join the Rio Grande). This small but important stream and its associated canyon, *Cañon de los Frijoles,* likely were named for the *frijoles,* Spanish, "beans," that were an essential crop of the ancient Indians whose cliff dwellings are the main feature of Bandelier National Monument. The Tewa name for the stream means "where they scraped or wiped bottoms (possibly of pottery)". Both the Tewas and the Keresan-speaking Indians of Cochiti Pueblo, whose ancestors lived here, associate the creek with the famous abandoned pueblo called Tyuonyi (see entry). *Frijoles Falls,* on the El Rito de los Frijoles, about 1.5 mi below the monument headquarters, are two falls: *Upper Frijoles Falls* about 90 ft. high and *Lower Frijoles Falls,* 0.25 mi farther downstream, about 40 ft. high.

RITO DEL PADRE (Mora; at the headwaters of the Pecos River, heading E of North Truchas Peak and flowing S into the Pecos River). Spanish, "creek of the father." Apocryphal tales still circulate that Catholic priests once worked a gold mine near this creek, hence the name, despite gold never having been found in the Pecos high country. More likely, explained Elliott Barker, the name resulted from priests going into the mountains to say mass for sheepherders here, who prepared a makeshift altar of branches and flowers for the priest's arrival; on the SE side of *Cerrito del Padre* is a spot said to have been selected for the ceremony. "I like to think this is how the Cerrito del Padre and the Rito del Padre got their names, rather than through the gold-mine theory," said Barker. "It fits better in this divinely-favored setting." *Cerrito del Padre,* "little peak of the father," 10,875 ft., is just to the W of Rito del Padre.

RITO QUEMADO (Santa Fe; joins the Rio Medio, 4 mi S of Truchas). Spanish, "burned creek," likely because of a fire along its banks.

RITO SEBADILLOSES (Mora; enters the Rito del Padre just above Beattys Cabin, 7 mi N of Cowles). The stream likely bears a family name.

RIVERA (Valencia; settlement; 6 mi S of Los Lunas, on NM 6). A new settlement, established around 1985 and named for the Rivera family, whose members live here.

RIVERSIDE (Eddy; settlement; on US 82 E of Artesia, just E of the Pecos River). A recent inhabited community, organized around the local oil industry and named for its location near the Pecos River.

RIVERSIDE (Grant; settlement; 2 mi S of Cliff, on the E side of the Gila River). Thomas Jefferson Clark built a two-story hotel and store here in 1900 that served as a stage stop for early freighters traveling between Mogollon and Silver City. This later was called the *Riverside Store;* other enterprises have since followed.

RIVERSIDE (Lincoln; settlement; on US 380, 31 mi W of Roswell). When this trading point was first established, its owner, W.O. Norman, called it *Big Hill Filling Station* because it is located at the foot of a big hill, but when he sold the place in 1930 the name was changed to *Riverside Camp* and later simply to Riverside, because of the locale being on the Rio Hondo.

RIVERSIDE (Rio Arriba; settlement; along NM 68 in Española, immediately E of the Rio Grande). Named for its location, Riverside is one of Española's many "suburbs."

RIVERSIDE (San Juan; settlement; on NM 550, 1 mi S of the Colorado line; PO 1905–38, mail to Aztec). This inhabited community on the Animas River also has been called *Hendricks,* for reasons unknown.

ROAD CANYON (Colfax; between the Canadian River and the Vermejo River, in NE part of county). An early route into the Vermejo country came through this canyon, hence the name, and indeed NM 555 still passes through here.

ROAD CANYON (Colfax, Taos; in the Sangre de Cristo Mountains, between Red River and Elizabethtown). Laid out in the 1870s, this canyon once was the standard route between the Red River and Moreno Valley mining camps.

ROAD CANYON (Union; in NE part of county). The first road leading through Cimarron Canyon to Clayton passed through here.

ROAD FORKS (Hidalgo; settlement; 17 mi SW of Lordsburg, at the junction of I-10 and NM 80; PO 1925–55, mail to Lordsburg). Settled about 1925 and named by Mr. and Mrs. G. H. Porter, Road Forks continues to be a very active truck stop and service area.

ROANOKE (Chaves; settlement; W of the Pecos River, NE of Roswell; PO 1908–11, mail to Elkins). It's unknown why homesteaders on the High Plains chose to give their community the name of Sir Walter Raleigh's colony in North Carolina, but the naming proved prophetic: the NM settlement also was short-lived and has vanished.

ROBERTS (Lea). See *Nadine*.

ROBINSON (Sierra; settlement; in the Black Range, 4 mi NW of Winston; PO 1882–83, mail to Fairview). In the early 1880s, during the Black Range mining boom, it was anticipated the SF RR would extend a line to here, and in 1882 Robinson was laid out as a terminal. Two explanations exist for the name: one is that the town's hopeful organizers named the town for the man who was chief engineer of the AT&SF RR; the other is that it took its name from M.L. Robinson, an early resident of Chrloride. The town boomed, but when the RR branch did not materialize Robinson faded quickly, and less than 10 years after its birth Robinson was dead.

ROBINSON MOUNTAIN, 8,040 ft. (Colfax; 5 mi N of Capulin). Said to have been named for the Robinson-Hoover Commission Co. of Kansas City, MO, which served cattlemen of Colfax and Union Counties.

ROBLEDO (Doña Ana; historic site; between Doña Ana and Radium Springs, on the W side of the Rio Grande). On May 21, 1598, three weeks after the Oñate expedition had entered what is now NM, the colonists suffered their first casualty with the death of Pedro Robledo. Records of the expedition describe him as a man "of good stature, entirely gray, 60 years of age," a native of Toledo, Spain, who was bringing with him into the new land his wife and five children; see *Doña Ana*. The expedition buried Robledo where he died, and marked his grave with a cross. Thus the campground *La Cruz de Robledo*, "Robledo's Cross," later simply *Robledo*, came to be a landmark on the *Camino Real*, marking the S entrance to the Jornada del Muerto, and Robledo's name still marks the site. One league S of the Robledo *paraje* was another called *Robledo el Chico*, "the little Robledo," while immediately to the W *Robledo Mountain*, 5,890 ft., still overlooks the site of the old Spaniard's death.

ROCIADA (San Miguel; settlement; on NM 105, 27 mi NW of Las Vegas; PO as Tecolote 1874–75, as Rincon 1875–83, as Rociada 1883–present). When a PO was established here, it briefly took the name *Tecolote* and then *Rincon,* reflecting the community's early name, *Rincón de Tecolote,* because of the village's proximity to El Cerro del Tecolote, now called Hermit Peak (see entry). Eventually a new name was chosen for the PO, possibly by the postmistress, Emilie Pendaries (see Pendaries); the Spanish *rociada* means "sprinkled with dew" and is said to have been inspired by the abundance of *rocío*, "dew," in the early mornings here. In contrast to more arid parts of NM, this valley turns a brilliant green in May and has mild, moist weather throughout the summer. Though the entire area usually is called Rociada, the community actually is divided into two separate villages, about 2 mi apart: *Upper Rociada*, whose church is dedicated to *San José*; and *Lower Rociada*, whose religious title is *Santo Niño*; see *Santo Niño (general)*.

ROCK CANYON (Sierra; settlement; on the W side of Elephant Butte Reservoir). Diffuse residential settlement, located where *Rock Canyon* enters from the W.

ROCK HOUND STATE PARK (Luna; in the Little Florida Mountains, 12 mi SE of Deming). Perhaps the world's only park where visitors are encouraged to remove some of the landscape, Rock Hound State Park was created in 1966 to offer rockhounds an opportunity to collect such mineral specimens as geodes, jasper, agate, carnelian, rhyolite, pitchstone, and perlite.

ROCK HOUSE CANYON (Hidalgo; just S of Pyramid Peak). Named for the foundations of a rock building, likely built as a smelter associated with the nearby mining camp of Pyramid City (see entry).

ROCK ISLAND (Quay). See *Glenrio.*

ROCK SPRING (McKinley; settlement; 2 mi S of NM 264, 7 mi NW of Gallup). The Navajo name for this locality means "rough rock." The site, located on the military trail between Old Fort Wingate and Fort Defiance, originally was a military outpost, then later a trading post.

Now the *Rock Spring Navajo Mission* is here.

ROCK WALL (Taos; settlement; on the Rio Pueblo, 1 mi E of Vadito). Tiny inhabited locality.

ROCKY ARROYO (Eddy; crosses US 285, approximately 6 mi NW of Carlsbad). Major watercourse, conspicuously choked with boulders.

RODARTE (Taos; settlement; on NM 73, 1.5 mi SE of Peñasco; PO 1916–65, mail to rural branch of Peñasco). Cristóbal de Rodarte (sometimes the person is identified as Xavier de Rodarte) was among the first settlers of Santa Cruz in 1696, and this inhabited community likely owes its name to one of his descendants.

RODEO (Hidalgo; settlement; on US 80, 33 mi S of I-10, just E of the Arizona border; PO 1903–present). In 1902 the EP&SW RR extended its line from Douglas, AZ, to Antelope Pass in the Peloncillo Mountains, and this locality soon became an important shipping point for the numerous livestock operations in the area; the Spanish *rodeo* means "roundup, enclosure" and originally did not carry the meaning of a festive cowboy gathering, with bull-riding, cow-roping, etc., it has since acquired.

RODEY (Doña Ana; settlement; on NM 185, 3 mi SE of Hatch; PO as Colorado 1879–86, as Rodey 1904–27, mail to Hatch). Said to be the oldest village in the area, settled around 1865 and once walled for defense against Apaches, this village originally was near the Rio Grande and called *Colorado,* for the reddish hills just to the W; old-timers still recognize this name. A flood caused the villagers to move W, to higher ground, where the village is still inhabited. The name Rodey recalls Bernard Shandon Rodey, an Irishman who came to Albuquerque as a stenographer for the A&P RR and later became a lawyer and political figure. He was instrumental in the creation of the University of New Mexico, where Rodey Theatre in the Fine Arts Center also commemorates him.

ROEBUCK (Roosevelt; settlement; 3 mi E and 2 mi N of Causey). Roebuck, named for a local homesteader, was established when extra acreage was allotted for a school, but not much of a settlement ever developed; the schoolhouse was moved long ago, and all that remains today is the Roebuck Cemetery.

ROGERS (Roosevelt; settlement; on NM 235, 20 mi SE of Portales; PO 1908–present). In 1906, when many homesteaders were settling the eastern plains, the Rev. Andrew J. Maxwell left Rogers, AR, and came here for his health. In 1908 he laid out a townsite and established a PO, naming it for his hometown. He lived here until his death in 1929.

ROGERS (Santa Fe; settlement; NW of Madrid, at the foot of Waldo Mesa). Only foundations remain of this former community, shown on a 1905 map. Name origin unknown.

ROMERO (general). Bartolomé Romero, a native of Toledo, Spain, arrived in NM with Oñate in 1598, along with his wife, Lucia López, and their family. Romeros were among the colonists who returned to NM with the reconquest of 1692. Their descendants have given their name to 28 NM places (GNIS).

ROMERO (Santa Fe; settlement; S of Santa Fe, exact location unknown; PO 1895–1900, mail to Santa Fe). Abandoned community, named for Carlos Romero, first postmaster. See *Romero (general).*

ROMERO (San Miguel; settlement; location unknown; PO 1904–08, mail to East Las Vegas). Short-lived locality, named for the Romero family. See *Romero (general).*

ROMEROVILLE (San Miguel; settlement; on I-25, 5 mi S of Las Vegas; PO 1877–80, 1927–36, 1952–53, mail to Las Vegas). Trinidad Romero was the son of a wealthy Las Vegas merchant and freighter on the Santa Fe Trail. Trinidad continued his father's prominence by becoming a rancher and member of Congress. He built a $100,000 mansion in the community that bears his name wherein he entertained such guests as President and Mrs. Rutherford B. Hayes and Gen. William T. Sherman. The mansion burned in 1932, but the town named for him survives. *Romeroville Gap* is 6 mi S of Romeroville. See *Romero (general).*

ROOSEVELT (Quay; settlement; 4 mi SW of McAlister, near the Roosevelt County line; PO 1906–19, mail to McAlister). Established in 1906 during the administration of President Theodore Roosevelt and likely named for him, this community at one time had a store, blacksmith shop, hotel, and school, but by 1920 Roosevelt was a ghost town and today is all but forgotten.

ROOSEVELT COUNTY (eastern NM; county seat, Portales). Created from Chaves and Guadalupe Counties in 1903 while President Theodore Roosevelt was in office and named for him.

ROPES SPRING, DRAW (Doña Ana; in SW San Andres Mountains, 18 mi N of Organ). In 1885 Horace Ropes of Massachusetts bought the Goldenburg Ranch here (see *Goldenburg Canyon*) and began ranching. Ropes was a brother-in-law of Albert B. Fall and a professor of engineering at NM A&M in Las Cruces. In 1934, the site was developed as a recreation area by the Civilian Conservation Corps, with rock terraces and a swimming pool. It now is within White Sands Missile Range.

ROSA (Rio Arriba; settlement; on the San Juan River, now beneath Navajo Reservoir; PO 1888–99, 1900–29, mail to Arboles, CO). Either wild roses, which are indeed abundant in the area, or a family named Rosa would account for the name of this drowned settlement.

ROSEBUD (Harding; settlement; on NM 420, 29 mi E of Mosquero; PO 1909–49, mail to Hayden). Though the details vary slightly, the generally accepted story behind this name is that three sisters— Laura, Elsie, and Rena Maass—settled here in 1908 on adjoining 160-acre tracts. They built a barn and hired some men to paint it, and as a final flourish the men painted rosebuds on the building. This irritated the sisters, but it so amused M.T. Nix that when he established a PO he called it Rosebud. Today, the sisters, their barn, and almost everything else in Rosebud have vanished.

ROSEDALE (Socorro; settlement; in the foothills of the San Mateo Mountains, 6 mi W of NM 107, 24 mi S of Magdalena; PO 1899–1928, mail to Marcial). In 1882 J.W. "Jack" Richardson and his wife, Rose, were prospecting here when Mrs. Richardson found a promising piece of float; at her urging they had it assayed and found it rich with gold. Soon a mining camp sprang up and was named Rosedale, after Mrs. Richardson. Richardson sold his mine to others, but he and his wife remained in Rosedale, and both are buried in the Rosedale Cemetery. Mining ceased in 1937, and Rosedale now is a ghost town.

ROSILLA PEAK, 10,500 ft. (San Miguel; in the Sangre de Cristo Mountains, E of Terrero). Spanish, "pinkish," possibly referring to its color at sunset, but the name possibly also could come from *rosillo,* NM Spanish for the shrubby cinquefoil (*Potentilla fruticosa*), common in the area.

ROSING (San Juan; settlement; on US 550, 6 mi NE of Aztec; PO 1909–19, mail to Cedar Hill). *Center Point* was the first name of this inhabited community, taken from the name of the school here. When a PO was proposed, two names were submitted: Center Point and Rosing, for a resident by that name. The postal officials chose Rosing, but the name Center Point has outlasted it in local usage. Rosing, located on the highway, was across the RR tracks from the D&RGW RR locality of *Inca* (see entry).

ROSWELL (Chaves; settlement, county seat; on US 70, 380, and 285, on the Rio Hondo; PO 1873–present). In 1869, Van C. Smith and his partner, Aaron O. Wilburn, came west from Omaha, NB, and settled on the Rio Hondo near its junction with the Pecos River. They built two adobe buildings as a general store and an inn for travelers. The site was known to local Hispanic residents as *Río Hondo,* for the stream, but in 1872 Smith let it be known among his friends that he was calling his place Roswell, for his father, Roswell Smith, back in Nebraska, because mail addressed to Rio Hondo could be delivered anywhere along the long stream and would be delayed in reaching him. When a PO was established in 1873, with Smith as postmaster, the name was formalized and has remained ever since. In 1877, Capt. Joseph C. Lea (see *Lea County*) bought Smith's holdings, and during the next decade he and his family controlled the entire town. (Van Smith's name perhaps has been preserved in Lake Van—see entry—E of Dexter SE of Roswell.) Since then, Roswell, located in the nation's most important artesian basin, has developed into NM's fourth largest city. Hispanic residents in early Roswell recognized five neighborhoods: *Barrio de los Ricos,* "neighborhood of the rich folks," where the Anglos lived; *Chihuahita,* "little Chihuahua"; *El Alto,* "the height," on a hill on the W side; *La Gara,* "the rag," because poor people hung their ragged laundry outdoors; and *Zaragosa,* the name of a city either in Mexico or Spain.

ROUGH AND READY HILLS (Doña Ana; 15 mi NW of Las Cruces). The origin of this name is obscure, for it appeared not only on the hills but also on the station here of the Butterfield Overland Mail, and it's unclear which was named first. The station, established in 1858 on the E side of the hills, consisted of an adobe corral and an adobe-and-stone building with two prominent chimneys, for which it was known locally as *Los Hornillos,* "the little fireplaces, ovens."

ROUND HOUSE (McKinley). See *Cousins.*

ROUND MOUNTAIN, 10,809 ft. (Mora; in SW part of county, in the Sangre de Cristo Mountains, 3 mi N of Cowles). Descriptive name.

ROUND MOUNTAIN (Sierra; settlement; location unknown; PO 1878–79). Ephemeral postal locality. This likely is the Round Mountain mentioned by George Adlai Feather, who said it was a station on the AT&SF RR route through the Jornada del Muerto, 18 mi S of Paraje, 15 mi E of the Rio Grande; Feather said the site originally was called *Toussaints Station,* for H.G. Toussaint. A Round Mountain exists in SW Sierra County, NW of Nutt, but it's unknown whether any connection exists between that name and this.

ROUND MOUNTAIN (Union). See *Mount Clayton.*

ROUNDTOP (Torrance; settlement; SW of Willard). Abandoned homesteader community, named either for its location or a nearby landform.

ROUNDVILLE (Sierra). See *Rendezvous.*

ROUNTREE (Quay). See *Montoya.*

ROWE (San Miguel; settlement; on I-25, 6 mi S of Pecos; PO 1884–present). Established in 1876 and named for a RR contractor. *Rowe Peak,* 8,053 ft., is 2 mi NW.

ROY (Harding; settlement; on NM 39 and 120, 9 mi E of the Canadian River; PO 1901–present). In 1901 Frank Roy and his three brothers came to NM from Canada, and soon Frank Roy had established a rural PO NW of the present townsite, giving it his family name. When the EP&SW RR was laying its tracks, Roy spotted a potential opportunity and moved his PO to the most probable station site and added a general store. Stimulated by land-hungry homesteaders arriving via the RR, the town bearing his name grew. Like other agricultural communities in this region, Roy has never recovered from the Dust Bowl, and though the town named for the Roy family survives, their descendants live elsewhere.

RUDOLPH (De Baca). See *Sunnyside, Fort Sumner.*

RUDULPH (Quay). See *Lesbia.*

RUDY TOWN (San Miguel). See *Terrero.*

RUIA (Grant; settlement; 9 mi W of Gage, on the SP RR; PO 1917–19, mail to Gage). When the RR section house known as *Wilna,* name origin unknown, applied for a PO, the postal authorities would not accept that name, so the name Ruia was adopted instead, origin also unknown. The PO was operated out of a nearby ranch house, which like the section house has been abandoned.

RUIDOSO (Lincoln; settlement; on NM 48 and US 70, 33 mi NE of Tularosa; PO 1882–90, 1891–present). This pleasant mountain village originally was called *Dowlins Mill,* for Paul Dowlin's grist mill, which still stands here. Dowlin had been an officer in the NM Volunteers during the Civil War in NM. Later he became post trader at Fort Stanton, where he had the right to sell liquor. Because of problems this created with the Indians, the post commander ordered Dowlin to move his operations. Dowlin prospered in his new location, acquiring not only a mill but also a store and other property, but in 1877 he was killed by a former employee. When a PO was established, the community took the name Ruidoso, for the *Río Ruidoso* (see entry), the "noisy river" running through the town. It since has become a tourist and vacation center.

RUIDOSO DOWNS (Lincoln; settlement; 2 mi SE of Ruidoso on US 70; PO as Green Tree 1947–58, as Ruidoso Downs 1958–present). During the 1930s, Heck Johnson sold water rights and lots around Hale Spring, and the community took the Spanish name *Palo Verde*. But when a PO application was submitted in 1947, the postal authorities translated the name to *Green Tree*. In the meantime, the Ruidoso Downs Race Track was developing across the road, and eventually included the All-American Quarter Horse Futurity. In 1958, Eugene V. Hensley, originator of the race and secretary-treasurer of the track, felt it would add to the prestige of the track if it had a postmark, so in a special election the citizens of Green Tree voted by a large margin to change their town's name to Ruidoso Downs.

RUIZ (Bernalillo; settlement; exact location unknown). Little is known about this locality, which appears in some early records; *Las Vegas de Ruiz* is mentioned as a boundary, and the Spanish census of 1790 records a Don Antonio Ruiz, a native of Puebla, Mexico, who married into the powerful Armijo family. The first Ruiz to appear in NM history was Pedro Ruiz, who in 1608–09 was among the soldier escorts to NM.

RUNNING WATER DRAW (Curry; heads in NW part of county and runs SE into Texas). Running Water Draw is one of few watercourses in Curry County, and even this is but a wide arroyo with only a trickle of water for most of its length. Nonetheless, several disastrous flash floods have been recorded on it, and its name is deserved.

RUNNING WATER DRAW STATE PARK (Curry; on NM 209, 7.5 mi N of Clovis). This includes 3,320 acres on both sides of *Running Water Draw* (see entry) and features fish ponds and shady recreation areas. Authorized by the state legislature in 1949, the locality has since 1954 been developed and operated by the City of Clovis as *Ned Houk Memorial Park* and is far better known by that name; Houk was mayor of Clovis in the 1950s and was instrumental in the park's creation.

RUSSIA (Otero; settlement; in the Sacramento Mountains, 5 mi S of Cloudcroft; PO 1904–06, mail to Cloudcroft). Russia was created when the EP&SW RR ran a line S from Cloudcroft to bring out logs; the settlement consisted of a depot, a loading dock, a storeroom, and a PO. Located at 9,300 ft., it is said to have been named for the severity of its winters. Only ruins remain today.

RUSTLER (general). Appropriating other peoples' livestock has not been unheard of in NM, and 5 names, in Eddy, Grant, Hidalgo, and Otero Counties, recall this (GNIS). See *Ladron, Ladrones (general)*.

RUTH (Guadalupe; settlement; 6 mi W of Ima, on Alamogordo Creek; PO 1905–17, mail to Haile). Ruth never consisted of more than a store and a PO. It is said to have been named by the first postmaster for his daughter.

RUTHERON (Rio Arriba; settlement; on NM 95, 13 mi S of Chama; PO 1927–present). The rancher K.A. Heron established the PO here and named it for his wife, Ruth. See also *Heron Lake*.

RYADO (Colfax). See *Rayado*.

SABINO, SABINAL, SABINOSO, SABI-
NOSA (general). Spanish, "juniper"; see
Juniper (general).

SABINAL (Socorro; settlement; on I-25, 15
mi S of Belen; PO 1866 intermittently to
1907, mail to Bernardo). Sabinal, "place
of the junipers," was settled in 1741,
reportedly by people from the nearby
community of Las Nutrias (see entry). It
appeared on Miera y Pacheco's 1779
map as *El Savinal;* the Spanish census of
1790 called it *San Antonio de Sabinal*
and listed 223 residents. The plaza here
also has been referred to as *Tabalopa* (see
entry), which was the name of a nearby
community. Despite the constant threat
of Indian attacks, Sabinal was continu-
ously inhabited, though a flood around
1868 forced a relocation of community
to its present location. See *Juniper (general)*.

SABINO (Harding; settlement; 21 mi E of
Roy). Abandoned trading point. See
Juniper (general).

SABINO (Bernalillo; settlement; 4 mi SE of
Tijeras, 1 mi E of NM 337). Tiny inhabited
locality; *Sabino Canyon* and the village of
Cedro are nearby. See *Juniper (general)*.

SABINO (Socorro; settlement; on the E
bank of the Rio Grande, NE of Socorro,
S of Lemitar). The origins of this abandoned hamlet are obscure; the first certain reference is in Escudero's *Noticias* of
1849, where it appears as *Sabinito*. It
later appeared as *Sabino* and *Sabina* in
19th-century US records, but even then
it was described as deserted. See *Juniper
(general)*.

SABINOSO (San Miguel; settlement; 5 mi
N of NM 419, on the Canadian River;
PO 1913–24, 1926–28, 1939–74). Tiny,
extremely isolated inhabited community. See *Juniper (general)*.

SACATE, SACATON (general). *Sacaton* is a
common misspelling of *zacatón*, a NM
Spanish term for a fodder grass. *Sacate*,
NM Spanish for shortgrass, also comes
from this term. See *Zacaton (general)*.

SACATON PEAK, 10,658 ft. (Catron; in the
Mogollon Mountains, 5 mi W of
Mogollon Baldy). See *Sacaton (general)*.
Sacaton Creek heads on the S side of this
mountain and runs S into Duck Creek at
Buckhorn.

SACRAMENTO (general). Spanish, "sacrament," in NM referring specifically to
the Holy Eucharist, the "most blessed
sacrament."

SACRAMENTO (Otero; settlement; 15 mi
SE of Cloudcroft, on NM 521; PO as
Chiquita 1935, as Sacramento
1935–present). This community, named
for the *Sacramento Mountains* in which
it's located, originally was called
Chiquita, because the Agua Chiquita
runs through it.

SACRAMENTO CITY (Otero; settlement;
about 40 mi S of Alamogordo, 3 mi E of
Orogrande). This was a short-lived promotional town laid out just E of the
EP&NE RR tracks. The Sacramento Valley Irrigation Co. sponsored the venture,
and an ephemeral cement and plaster
plant was established. Lots were adver-
tised and sold as far away as Kansas, Nebraska, and Iowa, but the "city" never
materialized, and only a few tents and
shacks were ever erected.

SACRAMENTO MOUNTAINS (Otero; see
below). Why this name, appearing in
early records as *Sierra del Sacramento,*
was applied to these mountains is unknown. Some maps designate only the
mountains S of US 70 as the Sacramento
Mountains, but USGS maps include all
the mountains from a point 40 mi N of
the Texas border to the N end of the
Jicarilla Mountains as the Sacramentos,

with the Jicarilla, Capitan, White Mountain, and Sacramento Mountains as subranges. *Sierra Blanca,* 12,003 ft., is the highest summit of the larger group, *Alamo Peak,* 9,685 ft., the highest in the smaller.

SACRAMENTO RIVER (Otero; heads in the southern Sacramento Mountains and flows S to disappear in the flats). Likely named for the mountains where it heads.

THE SADDLE MOUNTAIN, 5,818 ft. (Doña Ana; in W part of county, 13 mi SW of Hatch). Resembles a saddle.

SADDLEBACK MESA (Quay; 15 mi S of Tucumcari and 5 mi W of Quay). Has a sway in it resembling a saddle.

SAIL ROCK (Colfax; in Cimarron Canyon). Resembles a sail.

SAINT CHARLES (Sierra; settlement; on the E side of the Black Range, between Grafton and Winston). According to George Adlai Feather, this was a short-living mining camp, adjacent to the Occidental Mine and Mill and named for a superintendent, Kean St. Charles.

SAINT PATRICK (San Miguel; settlement; location unknown; PO 1892–94, mail to Las Vegas). Ephemeral locality, circumstances of naming unknown.

SAINT PETERS DOME, 8,463 ft. (Sandoval; in the Jemez Mountains, 1 mi W of Bandelier National Monument). Commanding dome-shaped mountain, with a watchtower on its summit. Said to resemble the dome on St. Peter's Basilica in Rome. See *Dome Wilderness.*

SAINT VRAIN (Curry; settlement; on US 60-84, 8 mi E of Melrose; PO 1907–present). Two explanations, both plausible and both due to the RR, exist for this tiny community's name. One is that it honors the father of a SF RR official's wife. The other, and the one believed in the community itself, is that the SF RR named the community to honor Ceran St. Vrain, the early guide, trapper, explorer, and colonel of the First NM Volunteer Infantry. St. Vrain was a partner of Charles Bent, first territorial governor of NM. St. Vrain died in 1870 at Mora, where he had a store. This version is bolstered by the SF RR likely naming La Lande (see entry), along the

line W of Saint Vrain, also for an early trapper. The town of Saint Vrain was born around 1907; by 1909 it was a thriving community, with a weekly newspaper, the *St. Vrain Journal.* The village has shrunk considerably since then but still survives.

SAIS (Valencia; settlement; on AT&SF RR, 20 mi SE of Belen). The progenitor of the family for whom this abandoned community was named was Ambrosio Saiz, a native of San Bartolome in New Spain, who came to NM shortly after 1665. His son and family returned with the reconquest of 1692. Though the village is gone, *Sais Spring* here perpetuates the family's name.

SAKETON (San Juan; settlement; W of Farmington, near the San Juan River; PO 1900–01, mail to Jewett). Abandoned community, named for local grass; see *Sacate, Sacaton (general).*

SALADO (general). Spanish, "salty," a common name element for water bodies in the arid Southwest where intermittent dryness concentrates mineral salts. *Salado* appears 63 times in GNIS, sometimes as the diminutive *Saladito.*

SALADO (De Baca; settlement; 3 mi N of Guadalupe, on the W side of the Pecos River; PO 1892–1919, mail to Guadalupe). Abandoned community, named for its location on *Salado Creek.*

SALAZAR (general). The first Salazar to appear in NM records was Francisco de Salazar, who was here in 1625. Unfortunately, his career here ended with his being beheaded for his involvement in the Governor Rosas murder affair. Another Salazar, Bartolomé de Salazar, was *alcalde mayor* of Zuni prior to his death here in 1662. And as Fray Angélico Chávez pointed out, women who were descended from the step-daughters of Antonio de Sala sometimes stretched the name to Salazar.

SALAZAR (Sandoval). See *Casa Salazar.*

SALAZAR CANYON (Lincoln; heads in the Capitan Mountains E of Capitan and runs SW into the Rio Bonito). Formerly known as *Baca Canyon,* because of the family and the settlement by that name, it now is called Salazar Canyon because the Salazars, still residents in the area, owned land here.

SALEM (Doña Ana; settlement; on US 85, 5 mi NW of Hatch; PO 1908–present). When a group of New Englanders arrived here in 1908 and established a PO, they named it for their native Salem, MA. This replaced the name the earlier Hispanic settlers had for the region, *Plaza,* though some old-timers say the original name was *Gallina.*

SALINAS (Otero). See *Three Rivers.*

SALINAS BASIN (Torrance). See *Estancia Valley.*

SALINAS PUEBLO MISSIONS NATIONAL MONUMENT (Torrance; archaeological-historic sites; in W and SW part of county). The three units—*Abo, Quarai,* and *Gran Quivira* (see entries)—of Salinas Pueblo Missions National Monument preserve the ruins of pre-European Indian pueblos as well as the missions the Spaniards established at each of them. By the time the Spanish arrived in the 1600s, the pueblos had become important trading centers, in part because of their access to salt deposits in the saline lakes, called *Las Salinas,* to the E (see *Estancia Valley*); for this reason the pueblos were called the *Saline Pueblos.* But despite this fortuitous location, drought, famine, disease, cultural conflict with the Spaniards, and deteriorating relations with nomadic Indians resulted in the pueblos and the missions being abandoned by the 1670s.

SALIZ MOUNTAINS (Catron; begin 6 mi SW of Reserve and lie NW of the Kelly Mountains, E of US 180). This subrange of the Mogollon Volcanic Plateau likely was named for a family with this surname, though the name also could refer to willows here, for "willow" is *sauz* in Spanish and *salix* in Latin. Highest elevation, unnamed summit, 7,581 ft.

SALMON RUIN (San Juan; S of US 64, just W of Bloomfield). This imposing Anasazi ruin was named for homesteader George Salmon (pronounced SAL-mun, not like the fish), who owned the property including the ruin and who had the foresight to prevent its plunder by treasure hunters. Eventually the San Juan County Museum acquired the property and also rebuilt the Salmon homestead after the original building burned. The locality was settled by the Anasazis as early as A.D. 1089, making it one of the earliest Chacoan settlements in the Aztec-Bloomfield area; see *Chaco Culture National Historical Park.*

SALT CREEK WILDERNESS (Chaves; within Bitter Lake National Wildlife Refuge, NE of Roswell). *Salt Creek* enters the Pecos River here from the W. Administered by the USFWS; see also *Bitter Lake National Wildlife Refuge.*

SALT LAKE (Catron). See *Zuni Salt Lake.*

SALT LAKE (Eddy; 2 mi E of the Pecos River, 15 mi SE of Carlsbad, 6 mi NE of Loving). This large water body has been known as *Grande Sal, Laguna Grande, Laguna Grande de la Sal,* and *Sodal Lake,* but Salt Lake was the form accepted by the USBGN in 1968.

SALTPETER MOUNTAIN, 7,269 ft. (Colfax; 1 mi N of US 64, 5 mi SE of Dawson). Named for the mineral. *Saltpeter Creek* runs just to the W.

SALYERS CANYON (Colfax; in NW part of county, runs SE into Vermejo River). Preserves the surname of an early settler here.

SAMPSON (Union; settlement; exact location unknown; PO 1912–16, mail to Grenville). Abandoned community, name origin unknown.

SAN ACACIA (Socorro; settlement; just E of I-25, 14 mi N of Socorro; PO 1881–present). San Acacio is said to have been a Roman soldier martyred for his faith in early Christian times; NM *santeros* depicted him as crucified dressed in a Spanish military uniform. This village named for him apparently came into existence around 1880 with the arrival of the AT&SF RR; the change from the terminal *o* to *a* dates from the establishment of the PO and perhaps arose from confusion with the acacia shrub or, more likely, ignorance of Spanish; residents of the village insist on the correct form, *San Acacio,* and interest has been shown in formally changing the name, though at this writing that has not occurred. Much of the original village was destroyed by the flood of 1929, though a portion of the late 19th-century village lies NE of the present village.

SAN AGUSTIN (general). St. Augustine (A.D. 354–430) was among the great founders of the Roman Catholic Church. He converted to Christianity in A.D. 386 and rose quickly in church affairs. His *Confessions* and *City of God* are major works of theology, and he has been called the "Christian Aristotle." In NM the name appears once as *San Agustin,* 6 times as *San Augustin,* 9 times as *Augustine* (GNIS).

SAN AGUSTIN PLAINS (Catron, Socorro). See *Plains of San Agustin.*

SAN AGUSTIN (San Miguel; settlement; 9 mi SE of Las Vegas, on the Gallinas River; PO as Lourdes 1918–66, mail to Las Vegas). This tiny inhabited village appears on most maps as *San Agustin,* or more formally, *Los Valles de San Agustín;* a prominence named *San Agustin* is 2 mi NE. The name of the village's PO, *Lourdes,* came from the shrine in SW France where a healing spring is located, but why this name appears in this NM village is unknown.

SAN ALBINO (Sierra; settlement; on the E bank of the Rio Grande, at the foot of the Fra Cristobal Range). Little is known about this tiny settlement, which appears on an 1887 map. St. Alban was a Roman-Briton soldier martyred in Britain circa A.D. 209.

SAN ANDRES MOUNTAINS (Doña Ana, Sierra; long linear N-S range between the Jornada del Muerto and the Tularosa Valley). Vargas in his campaign journal of 1692 mentioned seeing the *sierra* of *Peñuelas,* "large rock without earth," which describes these barren mountains. On a Miera y Pacheco map of the 1770s the mountains are identified as *Las Petacas,* "skin-covered chests," and indeed the blocklike summits of these mountains, when viewed from the W, can be thought to resemble the traveling trunks of the colonial era. Numerous features in southern NM take their name from their association with the San Andres Mountains, which in turn were

named for St. Andrew, brother of St. Peter and one of the 12 disciples of Jesus; he is depicted in Christian art as an old man with long, white hair and beard. The particular inspiration for the name here is unknown. In the 19th and early 20th centuries, the name appeared as San Andres and *San Andreas,* but in 1920 the USBGN approved a request by the Hon. Philip S. Smith of NM to formalize the name San Andres. Highest elevation, *Salinas Peak,* 8,958 ft., in the N part of the range. *San Andres Peak,* 8,239 ft., is the highest in the range's southern portion.

SAN ANDRES NATIONAL WILDLIFE REFUGE (Doña Ana; in the southern San Andres Mountains, W and SW of White Sands National Monument). This 57,215-acre refuge was established in 1941 to protect and restore a remnant population of desert bighorn sheep, as well provide habitat for other species. Located within White Sands Missile Range, it has no public access.

SAN ANTONIO (general). Though there are several St. Anthonys, it was St. Anthony of Padua, disciple of St. Francis, that the people of NM favored as a patron. His name appears on 36 NM places, more than that of any other saint (GNIS).

SAN ANTONIO (Bernalillo; settlement; on NM 14, 1 mi N of Tijeras). Named for its patron saint, this community, still active, was a trading point when ox carts made their way over the route here to Santa Fe. See *San Antonio (general).*

SAN ANTONIO (Grant; settlement; in W part of county, exact location unknown). A 1915 newspaper account mentioned this as a small settlement.

SAN ANTONIO (McKinley; settlement; on NM 371, 6 mi NE of Thoreau). Sometimes called *San Antone,* this Navajo community has been centered on *San Antonio Mission* here. Nearby is *San Antonio Spring.* The Navajo name for this locality means "yellow water." See *San Antonio (general).*

SAN ANTONIO (Mora; settlement; 3 mi SW of Mora). Former sheep-raising community. See *San Antonio (general).*

SAN ANTONIO (Rio Arriba; settlement; in

NE part of county, 6 mi W of San Antonio Mountain). Abandoned settlement. See *San Antonio Mountain* and *Río San Antonio;* see also *San Antonio (general).*

SAN ANTONIO (San Miguel; settlement; 2 mi NW of Las Vegas, on the E bank of the Gallinas River). Small inhabited community. See *San Antonio (general).*

SAN ANTONIO (Socorro; settlement; on US 60-85, 11 mi S of Socorro, 1 mi E of I-25; PO 1870–73, 1874–present). It's possible the site of the present village was known as San Antonio as early as 1600, for a document dated then mentions an *Estancia de San Antonio.* With more certainty the name can be traced to 1629, when Fray García de Francisco de Zuñiga and Fray Antonio de Arteaga founded the mission of *San Antonio de Senecú* at the Piro Indian pueblo of that name, located S of the present village. After the Pueblo Revolt of 1680, however, and throughout the 17th century, the region was generally depopulated.

Around 1820, Hispanic settlers from northern NM reoccupied the area, naming their settlement after the old mission. Later the AT&SF RR established a station. It was here, sometime in the 1880s, that A.H. Hilton arrived, and it was here that his son, Conrad Hilton, born in 1887, got his start in the hotel business, carrying luggage from the train station to his father's hotel. Today, the once-prosperous Hilton section of San Antonio is in decay, while business activity has shifted N to the present townsite. See *Senecu;* see also *San Antonio (general).*

SAN ANTONIO (Taos). See *Valdez.*

SAN ANTONIO DEL EMBUDO (Rio Arriba). See *Embudo.*

SAN ANTONIO DE LO DE MORA (Mora). See *Mora.*

SAN ANTONIO DE SENECU (Socorro). See *Senecu.*

SAN ANTONIO MOUNTAIN, 9,986 ft. (Sandoval; in the Jemez Mountains, 6 mi NW of Redondo Peak). One of several volcanic summits surrounding the Valle Grande caldera. *San Antonio Creek* heads W of here and flows S into the Jemez River. *San Antonio Hot Spring* also is just to the NW. See *San Antonio (general).*

SAN ANTONIO MOUNTAIN, 10,908 ft. (Rio Arriba; in NE part of county, 3 mi W of US 285, 10 mi S of the Colorado border). Huge, hulking volcanic mass. Tewas know the mountain by names meaning "bear mountain"; it is their cardinal mountain of the N. See *Río San Antonio;* see also *San Antonio (general).*

SAN ANTONITO (Bernalillo; settlement; on NM 14, 6 mi N of Tijeras). Active community, likely named for its association with the older community of *San Antonio* 5 mi S on NM 14.

SAN AUGUSTIN (Doña Ana; settlement; NE of teh Organ Mountains, E of Aguirre Spring; PO 1876–88, mail to Organ). In the latter half of teh 19th century, Warren Shedd acquired land on the E side of the Organ Mountains from Thomas Jefferson Bull and at *San Agustin Springs* founded the famous San Agustin Ranch, which as the Cox Ranch continues in operation today, though much of the original property is within the Organ National Recreation Area (see *Organ Mountains*).

SAN AUGUSTIN MOUNTAINS (Doña Ana; small spur of the San Andres Mountains, 3 mi NE of Organ). Highest elevation, *San Augustin Peak,* 7,030 ft. See *San Agustin (general).*

SAN AUGUSTIN PASS, approximately 5,700 ft. (Doña Ana; separates the Organ Mountains from the San Andres Mountains, on US 70, 13 mi NE of Las Cruces). *San Augustin Peak,* 7,030 ft., is just to the N. *San Augustin Springs* is here also. See *San Agustin (general).*

SAN BUENAVENTURA DE CHIMAYO (Santa Fe). See *Chimayo.*

SAN CARLOS (Bernalillo). See *Alameda.*

SAN CARLOS (Socorro; settlement; NE part of county; PO 1875–76, 1877–78, mail to Lemitar). Little is known about this locality.

SAN CLEMENTE (Valencia; settlement; near Los Lunas). The name of this 18th-century *rancho* honors St. Clement I, Bishop of Rome and Pope in A.D. 92–101. The *San Clemente Grant* was granted to Don Felix Candelaria in 1716.

SAN CRISTOBAL (general). These names honor St. Christopher, the legendary giant who carried the Christ child over a brook. Catholics look to him for protection against natural disasters.

SAN CRISTOBAL (Santa Fe; settlement; 1 mi E of US 285, E of Galisteo). This was one of the early 17th-century missions among the Tano Indians of the Galisteo Basin; the name here often is spelled *Cristoval. San Cristobal Arroyo* runs W from here to Galisteo Creek at Galisteo. See *San Cristobal (general)*.

SAN CRISTOBAL (Taos; settlement; on NM 522, 14 mi N of Taos; PO 1932–present). The *San Cristobal Grant* here was given to Severino Martínez in 1815; the agricultural community of San Cristobal was founded around 1860. *San Cristobal Creek* flows W through here to the Rio Grande. See *San Cristobal (general)*.

SAN DIEGO (general). St. Didacus was a 15th-century Franciscan lay-brother at Alcalá in Spain whose name is very popular in Hispanic regions. He was notable for ministering to the poor.

SAN DIEGO CANYON (Sandoval; parallels NM 4, between Cañones and Jemez Springs). According to legend, Indians living on the mesa to the W (see *Mesa de Guadalupe*) killed a priest and ignored warnings that armed Spaniards in the canyon below would retaliate. When the Spaniards attacked them at night, the Indians began trying to hurl the Spaniards from the cliffs, but at that moment a vision of San Diego appeared from the direction of the canyon named for him—the Virgin of Guadalupe appeared from the canyon named for her—and the Indians fled.

SAN DIEGO, TONUCO (Doña Ana; settlement; on the E bank of the Rio Grande, 10 mi SE of Hatch). The *Paraje de San Diego* was an important early *paraje,* or campground, on the Camino Real; it was at an important ford across the Rio Grande; on early maps it was shown as being on the W side of the river. San Diego was mentioned by Otermín in 1682 and later in the Vargas campaign journal of 1692. The site also has been called *Tonuco,* a name of unknown meaning and origin; a settlement by that name appears on the 1828 *Mapa de los*

EUM, and a RR siding here also took that name.

San Diego Mountain, 4,949 ft., is a hulking volcanic mass, just E of San Diego/Tonuco; it also is known as *Tonuco Mountain,* though the USBGN recognizes San Diego. The hills around here are called the *Tonuco Mountains.*

SAN FELIPE (general). St. Philip the Apostle was one of the 12 disciples and a missionary of the early church, martyred in Phrygia. Many of the early San Felipe names in NM honored not only the saint but also one of five Spanish kings named Philip, though the well-known Catholic church of San Felipe Neri (see *Albuquerque*) on Albuquerque's Old Town Plaza honors St. Philip Neri, a 16th-century priest of Rome and founder of a religious congregation. San Felipe appears 13 times on NM places (GNIS).

SAN FELIPE PUEBLO (Sandoval; settlement; 10 mi N of Bernalillo, 4 mi NW of I-25; PO 1928–36, mail to Algodones). The Keresan-speaking inhabitants of this pueblo explain their history thus: "Our village, *Katishtya,* was located at the foot of Black Mesa, *Tamita,* when Coronado and his party arrived in 1540. Centuries before this first visit by Europeans our people lived at El Rito del los Frijoles (see entry). When they left that site they moved S, building and occupying villages along the way and, finally, settling at Tamita. After the Pueblo Revolt of 1680 they moved to Potrero Viejo along with the Cochiti, Santo Domingo, Tano, Taos, and Picuris. They returned to the vicinity of Tamita in 1693, and early in the 18th century our ancestors built the present village of Katishtya on the W bank of the Rio Grande. The name San Felipe was given to us by Castaño de Sosa in 1591."

SAN FELIPE PUEBLO (Socorro; settlement; S of Socorro, probably near the confluence of Milligan Gulch and the Rio Grande). San Felipe was the first Piro Indian pueblo encountered by the Spanish moving N along the Rio Grande in NM, and they dubbed it *La Cabeza de la Provincia,* "the head of the province."

Though the pueblo was already abandoned and in ruins when Chamuscado arrived here in 1581, it nonetheless was the site where he took possession of the entire province, which he called the "Kingdom of San Felipe," on behalf of Philip II, King of Spain.

SAN FERNANDO, SAN FERNANDEZ (general). The parochial saint Ferdinand III was a 13th-century king of Castile and member of the Third Order of St. Francis.

SAN FERNANDEZ (Valencia; settlement; between Tome and Valencia, 3 mi SE of Los Lunas). This former settlement, now absorbed into Tome, originally was called *San Fernando de los Silvas,* "St. Ferdinand of the Silvas." Francisco Silva and Rosa de Chávez settled in the Tome area in the 17th century, and the 1790 Spanish census referred to the site as San Fernando de los Silvas. In the 1802 Spanish census it was called the *Plaza de San Fernando.* The locale also is said to have been called *La Ciénega de San Fernando Rey,* "the marsh of St. Ferdinand the King."

SAN FERNANDO (Valencia; settlement; on the Rio Puerco). Former community, inhabited around 1855 but abandoned soon thereafter.

SAN FIDEL (Cibola; settlement; on NM 124, 18 mi E of Grants; PO as Ballejos 1910–19, as San Fidel 1919–present). About 1868 Baltazar Jaramillo and his family settled here. An early name for the locality was *La Vega de San José,* "the meadow of St. Joseph," a reference to the *Río San José* just to the S. A tiny residential cluster about 1 mi N of present San Fidel still is called *San José* and may be the community sometimes referred to as *Old San José.* Another early name for the area now called San Fidel was *Rinconada,* "box canyon, or junction." The PO here took the name *Ballejos,* a variant of the Spanish family name Vallejos. Later it was changed to San Fidel, honoring the saint, a name said to have been suggested by the pastor of the church here, Fr. Robert Kalt, O.F.M.

SAN FRANCISCO (general). As T.M. Pearce explained, "Franciscan pioneers of NM named many places for the founder of their order, St. Francis of Assisi, who lived from 1182 to 1226. The first was the extinct pueblo of Puaray, which was originally selected as headquarters for the missions; from it the patronage was transferred to its successor, the 17th-century pueblo of Sandia." The name San Francisco occurs 14 times in NM (GNIS).

SAN FRANCISCO (Catron; settlement; exact location unknown; PO 1879–82, mail to Horse Springs). Little is known about this former community.

SAN FRANCISCO (Rio Arriba). See *El Duende.*

SAN FRANCISCO (Sandoval; settlement; 17 mi N of the Rio Puerco I-40 interchange, on the west side of the Rio Puerco). Abandoned 19th-century Hispanic community.

SAN FRANCISCO (Socorro; settlement; N of Socorro, on the W bank of the Rio Grande, where the Rio Puerco enters the Rio Grande). The 1873–78 Wheeler Survey put this village on the E bank of the Rio Grande, but the village later moved to the W bank, the former location taking the name *Los Ranchos de la Joya* (see *La Joya*). Census records from 1885 to 1920 showed populations from 40 to 264. A single family still resides in the locality, but the church and plaza are in ruins; the name, however, is still recognized and used.

SAN FRANCISCO MOUNTAINS (Catron; in W part of county, NW of Reserve). Likely named for the *San Francisco River* (see entry) to the N.

SAN FRANCISCO PLAZA (Catron; settlement; along the San Francisco River, beginning at Reserve and going 3 mi S). This name has been attached to three separate settlements along the San Francisco River: *Upper San Francisco Plaza,* now *Reserve* (see entry); *Middle San Francisco Plaza,* 1 mi S of Reserve, often called *San Francisco Plaza,* or even more simply, *Frisco;* and *Lower San Francisco Plaza,* 3 mi S of Reserve.

SAN FRANCISCO RIVER (Catron; heads in the San Francisco Mountains NW of Reserve and flows E and then S and then SW into Arizona to empty into the Gila

River). Most of the features named San Francisco in this area likely derive their names from this river. The circumstances of its naming are unknown. See *San Francisco (general)*.

SAN FRANCISCO XAVIER (Bernalillo). See *Albuquerque*.

SAN GABRIEL (general). The name of this saint translated from Hebrew means "man of God." One of the archangels, Gabriel sometimes has been regarded as the angel of death, the prince of fire and thunder, but more often as one of God's chief messengers. He is expected to sound the trumpet on Judgment Day.

SAN GABRIEL (Rio Arriba; settlement; at the confluence of the Rio Chama and the Rio Grande). When Oñate's expedition arrived at the confluence of the Rio Grande and the Rio Chama on July 11, 1598, they found on the E bank of the Rio Grande a Tewa pueblo its inhabitants called by a name often transliterated as *Ohke*. Oñate christened the pueblo *San Juan* (see *San Juan Pueblo*), then added *de los Caballeros* as a tribute to the Spanish gentlemen who accompanied his mission. Oñate established his military headquarters here. Less than a year later, however, Oñate and his men moved to the W bank, to another Tewa pueblo whose name has been spelled *Yungueingge*, "mockingbird place pueblo." The Spaniards christened their new headquarters *San Gabriel de Yunque Yunque*, while the previous site retained the name San Juan. The new site also was called *San Gabriel de los Españoles*, a name some people believe survives, though abbreviated, in the modern name Española. As headquarters of the Spanish colonizers, San Gabriel thus was the first Spanish capital of NM, but the distinction was short-lived; about 1610 the Spaniards moved to what is now Santa Fe, and San Gabriel, whose Tewa inhabitants already had moved to San Juan, was abandoned.

SAN GERONIMO (general). St. Jerome was a father of the Catholic Church and translator of the *Vulgate Bible*. He is generally represented as an aged man in a cardinal's dress, writing or studying. His name occurs only three times in NM (GNIS).

SAN GERONIMO (San Miguel; settlement; 9 mi W of Las Vegas, on Tecolote Creek; PO 1919 intermittently to 1944, mail to Las Vegas). San Geronimo was founded about 1835 when 400,000 acres were granted to a group of settlers, most of whom had come from nearby San Miguel del Bado and Tecolote. Local tradition is that San Geronimo was founded on the site of a pre-Spanish pueblo, and a hill on the W side of Tecolote Creek is called *Pueblecito*, "little pueblo." During the 19th century the village was called *Los Valles de San Gerónimo del Tecolote*, "the valleys of St. Jerome of the Tecolote." San Geronimo became an important trading center in the 19th century, especially with the arrival of the RR, but in the 20th century San Geronimo has declined, and many residents have left to seek employment elsewhere. See *Mineral Hill*.

SAN GERONIMO (Socorro; settlement; on the W bank of the Rio Grande, across from La Joya). This tiny settlement, long abandoned, consisted of only a few houses and does not appear on maps or census records.

SAN GERONIMO DE TAOS (Taos). See *Taos Pueblo*.

SAN GREGORIO LAKE (Rio Arriba). See *Gregorio Lake*.

SAN HILARIO (San Miguel; settlement; near Conchas Dam; PO 1878–86, mail to La Cinta). Though this name commemorates St. Hilary, a 4th-century Doctor of the Catholic Church, this former locality often was called simply *Hilario* and could in fact recall one Hilario González.

SAN IGNACIO (general). Though Catholics have beatified two persons named Ignatius, the only one known to New Mexicans was the Spaniard, St. Ignatius Loyola, founder of the Jesuits. He was a son of the Spanish ducal house of Loyola, and after being severely wounded at the siege of Pampeluna (now Pamplona) in 1521 he left the army and dedicated himself to the service of the Virgin. His Order of the Society of Jesus, which he projected in 1534, was confirmed by Paul III in 1540. The name San Ignacio appears 8 times in NM (GNIS).

SAN IGNACIO (Bernalillo; settlement; in W part of county, N of I-40 and E of the Rio Puerco). One of several tiny villages, now abandoned, along the Rio Puerco. See *San Ignacio (general)*.

SAN IGNACIO (Guadalupe; settlement; 4 mi S of I-40, 18 W of Santa Rosa; PO 1908 intermittently to 1946, mail to Pastura). The settlement here has vanished, but ranches are still in the area, and the church and the name are still used. See *San Ignacio (general)*.

SAN IGNACIO (San Miguel; settlement; on NM 266, 5 mi W of Sapello, on the Sapello River; PO as San Ignacio 1886–1901, as Koogler 1920–31, as Tecoloteños 1931–45, mail to Sapello). This tiny inhabited community has been known under four names: San Ignacio, honoring its patron saint; *Koogler,* for reasons unknown but likely having a connection with the Koogler who edited the *Las Vegas Gazette* in the 1870s; *Tecoloteños,* "Tecolote folks," because it was settled by people from Tecolote; and related to this *Rincón de Tecolote,* a name that appears on late 19th-century maps. It appears on most contemporary maps as San Ignacio. See *San Ignacio (general)*.

SAN ILDEFONSO PUEBLO (Santa Fe; settlement; just N of NM 502, 6 mi W of Pojoaque). The inhabitants of this Tewa pueblo explain its history thus: "The name of our pueblo is *Pokwoghayungwee,* 'where the water cuts through.' Our ancestors...came from the N, some say Mesa Verde, and moved S and occupied the villages of *Potsuwi, Sankewi,* and *Otowi* in the high mountains of the Pajarito Plateau. Later, because of drought, they moved into the Rio Grande valley. Our ancestors were living about a mile S of where we live today when they saw Europeans for the first time. After the Pueblo Revolt, about 1694, they moved to the top of Black Mesa, where they defended themselves against the Spanish leader Vargas. Finally, they returned to their village and in 1717 the pueblo, where we now live,

was built." Navajos know the pueblo by a name meaning "houses between the rocks, referring to the space between Round Mountain and La Mesita. When Oñate passed through here in 1598, he called the pueblo *Bove,* for reasons unknown, but later changed the name to commemorate St. Ildephonse, 7th-century Archbishop of Toledo. The Spanish built their mission here in 1617, and St. Ildephonse has been the pueblo's patron ever since.

San Ildefonso Mesa, see *Black Mesa*.

SAN JON (Quay; settlement; on I-40 and NM 469, 24 mi E of Tucumcari; PO 1906–present). The first building in what was to become San Jon was built in 1902, and RR construction in 1904 caused the little settlement to boom. When a PO was established in 1906, the first postmaster, W.D. Bennett, named it San Jon, an name that has puzzled people ever since, as the Spanish-sounding name in fact makes no sense in Spanish. The consensus is that it's a corruption of the Spanish *zanjon,* "deep gully." *San Jon Creek* heads S of here and flows E into Texas.

SAN JOSE (general). Joseph, husband of Mary, is among the most popular saints in Spanish Christendom. He was the patron of the first Jemez Indian mission, established in 1617. When the Spanish returned to NM in 1692 he was the patron of the new church at Laguna Pueblo. St. Joseph looks over carpenters and is depicted in art as an aged man with a budding staff in his hand. After San Antonio, San Jose is the saint most commonly represented in NM place names, appearing 33 times (GNIS).

SAN JOSE (Bernalillo; settlement; in S Albuquerque, E of the Rio Grande). The little community of San Jose was well-established by the 1860s, with 40–50 residences and small farms, with Antonio Sandoval the village's *patrón.* San Jose has since been absorbed into Albuquerque, but two parks and an elementary school preserve the name. See *San Jose (general)*.

SAN JOSE (Eddy; settlement; S of Carlsbad). Early records mention a

"Mexican village" named San Jose immediately S of Carlsbad. Today the village is gone, but the area still has that name, and San Jose Blvd. and San Jose Parish are still found in Carlsbad. See *San Jose (general)*.

SAN JOSE (Grant). See *Dwyer*.

SAN JOSE (Mora). See *Ledoux*.

SAN JOSE (Rio Arriba; settlement; on US 84-285, 1.5 mi SE of Hernandez). Inhabited community, that like its neighbor, Hernandez, has San Jose as its patron. See *San Jose (general)*.

SAN JOSE (San Miguel; settlement; just S of I-40, on the W bank of the Pecos River; PO 1858 intermittently to present). One of the county's oldest communities, this was founded by colonists from Santa Fe in 1803. See *San Jose (general)*.

SAN JOSE (Sierra; settlement; originally on the W side of the Rio Grande, now beneath Elephant Butte Reservoir). See *San Jose (general)*.

SAN JOSE (Socorro; settlement; in N part of county, exact location unknown; PO 1892–96, mail to Sabinal). Abandoned community. See *San Jose (general)*.

SAN JOSE (Valencia). See *Correo*; see also *San Jose (general)*.

SAN JOSE ARROYO (Sierra, Socorro; heads in the San Mateo Mountains, SE of Vicks Peak, and runs SE to Elephant Butte Reservoir in Sierra County). Also called *Pankey Canyon*, for the Pankey family whose ranch is here.

SAN JOSE DE CHAMA (Rio Arriba). See *Hernandez*.

SAN JUAN (general). Several St. Johns exist in the Catholic panoply of saints, but the two most likely eponymns in NM are St. John, one of the 12 disciples and brother of James, and St. John the Baptist, who baptized Jesus and is the patron of missionaries. Just after San Antonio and San Jose, San Juan is the saint whose name is most often found on place names in NM, appearing 31 times (GNIS).

SAN JUAN (Doña Ana). See *Tortugas*.

SAN JUAN (Grant; settlement; on the Mimbres River and NM 61, 3 mi S of San Lorenzo; PO as Sherman 1894–1967, mail to San Lorenzo). This inhabited settlement took the name of the patron of its Catholic church and parish; see *San Juan (general)*. Its PO was called *Sherman*, said to have been named for a trader in the area who in 1852 obtained a license to trade with the Apaches near Fort Webster.

SAN JUAN (San Miguel; settlement; on Arroyo Blanco, W of La Cabra Mesa). In 1823 Gov. Bartolomé Baca made to Juan Estevan Pino a grant known as *Hacienda de San Juan Bautista del Ojito del Río de las Gallinas*—"Estate of St. John the Baptist of the little spring of the Gallinas River," possibly NM's longest place name. The village, now abandoned, was more succinctly known simply as San Juan.

SAN JUAN (Socorro). See *Veguita*.

SAN JUAN COUNTY (NW NM; county seat, Aztec). Until 1887 Rio Arriba County extended to the Arizona border, and residents in this area were 75 to 100 miles over rough country from Tierra Amarilla, the county seat, so in 1887 this county was created; it was named for the San Juan River (see entry). Selection of a county seat was fiercely contested (see *Aztec* and *Junction City*), but Aztec finally won in 1892.

SAN JUAN DRAW (Chaves). See *Hernandez Draw*.

SAN JUAN MESA (Chaves; in NE part of county). Major landform, specific circumstances of naming unknown.

SAN JUAN MOUNTAINS (Rio Arriba). See *San Juan River*.

SAN JUAN PUEBLO (Rio Arriba; settlement; just W of NM 68, 7 mi N of Española, on the E bank of the Rio Grande; PO as San Juan 1870–81, as Chamita 1881–1944, as San Juan Pueblo 1944–present). The residents of this pueblo explain their history thus: "Our Tewa name is *O'ke*, which means 'we are the brothers.' According to our history, the present pueblo is the third one that has been called O'ke. The first was located about a mile N of the present San Juan; when it was destroyed by a flood the inhabitants built a second pueblo called O'ke at *Kutigii*, only a few hundred yards NW of the present pueblo. Other villages occupied by our ancestors include *Pioge, Pojiu-uingge,* and *Sajiuwingge.*" The anthropologist Alphonso Ortiz, a member of the pueblo, says that in addition to the everyday name, O'ke, the pueblo also is known by a ceremonial name meaning "village of the dew-bedecked corn structure." The name San Juan dates from July 12, 1598, when Oñate formally took possession of the pueblo and christened it *San Juan de los Caballeros,* honoring his personal patron saint, St. John the Baptist, and also the *caballeros,* or "gentlemen," who had accompanied him on his expedition; Oñate headed his official correspondence from here *San Juan de Nuevo México.* This complimentary title also is said by Villagra, Oñate's chronicler, to have recognized the courtesy and hospitality the Indians showed the Spanish colonists. Less than a year later, the Spaniards moved across the river, to another Tewa pueblo the Indians called *Yungueingge* but which the Spaniards christened *San Gabriel* (see entry); the first pueblo where the Spaniards stayed retained the name San Juan, which it has today.

SAN JUAN RIVER (Rio Arriba, San Juan; flows into Rio Arriba County from Colorado, runs W through Navajo Reservoir, past Farmington, then returns to Colorado in extreme NW San Juan County). Jerold G. Widdison has explained the evolution of this major river's name thus: "The Domínguez-Escalante expedition of 1776 came upon the San Juan River and its tributary, the Navajo River, at their confluence just N of the present CO-NM boundary. At that time the names of both streams already were known; indeed, some accounts say that the San Juan River's name had been bestowed about a hundred years earlier by Fray Alonso de Posada. But then one of the leaders of the 1776 expedition, Fray Silvestre Vélez de Escalante, used the name *Río Grande de Navajo* for all that portion of the San Juan downstream from the Navajo's confluence, stating that he did so because the river separated the homelands of the Navajo Indians from those of the Utes. The soldier-cartographer who accompanied Escalante, the redoubtable Capt. Bernardo Miera y Pacheco, somewhat similarly labelled the stream on his map as *Río de Nabajoó.* Thirty years later, Baron Von Humboldt's map still showed the San Juan as *Río Navajoa.* Yet as the years went by, the name San Juan returned to use."

Present day Navajos have several names for the river, including "Utes' river," "old age river," "male river" (the Rio Grande is "female river"), and simply "river." Navajos call much of this region and adjacent areas in Arizona and Utah by a name meaning "ancient land of the Navajos"; see *Dinetah.*

The San Juan River and its larger tributaries—the Animas, Los Pinos, and Piedra rivers, as well as the Navajo River—flow from the *San Juan Mountains,* mostly in SW Colorado but extending into NW NM. S of the mountains is the *San Juan Basin,* known for its gas and oil deposits, drained by two other San Juan tributaries, the Chaco River and Cañon Largo (see entries). San Juan Basin also denotes a cultural region, including parts of NM, Arizona, Colorado, and Utah, with Farmington as its economic center.

SAN LAZARO (Santa Fe; settlement; in the Galisteo Basin). This name, honoring St. Lazarus, whom Christ raised from the dead, was given to one of the early Tano missions in the Galisteo Basin. According to the Otermín documents, this pueblo participated in the Pueblo Revolt of 1680. See *Ortiz Mountains.*

SIERRA DE SAN LAZARO (Santa Fe). See *Ortiz Mountains.*

SAN LORENZO (general). St. Lawrence, patron of curriers, was deacon in the 3rd Century to Sextus I and was charged with the care of the poor, orphans, and widows. Spanish born, he has always been popular among Hispanic peoples. His name appears on 11 NM places (GNIS).

SAN LORENZO (Cibola). See *Tinaja.*

SAN LORENZO (Grant; settlement; on the E bank of the Mimbres River, just N of NM 152; PO 1886–1963, mail to rural station of Santa Rita). The site of this samll inhabited community is said to have been visited in 1714 by Gov. Juan Ignacio de Flores Mogollón. Later it was closely affiliated with Fort Webster (see entry), but when the fort was decommissioned in 1853 the area was ravaged by Apaches and abandoned. The modern community dates from 1869, when it was settled by persons from Pinos Altos. See *San Lorenzo (general)*.

SAN LORENZO (San Miguel; settlement; in E part of county, near Conchas Lake; PO 1876–77). A military outpost during the American occupation, this settlement, now abandoned, was named by Lorenzo López to commemorate his patron saint and also his own name. López was San Miguel County sheriff in the late 1880s. See *San Lorenzo (general)*.

SAN LUIS (general). St. Louis IX was King of France in the 13th century and the son of Louis VIII and Blanche of Castile. His name appears 11 times in NM (GNIS).

SAN LUIS (Sandoval; settlement; 6 mi W of NM 44, on the E side of the Rio Puerco). The scissors-like crossing of roads here gave this small ranching community, still inhabited, its first name, *Las Tijeras,* "the scissors." Father George Julliard named the village San Luis in the 1890s; see *San Luis (general)*. Navajos call the locality by a name meaning "rock coming up wide."

SAN LUIS (San Miguel; settlement; on the S bank of the Mora River, SW of Loma Parda). Abandoned community, shown on an 1870 map. See *San Luis (general)*.

SAN LUIS MOUNTAINS (Hidalgo; in S part of county, running N from the Mexican border). Small range but with considerable relief. Highest elevation, *Lang,* 6,751 ft. *San Luis Pass* is at the N end of the range. See *San Luis (general)*.

SAN MARCIAL (Socorro; settlement; on NM 178, 3 mi E of I-25, 17 mi S of San Antonio; PO 1869–1944, mail to San Antonio). Around 1854, Pascual Joyla, a farmer, moved his family to an adobe dwelling on the E side of the Rio Grande, at the N base of Black Mesa. He found a ready market for his produce and firewood at Fort Conrad to the N, and soon a little community sprang up called *La Mesa de San Marcial,* or often simply *La Mesa,* honoring the 3rd-century saint, Martial of Limoges, France. In 1866 a flood devastated the little community, so the village moved across the river, taking the name *San Marcial* with it. In the 1880s the village underwent a boom with the arrival of the RR, and soon another community sprang up near the RR station to the W. This was called *New San Marcial;* between this and *Old San Marcial* was still another settlement, called *Midway,* also known as *Torres Junction.* New San Marcial retained the PO name San Marcial; the PO at Old San Marcial took the name *Milligan* (PO 1907–13, mail to San Marcial); see *Milligan Gulch.* From 1890–1920, San Marcial was the second largest town in Socorro County. Throughout this period, the E bank village of La Mesa continued to be inhabited. But then in 1929 another disastrous flood devastated both villages—and this time they did not recover. Later the area was flooded to create *Lake San Marcial,* and today only ruins and the cemetery remain.

SAN MARCOS (general). St. Mark was author of the Gospel of St. Mark, second book of the *New Testament.* Little is known of his life. He is famed as the patron of Venice. Three NM places bear his name (GNIS).

SAN MARCOS (Santa Fe; settlement; in the Galisteo Basin). This name was bestowed by the Spanish upon one of several 17th-century missions among the Tano Indians of the Galisteo Basin. The *San Marcos Pueblo Land Grant* was given in 1754. See *San Marcos (general)*.

SAN MATEO (general). St. Matthew, or Levi, was one of the 12 Disciples of Jesus and author of the *Gospel of St. Matthew,* first book of the *New Testament.* His name has been placed on 16 NM features (GNIS).

SAN MATEO (Cibola; settlement; on NM 605, on the N slopes of Mount Taylor; PO 1876–present). In 1768 Governor Mendinueta gave the *San Mateo Springs*

Grant to Santiago Duran y Cháves, but credit for founding the village of San Mateo usually goes to Roman A. Baca, born in Cebolleta in 1833, who is said to have led a group of colonists here in 1855 following an expedition against the Ute Indians. Baca had a long career as a soldier, statesman, and political leader; he died in 1899 and is buried in San Mateo. The village took the name of the nearby mountains; see *San Mateo Mountains (Cibola, McKinley). San Mateo Creek* heads near San Mateo and flows E and S to join Bluewater Creek N of Grants to form the Rio San Jose. See *San Mateo (general)*.

SAN MATEO MOUNTAINS (Cibola, McKinley). On some maps, this name is applied to the entire upland complex topped by 11,301-foot Mount Taylor, but more often only the southern part, including Mount Taylor, bears this name, the northern part still called the *Cebolleta Mountains* (see entry), the name used for the complex in Spanish colonial times. Application of both these names has been confusing and inconsistent. The village of *San Mateo* (see entry) took its name from the San Mateo Mountains. See *San Mateo (general)*.

SAN MATEO MOUNTAINS (Socorro; in SW part of county, between NM 52 and NM 107). Highest elevations, *West Blue Mountain,* 10,336 ft. and *Blue Mountain,* 10,309 ft., *San Mateo Peak,* 10,139 ft., is in the southern part of the San Mateo Mountains; *San Mateo Mountain,* 10,145 ft., is 3 mi farther S. An 1870 map of NM labels these mountains the *Tucson Mountains,* though the mountains generally accepted as having that name are NE of Carrizozo. See *San Mateo (general)*.

SAN MIGUEL (general). In Roman Catholicism, St. Michael is the great prince of all the angels and leader of the heavenly armies. He is looked upon as bringing the gift of prudence to humankind. In portrayals of the final judgment he is represented with scales, with which he weighs the souls of the risen dead. One of the most popular saints in NM, his name appears on 27 places (GNIS).

SAN MIGUEL (Doña Ana; settlement; on NM 28, 10 mi S of Mesilla; PO as Telles 1894 intermittently to 1952, as San Miguel 1952–present). This small Hispanic village dates from 1850. San Miguel likely is its original name, but when a landowner named Telles opened a store and PO, postal officials listed the PO by his name until 1952. (It is interesting to note that when Nicolás Lafora, journeying N from El Paso, arrived here in 1766, he referred to a locality in this area as *Ancón de la Cruz de Juan Téllez,* "Narrow of the Cross of Juan Téllez"; whether any connection existed between the earlier name and the later one is not known.) See *San Miguel (general)*.

SAN MIGUEL (Rio Arriba; settlement; in NE part of county, on the Rio de los Pinos, 2 mi from the Colorado border). Tiny inhabited community. See *San Miguel (general)*.

SAN MIGUEL (Sandoval; settlement; 4 mi E of NM 44, 9 mi SE of Cuba). Inhabited locality, located in *San Miguel Canyon; San Miguel Spring* is 3 mi SE; *San Miguel Mountain,* 9,473 ft., where the canyon heads, is 6 mi SE. See *San Miguel (general)*.

SAN MIGUEL (Sierra; settlement; on Palomas Creek, 6 mi SW of Cuchillo). A church and a few scattered buildings are all that remain of this tiny community. See *San Miguel (general)*.

SAN MIGUEL COUNTY (NE NM; county seat, Las Vegas). Created by the Republic of Mexico in 1844 and named for *San Miguel del Bado* (see entry), one of the area's oldest communities and the county seat until this was moved to Las Vegas in 1864.

SAN MIGUEL DEL BADO (San Miguel; settlement; on the Pecos River, on NM 3, 3 mi S of I-25; PO 1851 intermittently to 1910, mail to Ribera). This, after Pecos one of the oldest communities in this part of NM, was founded about 1794 by *genízaros,* Hispanicized Indians, on a land grant given by Governor Chacón. The church was built in 1805, and the community, located at an important crossing of the Pecos River, took the name *San Miguel del Bado,* "St. Michael of the Ford." The name often is simply

San Miguel on maps, and *bado* often appears as *vado*. San Miguel del Bado served as an outpost against raiding Plains Indians, then as a lookout for French and later American interlopers into Spanish territory, but after Mexican Independence in 1821 and the opening of the Santa Fe Trail, the village became an important way-stop; the 1827 Mexican census listed 2,893 inhabitants. When *San Miguel County* was created in 1844, this village not only was its eponymn but also its first county seat. But in the meantime, Las Vegas, settled by persons from San Miguel del Bado, was burgeoning to the N; the county seat went there in 1864, and with the arrival of the RR there in 1879 the older town was further eclipsed. It survives today, but the present village gives no obvious hints of its past significance.

SAN MIGUEL MOUNTAINS (Sandoval; in the SE Jemez Mountains, straddling the western boundary of Bandelier National Monument). Small subrange, principal summit *St. Peters Dome*, 8,463 ft. To the Tewas of San Ildefonso Pueblo, these are the "bluebird tail mountains," while to the Keresan-speaking Indians of Cochiti Pueblo they are the "cottontail rabbit mountains."

SAN NICOLAS (Doña Ana; settlement; in SE San Andres Mountains, in San Nicolas Canyon). George Adlai Feather described this locality, now within White Sands Missile Range, as primarily a water stop on an old route where a merchant sold goods to travelers and prospectors. *San Nicolas Spring* is about 3 mi S.

SAN PABLO (general). San Pablo names honor St. Paul, author of the principal *Epistles* of the New Testament whose missionary activities are described in the *Acts of the Apostles*. As Saul of Tarsus, he originally was one of the most bitter persecutors of the early Christians, but he was converted by a vision on the road to Damascus. He is the patron of preachers and tentmakers. He changed his name from Saul to Paul in honor of Servius Paulus, whom he converted. Paul was martyred in Rome in A.D. 66.

SAN PABLO (Doña Ana; settlement; on NM 28, about 2 mi SE of Mesilla). Tiny residential cluster on the E side of the Rio Grande. See *San Pablo (general)*.

SAN PABLO (Guadalupe; settlement; location unknown). Abandoned community. See *San Pablo (general)*.

SAN PABLO (Sandoval; settlement; E of the Rio Puerco, between Cuba and La Ventana). Abandoned community. See *San Pablo (general)*.

SAN PABLO (San Miguel; settlement; 12 mi SW of Las Vegas, 1.5 mi S of San Geronimo). A single residence remains at this former trading point. *San Pablo Creek* heads just to the SW and flows NE into Tecolote Creek. See *San Pablo (general)*.

SAN PASCUAL (general). St. Pascual is the patron of cooking, the kitchen, and finding lost domestic animals. That and him having been a Spaniard—he was a gatekeeper in the late 1500s for the Franciscans—have made him one of the most popular saints in the Southwest.

SAN PASCUAL (Socorro; settlement; 10 mi S of Socorro). This was a Piro Indian pueblo, abandoned in the 17th century; Bishop Pedro Tamarón in 1760 found only traces of the old pueblo. It likely took this name because of a Spanish mission here. The name was still used when Josiah Gregg passed through here in the early 1800s, but it applied only to a campground. See *San Pascual (general)*.

SAN PASCUAL WILDERNESS (Socorro; flanks both E and W sides of Bosque del Apache National Wildlife Refuge, 8 mi S of San Antonio). Named for the abandoned Piro Indian pueblo named *San Pascual* once here (see entry). Associated with the wilderness to the E are the *Little San Pascual Mountains,* a small group centered on *Little San Pascual Mountain,* 5,525 ft. Administered by the USFWS.

SAN PATRICIO (general). St. Patrick, patron of Ireland, was not Irish but rather a Romanized Briton, and he is honored throughout the Roman Catholic world, even in the Spanish Southwest, though often the naming was by Irish priests.

SAN PATRICIO (Lincoln; settlement; on US 70, 20 mi E of Ruidoso; PO 1904–present). When Ramon Olguin and others settled here, the community was called *Ruidoso,* for the Rio Ruidoso on which it's located, but when the local Catholic church was built around 1875 and named San Patricio, the community's name was changed to correspond with it. The church was built under the care of an Irish priest, whose patron was St. Patrick.

SAN PEDRO (general). St. Peter was one of the 12 disciples of Jesus. He was first called Simon, but Jesus changed his name and addressed to him the words upon which the authority of the Catholic papacy is based: "Thou art Peter, and upon this rock I will build my church...." He is one of the most frequently honored saints, his name appearing on 19 NM places (GNIS).

SAN PEDRO (Rio Arriba; settlement; an Española suburb located E of the Rio Chama and SE of Española proper). Active community. See *San Pedro (general).*

SAN PEDRO (Santa Fe; settlement; on NM 344, 3 mi SE of Golden; PO 1881–84, 1888–1918, mail to Golden). When Lt. James W. Abert visited here in 1846, he found San Pedro to be an active mining camp based on washing placer gold from the surrounding *San Pedro Mountains* (see entry), for which the community was named. Gold and copper mining remained important until after WW I. Mining continues intermittently, and the area remains inhabited. See also *Carnahan* and *San Pedro (general).*

SAN PEDRO (Socorro; settlement; on the E bank of the Rio Grande, 1 mi E of San Antonio, S of US 360). San Pedro, sister village of San Antonio, was established in the early 1840s. The village waxed and waned over the years, but the 1940s saw its final decline, and today only a few scattered residences remain.

SAN PEDRO MOUNTAINS (Rio Arriba; in SW corner of county, S of Gallina, NE of La Jara). Highest elevation, *San Pedro Peaks,* 10,592 ft., in the center of the range. Navajos know this by a name meaning "big buttocks place," for reasons unknown. See *San Pedro (general).*

SAN PEDRO MOUNTAINS (Santa Fe; E of the Sandia Mountains, SE of Golden).

This small range, which gave its name to the mining camp of San Pedro (see entry), likely took its name in turn from *San Pedro del Cuchillo,* "St. Peter of the Ridge," the mission at the pueblo of *Paako* (see entry), whose ruins are to the W of the mountains. The mountains have also been called the *Tuerto Mountains,* doubtless for *Arroyo Tuerto* to the N. *San Pedro Peak,* 8,242 ft., is the highest summit.

SAN PEDRO PARKS WILDERNESS (Rio Arriba; in the SW corner of the county, in the San Pedro Mountains). Atop the *San Pedro Mountains* (see entry) is a high, moist plateau of rolling mountains with alternating areas of dense spruce and open mountain meadows—"parks." The 41,132-acre San Pedro Parks Wilderness, administered by the Santa Fe NF, was designated in 1931.

SAN RAFAEL (general). Raphael is one of the principal archangels, the one God chose to advise Adam of his danger. His name appears on six NM places.

SAN RAFAEL (Cibola; settlement; on NM 53, 4 mi SW of Grants; PO 1881–present). The community here originally was known as *El Gallo,* for nearby *Ojo del Gallo* (see entry). In 1863, Lt. J. Francisco Cháves established Fort Wingate (see entry) here. After Old Fort Wingate was abandoned in 1868, the Hispanic village of San Rafael grew up, taking its name from the patron of the local Catholic parish; see *San Rafael (general).*

SAN RAFAEL (San Miguel; settlement; on Trementina Creek, 3 mi NW of Old Trementina). Tiny Hispanic hamlet. See *San Rafael (general).*

SAN RAFAEL DEL QUIQUI (Rio Arriba). See *Quiqui.*

SAN RAMON (San Miguel; settlement; on NM 419, 5 mi N of Trementina). Diffuse scatter of buildings, long abandoned. St. Raymund of Peñafort (c. 1175–1275) was a Spanish academician and proselytizer.

SAN SIMON RIDGE, SINK, SWALE (Lea; in S-central part of county, SW of Eunice). In 1897 Francis (Frank) Divers sold his TAX Ranch here to Claiborne (Clabe) Merchant, co-owner of the San Simon Ranch in western NM and eastern Arizona. To stock his new ranch, Merchant brought 500 Texas longhorns from the San Simon Ranch, and with the cattle came the name of the ranch.

SAN SIMON RIVER (Hidalgo; heads in the San Simon Valley and heads NNW into Arizona). This watercourse has had numerous names, including *Río de Sauz, Río San Domingo, Río Suez, San Simon Creek, San Simon Wash, San River,* and *Solomonville Suauca,* but San Simon River is the form settled upon by the USBGN in 1962. See *San Simon Valley, Cienaga.*

SAN SIMON VALLEY, CIENAGA (Hidalgo; valley on the W side of the Peloncillo Mountains, straddling NM 9 W of Antelope Pass). This was first known as the *Sauz Valley,* (*sauz,* Spanish, "willow"). In 1883 J.H. Parramore and Claiborne "Clabe" Merchant, cattlemen from Abilene, TX, drove in 12,000 head of stock and set up headquarters of the San Simon Cattle Co. at the *ciénaga,* or "marsh," N of Rodeo. The valley and the *ciénaga* took the ranch's name, which is pronounced San See-MOHN. See *San Simon Ridge, Sink, Swale.*

SAN YSIDRO (general). Though St. Isidore of Seville, died 636, Spanish churchman and encyclopedist, is the most famous San Ysidro, the one most NM places honor was St. Isidore the farmer, who lived at Madrid, Spain, in the 11th century. He is the patron of farmers, gardeners, and sheepherders and thus has been popular in rural NM. He often is portrayed with a plow and oxen, sometimes also with an angel who does the plowing while the saint is at prayer. San Ysidro is widely honored in NM during May, when his image is carried through fields as a blessing for crops.

SAN YSIDRO (Doña Ana; settlement; 2 mi N of Las Cruces). Diffuse, inhabited community. See *San Ysidro (general).*

SAN YSIDRO, NORTH AND SOUTH (San Miguel; settlement; 23 mi SW of Las Vegas, just N of I-25). Small, inhabited villages, North San Ysidro 2 mi N of South San Ysidro, which is on the Pecos River. See *San Ysidro (general).*

SAN YSIDRO (Sandoval; settlement; at the junction of NM 4 and NM 44, 23 mi

NW of Bernalillo, 5 mi W of Jemez Pueblo; PO 1874–79, 1922–present). This old farming community on the Jemez River was settled in 1699 by Juan Trujillo and others. In 1786 Antonio Armenta and Salvador Sandoval were given a land grant here, but in 1936 much of the farming land went to Zia Pueblo. See *San Ysidro (general).*

SANCHEZ (general). In NM this Spanish family name dates from the arrival of the Oñate colonists in 1598, for a Pedro Sánchez de Monroy accompanied Oñate in 1598, along with his wife and children. The Sánchez name occurs on 25 NM places (GNIS).

SANCHEZ (San Miguel; settlement; on NM 419, 3 mi SW of the Canadian River; PO 1898 intermittently to 1927, mail to Sabinoso). Named for its first postmaster, Manuel A. Sánchez. A few people remain at this locality.

SANCHEZ CANYON (Sandoval; heads in the SE Jemez Mountains and runs SE to join the Rio Grande N of Cochiti Lake). This canyon's full name in Spanish is *Cañon de José Sánchez,* recalling a man who once owned land here. The Indians of Cochiti Pueblo know this canyon by a name meaning "canyon of the waterfall," referring to a small but lovely waterfall in the upper part of the canyon.

SANDIA (County unknown; settlement; exact location unknown; PO 1892–95, mail to San Pedro). Ephemeral locality, on the NE side of the Sandia Mountains.

SANDIA CANYON (Santa Fe; runs into the Rio Grande from the W between NM 4 and NM 508, N of White Rock). Tradition has it that *sandias,* "watermelons," or more likely, gourds resembling watermelons, grew in this canyon's upper reaches.

SANDIA KNOLLS (Bernalillo; settlement; N of NM 306, 2 mi E of San Antonito). Modern residential area, located among knolls E of the Sandia Mountains.

SANDIA MOUNTAINS, 10,678 ft. (Bernalillo, Sandoval; run 28 mi from Tijeras Canyon to Placitas, E of Albuquerque). Spanish, "watermelon." One explanation attributes this name to watermelons, or at least watermelon-resembling gourds, growing in canyons here. Another attributes it to being transferred from *El Corazón de la Sandia,* a mountain in the Spanish Sierra Nevada resembling the heart of a watermelon. The most popular explanation is that the Sandia Mountains, especially when viewed from the NW at evening, resemble a sliced watermelon, the granite pink with alpenglow, capped by a white limestone layer and covered with dark-green vegetation resembling a rind. But the most likely explanation is the one believed by the Sandia Indians: the Spaniards, when they encountered the pueblo in 1540, called it Sandia, because they thought the squash growing there were watermelons, and the name Sandia soon was transferred to the mountains E of the pueblo. And indeed, several mountain groups in NM have taken their names from nearby pueblos: the Taos Range, the Jemez Mountains, the Picuris Mountains, and the Zuni Mountains.

The Tiwas call the Sandia complex *Bien Mur,* "big mountain." The Tewas call it *Oku Pin,* "turtle mountain," for its shape. The Navajo name for the Sandia Mountains means "revolving (in a horizontal plane) mountains." The Sandias figure in the mythology of all the Indian groups.

Sandia Man Cave. Archaeological excavations revealed evidence of humans here at least 10,000 years ago, and possibly much earlier. Located in Las Huertas Canyon, in the N Sandias.

North Sandia Peak, 10,447 ft. The highest point along the northern Sandia Crest. Also known simply as *Sandia Peak.*

South Sandia Peak. At 9,782 ft., the highest summit of the southern Sandias.

SANDIA MOUNTAIN WILDERNESS (Bernalillo, Sandoval; along both sides of the crest of the Sandia Mountains, E of Albuquerque). This 37,232-acre wilderness covers primarily the mountains' western slopes but extends E of the crest at the N and S ends. The wilderness is split near its center by a corridor used by the Sandia Peak Tram. First designated in 1978, the wilderness is administered by the Cibola NF.

SANDIA PARK (Bernalillo; settlement; on NM 536 1 mi W of its junction with NM 14, 6 mi N of Tijeras; PO 1926–present). Inhabited residential community, named for its location in the E foothills of the Sandia Mountains.

SANDIA PUEBLO (Bernalillo; settlement; 13 mi N of Albuquerque, E of the Rio Grande, between I-25 and NM 313). The Tiwa Indian pueblo presently bearing this name is not the one encountered by Coronado in 1540. That unfortunate pueblo was razed by the Spaniards in reprisal for the Indians' protests against the Spanish occupation. Coronado gave the pueblo its Spanish name, meaning "watermelon." The Sandia Indians say this name was inspired by the Spaniards seeing gourds resembling watermelons in the village, though it's possible the name is linked to the *Sandia Mountains* (see entry) to the E. The Tiwa name for the pueblo means "dusty, or sandy place." During the Pueblo Revolt of 1680, the Sandia Indians fled to Hopi country and did not return until 1742. When Fray Francisco Atanasio Domínguez visited here in 1776, he counted 92 families, with 275 persons, most Tiwas but some Hopis. The name of the mission he founded here was *Nuestra Señora de los Dolores de Sandia,* "Our Lady of the Sorrows of Sandia."

SANDOVAL (Sandoval). See *Corrales.*

SANDOVAL COUNTY (central NM, W of the Rio Grande; county seat, Bernalillo). Created 1903 and named for the Sandoval family, whose members still live here. The first appearance of the Sandoval name in NM came with Sebastian de Sandoval, who was in Santa Fe in 1640, but he departed quickly from the scene, and the Sandovals active in NM after 1692 were descended from Juan de Dios Sandoval Martínez, a native of Mexico City, who arrived in NM with the reconquest; his immediate descendants dropped Martínez. See also *Corrales.*

SANDS (San Miguel; settlement; on AT&SF RR, 1 mi W of San Jose). Inhabited locality, before 1883 known as *McPherson,* origin unknown. Sands is said to have been the name of an AT&SF RR superintendent.

SANGRE DE CRISTO MOUNTAINS (E of

the Rio Grande, extending from E of Santa Fe N into Colorado). NM's highest summits are in this range, the southernmost extension of the great Rocky Mountain Chain. But while the mountains may be prominent, the origin of their present name is obscure. Numerous apocryphal legends explain the name, the most common being that a priest, mortally wounded in the Pueblo Revolt of 1680, begged God for a sign; looking E he beheld these mountains blood-red in the evening light and exclaimed, "Sangre de Cristo!" But as T. M. Pearce explained, the name Sangre de Cristo, "blood of Christ," actually dates from the early 19th century and likely is associated with the rise of the Penitente religious confraternity and its accentuated devotion to the Passion and Death of Christ; *Penitente Peak* NE of Santa Fe is a major southern summit in the Sangre de Cristo Mountains. Other scholars, however, have attributed the name variously to a creek, a pass, and a Spanish military outpost, all in the northern part of the range; all are plausible, deserving further investigation. Before the 19th century, early Spanish documents referred to the mountains as *La Sierra Nevada,* "the snowy range"; *La Sierra Madre,* "the mother mountains"; or simply as *La Sierra.* Early English-speaking trappers called the range *The Snowies.* Fray Francisco Atanasio Domínguez, describing Santa Fe in 1776, said the *Sierra Madre* lay to the E and was abundant in firewood and timber. The USBGN in 1965 chose to designate the group the Sangre de Cristo Mountains and not the *Sangre de Cristo Range.*

SANOSTEE (San Juan; settlement; 9 mi W of US 666, 30 mi SW of Shiprock). Inhabited Navajo community whose name can be translated variously as "rocks around it," "tilted stratum," and "crisscross rock extending out." According to Edward C. Beaumont of Albuquerque, USGS delayed putting the settlement on a map because of uncertainty about the spelling. Beaumont, a geologist for many years in the San Juan Basin, suggested the present spelling; it is pronounced sa-NOSS-tee.

SANTA ANA (Santa Fe). See *Galisteo.*

SANTA ANA COUNTY (NW NM)). When NM became an American territory in 1848, it included among its eight existing counties one named Santa Ana, that stretched from N of Bernalillo to the Arizona border. The county took its name from *Santa Ana Pueblo.* The county survived into the 1870s, when it was dissolved and its land included in an expanded Bernalillo County.

SANTA ANA PUEBLO (Sandoval; settlement; 2 mi NE of NM 44, 10 mi NW of Bernalillo). Catholic tradition says St. Anne was the mother of the Virgin Mary, and her name was given by the Spanish to this Keresan pueblo when they established a mission here. The Indians themselves know the pueblo as *Tamaya,* and they explain its history thus: "When Oñate visited our ancestors in 1598, our people were living on the *Mesa de Santa Ana.* After the Pueblo Revolt they moved, along with the Sandia, Zia, and Puaray, to the *sierra* of *Los Jemez.* Here, with the people of Zia, they built a new pueblo on the Cerro Colorado, about 14 mi from the old village of Zia. It was not until 1690 that we settled at our present location.

"Today, our village is divided into the old section [Tamaya] and the new section. The new area is called *El Ranchito,* and it lies on the E and W banks of the Rio Grande, adjacent to the town of Bernalillo." Other named settlements on the reservation include *Chical,* just E of US 85 in the new section, the name referring to a thicket of *chico,* or rabbit thorn, bushes; and *Rivajana,* 1 mi SW of El Ranchito, meaning unknown.

SANTA BARBARA (general). The patron of arsenals and powder magazines, St. Barbara also is invoked for protection against lightning, because she was saved from beheading when a lightning bolt felled her executioner.

SANTA BARBARA (Doña Ana). See *Fort Thorn.*

SANTA BARBARA, 12,662 ft. (Mora; in the Sangre de Cristo Mountains, E of the Truchas Peaks). Also known as *Santa*

Barbara Baldy, this summit appears on some maps by the intriguing name of *Trouble,* for reasons unknown. The three forks of the *Río Santa Barbara* (see entry) head just S and W of this peak. See *Santa Barbara (Taos).*

SANTA BARBARA (Taos; settlement; along the Rio Santa Barbara). In 1796, the *Santa Barbara Land Grant* was made to Valentin Martín, and the settlement of Santa Barbara was among the first in the valley, along with Llano and Llano Largo (see entries). The name survives on numerous features in the area.

SANTA CLARA (general). It was with the assistance of St. Clare of Assisi that St. Francis founded his second order, composed of cloistered nuns.

SANTA CLARA (Grant; settlement; 9 mi E of Silver City, 2 mi N of Bayard, on US 180; PO 1887–present). The establishment of Fort Bayard in 1866 stimulated a small village nearby called *Santa Clara,* whose residents provided services to the fort; see *Santa Clara (general).* In 1868 Grant County was created, and the thriving village, now called *Central City* because of its central location in the county, was designated the county seat. This status was short-lived, however, because in 1869 the county seat was moved to Pinos Altos. The settlement experienced a brief mining boom around 1900, and in 1947 property owners petitioned to be incorporated as the village of *Central.* Since then, the community has continued to grow, primarily because of its still-central location, though in 1996 the citizens voted to return to the original name of Santa Clara.

SANTA CLARA (Mora). See *Wagon Mound.*

SANTA CLARA PEAK (Rio Arriba). See *Chicoma Mountain.*

SANTA CLARA PUEBLO (Rio Arriba; settlement; on NM 30, 3 mi SW of Española, on the W bank of the Rio Grande). The Tewa-speaking inhabitants of this pueblo explain its history thus: "Our native name is *Kapo,* 'where the roses grow near the water.' Our ancestors lived in small settlements on the Pajarito Plateau and the cliffs at Puye. Because of drought and the hostility of nomadic Indians our ancestors were compelled to abandon these sites and move into the Rio Grande Valley. The pueblo we live in today was first inhabited before the Spaniards entered the Southwest in 1540." Santa Clara was formerly the seat of a Spanish mission church and monastery established in 1622–29 by Fray Alonso de Benavides. *Santa Clara Creek* heads in the E Jemez Mountains and runs E through Santa Clara Pueblo. See *Santa Clara (general).*

SANTA CRUZ (Santa Fe; settlement; on NM 76, 2 mi E of Española; PO as La Cañada 1852–57, as Santa Cruz 1878–82, 1886–present). Founded by Vargas in 1695, this village was the second *villa* formally decreed by the Spanish in NM; Santa Fe, decreed in 1609 was the first; Albuquerque, decreed in 1706, was the third. This *villa* was located near the confluence of the Rio Grande and the Rio Chama, not far from the first permanent Spanish settlement in NM, San Gabriel, and Vargas formally bestowed upon it the name *La Villa Nueva de la Santa Cruz de la Cañada,* "the new town of the holy cross of the canyon," but often the locality was called simply *La Cañada.* Now it's simply Santa Cruz. *Santa Cruz Reservoir* is on the Rio Medio and Rio Frijoles, 10 mi E of Española. The *Santa Cruz River* S of Santa Cruz flows W to enter the Rio Grande S of Española.

SANTA FE (Santa Fe; settlement, county seat, state capital; on US 84, 85, 285 and I-25, 20 mi E of the Rio Grande; PO 1849–present). In 1608 Don Pedro de Peralta succeeded Don Juan de Oñate as governor of NM, and in the following year he moved the colony's capital from San Gabriel (see entry) to the site of an abandoned Indian pueblo, situated on a little stream at the foot the great mountain chain later called the Sangre de Cristo Mountains; legend—and little more—says the Indian locality had been known as "the place of the dancing ground of the sun." Peralta was instructed by the viceroy of New Spain in Mexico City to establish the town as the capital of the "Kingdom of New

Mexico"; he named it *La Villa Real de Santa Fé*, "the Royal Town of Santa Fe," and for nearly a century it was the only officially established settlement of Spanish colonists in NM. Because the relocation of Spaniards at San Gabriel to Santa Fe took some time, most historians have declared 1610 as Santa Fe's founding date, though an obscure *conquistador* named Juan Martinez de Montoya may have established a plaza there as early as 1608.

In his naming, Peralta likely transferred to the new capital the name of the Santa Fe outside Granada in Spain that was the royal encampment from which the monarchs Ferdinand and Isabella oversaw the final conquest of the Moors in 1492. Indeed, persons who have visited the Spanish Santa Fe say its situation with the Sierra Nevada behind it strongly resembles that of the New Mexican city, with its Sangre de Cristo backdrop. Moreover, when a map was published by French cartographers circa 1673–82 with the cooperation of Don Diego de Peñalosa, who had been NM governor just 50 years after Santa Fe was established, it labeled the capital, albeit in French, *Santa Fe ou Granada*.

Somewhat countering Peralta's role in the city's founding is some information in recently discovered old documents. One document, a *testimonio* petition to Governor Oñate by one Juan Martínez de Montoya suggests that some of San Gabriel's settlers may have moved to the site of Santa Fe as early as 1606 or 1607 and that the place was known even then as Santa Fe. Thus it appears—as with several other towns founded later in NM's colonial period—that colonists took upon themselves the task of finding a suitable location for settlement, in this case three or four years ahead of official sanction. Soon, however, the incipient little community became the capital.

Santa Fe may have been the capital of a vast "kingdom," later a "province," but it was an impoverished one; its first inhabitants never referred to the town as "the capital" but rather simply as *La Villa*. That was distinction enough in the early days, for there were no other non-Indian

towns in NM until the *villas* of Albuquerque and Santa Cruz were established in the 1700s. To this day, Santa Feans often are referred to in Spanish as *villeros*.

A few other name-related events also occurred over the centuries. In 1717, after the reconquest of NM and the rebuilding of Santa Fe, a new patronal title was given to the parish church, *Nuestro Padre San Francisco*, "Our Father St. Francis." Accordingly, Santa Fe often has been called the "City of St. Francis." It also has been called the "City of the Holy Faith," a phrase that may first have been written by Albert Pike in his *Prose Sketches and Poems* (1834). Then, following the American conquest in 1846, the name frequently was misspelled *Santa Fee*. Though the name in proper Spanish takes an accent, *Santa Fé*, this usually is dropped. Finally, in modern times so much tourist romanticism has flourished in Santa Fe that various persons have claimed the city's original name to have been *La Villa Real de la Santa Fé de San Francisco de Asís*, "the Royal Town of the Holy Faith of St. Francis of Assisi." Documentation for this, however, is lacking. Nicknames for Santa Fe have been the "City Different" and the "City at the end of the Trail."

The Rio Grande Tewas call Santa Fe by names meaning "down at the water," and most of the pueblo Indian groups, as well as the Navajos, use names with the meaning "bead water," because beads were made from shells here. The Keresan-speaking inhabitants of Cochiti Pueblo have a fondness for directional names; they call the Santa Fe region "east corner."

SANTA FE BALDY, 12,622 ft. (Santa Fe; in the Sangre de Cristo Mountains NE of Santa Fe). This bare summit also has been known as *Baldy Peak* and *Old Baldy*. To the Tewas, this is "flower mountain."

SANTA FE COUNTY (N-central NM; county seat, Santa Fe). Created by the Republic of Mexico in 1844 and later redesignated by the territorial legislature in 1852.

SANTA FE FORKS (Colfax). See *Hoxie*.

SANTA FE LAKE (Curry; 1 mi SW of Clovis). Formerly owned by the SF RR.

SANTA FE LAKE (Santa Fe; SW of Lake Peak in the Sangre de Cristo Mountains NE of Santa Fe).

SANTA FE MOUNTAINS (San Miguel, Taos, Mora; from the Rio Fernando de Taos on the N to Glorieta Pass on the S). This subrange is the S end of the Sangre de Cristo Mountains, and thus the southernmost extremity of the great Rocky Mountain Chain. At least part of this group had been called the *Truchas Range,* and sometimes the mountains are called the *Santa Fe Range,* but in 1965 the USBGN established Santa Fe Mountains as the accepted form. They are the "eastern mountains" of the Tewas; the Jemez Mountains are the "western mountains." Highest summit, *Santa Fe Baldy* (see entry), 12,622 ft.

SANTA FE NATIONAL FOREST (includes the Jemez Mountains and the S Sangre de Cristo Mountains). First created in 1892 as the *Pecos River Forest Reserve,* with other units added later.

SANTA FE RIVER (Santa Fe; heads at Santa Fe Lake in the Sangre de Cristo Mountains NE of Santa Fe and flows S and then SW through Santa Fe to the Rio Grande). *Santa Fe River State Park,* created in 1935, is located on the N side of the creek for 3 blocks along East Alameda in Santa Fe.

SANTA FE TRAIL (NE NM). Immediately after Mexican Independence in 1821, a party of American traders led by William Becknell made the journey from Missouri over the trail soon to be known by its destination, Santa Fe. Becknell's success opened a floodgate of traders and later emigrants. The main trail entered NM over Raton Pass, while the shorter but more hazardous *Cimarron Cutoff* entered NE of Clayton. Hundreds of wagons traversed the trail, but when the RR reached Santa Fe in 1880, the trail became obsolete. Wagon ruts still remain at several points along the route, and in 1987 the Santa Fe Trail became a National Historic Trail.

SANTA LULU (San Juan; settlement; on the W bank of the Animas River, across from Aztec). This abandoned community once had a newspaper, the *Santa Lulu Independent,* but neither the community nor the paper lasted long.

SANTA MARIA DE ACOMA (Cibola). See *McCartys.*

SANTA RITA (Grant; settlement; S of NM 152, 7 mi NE of Central; 1881–1973, mail to Hanover). Copper was discovered here as early as 1800, and by 1803 Francisco Elguea, a Chihuahua businessman, had established a mining community he named *Santa Rita del Cobre,* "St. Rita of the copper." St. Rita (1381–1457) was an Italian nun to whom numerous supernatural events have been attributed. Apache attacks frequently plagued the little community, continuing after English-speaking settlers began to arrive in the 1870s. As mining expanded, the village several times was forced to move, and eventually the huge open pit—among the world's largest—engulfed what had been the settlement.

SANTA RITA (Socorro). See *Riley.*

SANTA ROSA (Guadalupe; settlement, county seat; on I-40 and US 54; PO 1873 intermittently to present). This community, settled in 1865, originally was on the west side of the Pecos River, where it was called *Agua Negra Chiquita,* "little black water," for the drainage 4 mi S. In 1873 the community acquired a PO, which took the name Santa Rosa; Tranquilino Labadie was the first postmaster and served, with a one-year absence, until 1898, when the PO was discontinued. In the meantime, in 1885 the community of Eden (see entry) on the Pecos River's E bank, had started a PO, called Eden, but when the Santa Rosa PO closed, the Eden PO changed its name to Santa Rosa—Celso Baca became postmaster—and since then the community's name and identity have been associated with the E side of the Pecos. Locally, Baca is credited with the name Santa Rosa, from a small chapel he built around 1890, the *Capilla de Santa Rosa,* for St. Rose of Lima, a maiden who was the first canonized saint of the New World. Rosa also was the name of Baca's wife, Doña Rosa Viviana Baca y Baca, who was buried beneath the chapel that was dedicated, at least in part, to her.

The town of Santa Rosa was a minor community—Puerto de Luna was Guadalupe County's first seat—until the coming of the RR in 1901. Since then, the city has continued as an important transportation service center. Billboards proclaim Santa Rosa to be "the City of Natural Lakes," because numerous artesian lakes are here. *Santa Rosa Creek* flows from Blue Hole at Santa Rosa into Municipal Lake.

SANTA ROSA LAKE STATE PARK (Guadalupe; on the Pecos River, 7 mi N of Santa Rosa). *Santa Rosa Lake* on which the park is centered was formed in 1980 by a dam built by the US Army Corps of Engineers in an area formerly known as *Los Esteros,* "the estuaries, swamps."

SANTA ROSA DE LIMA DE ABIQUIU. See *Abiquiu.*

SANTA TERESA (Doña Ana; settlement; NW of Hatch). See *Placitas.*

SANTA TERESA (Doña Ana; settlement; in SE part of county, 5 mi N of Sunland Park). Modern residential settlement, also the site of a recently established port of entry with Mexico. The name honors St. Theresa (1515–82), a Spanish nun famed for her trances and visions, who founded a number of convents and monasteries.

SANTIAGO (general). The Apostle St. James the Great, brother of John, is the patron saint of Spain; according to legend, the ship carrying his body beached on the Spanish coast. He was especially beloved by the Spanish *conquistadores,* whose war cry in battle was *Santiago!*

SANTIAGO (Mora). See *El Oro.*

SANTILLANES (general). Spanish family name. The earliest members in NM were Juan Simón de Santillan, living with his wife in the Isleta area in 1744.

SANTILLANES (San Miguel; settlement; in SE foothills of Sangre de Cristo Mountains, 3 mi W of San Geronimo). Abandoned community, named for the Santillanes family here.

SANTO DOMINGO PUEBLO (Sandoval; settlement; 1 mi W of NM 22, on the E bank of the Rio Grande; PO 1960–present). Spanish, "Holy Sunday." Tradition has it that Oñate gave this Keres pueblo the name because he ar-

rived here on a Sunday, but it's worth noting that the mission church here commemorates St. Dominic, 13th-century Spanish preacher who founded the Dominican order. He inveighed vehemently against heresy, and the pope called him "Inquisitor-General." A Keres account says that before the Spanish arrived the Indians lived at Potrero de la Cañada Quemada, from whence they moved successively to two villages, both named *Gipuy* (also transliterated *Quiqui* and *Quigui*). The earlier pueblo of Gipuy was W of the present village but was destroyed by floods. The present pueblo was established around 1770 and given the name *Kiva,* referring to the underground ceremonial chamber of Pueblo Indians. A 1776 census counted 528 persons here.

SANTO NIÑO (general). Throughout their history, Hispanic Catholics have shown devotion to the Baby Jesus through place names meaning "Holy Child"; among the most famous is Santo Niño de Atocha in Madrid, Spain.

SANTO NIÑO (Mora). See *Rociada.*

SANTO NIÑO (Rio Arriba; settlement; on NM 76, between Española and Santa Cruz). This is one of the many "suburbs" or "neighborhoods" making up what is commonly perceived as Española. See *Santo Niño (general).*

SANTO NIÑO (Rio Arriba; settlement; on US 64, E of the Jicarilla Apache Reservation). Abandoned community. See *Santo Niño (general).*

SANTO TOMAS (Doña Ana; settlement; on NM 28, approximately 6 mi S of Las Cruces). Small cluster of houses whose name recalls the *Santo Tomás de Iturbide* Spanish land grant here. Just to the W of the village is the *Black Mesa of Santo Tomas.*

SANTO TORIBIO (Sandoval). See *Ponderosa.*

SANTUARIO (Rio Arriba). See *Chimayo.*

SAN VICENTE (Grant). See *Silver City.*

SAPELLO (San Miguel; settlement; 13 mi N of Las Vegas, at the junction of NM 518 and 266; PO 1874–1975, mail to rural Las Vegas branch). Inhabited community, on the *Sapello River* (see entry), whose name it took.

SAPELLO RIVER (San Miguel; heads in the Sangre de Cristo Mountains, E of Spring Mountain, and flows E to join the Mora River at Watrous). The origin of this name is—and is likely to remain—a mystery. T.M. Pearce and Ina Sizer Cassidy exhaustively investigated this name and found several Spanish possibilities: *sapillo,* "little toad"; *sepilio,* "burial, interment"; and *sapello,* NM Spanish for a scrub brush. Stanley Crocchiola speculated that it might be a corruption of the NM Spanish *sapillo,* referring to the medicinal use of the "cotton" from cottonwood trees, which are indeed common along the river. But these words don't accent the last syllable, as local speakers do for Sapello (Sapelló); Pearce ultimately concluded it was likely of Indian origin, and local historians concur, pointing out that the name was in use before the area was settled and likely referred to the river; people would talk about settling "the Sapello." In 1839 a French priest, Pierre L'Esperance, applied for land at a place and river called *Shapellote,* and the historian Ralph Emerson Twitchell believed the place was Sapello. Still earlier, an 1821 reference in the Las Vegas Grant mentioned the *Chapellote River* as a N boundary, and 14 years later a conflicting grant mentioned the Sapello River as the boundary. Fray Angélico Chávez, who also has investigated the name, suggests the word comes from the Plains Indians, who frequented here. It resembles *Chapalote,* the name of a Kiowa, or French-Kiowa, who married in Taos. But all this evidence is, at best, circumstantial. A *Sapello River,* sometimes spelled *Sapillo,* also is found in Grant County, 15 mi N of Silver City, in the Pinos Altos Mountains. The origin of the name there also is unknown, though "little toad" is one plausible meaning.

SATAN PASS (McKinley; on NM 371, between Thoreau and Crownpoint). Navajos know this route by a name meaning "blue all the way up," referring to the color of the mud here. Early Spanish-speaking travelers called it *Cañon Infierno,* "hell canyon," likely because it was hellishly rough. And English-speak-

ers have called it Satan Pass, because it's a "devil" of a pass. The canyon through which it passes now is called *Satan Pass Canyon.* The road through the pass now is paved and gives little hint of the tribulations early travelers here endured.

SAUZ (Harding). See *Abbott.*

SAUZ CREEK (heads in Colfax County and flows SW through Abbott Lake to join the Canadian River). Spanish, "willow."

SAUZAL (Valencia; settlement; N of Belen, on the E side of the Rio Grande). Former community whose name meant "place of the willows."

SAVOYA (Cibola; settlement; 6 mi NE of Ramah, on Cebolla Creek; PO 1882–87, mail to Ramah). As early as 1874 the Mormon missionaries A.M. Tenney and R.S. Smith had arrived here and settled on Cebolla Creek. They soon were replaced by Lorenzo H. Hatch, but the first permanent Mormon settlers were Ernest Tietjen and Luther Burnham, who arrived here in 1877 from missionary work in Arizona. The Navajo chief José Pino showed them the most favorable location to settle. It was in a valley the Navajos called by a name meaning *"Stinking Grass Springs."* The "stinking grass" was wild onion, and the local Spanish-speakers called the valley *Cebolla,* meaning the same thing. The Mormons anglicized the spelling to Savoya, appearing on some maps as *Savoia.* Other Mormons arrived, but most soon left because of Indian troubles. Ernest Tietjen stayed, however, and began work on Ramah Reservoir (see *Ramah*). Eventually settlement shifted from Savoya to Ramah, and the earlier village was abandoned.

SAWMILL MOUNTAIN, 10,962 ft. (Taos; in the Taos Range, NW of Red River). B.J. Young had a steam sawmill near here that cut logs skidded off this mountain. Many buildings still standing in Red River have boards that came from this sawmill.

SAWTOOTH MOUNTAINS (Catron; western extension of the Datil Mountains, N of US 60, NW of Datil). Descriptive name. Highest elevation 8,950 ft.

SAWYER (Cibola; settlement; near the headwaters of Bluewater Creek, about 28 mi SW of Prewitt; PO as Kettner 1904–09, as Sawyer 1909–16, mail to Thoreau). In the early 1900s the American Lumber Co. established a small lumbering camp in a timbered valley of the Zuni Mountains. The first camp was known as Kettner (see entry), for a homesteader by that name, but in 1910 the headquarters moved to a camp with a name common to lumber camps throughout the US—Sawyer. Sawyer was small but active; eventually, however, the trees were cut, the sawmill closed, and by 1919 Sawyer was a ghost town.

SAWYERS CREEK (San Miguel; settlement; exact location unknown; PO 1909–16). Abandoned settlement, named for being on *Sawyers Creek*, which flows SE into the Pecos River 3 mi S of Terrero. The creek was either named for a person named Sawyer or, more likely, for lumbering operations along it.

SAWYERS PEAK, 9,668 ft. (Sierra; in the Black Range, 4 mi S of Emory Pass). Named for an engineer named Sawyer.

SAYDATOH (Sandoval; settlement; location unknown; PO 1918–22, mail to Haynes). Little is known about this ephemeral locality, including the origin of its name.

SCALESVILLE (Sierra; settlement; on the E slopes of the Black Range, 4 mi N of Grafton). Born about 1893, this mining camp, named for Thomas Scales, manager of the Elephant Mine, lasted only two years before being relocated 1 mi N to the mine.

SCHOLLE (Socorro, Torrance; settlement; on US 60, 32 mi SE of Belen, on Socorro-Torrance County line; PO 1908–11, 1917–75). Fred Scholle was one of the pioneer merchants of Belen, as well as sheep rancher and wine maker, and though the locality named for him has been abandoned, his name is still remembered in the area. During its heyday as a RR town, Scholle had a depot, two stores, a PO, a section gang, and a schoolhouse.

SCHOOLHOUSE MESA (Sandoval; NE-SW trending mesa S of Fenton Lake). During the lumbering era of the early 1900s, a schoolhouse was built here for children from the logging camps. *Schoolhouse Canyon* is just to the S of the mesa.

SCHROEDER (De Baca; settlement; in SW part of the county, NW of White Flat; PO 1908–13, mail to Buchannan). This homesteader community, now abandoned, took the surname of its first postmaster, August Schroeder.

SCHUREE CREEK (Colfax; tributary to Poñil Creek, NW of Cimarron). The Schuree Lodge (pronounced shur-REE) was in this area, and the immediate area around it was known as Schuree. It likely is a family name.

SCOTT (Lea; settlement; 6 mi SE of Tatum; PO 1909–21, mail to Tatum). Scott was named for C.C. Scott, an early district attorney. The village once had stores, a school, and a PO, but now all have vanished.

SEAMA (Cibola; settlement; on the Laguna Indian Reservation, 1 mi S of I-40, 3 mi S of Cubero; PO 1905–32, mail to Cubero). This locality originally was called *Cañada de la Cruz,* because the intersection here of the Cañada de la Cruz and the Rio San Jose forms a "cross." The present name comes from a Laguna Keres word meaning "door, passageway," because the topography, enclosing a wide valley, is a natural passageway.

SEBOLLA (Rio Arriba). See *Cebolla.*

SEBOYETA (Cibola; settlement; at end of NM 279, 13 mi N of Laguna; PO as Seboyeta 1885–92, 1893–present). The *Cebolleta Mountains* (see entry) to the N gave their name to this small Hispanic settlement, but when the settlement applied for a PO under this name, the name was rejected because several Cebolleta settlements already existed; the variant *Seboyeta* was chosen instead, and this was the form accepted by the USBGN in 1975. Seboyeta was settled in 1749 after a large contingent of Navajos journeyed to Santa Fe and agreed to the establishment of a mission on their lands; the site chosen was on the SE side of Cebolleta Mountain (now Mount Taylor), on an old Indian trail to the N. Though the Indians soon lost interest in the mission, they raided the resulting settlement frequently, and in 1804–08 a military outpost was here. At one time, the settlement, surrounded by a 10-foot wall, was beseiged by a large force of Navajos. In 1849, Lt. James H. Simpson mentioned Cebolleta and Cubero as notorious hangouts for Mexican traders dealing in slaves, whiskey, and guns, and from 1849–52 the military post that became Fort Wingate was here. Today, Seboyeta leads a more peaceful existence. Our Lady of Sorrows church is here, while about 1 mile to the N, in a cave, is a shrine known as *El Portal,* or *Los Portales.*

SECA, SECO (general). See *Dry (general).*

SEDAN (Union; settlement; on NM 421, 3 mi E of NM 402, 24 mi S of Clayton, 5 mi W of the Texas border; PO 1910–present). In 1908 A.B. "Bert" Christerson and his wife, Mattie, and their children, Kendall, Millard, and Lena, arrived on the plains here from Sedan, KS. They established a PO in their home, and they named it after their hometown. Sedan remains a tiny but tidy farming community.

MOUNT SEDGWICK, 9,256 ft. (Cibola; in the Zuni Mountains, W of Grants). The name of the highest summit of the Zuni Mountains is a mystery. As Sherry Robinson, historian of western NM, put it, "I found no homesteaders, railroaders, or ranchers here by that name." The most likely candidate, she says, is Gen. John Sedgwick, the Civil War hero who died in 1864 at the height of his fame. "Because it was popular then to remember war heroes with statues, libraries, and natural features bearing their names, it's entirely likely that Army officers then at Fort Wingate named the mountain for one of their own."

SEDILLO (Bernalillo; settlement; on NM 333, 14 mi E of Albuquerque). Named for the Sedillo family. Pedro de Cedillo, a native of Queretaro, Mexico, is the first person with that name recorded in NM, arriving here before the Pueblo Revolt of 1680; he was a captain in the Rio Abajo district, and his descendants returned to NM after the reconquest of 1692. *Sedillo Canyon* runs into the village from the S, while the long hill approaching it from the W is called *Sedillo Hill.*

SEELOCU (Socorro; settlement; on the E side of the Rio Grande, between the confluence of the Rio Puerco and the Rio Salado with the Rio Grande). Seelocu was among numerous Piro Indian pueblos the Spanish found along the Rio Grande S of Tiwa country. They established a mission here, *San Luis Obispo de Sevilleta de Seelocú,* but the settlement was ravaged by Apache raids, the mission was burned, later to be refounded at the nearby Piro *pueblo of Alamillo* (see entry), and Seelocu was abandoned. The meaning of its Piro name is unknown.

SEGREST DRAW (Otero, Eddy; heads in NE foothills of the Guadalupe Mountains, runs E into Eddy County then NE to join North Seven Rivers). Rufus P. Segrest, born in Switzerland, was a buffalo hunter and Indian fighter on the West Texas grasslands before becoming a rancher on the plains of SE NM. He had become one of the largest individual cattle and sheep ranchers on the open range by 1900 and claimed "waterings" throughout this area.

SELDEN (Doña Ana). See *Fort Selden.*

SELLERS (Luna; settlement; between Deming and Hatch, about 10 mi E of Nutt). Short-lived RR section settlement, sometimes called *Sellers Station.*

SEMINOLE DRAW (Lea; 1 mi NE of Hobbs). This was named by Lt. C.R. Ward in 1875 during an expedition against Indians. The name Seminole referred to the half-Indian, half–African-American scouts on the expedition.

SENA (San Miguel; settlement; on NM 3, 3 mi S of San Miguel, on the E bank of the Pecos River; PO 1895–present). This bears the name of the Sena family, the earliest NM member of which was Bernardo de Sena, who at age 9 came to NM in 1693 with his foster parents. In 1708 he was living in Pojoaque, then in Santa Fe, where *Sena Plaza* still preserves his memory, until his death. An 1857 source called the village *Puertecito,* "little gap."

SENECA (Union; settlement; on NM 406, 14 mi NE of Clayton; PO 1908–present). When freighters came over the Cimarron Cut-off of the Santa Fe Trail in the 1850s, they arrived here at an Hispanic settlement called *Ciénaga del Burro,* translated colloquially as *Jackass*

Swamp. When English-speaking settlers moved here after the Civil War, they corrupted Cienega to *Seneca*. The first PO was established in a dugout by Flora Blackwell and her son, Garrett. Once the hub of a heavily populated farming community, Seneca was depopulated by the Dust Bowl of the 1930s, but the community nonetheless has survived here.

SENECA CREEK (Union; heads E of Grenville and runs E into Clayton Lake, then E 4 mi S of village of Seneca into Oklahoma). Seneca is an Anglicized corruption of the Spanish *cienega*, "swamp, marsh." The original Spanish name for the watercourse was *Ciénega del Burro*, but freighters on the Santa Fe Trail Cimmaron Cut-off called it simply *Jackass Swamp*; the USBGN in 1974 approved Seneca Creek over numerous variants.

SENECU (Socorro; settlement; on the W bank of the Rio Grande S of Socorro, exact location unknown.) The Piro pueblo of Senecu was the southernmost inhabited pueblo in NM during the pre-Revolt era. The Piro name has been transcribed as *Tze-no-que, Tzen-o-cue*, and *She-an-ghua*; it has been translated as "eye socket, or spring hole." The Franciscan mission of *San Antonio de Senecú* was established in 1629 by Fray Antonio de Arteaga and Fray García de San Francisco, and the 1630 memorial of Fray Benavides mentioned Senecu and also the mission of *San Antonio de Padua*. But in 1675 the mission and the pueblo suffered the same fate as the Saline Pueblos farther N: it was abandoned after being beseiged by Apaches. Otermín in 1681 found it abandoned and burned. The ruins became a familiar landmark to travelers on the Camino Real during the 18th century, but after that traces faded, and now even the pueblo's exact location is unknown. The residents of Senecu and other Piro pueblos did not participate in the Pueblo Revolt of 1680 and fled S with the Spaniards to El Paso del Norte, where they established two pueblos, *Socorro del Sur* and *Senecú del Sur;* they did not return with the Spanish and eventually dispersed among other pueblo settlements along the lower Rio Grande.

SEÑORITO (Sandoval; settlement; on NM 126, 4 mi SE of Cuba; PO 1901–24, mail to Cuba). Around 1893 a small copper mining camp sprang up here and was called Señorito, "young gentleman, little master of the house," for reasons unknown. Eventually Señorito had 100 residents, a store, sawmill, PO, and mining facilities, but the mines closed, and though the PO lingered for several years, Señorito has all but vanished. *Señorito Canyon* enters the former camp from the NE.

SEPAR (Grant; settlement; on SP RR and I-10-70, 20 mi SE of Lordsburg; PO 1882–1960, mail to a rural Lordsburg branch). The Janos Trail crosses I-10 at Separ; established by the Spanish in the early 1800s, this route connected the copper mines at Santa Rita with northern Mexico. With the coming of the RR Separ became a cattle-loading station for nearby ranches. Folklore says it took its name from a RR construction camp called *Camp Separation*, but in fact, the station here originally was called *Sepas*, not Separ, possibly from the Spanish *cepas*, "tree stumps, shoots from the base of a tree." Little remains today of the settlement.

SERAFINA (San Miguel). See *Bernal*.

SERVILLETA (Taos; settlement; on US 285, 10 mi S of Tres Piedras; PO 1913–49, mail to Tres Piedras). Though this means "napkin, flat plain" in Spanish, it also is one of the commemorative titles of the Virgin Mary, *La Madona de la Servilleta*. The name here was first applied to *Servilleta Plaza* in Rio Arriba County, just over the county line to the W, but when the D&RG RR line was built here in 1880–85, the name was transferred to the siding around which a village grew. Now the RR has gone, and so has the village.

SETON VILLAGE (Santa Fe; settlement; 3 mi SE of Santa Fe, 1.5 mi W of I-25). This inhabited residential area was the home of Ernest Thompson Seton from 1930 until his death in 1946. World-famous naturalist and author, Seton wrote animal stories, many of which were set in NM, and he established his

Woodcraft League of America and School of Indian Wisdom here.

SEVEN LAKES (McKinley; settlement; in NE part of county, 4 mi NE of Whitehorse). This inhabited community began with oil exploration in the area. It was named for seven intermittent lakes.

SEVEN RIVERS (Eddy; settlement; on US 285, 15 mi NW of Carlsbad; PO 1877–95, mail to McMillan). As early as 1722 Spanish explorers mentioned the advantages of this locality, especially the water derived from seven springs to the W, but hostile Plains Indians made settlement impossible. Around the time of the Civil War, Anglo cowboys were herding in the area; because of the multiplicity of drainages, they subdivided the area in the *Upper Seven Rivers, Middle Seven Rivers,* and *Lower Seven Rivers.* In 1867 Dick Reed established a trading post, while Capt. Sam Samson established another trading post nearby. The locality is said to have been called *Dogtown* then, because of the numerous prairie dogs; *Ashland* has been mentioned as another early name for the locality; it was the earliest settlement in the area. In 1878 the name was changed to Seven Rivers; see *Seven Rivers;* see also *Belmont*). In 1883 a new town was built a mile W and called *Henpeck,* for reasons unknown, and later it moved again and changed its name to *White City,* for a rancher here by that name. By 1900 the old Seven Rivers was a ghost town, and the new settlement had assumed the name Seven Rivers, which the tiny inhabited settlement bears today. *Seven Rivers Hills* are 6 mi SW of village of Seven Rivers.

SEVEN RIVERS (Eddy; North, Middle, and South branches head W of village of Seven Rivers and flow E past the village into the Pecos River). Named for the seven springs that feed the streams.

SEVEN SPRINGS (Sandoval; settlement; in the Jemez Mountains, 1 mi NE of Fenton Lake). Large residential cluster, named for local springs.

SEVENTY-FOUR DRAW (Sierra; heads in the Black Range in NW part of the county and runs SW). Named for an early ranch brand.

SEVENTY-FOUR MOUNTAIN, 7,748 ft. (Grant; in the Diablo Range, 2 mi S of Catron County line). Named for an early ranch brand.

SEVILLETA (Socorro). See *La Joya.*

SEVILLETA NATIONAL WILDLIFE REFUGE (Socorro; in N-central part of county, straddling the Rio Grande). The entire 228,000-acre refuge has been designated a Long-term Ecological Research Site by the National Science Foundation and the USFWS. This area is ideal for ecological research, as it is bounded on the E by the Los Pinos Mountains and on the W by the Sierra Ladrones, with the Rio Grande in the center, and includes large expanses of desert grasslands.

SHABIK'ESHCHEE VILLAGE (San Juan; in Chaco Culture National Historical Park). The name for this Anasazi ruin is Navajo and means "sun's path across a petroglyph."

SHADY GROVE (Roosevelt; settlement; in center of county, SW of Dora). Abandoned community, likely named for its setting.

SHADYBROOK (Taos; settlement; on US 64, 7 mi E of Taos). Inhabited locality, named for the large cottonwoods shading the Rio Fernando de Taos here.

SHAGGY PEAK, 8,847 ft. (Santa Fe; in S Sangre de Cristo Mountains, 6 mi SE of Santa Fe). Descriptive name. This summit appears as *Peñacho Peak,* of obscure meaning, on an 1889 USGS map.

SHAKESPEARE (Hidalgo; settlement; at the N end of the Pyramid Mountains, 2 mi S of Lordsburg; PO 1897–85, mail to Lordsburg). In 1868, the National Mail and Transportation Co. sent John Evenson and Jack Frost W to locate stations. At *Mexican Springs,* where water was abundant, Frost established a mail stop; he initially named it *Pyramid Station,* for the nearby Pyramid Mountains, but with Gen. Ulysses S. Grant's popularity at its height then Frost soon renamed it *Grant.* In 1870, when William C. Ralston, founder of the Bank of California, became involved in silver-mining here, an ambitious townsite was laid out, and the village's name was changed to *Ralston.* But miners' and investors' hopes were disappointed; when the camp began to die, a fraudulent diamond scheme was attempted, but it was soon exposed. By this time, the community's reputation was tarnished, and it was losing population, so in 1879 citizens renamed the town *Shakespeare,* for the Shakespeare Mining Co., which had silver claims in the area. Eventually, the silver mines closed, and Shakespeare became a ghost town. In 1997, a fire devastated the town's remains.

SHALAM (Doña Ana; settlement; 8 mi N of Las Cruces). In 1885, Dr. John Ballou Newbrough of New York City led a small group of Faithists, a sect he had organized, to NM where they founded a small colony; they called it Shalam, for the chapter in *Oahspe,* the sect's religious tract, directing Newbrough to establish the colony. The Faithists at Shalam, a local newspaper reported, were a curious lot; they were strict vegetarians, they allowed their hair to grow and hang about their shoulders, and they wore sandals and long gowns. And Newbrough was even more striking: he was 6 feet 4 inches, weighed 275 pounds, and had a gleaming white beard. But he was a well-liked host to the many visitors and picnickers who soon flocked to Shalam. As the colony thrived, a suburb called *Levitica,* "joy of man," sprang up near Shalam. But when Newbrough died in 1891, the community lost its energy; disciples drifted away; Levitica vanished in a flood; and today Shalam is but ruins and a memory, though local people still use the name.

SHAMROCK (Otero). See *Valmont.*
SHANDON (Sierra). See *Pittsburg.*
SHEEP SPRINGS (San Juan; settlement; on US 666, about 50 mi N of Gallup). In 1892 1st. Lt. W. C. Brown visited the springs here and reported them a well-known camping place, and certainly Navajos' sheep would have watered here; the Navajo name for the locality means "sheep springs." In 1912 Charles Newcomb established a trading post 1.5 mi E of the springs that became the nucleus of the present settlement.
SHEEPSHEAD, 12,600 ft. (Rio Arriba; in the Santa Fe Range, S of the San Leonardo Lakes). Name origin unknown.

SHELL MOUNTAIN, 10,385 ft. (Sandoval; in the central Jemez Mountains, just W of Sandoval–Los Alamos line, NW of Cerro Rubio). Name origin unknown.
SHELLEY PARK, PEAK, 8,689 ft. (Grant; in the Mogollon Mountains, E of Seventy-four Mountain). In 1884 Peter M. Shelley and his family moved into the Gila country from Texas, driving a herd of cattle with them. They were among the area's earliest settlers.
SHERMAN (Grant). See *San Juan.*
SHILLINGBURG (McKinley; settlement; 7 mi NW of Crownpoint, W of NM 57). Abandoned community, named for T.P. Shillingburg, a trader in the area. Few people today recognize the name.
SHILOH DRAW, HILLS (Otero; in S part of county, 14 mi N of the Texas line). Around 1900 the rancher Oliver M. Lee (see *Oliver Lee Memorial State Park*) purchased for breeding a well-known race horse named Shiloh. Lee turned the stud out with a bunch of mares in this area, which cowboys soon referred to as "where Shiloh runs"; from this evolved Shiloh Draw and later Shiloh Hills.
SHIP ROCK (San Juan; in NW part of county, 9 mi SW of settlement of Shiprock). "Rock with wings" is how Navajos refer to this volcanic formation, though the "wings" are not the dramatic spires of Ship Rock itself but rather volcanic dikes radiating out from it. In their legends, Navajos tell that once their people dwelt on Ship Rock, a safe refuge from their enemies, but that lightning one day split the rock, barring descent by those still there. Navajos regard Ship Rock as sacred and refuse mountaineers permission to climb it. The formation, the eroded remnant of a volcanic core, was called *The Needle* by Capt. J.F. McComb in 1860, but by 1870 the name Ship Rock was appearing on USGS maps, though the name Needle persisted as late as 1905. Ship Rock is an apt image, for from some directions the rock does indeed resemble a full-rigged sailing schooner. A less dramatic *Shiprock Hill,* also named for its resemblance to a ship, exists in Union County near Clayton.

SHIPROCK (San Juan; settlement; on US 84 and 666, 30 mi W of Farmington; PO 1904–present). This Navajo community was established in 1903 when the US government established the San Juan School and Agency here, on land belonging to a Navajo named Tseheyabegay. Supt. William T. Shelton was its head. Described as a "stern disciplinarian and ruthless in his prosecution of moral lapse," he also was a staunch champion of the Navajos, who called him "Tall Boss," and even today many Navajos call Shiprock by that name, "Tall Boss," though they also use the name "River," for the San Juan River here. The present English name comes from the dramatic rock formation 9 mi to the SW. The one-word spelling of the town's name, as opposed to the two-word name of the rock, probably resulted from a postal policy, since rescinded, discouraging two-word postal names.

SHOEMAKER (Mora; settlement; on NM 97, 8 mi E of Watrous, on the Mora River; PO 1882 intermittently to 1957, mail to Valmora). This tiny diffuse farming community recalls Capt. W.R. Shoemaker, ordnance officer at Fort Union during the Civil War; the name is said to have been given to this community by Shoemaker's son. *Shoemaker Canyon* E of Fort Union also bears his name.

SHOOTING RANGE STATE PARK (Bernalillo; at the top of Nine-mile Hill, W of Albuquerque, N of I-40). As its name implies, this 4,500-acre park features ranges for target practice.

SIA (Sandoval). See *Zia Pueblo.*

SIBLEY (San Miguel; settlement; 3 mi N of Las Vegas; PO 1903–05, 1907–09, mail to Las Vegas). Abandoned settlement; name origin unknown, though possible eponymns include George Sibley, who in 1825 surveyed the Santa Fe Trail, or the Confederate general, Henry Hopkins Sibley, stationed at Fort Union before joining the Confederacy.

SIDE PRONG (Sierra). See *Holden Prong.*

SIERRA (general). Spanish, "mountain range," though the term sometimes is applied to individual peaks.

SIERRA BLANCA, 12,003 ft. (Otero; in the Sacramento Mountains, 7 mi NW of Ruidoso, on the Mescalero Apache Indian Reservation). Dominating the landscape of S-central NM, visible for many miles, and with the greatest relief of any mountain in NM, towering 7,000 ft. above the Tularosa Valley, Sierra Blanca, "white mountain," was named because its summit has snow when surrounding peaks do not; Sierra Blanca is the southernmost point in the US where the arctic life zone is found. The mountain also has been known as *Old Baldy,* for its treeless top, The name "white mountain" is the world's most common mountain name and appears, in various languages, on such distinguished peaks as Mont Blanc and the Weisshorn in the Alps, Dhaulagiri in the Himalayas, Snowdon in the British Isles, Elbruz in the Caucasus, Mauna Kea in Hawaii, and Aconcagua in the Andes. In the Spanish-speaking world, the name often appears as *Sierra Nevada,* "snowy range."

SIERRA CITY (Sierra). See *Lake Valley.*

SIERRA COUNTY (S-central NM, along the Rio Grande; county seat, Truth or Consequences). The creation of this county in 1884 was spearheaded by Nicholas Galles; he was born in Chicago but came to the West to become a miner, lawyer, and legislator. The name, "mountain range," likely came from the Black Range, focus of intense mining activity at the time, and the first county seat was at *Hillsboro* in the range's foothills. But the county includes other ranges as well: the San Andres, Caballo, and Fra Cristobal mountains, and the S tip of the San Mateos.

SIERRA DE LAS UVAS (Doña Ana; SW of Hatch). Spanish, "mountains of the grapes." These arid mountains hardly are conspicuous for their grapes, but at *Las Uvas Spring,* at the extreme N end of the range, there was a single vine of the common canyon grape that covered about an acre. From this vine the spring was named, and then the name spread, like the vine itself, onto the mountains. Highest elevation, *Magdalena Peak,* 6,625 ft.

SIERRA DE LOS PINOS (Sandoval). See *Vallecitos de los Indios.*

SIERRA DE CRISTO REY, 4,567 ft. (Doña Ana; just W of El Paso). Formerly known as *El Cerro de los Muleros,* "the mountain of the mule drivers," this mountain in 1935 became Sierra de Cristo Rey, "mountains of Christ the King," because of a 45-foot statue of Christ on its summit.

SIERRA GRANDE, 8,720 ft. (Union; 4 mi SW of Des Moines). A huge, sprawling shield volcano, this formation deserves its name, "big mountain."

SIERRA RICA (Hidalgo; NE of the Hachita Valley, just S of the Apache Hills). Small, low range, highest elevation, 5,495ft. Mineralization resulted in numerous mines here and the mountains' name, "rich mountains." A mining camp here, now abandoned, was called *Sierra Rica.*

SIERRA SOMBRERO (Sierra; near Lake Valley). Isolated summit, shaped like a sombrero.

SIGNAL PEAK (Luna). See *Cookes Peak.*

SIGNAL PEAK, 9,001 ft. (Grant; in the Pinos Altos Range, 12 mi NE of Silver City, E of NM 15). This and *Signal Knob,* 3.5 mi N of Bayard, were used by the US Army as heliograph stations in the late 1800s during campaigns agains the Apaches.

SILE (Sandoval; settlement; on the W bank of the Rio Grande, 4 mi S of Cochiti). Pronounced SEE-lay. A tiny Hispanic community, sandwiched between the Indian pueblos of Santo Domingo and Cochiti, Sile was founded in the early 1800s by Antonio de Sile, who was given a 4-square-mile grant by the Spanish governor. Over the years the grant has been reduced and has changed ownership several times.

SILTON ((Luna; RR stop; on SP RR 6 mi E of Deming; PO as Miesse 1914–18, as Silton 1918–24, mail to Deming). This was a tract of land opened to farmers during the 1910–14 land boom; Raymond E. Miesse organized the Southwestern Alfalfa Farms Co. here in 1913. The locality first was called *Miesse* and later Silton, origin unknown; a settlement never really developed, but a RR siding, a PO, and two place names did.

SILVER (GENERAL). As with gold, the allure of this precious metal has resulted in nu-merous place names in NM; GNIS lists 38, the Spanish form *Plata* appears 7 times.

SILVER CITY (Grant; settlement, county seat; on US 180 and NM 90; PO 1871–present). The little valley with its spring and marsh that was to become the site of Silver City long had been an Apache camping site, and the early Spanish miners, in negotiating with the Apaches to mine copper at nearby Santa Rita, wisely agreed not to settle in the Apaches' valley, which the Spaniards called *La Ciénega de San Vicente.* (St. Vincent, most celebrated of the Spanish martyrs, died at Valencia in 304.) English-speaking settlers, however, were less discreet, and their moving into the valley in 1869 ignited an already explosive situation with the Apaches. The first settlers were William M. Milby and John M. Bullard, but within a year 80 others were here. They called the resulting settlement Silver City, for silver mining in the area, and in 1871 Silver City became the seat of Grant County. The *Silver City Range* is a small mountain group just NW of Silver City; highest elevation, *McComas Peak,* 7,681 ft.

SILVER SPRINGS (Otero; settlement; NE of Cloudcroft). This and *Silver Springs Canyon* took the descriptive name of the springs here.

SIMPSON (San Juan; settlement; 12 mi SW of Farmington, W of Gallegos Canyon). The name of this former trading post recalls J.H. Simpson. The Navajo name means "streams coming together."

SIMPSON PEAK, 12,976 feet (Taos; in the Sangre de Cristo Mountains, on the ridge 0.6 mi S of Wheeler Peak). Smith H. Simpson came to Taos in 1859; when the Civil War broke out, he helped raise the Union Flag in the plaza of Taos. Simpson became a captain of spies and scouts in Kit Carson's campaign against the Navajos and Apaches. He married Josepha Valdéz of Taos and lived there until his death in 1916.

SITTING BULL FALLS (Eddy; 25 mi SW of Carlsbad, in the foothills of the Guadalupe Mountains). Lots of "bull" has been spread about the origin of this name. The most widely accepted story involves "Uncle Bill" Jones, who had come to the Seven Rivers area from Virginia. His brothers had accused him of telling tall tales about his wanderings in the Guadalupes, and when he told them of a waterfall in the arid mountains, they scoffed, saying, "Well, Sitting Bull, if there is a falls there we'll name it after you." There was, and they did. The canyon containing the falls is called *Sitting Bull Canyon.*

SIX SHOOTER SIDING (Quay). See *Tucumcari.*

SIXMILE CANYON (Socorro; on US 60, about 6 mi SW of Socorro).

SIXMILE CREEK (Colfax). See *Ninemile Creek.*

SIXMILE GATE (Colfax; settlement; on Poñil Creek at its junction with North Poñil Creek). Vanished community, named for its location at a gate 6 mi N of Cimarron.

SIXMILE HILL (Chaves; 6 mi W of Roswell, intersected by US 380-70). In the 1860s, this was called *Old Man Hill,* the "old man" being Robert Casey, for whom Old Man Spring also was named (see *Roswell*). The original road to Picacho and farther W passed just S of this hill.

SIXTEEN SPRINGS CANYON (Otero; in the Sacramento Mountains, 16 mi NE of Cloudcroft). This originally was called *Pleasant Valley* by ranchers who had cow camps here. The name was changed to Sixteen Springs Canyon, for the springs here, after the first official surveys were made during the early 1880s. Permanent settlers arrived in the mid-1880s.

SKARDA (Rio Arriba, Taos; settlement; 37 mi NW of Taos, on the Taos County line; PO 1922–42, mail to Tres Piedras). Skarda was a station on D&RG RR, the old "Chili Line." The name originally proposed for the PO here was *Clark,* but Skarda, the surname of a local rancher, was adopted instead. Homesteaders arriving after WWI made up most of the population, but dry years and hard times eventually led to Skarda's abandonment. In 1940 the PO was moved a short distance, from Taos County to Rio Arriba County.

SKELETON CANYON (Grant; in the Gila Wilderness, NE of Gila, NW of Turkey Creek). Local lore tells that in 1863 two prospectors discovered gold here but were frightened away by Apaches. The next year soldiers escorted them to the mouth of this canyon, but soon after the soldiers departed they heard shots and returned to find the naked bodies of the two prospectors, shot and stripped by Indians.

SKELETON CANYON (Hidalgo; heads in the S Peloncillo Mountains and runs W into Arizona). In 1882 Curly Bill Brocius and his outlaw gang ambushed a pack train of Mexicans who had been raiding and looting in Arizona and were returning with their booty to Mexico. Fifteen Mexicans were killed, their bodies left to the elements and predators; for many years their bones were collected as souvenirs. It was in Skeleton Canyon, at a site 1.25 mi W of the NM border, that Geronimo surrendered to Gen. Nelson Miles on September 3, 1886.

SLABTOWN (Otero; settlement; just above High Rolls, down in the canyon from US 82). A lumber mill was here—hence the name—that sawed logs brought down the upper Sacramento Mountains by the "Cloud-climbing" RR. Slabtown was destroyed by a flash flood.

SLABTOWN (Sierra; settlement; on the E side of the Black Range, at the head of Poverty Creek). In the late 1800s this was a lumber camp owned by lumbermen Anderson and McBride.

SLAGLE (Colfax; settlement; SE of Maxwell; PO 1901–02, mail to Chico). Abandoned community that took the surname of its first postmistress, Florence B. Slagle. *Slagle Canyon* is nearby.

SLATON (Lea). See *Pitchfork.*

SLAUGHTER CANYON CAVE (Eddy; in Slaughter Canyon, in Carlsbad Caverns National Park, 10 mi SW of Carlsbad Caverns). In 1983 NPS officials with Carlsbad Caverns National Park proposed changing the name of the major cave that since the 1930s had been known as *New Cave;* they wanted the cave to return to its original name of Slaughter Canyon Cave. The problem with the name New Cave, the officials pointed out, was that the cave was hardly "new"—the name New Cave had resulted when the cave was newly opened for guano mining following the closing of Carlsbad Caverns for that purpose—and that the cave was being confused with other caves, such as Lechuguilla, whose exploration was more recent. The NMGNC solicited the opinions of spelunkers, and while a few supported the name New Cave, saying it was long established and used in technical literature, most cavers agreed the name was potentially misleading, so in 1994 the USBGN followed the recommendation of the NMGNC and approved changing the name. *Slaughter Canyon* takes its name from the same Eddy County ranching family as *Slaughter Draw* (see entry).

SLAUGHTER DRAW (Eddy; near the Texas line, heads in the Yeso Hills and runs E). Charles Slaughter, brother of John Slaughter of Arizona, in 1882 had a ranch house E of the Black River. *Ben Slaughter Spring,* near the draw, also likely is named for the family.

SLAUGHTER MESA (Catron; 13 mi NE of Aragon). Named for the cattleman, John B. Slaughter, who ran cattle here in the 19th century.

SLEEPING LADY HILLS (Doña Ana; 15 mi NW of Las Cruces). Low hills said to resemble a recumbent lady with flowing tresses, especially when viewed while heading W on I-10. Neither the hills nor the resemblance is conspicuous.

SMITH (Eddy). See *Loco Hills.*

SMITH (Union; settlement; location unknown; PO 1914–17, mail to Malpie). Abandoned settlement, name origin unknown.

SMITH LAKE (McKinley; settlement; on NM 371, 13 mi NE of Thoreau). About 1916 a trader named L. C. Smith operated in this area, and his name appears on this intermittent lake, as well as on the active Navajo community named for the lake. Navajos call the locality "round house," for reasons unknown.

SMITHBURG (Rio Arriba). See *Gobernador.*

SMOKEY BEAR CAPITAN HISTORICAL STATE PARK (Lincoln; in Capitan, on US 385). In 1950 a badly singed bear cub was found in a tree that somehow had survived a 17,000-acre forest fire in the Capitan Mountains. The cub was taken to the Washington, D.C., zoo, where he assumed the identity of Smokey Bear and became the national symbol of fire prevention. Smokey lived there for 25 years, and after his death from natural causes he was returned to Capitan and ceremoniously buried here at the state park. The only NM resident ever to rival Smokey in national fame and recognition also was associated with Lincoln County—Billy the Kid.

SNAKE BRIDGE (San Juan; natural arch; in Sanostee Canyon on the Navajo Indian Reservation; 1.5 mi E of the Arizona border). In 1988, accurate measurements of this natural arch showed its opening to be 204 feet long, making it the world's ninth longest natural stone bridge (only 9 exceed 200 feet). Until then La Ventana Natural Arch (see entry), with an opening 165 feet long, was regarded as the longest in NM. The name Snake Bridge likely translates a local Navajo name.

SOCORRO (Socorro; settlement, county seat; on US 60-85 and I-25, 72 mi S of Albuquerque, on the W bank of the Rio Grande; PO 1852–present). On June 4, 1598, Don Juan de Oñate gave the Spanish name Socorro, meaning "aid, help," to the Piro pueblo of *Teypana,* in the vicinity of the present city of Socorro, because the Indians "gave us much corn." But while the Indians at Teypana inspired the name, it ultimately was planted upon the Piro pueblo of *Pilabó,* where by 1626 the mission of *Nuestra Señora de Socorro,* "Our Lady of Aid," had been established; the pueblo and its mission served as the administrative center for the area; the mission's name also has been given as "Our Lady of Assumption." When the Pueblo Revolt struck in 1680, most of Pilabo's 600 residents followed Governor Otermín S to present El Paso, where they established a new village, *Socorro del Sur,* "Socorro of the South," which still exists. When

Vargas led the Spaniards back to NM in 1692, he found Pilabo and its mission burned and abandoned; it remained thus throughout the 18th century. In 1800, Gov. Fernando Chacón ordered the locality resettled, and around 1815 the present church of *San Miguel de Socorro* was established, likely on the foundations of the old pueblo. The new settlement appears as Socorro on all 19th-century maps, and like many Hispanic settlements it includes numerous suburbs, such as *Cuba, Chihuahua, Rincon, La Vega, La Florida,* and *Park City.* Between 1867 and 1890 Socorro was the center of one of the nation's richest mining districts, and the NM Institute of Mining and Technology and the NM Bureau of Mines and Mineral Resources are located here. Navajos call Socorro *Sokwolah,* a corruption of the Spanish name.

SOCORRO COUNTY (central NM, along the Rio Grande; county seat, Socorro). This county was created by the Republic of Mexico in 1844 and designated by the territorial legislature in 1850; it takes its name from its principal city and county seat. Until the creation of Catron County in 1921, Socorro County stretched to the Arizona border.

SOCORRO MINES (Socorro). See *Magdalena.*

SOCORRO MOUNTAINS (Socorro; W of Socorro, bounded on the N by Nogal Canyon and on the S by Socorro Canyon). Other names have been *Mountains of Socorro, Sierra de Socorro,* and *Sierra Socorro,* but Socorro Mountains now is the accepted term. Highest elevation, *Socorro Peak,* 7,284 ft.

SODA DAM (Sandoval; on NM 4 and the Jemez River, 1 mi N of Jemez Springs). Springs here whose water is laden with calcium carbonate have formed a natural travertine dam across the river. *Soda* refers to the mineral-water.

SOFIA (Union; settlement; on NM 453 36 mi W of Clayton; PO 1914–26, mail to Grenville). Around 1911 several families from Bulgaria arrived here to homestead; they included George Belcheff, who named the community in 1914 for the capital of his native country. The descendants of these homesteaders still live here, and the name Sofia still is used throughout the area.

SOHAM (San Miguel; settlement; on US 84, 1.5 mi NW of San Jose; PO 1916–65, mail to San Jose). Former postal locality, name origin unknown.

SOLANO (Harding; settlement; on NM 39, between Roy and Mosquero; PO 1907–present). This homesteader community took the surname of Cipriano Solano, who once carried the mail from Springer to Raton.

SOLDIER HILL (Grant; in the Gila Wilderness, on Big Dry Creek, just E of US 180 and S of the Catron County line). In December 1885 Ulzana ambushed some US soldiers here, and several were killed.

SOLDIER HILL (Lea; 5 mi S of Caprock). Some US soldiers are said to have been killed here. A rural school here took this name, though it also was called *Caprock School.*

SOLDIERS FAREWELL HILL, 6,173 ft. (Grant; N of I-10, W of the Continental Divide). At least three legends—all dating from the late 1800s and all apocryphal—explain this romantic name. One is that soldiers manning a signal station here—mirrors by day, flares at night—were trapped by Apaches and, tormented by thirst, signalled a farewell, saying they were going down to battle the Indians; all were killed. Another story says a soldier from the East, despondent over separation from his sweetheart, killed himself here. The most widely accepted story says soldiers, escorting wagon trains and travelers en route to California, were ordered to go no farther than here, where they were forced to say "farewell."

SOLEDAD CANYON (Doña Ana; runs E from the Organ Mountains, 12 mi E of Las Cruces). Spanish, "solitude, loneliness." The canyon was named for a conspicuous and "solitary" thumb of granite at the canyon's mouth.

SOLEDAD PEAK (Doña Ana). See *Victorio Peak.*

SOLITARIO PEAK (San Miguel). See *Hermits Peak.*

SOMBRILLO (Rio Arriba; settlement; on US 84 and 285, 3 mi SE of Española).

One of many "suburbs" making up what is generally thought of as Española. Its name means likely is derived from the Spanish *sombrio,* "shady," doubtless referring to shade trees here.

SOMBRIO (Guadalupe; settlement; 28 mi W of Santa Rosa; PO 1936, mail to Pintada). Former settlement, whose Spanish name means "shady," likely a reference to shade trees.

SOUTH BALDY (Socorro). See *Magdalena Mountains.*

SOUTH CHISUM CAMP (Eddy). See *Artesia.*

SOUTH FORK (Otero). See *Mescalero.*

SOUTH FORK PEAK, 11,978 ft. (Taos; in the Sangre de Cristo Mountains, 3 mi W of Wheeler Peak). Named for the *South Fork of the Río Hondo,* which heads just E.

SOUTH GUAM (McKinley). See *Coolidge.*

SOUTH MOUNTAIN, 8,690 ft. (Santa Fe; in SW part of county, 2 mi S of San Pedro). This is the most southern summit of the mountain complex that also includes the Ortiz and San Pedro Mountains. The highest point on South Mountain is *Monte Largo,* "long mountain."

SOUTH SAN YSIDRO (San Miguel). See *San Ysidro.*

SOUTH SANDIA PEAK (Bernalillo). See *Sandia Mountains.*

SOUTH SPRING (Chaves; settlement; on AT&SF RR, 5 mi SE of Roswell, 0.5 mi W of the AT&SF RR; 1899–1900, mail to Roswell). In the 1860s this spring was known as *Dutch Spring,* because a German named Eisenstein lived here; in the American West of the 1800s, any non-English northern European tended to be known as a "Dutchman." Later, as South Spring, the spring became the site of the second ranch headquarters in Chaves County of John Chisum's cattle operations. In those days of self-sufficiency, a ranch and a settlement often were synonymous. Artesian pumping has depleted the springs, but a residential development called *South Spring Acres* is nearby and preserves the name. *South Spring River* heads at South Spring and flows just a few miles E to enter the Pecos River.

SOUTHSIDE (Colfax; settlement; location unknown; PO 1878–79). Ephemeral postal locality, name origin unknown.

SPAULDING (Grant; RR locality; on the AT&SF RR line between Deming and Faywood Hot Springs). This RR stop first was called *Crawford,* for reasons unknown, but the name later was changed to honor A.G. Spaulding, the baseball magnate who had interests in the area.

SPENCER VALLEY (McKinley; settlement; 8 mi W of Gallup). This inhabited area took the surname of a large Navajo family still living here.

SPIKES CREEK (Quay). See *Mesa Redonda.*

SPINDLE (Lincoln; settlement; on NM 246, 22 mi NE of Capitan; PO 1917–20, mail to Capitan). Former community; several families named Spindle lived here. At least one residence remains, and the name still is used in the area.

SPIRIT LAKE (Santa Fe; in the Sangre de Cristo Mountains, at the head of Holy Ghost Creek, 3 mi W of Cowles). Elliott Barker wrote that the lake's beauty might inspire thoughts of the Holy Spirit, hence the name. He also wrote: "I used to hear the old native Spanish Americans refer to the lake as *La Laguna del Espíritu Santo* (The Lake of the Holy Spirit), or Holy Ghost. It was, perhaps, originally so christened, and the creek naturally took the same name, while the lake's name was shortened to just Spirit Lake."

SPRING CANYON STATE PARK (Luna; in the NE Florida Mountains, SE of Deming). Probably named for a spring in the canyon.

SPRING HILL (Union; settlement; in Apache Valley, N of Clayton). Abandoned community, named for a spring issuing from the side of a hill.

SPRING HILL (Union; settlement; E of Des Moines, NW of Grenville; PO as Kimball 1890, as Spring Hill 1890–99, mail to Folsom). Little is known about this abandoned community, also known as *Kimball,* including the origin of either of its names.

SPRING MOUND VALLEY (Chaves; settlement; E of the Pecos from Dexter). Three springs existed here whose mineral-laden waters built up a mound, and a little homesteading community, now abandoned, took its name from this.

SPRING MOUNTAIN, 11,180 ft. (San Miguel; in NW part of county, in the Sangre de Cristo Mountains, 7 mi NE of Cowles). Elliott Barker wrote: "The name is appropriate because of the permanent ice cold spring at the N end of a long segment of the range, which is only slightly higher than the spring itself. It is nearer to the top of a mountain than any spring I know." In 1991, members of the Barker family proposed renaming Spring Mountain to Mount Barker, to honor Elliott Barker, but considerable local opposition existed, and such a change would have violated the USBGN's policies against changing names in wilderness areas, particularly long-established names of major features, so the NMGNC began a lengthy search for an alternative that culminated in 1994 when a previously unnamed summit 1 mi W of Elk Mountain was named Mount Barker (see entry), honoring not just Elliott Barker but the entire Barker family.

SPRINGER (Colfax; settlement; on I-25, US 56, and NM 21, 24 mi NE of Wagon Mound; PO as Dorsey 1879, as Springer 1879–present). Frank and Charles Springer moved to northeastern NM from Iowa in the late 1800s and played major roles in the region's development. Frank, a lawyer, was an official of the Maxwell Land Grant Co., while Charles was an influential rancher near Cimarron; he spearheaded the creation of Eagle Nest Dam. The community named for them briefly was called *Dorsey,* for nearby Dorsey Lake, named in turn for Stephen W. Dorsey, US Senator from Arkansas who had extensive holdings in this part of NM (see *Clayton*). Springer was the third county seat of Colfax County, until the seat was moved to its present location at Raton in 1887. *Springer Lake* is 3 mi NW of Springer.

SPRINGSTEAD (McKinley; settlement; on NM 566 between Pinedale and Church Rock). Inhabited residential community, bearing the name of a local family.

SPRINGTIME CANYON (Sierra; in the SE San Mateo Mountains). In the 1930s a small gold-mining camp was here; now it's the site of a USFS campground. Name origin unknown, though springs are in the area.

SPRUCE HILL, 10,313 ft. (Colfax; in SW part of county, 1.5 mi SE of Agua Fria Peak). Forested summit.

STABLE CANYON, MESA (Sandoval; in the Jemez Mountains, S of Schoolhouse Mesa, S of Fenton Lake). During the lumbering era, a stable for stock was here.

STAGECOACH CANYON (Santa Fe; 5 mi SW of Madrid, paralleling NM 14). The stagecoach route connecting Madrid with Golden and other points E of the Sandias passed through here.

STANBRO (Lea; NE of Lovington, 2 mi S of Prairieview; PO 1914–17, mail to Lovington). Ephemeral postal locality that took the name of its only postmaster, Orville C. Stanbro.

STANDING ROCK (McKinley; settlement; on the Navajo Reservation, 16 mi NW of Crownpoint). Inhabited Navajo community, located near a low sandstone pillar, whose English name merely translates its Navajo name. Another formation, also named *Standing Rock,* is just N of Mariano Lake.

STANLEY (Santa Fe; settlement; on NM 41 and 472, 10 mi N of Moriarty; PO 1907–present). Stanley began as a NMC RR siding and took the name of a RR official and engineer. The settlement originally was just a tent city and was located N of the present village, but the growing community soon had a hotel, restaurants, and general stores. Stanley also served numerous homesteaders and farmers in the area, but agriculture declined during the 1930s, the RR pulled out in the 1940s, and Stanley was left stranded. Nonetheless, the community survives.

STANOLIND (San Juan; settlement; 10 mi SE of Shiprock). Former oil community, named for the Stanolind Co., a wholly owned subsidiary of Standard Oil Co. of Indiana, the initial syllables of whose name created this name.

STAR (Guadalupe; settlement; in SE part of

county, exact location unknown; PO 1909–10, mail to Taft). History has largely forgotten this ephemeral community, including the origin of its name.

STAR LAKE (McKinley; settlement; in NE part of county, on NM 197). This active Navajo community owes its name to a trading post opened many years ago by "Old Man" Starr. Since then, an *r* has been dropped from his name, and sometimes the name is even rendered into Spanish as *Estrella*, "star." The Navajo name for the locality means "red oak."

STARKWEATHER CANYON (Catron; heads in San Francisco Mountains and runs SE into the San Francisco River at Reserve, paralleling NM 12). Likely named for a homesteader. One local source said this had been called *Stock Weather*, because livestock would seek shelter here during bad weather, but this smacks of a folk-etymology.

STARVATION PEAK, 7,042 ft. (San Miguel; SW of Las Vegas, 1.5 mi S of Bernal). This dramatic chisel-shaped butte, a conspicuous landmark on the Santa Fe Trail, has long been a magnet for legends, certainly before 1884 when the first published account appeared (in the *Detroit Free Press*!). Though the details vary, the legends all agree the name resulted from an incident in which travelers ambushed by Indians sought refuge on the summit and endured hunger there. In some versions, the travelers perished, in others they were rescued. Dr. Lynn Perrigo of Las Vegas researched the various versions and concluded, "In one form or another, the tradition persists, but nobody can cite documentary proof." But, he adds, this doesn't mean an incident didn't occur.

STATE COLLEGE (Doña Ana). See *University Park*.

STATE LINE PEAK, 12,867 ft. (Taos; in NE corner of county, in the Sangre de Cristo Mountains, on the NM–Colorado border). Named for its location.

STAUNTON (Union; settlement; on US 87 and C&S RR, 4 mi NW of Grenville; PO 1914–18). This was not so much a settlement as a RR passing site. Name origin unknown.

STEAD (Union; settlement; on NM 402 25 mi S of Clayton; PO 1916–present). Named for the father of L.R. "Rock" Stead of Clayton. Little but the PO is here, but it serves a widespread community whose members recognize and use the name. Local people pronounce it Steed.

STEAMBOAT BUTTE (Union; S of NM 325, E of Folsom). Sandstone strata here resemble a steamboat.

STEELE FLAT (Catron; near the Arizona line, 8.5 mi NW of Luna). The name *Stell Flat* has appeared on maps, but this is a misspelling of the name of the Steele family, former landowners here.

STEEPLE ROCK, 6,259 ft. (Grant; in W part of county, 5 mi E of the Hidalgo County line and 6 mi E of the Arizona line). Resembles a church steeple.

STEEPLE ROCK (Grant; settlement; 4 mi E of Arizona, 3 mi N of Steeple Rock; as Carlisle 1884–96, as Steeplerock 1896–1922, mail to Duncan, AZ). This abandoned mining camp originally was called *Carlisle*. Prospecting began here in 1881, and in 1883 the Carlisle Mine was located. It, like the community, was named for Claude Carlisle Fuller, the first child born in the camp. As with other mining boom towns, rumors of rich strikes swelled the local population, and at one time a few thousand persons were here. One of them was young Herbert Hoover, whose first job was as assistent superintendent of the Steeple Rock Mines. In 1896, the community's name was changed to Steeple Rock, for the formation to the S. Mining declined, but there was a pale resurgence in the 1930s that lasted 15 years. Now Steeple Rock is a ghost town.

STEGMAN (Eddy). See *Artesia*.

STEINS (Hidalgo; settlement; on I-10 21 mi SW of Lordsburg; PO as Steins Pass 1888–1905, as Steins 1905–44, mail to Lordsburg). Steins (locally pronounced Steens) was founded around 1880 with the extension of the SP RR through the Peloncillo mountains; the settlement originally was called *Steins Pass*, for the gap in the Peloncillo Mountains where it's located. (This RR community is not to be confused with Steins Station in

Doubtful Canyon to the N, on the Butterfield Overland Mail route.) A rock-crushing plant was built here in 1905, but the community always lacked water and eventually faded. A museum and store are at the site today. *Steins Mountain,* 5,492 ft., is at Steins Pass; *Steins Peak,* 5,867 ft., is 5 mi N. All these features bear the name of Maj. Enoch Steen of the US Dragoons who in 1856 camped in the area with his troops en route to the new Gadsden Purchase, and the pass became known as *Steins Pass* (sic). Some accounts claim the pass was named because Major Steen died defending it, but in fact he died of natural causes in 1880.

STELWORTH (Otero; settlement; in NE part of county, 6 mi SW of Mayhill; PO 1918–23, mail to Mayhill). Abandoned postal locality, name origin unknown.

STEVENS SAWMILL PLAZA (Catron). See *Rancho Grande Estates.*

STEWART PEAK, 7,130 ft. (Grant; just W of the Continental Divide, 6 mi NW of Silver City). The name has appeared on maps as *Steward Peak,* but the name actually recalls a man named Stewart, who while camped on the peak was confronted by Indians who pursued him around the mountain; Stewart killed one, the others fled.

STINKING DRAW (Eddy; heads in the eastern Guadalupe Mountains and runs E and NE into South Seven Rivers, W of Carlsbad). Local people say at least portions of this are indeed foul-smelling.

STINKING LAKE (Rio Arriba; on NM 95, 6 mi W of El Vado Lake). This lake, NM's largest natural water body, is known locally by the unflattering name Stinking Lake, a version of its earlier Spanish name, *La Laguna Grande Hedionda*; even the lake's Tewa name means "smelly lake." All these names are derived from an oderiferous sulphur-laden spring on the lake's west side. Some maps, however, label the lake *Burford Lake,* a name that resulted in 1918 when the Southwestern Geographic Society and the NM Game Protective Association rechristened it *Lake Burford,* to honor Miles W. Burford of Silver City, an early promoter

of game protection in the state. In 1939, the USBGN established Stinking Lake as the accepted form, but usage still seems divided. The lake's Navajo name simply refers to its location, "lake between ridges."

STINKING SPRING (De Baca; between Taiban and Tolar, 0.5 mi S of US 60-84, at the junction of Sand and Alamosa Creeks). During wet periods, groundwater brings bitter, foul-smelling alkali to the surface here, hence the name. At a rock house here, William "Billy the Kid" Bonney and three members of his gang on December 4, 1880, surrendered to Sheriff Pat Garrett following a gunfight in which a fifth outlaw, Charley Bowdre, was killed. Bonney later escaped but finally was killed by Garrett at Fort Sumner on July 14, 1881.

STOCKTON (Colfax; settlement; S of Raton and E of US 64, 1 mi E of the Canadian River; PO 1878). This was a PO in the ranch headquarters of William H. Stockton, whose descendants still live here.

STOCKTON (Roosevelt; settlement; in NW part of the county, exact location unknown; PO 1904–05, mail to Langton). Ephemeral community that took the name of its postmaster, John J. Stockton.

STOLEN TOWN (Sandoval; Indian pueblo; near the Rio Grande, near Coronado State Monument). In the winter of 1540–41, Coronado and his *conquistadores* commandeered this pueblo, telling its Tiwa inhabitants to move to other villages, hence the Tiwa name for the village, Stolen Town. See *Kuaua.*

STONE LAKE (Rio Arriba; 12 mi NW of El Vado, on the Jicarilla Indian Reservation). Also called *Boulder Lake,* both names derived from the stone parapet surrounding the lake. The lake's Tewa name means essentially the same as the English name.

STONEHAVEN (Union; settlement; in SE part of county, exact location unknown; PO 1910–13, mail to Hayden). Abandoned community, name origin unknown.

STONG (Taos). See *Taos Junction.*

STORRIE LAKE (San Miguel; 3 mi N of Las Vegas). This 1,100-acre lake bears the name of Robert C. Storrie, the contractor who in 1916 began work on the earthfill dam on the Gallinas River that created the lake. *Storrie Lake State Park,* established in 1960, is on the S side of Storrie Lake.

STOUT CANYON (Colfax; begins 7 mi N of Dawson and runs SW into Vermejo River Canyon). Named for a Pennsylvania pioneer who settled here.

STRAUSS (Doña Ana; settlement; 16 mi NW of El Paso, on the SP RR; PO 1894–97, 1918–43, mail to El Paso). Former RR section house, now just a siding. Origin of name unknown.

STRAWBERRY PEAK, 7,012 ft. (Socorro; 6 mi NW of Socorro). Resembles a strawberry.

SUGARITE (Colfax; settlement; on NM 526, 6 mi NE of Raton, in Chicarica Canyon; PO 1912–44, mail to Raton). In 1909 the Chicorica Coal Co. began developing deposits in Chicorica Canyon, and soon a company town sprang up that took the name Sugarite, an Anglo corruption of the canyon's name (see *Chicorica*). The town's population peaked just before the mines closed, in 1939. Most residents relocated in Raton, and now only ruins and foundations remain. These form the focus of *Sugarite Canyon State Park,* established in 1988.

SUGARITE CANYON, CREEK, MESA (Colfax). See *Chicorica*.

SUGARLOAF (general). Beginning in the 17th century, sugar was marketed not in its familiar granular form but rather was melted and poured into conical molds and when cool sold as "loaves." These "sugarloaves" subsequently became a descriptive metaphor for any conical-shaped landform. The Spanish form is *piloncillo.* NM has three *Sugarloaf Mountains,* three *Sugarloaf Peaks,* and one *Sugarloaf Butte.* See *Peloncillo Mountains.*

SUGARLOAF MOUNTAIN, 10,525 ft. (Rio Arriba; 5 mi SE of Chama). See *Sugarloaf (general).*

SULPHUR SPRINGS (Sandoval; settlement; in the Jemez Mountains, in the W part of Baca Location No. 1, 3 mi N of La Cueva; PO as Sulphur 1898–1909, as Sulphur Springs 1909–13, mail to Jemez Springs). This, one of many Jemez Mountains resorts built around a hot spring, took the English translation of the original Spanish name, *Ojo del Sufre,* from the Spanish *azufre,* "sulphur." The spring also has been called *Kidney Water Spring.* The Towa-speaking Jemez Indians call this "place of boiling water." The *Elk Mountain* residential development currently is located here.

SUMMIT (Hidalgo; RR locality; on the SP RR, 3 mi E of the Arizona line). Likely named for the *Summit Hills,* highest elevation 4,879 ft., just 1 mi NE.

SUMNER LAKE, SUMNER LAKE STATE PARK (De Baca, Guadalupe; on Alamogordo Creek, 16 mi NW of Fort Sumner). Sumner Lake originally was called *Alamogordo Lake,* because it was formed by the damming of Alamogordo Creek (see entry), but after the lake and much of the surrounding land became a state park in 1960, the name often was confused with that of the city of Alamogordo in Otero County, so in 1974 the name of the lake and state park were changed to Sumner, which honors Col. Edmond Vose Sumner, commander of NM's 9th Military District, who in the mid-19th century established Forts Craig, Fillmore, Union, and Thorn.

SUN VALLEY (Lincoln; settlement; 1 mi N of Alto, 0.5 mi W of NM 48). Modern residential development.

SUNDANCE (McKinley; settlement; 4 mi S of Rehoboth). Large inhabited subdivision named for the *Sundance Coal Mine* here, no longer active.

SUNDAY CONE (Sierra). See *Nutt Mountain.*

SUNLAND PARK (Doña Ana; settlement; on NM 273, 5 mi NW of El Paso; PO 1960–present). In 1960 this community assumed the name Sunland Park, for the horse race track here, just as an Otero County community took the name Ruidoso Downs. See also *Anapra.*

SUNNYSIDE (De Baca; settlement; just N of Fort Sumner; PO as Rudolph 1878, as Sunnyside 1878–1910, changed to Fort Sumner). Sunnyside was a RR construction town, a loose collection of shanties and saloons, on the N of what is now Fort Sumner. The PO here briefly was called *Rudolph,* for its postmaster, Milnor Rudolph, but after only one month it was changed to Sunnyside, for *Sunnyside Springs* (see entry) nearby. In 1908 a tornado struck Sunnyside, nearly obliterating the settlement, and the next year, at a special meeting, Sunnyside residents asked to be incorporated into Fort Sumner. Thereafter, what had been Sunnyside was known as the *Sunnyside Addition.*

SUNNYSIDE SPRINGS (De Baca; 1 mi N of Fort Sumner, about 100 yards E of US 84). These springs were named by Milnor Rudolph because they face S and thus are always in the sun. Still flowing, they drain into Truchas Creek.

SUNSET (Lincoln; settlement; on US 70-380 5 mi W of Picacho). Old-timers still recognize this name, but little else remains of this former community, and the name's origin has been forgotten.

SUNSHINE (Luna; settlement; on NM 11, 9 mi S of Deming). Inhabited residential area, named for its most abundant natural resource.

SUNSHINE VALLEY (Taos; settlement; 10 mi N of Questa, 3 mi W of NM 522; PO as Virsylvia 1909–14 mail to Cerro, as Sunshine Valley 1921–33 mail to Jaroso, CO). Active farming and ranching community, formerly called *Virsylvia,* for reasons unknown, now named for *Sunshine Valley* where it's located.

SUNSPOT (Otero; settlement; in the Sacramento Mountains, 16 mi S of Cloudcroft; PO 1953–present). Located on Sacramento Peak, this community originally was called *Sac Peak,* but when a PO was established here the residents, with wry humor, proposed the name Sunspot, because of the National Solar Observatory here.

SUWANEE (Valencia). See *Correo.*

SWAMP (Lea; settlement; 7 mi SW of Lovington; PO 1894–95, mail to Eddy). Research by Wade Shipley of Lovington has indicated this settlement grew up around a well dug in the High Plains by former buffalo hunters. A ranch at the site took the name Swamp Angel, "from the misty, heavenly appearance of the swamp on early mornings when the humidity was high, the water warm and the air cool." The site still is occupied by the Swamp Angel Ranch.

SWARTS (Grant; settlement; on the Mimbres River, on NM 61, 5 mi NE of Dwyer; PO 1887–1919, mail to Sherman). Inhabited hamlet, sometimes spelled *Swartz,* named for E. J. Swartz, merchant, saloon keeper, and postmaster here.

SWASTIKA (Colfax; settlement; 5 mi SW of Raton, in Dillon Canyon; PO 1918–40, changed to Brilliant). The word *swastika* comes from the Sanskrit and means "good fortune," an appropriate name for the coal-mining town the St. Louis, Rocky Mountain, and Pacific Co. established here as a sister community to Brilliant (see entry), a mile N. The two camps co-existed until 1935, when Brilliant closed; during WWI Swastika changed its name to *Brilliant II.* But by then the demand for coal was dwindling, and now both camps are abandoned.

SWEAZEVILLE (Catron). See *Omega.*

SWEETWATER (Colfax; settlement; on Sweetwater Creek, S of Rayado; PO 1878–82, mail to Springer). Now just a cow camp, Sweetwater was named for its location on *Sweetwater Creek,* which runs along the S border of the county and flows into Ocate Creek.

SYCAMORE CREEK (Grant; flows E to join the Gila River 3 mi S of Cliff). This major tributary of the Gila was named for the Arizona sycamore (*Platanus wrightii*) that grows along it. Its upper reaches consist of the *North Fork* and the *South Fork.*

SYLVANITE (Hidalgo; settlement; about 20 mi SE of Animas; PO 1908–13, mail to Lake). In 1908 "Doc" Clark discovered placer gold along the SW flank of the Little Hatchet Mountains, and within months the boom town tent camp of Sylvanite had sprung up, with 500 residents, taking the name of a gold-silver mineral. The camp's population reached 1,000, but eventually the mines played out, the camp died, and today only foundations remain.

T

TAAIYALONE MOUNTAIN (Cibola). See *Dowa Yalanne.*

TABALOPA (Valencia; settlement; just N of Tome). Former settlement, occupied during the 1800s, later abandoned. The name sometimes is spelled *Tavalopa;* its origin is unknown. This also was the original name for the plaza of *Sabinal* (see entry).

TABIRA (Torrance; settlement; in S part of county, NE of Gran Quivira). Like its neighbor Gran Quivira (see entry), Tabira was a pueblo of the Humanas Indians, and like its neighbor Tabira was plagued by drought, famine, and Apache raids; both eventually were abandoned, though the abandonment dates of Tabira are unknown. *Tabirá* is a Tompiro word, though its meaning is unknown.

TABLAZON (Bernalillo; settlement; just S of NM 333, 3 mi E of Tijeras). Recent housing development, whose Spanish name means "board, plank," likely referring to a sawmill here.

TABLE MESA (San Juan; 16 mi S of Shiprock). The specific (*table*) and generic (*mesa*) parts of this name both mean the same thing.

TAFOYA (general). The three sons of Juan de Tafoya Altamirano, natives of Mexico City, were the first persons by this name in NM, arriving shortly after the reconquest of 1692. Six NM places have this family's name (GNIS).

TAFOYA (Colfax; settlement; 8 mi N of Farley; PO 1936–53, mail to Raton). This community, now abandoned, was a junction on the Santa Fe Trail Cimarron Cutoff and a main freight junction after 1850.

TAFT (De Baca; settlement; 14 mi NE of Fort Sumner; PO 1909–27, mail to Fort Sumner). President Taft was inaugurated the same year this community applied for a PO, to be named for him. Taft, now vanished, was not really a village but did have a mercantile store, a school, and a church.

TAIBAN (De Baca; settlement; on US 60-84, 14 mi E of Fort Sumner; PO 1906–present). In 1906, during RR construction, the AT&SF RR staked out a townsite here and named it for *Taiban Creek,* which heads at *Taiban Spring* and flows SW to join the Pecos River S of Fort Sumner. (*Taiban Spring* was known locally in the early days as *Brazil Spring,* for a Portuguese immigrant who settled here in 1871.) Most sources agree Taiban is derived from an Indian word, but its meaning and origin are obscure. Some say it means "horsetail"; others say it means "three creeks," for the three tributaries of Taiban Creek, but its real meaning likely is lost. *Taiban Peak,* 4,418 ft., is 1 mi N of the village, while *Taiban Mesa* is 5 mi NW.

TAJIQUE (Torrance; settlement; on NM 55, 13 mi W of Estancia; PO 1885–1942, 1943–65, mail to rural Estancia branch). Settled in the early 17th century, Tajique was the first of several Spanish settlements in the eastern foothills of the Manzano Mountains. As with the others the Spaniards built their mission at the site of an existing Indian pueblo, which here was located on the S bank of *Tajique Creek* NW of the present village, and the Spanish settlement took the pueblo's Tiwa name, eventually corrupted to Tajique. In 1764 refugees from Indian raids at Quarai fled to here, but the next year Tajique, too, was abandoned. It was not resettled until 1834, when Manuel Sánchez successfully petitioned for a land grant here for himself and 19 other persons.

TAJO (general). Spanish, "mountain gap, cliff."

TAJO (Socorro; settlement; S of Socorro, on the E bank of the Rio Grande, at the junction with Arroyo del Tajo). The early history of this community is obscure. The *El Tajo Grant* was given to Diego Padilla in 1718, but the settlement doesn't appear in records until 1860 when the US Census recorded *El Tago,* with 129 residents; the 1870 census listed *Tajo* with 70 residents. Its settlement seems to coincide with the abandonment of *La Parida* (see entry), 4 mi N. By the end of the 19th century, Tajo also was abandoned. The village was named for its proximity to *Arroyo del Tajo,* named in turn because of a craggy narrow cleft called *El Tajo* 5 mi E of the arroyo's mouth.

TAJON (San Miguel; settlement; in E part of county, exact location unknown; PO 1889–92, mail to Bell Ranch). The Spanish name of this abandoned community could be translated as "gash, cutting edge," possibly a metaphor for a canyon or other landform. Or it could be a misspelling of *tejón,* "badger."

TALPA (Taos; settlement; on NM 518, 6 mi S of Taos; PO 1904–23, mail to Ranchos de Taos). Settled in the early 18th century as part of the general colonization of the Ranchos de Taos area, Talpa likely took the name of Talpa in Jalisco, Mexico, and thus is one of very few Hispanic transfer names in NM (see also *Santa Fe* and *Sevilleta*), though the name also means "knob" and could refer to a local feature. Also, a Señora Talpa Romero belonged to a prominent Taos family in the 19th century, and she could have inspired the name. *Quien sabe?* Formerly the village had been called Rio Chiquito, for the stream flowing through it.

TANDY (Roosevelt; settlement; NW of Melrose; PO 1908–09, mail to Melrose). Ephemeral homesteader community, named for Albert M. Tandy, first postmaster.

TANK CANYON (Cibola; S of El Malpais lava flow, 2 mi N of the Catron County line). The canyon was named for a small reservoir and stock tank in the center of the canyon, and in 1936 the WPA built a schoolhouse here to serve a scattered population of ranchers.

TAOS (Taos; settlement, county seat; on US 64 and NM 68, at the foot of the Sangre de Cristo Mountains; PO as Fernandez de Taos 1852–85, as Taos 1885–present). Although the Spanish were aware of this area and its Tiwa pueblo (see *Taos Pueblo*) as early as 1540–41, they did not settle a town here until early in the 1700s. Nevertheless, by the mid-1600s a few Spanish colonists had established farms and ranches not far from the pueblo. Prominent among these settlers was Don Fernando de Chávez. His family was slain during the Pueblo Revolt of 1680, and he did not return with the reconquest of 1692, yet when Cristóbal de la Serna in 1710 petitioned for a land grant here, he referred to Don Fernando, and the community that sprouted here soon was known as *Don Fernando de Taos.* This name persisted in various forms throughout the 18th and 19th centuries. Along the way, the name apparently became confused with the name of another local person, Don Carlos Fernández, for eventually the town's name appeared as *Fernandez de Taos.* When Josiah Gregg wrote about northern NM villages in 1844, he said, "The most important of these, next to the capital, is *El Valle de Taos,* so called in honor of the Taosa tribe of Indians, a remnant of whom still forms a pueblo in the north of the valley." He added that the term "Valley of Taos" actually referred to several closely related villages, the largest of which were *Fernandez de Taos,* the commercial center, and *Los Ranchos de Taos,* a residential and agricultural community a few miles to the S. In 1885, Fernandez de Taos formally changed its name to Taos, because of confusion among the numerous forms of the previous name; nevertheless, the stream running through the town still is called the *Río Fernando de Taos.* Residents of Taos are called *Taoseños.*

TAOS CONE, 12,227 ft. (Taos; in the Taos Range, E of Wheeler Peak and SW of Taos Peak). This peak is sacred to the Taos Indians; *Blue Lake,* site of Taos religious ceremonies, is on its SE side.

TAOS COUNTY (N-central NM, along the

Rio Grande; county seat, Taos). This was among the counties created by the Republic of Mexico in 1844 and named for its principal community.

TAOS JUNCTION (Taos; settlement; at the junction of US 285 and NM 567, 30 mi W of Taos; PO as Stong 1919–42, mail to Ojo Caliente). This stop on the D&RG RR line was originally called *Stong,* for the man who was a station agent when the old D&RG "Chili Line" was built here around 1885. Later, the RR built a spur line here to bring wood from the lumber community of La Madera, 16 mi away, but the line was abandoned when the timber was depleted, and eventually the main D&RG line was abandoned as well, though the locality and the name Taos Junction have survived.

TAOS PASS (Taos). See *Palo Flechado Pass.*

TAOS PEAK, 11,257 ft. (Colfax, Taos; in the Sangre de Cristo Mountains, on the Colfax-Taos County line, NE of Wheeler Peak).

TAOS PUEBLO (Taos; settlement; 8 mi E of the Rio Grande, 3 mi NE of the town of Taos). Long before Europeans arrived, Taos Pueblo was an important Native American locality, a trading center for both Pueblo and Plains Indians. In 1541, Francisco de Barrionuevo, one of Coronado's captains, became the first European to visit this, the northernmost of NM's Indian pueblos. The Spaniards with Coronado wrote that the pueblo was called *Braba,* a name of obscure origin but possibly a corruption of the Spanish *brava,* "brave, fearless." They chose, however, to name the pueblo *Valladolid,* after a fancied resemblance to the city in Spain, though Castañeda, Coronado's chronicler, also recorded the name *Teoas.* When Oñate arrived at the pueblo in 1605, he noted that it was called *Tayberon,* for reasons unknown, but a few years later, when a church was dedicated at the pueblo, it was given the title *San Gerónimo de los Taos* (sometimes spelled *San Jerónimo*), and the church at the pueblo still bears that name. (The pueblo ignored Oñate's choice for a patron saint, San Miguel, or St. Michael, and instead chose St.

Jerome, 4th-century translator of the Bible into Latin.) As for the name *Taos,* it is an approximation of a Tiwa word, sometimes rendered *Tua-tah,* often used by the Indians of the pueblo to mean "in the village." The Indians' own specific name for the pueblo is a different word, meaning "at the red willows," referring to willows along the Rio Pueblo de Taos running through the pueblo. As the Taos Indians explain: "Tua-tah is the Tiwa name of our village.... The Spaniards could not pronounce our name, and they called us Taos. There were many ruins surrounding our pueblo which were once thriving communities occupied by our ancestors. *Paimululuta* is the old Tua-tah which our tradition states was burned by the Spaniards." The Navajo name for the locality means "gurgling water."

TAOS RANGE (Taos; extends from Taos N to the Colorado border and the Culebra Range). This sub-range of the Sangre de Cristo Mountains includes some of NM's highest summits, including *Wheeler Peak,* 13,161 ft., *Old Mike,* 13,113 ft., and *Big Costilla Peak,* 13,005 ft. (see entries).

TAPIA (general). This is a Spanish word meaning "adobe or rock wall," but when used in a NM place name—it appears 12 times (GNIS)—it usually refers to a family name; Juan de Tapia was in NM as early as 1607; his wife was Francisca Robledo, daughter of Pedro Robledo; see *Robledo.* Tapia's descendants returned with the reconquest of 1692.

TAPIA (San Miguel; settlement; in the SW corner of the county, 5 mi N of Clines Corners and 1.5 mi E of US 285; PO 1927–39, mail to Stanley). Inhabited locality, named for the family. *Mesa las Tapias* is to the SE, 3 mi NE of Clines Corners.

TAPICITOS (Rio Arriba; settlement; on NM 595, 10 mi N of Lindrith; PO 1917–45, 1947–63, mail to Lindrith). NM Spanish, "little ridges," describing the topography around this inhabited community. *Tapicitos* Creek heads N of the settlement and flows W into Cañon Largo.

TATE (Union; settlement; on Carrizo Creek, 18 mi SW of Clayton; PO 1913–23). H.H. Tate about 1907 opened a store and later a PO at this locality on the old Clayton-Las Vegas trail. It is now a ranching area.

TATUM (Lea; settlement; on US 380 and NM 206, 19 mi N of Lovington; PO 1909–present). In 1909 James G. Tatum settled on land formerly part of the LFD Four Lakes Ranch and opened a store. To accommodate his customers, most of them recent homesteaders, Tatum brought their mail from Scott—another pioneer settlement—three times a week until he was granted a PO of his own; Mattie G. Tatum was the first postmistress. In 1934, Tatum sold all his NM holdings and moved to Lubbock, where he lived until his death in 1944. The town named for him survives as a tidy oil and ranching community.

TAWAPA (Sandoval; settlement; N of Placitas). This was a diffuse "hippie" community loosely strung out along Las Huertas Creek. The occupants of the owner-built houses, most constructed in the 1970s, claimed squatters' rights, but by 1990 they had either moved on or were being evicted by persons with legal title to the land.

TAYBERON (Taos). See *Taos Pueblo*.

MOUNT TAYLOR, 11,301 ft. (Cibola; NE of Grants). This giant extinct volcano, dominating the landscape here, is the Navajos' sacred mountain of the S, and in addition to an everyday name meaning "big, tall mountain" they also refer to the peak by a ceremonial name meaning "turquoise mountain"; in Navajo mythology, it was fastened from the sky to the earth with a great flint knife decorated with turquoise; the mountain is the home of Turquoise Boy and Yellow Corn Girl. Acoma Indians say it is the abode of the Rainmaker of the North. Zunis call a hole on the summit "lightning hole," and believe its closure leads to drought; they once made annual summer pilgrimages to keep it open. Early Spanish explorers called the mountain *Cebolleta*, "little onion," and it appears as *Sierra de la Zebolleta* on Miera y

Pacheco's 1778 map. Later Hispanic residents in the area called it *San Mateo*. The name Mount Taylor was given on September 1849, by Lt. James H. Simpson, a member of Lt. Col. John Washington's expedition into Navajo country. Simpson called it "one of the finest mountain peaks I have seen in this country," and in his journal he wrote: "This peak I have, in honor of the President of the United States, called Mount Taylor. Erecting itself high above the plain below, an object of vision at a remote distance, standing within the doman which has been so recently the theater of his sagacity and prowess, it exists, not inappropriately, an ever-enduring monument to his patriotrism and integrity." Though Taylor never saw the mountain named for him, the naming nonetheless was inadvertently appropriate, as Taylor soon became the bulwark against plans by Texans to annex NM, and it was through Taylor's determination, in the face of bitter southern opposition, that NM remained a territory until it could become a state in its own right.

TAYLOR MOUNTAIN, 5,936 ft. (Luna; in the NW corner of the county). Smooth, red mountain, named for the Taylor family who lived here.

TAYLOR RANCH (Bernalillo; settlement; NW Albuquerque, encompassing the intersection of Coors Rd. and Montaño Rd.). In 1918 Joel Taylor moved to NM from Texas; he and his wife, Nina, had two children here. In 1939, the Taylors bought approximately 800 acres of land on Albuquerque's West Mesa from two homesteaders. In 1970 the Taylors donated the land on which the Albuquerque Children's Home stands. Then in 1975, the Taylors sold 300 acres of their land to Bellamah, the land-development subsidiary of the Public Service Co. of NM, which applied the name Taylor Ranch to their housing development here. Bellamah paid the Taylors $1,750 an acre for their land—and nothing for their name.

TAYLOR SPRINGS (Colfax; settlement; 7 mi SE of Springer, on the Canadian

River near NM 56; PO as Taylor 1905–09, as Taylor Springs 1909–42, mail to Springer). In 1880 John C. Taylor came to NM and purchased from the Maxwell Land Grant Co. land that included the springs here. Taylor was primarily a rancher, but in 1905, in partnership with George G. King, he established the Aztec Mineral Water Co. The same year he opened the PO, with himself as postmaster. The PO was first called simply *Taylor,* but in 1909 the name was expanded to Taylor Springs.

TECHADO (Cibola; settlement; in S part of county, near the S end of El Malpais lava flow; PO as Trachado 1918–19, as Trechado 1924–47, mail to Fence Lake). Though the PO here was named *Trachado* and later *Trechado,* these were corruptions of the Spanish *techado,* "roofed over." The settlement was named for *Techado Mesa* nearby to the SE, which was named in turn for an Indian ruin with a covered well. *Techado Spring* also is at the foot of the mesa.

TECOLOTE (general). Mexican Spanish, "owl." This word, derived from the Nahuatl *tecolotl,* "ground owl," but the term was used in NM to denote any and all kinds of owls, to the exclusion of the other Spanish terms *buho* and *lechuza;* the linguist George Adlai Feather speculated that this was because the owl had religious significance among Mexican Indians, and their word supplanted the Spanish words. *Tecolote* and its diminutive *Tecolotito* occur 23 times in NM (GNIS). The name is less common in English, occurring 10 times in GNIS, but a *Hoot Owl Draw* exists in NE Chaves County.

TECOLOTE (San Miguel; settlement; just W of I-25, 10 mi SW of Las Vegas; PO 1851 intermittently to 1923, mail to Las Vegas). The name's origin here is unknown, though it probably is linked to *Tecolote Peak,* 7,240 ft., 4 mi N of the village, or possibly to *Tecolote Creek,* which heads in the Sangre de Cristo Mountains W of Las Vegas and flows SE through Tecolote. The inhabited Hispanic community of Tecolote, one of the oldest in the area, was settled in 1824 by

Salvador Montoya; he and his neighbors lived here only three or four years before Indian attacks drove them away. From 1850 to 1860, Tecolote was among a chain of posts established by the US Army to provide forage and corn during Indian campaigns. The RR station was named in 1883. See *Tecolote (general).*

TECOLOTE PEAK, 7,240 ft. (San Miguel; 1 mi E of village of Ojitos Frios). Though this locally is called *El Cerro del Salitre,* "saltpeter mountain," and also has been called *Ojitos Frios Peak,* probably for the nearby village, and *Sugarloaf Peak,* for its shape, the name accepted by the USBGN in 1965 was Tecolote Peak. This is not to be confused with *Cerro del Tecolote,* an early name for Hermit Peak. See *Tecolote (general).*

TECOLOTE (Sandoval; settlement; 1.5 mi NE of Placitas, on Las Huertas Creek). Tiny inhabited community, located on the site of a former Indian pueblo. See *Tecolote (general).*

TECOLOTEÑOS (San Miguel). See *San Ignacio.*

TECOLOTITO (San Miguel; settlement; on the Pecos River, on NM 386, 3 mi W of US 84). Though this name could be translated "little owl," the name actually was derived from this inhabited Hispanic community having been settled by persons from the larger village of Tecolote (see entry) to the N; thus the name here means "little Tecolote."

TEEL (Grant; settlement; just N of San Lorenzo; PO 1901–26, mail to San Lorenzo). Abandoned community that took the surname of its first postmistress, Alma E. Teel. Hugh A. Teel owned a store here.

TEJON (Sandoval; settlement; 4 mi NE of Placitas). Spanish, "badger." Located on the old route between Bernalillo and Golden, Tejon was in the center of the *Tejon Land Grant,* given to Salvador Barreras and others in 1840. By 1846 Tejon was an active little community, but it died when a non-resident bought legal title to the land grant and began dispossessing the residents, closing the grazing lands. The residents lost a bitter legal battle in the 1890s, and today Tejon is but foundations and a name.

TELEGRAPH (Grant; settlement; about 27 mi W of Silver City). Sometime before 1884 A.J. Kirby, a Texan, located the silver vein he called the Tecumseh Lode. The strike spawned the mining camp of Telegraph, likely named for being on *Telegraph Mountain,* 5,140 ft. The mountain derived its name from being an Army heliograph station in the 1880s. By 1884 Telegraph had 100 residents and was optimistic about the future, but within the year the Tecumseh closed; Telegraph died soon thereafter.

TELEPHONE CANYON (general). In Otero, Rio Arriba, and Taos Counties, this name recalls the first stringing of telephone lines.

TELESFORA (Union; settlement; in S part of county, on Ute Creek; PO 1901–03). This abandoned settlement likely bears a Spanish family name.

TELLES (Doña Ana). See *San Miguel.*

TELLTALE BLUFF (Eddy). See *Tracy Bluff.*

TEMPLE (Colfax; settlement; on the Rio del Plano, 18 mi NE of Springer). The Temple Ranch here, owned by the Temple family, became the nucleus of a small community, now abandoned. *Temple Peak,* 7,763 ft., is nearby.

TEMPORAL (Otero; RR locality; on the SP RR, between Tularosa and Three Rivers). Former RR station, named for *Temporal Canyon* to the E. *Temporal* is Spanish and can mean "storm, spell of rainy weather."

TENABO (Socorro; archaeological site; in NE part of county, S of US 60). Like its neighbor Abo (see entry), Tenabo was a Tompiro-speaking Indian pueblo, and like its neighbors it suffered drought and raids by nomadic Indians and eventually was abandoned. The meaning of the Tompiro word transliterated by the Spanish as *tenabó* is unknown.

TEQUESQUITE (general). New World Spanish, "alkali," derived from the Nahuatl language of the Aztecs.

TEQUESQUITE CREEK (Harding; rises E of Roy and flows SE from Albert into Ute Creek). Major drainage, named for alkali deposits along it.

TEQUESQUITE (Harding). See *Albert.*

TERRERO (San Miguel; settlement; on NM 63, 20 mi NE of the town of Pecos, on the Pecos River; PO as Tererro 1927–present). The Spanish *terrero* means "mound or dump for mine or smelter wastes," but its presence on this former mining community is the result of a mistake. The Hamilton, or Cowles, mines were in operation here as early as 1882, and at its peak the mining camp had 3,000 residents, most Spanish-speaking. An associated settlement was called *Rudy Town,* for reasons unknown. But as the local historian Leon E. McDuff tells it, the present name originated in 1927 when the community petitioned for a PO and solicited names from community members. One person suggested *Amco,* an acronym for the American Metal Co. of NM; many residents already were using this name, but a Mrs. Fisher, wife of the local forest supervisor, suggested Terrero. About a mile S of Willow Creek, just W of the Pecos River, was a depression that collected water—and that also collected trash from local residents, who had been calling the site *Terrero,* "dump." Later, the water evaporated, leaving salt deposits that attracted deer, and Mrs. Fisher mistakenly believed the name Terrero meant "deer lick." She compounded her error by submitting the name with the double *r* at the end of the word rather than at the beginning. Despite all this, her name was selected for the PO, which still retains her spelling—the USBGN in 1975 approved Tererro as the accepted spelling—though most maps and publications have corrected it to *Terrero.* McDuff points out that the American Metal Co. slag dump often credited as being the inspiration for the name did not exist when the name was adopted. Mining lingered at Terrero until 1939 when the mines closed permanently, and today the community is but a shadow of its former self.

EL TERROMOTE (San Miguel; settlement; 18 mi N of Las Vegas, about 6 mi W of Sapello). NM Spanish, "whirlwind, sandstorm." The origin of this name here is unknown, its use is fading.

TESUQUE (Santa Fe; settlement; on NM 590 and 591, 3 mi N of Santa Fe; PO 1938–present). Settled in 1740 and named for the Tewa pueblo (see entry) about 2 mi NW.

TESUQUE CREEK (Santa Fe; heads in the Sangre de Cristo Mountains, NE of Santa Fe, the North Fork on the W slopes of Tesuque Peak, the South Fork about 1.5 mi further S, Tesuque Creek flowing SW to join Little Tesuque Creek S of the village of Tesuque, where they become the Rio Tesuque). This and *Little Tesuque Creek* just to the S are tributaries of the *Río Tesuque*, all named for the Tewa Indian pueblo to the NW (see entry).

TESUQUE PUEBLO (Santa Fe; settlement; on US 84 and NM 591, 4 mi N of Santa Fe). This Tewa name has been spelled *Sayuque, Tezuque, Tesuqui, Tesuke,* and now *Tesuque*—all corruptions of the Tewa name for the pueblo whose ruins are 3 mi E of the present village. The name has been explained as combining Tewa words meaning "spotted dry place," describing water disappearing into the sand of *Tesuque Creek,* which flows through the pueblo, and reappearing in spots, but the pueblo's inhabitants say, "Our Tewa name is *Tay-tsoon-ghay,* 'place of the cottonwood trees.'" Navajos call the pueblo a name meaning "spotted grass," as well as *Suki,* derived from the Tewa word.

TESUQUE PEAK, 12,047 ft. (Santa Fe; in the Santa Fe Range, at the head of the Santa Fe Basin Ski Area). Named for the pueblo.

TETA, TETILLA (general). Throughout the world, a woman's breast (Spanish, *teta,* diminutive *tetilla*) is a common desriptive metaphor for mountains.

TETILLA PEAK, 7,206 ft. (Santa Fe; 14 mi SW of Santa Fe, 6 mi N of I-25 on La Majada Mesa). Spanish, "small breast," descriptive of this landform's shape. 2 mi NW of La Cienega and 3 mi SE of Tetilla Peak are some even smaller hills called *Las Tetillitas,* with a double diminutive.

TETILLA PEAK, 10,782 ft. (Taos-Colfax; in the Sangre de Cristo Mountains, 5 mi E of the village of Red River). Wooded summit named for its apparent resemblance to a "small breast"; see *Teta, Tetilla (general).*

TETILLAS PEAK, 9,380 ft. (Taos; 4 mi SE of Talpa). See *Teta, Tetilla (general).*

TEXICO (Curry; settlement; on US 84-70, 9 mi E of Clovis, on the Texas border; PO 1902–present). The oldest community in Curry County, Texico was founded soon after the first settler, Ira W. Taylor, arrived around 1900. This area was part of the XIT Ranch known as *Escavado,* Spanish, "dug out," but when a community developed in 1902 it acquired a name comprised of syllables from the names of the two states whose border it abutted. Farwell is Texico's sister community, just across the line in Texas.

TEYPANA (Socorro; settlement; on the W bank of the Rio Grande, exact location unknown). This name appears only in the Oñate expedition records, where it designates a Piro Indian pueblo. On June 4, 1598, Oñate christened the pueblo *Socorro,* "help, aid," because the Indians here supplied his expedition with food. Teypana is believed to mean "village flower" in the Piro language. Some sources place the pueblo at the present town of Socorro (see entry), while others place it 8 mi N. The name sometimes is spelled *Taypama.*

THAYER HILL, 5,547 ft. (Eddy; in the eastern Guadalupe Mountains, 2.5 mi N of Carlsbad Caverns National Park). Walter Thayer, born in Maryland, was a rancher here. He died of an accidental gunshot wound in 1915. His descendants still live in the area.

THERMA (Colfax). See *Eagle Nest.*

THIRTEEN MILE DRAW (Chaves; 13 mi S of Roswell). Likely named for its distance from Roswell rather than its length.

THOMAS (Union; settlement; W of NM 402, 17 mi S of Clayton; PO 1907–44, mail to Clayton). A school, store, and PO once were here. All have been abandoned, but the name still recalls the community's first postmistress, Laura F. Thomas.

THOMPSON PEAK, 10,554 ft. (Santa Fe; in the Sangre de Cristo Mountains, 5 mi E of Santa Fe). Arthur P. Davis of the USGS named this peak to honor A.H. Thompson, a USGS geographer.

THOREAU (McKinley; settlement; on I-40, 31 mi E of Gallup; PO as Chaves 1886–92, as Mitchell 1892–96, as Thoreau 1899–present). The arrival of the A&P RR in 1881 marked the beginning of Thoreau. The first name associated with the place was *Chaves,* a PO named for a local family who had a store here. (RR sidings E of Thoreau are still named *North* and *South Chaves.*) In 1890 the Mitchell brothers, Austin and William, from Cadillac, MI, bought timber land in the Zuni Mountains and intended to supply the entire Southwest with lumber. They laid out a townsite and called the place *Mitchell,* and by 1892 150 people lived here. Soon the A&P RR moved its station from Chaves nearby, and the PO came with it. But despite the Mitchell brothers' elaborate preparations, they soon abandoned their project. Then in 1896 Mitchell became a base for the Hyde Exploring Expedition. This developed into an extensive Indian trading operation, and the Hyde brothers renamed the place for the naturalist and philosopher, Henry David Thoreau. Local people, however, have said the name is that of a bookkeeper of the Mitchells (or of an army paymaster, or a railroad contractor), and they have altered the pronunciation to tho-ROO, or often THROO. The Navajo name for the place means "little prairie dog."

THORNE (Doña Ana). See *Rincon.*

THORNHAM (Roosevelt; settlement; 18 mi SE of Elida; PO 1910–15, mail to Valley View). Abandoned homesteader community, name origin unknown.

THORNTON (Sandoval). See *Domingo.*

THREE GUN SPRING (Bernalillo; at the S end of the Sandia Mountains, 3 mi N of Tijeras Canyon). This name originally appeared in Spanish as *Tres Pistoles,* and local lore tells that three ancient Spanish

pistols were found here. More recently, someone had carved the outline of three pistols into a wooden water tank, now gone, at this spring, possibly to commemorate the earlier discovery.

THREE RIVERS (Otero; settlement; on US 54, 17 mi N of Tularosa; PO 1883 intermittently to 1965, mail to rural Tularosa branch). In the late 1870s Patrick Coghlan established 2 mi E of here his ranch headquarters, which later became the Tres Ritos Ranch of Albert B. Fall. When a PO was established, *Salinas* was the name originally proposed, but this duplicated a PO name elsewhere; the name chosen instead was Three Rivers, for the *Three Rivers* watercourse (see entry) that passes by here. Three Rivers was prominent not only in Fall's cattle empire but also in those of John S. Chisum and Suzie McSween Barber, "Cattle Queen of NM." Charles B. Eddy's EP&NE RR reached here in 1899, yet few persons viewing the locale's present buildings would suspect the site's former prominence.

THREE RIVERS (Lincoln, Otero; rises in the Sierra Blanca complex and flows S and W to disappear in the sands of the Tularosa Valley). This and its two tributaries, *Indian* and *Golondrinas Creeks,* join 7 mi E of the village of Three Rivers.

THREE RIVERS PETROGLYPHS NATIONAL RECREATION SITE (Otero; 5 mi E of the settlement of Three Rivers, on the N side of Three Rivers Arroyo). More than 500 petroglyphs, made from A.D. 900 to 1200 by members of the Mogollon Culture, adorn a ridgetop here; remnants of dwellings are here also.

TIENDITAS (Taos; settlement; on NM 64, 12 mi E of Taos). Spanish, "little stores." The little stores here are gone, though a schoolhouse still stands, and local people still use the name.

TIERRA AMARILLA (Rio Arriba; settlement, county seat; on US 84, 14 mi S of Chama; PO 1866–68, 1870–present). The Tewa, Navajo, and Spanish names for this locality all mean the same thing—"yellow earth"—derived from yellow clay deposits; for generations the

Rio Grande pueblos used the yellow pigments here for pottery, ceremonies, and stuccoing. In the early days, the term *Tierra Amarilla* referred to the entire region, from Canjilon N to the Colorado border, W to the present Jicarilla Apache Reservation and E to Tres Piedras; the grant made in 1832 to Manuel Martínez and others was called the *Tierra Amarilla Grant*. Indian danger retarded Hispanic settlement of the area, and when Hispanics established a village here about 1862, they called it *Las Nutrias*, "the beavers," likely for beavers living along the *Rito de Tierra Amarilla*, which flows through the village, though the PO here has always been called Tierra Amarilla. In 1880 the state legislature moved the Rio Arriba County seat to here and at the same time formally changed the village's name to Tierra Amarilla.

TIERRA AZUL (Rio Arriba; settlement; on the S side of the Rio Chama, 3 mi E of Abiquiu). Spanish, "blue earth," a translation of the site's Tewa name, meaning "blue or green earth flats." Above this inhabited community is a hill with the letters TA on it.

TIERRA BLANCA (Quay). See *Liberty*.

TIERRA BLANCA (Sierra; settlement; 10 mi SW of Hillsboro; PO 1892–1903, mail to Lake Valley). Tierra Blanca was a small cluster of prospects and mines named for nearby *Tierra Blanca Mountain*, 7,142 ft., named in turn for its cap of white rhyolite; *tierra blanca* is Spanish and means "white earth." Rich but shallow gold and silver deposits were found here; in 1897 Tierra Blanca was but a PO and a few miners' shacks, with 35 residents. Today only the name remains. *Tierra Blanca Creek* heads near the crest of the Black Range and flows E past the mountain to the Rio Grande.

TIERRA BLANCA CREEK (Curry; heads 1 mi N of Broadview and flows SE into Texas). Spanish, "white earth," the stream likely named for alkali deposits along it.

TIERRA MONTE (San Miguel; settlement; at the junction of NM 94 and 105). Spanish, "mountain land," referring to this cluster of residences being located near the eastern foothills of the Sangre de Cristo Mountains.

TIFFANY (Socorro; settlement; on the Rio Grande's W bank, about 2.5 mi S of Bosque del Apache wildlife refuge). This locality, now just a RR siding, originally was a cluster of corrals; the site then was called *Arny*, a name that appears on a territorial map of 1908. This name possibly commemorates W.F.M Arny, NM Territorial Secretary, appointed by President Lincoln. Later, the Diamond A Cattle Co. established a farm here, and it was managed by one "Monsieur" Tiffany. The location was flooded in 1929. *Tiffany Canyon* heads N of I-25 and runs S into the Rio Grande at Tiffany.

TIGUEX PROVINCE (between present Bernalillo and Isleta). When Coronado arrived here in 1540, he found numerous Indian villages whose inhabitants all spoke the language now known as Tiwa. Modern Indians say the word heard by the Spaniards was *Shia-way*, but the visitors recorded it first as *Triquex*, then as *Tiquex*, and finally as *Tiguex*, and they used it to refer to the entire southern Tiwa region. In Coronado's time 12 to 16 villages were inhabited, but archaeologists say as many as 40 Tiwa villages once were here. Today, only two remain—*Isleta* and *Sandia*.

TIJERAS (Bernalillo; settlement; 7 mi E of Albuquerque, at the junction of NM 333, 337, and 14; PO 1888 intermittently to present). Spanish, "scissors." Two canyons come together here, like the blades of a pair of scissors, though some local sources say the blades were roads, not canyons. The site originally was inhabited by pueblo Indians, living in a pueblo, now called *Tijeras Pueblo*, whose ruins can be seen behind the USFS station at the S end of the village. Hispanic settlement did not occur until the 19th century. The deep canyon W of the village separating the Sandia and Manzano Mountains, traversed by I-40, now is called *Tijeras Canyon*, but it originally was *Cañon de Carnué*, for the older village at its W end (see *Carnuel*). The PO was established in 1888; in 1925 it changed its name to *Cedar Crest*, but then in 1947 the PO at *Zamora,* established in 1938 and named for a local family whose members included a postmaster, changed its name to Tijeras, which continues today.

TILDEN (Sandoval; settlement; 10 mi S of Cuba; PO 1930–32, mail to Cuba). Tilden was born in 1927 as the terminus of the SFNW RR, but the project failed; the depot and townsite were abandoned.

TILLOTSON CANYON (Chaves). See *James Canyon.*

TIMBER LAKE RANCH (McKinely; settlement; N of Ramah, near Ramah Lake). Recent residential development, named for its location.

TIMBER MOUNTAIN, 10,510 ft. (Socorro; in the southern Magdalena Mountains, 2 mi SE of South Baldy). Descriptive name.

TIMBERON (Otero; settlement; at S end of Sacramento Mountains, SE of Cloudcroft; PO 1982–present). Inhabited community, likely named by its developer inspired by its pleasant location in the forested mountains here.

TIN PAN CANYON (Colfax; enters Dillon Canyon from the NW, 5 mi NW of Raton). Said to be named for a shining tin pan a miner nailed to a post as a guide to his camp.

TINAJA (general). Spanish, "large earthen jar," but in place names of the Southwest it carries two other meanings: a low depression where water collects, a water hole; or, less frequently, a solitary, hemispherical mountain, somewhat resembling the bottom of a jar.

TINAJA (Cibola; settlement; on NM 53, 5 mi E of El Morro National Monument). When Pablo Candelaria and a brother-in-law, José María Marez, settled here soon after 1866, they called the place *San Lorenzo,* but eventually it came to be known as Tinaja, for a a nearby Indian ruin with a sunken depression resembling a jar; see *Tinaja (general).* Other Hispanic settlers arrived, and Tinaja became a stopping place for travelers; the village was described as a "Spanish town with a plaza in the center." By the 1920s, Tinaja was losing population; lacking title to their lands the Hispanic

settlers often were displaced by outsiders. Though the village became a logging camp during the Zuni Mountains lumber boom, by 1940 it was all but dead. Only a few residences remain.

TINAJA (Colfax; settlement; SW of Raton, 6 mi E of I-25, on the SE side of Eagle Tail Mountain). Tiny inhabited community, likely named for *Tinaja Mountain* (see entry), immediately to the E.

TINAJA MOUNTAIN, 7,805 ft. (Colfax; S of Raton, E of Eagle Tail Mountain). This prominent broad-based mountain, rising to a narrow, flat-topped neck, reminded travelers on the Santa Fe Trail of an earthen jar, or *tinaja;* see *Tinaja (general).* See also *Eagle Tail Mountain. Tinaja Arroyo* heads here and runs W into the Canadian River. The village of *Tinaja* (see entry) is just to the W.

TINGLE (Cibola; settlement; in SW part of county, on NM 36; PO 1932–39, mail to Fence Lake). Former community, named for a pioneer family.

TINKERTOWN (Bernalillo; settlement; in Sandia Park on NM 536, 1.3 mi W of its junction with NM 14). NM's smallest town, at least in area, is the whimsical miniature frontier community of Tinkertown, whose only residents are the apprxoximately 1,100 diminutive people and "critters" carved from wood by Ross Ward, artist, sign painter, and woodcarver. Ward became fascinated by roadside attractions when his parents took him to Knotts Berry Farm in California when he was 9 years old; returning home he began creating his own "town." The present Tinkertown was begun around 1962 and now is maintained as a museum and roadside attraction by Ward and his wife, Carla. As for the name, Ward says it just evolved from his having been "tinkering with it forever."

TINNIE (Lincoln; settlement; on US 70-380 and NM 368, 4 mi E of Hondo; PO as Analla 1903–09, as Tinnie 1909–present). Around 1876 José Analla settled here, and until 1909 this farming-ranching community on the Rio Hondo was called *Analla.* It also has been called *Las Cuevas,* "the caves," for some large caves in which early settlers lived, and later *Cuba*, "trough." In 1909 Steve and Oney Raymond bought out the Anallas; they built a new store and established a PO. At the request of the townspeople, they named it *Tinnie*, to honor their daughter. Raymond was postmaster at the time.

EL TINTERO, 7,222 ft. (McKinley; 6 mi E of Prewitt, S of Haystack Mountain, at the N end of El Malpais lava flow). Spanish, "inkwell," is an appropriate name for this extinct volcano from which black lava once flowed.

TIPTON (Quay; settlement; on Saladito Creek, 6 mi SE of San Jon; PO 1909–13, mail to San Jon). Abandoned homesteader community, name origin unknown.

TIPTONVILLE (Mora; settlement; 2 mi N of Watrous; PO 1876–1908, mail to Watrous). The area later called Tiptonville was at the center of the *Junta de los Ríos* land grant (see *Watrous*), and Hispanic and Anglo ranchers had long grazed livestock here. The settlement of Tiptonville was born around 1849 when William B. Tipton, an employee of Samuel B. Watrous, married Watrous's oldest daughter, and Tipton and his bride established a residence about 5 mi from the locality that would become Watrous but then was known simply as *La Junta*. Tipton platted a townsite, which became known as Tiptonville. A few people still live in the community named for the Tiptons; the name is still recognized and used in the area.

TOADLENA (San Juan; settlement; 12 mi SW of Newcomb; PO 1917–80). Toadlena approximates the name given by the Navajos who settled here, "water bubbling up," a reference to numerous springs nearby. A boarding school was established here in 1911. *Toadlena Lake* is 3 mi W in the Chuska Mountains.

TOBOGGAN (Otero; settlement; on US 82, 15 mi NE of Alamogordo; PO 1899–1900, mail to Cloudcroft). Toboggan was an end-of-the-line settlement created when the EP&SW RR—the "Cloud Climbing Railroad"—reached here in 1898. It was named for its loca-

tion in the tributary of Fresnal Canyon called *Toboggan Canyon*, likely named for some steep sledding here.

TOBOSA FLATS (Hidalgo; 9 mi W of Lordsburg, N of I-10). Spanish, referring to a tough grass, growing on rocky soil.

TOCITO (San Juan; settlement; 3 mi W of US 666, 9 mi NW of Newcomb). This is the Navajo equivalent of the common English and Spanish names *Hot Spring* and *Ojo Caliente*. This inhabited Navajo community, located on *Tocito Wash* that flows E to the Chaco River, likely was named for a hot spring in the vicinity.

TOE ROCK (Sandoval; 2 mi NW of Bernalillo, N of Coronado State Monument, on the Santa Ana Indian Reservation). This small but conspicuous rock formation, a volcanic plug, is also known as the *Bernalillo Plug*, but this name, a translation of its Tiwa name, is perhaps more appropriate. The toe-shaped rock is an important landmark among the pueblo peoples along the Rio Grande.

TOHATCHI (McKinley; settlement; 1 mi W of US 666, 25 mi N of Gallup; PO 1898–present). Tohatchi approximates Navajo words meaning "dig for water," likely referring to a dug well. George Washington "Gray Man" Sampson in 1890 opened a trading post here; a day school, the second on the Navajo Reservation, was established in 1895 under the name *Little Water*. (There was so little water here it had to be dug for.)

TOHATCHI WASH (San Juan; in extreme NW corner of state, crosses into Colorado to enter the San Juan River). Navajo, "dig for water." See *Escavada Wash*.

TOHDILDONIH WASH, PARK (McKinley; in NW part of county, 2.5 mi NE of Navajo). Derived from Navajo legend, this name refers to an earthen dam that trapped water here.

TOHLAKAI (McKinley; settlement; on US 666, 9 mi N of Gallup). This inhabited settlement, organized around the *Tohlakai Trading Post*, originally was called *Navata*, for reasons unknown, but it's now known by a Navajo name meaning "white water coming out." The name comes from whitish kaolin-laden water seeping from springs near the trading post.

TOKAY (Socorro; settlement; 2 mi S of US 380, 8 mi E of San Antonio; PO 1917–32, mail toCarthage). About 1918 Barney H. Kinney, a former mining official at the Cathage mines, organized the San Antonio Coal Co., and soon a little mining camp blossomed on the NM Midland RR. Kinney had wanted to name the camp *Kinney,* for himself, but the postal department rejected that name because of a possible conflict, and they rejected other names as well. One day while Kinney and a postal inspector were discussing names in the community's general store, Kinney looked at a case of Tokay grapes on the counter and asked, "How about Tokay?" The postal inspector agreed, the post office department approved, and about a year after its establishment the settlement had the name of a rich, sweet grape and a strong wine named for Tokay, Hungary. The community at one time had as many as 500 residents, but during the late 1940s mining ceased, and most of the buildings were moved to Socorro.

TOLAR (Roosevelt; settlement; on US 60-84, 18 mi W of Melrose; PO 1905–46, mail to Taiban). Like neighboring communities, Tolar (pronounced TOH-lar) was born with the construction of the RR, supplying sand and gravel. J.W. Coleman, the first postmaster here, named the community for Tolar, TX, where he had lived before coming to NM and where his daughter was still living. From its beginnings as a tent city, Tolar continued to develop, but in November 1944, a passing munitions train exploded, leveling the town; miraculously, only one man was killed. The sand and gravel industry are still here, but Tolar has never really recovered from the explosion.

TOLBY CREEK (Colfax; heads W of Tolby Peak and flows N into the Cimarron River at Eagle Nest Lake). The creek and nearby *Tolby Peak* (see entry) recall Rev. F.J. Tolby, a Methodist minister who became embroiled in the Colfax County land grant wars. He was murdered here

in September 1875.

TOLBY PEAK, 11,527 ft. (Colfax; in the Cimarron Range, 5 mi E of Eagle Nest Lake). See *Tolby Creek.*

TOLEDO, CERRO, VALLE, SIERRA DE TOLEDO (Sandoval; in NE corner of Baca Location No. 1, NW of Los Alamos). Spanish surname, common among Indian families in this area.

TOLL GATE CANYON (Union; tributary of the Dry Cimarron River, 8 mi from Folsom). Bill Metcalf built a toll road through the canyon in 1870–71.

TOLTEC (Rio Arriba; RR siding; 8 mi N of Chama, on the Colorado border). The D&RGW RR created and named this locality, but it's unknown why they chose the name of one of the earliest pre-Columbian civilizations in southern Mexico. The name survives through the present Cumbres and Toltec Scenic RR and also on *Toltec Gorge* nearby. A RR siding on the AT&SF RR 5 mi NW of Grants also is named *Toltec.*

TOME (Valencia; settlement; on NM 47, 5 mi NE of Belen; PO 1881–85, 1888–present). Around 1650, the aged Tomé Domínguez arrived in NM with his grown family and settled in the Sandia jurisdiction here; his sons later said he was 96 when he died in 1656; his wife, Eleña Ramírez de Mendoza, died around the same time. One of their three sons was Tomé Domínguez de Mendoza, and around 1661 he established an *hacienda* near the volcanic hill later called *El Cerro de Tome* (see entry). Mendoza, who was Gov. Otermín's *maese de campo,* lost everything in the Pueblo Revolt and did not return with the 1692 reconquest—he departed for Spain instead—but his name persisted when settlers took possession of the land grant made by Governor Mendoza in 1739. An earlier name for the site, however, had been *Fonclara,* a word from the Catalonian language of Spain and meaning "at the point of a clear spring or brook." The name Fonclara appears as a reference point in the grant documents, and as late as 1814 Fonclara referred to the site now known as Tome. The associated village of *Los Ranchos de Tome* was located about 1 mi S of Tome, N of Adelino.

TOMERLIN (Luna; RR locality; on the old EP&SW RR, 24 mi SW of Deming). Named for George Tomerlin, grocer and saloon keeper here. The locality served ranchers and miners in the area.

TONQUE ARROYO (Sandoval; on the E side of the Rio Grande, SE of San Felipe Pueblo). This name likely is derived from *Tunque,* a pre-Spanish pueblo at the NE edge of the Sandia Mountains; the word is Tewa for "village of the basket."

TONUCO (Doña Ana). See *San Diego.*

TOOTH OF TIME MOUNTAIN, 9,003 ft. (Colfax; in E foothills of the Cimarron Range, 3 mi W of Philmont Scout Ranch). In 1881 some hikers referred to this dramatic rock formation as *El Capitan,* for its resemblance to the Yosemite landmark, but the name that has persisted, Tooth of Time, is less easy to explain. One local version is that travelers approaching from the E and knowing water was ahead would say, "Time for water." But even persons long familiar with the area concede the name's real origin is unknown.

TOP O' THE WORLD (McKinley). See *Continental Divide.*

TORRANCE (Torrance; settlement; 29 mi SW of Vaughn, 0.5 mi S of US 54; PO 1902–07, 1935–42, mail to Corona). Born as the terminus of the NMC RR, Torrance was named for the RR's promoter, Francis J. Torrance; see *Torrance County.* Bean farming and cattle ranching here once supported 1,500 residents, but today only a single residence remains.

TORRANCE COUNTY (central NM; county seat, Estancia). Created in 1903 from parts of Lincoln, San Miguel, Socorro, Santa Fe, and Valencia Counties, Torrance County was named for the RR developer Francis J. Torrance. Around 1900 he and William H. Andrews, both from Pennsylvania, and their associates established what became the NMC RR; by 1902 grading was in full swing and a townsite laid out at Estancia. The first county seat, however,

was at Progresso, the sheep ranch of Col. J. Francisco Cháves, political leader for whom Chaves County was named. Estancia did not become the Torrance County seat until 1905.

TORREON (general). Spanish, "fortified tower." Because of constant Indian danger, many early Hispanic communities constructed towers as lookouts and refuges. 15 places named Torreon still recall this period in NM history (GNIS).

TORREON (Sandoval; settlement; on NM 197, 27 mi SW of Cuba). Navajos living here call the community by a name meaning "black or dark pinnacle above the horizon," referring to the black "tower" of Cabezon to the SE. The Spanish name, however, refers not to the volcanic tower but to a dwelling-fort, the ruins of which are on a promontory nearby.

TORREON (Torrance; settlement; on NM 55, 15 mi SW of Estancia; PO 1895 intermittently to present). Established on the site of an Indian pueblo, Torreon was named for fortified towers the Spanish built at Manzano to the S. Niño Antonio Montoya and 27 others received a land grant here in 1841.

TORRES, TORREZ (general). Juan de Torres, a native of Mexico City, appears on the Oñate lists of 1598 and is the earliest known New Mexican by that name, though other Torreses arrived soon after. A Francisco Gómez de Torres was listed as captain of the wagon train escorts in 1619 and 1621; other persons with this name are mentioned in reports after the reconquest of 1692. The name appears on 15 NM places (GNIS).

TORRES (San Miguel). See *Los Torres.*

TORRES JUNCTION (Socorro). See *Midway (Socorro).*

TORIETTE LAKES (Catron; 7 mi NW of village of Apache Creek). A homesteader named Toriette lived near here.

TORO (general). Spanish, "bull," whose appearance in 13 NM place names (GNIS) is a reminder that many early Hispanic residents here were involved in cattle ranching.

TORTUGAS (Doña Ana; settlement; 4 mi SE of Las Cruces, 0.5 mi SE of Mesilla

Park). Spanish, "turtles," and numerous folktales exist explaining why this Indian community bears this name. One says the name was derived from the flight S in 1680 by Governor Otermín; the aged and ill Tiwa Indians accompanying him—the "slow ones" or "turtles"-could go no farther and stopped here and founded the village. This, however, is pure folklore, as the village in reality was not founded until the 1850s by Indians from Isleta del Sur near Juarez. More likely, the village was called Tortugas either because of turtles the settlers found here or for *Tortugas Mountain,* 4,931 ft., to the W, which does resemble a turtle. This hill also is known as *Turtle Mountain* and *A Mountain,* for the A on its side betokening the agricultural school, NM State University. The Indians themselves call the settlement *Nuestra Señora de Guadalupe,* or simply *Guadalupe;* it's divided into two parts: *Guadalupe* and *San Juan.*

TOTAVI (Santa Fe; settlement; on San Ildefonso Reservation, on NM 502, 6 mi E of Los Alamos; PO 1949–53, mail to Santa Fe). This was a short-lived trailer camp established in 1949 and abandoned by the mid-1950s. Its name is from a Tewa word meaning "quail."

TOUCH-ME-NOT MOUNTAIN, 12,045 ft. (Colfax; in the Cimarron Range, NE of Eagle Nest, S of Baldy Mountain). The former landowners were reluctant to grant access to this mountain, hence the name.

TOWNDROW PEAK, 8,624 ft. (Colfax; on W part of Johnson Mesa, E of Raton). Named for an early family in the area.

TOWNER (Harding; settlement; exact location unknown; PO 1877–78). This appears on maps from the 1870s; it was named for its postmaster, John C. Towner.

TRACHADO (Cibola). See *Techado.*

TRACY (Curry; settlement; 6 mi NE of St. Vrain, 8 mi N of Grier; PO 1910–12, mail to St. Vrain). Few local people remember Tracy—and certainly not the origin of its name.

TRACY BLUFF (Eddy; on the E bank of the Pecos River, 2 mi SE of Carlsbad). Francis G. Tracy Sr. arrived from the East in 1890,

planted a peach orchard, and later pioneered the growing of cotton in this area. He was an important figure in Carlsbad's early history. The bluff bearing Tracy's name appears on some maps as *Telltale Bluff,* for reasons unknown.

TRAIL PEAK, 10,242 ft. (Colfax; in the Cimarron Range, within Philmont Scout Ranch). Named for a trail.

TRAILS END (Chaves; settlement; in SW part of county, on the Rio Peñasco; PO 1921–22, mail to Artesia). This ephemeral postal locality was established by men named Garner and Willingham at the same location as *Lower Peñasco* (see entry). The name's origin is unknown, but it has been suggested the name was inspired by the Trails End that was the country estate of James Cox, the 1920 Democratic candidate for President.

TRAMPAS (Taos). See *Las Trampas.*

TRAMPAS PEAK (Rio Arriba). See *Las Trampas.*

TRAMPERAS (Union). See *Louis.*

TRAMPEROS CREEK (Union; heads about 25 mi SW of Clayton and flows SE into Texas). Spanish, "trappers." This drainage also has been called *Major Longs Creek,* a name recalling Maj. Stephen H. Long, the American explorer and engineer who in 1819–20 led a US Army expedition to the Rocky Mountains and returned by way of the Canadian and Arkansas Rivers. Longs Peak in Colorado's Front Range also is named for him.

TRAMPEROS PLAZA (Union). See *Louis.*

TRAP CORRAL CANYON (Catron; in SE corner of county, 9 mi NE of Gila Cliff Dwellings, runs into the East Fork of the Gila River). The canyon could be closed off after wild horses were driven into it and thus trapped and corralled.

TRAVESILLA (Union; settlement; in NE part of county; PO 1892–94, mail to Veda). Spanish, "shortcut." The specific inspiration of the name of this abandoned community is unknown, though the name possibly is a corruption of the Spanish *traviesa,* "crossing, voyage."

TRAVESSER CREEK (Union; heads in NE part of county, near NM 370, and runs N into the Dry Cimarron River). Also spelled *Travasier Creek,* this name likely is a corruption either of the Spanish *travesilla,* "shortcut," or *traviesa,* "crossing, voyage."

TREASURE MOUNTAIN, 6,983 ft. (Grant; 6 mi NW of Silver City, N of the Little Burro Mountains). Named by early prospectors.

TREMENTINA (San Miguel; settlement; at junction of NM 104 and 419, 15 mi E of Trujillo; PO 1901–present). In 16th- and 17th- century Spanish *trementina* meant simply "pine trees," but later in NM the term evolved to refer specifically to pine resin, from which turpentine could be obtained. In NM the term also was applied to *Gutierrezia sarothe,* a shrub whose common names include snakeweed and turpentine bush; a semi-desert shrub, *Haplopappus laricifolius,* also is called turpentine bush.

The Trementina Apache band once lived along *Trementina Creek;* they were succeeded by Hispanic settlers, who supplemented their subsistence agriculture by selling pine oil and turpentine. An actual settlement didn't develop until around 1900, but by 1910 Trementina had 300 residents, as well as a PO, school, church, and hospital. But the population drifted away with WWI, drought, and the Depression; now the old town, located on the banks of Trementina Creek 4 mi E of NM 104, is in ruins. A new Trementina, however, has formed to the W, keeping the old name. *Trementina Creek* heads 5 mi E of Trujillo, flows E and SE into Conchas Creek.

TRENTON (Curry; settlement; 6 mi SE of Broadview; PO 1907–08, mail to Hollene). Abandoned homesteader community, name origin unknown.

TRES ALAMOS (Valencia; settlement; at the southern end of the Tome land grant). Documents detailing the boundaries of the Tome and Las Nutrias land grants mention as a landmark "the ancient pueblo of Tres Alamos [Spanish, 'three cottonwoods']." This pueblo, probably Piro, likely was abandoned by the time the Spanish arrived. Otermín around 1680 mentioned a *Pueblo del Alto,* "pueblo of the stopping place,"

which is believed to be at the same site as Tres Alamos.

TRES HERMANAS, North Peak, 5,801 ft.; Middle Peak, 5,786 ft.; South Peak, 5,614 ft. (Luna; 6 mi NW of Columbus). Spanish, "three sisters." An 1880 source said the sisters were Alice, Kate, and Lou, but the name Tres Hermanas likely antedates these women.

TRES HERMANOS (Otero; 10 mi SW of Alamogordo). Spanish, "three brothers." Three distinct summits, rising conspicuously above the flat valley floor. Sometimes called *Tres Montosos,* "three brushy hills," they are known locally as *Twin Buttes,* 4,553 ft. and 4,408 ft., and *Lone Butte,* 4,352 ft., sometimes called *One Butte,* 4 mi SE of the twins. Highest elevation, 4,552 ft.

TRES HERMANOS (Socorro; in NW part of county, just NW of the Alamo Band Navajo Reservation). Spanish, "three brothers." Three closely related peaks, whose elevations are 6,962 ft., 6,920 ft., and 6,847 ft.

TRES LAGUNAS (Catron; settlement; 6 mi NE of Pie Town; PO 1923–61, mail to Pie Town). Spanish, "three lakes." Tiny ranching community, named for a group of small lakes 3 mi SW of the settlement.

TRES LAGUNAS (San Miguel; settlement; on the Pecos River, on NM 63, 1.5 mi S of Terrero). Spanish, "three lakes." Tiny locality, once the site of a resort, named for three small lakes.

TRES MONTOSAS, 8,531 ft. (Socorro; 1 mi N of US 60, 12 mi W of Magdalena). Spanish, "three brushy hills." Conspicuous hills that would have been prominent landmarks on the old stock trail passing just to the S.

TRES OREJAS, 7,976 ft. (Taos; on the W side of the Rio Grande, 14 mi W of Taos). Spanish, "three ears." The Tewa name for the formations means "coyote ear mountains," because they are said to resemble coyote ears. Sometimes called *Orejas Mountain.*

TRES PIEDRAS (Taos; settlement; on US 285, 28 mi S of the Colorado border; PO 1880–present). Spanish, "three rocks." Settled in 1879, this lumbering and ranching community was named for three large granite formations to the W. The rocks were a favorite hunting ground of the Tewa Indians, whose name for the site means means "mountain sheep rock place."

TRES RITOS (Taos; settlement; in the Sangre de Cristo Mountains, on NM 518; PO 1915–27, 1937–40, mail to Vadito). Originally a camping ground for freighters on the old Taos–Las Vegas Trail, Tres Ritos was established as a mining and lumbering camp around 1900. It now is a resort community. Its Spanish name, "three creeks," derives from the site being at the confluence of the Rio La Junta, the Rio Pueblo, and Agua Piedra Creek.

TRIGO CANYON (Valencia; on the W side of the Manzano Mountains, E of Belen). Spanish, "wheat," because wheat once grew near the canyon's mouth. The canyon now is associated with the USFS John F. Kennedy Campground and a trail leading to the Manzano crest.

TRINCHERA PASS, 7,101 ft. (Colfax; at NE corner of county, at E end of Johnson Mesa). Spanish, "cut, trench," the pass cutting trenchlike through the mountains here into Colorado. *Trinchera Creek* flows from here into Colorado.

TRINCHERA (Colfax; settlement; in NE part of county; PO 1882–83, mail to Madison). Former locality, named for *Trinchera Pass* nearby.

TRINITY SITE (Socorro; historical site; on White Sands Missile Range, on the W side of the Oscura Mountains, 15 mi S of US 380). Here, on July 16, 1945, the atomic age began with the detonation of the world's first atomic bomb. Physicist J. Robert Oppenheimer was director of the Los Alamos nuclear physics laboratory that had developed the bomb, and in December 1944, while he was relaxing at home, he received a phone call from Kenneth Bainbridge, the scientist responsible for the experimental detonation, saying a site had been selected and a code name was needed immediately. Oppenheimer glanced at the book he had been reading, poems by John Donne, and then at the opening lines of the poem he had just read:

> Batter my heart, three-person'd God; for you
> As yet but knock, breathe, shine, and seek to mend....

"Trinity," replied Oppenheimer. "We'll call it Trinity."

TROUBLE (Mora). See *Santa Barbara.*

TROUT CREEK (Catron). See *Hellroaring Mesa.*

TROY, TROYBURG, TROYBURGH (Colfax). See *Parton.*

TRUCHAS (general). Spanish, "trout."

TRUCHAS (Rio Arriba; settlement; on NM 76, 18 mi NE of Española; PO 1894–1966, mail to rural Española branch). Like the Truchas Peaks to the SE (see entry), this village in the Sangre de Cristo foothills was named for nearby *Río de Truchas,* "trout river," (see entry). A document in Spanish archives dated 1752 refers to the village as *Nuestra Señora de Rosario de las Truchas,* "Our Lady of Rosary of the Trout." In 1770 the village had 26 families, 122 residents. Today it has more, but it remains small and isolated. The movie version of John Nichols's book *Milagro Beanfield War* was filmed in Truchas.

TRUCHAS CREEK (Quay, De Baca; heads in SW Quay County, flows SW into the Pecos River just N of Fort Sumner). Though the Spanish *truchas* means "trout," here it more likely refers to minnows in this intermittent watercourse.

TRUCHAS LAKES (Mora; in the Sangre de Cristo Mountains, at the head of the Rio de los Chimayosos, E of the Truchas Peaks). Spanish, "trout," but the lakes most likely were named for the nearby *Truchas Peaks* rather than for trout in the lakes themselves. One of the lakes has been called *Lone Tree Lake.*

TRUCHAS PEAKS (Rio Arriba, Mora; in the Sangre de Cristo Mountains, E of Española). Several closely related summits, all named for the *Río de Truchas,* Spanish, "river of trout," (see entry), which heads on their W slopes. *North Truchas,* 13,024 ft.; *Middle Truchas,*

13,070 ft.; *West Truchas,* 13,066 ft.; *South Truchas,* often called simply *Truchas Peak,* 13,102 ft. "Rock horn mountain" is the Tewa name, though it's not known which summit is meant. Until 1948, when more precise measurements were made of Wheeler Peak, Truchas Peak was believed to be the state's highest mountain.

TRUJILLO (general). The first Trujillo recorded in NM was Diego de Trujillo, a native of Mexico City, who arrived in 1632; he was among the refugees from the Pueblo Revolt who fled to Mexico, where he died in 1682. His descendants gave their names to 33 NM places (GNIS).

TRUJILLO (San Miguel; settlement; in center of county, on NM 104, 31 mi E of Las Vegas; PO as Trujillo 1912–18, as Ventanes 1918–27, as Trujillo 1927–74). Settled about 1836, this diffuse inhabited community has been called *La Ventana,* "the window," for a window-like opening in a nearby rock; *Cañon Ventanas* heads N and runs S through here. The settlement's name sometimes appears as *Los Trujillos,* for the Trujillo family here; a member of this family said the site became called Trujillo with the establishment of a PO here; Delfido Trujillo was the most literate member of the community, so to him fell the role of postmaster—and eponymn.

TRUTH OR CONSEQUENCES (Sierra; settlement, county seat; on I-25 and the Rio Grande, SW of Elephant Butte Reservoir; PO as Hot Springs 1914–51, as Truth or Consequences 1951–present). Truth or Consequences, often abbreviated to *TorC,* probably is NM's most often asked about and persistently controversial name. An early Spanish name for the locality has been reported to be *Alamocitos,* "little cottonwoods." As English-speaking settlers moved into the area, the locality came to be called *Hot Springs* (see entry), for the thermal springs here—the early Spanish name was *Ojo de Zoquete,* "mud spring"—and when a more formal settlement sprang up with the construction of Elephant

Butte Dam in 1912–16, it took the name Hot Springs. But then in 1951 Ralph Edwards, host of a popular TV game show, as a promotional gimmick offered to broadcast the show from a town that would adopt the show's name—Truth or Consequences. The NM State Tourist Bureau relayed the news to NM Sen. Burton Roach, also head of the Hot Springs Chamber of Commerce. Not only would the community garner national publicity, but also it no longer would be confused with the numerous other towns named Hot Springs (GNIS lists 78 populated places in the US named Hot Springs). In a special election, the matter was put to a vote, and the change was approved 1,294 to 295. A protest was filed and another vote held; again the change won 4 to 1. In 1964 the town's citizens again voted on the name, and again the citizens approved the change. And then in 1967 still another vote was held, with the same outcome. Yet throughout NM Hot Springs partisans shun and ridicule the new name as a promotional novelty, while Truth or Consequences partisans point to the worldwide recognition it has given their community. And Ralph Edwards kept his word; long after the TV show had been cancelled, he continued to visit and lend his celebrity status to the town that took him up on his offer.

TSANKAWI (Santa Fe; archaeological site; just S of NM 4, near its junction with NM 502). This abandoned pueblo on a mesa at the E edge of the Pajarito Plateau was first settled in the late 1100s; it was inhabited until the late 1500s. Residents of the modern Tewa pueblo of San Ildefonso say their ancestors once lived at Tsankawi, and they say its name means "gap of the sharp, round cactus."

TSAYA (San Juan; settlement; in S part of county, just N of the Chaco River; PO 1921–26, mail to Crownpoint). This inhabited Navajo community, along with *Tsaya Canyon* and *Tsaya Trading Post,* bears a Navajo name meaning "under the rocks."

TSAYATOH (McKinley; settlement; on the

NM–Arizona line, near Window Rock). Inhabited Navajo community, whose Navajo name means "water beneath rock."

TSE BONITO WASH (McKinley; NW of Gallup, just E of the Arizona border, crossing NM 264). This name combines the Navajo *tse,* "rock," with the Spanish *bonito,* "pretty," an appropriate name because of the scenic rock formations here. But more likely the *bonito* part of the name actually is a corruption of the Navajo *toh,* "water," the Navajo name for the wash meaning "water underneath the rock" or "water beneath the sand," also appropriate.

TSIPING (Rio Arriba; archaeological site; on Pueblo Mesa, about 1 mi S of Cañones). Prehistoric pueblo ruins whose Tewa name means "flaking stone mountain," referring to flint deposits on nearby Cerro Pedernal, whose Spanish name also means "flint mountain." Tsiping was occupied from A.D. 1300 to 1325.

TUCSON MOUNTAINS (Lincoln; NW of Capitan). This subrange of the Sacramento Mountains bears a name that is a corruption of a word used by an Arizona Indian group to mean "dark or brown spring," but why the name appears here in NM is unknown. Sometimes the group is called the *Vera Cruz Mountains,* for the Vera Cruz Mine; see *Vera Cruz.* Highest summit *Tucson Mountain,* 8,308 ft.

TUCUMCARI (Quay; settlement, county seat; at junction of I-40, US 54, NM 104 and 209; PO as Douglas 1901–02, as Tucumcari 1902–present). First, some clarification: the often-quoted tale that the name arose from an incident in which an Apache chief's daughter, Kari, was beloved by a brave called Tocom is pure fiction. The name's real origin is obscure, but the consensus is that it comes from a Plains Indian word meaning "lookout" and was applied to *Tucumcari Mountain,* 4,956 ft., the dramatic natural lookout just 2 mi S of town. Efforts to trace the name to specific words in a specific Indian language, however, have been inconclusive. As T.M. Pearce summarized after his inves-

tigation: "The most convincing explanation is contributed by Elliott Canonge, Oklahoma linguist, who writes that the name is Comanche *tukamukaru,* 'to lie in wait for someone or something to approach.' According to Felix Kowena, his Comanche informant, this particular mountain was frequently used as a lookout by Comanche war parties." Fray Angélico Chávez discovered a 1777 burial record mentioning a Comanche woman and her child captured in a battle at *Cuchuncari,* apparently an early version of Tucumcari. But other etymologies also are possible; a West Texas anthropologist believes it comes from a Kiowa word meaning "breast."

The town of Tucumcari appeared much later than the name. In 1901 the CRI&P RR extended its line to here, and half the population of nearby Liberty (see entry) moved to the unnamed tent city. Prairie winds caught clothing and rags and scattered them among the brush, giving the town its first nickname, *Ragtown.* The camp's saloons and gambling halls soon attracted outlaws and rowdies, and before long the camp had another nickname, *Six-shooter Siding.* The town's first formal name was *Douglas,* given for reasons unknown, but this was short-lived, and soon the name Tucumcari was adopted. *Tucumcari Creek* heads in the S part of the county near Ragland and flows NW E of Tucumcari to join the Canadian River at Logan. *Tucumcari Lake,* immediately N and E of Tucumcari, is a large natural lake, for centuries a watering place for Indians, *comancheros,* and cattle drivers on the Goodnight-Loving Trail.

TUERTO (Santa Fe). See *New Placers,* also *Arroyo Tuerto.*

ARROYO TUERTO (Santa Fe; heads between the Ortiz and San Pedro Mountains NE of Albuquerque and runs W into Arroyo Cuchillo SE of Hagan). Spanish, "crooked," and portions of this drainage indeed fit the description.

TUERTO MOUNTAINS (Santa Fe). See *San Pedro Mountains.*

TULAROSA (general). Southwest Spanish,

"having reeds, cattails," from the Mexican Spanish *tule,* "reed, cattail," derived in turn from the Nahuatl *tullin,* "cattail"; *tularosa* refers to a "reedy place."

TULAROSA (Otero; settlement; at the junction of US 54 and US 70, 13 mi N of Alamogordo; PO 1868–69, 1873–present). In 1862 Hispanic settlers arrived at the edge of the marshy land where *Tularosa Creek* fans out and loses itself among reeds and marsh grass about a mile from the mouth of *Tularosa Canyon.* It was those marsh plants, or *tules,* that gave place its name; see *Tularosa (general);* see also *West Tularosa.*

TULAROSA CREEK (Otero; rises in the Sacramento Mountains NE of Cloudcroft, flows NW to Mescalero then SW through Tularosa Canyon to the town of Tularosa). Sometimes labelled *Río Tularosa* or *Tularosa River,* this stream was formally designated *Tularosa Creek* by the USBGN in 1982. The stream was named for marsh plants at its mouth; see *Tularosa (general).*

TULAROSA MOUNTAINS (Catron; W of the Continental Divide, E of Reserve). Named for the *Tularosa River* (see entry) to the W. Highest elevation, *Eagle Peak,* 9,786 ft.

TULAROSA PEAK, 4,390 ft. (Otero; 6 mi SW of Tularosa, overlooking the Tularosa Valley). In 1863, during the Indian wars, several sheepherders were killed near this cone-shaped hill, causing it to be called *Dead Mans Hill.* Then in 1868, a Sergeant Glass defeated a group of Apaches here. In 1980, the USBGN accepted Tularosa Peak from among several local variants.

TULAROSA RIVER (Catron; heads S of NM 12 E of Aragon and flows SW to join the San Francisco River 2 mi S of Reserve). Spanish, "reedy river"; see *Tularosa (general).*

TULAROSA VALLEY (Otero; huge, broad basin separating the San Andres and Sacramento Mountains). Named for *Tularosa Creek* (see entry) at its northern end.

TULE LAKE (Curry; 6 mi S of Melrose). In Southwest Spanish *tule* refers to "reeds,

cattails"—see *Tularosa (general)*—marsh plants that would grow around this lake. Locally this name sometimes is given an Anglo pronunciation, TOOL. *Little Tule Lake* is immediately to the W. About 2 mi S is *Cañada del Tule.*

TULLOCH PEAK, 6,374 ft. (Grant; just E of NM 90, 15 mi SW of Silver City). In 1990, the USBGN followed the NMGNC's recommendation and changed this name from *Tullock Peak* to Tulloch Peak, reflecting the correct spelling of the surname of the settlers for whom the peak was named.

TULOSA (San Miguel; settlement; 28 mi SE of Las Vegas). Spanish, "reedy place"; see *Tularosa (general).* Abandoned community.

TUNIS (Luna; settlement; on SP RR, 6 mi W of Deming). Former community organized around a school and RR section house; now just a RR siding. Name origin unknown.

TUNITCHA MOUNTAINS (San Juan; in SW part of county, in the W Chuska Mountains). Navajo, "large water," for reasons unknown. The name sometimes appears as *Tunicha Mountains.*

TUNNEL HILL, 11,668 ft. (Taos; in the Sangre de Cristo Mountains, 5 mi W of village of Red River). Probably named for a mining tunnel.

TUNQUE PUEBLO (Sandoval). See *Tonque Arroyo.*

TUNSTALL CANYON (Lincoln; heads S of US 70 and runs N to the Rio Ruidoso at Glencoe). The Englishman John H. Tunstall was killed here on February 13, 1878, while going from his ranch on the Rio Felix to Lincoln with a party of friends that included Billy the Kid. It was this killing, among other incidents and tensions, that triggered the Lincoln County War.

TURKEY (general). Wild turkeys are among NM's most common eponymns, occurring in English in 81 place names and appearing in Spanish as *gallina* 45 times; see *Gallina (general).*

TURKEY MOUNTAINS (Mora; 8 mi SW of Wagon Mound). Wild turkeys abound here. Sandstone hills, highest elevation 8,423 ft.

TURLEY (San Juan; settlement; on NM 511, 4 mi NE of Blanco, on the S side of the San Juan River; PO 1906–41, mail to Blanco). The inhabited community of Turley recalls the Turley family. Urban B. Turley was first postmaster here, and J. Turley was an engineer and surveyor who was an early proponent of Navajo Dam. The Navajo name for the locality means "wildcat's house" and refers to a local Hispanic man with a long moustache.

TURN (Valencia). See *Casa Colorada*.

TURNER (Roosevelt; settlement; near Arch, SE of Portales; PO 1908–11, mail to Eiland). Short-lived homesteader community, named for W.A. Turner, an early settler.

TURNER PEAK, 9,453 ft. (Catron; 7 mi NW of Luna, just E of the Arizona border). Named for a homesteader.

TURNERVILLE (Grant; settlement; on NM 152, 5 mi NE of Central; PO 1945–present). A Mr. Wimsatt filed a mining claim here, but it proved disappointing, so he built a store instead, around which a small village grew; it was called *Wimsattville*. In 1928 the Wimsatts moved to Otero County, founding the settlement of Wimsatt (see entry). When the Grant County village established a PO, they called it *Turnerville*, for the Turner family, who also operated a store here and whose members still live in the area. In the 1970s, the community known as Turnerville was dismantled, its site now covered by mine dumps. What remains still is called Wimsattville.

TURQUESA, TURQUOISE CITY (Santa Fe; settlement; 5 mi S of Bonanza, in the center of the Los Cerrillos Mining District; PO as Carbonateville 1879–80, as Turquesa 1880–89, mail to Cerrillos). Although turquoise had been mined in this region since prehistoric times, it was the discovery of gold in the region by Anglo prospectors that led to the founding of *Carbonateville* in 1879 and its naming for the mineral carbonate. A year later the village had 40 houses, and the PO name was changed to *Turquesa*; subsequently the settlement was referred to as *Turquesa* or *Turquoise City*, though newspapers continued to use Carbonateville. By 1884 the town had 500 people, and Gov. Lew Wallace read the proofs of his best-selling novel *Ben Hur* while staying in a Turquesa hotel. But by 1885 mining was declining, Turquesa/Carbonateville with it, and today nothing remains of the former mining camp.

TURQUILLO (Mora; settlement; 11 mi NE of Mora, on NM 434; PO 1910–13, mail to Guadalupita). Inhabited residential cluster, whose Spanish name means "little Turk," for reasons unknown.

TURQUOISE HILL, 6,462 ft. (Santa Fe; just N of Cerrillos). Site of pre-Spanish turquoise mines.

TURQUOISE MOUNTAIN, 5,023 ft. (Grant; in the eastern Little Hatchet Mountains). Small mountain, site of numerous prospects and mines.

TURQUOISE TRAIL (Bernalillo, Sandoval, Santa Fe; coincides with NM 14 from Tijeras to Santa Fe). This historic route was named for turquoise mines in the Cerrillos area.

TURTLE MOUNTAIN (Doña Ana). See *Tortugas*.

TURTLEBACK MOUNTAIN, 6,091 ft. (Sierra; at the N end of the Caballo Mountains, 2 mi SE of Truth or Consequences). Though maps label this northernmost extension of the Caballo Mountains *Turtle Mountain* and call the actual summit *Caballo Cone*, the people in Truth or Consequences know the peak by just one name—Turtleback Mountain—and they willingly point out the rock formation capping the summit that does indeed resemble a turtle.

TUSAS (general). Spanish, "prairie dogs." The name appears 10 times in GNIS, mostly in Rio Arriba County; it appears 9 times as Prairie Dog.

TUSAS (Rio Arriba; settlement; on US 64, 6 mi W of Tres Piedras). Former trading point, located on the *Río Tusas*.

TUSAS MOUNTAINS (Rio Arriba; in NE part of county, extending 50 mi NNW from Ojo Caliente, W of Tres Piedras and E of Tierra Amarilla). The Tusas group, consisting of mountains and a high plateau of forests and alpine meadows, also has been called the *Brazos Mountain Range* and *Cumbres Mountains,* but Tusas Mountains is the name agreed to by the USBGN. Highest elevation, *Grouse Mesa,* 11,403 ft.; *Tusas Mountain,* 10,143 ft., in the S Tusas Mountains, is 3 mi S of US 64. The Cruces Basin Wilderness (see entry) is in the range, just S of the Colorado line.

TWIN BUTTES (McKinley; settlement; just S of NM 118, 6 mi SW of Gallup). Residential community, named for local landforms that are disappearing because of gravel excavation.

TWIN LAKES (McKinley; settlement; 12 mi N of Gallup, on US 666). Active community, origin of name unknown as no lakes are nearby, twin or otherwise. The Navajos' name for the locality means "lines of rock in different directions."

TWIN SISTERS, 8,340 ft. (Grant; 3 mi NE of Pinos Altos). Conspicuous double summit. *Twin Sisters Creek* heads here and flows S into San Vicente Arroyo.

TWINING (Taos; settlement; 15 mi NE of Taos, at the site of the Taos Ski Valley; PO 1902–10, mail to Valdez). When mining declined at the camp of *Amizette* around 1895, the miner and promoter William Frazer (see *Frazer Mountain*) located ore farther E in the Rio Hondo valley. He convinced Albert C. Twining, a New Jersey banker, to invest in the area, but disappointment along with disaster halted mining by 1903. The camp was abandoned; Albert Twining was convicted of embezzling New Jersey bank funds and served a prison term. Frazer was shot to death in a dispute. By 1932, following fires and the wrecker, Twining had vanished. Now snow, not minerals, keeps the locality, if not the name, alive.

TWO GREY HILLS (San Juan; settlement; in SW part of county, 7 mi SW of Newcomb; PO as Crozier 1903–19, mail to Shiprock). About 1887 Joseph R. Wilkin and Henry P. Noel set up a trad-

ing post here; it took the name of twin landforms 1.5 mi NW called *Two Grey Hills,* 6,584 ft. and 6,345 ft. (Curiously, the Navajo name for the locality means "yellow clay standing up," referring to two yellow sandstone crags.) When a PO was established, it took the surname of Capt. Tom Crozier, who in 1858 led troops through here en route to the Chuska Mountains. Other names for the locality have been *Davies* and *Williams,* for reasons unknown, but in 1968 the USBGN accepted Two Grey Hills. The name Two Grey Hills has become associated with a famous style of Navajo rugs.

TYRONE (Grant; settlement; on NM 90, 5 mi SW of Silver City; PO 1906–present). Soon after 1900 a small copper mining camp sprang up in the Burro Mountains; it was named Tyrone by a Mr. Honeyky for his native Tyrone, Ireland. In 1909, the mining magnate Phelps Dodge began buying up claims around Tyrone and the nearby camp of Leopold. Dodge created a new townsite 1.5 mi NE of the original site, keeping the original name. Dodge made his new Tyrone into the world's most luxurious, well-planned mining camp, but he couldn't control the copper market, and in 1921 mining ceased; the town of 7,000 died. In 1969, copper mining resumed, but the old town was sacrified to stripmining, and Tyrone moved once again, a few miles N of the old Tyrone.

TYUONYI (Sandoval; archaeological site; in Cañon de los Frijoles). Once three stories high, the ruins of Tyuonyi Pueblo are still the showcase of Bandelier National Monument. The name is Keresan, but its meaning is unknown, though Adolph Bandelier claimed it meant "treaty place," referring to an ancient boundary pact between the Tewa and Keres Indians. Cochiti Pueblo residents believe their ancestors lived at Tyuonyi. The Tewa name for the pueblo means "old pueblo where the bottoms of the pottery vessels were smoothed thin."

U

ULMORIS (Hidalgo; settlement; on SP RR, 5 mi E of Lordsburg). This is a RR siding that during WW II was a loading point for a POW camp here. People living here still recognize the name, though its origin is unknown.

UÑA DE GATO (general). Spanish, "cat's claw," a colloquialism for the catclaw acacia (*Acacia roemeriana*), whose curved thorns resemble a cat's claws.

UÑA DE GATO (Colfax; settlement; 13 mi SE of Raton, N of US 64-87; PO 1880–82, mail to Raton). Former settlement, named for being on *Uña de Gato Creek,* which rises on Johnson Mesa and flows SW to join Chicarica Creek. See *Uña de Gato (general).*

UÑA DE GATO (Sandoval; settlement; 1 mi S of Hagan, 5 mi E of Placitas). Abandoned locality, named for its location on *Arroyo Uña de Gato,* which heads near Hagan and runs NW. The site at one time also was called *Dover,* for reasons unknown. See *Uña de Gato (general).*

UNDERWOOD LAKE (Catron; 8 mi NW of Luna). Natural lake, named for a settler here.

UNION COUNTY (NE NM; county seat, Clayton). D. Ray Blakely in the *Union County History* explained the name thus: "There are a couple of romantic notions about why this county came to be called Union. One is that the people were 'united' in their desire to form a new local governmental unit. This is true. The second notion is that the new county was created by a 'union' of portions of three existing NM counties: Colfax, Mora, and San Miguel. This is also true. The fact is, of course, that those united to form a new county union could not possibly have agreed upon a 'proper' name; so, Union it was and Union it is." The county was created in 1893.

UNIVERSITY PARK (Doña Ana; settlement; surrounding NMSU, in SE part of Las Cruces; PO as Agricultural College 1905–12, as State College 1912–59, as University Park 1959–present). PO and settlement associated with NM State University, the PO changing its name to match that of the university.

UPHAM (Sierra; RR locality; on AT&SF RR, in SE part of county, at the S end of the Jornada del Muerto). Once a RR depot and stockyards, Upham was named for C.C. Upham, a RR surveyor. Said to be pronounced YOO-fam.

UPPER ANTON CHICO (Guadalupe). See *Anton Chico.*

UPPER COLONIAS (San Miguel). See *Colonias.*

UPPER DILIA (Guadalupe). See *Dilia.*

UPPER FRISCO PLAZA (Catron). See *Reserve.*

UPPER MIMBRES (Grant; settlement; exact location unknown; PO 1877–82, mail to Santa Rita). Abandoned community, associated with the Mimbres River. The locality also was called *Thompsons* and appeared as such on an 1887 map. Lee Thompson had a store and orchard here and was postmaster.

UPPER MORA (Mora; settlement; in vicinity of Mora; PO 1868). Part of Mora.

UPPER PEÑASCO (Otero). See *Mayhill.*

UPPER SAN FRANCISCO PLAZA (Catron). See *Reserve.*

UPTON (Roosevelt; settlement; 20 mi W of Portales; PO 1907–30, mail to Elida). W.G. Upton was an early settler in this community, now abandoned.

URRACA (general). Spanish, "magpie."

URRACA (Colfax; settlement; on NM 21 NW of Springer). Former community, likely named for its proximity to *Urraca Creek*—see *Urraca (general)*—which heads in the Cimarron Range and flows SE S of Philmont Scout Ranch to join Rayado Creek N of Miami. *Urraca Mesa* is 3 mi NW of Rayado.

URTON (Roosevelt). see *Kenna.*

URTON LAKE (De Baca; 25 mi S of Fort Sumner). Large intermittent lake, named for W.G. Urton, who came to NM in 1884 from Missouri with his brother, George. W.G. was foreman of the old Bar V Ranch, which covered this area then. See *Kenna.*

US HILL (Taos; on NM 518 between Talpa and NM 75). It's said the tortuous curves of this winding grade resemble the letters U S, but more likely the name comes from the USFS having completed the road. US Hill also was the name of the old military road farther W between Taos and Embudo. This is said to have been named in January 1847 when US Army troops marched N from Santa Fe to put down the Taos Rebellion; a snowstorm caught them here and halted their advance.

UTE (general). As with many Native American peoples, the name by which the Ute Indians are popularly known is not the name by which they call themselves; *Ute,* which earlier had been transliterated *Eutaw* and *Yutah,* comes from a word from another Indian group meaning "dwellers in the tops of mountains," a reference to Ute territory being among the high peaks of the Rocky Mountains; the Ute Indians call themselves *Nunt'z,* "the people." Originally a Plains tribe, the Utes were driven by other tribes into the S-central Rocky Mountains; their trading and hunting territory extended from Wyoming to Taos in northern NM. Like many other nomadic peoples, their economy included raiding agricultural settlements, such as those in NM, and this led to frequent conflict between them and the Pueblo Indians, the Span-

ish, and the Anglos of northern NM. The Utes also were traditional enemies of the Navajos. Though only a part of their reservation, the *Ute Mountain Indian Reservation* (see entry), located NW of Farmington, is in NM, 19 places in the state bearing their name recall their once more extensive habitation here (GNIS).

UTE MOUNTAIN INDIAN RESERVATION (San Juan; begins 6 mi NW of Farmington and extends N into Colorado and W to adjoin the Navajo Indian Reservation).

UTE CREEK (Colfax; settlement). See *Ute Park.*

UTE CREEK (Colfax, Harding, Union; rises in SE Colfax County and flows SE into Union and then Harding Counties to the Canadian River at Ute Lake). Appears as *Alamo Creek* on some old maps. The drainage once was within the territory of the Ute Indians; see *Ute (general).*

UTE LAKE STATE PARK (Quay; on the Canadian River, just W of Logan). Manmade lake named for *Ute Creek* (see entry), a major tributary of the Canadian that enters the river just N of the lake.

UTE MOUNTAIN, 10,093 ft. (Taos; 9 mi SW of Costilla). Huge extinct volcano, named for the Indians who once lived here; see *Ute (general).* The name often appears as *Ute Peak.*

UTE PARK (Colfax; settlement; in Cimarron Canyon on US 64, 10 mi E of Eagle Nest; PO as Ute Creek 1868–74, 1876–95 mail to Baldy, as Ute Park 1908–present). This was within Ute Indian territory—see *Ute (general)*—and Utes once lived here, to be near the government Indian agency at Cimarron that provided supplies. Anglo settlers moved in about 1867 and named the settlement *Ute Creek,* for its location at the confluence of Ute Creek and the Cimarron River. Later the name became Ute Park, which the inhabited community retains today.

V

VACA (general). See *Cow (general)*.

VADITO (Taos; settlement; on NM 75, 2 mi E of Picuris Pueblo). Spanish, "little ford," doubtless because of a crossing here of Embudo Creek, which flows by this inhabited village.

VADO (Doña Ana; settlement; on NM 478 15 mi SE of Las Cruces; PO as Herron 1886–88, as Earlham 1888–1911, as Vado 1911, as Center Valley 1913–19, as Vado 1927–67, mail to rural La Mesa branch). Vado, Spanish, "ford," likely for a crossing of the Rio Grande to the W, probably is the orignal Spanish name of this inhabited Hispanic farming community. By the end of the Civil War, the population consisted of Hispanics and a few African-Americans mustered out of the Army. When a PO was established here, it was first called *Herron,* for Samuel Herron and his family, who opened a broom factory here. The PO returned briefly to Vado, but it soon changed its name again, to *Earlham,* for the Indiana town from which some Quaker residents had come, but then a postmaster changed the name yet again, to *Center Valley,* possibly because of Vado's location in the central part of the Lower Mesilla Valley, though the portion of Doña Ana County that includes the village today is called *South Valley.* Still later, the RR, at the suggestion of the prominent Las Cruces attorney, W.A. Sutherland, changed the name yet again, back to Vado. In 1920, Francis and Ella Boyer, along with numerous other African-American residents from the failing community of Blackdom (see entry) moved here, and for many years Vado was NM's only predominantly African-American community.

VALDEZ (Taos; settlement; N of Taos, on NM 230, 6 mi E of NM 522; PO 1895– present). Settled between 1750 and 1800, Valdez takes its name from the descendants of José Luis Valdéz, a native of Mexico City, who came to NM with the reconquest of 1692 and settled at Santa Cruz. This village's full name is *San Antonio de Valdez,* for the Catholic chapel here.

VALEDON (Hidalgo; settlement; 3 mi SW of Lordsburg; PO 1917–32, mail to Lordsburg). The mining camp of Valedon grew up around some mining claims located in 1885. Around 1913 the SP RR put a spur line to the camp, and by 1926 Valedon, a company town, had 2,000 residents. Phelps Dodge Corp. bought the property in 1931 and a year later discontinued the mining here; residents were ordered to leave, and many of the buildings were immediately razed or moved; little remains today. The name's origin is unknown.

VALENCIA (Valencia; settlement; on NM 47 and 263, 14 mi N of Belen, 2 mi E of Los Lunas; PO 1884 intermittently 1939, mail to Los Lunas). Notes from the Chamuscado-Rodríguez expedition of 1580 indicate that the site of present Valencia had been occupied previously by a Tiwa pueblo whose name the Spaniards recorded as *Caxtole.* Blas Valencia, 20 years old, with a round face and light beard, entered NM in 1598 as a soldier with Oñate, and as early as 1660 Blas Valencia's grandson, Juan de Valencia, had an *hacienda* here. He and some of his family may have returned to NM with Vargas in 1692, and Vargas in his records was the first to mention Valencia as a place name. Valencia as a community had two plazas, about 2 mi apart: Plaza Number 1, the largest, was called Valencia, while Plaza Number 2 was called *Aragontown,* because Aragón was the dominant family there. Valencia at one time was the seat of the county and gave the county its name.

VALENCIA COUNTY (central NM, along the Rio Grande; county seat, Los Lunas). Created by the Republic of Mexico in 1844, this was named for the village of *Valencia* (see entry), its first county seat. Later the county seat moved to Tome, then in 1876, through the influence of the powerful Luna family, to Los Lunas.

VALLADOLID (Taos). See *Taos Pueblo*.

VALLE ESCONDIDO (Taos; settlement; just S of US 64, 12 mi E of Taos). Spanish, "hidden valley," inhabited residential development, named for its location in a secluded valley.

VALLE GRANDE (Sandoval; in the Jemez Mountains, immediately N of NM 4, SW of Los Alamos). This spectacular 176-sq-mi grassy valley, 16 mi across, in the caldera of an ancient volcano, ringed by mountains, deserves its Spanish name, "big valley." The East Fork of the Jemez River heads here with *Valle Grande Creek*.

VALLE VIDAL (Colfax, Taos; in the Sangre de Cristo Mountains, straddling the Colfax-Taos line). *Valle Vidal* can be translated from the Spanish to mean "valley of abundant life," appropriate because this unit of the Carson NF is known for being excellent wildlife habitat. Vidal also is a fairly common Spanish surname, though less so in NM than elsewhere. Which meaning resulted in this place name is unknown.

VALLECITO MOUNTAIN, 12,643 ft. (Taos; in the Sangre de Cristo Mountains, 6 mi E of Valdez). Spanish, "little valley."

VALLECITOS (Rio Arriba; settlement; on NM 111, 16 mi N of Ojo Caliente; PO 1886–present). Founded in 1776 and named either for "little valleys" nearby or more likely for the *Río Vallecitos* (see entry), which flows through here.

VALLECITOS (Sandoval). See *Ponderosa*.

VALLECITOS CREEK (Sandoval; rises in Paliza Canyon in the SW Jemez Mountains and flows SW through the village of Vallecitos to the Jemez River N of Jemez Pueblo). Spanish, "little valleys."

VALLECITOS DE LOS INDIOS (Sandoval; settlement; just S of NM 4, 8 mi E of La Cueva). Early Spanish explorers found an inhabited Indian pueblo here, later abandoned, and they called locality "little valleys of the Indians." In the 20th century a sawmill was here, but it moved to what is now Ponderosa (see entry). Most recently, a residential development has been built, and it bears the name given by the developer, *Sierra de los Pinos*, "mountains of the pines," which is gradually replacing the old name Vallecitos de los Indios.

VALLEY (Union; settlement; on NM 456, 2 mi from the Colorado line, on Dry Cimarron River; PO as Exter 1890–1903, as Valley 1903–26, mail to Folsom). Settled in 1879 and named for its location, Valley was never much more than a store and a PO, and it's even less now. The PO originally was called *Exter*, for reasons unknown.

VALLEY OF FIRES RECREATION AREA (Lincoln; on US 380, 3 mi W of Carrizozo). About 1,500 to 2,000 years ago, molten lava issued from a vent now called Little Black Peak (see entry) and flowed 44 mi SW through this valley. Known as the *Carrizozo Malpais*, this is one of the youngest and best preserved lava fields in the continental US. The *Valley of Fires State Park* was established in 1966; the site now is administered by the BLM.

VALLEY RANCH (San Miguel; settlement; 1 mi N of Pecos; PO 1908–49, mail to Pecos). Former locality.

VALLEY VIEW (Roosevelt; settlement; 14 mi S of Elida; PO as Wooten 1909–11, as Valley View 1911–18, mail to Elida). This abandoned homesteader community originally was named *Wooten*, for its first postmaster, Thomas J. Wooten, but it later changed its name to describe its location.

VALMONT (Otero; settlement; on US 54, 10 mi S of Alamogordo; PO as Camp 1908–1910, as Shamrock 1910–1916, as Valmont 1916–1921, mail to Alamogordo). This trading point and settlement has had many names. First it was called *Dog Town*, probably for Dog Canyon just to the E but possibly for local prairie dogs. Then it became *Camp City,* or simply *Camp,* for a rancher by that name. Around 1910, it became *Shamrock,* for reasons unknown, and finally in 1915 the community acquired its present name, *Valmont,* combining the words for "valley" and "mountain," aptly describing its location in the Tularosa Valley near the Sacramento Mountains. During its heyday, Valmont about about 40 residents, a school, and a PO, but now it's just a locality on the RR line.

VALMORA (Mora; settlement; on NM 97 and 446, 4 mi NE of Watrous; PO 1916–present). In 1916 the salubrious NM climate led to an extensive tuberculosis sanatorium—village being established here; it was named for its location in the valley of the Mora River. Though the hospital and patients' cabins remain, the sanatorium has closed.

VALVERDE (Socorro; settlement; 29 mi S of Socorro, at the N end of the Jornada del Muerto; PO as Clyde 1897–1938, mail to San Marcial). Though Valverde can be translated as "green valley," the name here is said to refer to Capt. Don Antonio Valverde y Cosío, acting governor of NM from 1717 to 1722. In 1805 a surgeon mentioned vaccinating four children at *el Paraje de Balberde, paraje* referring to a campground. By 1822 Valverde was being described as a new settlement, but Navajo raids soon caused its abandonment. It was resettled in the 1850s with the establishment of Fort Conrad (see entry), and in 1862 Confederate forces narrowly defeated Union troops in battle here. The RR arrival in 1881 at nearby San Marcial stimulated Valverde, and the village had a PO, named *Clyde,* for the Clyde family, pioneer homesteaders in the area. But while Valverde survived many floods, the disastrous deluge of 1929 spelled its doom, and today the village is abandoned.

VAN BREMMER CREEK (Colfax; heads in Van Bremmer Park NE of Cimarron and flows SE to join the Vermejo River 10 mi W of Maxwell). This name's origin is obscure. It appears as *Ken Brimmer*

Creek on an 1870 map, and it has appeared as *Van Brimmer Creek,* but the 1889 Surveyor General and Maxwell Land Grant Map labeled it Van Bremmer Creek. Van Bremmer's identity is unknown. *Van Bremmer Park* is at the head of Van Bremmer Creek, 6 mi E of Costilla Peak.

VAN DIEST PEAK, 11,223 ft. (Taos; in the Sangre de Cristo Mountains, NE of the village of Red River). E.C. Van Diest was manager of the Costilla Grant, as well as manager of the US Freehold and Emigration Co. He also was active in the development of the mining camp of La Belle (see entry).

VAN HOUTEN (Colfax; settlement; 6 mi W of US 64 and 11 mi SW of Raton; PO 1902–52, mail to Raton). *Willow* was the original name of this coal-mining camp, named for the Willow Coal Mine here. In 1902 the St. Louis, Rocky Mountain, and Pacific Co. revived mining here and changed the name to Van Houten, for Jan Van Houten, the company's president who also was the American representative of the Dutch syndicate that had purchased the Maxwell Land Grant. When mining peaked around 1915, the community of Van Houten had 1,500 residents, but it declined from there, and in 1954 mining ceased. Today Van Houten has vanished.

VAN PATTENS (Doña Ana). See *Dripping Springs.*

VANADIUM (Grant; settlement; on NM 356, 1.5 mi N of Bayard; PO 1912–present). Inhabited community, named for deposits here of the mineral vanadium, used in alloying steel.

VANCE (Union; settlement; in SE part of county, near Sedan; PO 1908–20, mail to Sedan). Vance, now abandoned, was never really a settlement, just a PO in the farmhouse of Willis R. Vance.

VANDER WAGEN (McKinley; 18 mi S of Gallup, on NM 602; PO 1951–present). In 1896 the Christian Reformed Church sent two Dutch missionaries to this area; one, Andrew VanderWagen (sometimes spelled Vanderwagen), settled first at Fort Defiance, then at Zuni, where his wife, Effa VanderWagen, a trained nurse, helped the Indians deal with a smallpox epidemic. Eventually the VanderWagens abandoned their missionary efforts but remained in the area as traders serving the Indians they had grown to like. In succeeding years, the couple's sons and other family members operated trading posts at Zuni and in Navajo country; their descendants still live in the area. One of the stores was at a place called *White Water,* for nearby *White Water Creek;* the name White Water survives on many maps, but when a PO was established the name adopted was Vanderwagen. There seems to be no local consensus as to the correct form of the name—common variants are *Vanderwagen, Vander Wagen,* and *VanderWagen;* the USBGN in 1975 chose Vander Wagen as the accepted form.

VANDORITOS (Mora). See *Halls Peak.*

VAQUEROS (Rio Arriba; settlement; in NW part of county, exact location unknown; PO 1900–22, mail to Dulce). Spanish, "cowboys." Abandoned settlement, about which little is known, including the origin of its name, but it likely is derived from *Vaqueros Canyon,* a tributary of La Jara Creek, E of Gobernador.

VARIADERO (San Miguel; settlement; on Conchas River and NM 104; PO as Variadero 1907 intermittently to 1923, mail to Trementina; PO as Variadero 1900 intermittently to 1919, as Garita 1919–present). Jesús Angel of Bernal founded this community about 1872. The name is a local coinage from the Spanish, *variar,* "to vary, to change," referring here to frequent changes in the course of the Conchas River. The *Garita* PO currently is at Variadero; the Spanish *garita* has been translated variously as "lookout," "watchtower," "jail," and "sentry box or entrance to a town" but perhaps means simply "government building." Though the village at Variadero is all but gone, the name still is recognized and used.

VARNEY (Torrance; settlement; on SP RR, 4 mi NE of Corona; PO 1914–18, mail to Corona). This abandoned RR locality was named about 1910 for the bookkeeper of the Corona Trading Co.

VAUD (Eddy). See *Loving.*

VAUGHN (Guadalupe; settlement; at the junction of US 54, 60 and 285 and SP RR and AT&SF RR; PO 1907–present). Transportation has nurtured Vaughn throughout its history. It originally was a site on the Stinson cattle trail from Texas to the Estancia Valley, pioneered by Jim Stinson in 1882. Later it was given a huge boost—and its name—when the EP&RI RR joined the AT&SF RR; it was named for Maj. G.W. Vaughn, a civil engineer for the AT&SF RR. At that time the community consisted of two closely related settlements, *East Vaughn* and *West Vaughn,* that eventually fused to create the present town.

VAUR (Harding). See *Leon.*

VEDA (Union; settlement; in N central part of county, on Corrumpa Creek; PO 1890–1907, mail to Corrumpa). Abandoned community, name origin unknown.

VEGA (general). Spanish, "meadow," derived from the Arabic *betha,* "pleasant meadow or valley." Diminutive, *veguita.* Vega and variants such as *vegoso* appears 34 times in NM (GNIS).

VEGA BLANCA (Santa Fe; RR locality; S of Santa Fe). Spanish, "white meadow." Vega Blanca was a station located N of Kennedy on the long-abandoned NMC RR; it is said to have been named for the ranch home near Hillsboro of Willard Hopewell (see *Willard*), promoter of the RR.

VEGUITA (Socorro; settlement; on the E side of the Rio Grande, on NM 304, 12 mi SE of Belen; PO as Moorad 1914–17, as Veguita 1917–present). The PO here originally was called *Moorad,* for reasons unknown, but Veguita, Spanish "little meadow," likely is the original name of this farming community and is the name that has survived. The community also has been known by the name of the patron saint of its Catholic church, *San Juan,* though it's possible that Veguita and San Juan at one time were separate settlements.

VELARDE (Rio Arriba; settlement; on NM 68, 14 mi NE of Española; PO 1885–present). Juan Antonio Pérez

Velarde was a Spaniard who by 1725 had settled at Guadalupe del Paso, from whence his descendants migrated into northern NM. In 1875 one Matías Velarde founded this farming community on the Rio Grande. It originally was called *La Jolla,* a misspelling of the Spanish *La Joya,* "the basin." This possibly translated the Tewa name for the locality, which means "basin of the chico bush." But when a PO was established, with David Velarde its first postmaster, the community took the Velarde family name.

VENADO PEAK, 12,734 ft. (Taos; in the N Sangre de Cristo Mountains, NE of Questa). Spanish, "deer."

VENTANES (San Miguel). See *Trujillo.*

VENTURA, VENTERO (Taos; settlement; in N part of county, 7 mi E of Costilla). Though this appears as *Ventura,* Spanish, "luck, chance, happiness," on some maps, it likely is derived from *Ventero,* "innkeeper."

VENUS (Santa Fe; settlement; 10 mi NW of Moriarty; PO 1909–28, mail to Moriarty). Abandoned trading point on the NMC RR, named for the Venus Mercantile Co., a general store here.

VERA CRUZ (Lincoln; settlement; 10 mi SE of Carrizozo, 1.5 N of US 380; PO 1881–83, mail to Nogal). In 1880 a small gold-mining camp sprang up on the W side of the Tucson Mountains, most of its residents miners working at the Vera Cruz Mine. But the ore deposits proved to be of low grade, the camp faded, and today only the dump of the Vera Cruz Mine remains, high on the slope of *Vera Cruz Mountain,* 7,801 ft. The Tucson Mountains sometimes are called the *Vera Cruz Mountains.*

VERMEJO (general). Spanish, "brown, auburn."

VERMEJO (Colfax; settlement; on the Vermejo River, about 1 mi N of its junction with US 64; PO as Vermejo 1874–82, as Cimilorio 1882–98). This locality began as a stop on the Barlow-Sanderson stage route, when it was called *Vermejo Swing Station.* Later the PO here changed its name to *Cimilorio,* for reasons unknown but likely manu-

factured from the name Cimarron.

VERMEJO PARK (Colfax; settlement; in NW part of county, near the headwaters of the Vermejo River; PO as Vermejo 1902–07, as Vermejo Park, 1907–66, mail to Weston, CO). Vermejo Park, named for the river (see entry) was the center of the old Bartlett Estate, a 350,000-acre ranch with palatial resort homes.

VERMEJO PEAK, 11,610 ft. (Colfax, Taos; in the Sangre de Cristo Mountains, on the Colfax-Taos line, 4 mi N of Little Costilla Peak). Likely named for the *Vermejo River* (see entry), whose headwaters are to the E.

VERMEJO RIVER (Colfax; rises in Colorado and flows SE to join the Canadian River S of Maxwell). Spanish, "brown, auburn." The earliest settlers in NE NM made their homes along the Vermejo River.

VERNON (Colfax; settlement; on the SP RR, N of Abbott; PO 1911–17, mail to Taylor Springs). Because the nearby community of Abbott had no RR loading facilities, that role fell to this community, where a stockyard was built and still remains. Name origin unknown.

VERY LARGE ARRAY (Socorro; on the Plains of San Agustin, between Datil and Magdalena). Operated by the National Radio Astronomy Observatory and funded by the National Science Foundation, the Very Large Array (VLA) is the world's largest radio telescope, consisting of 27 2.5-ton movable antennas arranged—hence the name—to receive radio signals from space.

VETEADO MOUNTAIN, 8,525 ft. (Catron; 3 mi S of NM 117, at the S end of El Malpais lava flow). Spanish, "striped, veined."

VICKS PEAK, 10,252 ft. (Socorro; in the San Mateo Mountains, 4 mi S of San Mateo Peak). The San Mateo Mountains were used for hunting and refuge by the Apaches, particularly the chief Victorio. See *Victorio (general).*

VICTOR (Valencia; settlement; in S part of county, on E side of the Rio Grande; PO 1910–14, mail to Belen). Victor probably was less an actual settlement than a short-lived postal locality. It was located just across from the Casa Colorada school, 0.5 mi S of Casa Colorada. The origin of the name Victor is unknown.

VICTORIA (Doña Ana). See *La Mesa.*

VICTORIO (general). Victorio was a Mimbreño Apache leader whose territory included much of S and SW NM. Though less well known among Europeans than Geronimo or Cochise, he is at least as highly regarded among Apaches. He was born around 1820, and in 1879, defying orders to relocate to the despised San Carlos Apache Reservation in Arizona, Victorio fled the reservation at Ojo Caliente and led his warriors on a two-year reign of terror before he was killed by Mexican troops in Mexico. It has been said his Spanish name, Victorio, is a corruption of his Apache name, which has been transliterated as *Beduiat.* Numerous places in NM recall his presence here.

VICTORIO MOUNTAINS (Luna; just S of I-10, 5 mi E of Hidalgo County line). Small range, highest elevation *Cone Summit,* 5,382 ft. A small mining camp named *Victorio* existed here in the 1880s. See *Victorio (general);* see also *Gage.*

VICTORIO PARK (Sierra; in the eastern Black Range, N of Kingston, N of Las Animas Creek). The Apache leader Victorio—(see *Victorio (general)*—had a camp at this relatively level clearing that once was watered by a spring. Nearby are *Victorio Park Mountain,* 8,957 ft., and *Victorio Park Canyon,* as well as Massacre Canyon (see entry), where Victorio ambushed Army troops. For many years the park was incorrectly labelled *Victoria Park* on maps until rangers with the Black Range Ranger District of the Gila NF in 1993 asked the USBGN to change it. Bob Julyan, chairman of the NMGNC, visited the area and discovered that no local people used the Victoria form—indeed, most simply called the park *Vicks Park*—so the NMGNC concurred with Black Range rangers and voted to recommend changing the name, which the USBGN did in 1994.

VICTORIO PEAK, 5,525 ft. (Doña Ana; in the W San Andres Mountains). Small isolated peak, site of a persistent but likely fraudulent treasure legend.

VICTORY (Curry; settlement; at Cannon Air Force Base; PO 1943–47). A rural PO rather than a settlement, Victory probably was named for the war effort at the time of its establishment.

VIGIL (general). Francisco Montes Vigil and his wife, María Jiménez de Ancizo, arrived in Santa Fe as early as 1695; in 1710 he received a land grant at Alameda. Since then, the Vigils' descendants have spread throughout NM, giving their name to 17 places (GNIS).

VIGIL (Harding). See *Bueyeros.*

VIGIL (Quay; settlement; 14 mi W of Tucumcari; PO 1882, mail to Fort Bascomb). Abandoned settlement, named for the Vigil family.

VILLANUEVA (San Miguel; settlement; on NM 3, 12 mi S of I-25, on the E bank of the Pecos River; PO 1890–present). Mariano Baros and José Felipe Madrid in 1808 founded this community on a bluff overlooking the Pecos River. They called their village *La Cuesta,* "the hill, slope," and this easily defended location was important because the village was intended to be an outpost guarding neighboring farming communities against attacks by Plains Indians. In 1890, when a PO was established, the villagers petitioned that it be called Villanueva, for the Villanueva family whose members still live here.

VILLANUEVA STATE PARK (San Miguel; 1 mi E of the village of Villanueva). Created in 1967, this scenic state park straddles the Pecos River, in a narrow canyon of red and yellow sandstone cliffs dotted with caves.

VIRDEN (Hidalgo; settlement; on NM 92 and the Gila River, 30 mi NW of Lordsburg). When the NM Mining Co. in 1870 created the town of Ralston (see *Shakespeare*), the promoters needed more water for their ambitions, so they located a site on the Gila River; they called the area the *Virginia Mining District* and named the resulting town *Richmond,* for Virginia's capital. Richmond became an Hispanic settlement and trading center for area ranchers, with the Gila Ranch Co. a large landowner. In 1912, when Mormons immigrating from Mexico arrived seeking new homes, they negotiated with the Gila Ranch Co. for local land, and Earnest W. Virden, the company's president, sold them the valley for $50,000—$5,000 down and $500 a year; in 1916 the community's name was changed to honor him. About 200 persons, most of them descendants of the Mormon immigrants, live here.

VIRGIN MESA, 8,365 ft. (Sandoval; in the SW foothills of the Jemez Mountains, W of Jemez Springs). This long finger-mesa likely takes its name from *Mesa de Guadalupe* (see entry), an outlier of Virgin Mesa at its S end. Both names refer to the Virgin of Guadalupe; see *Guadalupe (general).*

VIRGINIA CITY (Colfax; settlement; on Willow Creek, 3 mi NE of Eagle Nest; PO as Virginia 1868–69). This short-lived mining camp was born during the same gold fever that soon spawned Elizabethtown and Baldy (see entries). The camp was within the Maxwell Land Grant, so to Lucien B. Maxwell fell the privilege of naming it; he named it for his daughter, Virginia. By calling the hastily and crudely constructed scatter of shanties a "City," Maxwell clearly had high hopes for the camp, but before these could be realized, Virginia City was overshadowed by more exciting prospects at Elizabethtown, and today Virginia City is only mine dumps and a cemetery.

VIRSYLVIA (Taos). See *Sunshine Valley.*

VIRSYLVIA PEAK, 12,594 ft. (Taos; in the Sangre de Cristo Mountains, in the Latir Peak complex, NE of Questa). Name origin unknown.

VOCANT (Chaves; settlement; S of Roswell, W of Hagerman; PO 1908–13, mail to Hagerman). Vocant was not really a settlement but rather a rural PO; among the people it served were the residents of Blackdom (see entry), 4 mi to the E. Name origin unknown.

VOLCANO (Hidalgo; settlement; in W part of county, 6 mi N of Steins on I-10). A mining camp sprouted here around 1887 and soon had 2 general stores, 7 saloons, a drug store, and numerous other shops. *Volcano Draw* is a reminder of the vanished camp.

VOLCANO (Taos; settlement; N of Tres Piedras, opposite San Antonio Mountain; PO 1922–23, mail to Skarda). Volcano, likely named for its association with volcanic San Antonio Mountain to the W, was never a village but rather a station and PO on the old D&RG RR, the "Chili Line." When the RR died, the community, like the volcano for which it was named, became extinct.

VULCAN, 6,033 ft. (Bernalillo; on Albuquerque's West Mesa). Vulcan, the largest of the extinct volcanoes along the crest of the mesa W of Albuquerque, was named appropriately for the Roman god of fire. The volcano once was known as *J* cone because in 1951 St. Josephs College students painted a large white J on its side. The other volcanoes are named *Butte, Bond, Cinder, Black,* and *JA.* All were formed approximately 190,000 years ago.

WAGNER (Torrance; settlement; exact location unknown; PO 1908, mail to Mountainair). Ephemeral community, name origin unknown.

WAGON MOUND (Mora; settlement; on I-25 and NM 120, 25 mi SW of Springer; PO as Pinkerton 1881–82, as Wagon Mound 1882–present). The community now known as Wagon Mound began as a locality on the Santa Fe Trail; after 1836 it was a Mexican customs post. *Los Cuernos,* "the horns," has been mentioned as an early name, possibly because of association with *Las Mesas del Canjelon,* "mesas of the deer antler," to the E. The first settlement here was called *Santa Clara,* because of association with *Santa Clara Spring,* an important water source, on *Santa Clara Hill* just to the NW; several buildings in Wagon Mound still preserve the Santa Clara name; see *Santa Clara (general).* When a PO was established, it briefly was called *Pinkerton,* because detectives with the Pinkerton detective agency set up shop here guarding RR equipment, but the name soon was changed to *Wagon Mound,* for the butte just to the E strongly resembling a covered wagon. How long this name had been in use is unknown, but it likely dates from the early days of the Santa Fe Trail.

WAGON WHEEL (Torrance; 60 mi E of Albuquerque, on N side of I-40). Small service community.

WAITE PHILLIPS MOUNTAIN, 11,711 ft. (Colfax; in the Cimarron Range, in the W part of Philmont Scout Ranch, SW of Comanche Creek). This peak was known as *Clear Creek Mountain* prior to 1960 when Arthur A. Schuck renamed it for Waite Phillips, with whom Schuck had previously worked closely. Phillips was the philanthropist responsible for donating to the Boy Scouts the property that became Philmont Scout Ranch (see entry). He had been born on a farm in Iowa in 1883, developed a love of nature, studied business, moved to Oklahoma, got involved in the oil industry, became extremely wealthy, and eventually acquired Philmont. Phillips died in 1964.

WALDO (Santa Fe; settlement; on AT&SF RR, 2 mi NW of Cerrillos; PO 1900–36, mail to Cerrillos). Born in the 1890s, Waldo owed its existence to mining at Cerrillos and Madrid; from 1918 to 1924 a zinc oxide plant was here. The name recalls Henry L. Waldo, who came to Santa Fe from Missouri in 1862 and in 1881 was appointed chief justice of the territorial supreme court. An apocryphal story says that Judge Waldo and Atty. Ralph E. Twitchell were passing by on a train when odor from stockpens here assaulted them. Waldo looked out and saw "Twitchell" on a sign and teased his friend, saying, "I can't think of a more appropriate name for a bull-shipping point." But Twitchell had the last laugh; he used his political influence to change the name to Waldo. Now nothing but foundations remains.

WALKER AIR FORCE BASE (Chaves; at Roswell). Established in 1942, this was first called the *Roswell Army Flying School,* then the *Roswell Army Airfield* and the *Roswell Air Field* before finally being renamed Walker Air Force Base in 1948, to honor Brig. Gen. Kenneth N. Walker, killed in the air battle for New Guinea. The base closed in 1967; the site now is occupied by the *Roswell Industrial Air Center.*

WALL LAKE (Catron; in SE part of county). Lloyd Wall and property owner Art Fowler were good friends, and when the state built the dam creating the lake on property owned by Fowler, he requested that they name it for Wall.

WALLACE (Sandoval). See *Domingo*.

WALLACE (San Juan; settlement; location unknown; PO 1879–81). Ephemeral postal locality, name origin unknown.

WALNUT (general). This name refers to the Arizona walnut (*Juglans major*), an infrequent species found in canyons and along streams. Walnut appears in 26 NM place names; in its Spanish form *nogal* the word appears in 21 names (GNIS).

WALNUT WELLS (Hidalgo; settlement; on the E side of the Alamo Hueco Mountains; PO 1913–19, mail to Hachita). This was established around 1858, perhaps as a stage stop; the name probably refers to local walnut trees; see *Walnut (general)*. The Diamond A Cattle Co. owned the well here.

MOUNT WALTER, 13,133 ft. (Taos; in the Sangre de Cristo Mountains, on the N shoulder of Wheeler Peak). Harold D. Walter was a Santa Fe accountant, but his avocations were mountaineering and photography. Prior to 1948 it was widely accepted in NM that the Truchas Peaks were the state's highest summits, but that year Walter borrowed elevation-measuring equipment and determined that Wheeler Peak was higher; his observations were later confirmed. Knowing that the knob N of Wheeler was unnamed, Walter began calling it Mount Walter, for himself, but the name could not become official until after his death in 1958. A plaque on the mountain commemorates Walter, "who loved these mountains."

WANETTE (Union; settlement; NW of Clayton; PO 1910–16, mail to Seneca). A Doctor Carpenter, owner of a general store here, combined the name of his daugther, Nette, with that of a freighter, Walter Ciser, to create this name. Wanette has long vanished, but the name is still recognized and used.

WARM SPRINGS APACHE RESERVATION (Socorro; at Ojo Caliente on the Alamosa River, NW of Truth or Consequences). In 1875–76 this was home for 1,500–2,000 Apaches, but by 1877 most of the Indians had decamped for their traditional tribal homelands. In spring

1877 Geronimo was captured at the Ojo Caliente military installation here and taken to Arizona in chains, but he escaped three weeks later.

WARREN (Lea). See *Gladiola*.

MOUNT WASHINGTON, 7,116 ft. (Bernalillo; in the W Manzano Mountains, N of the Isleta Indian Reservation). Specific origin of name unknown.

WASHINGTON PASS (San Juan). See *Narbona Pass*.

WATER CANYON (Socorro; settlement; in the NE foothills of the Magdalena Mountains; PO 1887 intermittently to 1929, mail to Magdalena). This was a railhead and water station on the AT&SF RR located on the flats and serving mines in *Water Canyon* to the S, for which it was named. The name appeared variously as *Watercañon, Water Cañon,* and *Water Canyon.*

WATERFLOW (San Juan; settlement; on US 64, 13 mi W of Farmington; PO 1900–present). This community is said to have had in its early days the nickname *Kentucky Mesa,* for a group of settlers from Kentucky who homesteaded here; a local school was named Kentucky Mesa. But when a more formal name was needed, as for a PO, Waterflow was chosen, because the waters of three rivers—the San Juan, the Animas, and the La Plata—flow through the valley here. The Navajo name for the locality means "red devil" or "red ghost" and refers to Walter Stallings, a former trader here.

WATERLOO (Luna; settlement; 1 mi W of NM 11, 10 mi NW of Columbus; PO 1911–22, mail to Deming). This community, now all but abandoned, was established about 1910, but it faded during the Depression. The name doubtless refers to the battle in which Wellington defeated Napoleon, but why it was applied here is unknown.

WATROUS (Mora; settlement; 20 NE of Las Vegas, on I-25; PO as La Junta 1868–79, as Watrous 1879–present). The original name for this site was *La Junta de los Ríos Mora y Sapelló,* "the confluence of the rivers Mora and Sapello," and in 1843 several persons successfully petitioned for a land grant here. Early travelers on the Santa Fe Trail knew this locality simply as *La Junta.* In 1879, however, when the AT&SF RR pushed its line through here, the RR named the station Watrous, for Samuel B. Watrous, who had come to NM from Vermont in 1835 and become an influential merchant, rancher, and landowner; he had donated land for a RR right-of-way. When Mr. Watrous asked why the name La Junta was not chosen, RR officials told him it duplicated the name of a settlement in Colorado. Watrous died in 1886, but the community still bears his name. See also *Tiptonville.*

WEAVER (McKinley; settlement; N of Gallup). This was a little mining camp of the Gallup American Coal Co. It was named for Wiley Weaver, a mine official. The camp has vanished.

WEBER (Mora; settlement; on the N bank of the Mora River, between Mora and Loma Parda; PO 1898–1905, mail to La Cueva). George Adlai Feather said that in 1851 a soldier named Frank Weber, of German ancestry, settled here and later was joined by other Germans in forming a small community, now abandoned.

WEBER CITY (Curry; settlement; on NM 268, 15 mi N of Melrose). According to at least some old-timers, an early radio show mentioned a community named Weber in which there was "very little business," and as there was very little business here either, this place was called Weber too, with "City" added as a further ironic touch. A grocery—gas station survive here, and the name survives in the Weber City telephone district.

WEBSTER LAKE (Colfax; on Philmont Scout Ranch, on Cimarroncito Creek, 4 mi SW of Cimarron). George H. Webster Jr. was a rancher, politician, and promoter among whose many projects was irrigation in this area, and in 1908 he began construction on the dam creating this lake. He called it simply *Reservoir No. 1,* but now it appropriately bears his name.

WEDDING CAKE BUTTE (Union; N of US 64, 12 mi W of the Oklahoma line). A rock formation composed of varicolored strata topped by a rounded dome, resembling a wedding cake.

WEED (Otero; settlement; on NM 24, 10 mi S of Mayhill, on the E slope of the Sacramento Mountains; PO 1885–present). In 1884 George and Elizabeth Lewis and their nine children settled in Perk Canyon—named for an early settler—and soon a small community evolved. It took the name of William H. Weed, the White Oaks merchant who established a branch store here.

WEREWOLF HILL (Eddy; NW of Carlsbad). This name doesn't appear on any map, and no one seems to know where it comes from, but for at least 50 years Carlsbad residents have known this as a well-known place for necking and partying; they tell stories about parkers seeing a werewolf-like creature scratching at car windows.

WEST (Quay; settlement; 10 mi W of Quay; PO 1908–25, mail to Montoya). West took its name from one of its earliest settlers, James T. West,, who with his two sons, Add and Eurie, operated the West Sheep Co. Though the settlement of West has long been abandoned, old-timers remember it as a lively place, whose Easter egg hunts attracted more than 100 people.

WEST EL PASO (Doña Ana). See *Anapra.*

WEST GRAND PLAINS (Chaves). See *East Grand Plains.*

WEST LAS VEGAS (San Miguel). See *Las Vegas.*

WEST MALPAIS WILDERNESS (Cibola; on the W side of El Malpais National Monument, S of Grants). This 39,700-acre BLM wilderness was designated in 1987 as part of El Malpais National Conservation Area. It includes old lava flows, as well as a ponderosa parkland island surrounded by more recent lava. See also *Cebolla Wilderness* and *El Malpais National Monument.*

WEST TULAROSA (Otero; settlement; 1.25 mi W of Tulsarosa; PO 1911–12, mail to Tularosa). Originally called *Monterrey,* for reasons unknown, this community became West Tularosa and since has been absorbed into Tularosa.

WESTWATER (Eddy; settlement; in W part of county, on W slopes of the Guadalupe Mountains, exact location unknown; PO

1902–03, mail to Carlsbad). Little is known about this ephemeral locality; George Adlai Feather said the name resulted from the settlement being at the head of a canyon from whence water flowed W.

WESTYARD (McKinley). See *Williams Acres.*

WETHERLY LAKE (Union; on Corrumpa Creek, 8 mi SE of Des Moines). This large artificial lake originally was called *James Dam,* because it was at the former headquarters of the Thomas P. James Ranch. When A.D. Wetherly acquired the property, the lake took his name instead.

WHEATLAND (Quay; settlement; on NM 469 16 mi S of San Jon). Wheatland was settled about 1915; its name was selected by ballot when three school districts were consolidated here; Wheatland refers to the crop cultivated in the area. Most residents have moved away from Wheatland, most buildings are abandoned, but the village and the name survive.

WHEELER PEAK, 13,161 ft. (Taos; in the Sangre de Cristo Mountains E of Taos). The highest summits in five western states were named for geologists and surveyors involved in the mapping and exploration of the American West; Mount Whitney in California, Gannett Peak in Wyoming, Humphreys Peak in Arizona, Kings Peak in Utah—and this mountain in NM. Between 1871 and 1878 Maj. George M. Wheeler of the US Army was in charge of surveys W of the 100th meridian; he was inolved in mapping of NM, and the state's highest summit now bears his name. The name Wheeler Peak also appears on Nevada's second highest summit, and in California are four orographic features named Wheeler, including a Wheeler Peak in the Sierra Nevada; most, if not all, also were named for Major Wheeler. Until 1948, however, the pre-eminence of the NM mountain was not recognized. In that year a Santa Fe mountaineer and photographer—see *Mount Walter*—made accurate measurements that established Wheeler Peak as the state's highest summit.

WHEELER PEAK WILDERNESS (Taos; surrounds Wheeler Peak). Named for its focal point, 13,161-foot *Wheeler Peak* (see entry), this wilderness was designated in 1960 and in 1980 expanded to its present 19,663 acres. In addition to preserving high-country habitat, the area also is the headwaters of several streams vital to downstream users. Administered by the Carson NF.

WHISKEY (general). The four Whiskey Creeks in NM, as well as 7 other places named Whiskey (GNIS), likely take their names from bootlegging and moonshine operations, as do several places named *Bootleg.*

WHISKEY CREEK (Grant). See *Río de Arenas.*

WHISKEY LAKE (McKinley; in NW part of county at San Juan County line). This is a somewhat loose translation of the Navajo name, which means "murky," or "of the color of whiskey."

WHISPERING CEDARS (McKinley; settlement; near Ciniza, E of Gallup, N of I-40). Inhabited residential subdivision, bearing a fanciful developer's name.

WHITE (general). See *Blanca, Blanco (general).*

WHITE FLAT (De Baca). See *Gramma Valley.*

WHITE HORSE (McKinley; settlement; on NM 509 25 mi NE of Crownpoint). This active trading point originally was known as *Buck Store,* for the woman named Buck who owned it. The name White Horse is said to be derived from a pair of white horses owned by a Navajo rancher here. The locality's Navajo name means "water, one was killed by it."

WHITE LAKES (Santa Fe; settlement; on US 285, 15 mi NW of Clines Corners). A basin containing several intermittent lakes is near this community, now all but abandoned.

WHITE MESA (Sandoval; 3 mi SW of San Ysidro). Named for white gypsum deposits.

WHITE MOUNTAIN (Otero; settlement; 10 mi E of Three Rivers, at the base of Sierra Blanca; PO 1912–22, mail to Three Rivers). Less a community than simply a PO, named for *Sierra Blanca* (see entry).

WHITE MOUNTAIN WILDERNESS (Lincoln; in the Sacramento Mountains, just

N of Sierra Blanca). Beginning with desert grassland at 6,000 ft. and rising to subalpine conifers at 11,400 ft., the 48,873-acre White Mountain Wilderness includes five life zones. It is adjacent to 12,003-foot *Sierra Blanca* (see entry), for which it was named. Administered by the Lincoln NF.

WHITE OAKS (Lincoln; settlement; on NM 349, 12 mi NE of Carrizozo; PO 1880–1954, mail to Carrizozo). In 1879 three prospectors discovered gold near here, and soon a mining camp sprouted that was named for *White Oaks Spring* (actually two springs), 2.5 mi from the town. Mining and the camp grew quickly together, and by 1884 White Oaks had 1,000 residents; during the 1890s White Oaks was known as the liveliest town in the territory. But the RR did not lay tracks to White Oaks as hoped, the mines played out, and people began drifting away. Today only a few residents remain to keep the town alive.

WHITE ROCK (Los Alamos; settlement; on NM 4, SE of Los Alamos). This inhabited village began in 1948 as a construction camp for workers on government projects at nearby Los Alamos. It was named for nearby *White Rock Canyon,* a stretch of the Rio Grande above Cochiti Lake named for rocks in the river stained white by mineral deposits.

WHITE SANDS (Otero; in the Tularosa Valley W of Alamogordo). Gypsum eroding from the San Andres Mountains to the W has been deposited in the intermittent lake known as Lake Lucero (see entry). Prevailing winds have then blown these deposits northward, creating huge dunes of snow-white gypsum covering 275 sq mi and creating a natural feature found nowhere else in the world.

WHITE SANDS NATIONAL MONUMENT (Otero; 15 mi SW of Alamogordo, on US 70-82). Established in 1933.

WHITE SANDS MISSILE RANGE (Otero, Sierra; includes most of the San Andres Mountains and the Sierra Oscura and most of the valleys to the E and W). Created in 1945 for rocket research and originally called the *White Sands Proving Ground,* later given its present name.

WHITE SIGNAL (Grant; settlement; on NM 180, NW of Silver City; PO 1909–33, mail to Tyrone). Many Grant County residents still remember this former trading point, still a residential cluster. The *White Signal School* was 0.25 mi N. The name is said to have been inspired by a large white quartz outcrop on a hill to the W, from which would shine signal-like reflections in the early morning sun.

WHITE SULPHUR SPRINGS (Otero). See *Mescalero.*

WHITES CITY (Eddy; settlement; on US 62-180, at the entrance to Carlsbad Caverns National Park; PO 1942–present). About 1927 Charlie White, originally from Kentucky, homesteaded S of Carlsbad and started a small store and filling station. This grew into a larger tourist and trading center and took the name Whites City. White's descendants continue in business here.

WHITETAIL (Otero; settlement; in the N part of the Mescalero Apache Reservation, NE of Mescalero and E of US 70; PO 1915–26, mail to Mescalero). Named for nearby *Whitetail Draw,* where whitetail deer abound. Associated features include *Whitetail Lake, Whitetail Canyon,* and *Whitetail Spring.*

WHITEWATER (Catron). See *Glenwood.*

WHITEWATER (Grant; settlement; 3 mi W of US 180, 8 mi S of Hurley; PO 1883–1955, mail to Hurley). Whitewater, now abandoned, was a station on the AT&SF RR. A Civilian Conservation Corps camp once was here. The locality was named for *Whitewater Creek,* 3 mi to the E. An early name for the site was *Calsnachs Ranch.*

WHITEWATER (McKinley). See *Vander Wagen.*

WHITEWATER BALDY, 10,895 ft. (Catron; in the Mogollon Mountains, at the head of Whitewater Creek). Named for *Whitewater Creek,* which flows NW from here then SW to join the San Francisco River at Glenwood.

WHITFIELD (Socorro). See *Patterson.*

WHITMIRE CANYON, CREEK (Hidalgo; head in the S Peloncillo Mountains, NW of Cloverdale, and run E). J.P. Whitmire was a rancher here in the 1880s; he sold out and moved on, but his name remains on these features.

WHITNEY (Hidalgo; RR locality; on the SP RR, about 2 mi W of Lordsburg). Long-abandoned RR site; name origin unknown.

WHITSON (Colfax; settlement; exact location unknown; PO 1878). Ephemeral PO, origin of name unknown.

WIJIJI (San Juan; archaeological site; in Chaco Culture National Historical Park). Like many names in Chaco Canyon, this first appeared in 1849 when Lt. James Simpson recorded in his journal that this was the name given this ruin by his New Mexican guide, Carravahal. The name has been variously spelled, but it's believed to be a corruption of a Navajo word; among possible meanings are "turquoise house," "greasewood house," and "black greasewood."

WILD COW MESA (Eddy; in the Guadalupe Mountains). Named because of wild cattle here, the progeny of stolen stock.

WILDCAT (McKinley; settlement; 2 mi E of Black Hat on NM 264). Inhabited Navajo community, whose name translates the Navajo name of a nearby butte.

WILLARD (Torrance; settlement; on US 60 and NM 42, 14 mi NE of Mountainair; PO 1902–present). Willard was born in 1902 with the arrival of the AT&SF RR in Torrance County, and RR promoter Willard Samuel Hopewell named the fledgling station for his son, Willard Samuel Hopewell Jr. Among the first families to settle here were Marcelino Gallegos, his wife, Marillita, and their family; they lived in a tent while building their house. Willard thrived until the RR began to scale back its operations and agriculture declined in the area, causing Willard to lose population.

WILLIAMS ACRES (McKinley; settlement; 5 mi W of Gallup). Originally a RR settlement called *Westyard,* this inhabited subdivision now goes by the name Williams Acres, likely for a property owner or developer.

WILLIAMS LAKE (Taos; in the Sangre de Cristo Mountains, S of the Taos Ski Valley, at the NW foot of Wheeler Peak).

Name origin obscure, but this small tarn at 11,000 feet possibly recalls William S. Williams, an ex-preacher who arrived in Taos in the fall of 1825 and became a consummate hunter and trapper.

WILLIAMSBURG (Sierra; settlement; on I-25, 3 mi W of Truth or Consequences; PO 1951–present). This has been a neighboring community of Truth or Consequences, and when Truth or Consequences changed its name from *Hot Springs* in 1951, Williamsburg obligingly adopted the orphan name, but a year later it returned to Williamsburg, which honors Dr. Thomas B. Williams, the village's first mayor.

WILLIS (San Miguel; settlement; on the Pecos River, 15 mi N of Pecos; PO 1896–1905, mail to Pecos). Abandoned community, name origin unknown.

WILLOW (general). A common name element in NM, whether in English or in one of several Spanish forms. 57 NM places have Willow in their names, 86 have the Spanish form *Jara* or one of its variants (GNIS). See *Jara (general).*

WILLOW (Colfax). See *Van Houten.*

WILLOW (Union). See *Otto.*

WILLOW SPRINGS (McKinley). See *El Dado.*

WILLOW SPRINGS (Union; settlement; location unknown; PO 1914–16, mail to Corrumpa). Abandoned community, named for local springs.

WILNA (Grant). See *Ruia.*

WIMSATT (Otero; settlement; 8 mi E of Cloudcroft). The Wimsatt family settled originally in Grant County, where they gave their name to Wimsattville, later Turnerville (see entry), but in 1928 they moved here, where they gave their name to this inhabited community.

WIMSATTVILLE (Grant). See *Turnerville.*

WINDMILL (Hidalgo; settlement; 0.5 mi N of NM 9, 11 mi E of Animas). Inhabited community, established in the 1970s. Located on an open, windy plain, but ironically, in 1991 no windmill was to be seen here.

WINGATE (McKinley). See *Fort Wingate.*

WINSTON (Sierra; settlement; on NM 52, 31 mi E of I-25; PO as Fairview 1881–1930, as Winston 1930–present).

In 1881, following mineral discoveries—see *Chloride*—two neighboring mining camps sprang up—Chloride and 3 mi to the NE *Fairview*. Despite Indian threats, Fairview grew, and in 1886 Frank H. Winston arrived and established a mercantile business here. Winston, originally from Wisconsin, lived in Grafton NM before coming to Fairview, but until his death in 1929 he was Fairview's leading citizen—a state legislator, a miner, a rancher, and a businessman. When times were hard, as they often were, he gave credit at his general store, knowing he had little chance of being repaid. In 1930, one year after Winston's death, the town changed its name to honor him.

WIRE LAKE (Chaves; in NW corner of county). Around 1890 the rancher W.G. Urton fenced this lake with wire, which stock often dragged into the water.

MOUNT WITHINGTON, 10,116 ft. (Socorro; at the N end of the San Mateo Mountains). Repeated attempts to discover the identity of the person for whom this major summit was named all have been unsuccessful. It has been suggested the mountain might have been named by Maj. George M. Wheeler (see *Wheeler Peak*); if so, the most likely eponymn would have been William Herbert Withington (1835—1903), Union officer in the Civil War, later Michigan manufacturer and capitalist.

WITHINGTON WILDERNESS (Socorro; on the E slopes of the San Mateo Mountains, at the N end of the range). Designated in 1980, this rugged 18,869-acre wilderness was named for *Mount Withington,* its dominant feature.

WITT (Torrance; settlement; on NM 41, 5 mi N of Estancia). Former settlement associated with the dry-ice plant built on the old NMC RR by the Witt Ice Co.

WOLF (general). At one time four species of wolves lived in NM; all have been exterminated, except the Mexican wolf, which survives in zoos. Their names in English, however, remain on at least 11 places in NM, 25 in the Spanish form *Lobo* (GNIS).

WOLF CANYON (Sandoval; settlement; in NW part of county, exact location un-known; PO 1913–15, mail to Señorita). Little is known about this short-lived postal locality.

WOODBURY (Sandoval; settlement; N of Cochiti Pueblo; 1899–1903, mail to Bland). Woodbury was an ephemeral community organized around a mining mill built here in 1896 by the Cochiti Reduction and Improvement Co. of Denver; R.W. Woodbury was the company's president, and A.J. Woodbury was the community's first postmaster. Woodbury likely occupied the site earlier known as *Allerton.*

WOODROW (Quay; settlement; SW of Quay, 5 mi NW of Ragland; PO as Looney 1908–13, 1913–16, mail to Tucumcari). The homesteader era saw numerous small settlements in the Quay Valley, and one of them was *Looney,* named for Henry Looney, who in 1908 put up a store and established a PO, which he named for himself. But Henry Looney later left the area, and eventually Emma Stephenson acquired the PO. She believed the name Looney connoted "crazy," and because Woodrow Wilson was then US President, she wrote to him asking permission to use his name for the PO. Permission was granted. Now nothing remains of Looney/Woodrow but the names and memories.

WOODROW CANYON (Grant; in the W Diablo Range, runs N into Mogollon Creek). This short canyon recalls Henry Woodrow, who for 27 years was a wilderness ranger with the Gila NF and who wrote about its history.

WOOTEN (Otero; settlement; NE of Alamogordo, on the RR route between Mountain Park and Cloudcroft). Short-lived locality, name origin unknown.

WOOTEN (Roosevelt). See *Valley View.*

WRIGHT (Otero; settlement; 4.5 mi N of Weed, up Wills Canyon; PO 1904–09). Abandoned settlement, named for an early settler.

WYLIE DRAW (Chaves, De Baca; joins the Pecos River from the W, just N of the Chaves County line). Sometimes called *Wiley Creek,* this takes its name from "Old Man" Wiley, who settled here in the early 1900s.

X RAY (Torrance; settlement; 12 mi SE of
Mountainair; PO 1916–20, mail to
Mountainair). Alas, the inspiration of
this intriguing name is unknown.

YAH-TA-HEY (McKinley; settlement; 7 mi N of Gallup, and the junction of US 666 and NM 264). Transliteration of the traditional Navajo greeting. This active community is organized around the *Yah-ta-hey Trading Post,* established by J.B. Tanner. To local people, the names *Yah-ta-hey Junction* and *J.B. Junction* are synonymous.

YANKEE (Colfax; settlement; on NM 72 8 mi NE of Raton; PO 1906–22, mail to Raton). The coal-mining camp of Yankee was founded in 1904 by the Chicorica Coal Co. and named because several Boston financiers—Yankees— were involved in the venture. By 1907 2,000 persons lived in or around Yankee, but in 1914 the mines began to close, and the population dwindled steadily after that. Today Yankee has vanished. NM 72 winds through *Yankee Canyon* onto Johnson Mesa.

YAPASHI (Sandoval; archaeological site; in Bandelier National Monument, 5 mi W of Rito de los Frijoles). This abandoned pueblo has for its name a Keresan word meaning "place of the sacred enclosure," because near here, at the site known as the *Shrine of the Stone Lions,* enclosed by a low stone wall, are the weathered stone figures of two lions.

YATES (Harding; settlement; NE of Roy on NM 120, 4 mi S of Union County line; PO 1923–31, mail to Roy). "Uncle Jim" Yates settled here in 1908. People still live here and use the name.

YERBA MANSA (Doña Ana; settlement; along the Rio Grande, between Doña Ana and Robledo, exact location unknown). This former locality likely takes its name from the medicinal plant *Anemopsis californica,* whose common name is yerba mansa, that sometimes grows near waterways.

YESO (De Baca; settlement; on US 60, 20 mi W of Fort Sumner; PO as Yesso 1909, as Yeso 1909–present). Yeso was born in 1906 with construction of the AT&SF RR line; the settlement was named for *Yeso Creek* to the S, named in turn for the gypsum (Spanish, *yeso*) deposits there. *Mesa del Yeso* is 2 mi S of the village. At one time Yeso vied to become seat of De Baca County. Now all but a few buildings are abandoned.

YORK (Chaves; settlement; near the mouth of the Agua Chiquita on the Rio Peñasco, upriver from Elk). York, now abandoned, consisted of a small general store owned by William York; the store opened in 1892 and lasted about 15 years. *Yorktown* has been mentioned as an alternative name.

YOUNGSVILLE (Rio Arriba; settlement; on NM 96 18 mi W of Abiquiu; PO as Coyote 1888–1913, as Youngsville 1913–present). Established early in the 20th century, this Hispanic settlement has been called *Coyote* and also *Plaza de los Encinos,* "town of the evergreen oak," but these names have been replaced by Youngsville, whose origin is unknown.

YRISARRI (Bernalillo; settlement; S of Tijeras, on NM 217, 1 mi E of NM 337). This locality, still inhabited, is said to have been established by one Pablo Yrisarri after he, a Spanish loyalist, was driven out of Veracruz by Mexican patriots. He moved to the Rio Grande valley and married into local families, and some of the people who had come N with him settled here. Old-timers here recall an old and a new Yrisarri, the old 3 mi E of the present site. The ephemeral *Miera* PO (1935, mail to Chilili) coincided with Yrisarri.

YUNQUE YUNQUE (Rio Arriba) See *San Gabriel.*

Z

ZACATES (Bernalillo; settlement; exact location unknown). George Adlai Feather encountered this name, spelled *Xacates,* on an 1828 map, which showed a settlement W of the Rio Grande, N of the Rio Puerco. See *Sacate, Sacaton (general).*

ZACATON (general). See *Sacate, Sacaton (general).*

ZAMORA (Bernalillo). See *Tijeras.*

ZARCA (general). Common misspelling of the Spanish *sarca,* "light blue," appearing often in the names of water features.

ZELLER PEAK, 7,313 ft. (Hidalgo; at the N end of the Big Hatchet Mountains). Following his death in an airplane crash in eastern Arizona in 1970, Robert A. Zeller Jr. was described as "one of the most able geologists ever to live and work in the state of NM." He lived in Hachita, "in sight of his beloved Big Hatchet Mountains, the subject of his Ph.D. dissertation." The USBGN in 1979 approved naming this peak for him.

ZIA PUEBLO (Sandoval; on the E bank of the Jemez River, 1 mi E of NM 44, 8 mi NW of Santa Ana Pueblo). The name of this pre-Spanish Keresan pueblo has been spelled variously as *Cia, Zia, Chia, Tsia,* and *Tria* over the years, but the names all designate the same place on the Jemez River. As the pueblo's inhabitants explain: "*Tsiya* is located in same area today as it was when Coronado visited in 1540.... The province in which our ancestors lived was called *Puname* [Antonio de Espejo recorded this name as meaning 'people of the west'], and Tsiya was the chief village among the five in the province. Like many of the other Pueblo people, our ancestors deserted their village during the period of the revolt and reconquest and sought refuge in Cerro Colorado near Jemez; the Zia people were the first to return to their homes and establish relations with the Spanish government."

ZILDITLOI MOUNTAIN, 8,573 ft. (McKinley; in NW part of county, NW of Tohatchi). The variant name, *Fuzzy Mountain,* translates this Navajo name; cedars and piñons around the base of this extinct volcano give it a "fuzzy" appearance. Other variants have included *Fluffy Mountain, Baigaichi, Dzilditloi,* and *Zildigloi,* but Zilditloi is the form approved by the USBGN in 1915. *Zilditloi Wash* runs through the village of Navajo.

ZORA (Otero; RR locality at Orogrande). Ephemeral name associated with the SP RR near Orogrande; origin unknown.

ZUNI (general). As the inhabitants of Zuni Pueblo explain the name: "Our ancestors called themselves *A'shiwi,* 'the flesh,' and their territory *Shilwon,* 'the land that produces flesh,' but the Spaniards called us Zuni, which is their version of the Keresan *Sunyitsi* (unknown meaning)." The name was first applied by Chamuscado in 1580; he spelled it *Cuni.* In 1583 Espejo used the present form. See *Zuni Pueblo.*

ZUNI BUTTES, 7,225 ft. (McKinley; 5 mi NW of Zuni). Twin peaks, called by the Zunis "two mountains."

ZUNI MOUNTAINS (McKinley, Cibola; NE of Zuni). Highest elevation *Mount Sedgwick,* 9,256 ft, (see entry).

ZUNI PLATEAU (Cibola; in SW corner of county).

ZUNI PUEBLO (McKinley; 32 mi S of Gallup, on NM 53; PO 1879–intermittently to present). Residents of this pueblo refer to it by the name *Halona weh,* "place of the ants," a name with mythological meanings denoting it as the center of the Zuni universe. When the Spanish came here in 1539, the first pueblo they encountered was *Hawikuh* (see entry), one of 7 Zuni villages in a 20-mi radius. The name Zuni appeared in 1580; see *Zuni (general)*.

ZUNI RIVER (Cibola, McKinley; rises in the Zuni Mountains and flows SW through Zuni to enter the Little Colorado River in Arizona).

ZUNI SALT LAKE (Catron; in NW part of county, NW of Quemado). Although several Indian tribes consider this saline lake a sacred source of salt, the lake belongs to the Zunis. Oñate visited the lake in 1598, and it appears as *Salina de Zuni* on Miera y Pacheco's 1775 map. It appears in other documents by its Spanish name, *Laguna Salada*. When the boundaries of the Zuni Reservation were drawn in 1877, the lake was excluded

and commercial operations were begun; a PO named Salt Lake was here from 1902 to 1940. In 1970, however, the Zunis resumed ownership.

ZUZAX (Bernalillo; settlement; on I-40, 3 mi E of Tijeras). Herman Ardans, who has been described by a competitor as "the cleverest retail man I ever knew," opened a curio shop on US 66 here around 1956 and made up the name Zuzax so it would capture people's attention and also be the last entry in the phone book (as it is the last entry in this book). When asked by customers about the origin of the name, he often told then it referred to the Zuzax Indians. Ardans eventually left the curio business, and his curio shop is gone, but the name he created still intrigues travelers passing the Zuzax exit on I-40.